The Philosophy of Sex

The Philosophy of Sex

Contemporary Readings

Seventh Edition

Raja Halwani, Alan Soble, Sarah Hoffman,
and Jacob M. Held

ROWMAN & LITTLEFIELD
Lanham • Boulder • New York • London

Published by Rowman & Littlefield
A wholly owned subsidiary of The Rowman & Littlefield Publishing Group, Inc.
4501 Forbes Boulevard, Suite 200, Lanham, Maryland 20706
www.rowman.com

Unit A, Whitacre Mews, 26-34 Stannary Street, London SE11 4AB

British Library Cataloguing in Publication Information Available

Library of Congress Cataloging-in-Publication Data

Names: Halwani, Raja. editor.
Title: The philosophy of sex : contemporary readings / edited by Raja Halwani, Alan Soble, Sarah Hoffman, and Jacob M. Held.
Description: Seventh Edition. | Lanham, Md. : Rowman & Littlefield, 2017. | Includes bibliographical references and index.
Identifiers: LCCN 2017023431 (print) | LCCN 2017032952 (ebook) | ISBN 9781442261440 (electronic) | ISBN 9781538100905 (cloth : alk. paper) | ISBN 9781442261433 (pbk. : alk. paper)
Subjects: LCSH: Sex. | Sexual ethics.
Classification: LCC HQ12 (ebook) | LCC HQ12 .P47 2017 (print) | DDC 306.7—dc23
LC record available at https://lccn.loc.gov/2017023431

Printed in the United States of America

Raja Halwani
For Helkin Gonzalez

Alan Soble
For Gary and Andres, with gratitude

Sarah Hoffman
For Mark

Jacob M. Held
For my students, who remind me that there are critical, smart, and engaged people all around us

Contents

Preface

The seventh edition of *The Philosophy of Sex* has quite a few changes. First, it has nine new essays specifically written for this volume: Talia Mae Bettcher's "Trans 101" and Burkay Ozturk's "The Negotiative Theory of Gender Identity and the Limits of First-Person Authority" deal with transgender issues, the former going over some basics and the latter questioning the view that a person has a non-defeasible epistemic and ethical decision regarding what their gender is. Raja Halwani's "Racial Sexual Desires" tackles the question of whether there is something morally lacking in someone who sexually prefers (or does not prefer) members of a particular race or ethnic group (Halwani says "no"); Elizabeth Brake's "Is 'Loving More' Better? The Values of Polyamory" addresses some crucial issues surrounding polyamory: what it is, the important objections to it, and its value and importance; Robin Dembroff's "What Is Sexual Orientation?" defends a new conception of sexual orientation that is disconnected from the person's own gender; and Kim Q. Hall's "Thinking Queerly about Sex and Sexuality" explains the basics of queer theory and what it contributes to a discussion of sexuality and other connected issues, such as disability and zoophilia. Lina Papadaki's "Sexual Objectification" discusses in depth the concept of "objectification" and offers a new account of the concept that departs in important ways from existing ones. Shaun Miller's "BDSM" goes beyond responding to the main objections against BDSM to offer ways in which BDSM practitioners can live good lives *because* they are practitioners of BDSM. Finally, Alan Soble's "Gifts and Duties" provocatively explores the ideas of sexual duties and sexual supererogation (especially to strangers) and shows us how rich and complex a proper treatment of them is.

The seventh edition also has three essays that are new to the volume, though they have been published elsewhere before: Robert Gray's "Sex and Sexual Perversion" is a classic that we have decided to bring back to this edition (it was printed in the first, third, and fourth editions). Kathy Rudy's "LGBTQ . . . Z?" brings Rudy's knowledge of queer theory and love of nonhuman animals to bear on the question of human–animal sexual intimacy. Finally, Seiriol Morgan's "Dark Desires" argues that, contrary to what some liberal philosophers believe, the consent of the parties to a sexual act is not sufficient for the moral permissibility of the act.

The seventh edition also has three revised essays from the sixth one: both Alan Soble's "An Essay on Masturbation" and "Sexual Use" are shorter and leaner, yet no less acute and incisive, versions of his earlier essays on these topics. Kayley Vernallis's "Bisexuality and Bisexual Marriage" is a revised version of "Bisexual Marriage," containing more on the nature and types of bisexuality and less on bisexual marriage, while still defending the bold view that a marriage respecting the rights of bisexuals should comprise at least four bisexual partners, two men and two women. (Sadly, except for the title, Raja Halwani's "Casual Sex, Promiscuity, and Objectification" in this edition is the same as his "On Fucking Around" from the sixth.)

Thus, with a bit of justified cheating (by counting previously published essays and revised ones from the sixth edition as new), the majority of the essays of the seventh edition of *The Philosophy of Sex* (fifteen out of twenty-five) are new.

But "old" does not mean "bad": the essays of the seventh edition retained from the sixth are all classics or masterpieces (or both): Greta Christina's "Are We Having Sex Now or What?," Thomas Nagel's "Sexual Perversion," Alan Goldman's "Plain Sex," John Portmann's "Chatting Is Not Cheating," Thomas Mappes's "Sexual Morality and the Concept of Using Another Person," Alan Wertheimer's "Consent and Sexual Relations," Robin West's "The Harms of Consensual Sex," and David Benatar's "Two Views of Sexual Ethics" are by now (thanks partly to previous editions of this anthology) essential readings in the field of the philosophy of sex.

Because Alan Soble's introduction for the sixth edition, "The Analytic Categories of the Philosophy of Sex," is a gem of a stand-alone essay about some of the basic themes of the field, and because Alan has made this book what it is, we decided to retain his introduction but with additions by Raja Halwani addressing issues of character and preferences and of the importance of the field of the philosophy of sex.

The editors, of course, had to also make the (often) painful decision to not retain some essays from the previous edition (alas, such is the nature of change), and to drop entire topics, most notably those of same-sex marriage, pornography, and prostitution. Now that same-sex marriage is the law of the land in the United States of America and is gaining ground in other countries, and given how much has been written on the latter two topics, we decided to skip them over in favor of other issues to which philosophers are paying more attention (e.g., polyamory, race and sex, transgenderism), and issues into which fresh insight is badly needed (e.g., BDSM, zoophilia, queer theory). Of course, we retained the ever-important themes of what sexual desire and activity are, and of consent, use, and objectification.

We also decided to not divide the book into parts. This allows the essays to flow more smoothly into one another and the reader to not feel constrained, no matter how mildly, by such parts. Granted that deciding on the order of the essays was not easy, the existing order makes sense (though different orders would have as well): begin with a cluster of essays on sexual desire, activity, and perversion (chapters 2 through 7), move to essays that huddle around the notions of character and orientation (chapters 8 through 13), to essays on queer theory and its application (chapters 14 and 15), to essays on consent, use, and objectification (chapters 16 through 24), then to, finally, an essay (chapter 25) on sexual duties and supererogatory acts.

The seventh edition also has a large bibliography for those who wish to further pursue some of the themes of the philosophy of sex. The bibliography is arranged by category, such as "Consent, Power, and Rape," "Fantasy and Masturbation," "Internet and Technology," "LGBTQ," "Marriage and Relationships," "Pornography," and "Prostitution." We hope that it is of use and that it is as exhaustive as possible—if we have missed any crucial entries, please email Raja Halwani (rhalwa@saic.edu) and supply him with what you think is missing. We are constantly updating the bibliography.

In philosophy, it is unusual to see four editors to an anthology. However, ours had a good reason. We started with three: Halwani, Hoffman, and Soble, but, soon after, Sarah had to attend to some pressing issues, so we invited Jacob Held to join us.

The editors wish to thank all those who participated in surveys and questionnaires that have helped us decide on the content and direction of this new edition. We thank also the good people at Rowman & Littlefield who helped this book see the light of day, especially Jon Sisk and Kate Powers for their support and encouragement. We, of course, also thank all the contributors to the book (especially those who wrote new essays, for their patience with the process of revisions that new essays undergo). We thank our families, friends, and loved ones for their love and their support. We thank the readers of this book—the teachers, the students, the researchers, the philosophy-of-sex-curious, among others—for their continued interest and, well, reading.

Halwani, Held, and Hoffman wish to give special thanks to Alan Soble, who started this book in 1980 and who edited the first four editions by himself, the fifth with Nicholas Power, the sixth with Power and Halwani, and now this edition. He has shown us the importance of the field of the philosophy of sex and has placed it on equal footing with other fields in philosophy. He has also demonstrated how to do it excellently. Thank you, Alan.

We hope that readers enjoy reading this book and find it valuable. Their suggestions for improvement are welcome. The process of starting the eighth edition is already underway, though only mentally for now.

ONE

Introduction

The Analytic Categories of the Philosophy of Sex

Alan Soble, with Raja Halwani

In this introductory essay, **Alan Soble** *and* **Raja Halwani** *discuss the importance of the field of philosophy of sex and exhibit the range of topics that are studied—analytic, normative, and metaphysical—in it. Analytic questions have to do with defining the central concepts in the field: sexual desire, sexual activity, and sexual pleasure. The goal of this analysis is to define each concept separately from each other (to avoid circularity) or, alternatively, to demonstrate that all the concepts can be defined in terms of just one of them, which would then be the basic concept in the philosophy of sex. Of particular interest is the analysis of the concept of sexual perversion and laying out the difference between the sexually natural and the unnatural. The analysis of sexual perversion requires that we be able to state what makes a desire, activity, or pleasure sexual to begin with, and then to identify the specific features of sexual desires, activities, or pleasures that make them sexually perverted. Other concepts that are important to analyze in the philosophy of sex are issues surrounding sexual orientation and gender. Still other issues, such as consent and coercion, are important in other areas of philosophy as well: applied ethics (e.g., medical ethics), social and political philosophy, and the philosophy of law.*

The fact that the philosophy of sex often discusses the natural and the unnatural and utilizes the concepts of consent and coercion means that normative issues make up a large part of the philosophy of sex. Natural Law ethics asserts that there are significant connections between the naturalness of sexual desire or a sexual act and its morality; this is denied by philosophies that emphasize, for moral judgments, the importance of the presence of consent and the absence of

1

coercion. When we add the ethics of Immanuel Kant, which focuses on the wrongs of using people and treating them as objects, and when we add the ethics of character, of virtues and vices, and of living well, sexual ethics becomes complicated territory.

THE PHILOSOPHY OF SEX: WHAT IT IS AND ITS IMPORTANCE

Among the topics explored by the philosophy of sex are procreation, contraception, celibacy, marriage, adultery, casual sex, flirting, prostitution, homosexuality, masturbation, seduction, rape, sexual harassment, sadomasochism, pornography, bestiality, pedophilia, and sometimes birds.[1] What do all these activities or phenomena have in common? All are included in the vast domain of human sexuality, that is, they are related, on the one hand, to the human desires and activities that involve the search for and attainment of sexual pleasure and satisfaction and, on the other hand, to the human desires and activities that involve the creation of new human beings. It is a natural feature of humans that certain sorts of behaviors and certain bodily organs can be employed for pleasure or for reproduction, or for both, either at the same or at different times.

The philosophy of sexuality explores these topics both conceptually and normatively. Conceptual analysis is carried out in the philosophy of sex in order to clarify fundamental notions, including *sexual desire* and *sexual activity*. Defining these concepts is no easy task. What are the distinctive features of an act (or desire) that make it a sexual act (desire) instead of some other kind of act (desire)? Conceptual analysis is also carried out to arrive at satisfactory definitions of specific sexual practices, such as adultery, rape, and prostitution. In what ways does seduction differ from rape? Is it conceptually plausible to say that women who are paid to engage in sexual activities in the making of hardcore pornographic films are prostitutes?

Normative philosophy of sexuality inquires about the value of sexual activity and sexual pleasure and of the various forms they take. It is concerned with the perennial questions of sexual morality and constitutes a large branch of applied ethics. Normative philosophy of sex inquires about the possible contribution made to the good or virtuous life by sexuality and tries to determine what moral duties we have to refrain from performing certain sexual acts and what moral permissions we have to engage in others. Moral issues surrounding same-sex sexual activity, abortion, date rape, sexual harassment, pornography, and prostitution, among other things, have been widely discussed by philosophers of sex.

Why is the philosophy of sex an important field? *Is* it an important field? In his essay "Plain Sex" (reproduced in this volume), Alan Goldman states that "Sex affords us a paradigm of pleasure, but not a cornerstone of value. . . . [The pleasures of sex] give value to the specific acts which generate them, but not the lasting kind of value which enhances one's whole life. The briefness of the pleasures contributes to their intensity (or perhaps their intensity makes them necessarily brief), but it also relegates them to the periphery of most rational plans for the good life" (see page 66 in this volume). Goldman is claiming that sexual desire and activity, unlike their kin romantic love, are not important enough to ground a crucial value or on which to build one's life plan. These claims raise important issues in regards to the field of the philosophy of sex: they are claims important on their own and lead to questions about the importance of the field of philosophy that addresses them.

Even if Goldman is right about sexual desire and sexual activity, his claim cannot be extended to sexuality in general ("sexuality" is an ambiguous term with multiple referents, but it is quite serviceable in this context). Sexuality grounds crucial values: a quick look at the above list that opens this chapter assures us that procreation, celibacy, rape, and sexual harassment, for example, are no trivial matters. Whether one decides to reproduce, to stay celibate, or to engage in rape or sexual harassment are grave decisions with serious repercussions for others (that some people make decisions lightly in these areas does not affect this point). Consider that according to some philosophers, bringing children into this world does them great harm. Deciding on bringing children into this world is a serious decision, and so is the (different) decision of becoming a parent; both involve serious life plans. Other life plans that are based on sexuality come to mind: being a model is one, and being a prostitute is another. Deciding on one's gender is also intimately connected to sexuality. Let's also remember that being a practitioner of BDSM is not just a matter of engaging in sex with whip in hand; it is usually a complete lifestyle.

Furthermore, sexuality is deeply implicated in how one lives one's life in ways not involving life plans, especially if we do not understand "life plan" narrowly as referring only to how someone decides (deliberately or not so deliberately) to live his or her life. No one sets out to be a rapist or a pedophile, yet one act of rape or pedophilia is often enough to turn one into a rapist or a pedophile. Committing adultery can completely change an otherwise good (or bad) marriage into something else. Thus, sexuality in general is connected in myriad and profound ways to how people decide to live their lives and to how they end up living them.

However, there is the specific question about the pleasures of sex and sexual activity. Are these pleasures trivial, as Goldman suggests? Do sex-

ual activity and pleasure not afford us a cornerstone of value? As a descriptive claim, it is false. The amount of time that people spend on trying
to look sexually attractive and to attain sexual pleasure through sex with
others (not to mention masturbating, watching pornography, among other examples), indicates that in general sex and sexual pleasure are important to many people.[2]

Perhaps, however, Goldman meant his claim as a normative or pre-
scriptive one—that pursuing sexual pleasure and activity *should* not be of
much concern to people. Here, the fact that people pursue it often need
not belie Goldman's claim by indicating that there is some hidden value
yet to be uncovered—such adamant pursuit might be our culturally me-
diated biology at work, combined with the fact that the pleasures of sex
can be so intense and forbidden that wanting to experience them over
and again is a near obsession for many people. The cliché uttered by a
cheating spouse that "It meant nothing" in an attempt to assuage the pain
of the cheated-on partner can be translated into Goldmanian language as
follows: "You should not feel sad over this because what happened was
just sex and it has no deep value."

Goldman might be right on this point (but within limits—see below).
Common conceptions of sexual pleasure, even liberal ones, seem to con-
cur: liberal philosophers might claim that people are free to pursue sexual activity as they see fit, including casual sex, promiscuous sex, and sex
with prostitutes (all within the usual moral constraints) but to plan one's
life around them is irrational in that it accords sexual activity and pleasure undeserved weight. Even people who frantically pursue sex would
themselves admit that being a sex-starved maniac is one thing, yet deciding on which job to have based on how many good-looking people one
finds in it is too much. Note that thinking of sexual pleasure as not too
important, as trivial, as not providing a "cornerstone of value" does not
entail that it is not an intrinsic pleasure; it can be an intrinsic pleasure but
an unimportant one, like scratching an itch.

This leaves us with an interesting question: if the central concepts of
the field of philosophy of sex or their referents—the triumvirate of sexual
desire, activity, and pleasure—are not of profound value, how can we
justify the importance of the field? There are a few answers to this question. For one thing, it is fallacious to assume that just because the triumvirate does not itself reflect profound values, it does not involve itself, as
mentioned above, with ones that do. Second, sexual pleasures, though
brief, are intense, often leading people to do irrational and immoral
things in their pursuit (see the discussion of sexual pessimism below).
This alone makes their analytical and normative study an imperative.
Third, and connected to the previous points, is a Freudian view about the
pervasiveness and significance of sexuality and how it underlies much of
what we do. Such a view might take various forms—sexual desire and
pleasure is connected to the disgusting, to the forbidden, to the perverse,

to love, to eternal frustration and recurrence—but what they share in common is seeing a depth or complexity to sexual desire and pleasure that other views do not. They all sense something about sexual desire and pleasure that take them to be more than mere appetite. If some such views are right, we are then dealing with a phenomenon that is both basic but also necessitating complex philosophical inquiry, not all of it from the analytic tradition. Perhaps sex should not be a cornerstone of value, but, alas, given who we are, it is.[3]

Finally, and though die-hard optimists would resist this point, life is difficult and contains much irremediable suffering. This makes the presence of pleasure in our lives crucial—a matter of survival, really. To have as many moments of pleasure might be all that we can ultimately ask for in a good life (this would not justify the truth of an unsophisticated utilitarianism).[4] Sexual pleasures in this respect would not be special; they are just one type of pleasure among many others. But they are intense pleasures with an almost unique feel to them (especially the pleasures of orgasm), and they often involve a kind of intimacy that many people crave. It is in this way then that sexual pleasure can be a cornerstone of value. The philosophy of sex emerges as a crucial field in philosophy.

SEXUAL METAPHYSICS

Our moral evaluations of sexual activity are often influenced by our views about, or our emotional reactions to, the nature of the sexual impulse or sexual desire. In this regard there is a deep divide between those philosophers that we might call the metaphysical sexual "optimists" and those we might call the metaphysical sexual "pessimists."

The pessimists in the philosophy of sexuality, such as St. Augustine, Immanuel Kant, and, sometimes, Sigmund Freud, perceive the sexual impulse and acting on it to be things that are nearly always, if not necessarily, unbefitting the dignity of the human person. They see the essence and the results of the sexual drive to be incompatible with more significant and lofty goals and aspirations of human existence. They fear that the power and demands of the sexual impulse make it a danger to harmonious civilized life. And they find in a person's sexuality a severe threat not only to his or her proper relations with, and moral treatment of, other persons but also to his or her own dignity and humanity.

On the other side are the metaphysical sexual optimists (Plato, in some of his works; Bertrand Russell; Albert Ellis; and sometimes Sigmund Freud) who perceive nothing especially obnoxious in the sexual impulse. They frequently view human sexuality as merely another and mostly innocuous dimension of our existence as embodied or animal-like creatures (similar to the impulse to eat). They judge that our sexuality, which in substantial measure has been given to us by evolution, cannot but be conducive to our well-being. And they applaud rather than fear the power of an impulse that can lift us to high and exhilarating forms of happiness.

The particular metaphysics of sex a person holds, for either rational or emotional reasons, will influence his or her subsequent judgments about the value and role of sexuality in the virtuous or good life and about which sexual activities are morally wrong and which are morally permissible.

An extended version of metaphysical sexual pessimism might make the following claims:

1. Due to the nature of sexual desire, a person who sexually desires another person objectifies that other person, both before and during sexual activity. (Afterward, too, if he immediately reaches for the clicker.) Sexual desire, says the German philosopher Immanuel Kant, "makes of the loved person an Object of appetite. . . . Taken by itself it is a degradation of human nature."[5] Our sexual desire for another person tends to make us view and treat him or her merely as a thing, as an object, as an instrument by which we attain our own goal of sexual pleasure. When one person sexually desires another, what is desired is the other person's body and the pleasure to be derived from it; this truncating attitude toward the other is demeaning.

2. Furthermore, certain types of deception seem required prior to engaging in sex with another person (these are, I would argue, arranged by our social systems as well as by our evolutionary biology). We go out of our way to make ourselves look more physically attractive and more socially desirable to the other person than we think we really are, and we go to great lengths to conceal our physical, personality, and philosophical (or ideological) defects. Trying to make a good and hence misleading impression, we are never our true selves (or what we think our true selves are) on a first date. While it might be the case that men sexually objectify women more than women objectify men, it is undeniable that both men and women engage in deception in trying to elicit positive responses from other people.

3. The sexual act itself is peculiar, with its uncontrollable arousal, involuntary jerkings, and its yearning to master and consume the other person's body. This is part of what Augustine had in mind when he wrote, "lust . . . is the more shameful in this, that the soul does neither rule itself . . . nor the body either."[6] During sexual activity, a person both loses control of himself or herself and loses regard for the humanity of the other person. Our sexuality threat-

ens the other's personhood, but when we are in the grip of desire we also lose, or are on the verge of losing, our personhood.

4. Moreover, a person who gives in to another's sexual desire makes an instrument of himself or herself. As Kant makes the point, "For the natural use that one sex makes of the other's sexual organs is *enjoyment*, for which one gives oneself up to the other. In this act a human being makes himself into a thing."[7] Those engaged in sexual activity make themselves into objects or tools for each other merely for the sake of sexual pleasure. Both persons are reduced to the level of an animal (or a fungus).

5. Finally, once things get going it is often hard to stop them in their tracks, and as a result we often end up doing things sexually that we had never planned or wanted to do. Such is the "positive feedback" nature of the sexual impulse. Sexual desire is also powerfully inelastic, one of the passions most likely to challenge reason, compelling us to seek satisfaction even when doing so involves obvious physical, psychological, and social dangers (which extend, of course, into the inner chambers of the White House). The person who sexually desires another depends on the whims of that other person to gain satisfaction, and thereby becomes susceptible to the demands of the other. People who are caught up in sexual desire and arousal can be easily exploited and manipulated. (From which it follows that the most effective strategy is to make the other think that he or she desires you more than you desire them.)

Given this pessimistic metaphysics of human sexuality, one might conclude that acting on the sexual impulse is always morally wrong, or that for purely prudential reasons one would do best by eschewing sexuality and embracing celibacy. That might be precisely the conclusion to draw, even if it implies the end of *Homo sapiens*. (This result, the extinction of humanity, is also implied by St. Paul's praising celibacy as the ideal state in 1 Cor 7.) More often, however, the pessimistic metaphysicians of sexuality conclude that sexual activity is morally permissible and prudentially wise only within lifelong, monogamous, heterosexual marriage. Some pessimists go further, insisting that sexual activity should be engaged in only or primarily for the purpose of procreation. Regarding bodily acts that are procreative and produce sexual pleasure, it is their procreative potential that is singularly significant and bestows value on these activities; seeking pleasure for its own sake, apart from procreation, is an impediment to morally virtuous sexuality, and should not be undertaken deliberately. Sexual pleasure at most has instrumental value, in inducing us to engage in an act that has procreation as its main purpose. Such views have been common among Christians. For example, here is Augustine again: "A man turns to good use the evil of concupiscence, and is not overcome by it, when he bridles and restrains its rage . . . and never relaxes his hold upon it except when intent on offspring, and then controls and applies it to the carnal generation of children . . . not to the subjection of the spirit to the flesh in a sordid servitude."[8]

Metaphysical sexual optimists suppose that instead of dividing people through various processes of objectification, sexuality is a natural bonding mechanism that joins people together both sexually and nonsexually. Sexual activity involves pleasing the self and the other at the same time, and these joint efforts to exchange pleasure proceed from affection and generate gratitude and more affection, which in turn deepen human relationships, making them more satisfying and emotionally substantial. Furthermore, and this may be the most important point, sexual pleasure is, for a metaphysical optimist, a valuable thing in its own right, something to be cherished and promoted because it has intrinsic and not merely instrumental value. Hence the pursuit of sexual pleasure does not require any intricate or special justification. Nor must we make excuses for it; because sexual pleasure is an intrinsic good it surely need not be confined to marital sexual acts or acts that are directed at procreation. The good and virtuous life, while including much else, can also (logically, psychologically, and morally) include plentiful sexual relations.[9] Irving Singer is a contemporary philosopher who expresses metaphysical optimism: "For though sexual interest resembles an appetite in some respects, it differs from hunger or thirst in being an *interpersonal* sensitivity, one that enables us to delight in the mind and character of other persons as well as in their flesh. Though at times people may be used as sexual objects and cast aside once their utility has been exhausted, this is [not] . . . definitive of sexual desire. . . . By awakening us to the living presence of someone else, sexuality can enable us to treat this other being as just the person he or she happens to be. . . . There is nothing in the nature of sexuality as such that necessarily . . . reduces persons to things. On the contrary, sex may be seen as an instinctual agency by which persons respond to one another *through* their bodies."[10]

MORAL AND NONMORAL EVALUATIONS OF SEXUALITY

We often evaluate sexual activity *morally*: we inquire whether a sexual act—either a particular occurrence of a sexual act (the act we are doing or want to do right now) or a general type of sexual act (say, all instances of male-male fellatio)—is morally good or right or morally bad or wrong. More specifically, we evaluate or judge sexual acts to be morally obligatory, morally permissible, morally wrong, or even morally supererogatory. For example: a spouse might have a moral obligation to engage in sex with the other spouse; it might be morally permissible for married couples to employ contraception while engaging in pleasurable coitus; rape and prostitution are commonly thought to be morally wrong (or immoral); and one person's agreeing to have sexual relations with another person when the former has no sexual desire of his or her own but only wants to please the other might be supererogatory. "Morally supereroga-tory" sexual activity is a category that is infrequently discussed by sexual ethicists. Raymond Belliotti has this to say about it: "We cannot fully describe this type of sex, but we can say generally that it goes above and beyond the call of moral duty. It is sex that is not merely morally permis-sible, but morally exemplary. It would involve some extraordinary moral benefits to others not attainable in merely morally permissible sex."[11] I hope the nurse's aide who cares for me when I am ninety and terminally ill knows Belliotti.

Note that if a specific type of sexual act is immoral (say, homosexual fellatio), then every instance of that type of act is morally wrong. Howev-er, from the fact that the particular sexual act we are now doing or con-template doing is morally wrong, it does not follow that the specific type of act we are performing is morally wrong, in all cases; the sexual act that we are contemplating might be wrong for lots of reasons having nothing to do with the type of sexual act it is. For example, suppose a couple is engaging in heterosexual coitus, and that this particular sexual act is wrong because it is adulterous. The wrongfulness of this sexual activity does not imply that heterosexual coitus in general, as a type of sexual act, is morally wrong. In some cases, of course, a particular sexual act will be wrong for several reasons at once: not only is it wrong because it is an act of a specific type (say, it is an instance of male-female anal coitus), but it is also wrong because at least one of the participants is married to some-one else (it is wrong also as adultery).

In addition to evaluating sexual acts morally, we can also evaluate sexual activity (again, either a particular occurrence of a sexual act or a specific type) *nonmorally*. Let us define "nonmorally good" sex as sexual activity that provides sexual pleasure to the participants or is physically or emotionally satisfying, while "nonmorally bad" sex is unexciting, tedi-ous, boring, unenjoyable, or even unpleasant. (Be careful: "nonmoral" is not the same as "immoral," and "nonmorally bad sexual activity" does not mean "immoral sexual activity.") Two analogies will clarify the dif-ference between morally evaluating something as good or bad and non-morally evaluating it as good or bad. This radio on my desk is a good radio, in the nonmoral sense, because it does what I expect from a radio: it consistently provides clear tones. If, instead, the radio hissed and crack-led most of the time, it would be a bad radio, nonmorally speaking, and it would be senseless for me to blame the radio for its faults and threaten it with a trip to hell if it did not improve its behavior. Another analogy involves the human activities surrounding eating. For some people, eat-ing animal flesh (in the form of steaks or hamburgers) provides a great deal of pleasure, and for that reason eating meat is nonmorally good. For other people, eating a burger results in nausea and vomiting. They cannot "stomach" this meat; the displeasure they experience means that, for them, the activity is nonmorally bad. The question of whether eating meat is nonmorally good or bad is distinct from the question of whether it is morally permissible or morally wrong. Someone who enjoys eating baby back ribs might believe that doing so is, nevertheless, morally wrong (maybe because the factory farming of animals is cruel). Someone who dislikes eating meat can still claim, without contradiction, that doing so is morally permissible.

Similarly, sexual activity can be nonmorally good if it provides for us what we expect sexual activity to provide, which is usually sexual pleasure. But that sexual activity is or can be nonmorally good or bad does not necessarily generate any moral implications. For example, that a sexual activity is nonmorally good, by abundantly satisfying both persons, does not necessarily mean that the act is morally good: some adulterous sexual activity might be sexually pleasing to the participants, yet be morally wrong. Furthermore, that a sexual activity is nonmorally bad, does not produce sexual pleasure for the persons engaged in it, does not mean that the act is morally wrong. Unpleasant sexual activity might occur between persons who have little experience engaging in sexual activity (they do not yet know how to do sexual things, or have not yet learned what their likes and dislikes are); their failure to provide pleasure for each other does not mean that they are performing morally wrongful acts.

So the moral evaluation of sexual activity is distinct from the nonmoral evaluation of sexual activity, even if there are sometimes important connections between them. For example, the fact that a sexual act provides pleasure to both participants, and is thereby nonmorally good, might be taken (especially by a metaphysical sexual optimist) as a strong, but only prima facie strong, reason for thinking that the act is morally good or has moral value. (A utilitarian moral philosopher, such as Jeremy Bentham, would say that, in general, the nonmoral goodness of sexual activity goes a long way by itself toward justifying it.) Another example: If one person never attempts to provide sexual pleasure for his or her partner, but selfishly insists on experiencing only his or her own pleasure, that person is behaving in a morally suspicious way. That moral judgment might not rest simply on the fact that he or she did not provide pleasure for the other person—that is, on the fact that the sexual activity was for the other person nonmorally bad. The moral judgment might rest, more precisely, on his or her motives for not providing any pleasure, for not making the experience nonmorally good for the other person.

It is one thing to point out that as evaluative categories, moral goodness/badness is distinct from nonmoral goodness/badness. It is another thing to wonder, nonetheless, about the psychological connections between the moral quality of sexual activity and its nonmoral quality. Perhaps morally good sexual activity tends also to be the most satisfying sexual activity, in the nonmoral sense. Whether that is true likely depends on what we mean by morally "good" sexual acts and on certain features of human moral psychology. What would our lives be like if there were always a neat correspondence between the moral quality of a sexual act and its nonmoral quality? Examples that violate such a neat correspondence are easy to come by. A sexual act might be morally good and nonmorally bad: consider the routine, bland sexual acts of a couple married for ten years ("bedroom death"). Furthermore, a sexual act might be morally bad yet nonmorally good: one spouse in that couple, married for ten years, commits adultery with another married person and finds the sexual activity to be extraordinarily satisfying. A world in which there was little or no discrepancy between the moral quality and the nonmoral quality of sexual activity might be a better world than ours, or it might be a worse world. I would refrain from making such a judgment unless I were pretty sure what the moral goodness and badness of sexual activity amounted to in the first place and until I knew a lot more than I now do about human psychology. Sometimes that a sexual activity is acknowledged to be morally wrong by its participants actually contributes to its being, for them, nonmorally good, that is, sexually exciting. In this sense, the metaphysical sexual pessimists, by issuing moral prohibitions against all sorts of sexual activities, might, ironically, be keeping our sexual lives satisfying.

DANGEROUS SEX

Whether a particular sexual act, or type of sexual act, provides pleasure is not the only factor in judging its nonmoral quality: pragmatic considerations also figure into whether a sexual act, all things considered, has a preponderance of nonmoral goodness or badness. Many sexual activities can be physically or psychologically harmful, risky, or dangerous. Anal coitus, for example, whether carried out by a heterosexual couple or by two gay males, can damage tissues and is a mechanism for the potential transmission of pathogens. The same can of course be said about ordinary heterosexual genital intercourse. Thus, in evaluating whether a sexual act is overall nonmorally good or bad, we must take into account not only its anticipated pleasure but all sorts of negative or undesired side effects: whether the sexual act is likely to damage the body, as in some sadomasochistic acts, or transmit a venereal disease, or result in an unwanted pregnancy, or even whether one might feel regret, anger, or guilt afterward. Note that when we condemn a sexual act morally, we impugn a person's moral character; when we condemn a sexual act on pragmatic grounds, we impugn a person's intelligence or self-control. Is it recklessness or stupidity that leads politicians into sexual liaisons that they cannot really hope to keep secret? All these prudential factors may also figure into the moral evaluation of sexual activity: intentionally causing unwanted pain or discomfort to one's partner, or not taking adequate precautions against the possibility of pregnancy, or not informing one's partner of a suspected case of genital infection, might very well be morally wrong.[12] The metaphysical sexual pessimist will emphasize these problems: we must always be vigilant about the sexual urge, and keep it on a short leash, on account of its power to lead us into disaster. It may not be recklessness or stupidity alone that leads any of us into prudentially dangerous sexual activity. When we experience sexual desire and become sexually aroused, our "brains go out the window," as a Yiddish joke puts it.

SEXUAL PERVERSION

In addition to inquiring about the moral and nonmoral quality of sexual acts, we can also ask whether the act or type is natural or unnatural ("perverted"). Natural sexual acts—to provide a broad definition—are acts that either flow naturally from human sexual nature or do not frustrate, counteract, or interfere with sexual tendencies that flow naturally from human sexual desire. An account of what is natural in human sexuality is part of a philosophical account of human nature in general (or philosophical anthropology), which is a large undertaking.

Evaluating a particular sexual act or type of sexual activity as being natural or unnatural is often distinct from evaluating the act or type either as being morally good/bad or as being nonmorally good/bad. Suppose we assume, for the sake of discussion only, that heterosexual coitus is a natural human sexual activity and that male-male fellatio is not. Even so, it does not follow from the judgment that heterosexual coitus is natural that it is also morally good or right. (Some natural sexual acts might be adulterous or rape.) Nor does it follow that all male-male fellatio is morally bad or wrong (e.g., if engaged in by consenting adults, it might be morally permissible even if, *ex hypothesi* only, it is unnatural). Furthermore, from the judgment that heterosexual coitus is natural, it does not follow that acts of heterosexual coitus are nonmorally good (sexually pleasurable); nor does it follow from the judgment that male-male fellatio is unnatural that it is incapable of producing sexual pleasure for those who engage in it. Of course, both natural and unnatural sexual acts can be medically, psychologically, or socially risky or dangerous. It is nonsense to assume that natural sexual acts are in general less dangerous or risky than unnatural sexual acts. Unprotected heterosexual intercourse (sans condom) is dangerous in ways in which mutual male-male masturbation is not.

Because there are no necessary links between the naturalness of sexuality and its moral and nonmoral quality, why should we wonder about and investigate the sexually unnatural? Many philosophers suggest that we abandon the term "perversion" and hence the concept of the unnatural in talking about sexuality.[13] One reason for continuing to discuss the natural/unnatural distinction is that understanding what is sexually natural may help complete our picture of human nature in general and allows us to understand our species more fully. With such deliberations, human self-reflection (the heart of philosophy) about the human condition becomes more thorough. A second reason is that an account of the sexually natural/unnatural distinction might be useful for the discipline of psychology, if a desire or tendency to engage in unnatural sexual activities is a symptom of underlying mental pathology. (The American Psychiatric Association no longer considers a preference for same-sex sexual activity to be a mental disorder.)[14] A third reason: Even though (un)natural sexual activity is not on that score *alone* morally good or bad, it is still possible to argue that whether a sexual act is (un)natural does contribute, to a greater or lesser extent, to the moral goodness or badness of the act, just as whether a sex act is nonmorally good or bad may be a factor, sometimes an important one, in the morality of the act (although it may also have little or no moral impact at all). Roman Catholic sexual ethics might be unique in claiming that the unnaturalness of a sexual act certainly makes it immoral, and it does so without our having to appeal to any other considerations.

A comparison of the sexual philosophy of the medieval Catholic theologian St. Thomas Aquinas (ca. 1225–1275) with that of the contemporary secular philosophy of Thomas Nagel is, in this matter, instructive. Both Aquinas and Nagel make the innocuous assumptions that what is sexually unnatural is perverted and that what is unnatural in human sexuality is that which does not conform with or is inconsistent with natural human sexuality. But beyond these trivial areas of agreement, there are deep differences between Aquinas and Nagel.

Based partly on a comparison of the sexualities of humans and lower animals (birds and dogs, for example),[15] Aquinas concludes that what is natural in human sexuality is the impulse toward heterosexual coitus, which is the mechanism designed by God to ensure the preservation of animal species, including the human species. Hence engaging in this activity is the primary natural expression of human sexuality. Furthermore, God designed each of the parts of the human body to carry out specific functions and, on Aquinas's view, God designed the male penis to implant or inject sperm into the female's vagina to effect procreation. It follows, for Aquinas, that ejaculation elsewhere than inside a human female's vagina is unnatural: it is a violation of God's sagacious design. For this reason alone, on Aquinas's view, such activities are immoral, a grave offense to the Almighty. Seeking sexual pleasure is permissible, for Aquinas, but only during sexual activities that involve the proper use of the sexual pleasure organs.

Sexual intercourse with lower animals (bestiality), sexual activity with members of one's own sex (homosexuality), and masturbation, for Aquinas, are unnatural sexual acts. They are also immoral (if committed intentionally) exactly because they are unnatural; they disrupt the natural order of the world as created by God and which He commanded to be respected.[16] In none of these activities is there any possibility of procreation, and the sexual organs are used (misused) for purposes other than those for which they were designed. Although Aquinas does not say so explicitly, but only hints in this direction, it follows from his philosophy that fellatio, even when engaged in by a married heterosexual couple, can be unnatural and so morally wrong. At least in those cases in which male orgasm occurs by means of this act, the sperm is not being placed where it should be placed and procreation is therefore not possible.[17] If the penis entering the vagina is the paradigmatic natural act, any other combination of anatomical connections will be unnatural and hence immoral—for example, the penis or a finger entering the anus. Aquinas's criterion of a sexually natural act, that it must be procreative in form or potential, makes no mention of human psychology. His line of thought yields an anatomical or physiological criterion of natural and perverted sexuality that refers only to bodily organs, to where they are, or are not, put in relation to each other, and what they might accomplish as a result.

The contemporary philosopher Thomas Nagel denies Aquinas's presupposition that in order to discover what is natural in human sexuality we should emphasize what is *common* sexually between humans and lower animals.[18] Applying this formula, Aquinas concludes that the purpose of sexual activity and the sexual organs in humans is procreation. Everything else in Aquinas's sexual philosophy follows more or less logically from this. Nagel, by contrast, argues that to discover what is distinctive about natural human sexuality, and hence what is unnatural or perverted, we should focus, instead, on what humans and lower animals do *not* have in common. We should emphasize the ways in which humans are different from animals, the ways in which humans and their sexuality are special. As a result, Nagel argues that human sexual perversion should be understood as a psychological phenomenon rather than, as in Aquinas, an anatomical or physiological phenomenon. For it is human psychology that makes us different from other animals; an account of natural human sexuality must acknowledge the role of human psychology in sexuality.

Nagel proposes that sexual interactions in which each person responds with sexual arousal to noticing the sexual arousal of the other person exhibit the psychology that is natural to human sexuality. In such an encounter, each person becomes aware of himself or herself and the other person as both the subject and the object of their joint sexual experience. I am sexually aroused not only by your physical attractiveness or your touch but also by the fact that you are aroused by me and my touches; we become sexually aroused by recognizing that we are aroused. Nothing as complex as this occurs among the lower animals. Perverted sexual encounters are, on Nagel's view, those in which this mutual recognition of arousal is absent and in which a person remains fully a subject or fully an object of the sexual interaction. Sexual perversion, then, is a departure from or a truncation of a psychologically "complete" pattern of arousal.[19] (On Nagel's view, a person is sexually perverted only if he or she prefers to perform sexually perverted acts.) Nothing in Nagel's psychological account of the natural and perverted refers to bodily organs or physiological processes. For a sexual encounter to be natural, it need not be procreative in form, as long as the requisite psychology of mutual recognition is present. Whether a sexual activity is natural or perverted does not depend, on Nagel's view, on what organs are used or where they are put, but only on the character of its psychology. Thus Nagel disagrees with Aquinas that same-sex sexual activity is unnatural, for homosexual fellatio and anal intercourse can be accompanied by the mutual recognition of and response to the other person's sexual arousal.

Note that Aquinas and Nagel agree about other things; for example, that fetishism is unnatural. But they disagree about the grounds of that evaluation. For Aquinas, masturbating while fondling shoes or undergarments is unnatural because the sperm is not deposited where it should be; the act has no procreative potential. For Nagel, masturbatory fetishism is perverted for a different reason: there is no possibility of a person noticing and being aroused by the arousal of another person. In this example, there is one more difference between these two philosophers: Aquinas would judge the sexual activity of the fetishist to be immoral precisely because it is unnatural, while Nagel would not conclude that it is morally wrong (even though it is unnatural). After all, a fetishistic sexual act can be carried out without harming anyone. The move from a Thomistic moralistic account of sexual perversion to a morality-free psychological account such as Nagel's is one aspect of a more widespread phenomenon: the gradual replacement of religious or moral judgments, about all sorts of deviant behavior, by medical, psychiatric, or psychological judgments and interventions.[20]

A different kind of disagreement with Aquinas is registered by Christine Gudorf, a Christian theologian who otherwise has much in common with Aquinas. Gudorf agrees with Aquinas that the study of anatomy and physiology yields insights into God's design and that human sexual behavior should conform with God's creative intentions. Gudorf's philosophy is squarely within the Thomist or Natural Law tradition. But Gudorf argues that if we take a more careful look at the anatomy and physiology of the female sexual organs, especially the clitoris, instead of focusing exclusively on the sexual role of the male's penis and ejaculate (which is what Aquinas did), we arrive at very different conclusions about God's design. As a result, Christian sexual ethics turns out to be less restrictive. In particular, Gudorf claims that the clitoris is a tissue or organ whose only purpose is to yield sexual pleasure. Unlike the penis, which has three functions (elimination of urine, production of sexual pleasure, insertion of the seed into the vagina), the clitoris has no connection with procreation. Gudorf concludes that the existence of the clitoris in the female body suggests that God intended that the purpose of sexual activity was as much for sexual pleasure *for its own sake* as it was for procreation. Hence, according to Gudorf, pleasurable sexual activity apart from procreation does not violate God's design, is not unnatural, and is not morally wrong, as long as it occurs within a monogamous marriage (even a same-sex monogamous marriage).[21] Gudorf, it seems, is advancing a Christian semi-optimistic sexual metaphysics. Today we are not as confident as Aquinas was that God's design can be discovered by a straightforward examination of human and animal bodies. However, this healthy skepticism about our ability to discern God's intentions and design from the facts of the natural world applies to Gudorf's proposal as well. That the clitoris, through its ability to provide sexual pleasure, plays a role in leading to procreative heterosexual sexual activity, is not obviously false.

DEBATES IN SEXUAL ETHICS: CONSENT

The ethics of sexual behavior, as a branch of applied ethics, is no more and no less contentious than the ethics of anything else. Think of the notorious debates over euthanasia, welfare entitlement, capital punishment, abortion, environmental pollution, and our treatment of animals for food, clothing, entertainment, and scientific research. It should come as no surprise that even though a discussion of sexual ethics might remove some confusions and clarify some of the issues, few final or absolute answers to questions about the morality of sexual activity are likely to be forthcoming from studying the philosophy of sex. Of course, everyone, except the Marquis de Sade, agrees that rape is seriously morally wrong. Yet debates remain even here: What, exactly, is a case of rape? How can its occurrence be reliably identified? And *why* is it wrong? Some ethical systems assert that adultery is morally wrong. But, again, what counts as adultery? Is it merely having lustful thoughts, as claimed by Jesus in Matthew 5:28?

There are several important topics that have received much attention from philosophers of sex. We have already encountered one of them: the dispute between a Natural Law approach to sexual morality and a liberal-secular outlook that denies a connection between what is unnatural and what is immoral. Secular liberal philosophers emphasize the values of autonomous choice and self-determination in arriving at moral judgments about sexual behavior, in contrast to the Thomist tradition that justifies a more restrictive sexual ethics by invoking a divinely imposed scheme to which human action must conform. For a secular-liberal philosopher of sex, rape is the paradigmatically morally wrong sexual act: one person forces himself or herself on another or uses threats to coerce another to engage in sexual activity. By contrast, for the liberal, anything done voluntarily or consensually between two or more people is generally morally permissible. Thus a sexual act is morally wrong only if it is coercive, dishonest, or manipulative. Natural Law theory agrees that the use of coercion (and so forth) makes sexual activity morally wrong. It adds, however, that a sexual act's being unnatural is another, independent reason for condemning it morally, as in masturbation and same-sex sexual activity.[22] The sexual liberal finds nothing morally wrong with either masturbation or same-sex sexual activity. These activities might be unnatural, and perhaps sometimes prudentially unwise, but they can be carried out without harm being done to anyone else or to the participants. Despite the current popularity of secular-liberal sexual ethics, Natural Law is still alive and well among some philosophers of sex, even if the details do not precisely match Aquinas's original version.[23]

When no harm is done to third parties (nonparticipants), is the free and informed consent of the people who together engage in sexual activity necessary and sufficient for making their interaction morally permissible? The Natural Law tradition denies that consent is sufficient; to willingly, voluntarily engage in unnatural sexual acts is (still) morally wrong. Natural Law is not alone in reducing the moral significance of consent. Sexual activity between two persons might be harmful to one or both participants, as in some sadomasochism, and a moral paternalist or perfectionist might claim that it is wrong for one person to harm another, or for the latter to allow the former to engage in harmful behavior, even when both persons provide free and informed consent to their joint activity. Consent, on this view, is not sufficient, even if the participants in, say, sadomasochism, deny that they are really being harmed or causing harm. Philosophers who claim that only in a committed relationship or marriage is sexual activity between two people morally permissible also deny that free and informed consent is sufficient. The consent of both parties may be a necessary condition for the moral goodness of their sexual activity, but in the absence of some other magical ingredient (love, marriage, devotion, and the like) their sexual activity remains mere mutual use or objectification and hence is morally objectionable.

About casual sex, for example, it might be said that two people are merely using each other for their own separate sexual pleasure; even when genuinely consensual, these mutual sexual uses do not yield a virtuous sexual act.[24] Kant and Karol Wojtyla (Pope John Paul II) take this position: willingly allowing oneself to be used sexually by another person makes an object of oneself. Hence mutual consent is not sufficient for the moral rightness of sexual acts. For Kant, sexual activity avoids treating a person merely as a means only in marriage, because in such a state both persons have surrendered their bodies and souls to each other.[25] For Wojtyla, "only love can preclude the use of one person by another," because love is a unification of persons resulting from a mutual gift of their selves.[26] Note, however, that the thought that a unifying love is the ingredient that justifies (beyond consent) sexual activity has an interesting implication: gay and lesbian sexual relations would be permissible if they occur within homosexual marriages that are loving, committed, and monogamous. At this point, defenders of the view that sexual activity is justifiable only in marriage commonly appeal to Natural Law to rule out same-sex marriage. "God made Adam and Eve, not Adam and Steve," goes the slogan.

On another view of these matters, if sexual activity is carried out voluntarily by all persons involved (assuming no harm to third parties), the sexual activity is morally permissible. In defending the sufficiency of free and informed consent for the moral goodness of sexual activity, Thomas Mappes writes that "respect for persons entails that each of us recognize the rightful authority of other persons (as rational beings) to conduct their individual lives as they see fit."[27] Allowing the other person's consent to control when the other engages in sexual activity with me is to respect that person by taking seriously his or her autonomy, his or her ability to reason and make choices, while not to allow the other to make the decision about when to engage in sexual activity with me is disrespectful. According to such a view of the power of consent, there can be no moral objection in principle to casual sexual activity, to sexual activity with strangers, to promiscuous sexual behavior, or to sexual activity involving "monstrous techniques" or unusual organs and apertures, as long as the participants genuinely agree to engage in their chosen sexual acts.

Even if Mappes's consent criterion is correct, difficult questions remain. How *specific* must consent be? When one person agrees vaguely, and in the heat of the sexual moment, with another person, "yes, let's have sex," has the speaker consented to every type of sexual caress or coital position the other person has in mind? How *explicit* must consent be? Can consent be reliably implied by involuntarily behavior (moans, for example), and do nonverbal cues (erection, lubrication, insistent tongue-kissing) decisively show that another person has consented to sex? Some insist that consent must be exceedingly specific as to the sexual acts to be carried out, and some would permit only explicit verbal consent, denying that body language can do an adequate job of expressing desires and intentions.[28]

Another debate concerns the meaning of "free" (or "voluntary") in the expression "free and informed consent." Whether consent is only necessary for the moral goodness of sexual activity, or also sufficient, any principle that relies on consent to make moral judgments assumes a clear understanding of the voluntary nature of consent. Participation in sexual activity ought not to be physically forced on one person by another. But this obvious and imprecise truth leaves matters wide open. The philosopher Onora O'Neill, for example, believes that much casual sex is morally wrong because the consent it involves is not likely to be sufficiently voluntary, in light of subtle pressures people commonly put on each other to engage in sexual activity. On her view, these people who engage in casual sex are merely using each other, not treating each other with respect as persons in a Kantian sense.[29] We might want to go further than O'Neill and claim that if she is right that in casual sex the genuineness of consent is doubtful, then this casual sex is (acquaintance) rape.[30]

One moral ideal is that genuinely voluntary participation in sexual activity requires not a hint of coercion or pressure of any sort.[31] Because engaging in sexual activity can be risky or dangerous in many ways (physically, psychologically, or socially), we would like to be sure, according to this moral ideal, that anyone who engages in sexual activity does so with perfectly voluntarily and informed consent. Some philosophers have argued that this ideal can be realized only when there is substantial economic and social equality between the persons involved in a given sexual encounter. For example, a society that exhibits disparities in income or wealth is one in which some people will be exposed to economic coercion. If some groups of people (women and members of ethnic minorities, in particular) have less economic and social power than others, members of these groups will be exposed to sexual coercion, among other kinds.

One immediate application of this thought is that prostitution, which to many sexual liberals is a business bargain made by a provider of sexual services and a client and is largely characterized by adequately free and informed consent, may be morally wrong, if the economic situation of the prostitute acts as a kind of pressure that negates the voluntary nature of his or her participation in the transaction. Furthermore, women who have children and who are dependent economically on their husbands may find themselves in the position of having to engage in sexual activity whether they want to or not, for fear of being abandoned; these women, too, may not be engaging in sexual activity fully voluntarily. The woman who allows herself to be nagged into sex by her husband worries that if she says "no" too often, she will suffer economically, if not also physically and psychologically.[32]

The view that the presence of any kind of pressure is coercive and negates the voluntary nature of participation in sexual activity, and hence is morally objectionable, has been expressed by, among others, Charlene Muehlenhard and Jennifer Schrag.[33] They list—to provide only two of their examples—"status coercion" (women are coerced into sexual activity or marriage by a man's occupation) and "discrimination against lesbians" (which compels women into having sexual relationships only with men) as forms of coercion that undermine the voluntary nature of partici-pation by women in sexual activity with men. But depending on the kind of case we have in mind, it might be more accurate to say either that some pressures are not coercive and do not appreciably undermine voluntari-ness or that some pressures are coercive but are nevertheless not morally objectionable. Is it true that the presence of any kind of pressure put on one person by another amounts to coercion that negates the voluntary nature of consent, so that any subsequent sexual activity is morally wrong? I wonder whether a woman who says to her husband, "Buy me that mink coat or you will sleep on the couch for a month," is engaging in any objectionable behavior.

DEBATES IN SEXUAL ETHICS: BEYOND CONSENT

Consent has loomed large in debates in sexual ethics, and rightly so. Note that its importance goes beyond act evaluation and enters into the evalu-ation of practices, such as BDSM, pedophilia, zoophilia, prostitution, par-ticipating in pornography (e.g., being a porn star), and promiscuity. While one criterion of evaluation would surely be the social effects that a widespread practice of, say, BDSM, might have, another crucial criterion in evaluating such practices is consent. Indeed, if the parties to the prac-tice tend to be coerced into it, the social effects of the practice, no matter how good, would diminish by comparison.

Granted the importance of consent, a plethora of other ethical aspects remain in need of discussion. Some have already been mentioned: the harm that might result to the parties to the act or practice or to third parties from the activity. For instance, one can argue that people with racial desires for members of other racial groups harm the latter by fos-tering in them doubts and anxieties about why the former are with them.[34] There is no issue with consent here: all parties to the relationship consent, yet, if the argument is sound, the harm still occurs.

An entirely different set of ethical questions concerns the idea of liv-ing well, of flourishing: Do some sexual practices allow one to live a good life, not in the sense that they make the person less sexually frustrated and thus able to pursue one's projects unhindered, but in the sense that their presence is a positive contribution to that life? And would this posi-tive contribution be a universal thing that any person can benefit from, or would it depend on the person's preferences in lifestyle? It is crucial not to confuse two things. Suppose that William has a fetish for shoes. He likes to smell or fondle them as he masturbates or as he has sex with someone else. Smelling or fondling shoes enhances William's pleasure and satisfies his sexual fantasies (remember that because many people are probably "weirded out" by this desire, fulfilling it is hard for William, which in turn converts it into a fantasy for him). Suppose that he finds a group of like-minded people on an Internet website and he is able to satisfy his desire on a regular basis. This no doubt contributes positively to William's happiness, thereby making his life, everything else being equal, better.

But if William's desires for shoes are like others' sexual preferences, not satisfying them (at least on a regular basis) is not likely to put a serious dent in William's life. He can continue to have quite satisfying shoe-less sex, even if he would have preferred shoe-full sex. The point is that although a sexual life with shoes is likely to make William's life better, this better-ness is not so deep as to merit the description that "smelling or fondling shoes during sex allows William to flourish."

Well, which practice would? Consider polyamory as an example.[35] If, as most would agree, love is important to us, and if, as many would agree, we are not sexually monogamous by nature, it behooves us, or some people at least, to cultivate relationships that preserve both love and sexual variety. This can be done by having monogamous love, yet non-monogamous sex ("open relationships"), or by having multiple lovers simultaneously. Either of these would allow the partners to love one another, to increase their sources of love and support to more than one partner, to trust one another, to let go of unhealthy forms of jealousy, and to enjoy sexual variety. These values deeply enhance a life. Moreover, on the way to that life, partners would need to develop particular character traits that would help them get there: courage, fairness, trust (especially the trust needed to get one to being comfortable with one's partners), and fortitude, among others. None of them of course guarantees a flourishing life, but then again nothing really can.

There is the further interesting and connected question as to whether such a life is desirable for everyone or only for those who desire it. Although it is tempting to argue for the latter for obvious reasons, arguing for the former is more interesting. If we all need love, if it is better for us to get love from multiple sources (so if we lose one source we are not left bereft), and if we all enjoy sexual variety (how *much* sexual variety would be a personal preference), then a case can be made that polyamory is an ideal to which we must aspire. Those who say, "It is not my thing," might be squeamish or in the grip of social and cultural ways that have affected them so deeply that their very desires revolt at the idea. The point is not that this argument is sound, but that it goes in the direction of where the tough and rich issues are. It also leads to the question of which criteria to use to decide whether a life-enhancing sexual practice is life-enhancing for all or for some.

There is also the flip side: Which sexual practices detract from or even block flourishing and why? Might pedophilia or zoophilia prevent one from flourishing? Might they make someone's life worse? The issue is not making a life worse because the person gets caught, feels shame, or is shunned by society, although these are important factors. The issue is whether there is something about such practices that negatively affects the person's character or, more poetically, erodes his or her soul: they might cause the agent to come to have (or to entrench) vices that no person with a good life would have, such as intemperance, cruelty, injustice, and insensitivity. BDSM is an interesting case here, because even though many of its forms seem harmless in this respect and might even help the practitioners build virtues given the amount of trust they need (trust), the social condemnation they unjustly face (courage, fairness), and the self-exploration that they require (wisdom, courage),[36] other forms of BDSM might be problematic: being another's slave or tethered to a leash for a few days, despite the consent, could have negative effects on the character of the practitioner. These issues bear further exploration, philosophically and empirically.

BDSM, though not only BDSM, raises another crucial issue—namely, the question of character and its connection to fantasy. Some BDSM scenes (as they are called) involve role play that might be considered morally problematic: a white man playing the role of a Nazi officer and "raping" a woman who plays the role of a Jew, or a white man playing a slave master with a black woman playing the slave. Even though the parties to the act consent to it (as many writers on BDSM emphasize), the question remains as to whether something is defective with their characters. Many would claim that there is something morally wrong with the character of a man who has rape fantasies even if he never acts on his desires (or is not tempted to act on them, even reacting with horror at the thought of acting on them), so why not believe the same about those BDSM practitioners who play such seemingly compromised moral personas? Put slightly differently, people who sexually desire such acts seem to be defective because their desires are defective, and having defective desires is having, to that extent, a defective character.

Questions about the character of a person with morally suspicious desires apply to people other than BDSM practitioners. For instance, people who desire members of other races or ethnic groups are often thought of as racist or morally defective in some way because of stereotypes that they have or because they "exoticize" members of the races they desire.[37] Pedophiles, zoophiles, necrophiliacs, and others also raise similar questions.

It would be philosophically impoverished to address these questions without looking into another crucial theme, that of fantasy. This is not just because of the intimate connection between fantasy and sexual desire but also because in the case of the above-mentioned controversial desires, fantasy is key in seeing how they might not be as morally compromised as some believe. Consider a BDSM practitioner who plays the role of a "rapist" but who in every other aspect of his life is a decent fellow. His desires for "rape" might be special forms of desire: desires to engage in simulations of rape, not rape itself.[38] If true, then at least some BDSM desires get off the immoral hook. But not all such desires are for simulations: perhaps some BDSM practitioners desire to embody (temporarily) the persona of a rapist, and they desire this very embodiment, in which case their desire is not for simulation but for an action that is as close as possible to the real thing, delimited by some moral considerations (e.g., consent). Moreover, many non-BDSM practitioners have such desires: What to say about someone who masturbates while fantasizing about sex with young boys? What to say about the man with the rape fantasies?

Fantasy is key here because it works in interesting ways. It often inhabits a region of its own in our psyches: it surfaces when someone is feeling sexual, and then recedes to its isolation once the sexual desire is satisfied (or something else happens to distract the agent). Moreover, the content of such fantasies might not extend to the actual sexual acts of the person with other people, if the person understands that the fantasies are problematic and should not be acted on, or if they conflict with other ideals the person has (e.g., being a feminist). But there are gradations between characters. For instance, people's sexual fantasies can be confined to their own psychic regions with no strong pull on their agents outside the duration of the fantasy, they can exercise a strong pull on some people almost constantly, with some resisting this pull while others not resisting. Moral psychology and empirical studies are needed to help distinguish the various forms of character.

No proper discussion of sexual desire and pleasure can be complete without discussing the notions of character, fantasy, beliefs, virtues, vices, and the ethics of the person. Whether dealing with a pedophile, a BDSM practitioner, a person with racial desires, or someone with rape fantasies, to give a few examples from across the moral spectrum, questions about the agent's desires, beliefs, fantasies, their inter-connections, the role that they play in the person's psyche, and their connections to the agent's other character traits, form an important network of themes that any philosophy of sex worthy of its name must investigate.

We might tie the above points together by looking into a topic that has yet to be given its proper due: sexual tastes and preferences and their connection to moral ideals or obligations. Except perhaps for asexual people, all people have sexual preferences, ranging from basic ones, such as sexual orientations, to less basic (yet hefty) preferences, such as for young people or members of a specific race or ethnic group, to mere preferences (for blondes, particular sexual positions, specific body parts, length of hair, and so forth). The question is whether people have obligations or should aspire to vary, as much as possible, their sexual preferences and tastes. Some such obligations are moral: to shed, say, problematic preferences or to cultivate more democratic ones, especially in a world deeply divided by a history of racism and oppression. A person with pedophiliac desires should try to get rid of them. A person who has no sexual preferences for members of a particular group might also have to try to change that, though whether the reasons are morally obligatory remains to be seen. Even with sexual orientation we should ask whether it behooves humanity to move toward the ideal of some kind of poly-sexuality, a state in which we desire all genders, trans or cis. The reasons for such changes might well be moral: one can argue that even though we have no moral *obligations*, we do have strong moral reasons to change: to move away from a history of racism, sexism, and homophobia that has probably helped entrench these divides in our orientations and basic preferences. Here, of course, conceptual work in the areas of sexual orien-tation and gender identity (how to understand and define them, say) is important on its own but also needed for the evaluative investigation.

There are, of course, pragmatic reasons: being more flexible in one's preferences means more options for one, which in turn means more ease in the satisfaction of one's sexual desires. More important, though per-haps more obscure, there might be aesthetic reasons: people are often urged to develop their tastes in wine, food, clothing, art, and a bevy of other kinds of objects. Why not improve their sexual tastes? Here a pleth-ora of issues comes up: What does it mean to improve one's sexual tastes? We distinguish between high and low art (not to be confused with good and bad art), between high cuisine and low cuisine, and so forth. Are there sexual counterparts to these distinctions? Some traditions have ele-vated sexual activity to a skill or an art—might this correspond to high and low ways of having sex? Are there such distinctions among the ob-jects of sexual desire? Would developing our sexual taste for people not normally considered attractive be a desirable goal? For aesthetic or moral reasons or both? Or does sexuality consist of its own ideals, such that developing sexual taste is subsumed under neither the aesthetic nor the moral, but under its own category?

The fact that the above discussion is housed in questions instead of assertions indicates how little work has been done in this area, and how philosophy of sex and aesthetics (not just ethics) need to be in dialogue. Of course, as soon as we discuss character and development of character we encounter the issue of responsibility and the extent to which we, individually, are responsible for the sexual preferences and tastes that we have, and the extent to which we have direct and indirect control over them. It seems hard to deny that one can develop a sexual taste for mem-bers of a racial group were one not to have this desire already. But it seems harder to say the same about developing sexual preferences for members of the gender one does not desire or for people who are not sexually attractive because of their age, physical deformities, and so forth. Preferences for the latter groups might change, but they might change as a result of cultural shifts and over time (assuming that our biology does not play a strong role here), not as a result of individual efforts (at least in general).

CONCLUDING REMARKS

This chapter did not introduce the reader to the different claims and arguments made in the individual essays of this book (though it touched on some), but to the different themes of the field of the philosophy of sex. It shows that the field is rife with important topics, old and new, that are still in need of further research. Once we remember that analytic philosophy, as valuable as it is, can be combined with a continental approach, especially queer theory (as we hope two of the essays in this book demonstrate), we see how vast, deep, and promising the field is, with plenty of opportunities for further scholarship.[39]

NOTES

1. The writers, philosophies, and topics mentioned or discussed in this essay are covered in Alan Soble, ed., *Sex from Plato to Paglia: A Philosophical Encyclopedia* (Westport, Conn.: Greenwood Press, 2006). See also Alan Soble, *The Philosophy of Sex and Love*, 2nd ed. (St. Paul, Minn.: Paragon House, 2008) and Raja Halwani, *Philosophy of Love, Sex, and Marriage* (New York: Routledge, 2010).

2. There might be general differences among people relating to age, gender, and other such factors—not to mention different individual preferences—which we need to set aside.

3. The third point indicates that Goldman might be mistaken to think of sexual desire as "plain" as he thought, which in turn might show that he is mistaken that sex is not a "cornerstone of value," though how this cornerstone is to be understood is unclear.

4. A comparison with our experiences with art is instructive here, inasmuch as art also affords us moments of pleasure, regardless of how highly we think of art's value in general or how important a role we believe that it plays cognitively, historically, or morally.

5. Immanuel Kant, *Lectures on Ethics*, trans. Louis Infield (New York: Harper and Row, 1963), 163. Kant, I think, uses the phrase "loved person" euphemistically, the way we sometimes use "make love" euphemistically for "have sex."

6. Augustine, *The City of God*, vol. 2, trans. John Healey (London: J. M. Dent, 1945), bk. 14, sec. 23.

7. Immanuel Kant, *The Metaphysics of Morals*, trans. Mary Gregor (Cambridge: Cambridge University Press, 1996), 62.

8. Augustine, *On Marriage and Concupiscence*, in *The Works of Aurelius Augustine, Bishop of Hippo*, vol. 12, ed. Marcus Dods (Edinburgh, Scot.: T. & T. Clark, 1874), bk. 1, chap. 9.

9. See Russell Vannoy's defense of the value of sexual activity for its own sake, in *Sex Without Love: A Philosophical Exploration* (Buffalo, N.Y.: Prometheus, 1980).

10. Irving Singer, *The Nature of Love*, vol. 2: *Courtly and Romantic* (Chicago: University of Chicago Press, 1984), 382. As we leave the metaphysics of sexuality, I must acknowledge my debt to Murray Davis, *Smut: Erotic Reality/Obscene Ideology* (Chicago: University of Chicago Press, 1983). I recommend the book for those who wish to learn more (and better) about the metaphysics of sex.

11. Raymond Belliotti, *Good Sex: Perspectives on Sexual Ethics* (Lawrence, Kans.: University Press of Kansas, 1993), 210. For a brief review of *Good Sex*, see Alan Soble, "Book Note," *Ethics* 105:2 (1995), 447–48.

12. The philosopher David Mayo argues that we do not necessarily have a moral obligation to reveal our HIV status to potential sexual partners. See his provocative

essay "An Obligation to Warn of HIV Infection?" in Alan Soble, ed., *Sex, Love and Friendship* (Amsterdam: Rodopi, 1997), 447–53.

13. Michael Slote argues that "sexual perversion" is an "inapplicable concept" ("Inapplicable Concepts and Sexual Perversion," in *Philosophy and Sex*, 1st edition, Robert Baker and Frederick Elliston, eds. [Buffalo, N.Y.: Prometheus, 1975], 261–67, at 266); Graham Priest also calls it "inapplicable" and adds that "the notion of sexual perversion makes no sense" any longer ("Sexual Perversion," *Australasian Journal of Philosophy* 75:3 [1997], 360–72, at 370–71); Igor Primoratz thinks that "sexual perversion" is "a concept best discarded" (*Ethics and Sex* [London: Routledge, 1999], 63–66); Linda LeMoncheck wants to replace "sexual perversion" with "sexual difference" (*Loose Women, Lecherous Men: A Feminist Philosophy of Sex* [New York: Oxford University Press, 1997], 72, 80, 82–83); and Robert Gray submits that "sexual perversion" should "be dropped from our sexual vocabulary altogether" ("Sex and Sexual Perversion," *Journal of Philosophy* 75:4 [1978]: 189–99, at 199 [82 in this volume]).

14. See the *Diagnostic and Statistical Manual of Mental Disorders*, 4th edition (Washington, D.C.: American Psychiatric Association, 1994), 493–538. For discussion of how "sexual disorder" is handled in the *DSM*, see Alan Soble, "Paraphilia and Distress in *DSM-IV*," in *The Philosophy of Psychiatry: A Companion*, edited by Jennifer Radden (New York: Oxford University Press), 54–63.

15. Aquinas found the analogy between birds and humans with respect to monogamy to be illuminating. See his *Summa contra gentiles*, III/2: 122.8, 123.2; and *Summa theologiae*, IIa–IIae: 154.2. By the way, the Hebrew view of sexual perversion is not far from Aquinas's. See Louis M. Epstein, *Sex Laws and Customs in Judaism* (New York: Ktav, 1948), chap. 5.

16. Aquinas, *Summa theologiae*, IIa–IIae: 153–54.

17. Aquinas condemns heterosexual sexual acts in which "the natural style of intercourse is not observed, as regards the proper organ or according to rather beastly and monstrous techniques" (IIa–IIae: 154.11). I believe that he is referring to heterosexual oral-genital, genital-anal, and oral-anal sexual acts. Depending on the theological leanings of your corner clergyman, these acts may be prohibited, or they may be forgiven or even allowed as foreplay—that is, as acts (just like kissing and caressing) that lead to and culminate in heterosexual coitus. For example, St. Paul's idea in 1 Cor 7:4, that the central, even only, purpose of marital sexual activity is as a "remedy against sin"— in other words, to provide sexual satisfaction so that neither spouse has any motive or inclination to commit adultery—might be interpreted as blessing the unnatural heterosexual acts that Aquinas condemns. Maximizing the sexual satisfaction of the spouses might require, say, oral-genital sexual activity, and thus these acts serve well as a remedy against sin. See Alan Soble, *Sexual Investigations* (New York: New York University Press, 1996), 8. One student of mine replied to this "theory of acceptable unnatural acts" by quipping: A married Catholic couple may engage in anal intercourse as long as it is followed by ejaculatory vaginal intercourse (and the penis is washed in between).

18. On the advantages and pitfalls of employing an animal model to understand human sexuality, see Jeffrey Hershfield, "Animal Sexuality," in Soble, *Sex from Plato to Paglia*, 45–50.

19. See Thomas Nagel's "Sexual Perversion," in this volume, and Soble, *The Philosophy of Sex and Love*, 78–82.

20. See Soble, *Sexual Investigations*, chap. 4; and Peter Conrad and Joseph W. Schneider, *Deviance and Medicalization: From Badness to Sickness* (St. Louis, Mo.: C. V. Mosby, 1980), especially "Homosexuality: From Sin to Sickness to Life-Style," 172–214.

21. Christine Gudorf, *Sex, Body, and Pleasure: Reconstructing Christian Sexual Ethics* (Cleveland, Ohio: Pilgrim Press, 1994), 65. For another Christian defense of same-sex marriage, see Patricia Jung and Ralph Smith, *Heterosexism: An Ethical Challenge* (Albany, N.Y.: State University of New York Press, 1993).

22. Kant also held that masturbation "is abuse of the sexual faculty. . . . By it man sets aside his person and degrades himself below the level of animals. . . . Intercourse

between *sexus homogenii* . . . too is contrary to the ends of humanity" (*Lectures on Ethics*, 170).

23. See, for example, John Finnis, "Law, Morality, and 'Sexual Orientation,'" *Notre Dame Law Review* 69:5 (1994), 1049–76.

24. On the morality of casual sex, in particular, see Raja Halwani's essay "Casual Sex, Promiscuity, and Objectification," in this volume. See also, in this volume, the essays by Alan Goldman and Thomas Mappes.

25. For the details, see Alan Soble, "Sexual Use," in this volume.

26. Karol Wojtyla (Pope John Paul II), *Love and Responsibility* (New York: Farrar, Straus and Giroux, 1981), 30.

27. "Sexual Morality and the Concept of Using Another Person," in this volume (274). Also defending the sufficiency of consent is Bernard Baumrin's "Sexual Immorality Delineated," in *Philosophy and Sex*, 2nd ed., edited by Robert Baker and Frederick Elliston (Buffalo, N.Y.: Prometheus, 1984), 300–311; and Igor Primoratz, "Sexual Morality: Is Consent Enough?" *Ethical Theory and Moral Practice* 4:3 (2001), 201–18. An important essay arguing against the sufficiency of consent is Seiriol Morgan's "Dark Desires," *Ethical Theory and Moral Practice* 6:4 (2003), 377–410 (reproduced in this volume). See also Morgan's discussion of Alan Goldman in "Sex in the Head," *Journal of Applied Philosophy* 20:1 (2003), 1–16, reprinted in *The Philosophy of Sex*, 6th ed., edited by Nicholas Power, Raja Halwani, and Alan Soble (Lanham, Md.: Rowman & Littlefield, 2013), 101–22.

28. See Alan Soble, "Antioch's 'Sexual Offense Policy': A Philosophical Exploration,"*Journal of Social Philosophy* 28:1 (1997), 22–36, reprinted, revised, in Alan Soble, ed., *Philosophy of Sex*, 4th edition (323–40), and Soble and Powers, eds., *Philosophy of Sex*, 5th edition (459–77). For criticisms, see Eva Feder Kittay, "Ah! My Foolish Heart," in Soble and Powers, eds., *Philosophy of Sex*, 5th edition (479–87).

29. Onora O'Neill, "Between Consenting Adults," in her *Constructions of Reason: Explorations of Kant's Practical Philosophy* (Cambridge: Cambridge University Press, 1989), 105–25.

30. On date rape, see Lois Pineau, "Date Rape: A Feminist Analysis," *Law and Philosophy* 8:2 (1989), 217–43, reprinted in Nicholas Power, Raja Halwani, and Alan Soble, eds., *Philosophy of Sex*, 6th edition, 461–83.

31. See Alan Soble, "Ethics, Sexual," in *Sex from Plato to Paglia*, 273–79.

32. See also the points made by Robin West, "The Harms of Consensual Sex," in this volume.

33. Charlene Muehlenhard and Jennifer Schrag, "Nonviolent Sexual Coercion," in *Acquaintance Rape: The Hidden Crime*, edited by Andrea Parrot and Laurie Bechhofer (New York: John Wiley, 1991), 115–28. In this context, read Alan Wertheimer, "Consent and Sexual Relations," in this volume.

34. See Robin Zheng, "Why Yellow Fever Isn't Flattering: A Case Against Racial Fetishes" (*Journal of the American Philosophical Association* 2:3 [2016], 400–419. For criticism of her view, see note 1 in Raja Halwani's "Racial Sexual Desires" in this volume.

35. It is unclear whether "polyamory" refers (or should refer) to simultaneous multiple loves, simultaneous multiple sexual partners, or both (see Elizabeth Brake's "Is 'Loving More' Better? The Values of Polyamory" in this volume). It probably refers (or should refer) to both, going just by the name.

36. See Shaun Miller's "BDSM" in this volume.

37. For discussion, see Halwani, "Racial Sexual Desires."

38. See Patrick D. Hopkins, "Rethinking Sadomasochism: Feminism, Interpretation, and Simulation," *Hypatia* 9:1 (1994), 116–24, reprinted in Soble, ed., *Philosophy of Sex*, 3rd edition, 189–24.

39. For additional introductory material on the topics of this essay, see Alan Soble's "Philosophy of Sexuality," *Internet Encyclopedia of Philosophy*, edited by James Fieser (http://www.iep.utm.edu/sexualit/); "Sexuality and Sexual Ethics," *Encyclopedia of Ethics*, 2nd ed. (New York: Routledge, 2001), 1570–77; "Sexuality, Philosophy of," *Routledge Encyclopedia of Philosophy*, edited by Edward Craig (London: Routledge, 1998),

vol. 8, 717–30; and "Philosophy of Sex," *Encyclopedia of Philosophy*, 2nd ed., edited by
Donald Borchert (Detroit: Macmillan/Thomson, 2006), vol. 7, 521–32. See also Raja
Halwani's *Philosophy of Love, Sex, and Marriage: An Introduction* (New York: Routledge,
2010).

STUDY QUESTIONS

1. What are some of the thematic differences between metaphysical
   sexual optimism and metaphysical sexual pessimism? Which position do you think is right or more accurate? Can you provide convincing reasons for your choice?
2. How could it be decided whether specific sexual desires and sexual acts are natural or unnatural? If a sexual desire or a sexual act is
   unnatural (i.e., contravenes human sexual nature), is that fact always, often, not often, or never an important consideration in judging whether the desire or the act is morally wrong? See how deeply
   you can go in defending your answer.
3. How could we decide whether a particular sexual act has been
   performed with the full consent of both (or all) parties or has,
   instead, occurred because one party has been coerced? Is this, however, a false dilemma? That is, does the presence of coercion always mean that the act was not performed with consent, and does
   the absence of coercion always mean that the act was done consensually? Try to think of situations (analogous to the sexual) in which
   we coerce or put pressure on people to do things they prefer not to
   do, and yet our exerting pressure is not morally wrong.
4. Discuss to what extent and in what ways the nonmoral and pragmatic evaluations of sexual acts make a difference in evaluating
   them morally. If these evaluations do make a difference, and do so
   frequently, what might this mean about the difficulty of arriving at
   sound judgments in sexual ethics? Should we conclude that to be
   morally safe, we should never engage in sexual activity unless every single moral and nonmoral consideration points in its favor?
5. Does the marital status, age, gender, species, race, or ethnicity of
   one's sexual partner (or of oneself) make a difference to the morality of sexual acts carried out with that partner? Why or why not?
   What other features of potential partners might be added to this
   list? Their physical attractiveness? Their income? Certain features
   of their biography?
6. In a legal case decided by the U.S. Supreme Court (*Rose v. Locke*,
   423 U.S. 48 [1975]), the defendant was accused of forcing a woman,
   at knife point, "to submit to his twice performing cunnilingus
   upon her." What are the analytic criteria for individuating and
   counting sexual acts, such that it is possible, and makes sense to
   say, that X performed cunnilingus once, twice, or N times on an-

other person? Similarly, suppose that a man ties up a woman and proceeds to rape her—in other words, has penis–vagina intercourse with her without her consent and against her will. He stops for a while, going to the bathroom and then the kitchen, and afterward again has penis–vagina intercourse with her. Has the woman been raped once or twice? In the *Rose* case, the defendant was not charged with rape but only violating a Tennessee "crimes against nature" statute (by now, more than forty years later, abandoned). Did he commit an unnatural act? Should unnatural acts be illegal? Can you surmise why he was not charged with rape?

7. Should people develop their sexual preferences and tastes to include as many people as possible, and from as many categories (cultural, racial, age, gender, class, etc.) as possible? Why? And what type of "should" would be at stake—moral, aesthetic, pragmatic, or something else?

8. What do you think of the analogy between eating food and engaging in sexual activity? In what ways are hunger and sexual desire, or eating and having sex, similar to each other? In what ways are they not? Try to understand your answers in terms of the difference between pessimistic and optimistic metaphysical philosophies of sex, and in terms of the contribution that sexual desire and pleasure make to a well-lived life.

9. Is there something ethically defective about someone who has morally problematic fantasies but who does not act on them? Or should the realm of fantasy be immune from the scrutiny of morality? Why?

TWO

Are We Having Sex Now or What?

Greta Christina

Though sex, and the philosophy of sex, are often serious if not solemn affairs, it pays to approach them with a sense of humor, as **Greta Christina** *demonstrates. The philosophical topic at hand is what it is for a sexual act or encounter to be sexual (views about how to define "sex" properly are implicated in many issues, for example, in defining "rape" and "sexual harassment"). While laying out commonsensical definitions of "sexual activity" (say, that it must include penis-in-vagina coitus; that it requires that the participants be naked; that it involves sexual pleasure for all concerned), Christina reveals counterexamples, often from her own experience. This reflective exercise might lead us to be, as Christina is, skeptical about ever finding a final definition of "sexual activity." Her essay has the virtue of forcing us to ask the analytic question and to realize that everyday understandings of "sex" are not very satisfying. Christina's essay was reprinted by the magazine* Ms. *in its 1995 "Feminism and Sex" issue (November/December, 60–62). The essay's last two paragraphs are missing from that version, and there is no editorial warning that the essay was abridged. Those paragraphs, included here, are perhaps the most provocative in her essay: Christina admits to finding some sadomasochism "tremendously erotic," and she relates that when working as a nude dancer inside a peep show booth she had a "fabulous time" with one of her quarter-laden customers. These examples of "sex" are valuable to think about, both conceptually and normatively.*

Greta Christina's recent work includes the books *Comforting Thoughts About Death That Have Nothing to Do with God* (2015); *Coming Out Atheist: How to Do It, How to Help Each Other, and Why* (2014); and *Why Are You Atheists So Angry? 99 Things That Piss Off the Godless* (2012). She is also the author of *Bending*, an erotic novella published as part of a three-novella collection, *Three Kinds of Asking for It* (edited by Susie Bright, 2005), and has edited the eminently wise and good-natured *Paying for It: A Guide by Sex Workers for Their Clients* (2004). She blogs at http://freethoughtblogs.com/greta. Her website is http://gretachristina. com. A wonderful *Wikipedia* entry about Greta can be found at https://en.wikipedia.org/wiki/Greta_Christina.

This essay originally appeared in David Steinberg's anthology, *The Erotic Impulse: Honoring the Sensual Self* (New York: Tarcher/Penguin, 1992), 24–29. It is reprinted here with the permission of Greta Christina.

When I first started having sex with other people, I used to like to count them. I wanted to keep track of how many there had been. It was a source of some kind of pride, or identity anyway, to know how many people I'd had sex with in my lifetime. So, in my mind, Len was number one, Chris was number two, that slimy awful little heavy metal barbiturate addict whose name I can't remember was number three, Alan was number four, and so on. It got to the point that, when I'd start having sex with a new person for the first time, when he first entered my body (I was only having sex with men at the time), what would flash through my head wouldn't be "Oh, baby, baby, you feel so good inside me," or "What the hell am I doing with this creep?" or "This is boring, I wonder what's on TV." What flashed through my head was "Seven!"

Doing this had some interesting results. I'd look for patterns in the numbers. I had a theory for a while that every fourth lover turned out to be really great in bed, and I would ponder what the cosmic significance of the phenomenon might be. Sometimes I'd try to determine what kind of person I was by how many people I'd had sex with. At eighteen, I'd had sex with ten different people. Did that make me normal, repressed, a total slut, a free-spirited bohemian, or what? Not that I compared my numbers with anyone else's. It was my own exclusive structure, a game I played in the privacy of my own head.

Then the numbers started getting a little larger, as numbers tend to do, and keeping track became more difficult. I'd remember that the last one was *seventeen* and so this one must be *eighteen*, and then I'd start having doubts about whether I'd been keeping score accurately. I'd lie awake at night thinking to myself, well, there was Brad, and there was that guy on my birthday, and there was David and . . . no, wait, I forgot that guy I got drunk with at the social my first week at college . . . so that's seven, eight, nine . . . and by two in the morning I'd finally have it figured out. But there was always a nagging suspicion that maybe I'd missed someone, some dreadful tacky little scumball that I was trying to forget about having invited inside my body. And as much as I maybe wanted to forget about the sleazy little scumball, I wanted more to get that number right.

It kept getting harder, though. I began to question what counted as sex and what didn't. There was that time with Gene, for instance. I was pissed off at my boyfriend, David, for cheating on me. It was a major crisis, and Gene and I were friends, and he'd been trying to get at me for weeks and I hadn't exactly been discouraging him. I went to see him that night to gripe about David. He was very sympathetic, of course, and he gave me a backrub, and we talked and touched and confided and hugged, and then we started kissing, and then we snuggled up a little closer, and then we started fondling each other, you know, and then all heck broke loose, and we rolled around on the bed groping and rubbing and grabbing and smooching and pushing and pressing and squeezing. He never did actually get it in. He wanted to, and I wanted him to as well, but I had this thing about being faithful to my boyfriend, so I kept saying, "No, you can't do that; yes, that feels so good; no, wait that's too much; yes, yes, don't stop; no, stop, that's enough." We never even got our clothes off. Jesus Christ, though, it was some night. One of the best, really. But for a long time I didn't count it as one of the times I'd had sex. He never got inside, so it didn't count.

Later, months and years later, when I lay awake putting my list together, I'd start to wonder: Why doesn't Gene count? Does he not count because he never got inside? Or does he not count because I had to preserve my moral edge over David, my status as the patient, ever-faithful, cheated-on, martyred girlfriend, and if what I did with Gene counts then I don't get to feel wounded and superior?

Years later, I did end up fucking Gene and I felt a profound relief because, at last, he definitely had a number, and I knew for sure that he did in fact count.

Then I started having sex with women, and, boy, howdy, did *that* ever shoot holes in the system. I'd always made my list of sex partners by defining sex as penile-vaginal intercourse—you know, screwing. It's a pretty simple distinction, a straightforward binary system. Did it go in or didn't it? Yes or no? One or zero? On or off? Granted, it's a pretty arbitrary definition, but it's the customary one, with an ancient and respected tradition behind it, and when I was just screwing men, there was no compelling reason to question it.

But with women, well, first of all there's no penis, so right from the start the tracking system is defective. And then, there are so many ways women can have sex with each other, touching and licking and grinding and fingering and fisting—with dildos or vibrators or vegetables or whatever happens to be lying around the house, or with nothing at all except human bodies. Of course, that's true for sex between women and men as well. But between women, no one method has a centuries-old tradition of being the one that counts. Even when we do fuck each other there's no dick, so you don't get that feeling of This Is What's Important, We Are Now Having Sex, objectively speaking, and all that other stuff is just foreplay or afterplay. So when I started having sex with women the binary system had to go, in favor of a more inclusive definition.

Which meant, of course, that my list of how many people I'd had sex with was completely trashed. In order to maintain it I would have had to go back and reconstruct the whole thing and include all those people I'd necked with and gone down on and dry-humped and played touchy-feely games with. Even the question of who filled the all-important Number One slot, something I'd never had any doubts about before, would have to be reevaluated.

By this time I'd kind of lost interest in the list anyway. Reconstructing it would be more trouble than it was worth. But the crucial question remained: What counts as having sex with someone?

It was important for me to know. You have to know what qualifies as sex because when you have sex with someone your relationship changes. Right? *Right?* It's not that sex itself has to change things all that much. But knowing you've had sex, being conscious of a sexual connection, standing around making polite conversation with someone while thinking to yourself, "I've had sex with this person," that's what changes things. Or so I believed. And if having sex with a friend can confuse or change the friendship, think how bizarre things can get when you're not sure whether you've had sex with them.

The problem was, as I kept doing more kinds of sexual things, the line between *sex* and *not-sex* kept getting more hazy and indistinct. As I brought more into my sexual experience, things were showing up on the dividing line demanding my attention. It wasn't just that the territory I labeled sex was expanding. The line itself had swollen, dilated, been transformed into a vast gray region. It had become less like a border and more like a demilitarized zone.

Which is a strange place to live. Not a bad place, just strange. It's like juggling, or watchmaking, or playing the piano—anything that demands complete concentrated awareness and attention. It feels like cognitive dissonance, only pleasant. It feels like waking up from a compelling and realistic bad dream. It feels like the way you feel when you realize that everything you know is wrong, and a bloody good thing too, because it was painful and stupid and it really screwed you up.

But, for me, living in a question naturally leads to searching for an answer. I can't simply shrug, throw up my hands, and say, "Damned if I know." I have to explore the unknown frontiers, even if I don't bring back any secret treasure. So even if it's incomplete or provisional, I do want to find some sort of definition of what is and isn't sex.

I know when I'm *feeling* sexual. I'm feeling sexual if my pussy's wet, my nipples are hard, my palms are clammy, my brain is fogged, my skin is tingly and super-sensitive, my butt muscles clench, my heartbeat speeds up, I have an orgasm (that's the real giveaway), and so on. But feeling sexual with someone isn't the same as having sex with them. Good Lord, if I called it sex every time I was attracted to someone who returned the favor, I'd be even more bewildered than I am now. Even *being* sexual with someone isn't the same as *having* sex with them. I've danced and flirted with too many people, given and received too many sexy, would-be-seductive backrubs, to believe otherwise.

I have friends who say, if you thought of it as sex when you were doing it, then it was. That's an interesting idea. It's certainly helped me construct a coherent sexual history without being a revisionist swine: redefining my past according to current definitions. But it really just begs the question. It's fine to say that sex is whatever I think it is, but then what do I think it *is*? What if, when I was doing it, I was *wondering* whether it counted?

Perhaps having sex with someone is the conscious, consenting, mutually acknowledged pursuit of shared sexual pleasure. Not a bad definition. If you are turning each other on and you say so and you keep doing it, then it's sex. It's broad enough to encompass a lot of sexual behavior beyond genital contact/orgasm; it's distinct enough not to include every instance of sexual awareness or arousal; and it contains the elements I feel are vital—acknowledgment, consent, reciprocity, and the pursuit of pleasure. But what about the situation where one person consents to sex without really enjoying it? Lots of people (myself included) have had sexual interactions that we didn't find satisfying or didn't really want and, unless they were actually forced on us against our will, I think most of us would still classify them as sex.

Maybe if *both* of you (or all of you) think of it as sex, then it's sex whether you're having fun or not. That clears up the problem of sex that's consented to but not wished for or enjoyed. Unfortunately, it begs the question again, only worse: now you have to mesh different people's vague and inarticulate notions of what is and isn't sex and find the place where they overlap. Too messy.

How about sex as the conscious, consenting, mutually acknowledged pursuit of sexual pleasure of *at least one* of the people involved? That's better. It has all the key components, and it includes the situation where one person is doing it for a reason other than sexual pleasure—status, reassurance, money, the satisfaction and pleasure of someone they love, and so on. But what if *neither* of you is enjoying it, if you're both doing it because you think the other one wants to? Ugh.

I'm having trouble here. Even the conventional standby—sex equals intercourse—has a serious flaw: it includes rape, which is something I emphatically refuse to accept. As far as I'm concerned, if there's no consent, it ain't sex. But I feel that's about the only place in this whole quagmire where I have a grip. The longer I think about the subject, the more questions I come up with. At what point in an encounter does it *become* sexual? If an interaction that begins nonsexually turns into sex, was it sex all along? What about sex with someone who's asleep? Can you have a situation where one person is having sex and the other isn't? It seems that no matter what definition I come up with, I can think of some real-life experience that calls it into question.

For instance, a couple of years ago I attended (well, hosted) an all-girl sex party. Out of the twelve other women there, there were only a few with whom I got seriously physically nasty. The rest I kissed or hugged or talked dirty with or just smiled at, or else watched while they did seriously physically nasty things with each other. If we'd been alone, I'd probably say that what I'd done with most of the women there didn't count as having sex. But the experience, which was hot and sweet and silly and very, very special, had been created by all of us, and although I only really got down with a few, I felt that I'd been sexual with all of the women there. Now, when I meet one of the women from that party, I always ask myself: Have we had sex?

In another example, when I was first experimenting with sadomasochism, I got together with a really hot woman. We were negotiating about what we were going to do, what would and wouldn't be permitted, and she said she wasn't sure she wanted to have sex. Now we'd been explicitly planning all kinds of fun and games—spanking, bondage, obedience—which I strongly identified as sexual activity. In her mind, though, *sex* meant direct genital contact, and she didn't necessarily want to do that with me. Playing with her turned out to be a tremendously erotic experience, arousing and stimulating and almost unbearably satisfying. But we spent the whole evening without even touching each other's genitals. And the fact that our definitions were so different made me wonder: Was it sex?

For instance, I worked for a few months as a nude dancer at a peep show. In case you've never been to a peep show, it works like this: the customer goes into a tiny, dingy black box, kind of like a phone booth, puts in quarters, and a metal plate goes up; the customer looks through a window at a little room/stage where naked women are dancing. One time, a guy came into one of the booths and started watching me and masturbating. I came over and squatted in front of him and started masturbating too, and we grinned at each other and watched each other and masturbated, and we both had a fabulous time. (I couldn't believe I was being paid to masturbate—tough job, but somebody has to do it. . . .) After he left I thought to myself: Did we just have sex? I mean, if it had been someone I knew, and if there had been no glass and no quarters, there'd be no question in my mind. Sitting two feet apart from someone, watching each other masturbate? Yup, I'd call that sex all right. But this was different, because it was a stranger, and because of the glass and the quarters. Was it sex?

I still don't have an answer.

STUDY QUESTIONS

1. We seem to have objective, solid definitions of such things as chairs, dogs, asparagus. Why should defining "sex" be any different? Moreover, traditional definitions (if they can be called that) of "sex" and "sexual act" have been accused of being "phallocentric." Explain how Christina's essay gets us to move away from this form of centrism. Does it move away from other "centrisms," such as orgasm-centric and even touch-centric definitions?

2. Are there any differences between "having sex," "engaging in a sexual act," and "sex"? Would being more careful about these three expressions help Christina solve or overcome some of her worries about finding a definition? Genital kisses might not be, according to some plausible definition, "having sex"; yet it is still a "sexual act," and if your spouse committed only oral sex with a stranger, would you not be upset at his or her *sexual* infidelity? If not, why not?

3. Many of Christina's examples are sexual acts that cannot be procreative. What makes nonprocreative acts sexual—*if* they are sexual? That is, can you find one single feature that is shared by all sexual acts? Note that there is a difference in the way that contracepted heterosexual intercourse is not procreative and the way in which sadomasochist sexuality is not.

4. Would you count as "sex," as "having sex," or as a "sexual activity" (or none of these) the masturbatory encounter described by Christina at the end of her essay? (What *kind* of masturbation did the event involve? See Soble, "An Essay on Masturbation," in this volume, and Soble, "On Jacking Off, Yet Again," in *The Philosophy of Sex: Contemporary Readings*, 6th ed., edited by Nicholas Power, Raja Halwani, and Alan Soble [Lanham, Md.: Rowman & Littlefield, 2013], 77–99.) What judgment would you make about the morality of this sexual encounter? Why?

5. What are some possible explanations for the abridgment of Christina's essay by the editors of *Ms.*? Was it merely a pragmatic matter of constraints on space, which often plagues editors, or might there have been political reasons for the exclusion of touchy material?

THREE

Sexual Perversion

Thomas Nagel

The contribution of **Thomas Nagel** to the philosophy of sex cannot be overestimated. From his opening claim—"there is something to be learned about sex from the fact that we have a concept of sexual perversion"—to his final conclusion—that bad sex is preferable to no sex at all—the essay is full of controversial claims bravely asserted and defended. The essay brought the bedroom into rigorous analytic philosophy (and vice versa), invited existentialism along to help, and deepened our understanding of the distinction between the natural and the perverted that is central to the subsequent development of the philosophy of sex. Nagel offers a psychological account of unnatural sex, or sexual perversion, which many see as a refreshing departure from theological and biological approaches. Moving away from moralistic accounts of sexual perversion, Nagel focuses on its phenomenology—on what "it is like to have a perverted sexual desire-arousal system." For Nagel, a natural (psychologically "complete") sexual encounter for human beings results in the increasing mutual embodiment of both persons through a reciprocal awareness of their emotional responses. "Truncated" versions of this pattern constitute sexual perversion, as in sex with inanimate objects, animals, and young children. Consistent with contemporary psychiatry, Nagel insists that perversion lies not in the nature of the act performed but in the psychology of the person who performs it, and a necessary part of sexual perversion resides in this individual's preference for certain psychologically truncated sexual acts.

Thomas Nagel is university professor emeritus at New York University and the author of *The Possibility of Altruism* (Oxford University Press, 1970), *Mortal Questions* (Cambridge University Press, 1979), *The View from Nowhere* (Oxford University Press, 1986), *Concealment and Exposure and Other Essays* (Oxford University Press, 2002), and *Mind and Cosmos* (Oxford University Press, 2012). This essay is reprinted, with the

[perverse = psychological]

Thomas Nagel

permission of Thomas Nagel and Cambridge University Press, from Thomas Nagel, *Mortal Questions*, 39–52 (which is a revised version of the article that appeared in *Journal of Philosophy* 66:1 [1969], 5–17).

There is something to be learned about sex from the fact that we possess a concept of sexual perversion. I wish to examine the idea, defending it against the charge of unintelligibility and trying to say exactly what about human sexuality qualifies it to admit of perversions. Let me begin with some general conditions that the concept must meet if it is to be viable at all. These can be accepted without assuming any particular analysis.

First, if there are any sexual perversions, they will have to be sexual desires or practices that are in some sense unnatural, though the explanation of this natural/unnatural distinction is of course the main problem. Second, certain practices will be perversions if anything is, such as shoe fetishism, bestiality, and sadism; other practices, such as unadorned sexual intercourse, will not be; about still others there is controversy. Third, if there are perversions, they will be unnatural sexual *inclinations* rather than just unnatural practices adopted not from inclination but for other reasons. Thus contraception, even if it is thought to be a deliberate perversion of the sexual and reproductive functions, cannot be significantly described as a *sexual* perversion. A sexual perversion must reveal itself in conduct that expresses an unnatural *sexual* preference. And although there might be a form of fetishism focused on the employment of contraceptive devices, that is not the usual explanation for their use.

The connection between sex and reproduction has no bearing on sexual perversion. The latter is a concept of psychological, not physiological, interest, and it is a concept that we do not apply to the lower animals, let alone to plants, all of which have reproductive functions that can go astray in various ways. (Think of seedless oranges.) Insofar as we are prepared to regard higher animals as perverted, it is because of their psychological, not their anatomical, similarity to humans. Furthermore, we do not regard as a perversion every deviation from the reproductive function of sex in humans: sterility, miscarriage, contraception, abortion.

Nor can the concept of sexual perversion be defined in terms of social disapprobation or custom. Consider all the societies that have frowned upon adultery and fornication. These have not been regarded as unnatural practices, but have been thought objectionable in other ways. What is regarded as unnatural admittedly varies from culture to culture, but the classification is not a pure expression of disapproval or distaste. In fact, it is often regarded as a *ground* for disapproval, and that suggests that the classification has independent content.

I shall offer a psychological account of sexual perversion that depends on a theory of sexual desire and human sexual interactions. To approach this solution, I shall first consider a contrary position that would justify skepticism about the existence of any sexual perversions at all, and perhaps even about the significance of the term. The skeptical argument runs as follows: [*address those who don't believe in perversion*]

Sexual desire is simply one of the appetites, like hunger and thirst. As such it may have various objects, some more common than others per-haps, but none in any sense "natural."[2] An appetite is identified as sexual by means of the organs and erogenous zones in which its satis-faction can be to some extent localized, and the special sensory pleas-ures which form the core of that satisfaction.[3] This enables us to recog-nize widely divergent goals, activities, and desires as sexual, since it is conceivable in principle that anything should produce sexual pleasure and that a nondeliberate, sexually charged desire for it should arise (as a result of conditioning, if nothing else). We may fail to empathize with some of these desires, and some of them, like sadism, may be objection-able on extraneous grounds, but once we have observed that they meet the criteria for being sexual, there is nothing more to be said on *that* score. Either they are sexual or they are not: sexuality does not admit of imperfection, or perversion, or any other such qualification—it is not that sort of affection. *Sexuality ≠ Morality ≠ normalcy*

[Sexual desire = appetite]

[Sexual desire has an objection (≠ =) natural]

[dismissing the skeptic]

This is probably the received radical position. It suggests that the cost of defending a psychological account may be to deny that sexual desire is an appetite. But insofar as that line of defense is plausible, it should make us suspicious of the simple picture of appetites on which the skepticism depends. Perhaps the standard appetites, like hunger, cannot be classed as pure appetites in that sense, either—at least in their human versions.

Can we imagine anything that would qualify as a gastronomical per-version? Hunger and eating, like sex, serve a biological function and also play a significant role in our inner lives. Note that there is little tempta-tion to describe as perverted an appetite for substances that are not nour-ishing: we should probably not consider someone's appetite *perverted* if he liked to eat paper, sand, wood, or cotton. Those are merely rather odd and very unhealthy tastes: they lack the psychological complexity that we expect of perversions. (Coprophilia, being already a sexual perversion, may be disregarded.) If on the other hand someone liked to eat cook-books, or magazines with pictures of food in them, and preferred these to ordinary food—or if when hungry he sought satisfaction by fondling a napkin or ashtray from his favorite restaurant—then the concept of per-version might seem appropriate (it would be natural to call it gastronom-ical fetishism). It would be natural to describe as gastronomically per-verted someone who could eat only by having food forced down his throat through a funnel, or only if the meal were a living animal. What helps is the peculiarity of the desire itself, rather than the inappropriate-ness of its object to the biological function that the desire serves. Even an appetite can have perversions if, in addition to its biological function, it has a significant psychological structure.

Sex organs can be purely for pleasure — clit

In the case of hunger, psychological complexity is provided by the activities that give it expression. Hunger is not merely a disturbing sensation that can be quelled by eating; it is an attitude toward edible portions of the external world, a desire to treat them in rather special ways. The method of ingestion—chewing, savoring, swallowing, appreciating the texture and smell—all are important components of the relation, as is the passivity and controllability of the food (the only animals we eat live are helpless mollusks). Our relation to food depends also on our size: we do not live upon it or burrow into it like aphids or worms. Some of these features are more central than others, but an adequate phenomenology of eating would have to treat it as a relation to the external world and a way of appropriating bits of that world, with characteristic affection. Displacements or serious restrictions of the desire to eat could then be described as perversions, if they undermined that direct relation between man and food which is the natural expression of hunger. This explains why it is easy to imagine gastronomical fetishism, voyeurism, exhibitionism, or even gastronomical sadism and masochism. Some of these perversions are fairly common.

If we can imagine perversions of an appetite like hunger, it should be possible to make sense of the concept of sexual perversion. I do not wish to imply that sexual desire is an appetite—only that being an appetite is no bar to admitting of perversions. Like hunger, sexual desire has as its characteristic object a certain relation with something in the external world; only in this case it is usually a person rather than an omelet, and the relation is considerably more complicated. This added complication allows scope for correspondingly complicated perversions.

The fact that sexual desire is a feeling about other persons may encourage a pious view of its psychological content—that it is properly the expression of some other attitude, like love, and that when it occurs by itself it is incomplete or subhuman. (The extreme Platonic version of such a view is that sexual practices are all vain attempts to express something they cannot in principle achieve: this makes them all perversions, in a sense.) But sexual desire is complicated enough without having to be linked to anything else as a condition for phenomenological analysis. Sex may serve various functions—economic, social, altruistic—but it also has its own content as a relation between persons.

The object of sexual attraction is a particular individual, who transcends the properties that make him attractive. When different persons are attracted to a single person for different reasons—eyes, hair, figure, laugh, intelligence—we nevertheless feel that the object of their desire is the same. There is even an inclination to feel that this is so if the lovers have different sexual aims, if they include both men and women, for example. Different specific attractive characteristics seem to provide enabling conditions for the operation of a single basic feeling, and the different aims all provide expressions of it. We approach the sexual attitude toward the person through the features that we find attractive, but these features are not the objects of that attitude.

This is very different from the case of an omelet. Various people may desire it for different reasons, one for its fluffiness, another for its mushrooms, another for its unique combination of aroma and visual aspect; yet we do not enshrine the transcendental omelet as the true common object of their affections. Instead, we might say that several desires have accidentally converged on the same object: any omelet with the crucial characteristics would do as well. It is not similarly true that any person with the same flesh distribution and way of smoking can be substituted as object for a particular sexual desire that has been elicited by those characteristics. It may be that they recur, but it will be a new sexual attraction with a new particular object, not merely a transfer of the old desire to someone else. (This is true even in cases where the new object is unconsciously identified with a former one.)

The importance of this point will emerge when we see how complex a psychological interchange constitutes the natural development of sexual attraction. This would be incomprehensible if its object were not a particular person, but rather a person of a certain *kind*. Attraction is only the beginning, and fulfillment does not consist merely of behavior and contact expressing this attraction, but involves much more.

The best discussion of these matters that I have seen appears in part III of Sartre's *Being and Nothingness*.[1] Sartre's treatment of sexual desire and of love, hate, sadism, masochism, and further attitudes toward others depends on a general theory of consciousness and the body which we can neither expound nor assume here. He does not discuss perversion, and this is partly because he regards sexual desire as one form of the perpetual attempt of an embodied consciousness to come to terms with the existence of others, an attempt that is as doomed to fail in this form as it is in any of the others, which include sadism and masochism (if not certain of the more impersonal deviations) as well as several nonsexual attitudes. According to Sartre, all attempts to incorporate the other into my world as another subject, in other words, to apprehend him at once as an object for me and as a subject for whom I am an object, are unstable and doomed to collapse into one or other of the two aspects. Either I reduce him entirely to an object, in which case his subjectivity escapes the possession or appropriation I can extend to that object, or I become merely an object for him, in which case I am no longer in a position to appropriate his subjectivity. Moreover, neither of these aspects is stable; each is continually in danger of giving way to the other. This has the consequence that there can be no such thing as a *successful* sexual relation, since the deep aim of sexual desire cannot in principle be accomplished. It seems likely, therefore, that the view will not permit a basic distinction between successful or complete and unsuccessful or incomplete sex, and therefore cannot admit the concept of perversion.

I do not adopt this aspect of the theory, nor many of its metaphysical underpinnings. What interests me is Sartre's picture of the attempt. He says that the type of possession that is the object of sexual desire is carried out by "a double reciprocal incarnation" and that this is accomplished, typically in the form of a caress, in the following way: "I make myself flesh in order to impel the Other to realize *for herself* and *for me* her own flesh, and my caresses cause my flesh to be born for me in so far as it is for the Other *flesh causing her to be born as flesh*" (*Being and Nothingness*, 391; Sartre's italics). This incarnation in question is described variously as a clogging or troubling of consciousness, which is inundated by the flesh in which it is embodied.

The view I am going to suggest, I hope in less obscure language, is related to this one, but it differs from Sartre's in allowing sexuality to achieve its goal on occasion and thus in providing the concept of perversion with a foothold.

Sexual desire involves a kind of perception, but not merely a single perception of its object, for in the paradigm case of mutual desire there is a complex system of superimposed mutual perceptions—not only perceptions of the sexual object but also perceptions of oneself. Moreover, sexual awareness of another involves considerable self-awareness to begin with—more than is involved in ordinary sensory perception. The experience is felt as an assault on oneself by the view (or touch, or whatever) of the sexual object. *Romeo & Juliet*

Let us consider a case in which the elements can be separated. For clarity we will restrict ourselves initially to the somewhat artificial case of desire at a distance. Suppose a man and a woman, whom we may call Romeo and Juliet, are at opposite ends of a cocktail lounge, with many mirrors on the walls which permit unobserved observation, and even mutual unobserved observation. Each of them is sipping a martini and studying other people in the mirrors. At some point Romeo notices Juliet. He is moved, somehow, by the softness of her hair and the diffidence with which she sips her martini, and this arouses him sexually. Let us say that X *senses* Y whenever X regards Y with sexual desire. (Y need not be a person, and X's apprehension of Y can be visual, tactile, olfactory, etc., or purely imaginary; in the present example we shall concentrate on vision.) So Romeo senses Juliet, rather than merely noticing her. At this stage he is aroused by an unaroused object, so he is more in the sexual grip of his body than she of hers.

Let us suppose, however, that Juliet now senses Romeo in another mirror on the opposite wall, though neither of them yet knows that he is seen by the other (the mirror angles provide three-quarter views). Romeo then begins to notice in Juliet the subtle signs of sexual arousal: heavy-lidded stare, dilating pupils, faint flush, and so forth. This, of course, intensifies her bodily presence, and he not only notices but also senses this. His arousal is nevertheless still solitary. But now, cleverly calculating the line of her stare without actually looking her in the eyes, he realizes that it is directed at him through the mirror on the opposite wall. That is, he notices, and moreover senses, Juliet sensing him. This is definitely a new development, for it gives him a sense of embodiment not only through his own reactions but also through the eyes and reactions of another. Moreover, it is separable from the initial sensing of Juliet, for sexual arousal might begin with a person's sensing that he is sensed and being assailed by the perception of the other person's desire rather than merely by the perception of the person.

But there is a further step. Let us suppose that Juliet, who is a little slower than Romeo, now senses that he senses her. This puts Romeo in a position to notice, and be aroused by, her arousal at being sensed by him. He senses that she senses that he senses her. This is still another level of arousal, for he becomes conscious of his sexuality through his awareness of its effect on her and of her awareness that this effect is due to him. Once she takes the same step and senses that he senses her sensing him, it becomes difficult to state, let alone imagine, further iterations, though they may be logically distinct. If both are alone, they will presumably turn to look at each other directly, and the proceedings will continue on another plane. Physical contact and intercourse are natural extensions of this complicated visual exchange, and mutual touch can involve all the complexities of awareness present in the visual case, but with a far greater range of subtlety and acuteness. ideally leads to sex – More) satisfaction

Ordinarily, of course, things happen in a less orderly fashion—sometimes in a great rush—but I believe that some version of this overlapping system of distinct sexual perceptions and interactions is the basic framework of any full-fledged sexual relation and that relations involving only part of the complex are significantly incomplete. The account is only schematic, as it must be to achieve generality. Every real sexual act will be psychologically far more specific and detailed, in ways that depend not only on the physical techniques employed and on anatomical details but also on countless features of the participants' conceptions of themselves and of each other, which become embodied in the act. (It is a familiar enough fact, for example, that people often take their social roles and the social roles of their partners to bed with them.)

The general schema is important, however, and the proliferation of levels of mutual awareness it involves is an example of a type of complexity that typifies human interactions. Consider aggression, for example. If I am angry with someone, I want to make him feel it, either to produce self-reproach by getting him to see himself through the eyes of my anger—and to dislike what he sees—or else to produce reciprocal anger or fear, by getting him to perceive my anger as a threat or attack. What I want will depend on the details of my anger, but in either case it will involve a desire that the object of that anger be aroused. This accom-

ideal Sex = mutual recognition
if missed = perversion

plishment constitutes the fulfillment of my emotion, through domination of the object's feelings.

Another example of such reflexive mutual recognition is to be found in the phenomenon of meaning, which appears to involve an intention to produce a belief or other effect in another by bringing about his recognition of one's intention to produce that effect. (That result is due to H. P. Grice,[2] whose position I shall not attempt to reproduce in detail.) Sex has a related structure: it involves a desire that one's partner be aroused by the recognition of one's desire that he or she be aroused.

It is not easy to define the basic types of awareness and arousal of which these complexes are composed, and that remains a lacuna in this discussion. In a sense, the object of awareness is the same in one's own case as it is in one's sexual awareness of another, although the two awarenesses will not be the same, the difference being as great as that between feeling angry and experiencing the anger of another. All stages of sexual perception are varieties of identification of a person with his body. What is perceived is one's own or another's *subjection* to or *immersion* in his body, a phenomenon which has been recognized with loathing by St. Paul and St. Augustine, both of whom regarded "the law of sin which is in my members" as a grave threat to the dominion of the holy will.[3] In sexual desire and its expression, the blending of involuntary response with deliberate control is extremely important. For Augustine, the revolution launched against him by his body is symbolized by erection and the other involuntary physical components of arousal. Sartre also stresses that the penis is not a prehensile organ. But mere involuntariness characterizes other bodily processes as well. In sexual desire the involuntary responses are combined with submission to spontaneous impulses: not only one's pulse and secretions but also one's actions are taken over by the body; ideally, deliberate control is needed only to guide the expression of those impulses. This is to some extent also true of an appetite like hunger, but the takeover there is more localized, less pervasive, less extreme. One's whole body does not become saturated with hunger as it can with desire. But the most characteristic feature of a specifically sexual immersion in the body is its ability to fit into the complex of mutual perceptions that we have described. Hunger leads to spontaneous interactions with food; sexual desire leads to spontaneous interactions with other persons, whose bodies are asserting their sovereignty in the same way, producing involuntary reactions and spontaneous impulses in *them*. These reactions are perceived, and the perception of them is perceived, and that perception is in turn perceived; at each step the domination of the person by his body is reinforced, and the sexual partner becomes more possessable by physical contact, penetration, and envelopment.

Desire is therefore not merely the perception of a preexisting embodiment of the other, but ideally a contribution to his further embodiment which in turn enhances the original subject's sense of himself. This explains why it is important that the partner be aroused, and not merely aroused, but aroused by the awareness of one's desire. It also explains the sense in which desire has unity and possession as its object: physical possession must eventuate in creation of the sexual object in the image of one's desire, and not merely in the object's recognition of that desire, or in his or her own private arousal.

Even if this is a correct model of the adult sexual capacity, it is not plausible to describe as perverted every deviation from it. For example, if the partners in heterosexual intercourse indulge in private heterosexual fantasies, thus avoiding recognition of the real partner, that would, on this model, constitute a defective sexual relation. It is not, however, generally regarded as a perversion. Such examples suggest that a simple dichotomy between perverted and unperverted sex is too crude to organize the phenomena adequately.

Still, various familiar deviations constitute truncated or incomplete versions of the complete configuration, and may be regarded as perversions of the central impulse. If sexual desire is prevented from taking its full interpersonal form, it is likely to find a different one. The concept of perversion implies that a normal sexual development has been turned aside by distorting influences. I have little to say about this causal condition. But if perversions are in some sense unnatural, they must result from interference with the development of a capacity that is there potentially.

It is difficult to apply this condition, because environmental factors play a role in determining the precise form of anyone's sexual impulse. Early experiences in particular seem to determine the choice of a sexual object. To describe some causal influences as distorting and others as merely formative is to imply that certain general aspects of human sexuality realize a definite potential whereas many of the details in which people differ realize an indeterminate potential, so that they cannot be called more or less natural. What is included in the definite potential is therefore very important, although the distinction between definite and indeterminate potential is obscure. Obviously a creature incapable of developing the levels of interpersonal sexual awareness I have described could not be deviant in virtue of the failure to do so. (Though even a chicken might be called perverted in an extended sense if it had been conditioned to develop a fetishistic attachment to a telephone.) But if humans will tend to develop some version of reciprocal interpersonal sexual awareness unless prevented, then cases of blockage can be called unnatural or perverted.

Some familiar deviations can be described in this way. Narcissistic practices and intercourse with animals, infants, and inanimate objects seem to be stuck at some primitive version of the first stage of sexual feeling. If the object is not alive, the experience is reduced entirely to an awareness of one's own sexual embodiment. Small children and animals

Sexual desire [handwritten]

permit awareness of the embodiment of the other but present obstacles to reciprocity, to the recognition by the sexual object of the subject's desire as the source of his (the object's) sexual self-awareness. Voyeurism and exhibitionism are also incomplete relations. The exhibitionist wishes to display his desire without needing to be desired in return; he may even fear the sexual attention of others. A voyeur, on the other hand, need not require any recognition by his object at all: certainly not a recognition of the voyeur's arousal. *[handwritten: — to go unnoticed]*

[handwritten in left margin: Wanky]

On the other hand, if we apply our model to the various forms that may be taken by two-party heterosexual intercourse, none of them seem clearly to qualify as perversions. Hardly anyone can be found these days to inveigh against oral-genital contact, and the merits of buggery are urged by such respectable figures as D. H. Lawrence and Norman Mailer. In general, it would appear that any bodily contact between a man and a woman that gives them sexual pleasure is a possible vehicle for the system of multilevel interpersonal awareness that I have claimed is the basic psychological content of sexual interaction. Thus a liberal platitude about sex is upheld.

The really difficult cases are sadism, masochism, and homosexuality. The first two are widely regarded as perversions and the last is controversial. In all three cases the issue depends partly on causal factors: do these dispositions result only when normal development has been prevented? Even the form in which this question has been posed is circular, because of the word "normal." We appear to need an independent criterion for a distorting influence, and we do not have one. *[handwritten: nothing wrong w. Homo]*

It may be possible to class sadism and masochism as perversions because they fall short of interpersonal reciprocity. Sadism concentrates on the evocation of passive self-awareness in others, but the sadist's engagement is itself active and requires a retention of deliberate control which may impede awareness of himself as a bodily subject of passion in the required sense. De Sade claimed that the object of sexual desire was to evoke involuntary responses from one's partner, especially audible ones. The infliction of pain is no doubt the most efficient way to accomplish this, but it requires a certain abrogation of one's own exposed spontaneity. A masochist on the other hand imposes the same disability on his partner as the sadist imposes on himself. The masochist cannot find a satisfactory embodiment as the object of another's sexual desire, but only as the object of his control. He is passive not in relation to his partner's passion but in relation to his nonpassive agency. In addition, the subjection to one's body characteristic of pain and physical restraint is of a very different kind from that of sexual excitement: pain causes people to contract rather than dissolve. These descriptions may not be generally accurate. But to the extent that they are, sadism and masochism would be disorders of the second stage of awareness—the awareness of oneself as an object of desire. *[handwritten: Both consenting ≠ perverse]*

Homosexuality cannot similarly be classed as a perversion on phenomenological grounds. Nothing rules out the full range of interpersonal perceptions between persons of the same sex. The issue then depends on whether homosexuality is produced by distorting influences that block or displace a natural tendency to heterosexual development. And the influences must be more distorting than those which lead to a taste for large breasts or fair hair or dark eyes. These also are contingencies of sexual preference in which people differ, without being perverted.

The question is whether heterosexuality is the natural expression of male and female sexual dispositions that have not been distorted. It is an unclear question, and I do not know how to approach it. There is much support for an aggressive-passive distinction between male and female sexuality. In our culture the male's arousal tends to initiate the perceptual exchange, he usually makes the sexual approach, largely controls the course of the act, and of course penetrates whereas the woman receives. When two men or two women engage in intercourse they cannot both adhere to these sexual roles. But a good deal of deviation from them occurs in heterosexual intercourse. Women can be sexually aggressive and men passive, and temporary reversals of role are not uncommon in heterosexual exchanges of reasonable length. For these reasons it seems to be doubtful that homosexuality must be a perversion, though like heterosexuality it has perverted forms.

Let me close with some remarks about the relation of perversion to good, bad, and morality. The concept of perversion can hardly fail to be evaluative in some sense, for it appears to involve the notion of an ideal or at least adequate sexuality which the perversions in some way fail to achieve. So, if the concept is viable, the judgment that a person or practice or desire is perverted will constitute a sexual evaluation, implying that better sex, or a better specimen of sex, is possible. This in itself is a very weak claim, since the evaluation might be in a dimension that is of little interest to us. (Though, if my account is correct, that will not be true.)

Whether it is a moral evaluation, however, is another question entirely—one whose answer would require more understanding of both morality and perversion than can be deployed here. Moral evaluation of acts and of persons is a rather special and very complicated matter, and by no means all our evaluations of persons and their activities are moral evaluations. We make judgments about people's beauty or health or intelligence which are evaluative without being moral. Assessments of their sexuality may be similar in that respect.

Furthermore, moral issues aside, it is not clear that unperverted sex is necessarily *preferable* to the perversions. It may be that sex which receives the highest marks for perfection *as sex* is less enjoyable than certain perversions; and if enjoyment is considered very important, that might outweigh considerations of sexual perfection in determining rational preference.

if masturbating is perverse, it could be 'normalized' →

That raises the question of the relation between the evaluative content of judgments of perversion and the rather common *general* distinction between good and bad sex. The latter distinction is usually confined to sexual acts, and it would seem, within limits, to cut across the other: even someone who believed, for example, that homosexuality was a perversion could admit a distinction between better and worse homosexual sex, and might even allow that good homosexual sex could be better sex than not very good unperverted sex. If this is correct, it supports the position that, if judgments of perversion are viable at all, they represent only one aspect of the possible evaluation of sex, even qua sex. Moreover, it is not the only important aspect: sexual deficiencies that evidently do not constitute perversions can be the object of great concern.

Finally, even if perverted sex is to that extent not so good as it might be, bad sex is generally better than none at all. This should not be controversial: it seems to hold for other important matters, like food, music, literature, and society. In the end, one must choose from among the available alternatives, whether their availability depends on the environment or on one's own constitution. And the alternatives have to be fairly grim before it becomes rational to opt for nothing.

NOTES

1. Jean-Paul Sartre, *L'Etre et le Néant* (Paris: Gallimand, 1943), translated by Hazel E. Barnes (New York: Philosophical Library, 1956).
2. H. P. Grice, "Meaning," *Philosophical Review* LXVI: 3 (July 1957), 377–88.
3. See Romans 7:23; and *Confessions*, bk. VIII, pt. v.

STUDY QUESTIONS

1. After stating and explaining clearly what Nagel's views are of natural sexual desire and of perverted sexual desire, explain the reasons that Nagel gives in support of these views. Why, for instance, should we be convinced that natural sexual desire involves the multi-levels of awareness on which Nagel insists?

2. Try to provide examples of sexual acts that would be judged perverted on Nagel's model but are not usually considered perverted, as well as psychologically complete sexual acts that may, nonetheless, be considered perverted by many people. If you can find such examples, what would this mean about the accuracy of Nagel's theory? In answering this question, keep in mind the connections (or lack thereof) between sexual acts and sexual desires.

3. On what grounds does Nagel argue against sexual desire's being an appetite, such as hunger (or the desire to eat food)? How does sexual desire differ from, and how is it similar to, the desire for

pizza? How do these comparisons or contrasts affect Nagel's argument? We can stay alive without eating pizza; we cannot stay alive if we do not eat at all. Can we stay alive without engaging in some sexual activities? Can we stay alive *well* (that is, flourish) if we are totally abstinent?

4. Nagel writes, "Let us say that X *senses* Y whenever X regards Y with sexual desire. (Y need not be a person, and X's apprehension of Y can be visual, tactile, olfactory, etc., or purely imaginary; in the present example we shall concentrate on vision.)" So Nagel claims that a person could become sexually aroused by someone who is "purely imaginary" (or fantasized). Might he be referring to fantasizing during solitary masturbation, which seems not to be complete sexuality? Indeed, consider also both "deviant" Nagelian patterns (a person is sexually aroused not by the sexual arousal of the other person, but by the other's fear or disgust), and "degenerate" Nagelian patterns (in which one person is aroused not by the genuine arousal of the other person but by the other person's feigned or pretended arousal).

5. Why does Nagel claim that "bad" sex may be better than none at all? Granted, he does not seem to mean that "morally bad" sex may be better than none. Still, does he claim that perverted sex (a kind of nonideal sex) may be better—more arousing? more satisfying?—than having no sex at all, or at least better than nonperverted, psychologically complete sex?

6. Nagel proposes that we need an account of the "distorting influences" that cause some people to have unusual sexual preferences. He also admits that this theoretical requirement has the potential of leading any model of sexual perversion into failure. Explain. What are the implications of this problem for a science of sexual perversion, or a medical/psychiatric account of sexual mental health and illness?

7. Nagel is careful to assert that a person who performs a perverted sexual act is not necessarily a perverted person or a pervert. (Someone who performs same-sex sexual acts is, likewise, not necessarily homosexual in orientation.) A sexual act rises to the level of a sexual perversion, or a person rises to the level of a pervert, only if psychologically incomplete (or truncated) sexual acts are the preferred route to sexual satisfaction. If so, how can we make sense of Nagel's parenthetical remark that "a chicken might be called perverted in an extended sense if it had been conditioned to develop a fetishistic attachment to a telephone"? Part of the issue is whether it makes sense to talk about a chicken's conditioned response as a preference. Further, should we understand the "distorting influences" and "contingencies of sexual preference" mentioned by Nagel in terms of "conditioning"?

8. To Nagel, perversions must involve a certain amount of psychological complexity. This is what (at least partly) animates his claim
   that desiring to eat paper is not a hunger perversion, but desiring
   to eat paper with pictures of food is. What is it about the former
   desire that does not make it complex enough to be a hunger perversion? And shouldn't sexual perversions be treated with parallel
   complexity? That is, shouldn't the perversion be desiring sex with
   a lingerie-wearing sheep instead of sex with a (regular) sheep?

FOUR

Plain Sex

Alan Goldman

Whereas many accounts of human sexuality connect, in some way or another, sexual activity to love, marriage, or progeny, **Alan Goldman** *believes that it is a mistake to focus on these contingent ends or purposes of sexual desire and activity as either conceptually or morally central for understanding sexuality. His "plain" account of sex is meant to capture the lowest common denominator of all sexuality, and to expose what is analytically central to sexuality per se. His proposal is that sexual desire is simply the desire for certain pleasures that are produced by bodily contact and that sexual activity is activity that "tends to fulfill" this desire for pleasurable contact. Goldman provides arguments that his account of sexual desire is neither overly broad (i.e., does not judge to be sexual desires that are not sexual) nor too narrow (i.e., does not fail to judge as sexual desires that are sexual). Based on his analyses of sexual desire and activity, Goldman explores the morality of sexual behavior and the notion of sexual perversion.*

Alan Goldman is Emeritus Kenan Professor of Humanities at the College of William and Mary. He is the author of *Justice and Reverse Discrimination* (Princeton, 1979), *The Moral Foundations of Professional Ethics* (Rowman & Littlefield, 1980), *Empirical Knowledge* (California, 1988), *Moral Knowledge* (Routledge, 1988), *Aesthetic Value* (Westview, 1995), *Practical Rules: When We Need Them and When We Don't* (Cambridge, 2002), *Reasons from Within: Desires and Values* (Oxford, 2010), and *Philosophy and the Novel* (Oxford, 2013). This essay was first published in *Philosophy and Public Affairs* vol. 6, no. 3 (1977), 267–87. It is reprinted here with the permission of Alan Goldman and Wiley Global Permissions.

I

Several recent articles on sex herald its acceptance as a legitimate topic for analytic philosophers (although it has been a topic in philosophy

53

since Plato). One might have thought conceptual analysis unnecessary in this area; despite the notorious struggles of judges and legislators to define pornography suitably, we all might be expected to know what sex is and to be able to identify at least paradigm sexual desires and activities without much difficulty.

Philosophy is nevertheless of relevance here if for no other reason than that the concept of sex remains at the center of moral and social consciousness in our, and perhaps any, society. Before we can get a sensible view of the relation of sex to morality, perversion, social regulation, and marriage, we require a sensible analysis of the concept itself, one that neither understates its animal pleasure nor overstates its importance within a theory or system of value. I say "before," but the order is not quite so clear, for questions in this area, as elsewhere in moral philosophy, are both conceptual and normative at the same time. Our concept of sex will partially determine our moral view of it, but as philosophers we should formulate a concept that will accord with its proper moral status. What we require here, as elsewhere, is "reflective equilibrium," a goal not achieved by traditional and recent analyses together with their moral implications. Because sexual activity, like other natural functions such as eating or exercising, has become embedded in layers of cultural, moral, and superstitious superstructure, it is hard to conceive it in its simplest terms. But partially for this reason, it is only by thinking about plain sex that we can begin to achieve this conceptual equilibrium.

I shall suggest here that sex continues to be misrepresented in recent writings, at least in philosophical writings, and I shall criticize the predominant form of analysis which I term "means–end analysis." Such conceptions attribute a necessary external goal or purpose to sexual activity, whether it be reproduction, the expression of love, simple communication, or interpersonal awareness. They analyze sexual activity as a means to one of these ends, implying that sexual desire is a desire to reproduce, to love or be loved, or to communicate with others. All definitions of this type suggest false views of the relation of sex to perversion and morality by implying that sex which does not fit one of these models or fulfill one of these functions is in some way deviant or incomplete.

The alternative, simpler analysis with which I will begin is that sexual desire is desire for contact with another person's body and for the pleasure which such contact produces; sexual activity is activity which tends to fulfill such desire of the agent. Whereas Aristotle and Butler were correct in holding that pleasure is normally a byproduct rather than a goal of purposeful action, in the case of sex this is not so clear. The desire for another's body is, principally among other things, the desire for the pleasure that physical contact brings. On the other hand, it is not a desire for a particular sensation detachable from its causal context, a sensation which can be derived in other ways. This definition in terms of the general goal of sexual desire appears preferable to an attempt to more explicitly list or define specific sexual activities, for many activities such as kissing, embracing, massaging, or holding hands may or may not be sexual, depending upon the context and more specifically upon the purposes, needs, or desires into which such activities fit. The generality of the definition also represents a refusal (common in recent psychological texts) to overemphasize orgasm as the goal of sexual desire or genital sex as the only norm of sexual activity (this will be hedged slightly in the discussion of perversion below).

Central to the definition is the fact that the goal of sexual desire and activity is the physical contact itself, rather than something else which this contact might express. By contrast, what I term "means–end analyses" posit ends which I take to be extraneous to plain sex, and they view sex as a means to these ends. Their fault lies not in defining sex in terms of its general goal, but in seeing plain sex as merely a means to other separable ends. I term these "means–end analyses" for convenience, although "means–separable–end analysis," while too cumbersome, might be more fully explanatory. The desire for physical contact with another person is a minimal criterion for (normal) sexual desire, but is both necessary and sufficient to qualify normal desire as sexual. Of course, we may want to express other feelings through sexual acts in various contexts, but without the desire for the physical contact in and for itself, or when it is sought for other reasons, activities in which contact is involved are not predominantly sexual. Furthermore, the desire for physical contact in itself, without the wish to express affection or other feelings through it, is sufficient to render sexual the activity of the agent which fulfills it. Various activities with this goal alone, such as kissing and caressing in certain contexts, qualify as sexual even without the presence of genital symptoms of sexual excitement. The latter are not therefore necessary criteria for sexual activity.

This initial analysis may seem to some either over- or underinclusive. It might seem too broad in leading us to interpret physical contact as sexual desire in activities such as football and other contact sports. In these cases, however, the desire is not for contact with another body per se, it is not directed toward a particular person for that purpose, and it is not the goal of the activity—the goal is winning or exercising or knocking someone down or displaying one's prowess. If the desire is purely for contact with another specific person's body, then to interpret it as sexual does not seem an exaggeration. A slightly more difficult case is that of a baby's desire to be cuddled and our natural response in wanting to cuddle it. In the case of the baby, the desire may be simply for the physical contact, for the pleasure of the caresses. If so, we may characterize this desire, especially in keeping with Freudian theory, as sexual or protosexual. It will differ nevertheless from full-fledged sexual desire in being more amorphous, not directed outward toward another specific person's body. It may also be that what the infant unconsciously desires is not physical contact per se but signs of affection, tenderness, or security, in which case we have further reason for hesitating to characterize its wants as clearly sexual. The intent of our response to the baby is often the showing of affection, not the pure physical contact, so that our definition in terms of action which fulfills sexual desire *on the part of the agent* does not capture such actions, whatever we say of the baby. (If it is intuitive to characterize our responses as sexual as well, there is clearly no problem here for my analysis.) The same can be said of signs of affection (or in some cultures polite greeting) among men or women: these certainly need not be homosexual when the intent is only to show friendship, something extrinsic to plain sex although valuable when added to it.

Our definition of sex in terms of the desire for physical contact may appear too narrow in that a person's personality, not merely her or his body, may be sexually attractive to another, and in that looking or conversing in a certain way can be sexual in a given context without bodily contact. Nevertheless, it is not the contents of one's thoughts per se that are sexually appealing, but one's personality as embodied in certain manners of behavior. Furthermore, if a person is sexually attracted by another's personality, he or she will desire not just further conversation but also actual sexual contact. While looking at or conversing with someone can be interpreted as sexual in given contexts, it is so when intended as preliminary to, and hence parasitic upon, elemental sexual interest. Voyeurism or viewing a pornographic movie qualifies as a sexual activity, but only as an imaginative substitute for the real thing (otherwise a deviation from the norm as expressed in our definition). The same is true of masturbation as a sexual activity without a partner.

That the initial definition indicates at least an ingredient of sexual desire and activity is too obvious to argue. We all know what sex is, at least in obvious cases, and do not need philosophers to tell us. My preliminary analysis is meant to serve as a contrast to what sex is not, at least not necessarily. I concentrate upon the physically manifested desire for another's body, and I take as central the immersion in the physical aspect of one's own existence and attention to the physical embodiment of the other. One may derive pleasure in a sex act from expressing certain feelings to one's partner or from awareness of the attitude of one's partner, but sexual desire is essentially desire for physical contact itself. It is a bodily desire for the body of another that dominates our mental life for more or less brief periods. Traditional writings were correct to emphasize the purely physical or animal aspect of sex; they were wrong only in condemning it. This characterization of sex as an intensely pleasurable physical activity and acute physical desire may seem to some to capture only its barest level. But it is worth distinguishing and focusing upon this least common denominator in order to avoid the false views of sexual morality and perversion which emerge from thinking that sex is essentially something else.

II

We may turn then to what sex is not, to the arguments regarding supposed conceptual connections between sex and other activities which it is necessary to conceptually distinguish. The most comprehensible attempt to build an extraneous purpose into the sex act identifies that purpose as reproduction, its primary biological function. While this may be "nature's" purpose, it certainly need not be ours (the analogy with eating, while sometimes overworked, is pertinent here). While this identification may once have had a rational basis which also grounded the identification of the value and morality of sex with that applicable to reproduction and childrearing, the development of contraception rendered the connection weak. Methods of contraception are by now so familiar and so widely used that it is not necessary to dwell upon the changes wrought by these developments in the concept of sex itself and in a rational sexual ethic dependent upon that concept. In the past, the ever-present possibility of children rendered the concepts of sex and sexual morality different from those required at present. There may be good reasons, if the presence and care of both mother and father are beneficial to children, for restricting reproduction to marriage. Insofar as society has a legitimate role in protecting children's interests, it may be justified in giving marriage a legal status, although this question is complicated by the fact (among others) that children born to single mothers deserve no penalties. In any case, the point here is simply that these questions are irrelevant at the present time to those regarding the morality of sex and its potential social regulation. (Further connections with marriage will be discussed below.)

It is obvious that the desire for sex is not necessarily a desire to reproduce, that the psychological manifestation has become, if it were not always, distinct from its biological roots. There are many parallels, as previously mentioned, with other natural functions. The pleasures of eating and exercising are to a large extent independent of their roles in nourishment or health (as the junk-food industry discovered with a vengeance). Despite the obvious parallel with sex, there is still a tendency for many to think that sex acts which can be reproductive are, if not more moral or less immoral, at least more natural. These categories of morality and "naturalness," or normality, are not to be identified with each other, as will be argued below, and neither is applicable to sex by virtue of its connection to reproduction. The tendency to identify reproduction as the conceptually connected end of sex is most prevalent now in the pronouncements of the Catholic Church. There the assumed analysis is clearly tied to a restrictive sexual morality according to which acts become immoral and unnatural when they are not oriented toward reproduction, a morality which has independent roots in the Christian sexual ethic as it derives from Paul. However, the means–end analysis fails to generate a consistent sexual ethic: homosexual and oral-genital sex is condemned while kissing or caressing, acts equally unlikely to lead in themselves to fertilization, even when properly characterized as sexual according to our definition, are not.

III

Before discussing further relations of means–end analyses to false or inconsistent sexual ethics and concepts of perversion, I turn to other examples of these analyses. One common position views sex as essentially an expression of love or affection between the partners. It is generally recognized that there are other types of love besides sexual, but sex itself is taken as an expression of one type, sometimes termed "romantic" love.[1] Various factors again ought to weaken this identification. First, there are other types of love besides that which it is appropriate to express sexually, and "romantic" love itself can be expressed in many other ways. I am not denying that sex can take on heightened value and meaning when it becomes a vehicle for the expression of feelings of love or tenderness, but so can many other usually mundane activities such as getting up early to make breakfast on Sunday, cleaning the house, and so on. Second, sex itself can be used to communicate many other emotions besides love, and, as I will argue below, can communicate nothing in particular and still be good sex.

On a deeper level, an internal tension is bound to result from an identification of sex, which I have described as a physical-psychological desire, with love as a long-term, deep emotional relationship between two individuals. As this type of relationship, love is permanent, at least in intent, and more or less exclusive. A normal person cannot deeply love more than a few individuals even in a lifetime. We may be suspicious that those who attempt or claim to love many love them weakly if at all. Yet fleeting sexual desire can arise in relation to a variety of other individuals one finds sexually attractive. It may even be, as some have claimed, that sexual desire in humans naturally seeks variety, while this is obviously false of love. For this reason, monogamous sex, even if justified, almost always represents a sacrifice or the exercise of self-control on the part of the spouses, while monogamous love generally does not. There is no such thing as casual love in the sense in which I intend the term "love." It may occasionally happen that a spouse falls deeply in love with someone else (especially when sex is conceived in terms of love), but this is relatively rare in comparison to passing sexual desires for others; and while the former often indicates a weakness or fault in the marriage relation, the latter does not.

If love is indeed more exclusive in its objects than is sexual desire, this explains why those who view sex as essentially an expression of love would again tend to hold a repressive or restrictive sexual ethic. As in the case of reproduction, there may be good reasons for reserving the total commitment of deep love to the context of marriage and family—the normal personality may not withstand additional divisions of ultimate commitment and allegiance. There is no question that marriage itself is best sustained by a deep relation of love and affection; and even if love is not naturally monogamous, the benefits of family units to children provide additional reason to avoid serious commitments elsewhere which weaken family ties. It can be argued similarly that monogamous sex strengthens families by restricting and at the same time guaranteeing an outlet for sexual desire in marriage. But there is more force to the argument that recognition of a clear distinction between sex and love in society would help avoid disastrous marriages which result from adolescent confusion of the two when sexual desire is mistaken for permanent love, and would weaken damaging jealousies which arise in marriages in relation to passing sexual desires. The love and affection of a sound marriage certainly differ from the adolescent romantic variety, which is often a mere substitute for sex in the context of a repressive sexual ethic.

In fact, the restrictive sexual ethic tied to the means–end analysis in terms of love again has failed to be consistent. At least, it has not been applied consistently, but forms part of the double standard which has curtailed the freedom of women. It is predictable in light of this history that some women would now advocate using sex as another kind of means, as a political weapon or as a way to increase unjustly denied power and freedom. The inconsistency in the sexual ethic typically attached to the sex–love analysis, according to which it has generally been taken with a grain of salt when applied to men, is simply another example of the impossibility of tailoring a plausible moral theory in this area to a conception of sex which builds in conceptually extraneous factors.

I am not suggesting here that sex ought never to be connected with love or that it is not a more significant and valuable activity when it is. Nor am I denying that individuals need love as much as sex and perhaps emotionally need at least one complete relationship which encompasses both. Just as sex can express love and take on heightened significance when it does, so love is often naturally accompanied by an intermittent desire for sex. But again love is accompanied appropriately by desires for other shared activities as well. What makes the desire for sex seem more intimately connected with love is the intimacy which is seen to be a natural feature of mutual sex acts. Like love, sex is held to lay one bare psychologically as well as physically. Sex is unquestionably intimate, but beyond that the psychological toll often attached may be a function of the restrictive sexual ethic itself, rather than a legitimate apology for it. The intimacy involved in love is psychologically consuming in a generally healthy way, while the psychological tolls of sexual relations, often including embarrassment as a correlate of intimacy, are too often the result of artificial sexual ethics and taboos. The intimacy involved in both love and sex is insufficient in any case in light of previous points to render a means–end analysis in these terms appropriate.

IV

In recent articles, Thomas Nagel and Robert Solomon, who recognize that sex is not merely a means to communicate love, nevertheless retain the form of this analysis while broadening it. For Solomon, sex remains a means of communicating (he explicitly uses the metaphor of body language), although the feelings that can be communicated now include, in addition to love and tenderness, domination, dependence, anger, trust, and so on.[2] Nagel does not refer explicitly to communication, but his analysis is similar in that he views sex as a complex form of interpersonal awareness in which desire itself is consciously communicated on several different levels. In sex, according to his analysis, two people are aroused by each other, aware of the other's arousal, and further aroused by this awareness.[3] Such multileveled conscious awareness of one's own and the other's desire is taken as the norm of a sexual relation, and this model is therefore close to that which views sex as a means of interpersonal communication.

Solomon's analysis is beset by the same difficulties as those pointed out in relation to the narrower sex-love concept. Just as love can be communicated by many activities other than sex, which do not therefore become properly analyzed as essentially vehicles of communication (making breakfast, cleaning the house, and so on), the same is true of the other feelings mentioned by Solomon. Domination can be communicated through economic manipulation, trust by a joint savings account. Driving a car can be simultaneously expressing anger, pride, joy, and so on. We may, in fact, communicate or express feelings in anything we do, but this does not make everything we do into language. Driving a car is not to be defined as an automotive means of communication, although with a little ingenuity we might work out an automotive vocabulary (tailgating as an expression of aggression or impatience; beating another car away from a stoplight as expressing domination) to match the vocabulary of "body language." That one can communicate various feelings during sex acts does not make these acts merely or primarily a means of communicating.

More important, to analyze sex as a means of communication is to overlook the intrinsic nature and value of the act itself. Sex is not a gesture or series of gestures, in fact not necessarily a means to any other end, but a physical activity intensely pleasurable in itself. When a language is used, the symbols normally have no importance in themselves; they function merely as vehicles for what can be communicated by them. Furthermore, skill in the use of language is a technical achievement that must be carefully learned; if better sex is more successful communication by means of a more skillful use of body language, then we had all better be well schooled in the vocabulary and grammar. Solomon's analysis, which uses the language metaphor, suggests the appropriateness of a sex-manual approach, the substitution of a bit of technological prowess for the natural pleasure of the unforced surrender to feeling and desire.

It may be that Solomon's position could be improved by using the analogy of music rather than that of language, as an aesthetic form of communication. Music might be thought of as a form of aesthetic communicating, in which the experience of the "phonemes" themselves is generally pleasing. And listening to music is perhaps more of a sexual experience than having someone talk to you. Yet it seems to me that insofar as music is aesthetic and pleasing in itself, it is not best conceived as primarily a means for communicating specific feelings. Such an analysis does injustice to aesthetic experience in much the same way as the sex-communication analysis debases sexual experience itself.[4]

For Solomon, sex that is not a totally self-conscious communicative act tends toward vulgarity,[5] whereas I would have thought it the other way around. This is another illustration of the tendency of means–end analyses to condemn what appears perfectly natural or normal sex on my account. Both Solomon and Nagel use their definitions, however, not primarily to stipulate moral norms for sex, as we saw in earlier analyses, but to define norms against which to measure perversion. Once again, neither is capable of generating consistency or reflective equilibrium with our firm intuitions as to what counts as subnormal sex, the problem being that both build factors into their norms which are extraneous to an unromanticized view of normal sexual desire and activity. If perversion represents a breakdown in communication, as Solomon maintains, then any unsuccessful or misunderstood advance should count as perverted. Furthermore, sex between husband and wife married for several years, or between any partners already familiar with each other, would be, if not perverted, nevertheless subnormal or trite and dull, in that the communicative content would be minimal in lacking all novelty. In fact, the pleasures of sex need not wear off with familiarity, as they would if dependent upon the communicative content of the feelings. Finally, rather than a release or relief from physical desire through a substitute imaginative outlet, masturbation would become a way of practicing or rehearsing one's technique or vocabulary on oneself, or simply a way of talking to oneself, as Solomon himself says.[6]

Nagel fares no better in the implications of his overintellectualized norm. Spontaneous and heated sex between two familiar partners may well lack the complex conscious multileveled interpersonal awareness of which he speaks without being in the least perverted. The egotistical desire that one's partner be aroused by one's own desire does not seem a primary element of the sexual urge, and during sex acts one may like

one's partner to be sometimes active and aroused, sometimes more passive. Just as sex can be more significant when love is communicated, so it
can sometimes be heightened by an awareness of the other's desire. But
at other times this awareness of an avid desire of one's partner can be
merely distracting. The conscious awareness to which Nagel refers may
actually impede the immersion in the physical of which I spoke above,
just as may concentration upon one's "vocabulary" or technique. Sex is a
way of relating to another, but primarily a physical rather than intellectual way. For Nagel, the ultimate in degeneration or perversion would have
to be what he calls "mutual epidermal stimulation"[7] without mutual
awareness of each other's state of mind. But this sounds like normal, if
not ideal, sex to me (perhaps only a minimal description of it). His model
certainly seems more appropriate to a sophisticated seduction scene than
to the sex act itself,[8] which according to the model would often have to
count as a subnormal anticlimax to the intellectual foreplay. While Nagel's account resembles Solomon's means–end analysis of sex, here the sex
act itself does not even qualify as a preferred or central means to the end
of interpersonal communication.

V

I have now criticized various types of analysis sharing or suggesting a
common means–end form. I have suggested that analyses of this form
relate to attempts to limit moral or natural sex to that which fulfills some
purpose or function extraneous to basic sexual desire. The attempts to
brand forms of sex outside the idealized models as immoral or perverted
fail to achieve consistency with intuitions that they themselves do not
directly question. The reproductive model brands oral-genital sex a deviation but cannot account for kissing or holding hands; the communication account holds voyeurism to be perverted but cannot accommodate
sex acts without much conscious thought or seductive nonphysical foreplay; the sex-love model makes most sexual desire seem degrading or
base. The first and last condemn extramarital sex on the sound but irrelevant grounds that reproduction and deep commitment are best confined
to family contexts. The romanticization of sex and the confusion of sexual
desire with love operate in both directions: sex outside the context of
romantic love is repressed; once it is repressed, partners become more
difficult to find and sex becomes romanticized further, out of proportion
to its real value for the individual.

   What all these analyses share in addition to a common form is accordance with and perhaps derivation from the Platonic-Christian moral
tradition, according to which the animal or purely physical element of
humans is the source of immorality, and plain sex in the sense I defined it
is an expression of this element, hence in itself to be condemned. All the

analyses examined seem to seek a distance from sexual desire itself in attempting to extend it conceptually beyond the physical. The love and communication analyses seek refinement or intellectualization of the desire; plain physical sex becomes vulgar, and too straightforward sexual encounters without an aura of respectable cerebral communicative content are to be avoided. Solomon explicitly argues that sex cannot be a "mere" appetite, his argument being that if it were, subway exhibitionism and other vulgar forms would be pleasing.[9] This fails to recognize that sexual desire can be focused or selective at the same time as being physical. Lower animals are not attracted by every other member of their species, either. Rancid food forced down one's throat is not pleasing, but that certainly fails to show that hunger is not a physical appetite. Sexual desire lets us know that we are physical beings and, indeed, animals; this is why traditional Platonic morality is so thorough in its condemnation. Means–end analyses continue to reflect this tradition, sometimes unwittingly. They show that in conceptualizing sex it is still difficult, despite years of so-called revolution in this area, to free ourselves from the lingering suspicion that plain sex as physical desire is an expression of our "lower selves" and that yielding to our animal natures is subhuman or vulgar.

VI

Having criticized these analyses for the sexual ethics and concepts of perversion they imply, it remains to contrast my account along these lines. To the question of what morality might be implied by my analysis, the answer is that there are no moral implications whatever. Any analysis of sex which imputes a moral character to sex acts in themselves is wrong for that reason. There is no morality intrinsic to sex, although general moral rules apply to the treatment of others in sex acts as they apply to all human relations. We can speak of a sexual ethic as we can speak of a business ethic, without implying that business in itself is either moral or immoral or that special rules are required to judge business practices which are not derived from rules that apply elsewhere as well. Sex is not in itself a moral category, although, like business, it invariably places us into relations with others in which moral rules apply. It gives us opportunity to do what is otherwise recognized as wrong, to harm others, deceive them, or manipulate them against their wills. Just as the fact that an act is sexual in itself never renders it wrong or adds to its wrongness if it is wrong on other grounds (sexual acts toward minors are wrong on other grounds, as will be argued below), so no wrong act is to be excused because done from a sexual motive. If a "crime of passion" is to be excused, it would have to be on grounds of temporary insanity rather than sexual context (whether insanity does constitute a legitimate excuse for certain actions is too big a topic to argue here). Sexual motives are among others which may become deranged, and the fact that they are sexual has no bearing in itself on the moral character, whether negative or exculpatory, of the actions deriving from them. Whatever might be true of war, it is certainly not the case that all's fair in love or sex.

Our first conclusion regarding morality and sex is therefore that no conduct otherwise immoral should be excused because it is sexual conduct, and nothing in sex is immoral unless condemned by rules which apply elsewhere as well. The last clause requires further clarification. Sexual conduct can be governed by particular rules relating only to sex itself. But these precepts must be implied by general moral rules when these are applied to specific sexual relations or types of conduct. The same is true of rules of fair business, ethical medicine, or courtesy in driving a car. In the latter case, particular acts on the road may be reprehensible, such as tailgating or passing on the right, which seem to bear no resemblance as actions to any outside the context of highway safety. Nevertheless, their immorality derives from the fact that they place others in danger, a circumstance which, when avoidable, is to be condemned in any context. This structure of general and specifically applicable rules describes a reasonable sexual ethic as well. To take an extreme case, rape is always a sexual act and it is always immoral. A rule against rape can therefore be considered an obvious part of sexual morality which has no bearing on nonsexual conduct. But the immorality of rape derives from its being an extreme violation of a person's body, of the right not to be humiliated, and of the general moral prohibition against using other persons against their wills, not from the fact that it is a sexual act.

The application elsewhere of general moral rules to sexual conduct is further complicated by the fact that it will be relative to the particular desires and preferences of one's partner (these may be influenced by and hence in some sense include misguided beliefs about sexual morality itself). This means that there will be fewer specific rules in the area of sexual ethics than in other areas of conduct, such as driving cars, where the relativity of preference is irrelevant to the prohibition of objectively dangerous conduct. More reliance will have to be placed upon the general moral rule, which in this area holds simply that the preferences, desires, and interests of one's partner or potential partner ought to be taken into account. This rule is certainly not specifically formulated to govern sexual relations; it is a form of the central principle of morality itself. But when applied to sex, it prohibits certain actions, such as molestation of children, which cannot be categorized as violations of the rule without at the same time being classified as sexual. I believe this last case is the closest we can come to an action which is wrong *because* it is sexual, but even here its wrongness is better characterized as deriving from the detrimental effects such behavior can have on the future emotional and sexual life of the naive victims, and from the fact that such behavior therefore involves manipulation of innocent persons without regard for their interests. Hence, this case also involves violation of a general moral rule which applies elsewhere as well.

Aside from faulty conceptual analyses of sex and the influence of the Platonic moral tradition, there are two more plausible reasons for thinking that there are moral dimensions intrinsic to sex acts per se. The first is that such acts are normally intensely pleasurable. According to a hedonistic, utilitarian moral theory they therefore should be at least prima facie morally right, rather than morally neutral in themselves. To me this seems incorrect and reflects unfavorably on the ethical theory in question. The pleasure intrinsic to sex acts is a good, but not, it seems to me, a good with much positive moral significance. Certainly I can have no duty to pursue such pleasure myself, and while it may be nice to give pleasure of any form to others, there is no ethical requirement to do so, given my right over my own body. The exception relates to the context of sex acts themselves, when one partner derives pleasure from the other and ought to return the favor. This duty to reciprocate takes us out of the domain of hedonistic utilitarianism, however, and into a Kantian moral framework, the central principles of which call for such reciprocity in human relations. Since independent moral judgments regarding sexual activities constitute one area in which ethical theories are to be tested, these observations indicate here, as I believe others indicate elsewhere, the fertility of the Kantian, as opposed to the utilitarian, principle in reconstructing reasoned moral consciousness.

It may appear from this alternative Kantian viewpoint that sexual acts must be at least prima facie wrong in themselves. This is because they invariably involve at different stages the manipulation of one's partner for one's own pleasure, which might appear to be prohibited on the formulation of Kant's principle which holds that one ought not to treat another as a means to such private ends. A more realistic rendering of this formulation, however, one which recognizes its intended equivalence to the first universalizability principle, admits no such absolute prohibition. Many human relations—most economic transactions, for example—involve using other individuals for personal benefit. These relations are immoral only when they are one-sided, when the benefits are not mutual, or when the transactions are not freely and rationally endorsed by all parties. The same holds true of sexual acts. The central principle governing them is the Kantian demand for reciprocity in sexual relations. In order to comply with the second formulation of the categorical imperative, one must recognize the subjectivity of one's partner (not merely by being aroused by her or his desire, as Nagel describes). Even in an act which by its nature "objectifies" the other, one recognizes a partner as a subject with demands and desires by yielding to those desires, by allowing oneself to be a sexual object as well, by giving pleasure or ensuring that the pleasures of the acts are mutual. It is this kind of reciprocity

which forms the basis for morality in sex, which distinguishes right acts
from wrong in this area as in others. (Of course, prior to sex acts one must
gauge their effects upon potential partners and take these longer-range
interests into account.)

VII

I suggested earlier that in addition to generating confusion regarding the
rightness or wrongness of sex acts, false conceptual analyses of the
means–end form cause confusion about the value of sex to the individual.
My account recognizes the satisfaction of desire and the pleasure this
brings as the central psychological function of the sex act for the individual. Sex affords us a paradigm of pleasure, but not a cornerstone of value.
For most of us, it is not only a needed outlet for desire but also the most
enjoyable form of recreation we know. Its value is nevertheless easily
mistaken by being confused with that of love, when it is taken as essentially an expression of that emotion. Although intense, the pleasures of
sex are brief and repetitive rather than cumulative. They give value to the
specific acts which generate them, but not the lasting kind of value which
enhances one's whole life. The briefness of the pleasures contributes to
their intensity (or perhaps their intensity makes them necessarily brief),
but it also relegates them to the periphery of most rational plans for the
good life.

By contrast, love typically develops over a long-term relation; while
its pleasures may be less intense and physical, they are of more cumulative value. The importance of love to the individual may well be central
in a rational system of value. And it has perhaps an even deeper moral
significance relating to the identification with the interests of another
person, which broadens one's possible relationships with others as well.
Marriage is again important in preserving this relation between adults
and children, which seems as important to the adults as it is to the children in broadening concerns which have a tendency to become selfish.
Sexual desire, by contrast, is desire for another which is nevertheless
essentially self-regarding. Sexual pleasure is certainly a good for the individual, and for many it may be necessary in order for them to function in
a reasonably cheerful way. But it bears little relation to those other values
just discussed, to which some analyses falsely suggest a conceptual connection.

VIII

While my initial analysis lacks moral implications in itself, as it should, it
does suggest by contrast a concept of sexual perversion. Since the concept
of perversion is itself a sexual concept, it will always be defined relative

to some definition of normal sex; and any conception of the norm will imply a contrary notion of perverse forms. The concept suggested by my account again differs sharply from those implied by the means–end analyses examined above. Perversion does not represent a deviation from the reproductive function (or kissing would be perverted), from a loving relationship (or most sexual desire and many heterosexual acts would be perverted), or from efficiency in communicating (or unsuccessful seduction attempts would be perverted). It is a deviation from a norm, but the norm in question is merely statistical. Of course, not all sexual acts that are statistically unusual are perverted—a three-hour continuous sexual act would be unusual but not necessarily abnormal in the requisite sense. The abnormality in question must relate to the *form of the desire* itself in order to constitute sexual perversion; for example, desire, not for contact with another, but for merely looking, for harming or being harmed, for contact with items of clothing. The concept of sexual abnormality is that suggested by my definition of normal sex in terms of its typical desire. However, not all unusual desires qualify either, only those with the typical physical sexual effects upon the individual who satisfies them. These effects, such as erection in males, were not built into the original definition of sex in terms of sexual desire, for they do not always occur in activities that are properly characterized as sexual, say, kissing for the pleasure of it. But they do seem to bear a closer relation to the definition of activities as perverted. (For those who consider only genital sex sexual, we could build such symptoms into a narrower definition, then speaking of sex in a broad sense as well as "proper" sex.)

Solomon and Nagel disagree with this statistical notion of perversion. For them the concept is evaluative rather than statistical. I do not deny that the term "perverted" is often used evaluatively (and purely emotively for that matter), or that it has a negative connotation for the average speaker. I do deny that we can find a norm, other than that of statistically usual desire, against which all and only activities that properly count as sexual perversions can be contrasted. Perverted sex is simply abnormal sex, and if the norm is not to be an idealized or romanticized extraneous end or purpose, it must express the way human sexual desires usually manifest themselves. Of course not all norms in other areas of discourse need be statistical in this way. Physical health is an example of a relatively clear norm which does not seem to depend upon the numbers of healthy people. But the concept in this case achieves its clarity through the connection of physical health with other clearly desirable physical functions and characteristics, for example, living longer. In the case of sex, that which is statistically abnormal is not necessarily incapacitating in other ways, and yet these abnormal desires with sexual effects upon their subject do count as perverted to the degree to which their objects deviate from usual ones. The connotations of the concept of perversion beyond those connected with abnormality or statistical deviation are derived more from the attitudes of those likely to call certain acts perverted than from specifiable features of the acts themselves. These connotations add to the concept of abnormality that of *sub*normality, but there is no norm against which the latter can be measured intelligibly in accord with all and only acts intuitively called perverted.

The only proper evaluative norms relating to sex involve degrees of pleasure in the acts and moral norms, but neither of these scales coincides with statistical degrees of abnormality, according to which perversion is to be measured. The three parameters operate independently (this was implied for the first two when it was held above that the pleasure of sex is a good, but not necessarily a moral good). Perverted sex may be more or less enjoyable to particular individuals than normal sex, and more or less moral, depending upon the particular relations involved. Raping a sheep may be more perverted than raping a woman, but certainly not more condemnable morally.[10] It is nevertheless true that the evaluative connotations attaching to the term "perverted" derive partly from the fact that most people consider perverted sex highly immoral. Many such acts are forbidden by long-standing taboos, and it is sometimes difficult to distinguish what is forbidden from what is immoral. Others, such as sadistic acts, are genuinely immoral, but again not at all because of their connection with sex or abnormality. The principles which condemn these acts would condemn them equally if they were common and nonsexual. It is not true that we properly could continue to consider acts perverted which were found to be very common practice across societies. Such acts, if harmful, might continue to be condemned properly as immoral, but it was just shown that the immorality of an act does not vary with its degree of perversion. If not harmful, common acts previously considered abnormal might continue to be called perverted for a time by the moralistic minority, but the term, when applied to such cases, would retain only its emotive negative connotation without consistent logical criteria for application. It would represent merely prejudiced moral judgments.

To adequately explain why there is a tendency to so deeply condemn perverted acts would require a treatise in psychology beyond the scope of this paper. Part of the reason undoubtedly relates to the tradition of repressive sexual ethics and false conceptions of sex; another part to the fact that all abnormality seems to disturb and fascinate us at the same time. The former explains why sexual perversion is more abhorrent to many than other forms of abnormality; the latter indicates why we tend to have an emotive and evaluative reaction to perversion in the first place. It may be, as has been suggested according to a Freudian line,[11] that our uneasiness derives from latent desires we are loath to admit, but this thesis takes us into psychological issues I am not competent to judge. Whatever the psychological explanation, it suffices to point out here that the conceptual connection between perversion and genuine or consistent moral evaluation is spurious and again suggested by misleading means–end idealizations of the concept of sex.

The position I have taken in this paper against those concepts is not totally new. Something similar to it is found in Freud's view of sex, which of course was genuinely revolutionary, and in the body of writings deriving from Freud to the present time. But in his revolt against romanticized and repressive conceptions, Freud went too far—from a refusal to view sex as merely a means to a view of it as the end of all human behavior, although sometimes an elaborately disguised end. This pansexualism led to the thesis (among others) that repression was indeed an inevitable and necessary part of social regulation of any form, a strange consequence of a position that began by opposing the repressive aspects of the means–end view. Perhaps the time finally has arrived when we can achieve a reasonable middle ground in this area, at least in philosophy (if not in society).

NOTES

1. Even Bertrand Russell, whose writing in this area was a model of rationality, at least for its period, tends to make this identification and to condemn plain sex in the absence of love: "Sexual intercourse apart from love has little value, and is to be regarded primarily as experimentation with a view to love." *Marriage and Morals* (New York: Bantam, 1959), 87.

2. Robert Solomon, "Sex and Perversion," in Robert Baker and Frederick Elliston, eds., *Philosophy and Sex*, 1st ed. (Buffalo, N.Y.: Prometheus, 1975), 268–87.

3. Thomas Nagel, "Sexual Perversion," *Journal of Philosophy* 66:1 (1960): 5–17. [The slightly revised version from *Mortal Questions* is reprinted in this volume—eds.]

4. Sex might be considered (at least partially) as communication in a very broad sense in the same way as performing ensemble music, in the sense that there is in both ideally a communion or perfectly shared experience with another. This is, however, one possible ideal view whose central feature is not necessary to sexual acts or desire per se. And in emphasizing the communication of specific feelings by means of body language, the analysis under consideration narrows the end to one clearly extrinsic to plain and even good sex.

5. Solomon, "Sex and Perversion," 284–85.

6. *Ibid.*, 283. One is reminded of Woody Allen's rejoinder to praise of his technique: "I practice a lot when I'm alone."

7. Nagel, "Sex and Perversion," 15 [original page number in *Journal of Philosophy*; this passage is omitted from the later version of Nagel's essay that is reprinted in this volume—eds.].

8. Janice Moulton made the same point in a paper at the Pacific (American Philosophical Association) meeting, March 1976. [See Janice Moulton's "Sexual Behavior: Another Position," reprinted in *The Philosophy of Sex: Contemporary Readings*, 6th ed., edited by Nicholas Power, Raja Halwani, and Alan Soble (Lanham, Md.: Rowman & Littlefield, 2013), 47–55—eds.]

9. Solomon, "Sex and Perversion," 285.

10. The example is like one from Sara Ruddick, "Better Sex," in *Philosophy and Sex*, 2nd ed., Baker and Elliston, eds., 96.

11. See Michael Slote, "Inapplicable Concepts and Sexual Perversion," in *Philosophy and Sex*, 1st ed., Baker and Elliston, eds., 261–67.

STUDY QUESTIONS

1. Goldman defines "sexual activity" as acts that "tend to fulfill" sexual desire. Devise counterexamples to this definition that turn on (a) the vagueness of "tends to fulfill" or, instead, (b) the purported link between activity and desire (e.g., if prostitutes do not desire their clients, are they not engaging in sexual activity when they have sex with them?). Do these counterexamples deal a decisive blow to Goldman's conceptual analysis?

2. Suppose that the ancient Greek philosopher Aristotle was right that "every art and inquiry" has an aim. Does Goldman run afoul of Aristotle's insight by understanding sexual desire as, at root, the desire for the pleasure of physical contact and not in terms of other goals, such as the expression of love or procreation? Review what Goldman says about the appropriateness of his "means–ends" terminology.

3. After claiming that sexual desire is desire for contact with another person's body and the pleasure such contact brings, Goldman states, "It is not a desire for a particular sensation detachable from its causal context, a sensation which can be derived in other ways." Explain what Goldman means and why this is important to his view.

4. Though disagreeing with Thomas Nagel's essay "Sexual Perversion" on several counts, Goldman identifies, as Nagel does, another person (or person's body) as the locus, object, or source of sexual pleasure. What are the drawbacks, if any, to the conceptual requirement that sexuality is, ontologically, a relation between two (or more) people? Or does this requirement make all the sense in the world to you? If so, how do you understand solitary masturbation? (See, in this volume, Alan Soble's "An Essay on Masturbation," and Soble's "On Jacking Off, Yet Again," in *The Philosophy of Sex: Contemporary Readings*, 6th ed., edited by Nicholas Power, Raja Halwani, and Alan Soble [Lanham, Md.: Rowman & Littlefield, 2013], 77–99.)

5. Goldman admits that if sexual desire is the desire for the pleasure of contact with another person's body, then sexual desire and its generated sexual activity at least prima facie involve treating the other person, in a negative moral sense, as an object or instrument. As Goldman concedes, sexual desire and activity seem to violate the ethics of Immanuel Kant, according to which it is morally wrong to treat other people merely as means or tools. Goldman tries to avoid this conclusion. Explain how he does so and evaluate the sexual morality that he espouses. (After trying to answer this question on your own, see Alan Soble's "Sexual Use," in this volume.)

6. There may be some tension between Goldman's analysis of sexual desire and his account of sexual perversion as "statistically abnormal desire." For example, on Goldman's view, is voyeurism a sexual perversion, because it involves an unusual sexual desire (merely to watch), or is it not even sexual to begin with, because it does not involve the desire for physical contact? What other desires and activities might give us reason to raise similar questions? On Goldman's view, is there room to argue that homosexual desire and activity do not have the right "form"?

7. In section VII of his essay, Goldman weighs in on the value of sex: "Sex affords us a paradigm of pleasure, but not a cornerstone of value." Sex is valuable, yes, but its value pales in comparison to other crucial things, such as love. Evaluate this claim by Goldman, and in doing so, try to understand the different ways it might be understood.

8. In his discussion of sex and morality, Goldman claims that there is "no morality intrinsic to sex" — that is, there are no wrong (or right) actions *because* they are sexual. Although Goldman seems willing to make an exception for the "molestation of children," he does not make an exception for rape. Is it consistent to exempt the molestation of children but not rape? More generally, is it true that there is no morality intrinsic to sex? Evaluate this claim.

FIVE

Sex and Sexual Perversion

Robert Gray

In this essay **Robert Gray** *accepts that the notion of "sexual perversion" might very well be viable, and that it is best understood in terms of sexuality's evolutionary adaptive function. However, Gray argues that, first, on this construal "sexual perversion" is a nonevaluative, descriptive concept, such that, and given its ordinary pejorative connotations, it is one better dropped from our language. He argues, second, that human beings' sexual adaptive functions, unlike those of fruit flies, are broad and even culture-sensitive, and thus that sexually nonperverted activities are likely to be highly varied. Along the way, Gray defines other crucial concepts, such as "sexual desire" and "sexual activity," contrasting his views with those of other philosophers, such as Thomas Nagel's and Sara Ruddick's.*

Robert Gray received a doctorate from McMaster University. After teaching philosophy for a couple of years, he changed disciplines to Management Information Systems, a business discipline concerned with the application of information technology to the information processing needs of organizations. He spent the majority of his career as a professor of Management Information Systems and in various management positions in the IT industry. His last such position was vice president of a computer manufacturer. After retiring, he returned to his first love, philosophy. He now teaches as a part-time professor of philosophy at Randolph-Macon College in Ashland, Virginia, focusing principally in the areas of moral, social, and political philosophy. This essay first appeared in the *Journal of Philosophy* vol. 75, no. 4 (1978), 189–99. It is reprinted here with the permission of Robert Gray and the *Journal of Philosophy*.

Sara Ruddick has suggested, what seems probable, that intrinsic to the notion of perversion is that of unnaturalness.[1] That and only that sexual activity which is unnatural is perverted. There are, of course, difficulties with the notion of unnaturalness itself. "Natural" may be used synonymously with "usual" or "ordinary," in which case perversion would appear to be entirely culturally relative. (We should have, perhaps, to except such things as adultery, which seem to be common to virtually all human societies.) On the other hand, "natural" may be used to describe particular activities as the outcomes of naturally occurring processes. Ignoring the circularity in this, such a definition would have as a consequence that all perversions are natural, since the fetishes of the coprophiliac are as much the outcome of his natural desires and propensities as those of the "normal" heterosexual. Even if it were argued that there has been some sort of breakdown in the control mechanisms governing the coprophiliac's behavior, still that breakdown itself could be accounted for ultimately only by an appeal to naturally occurring events (in this case, perhaps, biological laws). There is, however, a sense of "natural" which may allow an argument such as Ruddick's to get off the ground.

Typically, by "unnatural" we mean not just "unusual" but also something more like "contrary to nature." The question is: In what sense would anything be regarded as contrary to nature? To this, the best answer would appear to be that something is contrary to (its own) nature if it is counterproductive. What this requires, of course, is that there be some end or function of a given kind of behavior in terms of which we may say that a particular behavior is counterproductive or contrary to its nature as an instance of behavior of that kind, and the question is "How do we fix that end or function in a noncircular way?" The way Ruddick would seem to favor, and the only way I see if we are to avoid cultural relativism, is in terms of evolutionary theory. If, then, we are able to show that there is some adaptive function or end that sexual activity evolved to fulfill, we may speak of sexual activity that departs from that function and, more clearly, of sexual activity that, by departing from that function, is maladaptive, as counterproductive and, in that sense, contrary to nature or unnatural. Thus, if reproduction is the adaption function of sexual activity, those forms of sexual activity which are nonreproductive and, more clearly, those which are inimical to successful reproduction (for example, any nonreproductive sexual obsession) would be unnatural and perverted; they would constitute, as it were, a twisting of sexual activity away from its "natural" function or object. Put more simply, those forms of sexual activity would be perverted, which, in evolutionary terms, is dysfunctional.

This would, in fact, seem to be Ruddick's position. On her view, the adaptive function or, if one prefers, the natural end of sexual activity is reproduction, and she concludes that all and only those forms of sexual activity which may, under normal conditions, be expected to fulfill this end are natural.[2] All others are unnatural and perverted. However, this view raises some problems.

In the first place, one might ask how sexual activities are to be identified. If, for example, the natural function of sexual activity is reproduction, an end to which coprophilia has no relation at all, would that not by itself be ground for suggesting that the activities of the coprophiliac are *not* sexual activities at all, and so, of course, not sexual perversions? The problem may not be one whose solution is difficult, but for our question it is important, for in order to elucidate the notion of sexual perversion it would seem crucial that we be able to specify just what it is about an activity that makes it an instance of sexual activity. The coprophiliac's activities might well be perverted, but there need be nothing about them in virtue of which they are sexually perverted. I might, for example, have developed some sort of penchant for eating cow dung, doubtless disgusting, doubtless nonnutritive, almost certainly perverted, but what has this to do with sex? Clearly, if I regard the eating of manure simply as the only means of fulfilling my appetite for food—if, in other words, I eat because I am hungry and because it tastes good or better than the available alternatives or, if it tastes worse, because it leaves me feeling less hungry—my perversion is not sexual. Sexually, I might be entirely normal. Now the only thing I can see in this example that would constitute it as a nonsexual form of coprophilia and the only thing whose change could conceivably make it an example of coprophilia in the sexual sense, is the motive assigned. Hunger is a fairly distinct, clearly recognizable form of displeasure; as such, it gives rise, circumstances permitting, to activities that will remove or assuage it. In the same way, sexual desire (although, unlike hunger, it may be in itself pleasant or partially so) is a distinct, recognizable appetite, typically unpleasant if unfulfilled, which gives rise to activities that will remove or assuage it.

What is to be noted here is that neither hunger nor sexual desire is in itself a desire for a particular (kind of) object. In itself, each is a feeling which, all things considered, it would, at the time, be better not to have, or, better, which one would, when circumstances permit, so act as to remove. Hunger seems to be a desire for food because, typically, it is food that relieves it, and it is therefore food that the hungry person seeks. But it is entirely possible that someone should develop a food fetish for the coprolites of cattle; that is to say, it is entirely possible that, for whatever reason, someone's feeling of hunger might be relieved only by the ingestion of manure. Such a person we might well call a food pervert. But we would not call him a sexual pervert. The difference lies in his motive. His motive is hunger, not sex. On the other hand, if what he had eaten gave him sexual pleasure, his perversion, and therefore his activity, would have been sexual. Since the activities I have described here are otherwise identical (need the coprophiliac who is sexually perverted display any overt signs of sexual excitement?), I see no other way by which the one might be classed as sexual and the other not. Those activities, accordingly, are sexual which serve to relieve sexual feeling or, alternatively put, which give rise to sexual pleasure.

Of course, it might well be objected that sexual activity does not, in fact, serve so much to relieve as to heighten sexual feeling (which, for purposes of this discussion, we may take to refer, at least initially, to a physiological state, although many emotional and cognitive states may, and typically do, come to be intimately associated with it). The objection has some force; however, I believe it may be fairly easily answered, for, in much the same way, food, which typically serves to relieve hunger, may also serve to heighten it. There is, of course, a point at which the analogy between hunger and sexual feeling breaks down, for sexual feeling is typically relieved by intensifying it. Whereas a little food may, in some cases, be very satisfying, a little bit of sex often leaves an individual feeling less satisfied than he might otherwise have been. Accordingly, I prefer to speak of sexual activity in terms of sexual pleasure. The activities by which sexual feeling is removed are experienced as (an intensification of) pleasurable sexual feeling. When they cease to be pleasurable, that is to say, when the sexual feeling has been removed, the activities lose their specifically sexual character, and, unless there is some other reason for continuing, the behavior ceases.

Sexual perversions, then, will be all and only those activities which are dysfunctional (in the sense given above) in terms of sexual pleasure, or, as Thomas Nagel expresses it, "A sexual perversion must reveal itself in conduct that expresses an unnatural *sexual* preference."[3] However, as the quotation from Nagel shows, this is not adequate. Perversion, as a category, applies not only to activities but also to persons, in which case the perversion must reveal itself in an unnatural sexual *preference*. There are many sorts of activities from which we might derive sexual pleasure, some of which are undoubtedly perverted, but it is not the fact that a person might derive sexual pleasure from a given activity that makes him perverted; it is, rather, that he desires or prefers to engage in such sexual activities. We may say, accordingly, that a person will be sexually perverted if his sexual desires are for, or lead him to perform, activities which, given the adaptive function(s) of sexual activity (e.g., that it ends in reproduction), are counterproductive or maladaptive.

The definitions given here have some interesting implications, which may be best seen by contrasting them with the views taken by Ruddick. Ms. Ruddick is concerned not so much with sexual perversion as with what she calls "better sex," of which, on her account, pleasure, naturalness (nonpervertedness), and "completeness" are the three criteria.[4] As I have developed the notion of sexual activity, however, it is clear that pleasure is a criterion not so much of better sex as of sex itself. Those activities not serving to relieve sexual feeling, or from which no sexual pleasure is derived, would thus not be sexual activities at all. This at first sight seems counterintuitive, since we often speak, for example, of a person's not enjoying (in the sense of deriving pleasure from) sexual relations with his or her spouse. In this case, the difficulty lies, I think, with ordinary language. Sexual intercourse is thought to be, and is spoken of as, sexual activity, because it is that activity to which sexual desire paradigmatically leads. The unacceptability of the ordinary-language criterion is best shown, however, by the fact that, if we accept it, we are led to the unhappy conclusion that the rape victim has engaged in sexual activity, although, from her point of view, the activity may not have been sexual at all. It may make the analysis of sexual relations more difficult, but there is nothing intrinsically objectionable in the suggestion that what is, from the point of view of one of the participants, a sexual activity, may not be so from the point of view of the other. In fact, it would seem that ordinary language itself recognizes sexual pleasure as a criterion of sexual activity, at least implicitly and on some occasions. For example, ordinary persons are fond of bewailing the amount of sex and violence shown on commercial television. Just what constitutes sex in this case, however, is not clear, since neither nudity nor the portrayal of it is, in itself, a sexual activity. Were it so, the ordinary man, it seems to me, would be forced to conclude that he engages in sexual activity far more frequently than he might otherwise think (for example, in taking a bath or changing his clothes). The only thing I can see in this example in virtue of which televised nudity might be called sexual is the fact that it is intended to, and in fact does, arouse sexual feelings. The fact that it is so intended, however, may not be crucial. To take another example, Dr. David Reuben relates that, in the early days of the garment industry, women found that the operation of treadle sewing machines could be employed as a masturbatory technique,[5] and, to the extent that they so employed it, I think it is clear that they would, in ordinary parlance, be said to be engaging in sexual activity. We must assume, however, that at some point the sexual possibilities of operating a treadle sewing machine must have been discovered, presumably, at least in some cases, by accident. Those women who made this discovery would then have found themselves engaging in sexual activity quite unintentionally. They may or may not have found this a welcome discovery, but that is quite beside the point.

If these examples are compelling, and taken in sum I think they are, we are forced to the conclusion that what makes an activity a sexual activity, even in terms of ordinary language, is just the nature of the sexual pleasure deriving from it. Accordingly, it is quite possible that any activity might become a sexual activity and, as the last example shows, that it might become a sexual activity unintentionally. And, of course, it would follow too that no activity is a sexual activity unless sexual pleasure is derived from it. And, since no activity could be sexually perverted unless it were also a sexual activity, the same thing would hold for sexual perversion.

Although pleasure would thus seem to enter the analysis of sexual activity only as a matter of degree, as one means of determining the comparative worth, in sexual terms, of any given sexual experience, the notion of completeness would not appear to enter at all. Ruddick, who seems to take the notion principally from Nagel, defines it in this way:

A sex act is complete if each partner (1) allows himself to be "taken
over" by desire, which (2) is desire not merely for the other's body but
also for *his* desire, and (3) where each desire is occasioned by a response to the partner's desire.[6]

Though she offers a defense of sorts for the claim that, in a complete sex
act, the participant is "taken over" or "embodied" by his or her desire,
Ruddick would seem to have no real argument in support of the other
elements of her definition. In fact, she goes so far as to say at the end of
her discussion of completeness that "incompleteness does not disqualify
a sex act from being fully sexual."[7] Presumably, these other aspects of the
completeness of a sex act are just accidental components, characteristics
which may or may not be present but which serve to make the sex act
"better" when they are. It should be noted, however, that when Ruddick
comes to discuss the contribution that completeness makes to the sex act,
it is not the sex act itself that is said to be improved. (This will not hold
for the condition of "embodiment.") She argues, rather, that completeness contributes to the psychological and social well-being of the participants.[8]

For Nagel, by contrast, completeness would appear to be, at least
partially, constitutive of sexual activity. Completeness, on his view,
would appear to consist in a complex interaction between the desires of
the two participants ("It is important that the partner be aroused, and not
merely aroused, but aroused by the awareness of one's desire"[9]), and he
writes accordingly that "this overlapping system of distinct sexual perceptions and interactions is the basic framework of any full-fledged sexual relation and that relations involving only part of the complex are significantly incomplete."[10] That Nagel should have attached such significance to the notion of completeness (a perversion is, for him, simply an
incomplete sex act[11]) is fairly easily explained. Nagel has incorrectly assumed that "sexual desire is a feeling about other persons." It "has its
own content as a relation between persons."[12] Accordingly, on his view,
it is only by analyzing that relation that we can understand the conditions
of sexual perversion. This mistake, as has already been pointed out, is
understandable and is, furthermore, one we commonly make. Copulation is the paradigmatic object of sexual desire; it is just such a relation
between persons that sexual desire has as its "characteristic object." But it
is a mistake to go from this to the view that sexual desire has such an
object as its content (or to the view that, in the analysis of sexual activity,
the nature of sexual desire is in any way fundamental). A given desire is
sexual, not because it has a particular object but because it arises from a
particular kind of feeling. Put differently, it is the desire (or feeling) itself
that is sexual, and it is in terms of this that the activity it has as its object is
perceived as a sexual activity. The relationship is not the other way
around. If it were, it would be difficult, if not impossible, to see how

many of the more exotic perversions could be considered sexual. One might characterize an activity such as masturbation (which Nagel apparently regards as a perversion[13]) as sexual on the basis of some sort of family relation with coital activity, but this seems unlikely as a means of categorizing all sexual activities as sexual. Even in the case of masturbation this approach would raise problems (one could, for example, conceive of a situation in which a person might masturbate while feeling nothing at all—perhaps by using anesthetic ointments—for reasons having nothing to do with sexual desire or gratification—as part of a medical experiment, for instance; would this activity in that case be sexual?), but one wonders what the family resemblance might be in the admittedly strange case of coprophila described earlier.

This, however, is not the only difficulty with Nagel's notion of completeness, although I think it is the most serious. As Janice Moulton has argued, both Nagel and Robert Solomon (who sees the specific content of sexual desire in terms of interpersonal communication—sexual activity is a kind of "body language")[14] have "assumed that a model of flirtation and seduction constitutes an adequate model of sexual behavior in general," whereas, as she argues, "most sexual behavior does not involve flirtation and seduction, and . . . what characterizes flirtation and seduction is not what characterizes the sexual behavior of regular partners."[15] This itself, however, leads Moulton into difficulties. She is forced to conclude that it is impossible to characterize sexual behavior, because there are two kinds: "sexual anticipation," which includes "flirtation, seduction, and traditional courtship," and "sexual satisfaction," which "involves sexual feelings which are increased by the other person's knowledge of one's preferences and sensitivities, the familiarity of their touch or smell or way of moving, and not by the novelty of their sexual interest."[16] "However, anticipation and satisfaction are often divorced."[17] But even this classification is too narrow, for, to the extent that satisfaction is here defined in interpersonal terms, "the *other* person's knowledge . . . the familiarity of *their* touch," and so forth, masturbation and related types of sexual activities would, again, be excluded from the possible range of sexual behaviors. However, there is, as we have seen, a means, if not of characterizing, at least of identifying behavior as sexual, and the ground here, sexual feeling, is independent of any particular model of sexual activity. Note that this is not equivalent to saying that, as Solomon puts it, "sex is pure physical enjoyment."[18] To put it in Solomon's words again, "this enjoyment accompanies sexual activity and its ends, but is not that activity or these ends."[19] Sexual activity may have many ends, interpersonal communication among them, but if we take the view that it is the end that identifies it as sexual, then we are left squarely facing the problem that any sexual activity that does not have that specific end is not, in fact, sexual activity or is somehow less than fully sexual. Thus, on Solomon's communication model, masturbation turns out to be like "talking to

yourself" and therefore "clearly secondary to sexuality in its broader
interpersonal context." And "'Unadorned sexual intercourse' . . . becomes
the ultimate perversion, since it is the sexual equivalent of hanging up the
telephone without saying anything."[20] One is inclined to take the view, in
fact, that if Solomon has concentrated too narrowly on one model of
sexuality, it is not that of anticipation, but of satisfaction. Like most men,
Solomon seems to be fully persuaded of the fundamental role of genital-
genital intercourse (which is entirely satisfactory from a male point of
view) in human sexuality. There is evidence, however, to show that, at
least from the female point of view, it is not (this sort of) intercourse, but
masturbation that is crucial.[21] This may, of course, take place in an interpersonal context, and it may be preferable when it does. All it shows is
that our models must not be so constructed as to exclude it.

What the foregoing discussion will show is that the classification of a
given (type of) sexual behavior as perverted is purely descriptive. Which
activities are and are not perverted will depend on what we ultimately
discover the natural adaptive function of sexual activity to be, and this is
a question whose answer must be given by the scientist whose business it
is to study such things. Of course, if reproduction were, as some think,
the sole function of sexual activity, the scientist would have no further
questions to ask about the matter, and all nonreproductive sexual activity
might correctly be described as perverted. However, it would seem that
this is not the case. "Reproduction" is, as Nagel claims, a biological concept. As such, it includes such biological functions as conception, gestation, and birth, and, if men were fruit flies, sexual behavior might have
been just that behavior minimally sufficient to ensure reproduction in
this limited sense. Copulation, then, might have been enough to ensure
conception; conception enough to ensure gestation; and gestation enough
to ensure birth. The fact is, however (and the world may or may not be
better off for it), that men are not fruit flies, and reproduction in man
includes far more than just the production of new individuals. Reproductive activity in man must be construed as the sum of all those activities
minimally necessary to bring those new individuals to reproductive maturity. Among other things, this would seem to include the formation and
maintenance of well-organized, stable societies and the establishment
and maintenance of fairly stable male-female reproductive pairs. Since
the latter would seem ultimately to depend on sexual attraction and since
there is substantial evidence to show that many characteristics of human
sexual behavior contribute as well to the former, it would seem probable
at least that maintenance of that degree (and kind) of social organization
and stability requisite to the maintenance of human society is a function
that human sexual behavior has evolved to fulfill, and, if this is so, it is

clear that the range of nonperverted sexual activity will be much broader than it has traditionally been taken to be. It may turn out, too, that the natural adaptive functions of human sexual activity are not culturally independent. In this case, a behavior that is maladaptive in one society may not be so in another. Thus, for example, male homosexual behavior may be maladaptive in a society with a high ratio of females to males and a birth rate too low to make the society viable. In another society, however, where the sex ratios are reversed, male homosexual behavior, by reducing sexual rivalry, might be adaptive. A similar argument would serve to demonstrate the possible adaptive character of such activities as masturbation, whatever the techniques used, including "intercourse with . . . inanimate objects," which Nagel classes as a perversion. We could, perhaps, say then that variability of sexual objects is a natural characteristic, or natural adaptive function, of human sexual desire and that, where it contributes to (or, at least, does not detract from) the maintenance of the overall social order, or to the long-term viability of society, such variability is adaptive (or, at least, not maladaptive) and nonperverted.

Of course, it may well be that, as many stalwarts claim, all and only those sexual activities traditionally approved in our society are natural (or adaptive) and nonperverted, and what the discussion so far will show is that those who agitate against the increasing sexual permissiveness of contemporary society on the ground that it is destructive of the family, presumably the bulwark of modern social institutions, are at least on the right track. However, if the view of the nature of sexual perversion taken here is correct, to uphold the claim that such practices are sexually perverted, it will be necessary to show that societies that encourage divergent sexual behaviors are, for that reason, substantially less viable than our own (since evolutionary theory regards the reproductive group rather than the individual, it should be noted, too, that a particular practice detrimental to a given group or institution may benefit the society as a whole), or that our own society, with its peculiar institutions, would be made substantially less viable, and not merely different, if it permitted or encouraged other sexual practices. In any case, the judgment of whether a given activity is sexually perverted, to the extent that it is properly an answer to the factual question of whether the behavior is consonant with the natural adaptive function(s) of sexual activity, would be descriptive and nonevaluative and need not, therefore, carry any moral connotations.

This, of course, is not to say that sexual perversion is not immoral. In fact, depending on the moral view we take, there may well be ground for claiming that any and all sexual perversion is immoral. For example, one might adopt a moral view according to which the natural is the moral. This would not automatically brand sexual perversion as immoral, since it may be the case, as we have seen, that human sexual activity is naturally variable. If, however, this theory were cast in evolutionary terms, so that natural is taken to mean the naturally adaptive function of given behavior, sexual perversion would, by definition, be immoral. I am not myself inclined to such a moral view. I am, rather, inclined to take a somewhat Hobbesian view, according to which morality is the sum of those rules minimally necessary to social cohesion. On this view, all sexual activities that are perverted by virtue of the fact that they disrupt the cohesiveness of society, assuming social cohesion is a natural function of human sexual activity, would be immoral. But it should be noted that this judgment is logically independent of the judgment that those activities are perverted. One might, therefore, make the suggestion, since "perversion" has acquired such a strong pejorative connotation in our society, that the term be dropped from our sexual vocabulary altogether. Other clearer and less emotive terms may just as easily be substituted for it.

But whatever the moral implications, this much seems clear. If we have correctly defined what it is for behavior to be sexually perverted and, in that sense, "contrary to nature," as any practice or activity from which sexual pleasure is derived and which, given the natural adaptive function(s) of sexual activity, is counterproductive or maladaptive, we will at least have succeeded in putting the question "What specific activities are and are not perverted?" in terms amenable to investigation by the behavioral sciences. In such questions as these, no more can really be asked of the philosopher.

NOTES

1. Sara Ruddick, "On Sexual Morality," in *Moral Problems*, 2nd ed., edited by James Rachels (New York: Harper & Row, 1975), 16–34, at 23–24. See also Thomas Nagel, "Sexual Perversion," *Journal of Philosophy* 66:1 (1969), 5–17. [Reprinted in this volume from its revised version in *Mortal Questions*—eds.]

2. "On Sexual Morality," 24.

3. "Sexual Perversion," in this volume, 40.

4. "On Sexual Morality," 18.

5. David Reuben, *Everything You Wanted to Know About Sex* (New York: Bantam, 1971), 201–2.

6. "On Sexual Morality," 20.

7. "On Sexual Morality," 23.

8. "On Sexual Morality," 29–30.

9. "Sexual Perversion," in this volume, 47.

10. "Sexual Perversion," in this volume, 45.

11. "Sexual Perversion," in this volume, 47.

12. "Sexual Perversion," in this volume, 42.

13. "Sexual Perversion," in this volume, 47–48.

14. Robert Solomon, "Sexual Paradigms," *Journal of Philosophy* 71:1 (1974), 336–45, at 343.

15. Janice Moulton, "Sexual Behavior: Another Position," *Journal of Philosophy* 73:16 (1976), 537–46, at 538. [Reprinted in *The Philosophy of Sex: Contemporary Readings*, 6th ed., edited by Nicholas Power, Raja Halwani, and Alan Soble (Lanham, Md.: Rowman & Littlefield, 2013), 47–55—eds.]

16. "Sexual Behavior," 538–39.

17. "Sexual Behavior," 539.
18. "Sexual Paradigms," 343.
19. "Sexual Paradigms," 341.
20. "Sexual Paradigms," 343.
21. Shere Hite, *The Hite Report* (New York: Macmillan, 1976), 229–52.

STUDY QUESTIONS

1. Gray states, "It is entirely possible that, for whatever reason, someone's feeling of hunger might be relieved only by the ingestion of manure. Such a person we might well call a food pervert." Compare this claim to Thomas Nagel's example of a hunger perversion: someone who desires to eat paper containing pictures of food ("Sexual Perversion," in this volume). Do both philosophers give similar accounts of hunger perversions? In what ways do their accounts differ? Which is more plausible, do you think?

2. Gray claims that sexual activities are activities that "serve to relieve sexual feeling or, alternatively put, which give rise to sexual pleasure." Is this true? What does "serve" mean exactly? (Compare it to Alan Goldman's "tends to" in Goldman's definition of "sexual activity" in his essay "Plain Sex" in this volume.) And must an activity give rise to sexual pleasure for it to be sexual? In answering these questions, make sure to take into account what Gray says about the rape victim and about the sewing machines.

3. Gray defines a sexually perverted person as someone whose "sexual desires are for, or lead him to perform, activities which, given the adaptive function(s) of sexual activity (e.g., that it ends in reproduction), are counterproductive or maladaptive." Can you think of counterexamples to this view? Can you think of sexual desires for reproductive purposes that are still perverted? What about sexual desires for nonreproductive activities that are not perverted?

4. Gray claims that what makes a desire sexual is not its object but that "it is the desire (or feeling) itself that is sexual." Explain this view, especially as it contrasts with Nagel and Goldman's views. How, on Gray's view, do we differentiate between different types of desires? Would "motive" play a role?

5. How does Gray argue that even on a reproductive view of the naturalness of sex it might be that there is a broad range of nonperverted sexual activities? How does he argue that some of it might even be culturally relative?

6. Why does Gray suggest that the term "perverted" be dropped from our vocabulary altogether? Do you agree with him? Might the concept serve a good purpose that Gray has neglected to take into account?

7. Given Gray's concluding remarks, what role does philosophy play in a discussion of sexual (and nonsexual) perversion, and what role do the behavioral sciences (biology, psychology, etc.) play? What does Gray himself say about this?

SIX

Chatting Is Not Cheating

John Portmann

John Portmann *argues that our interacting verbally through erotically desig-*
nated Internet chat rooms does not count as our having sex, or as sex, because no
skin-against-skin physical contact occurs. Erotic keyboard chatting with another
person, which is akin to dirty talk, is no more having sex with that person than is
flirting visually with another person. By using the expression "chatting is not
cheating," Portmann means to deny that erotic chatting is adultery. Not only
does erotic chatting (whether done through the Internet or over the telephone)
not involve any penetration (an old, suspicious, but possibly unavoidable criter-
ion of adultery), but it also fails to be adultery because it is not having sex to
begin with on Portmann's criterion. Chatting allows us to satisfy sexual desires
by relying on our imaginations while also not violating the rules of marriage or
monogamy, much like viewing pornography provides sexual satisfaction while
not involving any real, physical sexual interaction with another person (and
hence is not cheating).

John Portmann studied philosophy at Yale and Cambridge and is professor of religious studies at the
University of Virginia. This essay is from John Portmann, editor, *In Defense of Sin*, 223–41, published in 2001,
reproduced here with John Portmann's permission and the permission of St. Martin's Press. (Readers are
hereby advised that in the process of preparing this chapter, a number of changes were made to the original
text.) "Chatting Is Not Cheating" and its author received national media attention in the summer of 2011, in
the wake of the Anthony Wiener scandal. Wiener, a Democratic member of the U.S. House of Representatives
from New York, was forced to step down after sexting a woman who wasn't his wife.

> Do you know what it is as you pass to be
>   loved by strangers?
> Do you know the talk of those
>   turning eye-balls?
>   —Walt Whitman, "Song of the Open Road" (1856)

A triumph of human imagination, the Internet has expanded and facilitated communication. Lust, an age-old focus of human imagination, now enjoys a new stage on which to triumph.

The Internet simplifies life in ways many people have noticed. It complicates life as well, though, particularly with regard to sexual morality. Anonymous dirty talk over the Internet presents what may seem to be a new moral puzzle: Is it sex? Does it amount to betrayal if your boyfriend, girlfriend, husband, or wife logs on to an erotic chat room? Your mother or father? Your son or daughter? A priest, nun, rabbi, or minister? No. The Internet has not given us a new way to *have* sex but rather an absorbing new way to *talk about* sex. Distinguishing between flirting and fidelity will show that talking dirty, whether on the Internet or over the phone, does not amount to having sex.

I make a case for the moral acceptability of anonymous dirty talk, which is no better or worse than viewing pornography. Along the way, I suggest that reflection on the erotics of the Internet usefully exposes the largely intuitive and pre-articulate anxiety with which most of us approach the topic of sex.

WAYS OF FLIRTING

Probably as long as *Homo sapiens* have been around they have been having dirty thoughts. Like some Greeks before them, many ancient Jews (Genesis 20:2 and Leviticus 18) and Christians suffered through lust as if it were a curse. Famously, Jesus taught that the man who lusted after a woman in his heart had already committed adultery (Matthew 5:28). When, some two thousand years later, Jimmy Carter confessed in a *Playboy* interview to having lusted after women other than his wife, Americans took the news badly. Carter lost the 1980 presidential election.

What's so bad about lust? Certainly it can lead to bad consequences, but so can love, charity, mercy, and a host of other decidedly laudable motivations. We might place the blame on how lust affects our relations to others, but Plato objects to how lust affects our relation to *ourselves*. The true philosopher doesn't concern himself with sexual pleasure, according to Plato, who refers to sexual desire as a disease of the personality. Plato counsels us to sublimate sexual energy in intellectual pursuits.[1] Many Jewish and Christian thinkers have endorsed Plato's denunciation. In 1 Cor. 7, a text that shaped Christian thinking about sexuality for many centuries, Paul warns married couples who refrain from sexual relations to resume intercourse, "lest Satan tempt you through lack of self-control." Augustine, perhaps the greatest Christian theologian of all, implored God to free him from the lust that controlled him: "Oh Lord, you will increase your gifts in me, so that my soul may follow me to you, freed from the concupiscence [that is, lust] which binds it, and rebel no more against itself."[2] Luther, among other theologians, regarded lust as a consequence of self-love or pride, an obstacle to be overcome.[3] Thomas More accused Luther, a common lecher, of having begun the Reformation simply because he could not control his own lust.

Lust prevents us from being who we really are, Augustine says. He cultivates an athletic ideal, one in which we become strong enough to surmount lust as a champion hurdler mechanically leaps over obstacles in his path. Augustine's reflections leave us to wonder whether he understood the harmful effects of repressing sexual desire. (Freud made a career out of detailing these effects.) Missing from Augustine is the idea that lust completes us (however temporarily), fills us with a vivid sense of being alive, and propels us along the way to self-fulfillment. (The zeal with which religious figures such as St. Teresa of Avila, St. John of the Cross, or St. Jerome have sought God approximates lust, it may sometimes seem.) Lust, like the treasures of the Louvre or the playfulness of children, lights up a rainy day.

Not surprisingly, dirty thoughts can terrorize those who condemn lust. Hemingway's short story "God Rest You Merry, Gentlemen" introduces a sixteen-year-old boy whose fear of lust drives him to castrate himself. Some parents subject their daughters to female genital mutilation in order to prevent lustful desires or, worse, succumbing to passion. An official document from the World Health Organization estimated in February 2012 that more than 92 million African girls and women had been subjected to the procedure.[4]

At the dawn of a new century, there is considerably less public fear of dirty thoughts than there used to be. In the 1990s the American press trumpeted the singer Madonna's confessing to fantasies of having sex in a Catholic church (her 1989 video "Like a Prayer," set in a church, stirred controversy upon its release).[5] And in that same decade, Americans largely forgave President Bill Clinton his now-famous extramarital misdeeds.

Even now, though, some conservative religious people will still insist that sex ought to be procreative, not merely recreational (as in adultery). As late as 1972, one of the better-known philosophers in the West insisted that this view is a necessary step if one is morally to oppose petting, prostitution, sodomy, and "homosexual intercourse."[6] People who morally object to dirty thoughts will naturally (and reasonably) object to talking dirty (in person) and chatting dirty (over the phone or on the Internet). My thoughts will do nothing to dissuade them. Here I address what must be the overwhelming majority of people who see some moral leeway in dirty thoughts and indeed dirty talk.

On the Internet, dirty talk passes as "chatting" (which is not to say that all chat rooms are erotically oriented). As if chatting were not already ambiguous enough, some people have taken to referring to it as "phone sex." What is phone sex? Do you need a phone for it? Will a chat room do? Is phone sex any different from what we call "talking dirty"?

For at least a decade before the advent of the Internet, pornographic magazines and subway advertisements (ubiquitous in Paris) offered the telephone numbers of professionals (in the sense that they got paid) available to explore sexual fantasies. A business transaction, this call entailed a fee, charged to your phone bill, based on time spent talking. You paid, and the pro profited.

By "phone sex," people seem to mean talking dirty on the phone. You may have a private phone conversation with an amateur you have "met" in a chat room, or you may call a "pro" and pay for his or her services, as advertised on the Internet or elsewhere. In any event, you do not meet, although you may have seen a photograph of him or her (or think you have—you may have exchanged pictures on the Internet, but he or she may have submitted a photo of someone else). "Phone sex" involves another person in a way that solitary sprints through pornographic magazines do not.

Is this talk a way of having sex? The idea that words can seduce others, or might serve as a kind of foreplay, has been around for centuries. Poets from around the world have left us some shining examples. With Freud came the idea that talking might be equivalent to sex itself. Certainly talking dirty falls within the realm of sexual harassment—it is not something a manager can do at work to subordinates, for example (although technically, the dirty talk must be unwelcome, severe, and protracted in order to win a lawsuit against an employer). The idea that "phone sex" is a "gateway drug" that will escalate to something much bigger and more dangerous does not seem obvious, though. Chat rooms are journeys that needn't lead to physical contact with another. Of course, they sometimes do.

What people call "phone sex" isn't really sex at all. Of crucial importance is the lack of touching (despite AT&T's commercial invitations to "reach out and touch someone"). Thinking of dirty talk over the phone as sex confuses moral evaluation. The verbal innovation "phone sex," clever as it may sound, ought to be abandoned. We already have a perfectly apt way of describing this activity: talking dirty. Anyone wishing to emphasize the phone's role in dirty talk would do better to speak of phone flirting. Flirting may or may not lead to sexual contact, but flirting itself is not sex.

Nor is voyeurism sex. Ogling pornographic images, either in an old-fashioned magazine or on the Internet, is a kind of voyeurism. It is not sex. Most of us are soft-core voyeurs to some extent (not just the prosaic husband with "a wandering eye"). Depending on the configuration of the shower room, lesbian, gay, and bisexual people can hardly avoid becoming voyeurs each time they wash off at the gym. Looking into other people's windows, what a peeping Tom does, is hardcore voyeurism. Although a peeping Tom can get into trouble with the law, what he or she does is not sex. People who talk dirty in Internet chat rooms are a new kind of peeping Tom—typing Toms we might call them. They are not having sex.

Whatever else flirting may be, it is not sex. Patting someone on the bottom or giving a hug may sometimes arouse us; neither amounts to sex, though. And what about dancing? Is that sex? Indeed, there is such a thing as "dirty dancing"—even a movie by that title. Flirting and dancing have long troubled religious leaders because of the confusing dynamic that these activities inaugurate. We want to insist that waltzing with the boss's husband or the boss's wife can be morally innocent, despite the close physical contact involved. Dancing, like flirting, is not sex.

It might be thought that flirting is intentional, that is to say that we flirt only if we intend to do so. But this view misses the ease with which we can hide behind our roles as sales clerks, waiters, and entertainers. We can flirt even when we pretend we are just doing what's expected of us. We can deceive others, even ourselves, about what we intend.

Waiters and sales clerks routinely report that flirting with customers is good for business. It is hard to deny that flirting becomes us. The stodgy butler from Ishiguro's novel *The Remains of the Day* ruminates on his refusal to flirt and the colorless, lonely existence to which it has led: "Perhaps it is indeed time I began to look at this whole matter of bantering more enthusiastically. After all, when one thinks about it, it is not such a foolish thing to indulge in—particularly if it is the case that in bantering lies the key to human warmth."[7] Flirting can build rapport with others. We understand what it means, for example, to dress for success in the workplace or to keep up with fashion trends when going to parties. We may find ourselves flirting by wearing clothing that fits our bodies closely or exposes a certain amount of leg, chest, or arm. We might wonder, what is the difference between the sight of a woman's cleavage emerging from an expensive French gown and the chat room journey of someone who never intends to have sex with anyone he meets in cyberspace? It may well be that flirting amounts to self-centered bragging or exhibitionism: "Look how beautiful I am," fashionably dressed people may be saying. Flirting may sometimes ask nothing more of others than admiration.

In contrast to flirting, it is possible to engage in another suspect kind of activity all by yourself: masturbation. Involving no mutuality, masturbation is known as a distinctly inferior form of sexual activity. In his early writings, Karl Marx derided what he took to be Hegel's extravagantly theoretical books through a mean analogy: Hegel is to "real" philosophy what masturbation is to "real" sex. Those who view anonymous cyberchatting as a new way of having sex would presumably conclude that chatting is a disappointing and even embarrassing substitute for a higher pleasure.

Long-standing opposition to pornography is rooted in an ancient fear of (male) masturbation. (Most moral thinking about masturbation has ignored female masturbation.) Chatting will likely (and reasonably) offend anyone who objects to pornography, in part because of the alleged link between pornography and masturbation.

Vilification of masturbation, or onanism, stretches back over two thousand years. Modern people often find the received reasons for condemning masturbation hilarious. Ancient Greeks and Romans, for example, thought of semen as costly horsepower. Ejaculation robbed a man of a vital fluid without which he could not roar or soar. As recently as a hundred years ago, some religious thinkers in the United States insisted that unused semen was reabsorbed by the body and then harnessed as energy. Proper religious devotion was impossible without the tremendous energy supplied by conserved semen. Frequent intercourse in a marriage was therefore discouraged and masturbation vilified (soldiers in the ancient world were cautioned against any ejaculations at all). Rabbinical Judaism and Roman Catholicism have long condemned the sin of Onan. The film *Monty Python's The Meaning of Life* even includes a musical send-up of Catholic reverence for semen called "Every Sperm Is Sacred."[8] To the extent that chatting, like pornography, induces masturbation, it is not surprising that a cultural tide of objection rises up to greet this cyber-innovation.

Men fantasize about sex roughly twice as frequently as women, according to studies in Japan, the United Kingdom, and the United States. Men are more likely to fantasize about strangers as well, which means that chatting might tempt men more than women.

But if Oscar Wilde is correct that women fall in love with their ears and men with their eyes, then the textual, nonpictorial world of chat rooms might appeal more to women than men. Some recent fiction (such as Sylvia Brownrigg's *The Metaphysical Touch*, Jeanette Winterson's *The Powerbook*, and Alan Lightman's *The Diagnosis*) prominently features women chatting. We are sure to see a steady stream of novels involving chatting in the near future, and these works may challenge the very idea that chatting appeals more to one gender than the other.

Women may risk more in chatting or flirting. Culture and law have long been men's domains. It is hardly surprising that religious and secular cultures both reflect a masculine bias. To be sure, there are words for men who "get around": We call them a Don Juan, a Casanova, a Lothario. We call women other names, names that should not be repeated in polite society. For millennia, fathers and husbands have made it difficult for their daughters and wives to flirt. The Internet makes it easier for anyone with access to cyberspace to flirt. As long as women remain economically dependent on men, though, they will risk more in chatting (assuming, of course, that those on whom they depend consider chatting cheating).

Flirting requires a certain comfort level with uncertainty. As the popular saying "flirting with disaster" indicates, we are on our way somewhere when we flirt. We have not arrived, nor will we necessarily. Augustine, who cast greater aspersion on sex than perhaps any other Western thinker, started out as an adventurous young man. His famous plea to God "Give me chastity and continence—but not yet" plays off of flirting. Augustine had not yet embraced the ideal moral life and so, his reasoning goes, did not deserve any credit for the desire. By the same reasoning, we do not deserve blame for flirting with attractive people.

We sustain our notion of fidelity by banishing uncertainty and policing its attendant complications, such as devouring porn magazines, a night at Chippendale's or a topless bar, and everyday flirting. We may understandably fear ambivalence once we have made a romantic commitment. Nonetheless, the idea that better or deeper erotic fulfillment lies elsewhere may nag at us. Through flirting, we enjoy uncertainty. Our comfort level with uncertainty (and love is notoriously unstable) drives our moral evaluation of online dalliances.

WAYS OF CHEATING

Strangers in the Net, exchanging glances, strangers in the Net, what are the chances? They'll be sharing love, before the night is through? The chances of falling in love online may not be any worse than in the street. Yet, as always, a person intent on remaining faithful to a spouse or partner must be careful to avoid crossing a certain line. Whatever else a monogamous commitment may entail, it forbids sex outside the couple.

As I have acknowledged, some people certainly do believe that talking dirty is a form of having sex.[9] In some arenas (such as the office), talking dirty qualifies as sexual harassment, but, as I have said, I don't think it makes sense to call this sex. I hold on to the notion, admittedly old-fashioned, that sex entails skin-to-skin contact. Peeping Toms may get into real legal trouble, but it doesn't make sense to say that voyeurism amounts to having sex. Like sexual harassment, voyeurism implicates the active party but not necessarily the passive one.

Ranking sexual misdeeds requires talent and time. Our legal system can help. "Adultery" signifies penal-vaginal penetration and applies to the illicit sexual activity of two or more people, at least one of whom is married. Only married people can be guilty of adultery: if an unmarried woman engages in vaginal intercourse with a married man, he is guilty of adultery, whereas she is guilty of fornication. "Fornication" is to unmarried people what "adultery" is to the married, which is not to say that married people can't fornicate. "Sodomy" applies to both the married and the unmarried and involves anal and/or oral sex. Because they cannot legally marry [this was true when this essay was first published — eds.], gay and lesbian couples can in principle never be guilty of adultery—only of fornication or sodomy. In the highly publicized Monica Lewinsky case, President Clinton (a married man) was guilty of fornication and Lewinsky was guilty of sodomy.

Moral distinctions loom behind such legal ones. There is nothing legally wrong with serial monogamy, for instance. Lots of people in their late teens and twenties devote themselves in earnest to a sexual relationship that they claim has long-term potential. After the break up, another relationship begins and then ends. The cycle continues. Morally speaking, such serial monogamy may not seem very different from fornication. And yet most of us will feel there has to be some difference between promiscuity and failing to carry through on good intentions.

It is important to recognize these distinctions as culturally conditioned. Not everyone agrees with American mores (not even in America). Throughout much of Asia, for example, married men have openly taken concubines with apparent impunity:

> A traditional Chinese or Japanese man could be branded as adulterous only if he slept with the wife of another man. This was taboo. Illicit sex with a married woman was a violation against the woman's husband and his entire ancestry. In China these lawbreakers were burned to death. If a man seduced the wife of his guru in India, he might be made to sit on an iron plate that was glowing hot, then chop off his own penis. A Japanese man's only honorable course was suicide. In traditional Asian agricultural societies, only geishas, prostitutes, slaves, and concubines were fair game. Sex with them was simply not considered adultery.[10]

Not surprisingly, extramarital sex in traditional East Asian cultures was strictly off limits to women, always. What is nonetheless interesting here is the notion that morality (like immorality) has a limit. Adultery doesn't signify *all* sex with someone other than your spouse, just some. This is roughly analogous to the idea that on the third Friday of every month, husbands and wives may morally have sex with anyone they like. If the analogy seems arbitrary, it is because so little of cultural practice is transparent to people who live beyond it.

And so the identity of the person one courted or bedded has figured into the ways other cultures have defined adultery. That identity counts for little in America, where *all* sex with someone other than your spouse qualifies as adultery. Where does cyberflirting fit into this schema? Legally, Internet flirting (what typing Toms do) does not fall into any of our three categories (adultery, fornication, or sodomy). And yet many people will maintain that chatting threatens, or could threaten, monogamous unions. If chatting did represent a kind of cheating, then it would have to be acknowledged as a genuinely new one. I do not think there is anything new under the sun.

Despite the criticism heaped upon Bill Clinton in the wake of his "rationalizations" of sexual adventures (or nonadventures, as he insisted) in the White House, still it remains that most of us agree there is a difference between all-out adultery, hanky-panky, and just talking about one or the other. I am not claiming that we should think of the ethics of virtual flirting on a case-by-case basis but that we should think of chat rooms as morally ambiguous—neither wholly bad nor wholly good.

Another way of thinking about online fidelity is to ask whether a virgin is still a virgin after chatting. In strict religious terms, certainly not.[11] He or she has affronted modesty—"sinned against purity," as Catholic theologians say. Nowadays it is hard to imagine such a view commanding much agreement, even among Catholics. It is still important to remember that rules in a given religion or society go far toward shaping cultural attitudes, though. We can tell something important about Catholicism, for example, from the fact that its greatest moral theologian of the past century maintained that fantasizing about someone else during sex (with your spouse) was a grave moral sin.[12]

Even virgins may burn with lust. The people whom chatting helps most are those committed to celibacy or monogamous relationships. We should expect these people to become the most ardent defenders of imaginative possibilities wrought by the Internet. An obvious advantage to chat rooms is that they keep people out of bars and clubs: away from actual (as opposed to virtual) adulterous possibilities, and away from sexually transmitted diseases as well. This is hardly a moral defense, admittedly.

A good way of defending chatting in the context of committed relationships (whether straight, gay, or religiously committed) is as a temporary "fix"—not unlike a sleeping pill or an antidepressant. Chatting can help you through the inevitable tough times in a relationship aiming at permanency.

Chatting is dangerous to the extent that it absorbs some of the energy required to make a couple a success. A double life carried out in veiled Internet spaces resembles the closet against which most gay and lesbian people develop a sense of self-identity. Chat rooms can become a new closet of sorts (at base, any deep secret can). Double lives can exhaust us, and the Internet can become a demanding mistress indeed, even an addiction. Until chat room adventures start taking up more time than the relationship from which they are a distraction, this danger has nothing to do with the moral acceptability of courting strangers in cyberspace.

While perhaps not the moral ideal, chat room adventures should not be considered adultery or infidelity. The possibility of deceit lurks here, as it does in so many other places. We may pretend to our spouses or spouse equivalents that we would not, could not, even look at another man or woman. There is no question that Romeos and Juliets would be guilty of deceiving their partners if they entered a chat room after having declared they couldn't conceive of doing so. How many among us pretend never to notice attractive strangers? How many of us feel threatened when our partners do notice attractive strangers (or familiars, for that matter)? Chiding chatters may reveal more personal insecurity than moral concern. In any event, it seems the only durable moral objection to chatting is deceit. There might be a good practical objection as well: that chatting will inure us to erotic pleasure with our spouses. If the mind could be so easily dulled by the computer screen, then chatting might in fact threaten a sexual tie to a spouse or spouse equivalent.

Some people are better at flirting than others, and some people are better at fidelity than others. Those who excel at flirting may strike us as cruel if they insist on pointing out our inferior charms and relative unattractiveness. And those who excel at fidelity might strike us as cruel if they were to demand perennial center stage in the thoughts of their spouses or spouse equivalents.

PENETRATION VENERATION

Why should penetration serve as the pivotal criterion for infidelity? Precision is a ready answer. It may seem impossibly difficult to ascertain what someone wants from flirting. She bats her eyelashes and he thinks he has a chance. Then she declines his invitation for a drink, and he furiously demands an explanation. She maintains that he misunderstood her attempt at civil conversation. Or another scenario: Eager to show her interest, she requests help repairing her car. He agrees to try. She cries when he leaves without having asked to see her again. Intentions and desires may sometimes drive our behavior, but others may quite understandably fail to see our motives.

Penetration is another story. A penis in a vagina or someone else's tongue in your mouth can be readily felt or observed. Even if we are under the influence of drugs or alcohol, we will almost certainly realize that penetration is taking place. Act and motive overlap, and so penetration lends itself to the certainty lacking in flirting.

Both formally in the law and informally in the streets, we have long venerated penetration as a reliable threshold for whether sexual intercourse is taking place. Two thousand years ago, for instance, the poet Ovid lamented his impotence. In a poem included in the "Amores" series, he wrote, "Although I wanted to do it, and she was more than willing, / I couldn't get my pleasure part to work. / She tried everything and then some."[13]

Ovid piques our curiosity through the terseness of this last line. Despite the diligence of his partner, Ovid tells us, "She left me, pure as any Vestal virgin / polite as any sister to her brother."[14] He leaves us to wonder how seriously Vestal virgins took their profession and also how well he knew his sister. Ovid's coquettishness aside, we should take him at his word here. He apparently believed that he had not had sex with this woman, who so exerted herself and with whom he tried "everything and then some." Anne Fausto-Sterling has woven this notion into a description of male identity: "Of course, we know already that for men the true mark of heterosexuality involves vaginal penetration with the penis. Other activities, even if they are with a woman, do not really count."[15] Other writers have used penetration as a dramatic psychological threshold. Entering another person may excite fear, a fear that even marriage may not dislodge:

> Among couples who come to a sex-therapy clinic, the prevalence of the madonna/whore or saint/sinner phenomenon is astonishingly high. It wears a proverbial coat of many colors and designs, and so has many disguises. A classic example is that in which the period of romance and courtship was intensely positive for both partners. They engage in much above-the-belt activity and some heavy petting of the genitals to the point of climax, but no genital union itself. They don't actually say that they are saving the dirty part of sex until after they are legally married. Their own explanation is that they are applying their own moral standards by postponing actual penovaginal penetration.
>
> Once they are legally married, they gradually reach the discovery that they can't have ordinary sexual intercourse. He blames himself for ejaculating too soon and for not being able to arouse her to have much active desire or enthusiasm for his penis. She goes along with his self-blame and keeps both of them blinded to the fact that she has a paralyzing fear of having anything actually penetrate into the cavity of her vagina. For her that would be as degrading as being a whore.[16]

Johns Hopkins psychologist John Money draws our attention to a primitive fear of one of the most sensitive boundaries of all—that between our bodies and the outside world. Religious anxiety blossoms on this boundary. This is how sex writer Lisa Palac recounts her furtive sexual debut while a Catholic high school girl in 1970s Chicago:

> Just before the big moment, I admitted that I didn't *exactly* know what to do. "Just open your legs and rock," he told me, which sounded remarkably like a Foghat song. It was over in minutes. Afterwards, I was extremely disappointed and felt sick with guilt. I kept torturing myself with the mantra "I am not a virgin I am not a virgin," which was stupid because I'd done practically everything else—as many oth-

er girls in my class had done—yet none of that constituted sex. It wasn't sex until he put it in.[17]

Penetration veneration finds itself covertly transmitted through the celebration of modesty in this confession. Later recounting one of her first online erotic encounters, Palac tells us of the terrible guilt she felt after the fact. She warned her chat man, "If you tell anyone what we just did, I'll never speak to you again!" She added, "I felt so uncontrollably Catholic. I shouldn't have had cybersex on the first date. Big sin. I should have waited. It would have meant more to me if I'd waited."[18]

Ironic chuckles aside, Palac contradicts herself. Her dirty talk, which in this case eventually progressed from the Internet to the telephone, was not sex, even on her own terms. But vestiges of Catholic school modesty surfaced and prompted guilty feelings.

Carnal contact cannot by itself distinguish flirting from cheating. Unlike exhibitionism or rape, flirting plays off of negotiation. We do not force ourselves on others in flirting; we toy with the exploration of another's opinion of us. It would be too simplistic to reduce flirting to sexual playfulness, though. The ancient Greeks and Romans were notoriously playful sexually. Ascetic Jews and then Christians challenged this playfulness and replaced it with *gravitas*, a high moral seriousness. It is difficult to ally flirtatiousness with either side of this divide. For the sexually playful will pursue flirting until sex, which is to say that the flirting is actually foreplay. The morally serious will swear off flirting generally but smile on a scripted version of chaste romance. Who, then, flirts?

Technically speaking, gregarious people who do not really intend to have sex are just flirting (using penetration as the criterion here). Of course, it is often difficult to predict whether any spirited conversation or eye exchange will lead to full-fledged physical contact. But people who know what they want will see the sense of setting foreplay off from flirting. Seduction can be a game that consciously starts with words and glances. Flirting is an end unto itself—a way of showing someone else that we know "how to play the game" or, perhaps, a test in which we prove to ourselves that we are still attractive. Happily (or even not so happily) married people flirt with colleagues and cocktail party strangers, and it is perfectly acceptable for them to do so. Chatting is the technological celebration of flirting. Adulterous impulses lurking in protected cyberspace will likely lead to penetration; curiosity, playfulness, or boredom, however, will just end in chatting.

The problem with penetration veneration, to which I myself fall victim, is that we end up saying that a man who receives anonymous fellatio has had sex, whereas two close friends who spend a night cuddling naked in bed have not. Even this position is easier to accept than the idea that typing amounts to having sex, though. In the second scenario, we might applaud whatever moral motivation prevented the two friends from consummating their passion. The first scenario, meaningless as it might have been, lacks this moral motivation.

Penetration veneration molds the mind of many a Westerner, sometimes to quite surprising effect. In *Been There, Haven't Done That*, recent Harvard graduate Tara McCarthy, also Catholic, tells us that she is a virgin, despite having been "touched, kissed, poked, prodded, rubbed, caressed, sucked, licked, bitten—you name it."[19] Reflection on this so-called virgin's way of seeing the world should remind us that sex, despite all the advertising it gets, is neither transparently obvious nor wholly intuitive. If it accomplished nothing else, the media coverage of the Monica Lewinsky scandal made clear the extent to which people can differ over the question of when sex begins and flirting ends.

In a sea of ambiguity, penetration emerges as the best single criterion of cheating we may expect to find.

INFIDELITY ONLINE?

Nothing prompts divorce so often as infidelity. We can't stand it when our partners go astray—"go astray" may mean sex, lying about having had sex, or both. Many of our most engaging plays and novels have relied on infidelity as a plot device.

Who cares about the ethics of cyberchatting? Many if not most couples naturally do, as well as those who worry about the moral health of the communities they inhabit. The sex lives of strangers have something to do with us, after all. Our children may someday attend school or play soccer with their children, and we want those meetings to be as constructive as possible. Our fear of lust affects our children, our neighbors, and our laws.

Moral evaluation of chatting colors the ways couples interact with one another as well as what we think of our teachers, colleagues, priests, and rabbis. It should go without saying that in order to care about the ethics of chatting, you first have to care about something else: fidelity, "sins against purity," or trust. I consider fidelity a moral ideal, one I certainly endorse.

We can remain agnostic as to whether or how often chatting will lead to a face-to-face encounter. My goal here is to isolate chatting from attendant activities and ask whether there is something intrinsic to chatting itself that qualifies as betrayal (of a promise to a lover or to God), as opposed to an exercise of the imagination (whether we can betray others through the free use of our imagination is a question I do not take up here). I have presented penetration as the decisive test of whether someone has cheated, while indicating the unsettling underside of flirting. I concede that a whole-hearted person, a saint of heroic integrity, would consistently avoid flirting of any sort.

Is cyberchatting the moral equivalent of talking to someone in a bar, then? Anonymous chatting is morally superior to the extent that it is less likely to lead to physical contact. Is Net naughtiness, even when it becomes a habit, morally worse than an actual (and physical) one-night stand? No. Net naughtiness enhances the sexual imagination. It teaches as it titillates. Giving in to lust and allowing ourselves to chat may provide the illusion of flying over personal limitations that reduce our attractiveness to others. So much of human industry (for example, cosmetics, fitness, fashion, and real estate) comes down to this goal that we really should look sympathetically on chatting. Moreover, we may deepen our sense of who we are and what we want from anonymous chatting. Net naughtiness challenges the sexual uniformity many take monogamy to impose. It shows us that something like sexual diversity is possible without shattering monogamous bonds.

Net naughtiness strains traditional ideas about what a person is. Are the faceless strangers we meet online real people? Can we hurt their feelings? Can they have us arrested? They understand that we do not know who they are; presumably they cannot be slighted by us over the Internet in the way they can in person. Given the way the Internet depersonalizes human contact (even as it increases the opportunities for locating other people), it is hard to say whether chatting involves another human being in the way that even a one-night stand does. How thinly can we stretch our notion of a person? Very thin indeed, chatting shows us. Those we chat with may seem no more human than the characters who populate the fiction we read.

In the course of defending it, I have recognized the danger of chatting. If it is true that "women are more forgiving and less upset if no emotional involvement accompanies their husband's affair,"[20] then extensive chatting might seem more threatening than a one-night stand. Pen pals or Net pals might seem to develop an emotional attachment to one another over time, an attachment unlikely to begin in a one-night stand. Time, or duration, has a lot to do with both the psychological and moral evaluation of chatting. A night of passion is for many fuming spouses easier to forgive than a cultivated attachment. Chatting certainly can fray our commitments to others, no less than our quest for self-fulfillment.

In sum, the Internet has given lust a new outlet. Fantasy life has always been possible, and pornography already abounded in ancient Greece and Rome (despite Plato's disapproval). Being human just got more exciting—and more complicated. The Internet and the phone may threaten fidelity, chastity, even integrity—but no more so than old-fashioned pornography. Chat rooms may in the long run facilitate fidelity, insofar as they can in themselves satisfy an active imagination.

A pleasure both simple and complex, chatting captures nicely the undying tension between trust and lust. Making room for chatting in a monogamous relationship honors both the promise of sexual exclusivity and the titanic power of the imagination.[21]

NOTES

1. Edith Hamilton and Huntington Cairns, eds., *The Collected Dialogues of Plato*, translated by Lane Cooper et al. (Princeton, N.J.: Princeton University Press, 1961), 64, 82 (the *Phaedo*, 485–88) (the *Phaedrus*, 237–42).

2. Augustine, *Confessions*, translated by R. S. Pine-Coffin (Baltimore, Md.: Penguin Books, 1961), 234.

3. See Richard Marius, *Martin Luther: The Christian between God and Death* (Cambridge, Mass.: Harvard University Press, 2000): "Our bodies, he said, are ordered for honorable marriage or still more honorable chastity, and the cure for lust is prayer" (109).

4. http://www.who.int/mediacentre/factsheets/fs241/en/index.html (accessed April 2, 2012).

5. This, despite the allowance of the highly influential eighteenth-century Roman Catholic theologian St. Alphonsus Liguori that having sex in a church or a public place might be allowed in a case of "necessity." See Peter Gardella, *Innocent Ecstasy: How Christianity Gave America an Ethic of Sexual Pleasure* (New York: Oxford University Press, 1985), 18.

6. G. E. M. Anscombe, "Contraception and Chastity," *The Human World*, no. 7 (1972), 22.

7. Kazuo Ishiguro, *The Remains of the Day* (New York: Vintage, 1990), 245.

8. *Monty Python's The Meaning of Life* (Celandine Films, 1983), starring Graham Chapman, John Cleese, Terry Gilliam, Eric Idle, Terry Jones, Michael Palin, Sydney Arnold, and Guy Bertrand. Kasy Moon provided the correct reference here.

9. "You can meet someone on-line. You can fall in love on-line. You can even consummate that love on-line." Paco Underhill, *Why We Buy: The Science of Shopping* (New York: Simon & Schuster, 1999), 212.

10. Helen Fisher, *Anatomy of Love* (New York: W. W. Norton, 1992), 79–80.

11. Bernard Häring, *The Law of Christ*, translated by Edwin G. Kaiser (Westminster, Md.: Newman Press, 1966), vol. III, 306.

12. *Ibid.*, 375–76.

13. Quoted in Elizabeth Abbott, *A History of Celibacy* (New York: Scribners, 2000), 354.

14. *Ibid.*

15. Anne Fausto-Sterling, "How to Build a Man," in Vernon A. Rosario, ed., *Science and Homosexualities* (New York: Routledge, 1997), 219–25. Quoted in Robert A. Nye, ed., *Sexuality* (New York: Oxford University Press, 1999), 238.

16. John Money, *The Destroying Angel* (Buffalo, N.Y.: Prometheus Books, 1985), 127.

17. Lisa Palac, *The Edge of the Bed: How Dirty Pictures Changed My Life* (Boston: Little, Brown, 1998), 20.

18. *Ibid.*, 106.

19. Tara McCarthy, *Been There, Haven't Done That: A Virgin's Memoir* (New York: Warner Books, 1997), 3.

20. David M. Buss, *The Evolution of Desire: Strategies of Human Mating* (New York: Basic Books, 1994), 155.

21. Pamela Karlan, Jerome Neu, and Anthony Ellis graciously provided comments on this essay, which Daniel Ortiz especially enriched.

STUDY QUESTIONS

1. Is Portmann's view of sexual desire and arousal—"lust completes us (however temporarily), fills us with a vivid sense of being alive, propels us along the way to self-fulfillment"—naively idealistic or implausibly optimistic? Compare his view to what the metaphysical pessimists might say about lust (as outlined in the introduction to this volume), and for which they use the term, often meant to be derogatory, "concupiscence."

2. Explicate the details of Portmann's major arguments, making sure to explain the role that concepts such as "adultery," "fornication," "serial monogamy," and "virginity" play in them. Ask, while reconstructing his arguments, whether his conclusion is that erotic chatting is not "sex," or that it is "sex" but a morally acceptable type.

3. Is physical touching, skin-to-skin, necessary for "sex" or for people to be "having sex," as Portmann believes? Consider the dual masturbation spoken of by Alan Soble ("An Essay on Masturbation," in this volume): two people masturbate, in the sense of "self-stimulation," in front of each other, without touching but aroused by the sight of each other. Is this "sex"? Is it "having sex"? Why or why not? Does the presence or absence of orgasm make a difference?

4. Evaluate Portmann's "penetration" criterion for "sex" (about which he does have some doubts, as does Greta Christina, "Are We Having Sex Now or What?" in this volume). Given that criterion, would lesbian couples not "have sex" unless they used objects with which to penetrate each other? Would penetration by tongues, fingers, or fists, rather than by dildos or vegetables, be the right amount or kind of penetration to make their acts "sex"? (On this topic see Marilyn Frye, "Lesbian 'Sex,'" in *Willful Virgin: Essays in Feminism, 1976–1992* [Freedom, Calif.: Crossing Press, 1992], 109–19.)

5. Even if cyberchatting is not sexual cheating, might it still not be a form of non-sexual (e.g., emotional) cheating or unfaithfulness? Following the words of Jesus (Matthew 5:28), might there be a metaphorical adultery *of* the heart, in terms of a person's character, their virtues, or even their spirituality? Imagine a woman coming home to find her boyfriend or husband masturbating furiously with one hand while typing (also furiously) with the other. Will she be much mollified by Portmann's philosophy? (Maybe, if she gave the guy permission.)

6. Note that Portmann uses the term "sexual activity" only twice in his essay, preferring to talk, instead, about whether a behavior is "sex" or "having sex." Is it possible that his language involves an equivocation or makes defending his theses too easy? Is it one

thing to say that to chat erotically is not "sex" or "having sex," and another (perhaps quite different) thing to say that to chat erotically is not (even) a "sexual activity"? The former seems trivial; the latter seems to be an important substantive thesis. Which one is Portmann's? Consider a similar linguistic problem that arises about Greta Christina's essay "Are We Having Sex Now or What?" in this volume.

SEVEN

An Essay on Masturbation

Alan Soble

Alan Soble *begins his essay by discussing the* Oxford English Dictionary's *definition of "masturbation," focusing on its three central concepts of "stimulation," "manually," and "for sexual pleasure." He finds that the attempted definition fails for a number of reasons, one being its inability to provide necessary conditions. Soble then segues into a discussion of social attitudes toward masturbation, and ponders why they tend to condemn the masturbation of men more than that of women. He then raises problems with the idea of mutual masturbation: if to understand it we should not insist on the necessity of the use of hands and genitals, then what differentiates it from other sexual acts, such as oral sex? Finally, after going over some unconvincing medical and psychological condemnations of masturbation, Soble ends the essay by praising the practice.*

If your right hand causes you to sin, cut it off and throw it away.
—Jesus according to Matthew, 5:30

If thy right hand causes thee to sin, use thy left hand instead.
—Philip according to Woody, 25:69

TACKLING THE *OXFORD ENGLISH DICTIONARY*

Many arguments have been fashioned to condemn masturbation—assuming, that is, that "masturbation" has been defined well enough so that one and the same thing is the object of all these arguments. It would be annoying if only family resemblances could be found to thread together the varieties of masturbatory activities. Analytic definitions that state necessary and sufficient conditions are elusive, but they promise both beauty and utility. I have been trying for over three decades (off and on, not continuously) to define "masturbation," often uncovering an illuminating tangle in the masturbatory landscape, but not finishing the task.

The *Oxford English Dictionary* does well to remind us that any philosophical essay on, say, masturbation may itself be an instance of masturbation:

> 1995 *Sun* (Baltimore) (Nexis) 19 Nov. 1 A, Is this art or isn't it? I remember all those intellectual, masturbatic discussions in the art community.[2]

This is good reason for not titling this essay the provocatively ambiguous "Masturbation."[3] It would have been commendable if the *OED* had also given us an accurate and helpful definition of the verb "to masturbate." Instead, we are given the limp

> masturbate, *v.* **1.** *intr.* To stimulate one's genitals manually, or by other means, for sexual pleasure.[4]

I admit that it would be lame to get bent out of shape over the word "stimulate." Still, I would prefer something weaker, such as "fool around with," "move around," or "apply pressure to," because "stimulate" implies *success* and some masturbatory acts go nowhere, for various reasons. One reply, in defense of "stimulate," would have it that the failure of stimulation implies that the act was only an attempt at masturbation, not a genuine case of masturbation. This is where some laypersons and philosophers sense the masturbatory nature of philosophy.

Nonetheless, the *OED*'s definition is suspicious for other reasons, and even intelligent laypersons and philosophers will be moved by a few simple points. The phrase "manually, or by other means" rules out absolutely nothing as being a technique of stimulating the genitals. That may be right, in principle; there is no limit to the Rube Goldberg contraptions I could set up to stimulate my genitals. (Wouldn't they all begin or end in quasi-manual stimulation?) Some "other means" would, however, be positively stupid and dangerous. Think *Robot Chicken*. As a result, the vacuity leaves me wondering what particular methods the *OED* had in its collective mind, besides the manual, which prompted it to tack on "by other means."

Another worry I have about "manual" is whether it betrays a phallo-centric perspective. I hate to speak for men, but I'm pretty sure that guys often make use of their hands, qua amalgam of fingers and palms, so "manually" is alright. I would doubly hate to speak for women, but it seems to me that masturbating women may sporadically use fingers more so than hands, in which case "digitally" is more appropriate. To be safe, the definition should be "manually, digitally, or by other means." Further, some guys use one or two dainty fingers, and some women employ a paw, fist, or fat dildo. "Manually or digitally" covers all these bases.

It might be thought that "by other means" is no cause for alarm, because the definition says that the masturbatory act is done for (*to achieve*) sexual pleasure. Thus "manually, digitally, or by other means that are aimed at yielding sexual pleasure" puts an intelligible limit on nonmanual and nondigital methods of masturbating. Simulating humping or coital motions against a mattress is another means. But if the purpose or goal of stimulating one's genitals is sexual pleasure, then the act of rubbing one's erect penis until it squirts fluid into a collection vessel, the fluid to be employed later in artificial insemination or to be assayed for sperm density and motility, is *not* masturbation. Pleasure may be attained in such acts, but it is not the goal.

This point sinks the *OED*'s definition. "Stimulate for sexual pleasure" may be a true *description* of many acts of masturbation, but it is not *definitional*, on pain of eliminating masturbation engaged in for medical reasons.[5] What are we to call medical masturbation, if not "masturbation"?—He's not jerking off, he's only providing a sperm sample. That's why the nurse didn't leave a copy of *Juggs Galore* or *Really Big Dicks* in the men's room.—It is one thing, and ignorable, to complain about "stimulate" that it snags us into a debate about failed vs. successful masturbations, and another thing (significant) that a paradigm case of masturbation is, after all, not masturbatory, due to defining the act in terms of an intended purpose. Now, if we avoid reference to the sexual goal of the act, the intelligible handle we thought we had on the specific nonmanual, nondigital "other means" is gone. "Other means" now floats untethered.

The *OED* proposes three features from which to fashion a definition of "masturbation": (i) stimulation of one's genitals, (ii) manually, and (iii) for sexual pleasure. I grant that if these three features are put together, they are jointly sufficient to pick out acts as masturbatory. Any person who manually stimulates his or her genitals in order to (try to) experience sexual pleasure from that manual stimulation *is* masturbating.[6] But none of the features is individually necessary for an act to be masturbatory: other body parts may be stimulated; the stimulation need not be manual, digital, or comprehensible; and the goal need not be sexual pleasure. If the three features are sufficient but not necessary, the definition is powerful enough to conclude that act *X* is a case of masturbation but too weak to conclude that act *Y* is not a case of masturbation. Make up your own example of masturbation (not figurative) that has none of the three *OED* features.

We have come across a genuine puzzle: What is masturbation? How should it be defined? In the paradigm case, which the *OED* likely considered, a person in a private place manually rubs the penis or clitoris and eventually reaches an orgasm. It seems simple enough. We have seen, however, that salient features of the paradigm case are inessential. A person can masturbate in the waiting room of a bus terminal, erect penis or engorged vulva exposed for all to see. (You are quickly put away for such things.) The hands or fingers do not have to be used as long as sexual areas of the body can be pressed against suitably shaped, comfortable items: a horse's back, the seat of a motorcycle, a rug. Orgasm need not be attained, nor need it be the goal. Prolonged, endless, pleasure may be the point, which is nipped in the bud by orgasm. The clitoris or *glans penis* need not receive the most or any attention; other sensitive areas can be touched or probed for pleasure: nipples, anus, thighs, lips. What remains in the paradigm case? All I see is that the person who, by touching the body's sexual areas causally produces the sensations, is the same person who experiences them. The rubber is the rubbed; the stroker is the stroked. The "solitary vice" is logically reflexive. (Don't bet on that.)

A DOUBLE STANDARD

In addition to funny phrases for masturbation (buttering the bagel, bashing the bishop),[7] there is also the derogatory "self-abuse." Social attitudes toward masturbation are especially strong and negative. In class, my students are comfortable talking about casual sex and gross perversions but are noticeably reticent when masturbation arises. Negative social attitudes may explain why we tend to keep our masturbatory practices to ourselves, except anonymously, as in reports to Shere Hite.[8] The sexual revolution of the 1960s and 1970s, as far as I remember it, made living together and engaging in sex outside matrimony socially acceptable; it encouraged the toleration, if not the celebration, of LGBT lifestyles (although they were not called that); it breathed respectful life into the colorful practices of the heterosexual and homosexual daughters and sons of the Marquis de Sade. Adultery, homosexuality, prostitution, sexual harassment, and premarital sex are by now standard fare in television dramas and sitcoms, but except for one episode of *Seinfeld*—Who in this motley group can resist doing it the longest?—masturbation is absent.[9] The masturbatic closet remains shut.[10]

It is primarily male masturbation that is the illustrious black sheep of the family of sex (though bestiality might literally be the black sheep, hidden in the B-movie territory of West Virginia). To call a man a "jerk off" or to insinuate that he masturbates is strongly critical. Bagel-buttering women avoid criticism because their masturbation is innocuous, not "wasting" any precious fluids or ova, as the male "wastes" his silver seed. This idea has a long history in the West.[11] Further, in singling out male masturbation for condemnation, the Hebrews and, later, Thomas Aquinas (ca. 1225–1275) may have thought that a man who masturbates loses control of himself and demonstrates weakness of will. He effaces himself and becomes, in effect, a woman, a creature with less rational autonomy.[12] Hence there was no reason for the patriarchs to complain about female masturbation. It is of no consequence not only because women do not waste anything but also because, already *being* women, they don't run the risk of *becoming* women. Women's masturbation is not an effeminizing disaster.

Male masturbation may receive worse press than female masturbation also because it is more prevalent, both among men as a group and for particular men, and is commonly associated with perversion.[13] Another take is Immanuel Kant's (1724–1804) argument that masturbation may be morally worse than suicide. Masturbation "makes man . . . a thing that is contrary to nature, that is, a *loathsome* object," while someone "who defiantly casts off life as a burden is at least not making a feeble surrender to animal impulse . . . murdering oneself requires courage."[14] Kant asserts a traditional cultural standard of masculinity: genuine men don't masturbate, as spineless, effeminate males do, even if genuine men, relying on their gender-linked courage (but afraid of *something*), occasionally commit suicide.

Male masturbation is useless in two ways. Because it wastes seed, it creates nothing. It is also a private affair in which the guy concentrates on his own pleasure; it is self-indulgent and as a result selfish by removing time and energy from socially productive labor. Masturbation is the idle production only of pleasure and for that reason worthless. But, as Ronald de Sousa writes, "Some things can be both valuable and useful, but only what is useless can be purely valuable."[15] In contrast to the disparaging view of masturbation as useless, we could praise it exactly because it is playfully idle. Here the difference between male and female masturbation arises again, that the male variety wastes seed while female masturbation is innocuous. Only female masturbation could be purely valuable because purely useless. It does not waste anything. It does not fail to be productive. True, male masturbation is often perfectly useless and enjoyable. But it is always haunted by the thought that the energy and resources are better employed by plowing the field or writing another book.[16]

Of course, there's always the suspicion that boys and men who wank, or wank the most, are those who have neither the resources nor the charisma to charm the ladies, or are positively physically or socially repulsive (*Family Guy*'s Neil Goldman). To be called a "jerk off," then, is to be accused of being an (effeminate) wimp who will never have sexual relations with a woman. His masturbation announces to the world and to himself that he doesn't fulfill the standards of masculinity that are socially expected of males. Women who masturbate do not violate a similar social standard of femininity.[17] (Some kind words for Neil: "Shock. Denial. Anger. Bargaining. Depression. Acceptance. Masturbation." Thank you, Garry Shandling, 11/29/1949–3/24/2016.)

TYPES OF MASTURBATION

Can one person masturbate another person—is it conceptually possible? According to the *OED*, the answer is "yes":

> masturbate, *v.* **2.** *trans.* To stimulate the genitals of (a person), esp. manually, for sexual pleasure.

Neither "manually" nor "for sexual pleasure" is essential, as we have seen. I wonder why "by other means" was omitted; surely I can create and set in motion a contraption that masturbates you (or bribe my cousin to do it). "A person" in parentheses is provocative; although I have never done so, I could gently masturbate a dog in an artificial breeding procedure. "To masturbate" as a transitive verb, however, causes headaches.

A sexology dictionary asserts that one person can masturbate another; indeed, which seems logical, two people can masturbate each other. Its "Masturbation" entry offers this definition:

> Self-stimulation of the genitalia (qv) by touch or pressure, usually with the hands or vibrator (qv), and with orgasm (qv) as a common but not inevitable or necessary outcome. In masturbating, many women may combine vaginal and breast stimulation with clitoral stimulation. . . . Mutual masturbation may be engaged in by a couple as an alternative to sexual intercourse (qv).[18]

Defining "masturbation" by mentioning a vibrator is silly. More general terms should be used that would include, for example, stuffing oneself (fore or aft) with an ivory dildo; the ancients did not have batteries. Who knows what the technology of masturbation (or sexuality itself) will be in 2101? To be fair, the authors realize that "vibrator" is only historically descriptive.

Something else troubles me more: if "masturbation" is *defined* as "self-stimulation," there could not *be* any such phenomena as Jack's masturbating Jill and Jack and Jill masturbating each other. What the sexologists (and the *OED*) may have in mind is that solitary masturbation often involves hand-genital contact, so masturbation occurs when one person manually rubs another person's crotch (sometimes called a *handjob*, on analogy with *blowjob*); and when two people use their hands on each other's genitals, these acts are "mutual" masturbation. Appealing to this rationale is awkward, because neither the hands nor the genitals are essential for an act's being solo masturbatic. Further, mutual masturbation would then include all sorts of acts between people (e.g., rubbing, tweaking, or licking the other's nipples or neck) which are not *called* "mutual" or any other kind of masturbation. The alternative is to assert that reflexivity is necessary for a sexual act to be masturbatory and jettison "mutual masturbation" as a confused misnomer. "Handjob" (and "footjob") can be kept for handjobs (footjobs) and mutual handjobs (footjobs).

In another sexology reference book, Lester Dearborn lists several types of masturbation, including:[19] (i) "dual" masturbation, in which two people masturbate themselves in the presence of the other, presumably looking at each other, with or without mirrors, or at least listening to their noises and words (else dual has no advantage over solo); (ii) "group" masturbation, which goes beyond the two people of dual masturbation; (iii) "nocturnal" masturbation, which is not involuntary emission but occurs when a person wakes up and finds his hands busy in his crotch; and (iv) "psychic" masturbation, where orgasm results from fantasy alone, without genital stimulation.[20] Dearborn observes about group masturbation that it may be "a contest to see which [boy] ejaculates first"; that's evidence that achieving pleasure need not be masturbation's goal. Later the boys will learn the virtues of finishing last or of settling for a tie.

About (v) "mutual masturbation," Dearborn candidly writes:

> This refers to two individuals, who practice manual masturbation of each other. Some laymen loosely use the term mutual masturbation to include any act other than penile-vaginal intercourse and would therefore consider fellation and cunnilinctus as masturbatory acts. But this is loose and inaccurate usage.[21]

I agree that this usage is suspicious; mutual oral sex is not ordinarily seen as masturbatory. Here's the headache. Once it is decided that genitals and hands need not be involved in masturbation, mutual masturbation cannot be restricted to the case in which the hands of Jack make contact with the genitals of Jill. Hence oral sex can be mutual masturbation — *if* we wish to continue to use "masturbate" as a transitive verb and masturbation can be a two-person sexual activity.[22] Indeed, every two-party sex act is masturbatory, because the friction of skin against skin that occurs during mutual masturbation is the same as any other two-person rubbing of skin against skin. There are no differences between solitary and mutual masturbation or between solo sexual activity and any paired sexual activity, even intercourse. All sex is the rubbing of surfaces. The only difference between some sexual acts and others is the number of people-surfaces $(1, 2, 3, \ldots, n)$ involved.

Here's another way of approaching the headache. Suppose that Jack, while engaging in coitus with Jill, deliberately elaborates private fantasies that add to his sexual pleasure. We might say that Jack is using Jill's body to masturbate in or with. What Jack is doing is significantly similar to what Jack would be doing were Jack fantasizing while solo masturbating. We could also say that the rapist who uses the body of his victim for his own pleasure is masturbating with her flesh. Much the same could be said about the inconsiderate husband who is concerned only with his own pleasure and is oblivious to what his spouse is experiencing. If these men are the authors of masturbatory sex acts, what divides the nonmasturbatory from the masturbatory in paired sex are not the physical features of the acts performed (manual, genitals, etc.) but whether the people are sharing the activity or one person is employing it at the other's expense. On this view, paired sexual acts are masturbatory if they involve gross selfishness, and no paired act that is designed to afford mutual pleasure is masturbatory. Solitary masturbation might then be seen as essentially self-centered. That may be true, but no moral judgment follows, whereas in the two-party case it is easier to derive moral judgments from the act's being masturbatory. (But what if each person consents to being so used by the other? Another headache.)

WHAT'S THE BIG DEAL?

In the thirteenth century, Aquinas laid the foundation for contemporary Catholic sexual ethics, according to which sexually unnatural acts, those having no procreative potential or those that are an obstacle to procreation, are sinful.[23] Hence masturbation (solo or mutual, to completion) is a mortal sin. I have never found Natural Law arguments that prohibit harmless (and victimless) sexual acts to be convincing, especially if the acts can be carried out with the spirit of *agape*.[24] Five centuries later, Kant, too, asserted the immorality of solo masturbation: "By it man sets aside his person [his *humanity*—AS] and degrades himself below the level of animals."[25]

Aside from Catholics, other Natural Law theologians, nearly all Protestants, a slew of proponents of Judaism or Islam, and secular conservative Kantians (vs. liberal Kantians, for whom J. S. Mill's "free and informed consent" is the moral gold standard), hardly anyone else bothers these days to rant morally against masturbation. However, there has been and still is the alternative vilification of masturbation on medical or psychological grounds. Keith Ward has suggested that Kant condemned masturbation in part by claiming that it "leads to sterility and early senility."[26] Masturbation, as do gluttony and drunkenness, for Kant, destroys the body and mind and hence undermines one's humanity (i.e., rational autonomy). Kant's medical views about the debilitating effects of masturbation do not appear in his *Lectures on Ethics* (where he condemns masturbation as a crime against nature), but are in *Pedagogie*.[27] Kant claims that if faced with the choice between masturbating and having unmarried sexual relations with a (disease-free?) girl, a young man should opt for the girl — thereby violating the Second Formulation of the Categorical Imperative[28] — so severe are masturbation's medical effects. In replying to Kant's disapproval of masturbation, Arthur Schopenhauer (1788–1860) wrote this obituary for ethics:

> To combat [masturbation] is much more a matter of diet than ethics; for this reason works against it are written by medical men . . . and not by moralists. If morality now wishes to take a hand in this matter after dietetics and hygiene have done their part and crushed it with irrefutable arguments, she finds so much already done that there is little left for her to do.[29]

Schopenhauer must have been thinking about Kant's moral criticism of masturbation in the *Lectures on Ethics* and *The Metaphysics of Morals*, not his medical critique in *Pedagogie*. Nevertheless, Schopenhauer was a sharp observer: he sensed that medicine was firmly grabbing control over masturbation and the rest of the domain of sexual behavior (including perversions) from theology and the bureaucracy of religion.[30] That commandeering is by the twenty-first century hegemonically complete.

In an earlier foray into the medicine of masturbation, Bernard Mandeville (1670–1733) had outdone Kant: "[T]here are three Ways by which lewd young Men destroy their natural Vigour, and render themselves impotent: First, By Manufriction, *alias* Masturbation."[31] What happens to these youngsters? A psychosomatic disaster:

> *Onanites* . . . so weaken their genitals, and accustom them to this violent Friction, that, tho' they have frequent Evacuations without an Erection, yet the common and ordinary Sensation which Females afford to those Parts, is not able of itself to promote this Evacuation: so that they are impotent to all Intents and Purposes of Generation.[32]

A few centuries later Sigmund Freud (1856–1939) also claimed that "on the basis of my medical experience I cannot rule out a permanent reduction in potency as one among the results of masturbation."[33] Whereas Kant had relied on the frightful effects of masturbation to excuse, but not fully bless, a young boy's engaging in sexual relations with an available, unmarried girl, Mandeville used the frightful effects to justify houses of prostitution: "To put a stop therefore to these clandestine Practices, and prevent young Men from laying *violent Hands* upon themselves, we must have recourse to the *Publick Stews*."[34] Mandeville's wisdom is not meant in the spirit of Jonathan Swift's "A Modest Proposal" (1729).

The contemporary sexual zeitgeist asserts not only that masturbation is innocuous but also that it actually has a beneficial effect: helping teenagers abstain from intercourse, which may yield unwanted or burdensome pregnancies (or abortion) and the transmission of disease.[35] Whereas from Kant and Mandeville we can extract the principle "*coitus ad remedium masturbationis*,"[36] and from St. Monica we heard the (eventually retracted) Pauline advice to her adolescent son, Augustine,[37] *"matrimonium ad remedium concupiscentiae [et masturbationis],"* the contemporary mind (with the exceptions noted a few paragraphs above) ironically proffers *"masturbatio ad remedium concupiscentiae."*

But the twentieth and twenty-first centuries have not been altogether kind to masturbation. In Freud's picture, "The masturbator forsakes reality, hindering the development of strong character traits. . . . The masturbator lives in accordance with the principle of lust and so is caught in psychical infantilism."[38] Contemporary philosophers have found esoteric defects in masturbation.[39] Alan Goldman claims, "[V]iewing a pornographic movie qualifies as a sexual activity, but only as an imaginative substitute for the real thing. . . . The same is true of masturbation as a sexual activity without a partner."[40] The "real thing" for Goldman is two-party sexual activity. Thomas Nagel argues that "narcissistic practices" are "truncated or incomplete versions of the complete [sexually natural] configuration."[41] Robert Solomon offers this ingenious account: "If sexuality is essentially a language, it follows that masturbation, while not a perversion, is a deviation. . . . Masturbation is not 'self-abuse' . . . but it is, in an important sense, self-denial. It represents an inability or a refusal to say what one wants to say. . . . Masturbation is the sexual equivalent of a Cartesian soliloquy."[42] And James Giles analyzes sexual desire as "the desire for mutual baring and caressing of bodies," thereby explicitly excluding (as does Goldman) masturbation from the realm of sexual desire and hence sexual activity.[43]

After reading such nonsense for years, and demolishing it in print,[44] I welcome the clever observation, which hits home for men (at least), that in terms of human development and growth, it is masturbation, solitary sexuality, that is primary, and precedes two-party sexuality by over a decade. Further, more solitary masturbation occurs in many (perhaps most) lives than two-party or three-party or *N*-party sex. If so, we should understand paired sex in terms of masturbation instead of concocting miserable understandings of masturbation in terms of paired sex. As Karl Kraus in 1907 famously made the point, "Intercourse with a woman is sometimes a satisfactory substitute for masturbation. But it takes a lot of imagination to make it work."[45] Returning to Neil Goldman, he has nothing to do with girls his age not because he's a loser whom they reject but because he knows that girls at that age (as much as they pretend world-sophistication otherwise) are pretty darn rotten in bed. A better example is Steve Smith (*American Dad*), who does have this deep instinct about girls, even if you insist that Neil is absolutely clueless. (Roger might quip: girls only pretend to be rotten in bed.) What makes all this speculation reality is the sociopsychological finding concerning 421 undergraduate subjects (as if ordinary people didn't already know it), that "Fantasizing during coitus," which was reported by a *majority* of the subjects, "is a normal component of sexual behavior."[46] We fantasize during sexual activity with our partners as if they were not there and as if we were solo masturbating with our favorite trigger images. When both sexual partners X and Y do this at the same time, they are engaged in mental dual masturbation.

NOTES

1. The first essay I wrote on masturbation, "Sexual Desire and Sexual Objects," was presented at the Pacific Division meetings of the American Philosophical Association (San Francisco, March 1978). I then published "Masturbation" in *Pacific Philosophical Quarterly* 61:3 (1980), 233–44. That essay was reprinted, unchanged (qua facsimile), in *Human Sexuality*, edited by Igor Primoratz (Aldershot, UK: Dartmouth, 1997), 139–50. Part of my introduction to *The Philosophy of Sex*, 1st edition (1980), was devoted to masturbation and was developed into another version of the essay, "Masturbation and Sexual Philosophy," which was included in my *The Philosophy of Sex*, 2nd edition (1991), 133–57. Additional thoughts on the topic emerged as chapter 2 of my *Sexual Investigations* (New York: New York University Press, 1996). Part of that chapter became "Masturbation" in my *The Philosophy of Sex*, 3rd edition (1997), 67–85. That version was reprinted in *Ethics for Everyday*, edited by David Benatar (New York: McGraw-Hill, 2002), 180–96. It was further modified to become "Philosophies of Masturbation," in *The Big Book of Masturbation: From Angst to Zeal*, edited by Martha Cornog (San Francisco, Calif.: Down There Press, 2003), 149–66. In most versions of my essays on masturbation, I make a distinction between "binary" and "unitary" theories of sexuality: those that assume that sexuality is ontologically or analytically a "two-person" affair and those that do not make this assumption, and I laid out the arguments for considering the "unitary" theory to be superior (for example, in empirical research on human sexuality). The first places I made this distinction were the 1980 *Pacific Philosophical Quarterly* essay and the introduction to the first edition of *Philosophy of Sex* in 1980.

The problem that arises here appears clearly if we examine an account of sexuality that has much in common with Goldman's but which attempts to overcome the main drawback of his theory—the fact that masturbation was excluded from the domain of sexual activity. This account would say that Goldman has not really exposed the bare level or core of sexuality, that there is a sexuality that is "plainer" than his plain sex. Sexual desire, on this view, is the desire for certain pleasurable sensations (*period*; no mention of contact with another body).

Please note my use here of both terms "plainer" and "period" ("Introduction," 18; see also 48*n*9, 49*n*10) well before other scholars in the philosophy of sex used these words, without providing proper citation or credit, for example, Igor Primoratz, *Ethics and Sex* (London: Routledge, 1999), specifically page 46, lines 15 and 18. Hence, when Seiriol Morgan ("Dark Desires," in this volume) critically discusses Primoratz's theory of sexuality, which is "plainer" than Alan Goldman's, Morgan was misled into thinking he was discussing Primoratz's invention, not mine.

2. From "Masturbatic," *OED* online (2015). A famous example of this figurative use of "masturbation" occurs in Karl Marx and Friedrich Engels's *The German Ideology* (ed. C. Arthur; New York: International Publishers, 1970, 103): "Philosophy and the study of the actual world have the same relation to one another as masturbation and sexual love." For an admirably clear and detailed discussion of this passage, see Luke Roelofs (blog), "Philosophy and Masturbation: Anatomy of a Metaphor," https://majesticequality.wordpress.com/2011/08/04/philosophy-and-masturbation-anatomy-of-a-metaphor/.

3. The wise editors the *Pacific Philosophical Quarterly* encouraged me to rethink the title of my first published article on masturbation (see note 1). For only four decades, I insufferably declined the invitation.

4. The *OED*'s definition of the noun "masturbation" is similar: "Masturbation, *n.* **1.** The stimulation, usually by hand, of one's genitals for sexual pleasure." Entries from the *OED* were kindly supplied to me by coeditor Sarah Hoffman.

5. "Masturbation is the primal moment in which a lesson in the rhythms of power and powerlessness is instilled, insofar as masturbation is an act of control indissociable from loss of control" must be descriptive of masturbation, not definitional (the words are Michael Uebel's [in "Striptopia?" *Social Semiotics* 14:1 (2004), 7–19, at 17*n*15], who paraphrases Leo Bersani). Any brave soul, please tell me what Uebel's Bersani *means* (asoble01@gmail.com).

6. The additional clause is added for this reason: a person may stimulate his or her genitals in order to experience sexual pleasure, but the actual cause of the pleasure is not the stimulation of the genitals but something causally independent of the stimulation (somewhat like an Edmund Gettier "counterexample"). Maybe this would be called an "accidental" rather than an "intentional" masturbation, but I can think of other cases that deserve to be called "accidental": a guy shakes it a few extra times (inadvertently, nonconsciously) after relieving himself at a urinal.

7. Links to "female masturbation words" and "male masturbation words" can be found at http://www.realsissyschool.com/words/words.html (the pages used to be hosted directly on the "Adult Toy Reviews" website).

8. *The Hite Report on Male Sexuality* (New York: Knopf, 1981), 485–525. Laumann and his colleagues, who conducted an extensive study of sexual behavior (Edward O. Laumann, John H. Gagnon, Robert T. Michael, and Stuart Michaels, *The Social Organization of Sexuality: Sexual Practices in the United States* [Chicago, Ill.: University of Chicago Press, 1994]), reveal that "the [survey questions] concerning masturbation . . . prompted significant negative responses from the government officials who were responsible for reviewing a variation of this survey instrument . . . they insisted that questions on masturbation be removed from the study" (81; see 40*n*2). The scholars did not fold, and sought other sources of funding.

9. The unlikely George won the bet. But in the penultimate episode of the program, when the four friends were sure they were plunging to their deaths in a nose-diving private jet, George confesses that he had cheated (or lied). I admit that I may have missed, over the decades, TV sitcom episodes or scenes about masturbation.

10. In "The Decloseting of Masturbation?" (*Journal of Sex Research* 41:3 [2004], 310–12), Martha Cornog expresses this optimism: "Can serious scholarship and publishing about masturbation finally be catching up to a millennia-old sexual practice? Perhaps masturbation is out of the closet at last." I believe that the act itself remains secretive; Cornog establishes only that scholarship about masturbation has been "decloseted." See her *Big Book of Masturbation: From Angst to Zeal* (San Francisco, Calif.: Down There Press, 2003).

11. Louis M. Epstein, *Sex Laws and Customs in Judaism* (New York: Ktav, 1967), 144–47; Mark D. Jordan, *The Ethics of Sex* (Oxford: Blackwell, 2002), 101–2; Michael L. Satlow, "'Wasted Seed': The History of a Rabbinic Idea," *Hebrew Union College Annual* 65 (1994), 137–69.

12. Note the (perhaps) Aristotelian conception of women's nature. See *Politics*, 1259a41–1260a11, in *Politics and Poetics*, trans. Benjamin Jowett (Cleveland, Ohio: Fine Editions Press, 1952).

13. Men's more frequent masturbation might be causally linked (by conditioning) with men's proclivity for sexual perversion: "Men masturbate to climax very liberally . . . making them particularly susceptible—in contrast to women—to developing deviations in [a] piecemeal fashion" (Dolf Zillmann, *Connections between Sex and Aggression* [Hillsdale, N.J.: Erlbaum, 1984], 182).

14. Immanuel Kant, *The Metaphysics of Morals*, trans. Mary Gregor (Cambridge: Cambridge University Press, 1996), 179.

15. Ronald de Sousa, *The Rationality of Emotion* (Cambridge, Mass.: MIT Press, 1987), 219.

16. In her review of Suzanne and Irving Sarnoff's *Sexual Excitement/Sexual Peace: The Place of Masturbation in Adult Relationships* (New York: Evans, 1979), Leonore Tiefer nicely observes, "The Sarnoffs want this book to be . . . about how 'people can use their inclinations to masturbate as a way of getting insights that will help them resolve their emotional conflicts.' In their world there'll be no more idle jerking off. Every masturbatory episode will provide an opportunity for self-analysis" (*Psychology of Women Quarterly* 8:1 [1983], 107–9, at 108).

17. The central claim of this section on a gendered masturbatic double standard is denied by Megan Adams in the introduction to her 2011 M.A. thesis: "For women in contemporary American society, masturbation, though a natural and common part of healthy sexuality, remains shrouded in secrecy and shame. When it is not denied and ignored completely, it is often discussed in hushed tones or with subtle winks" (*Flicking the Bean on the Silver Screen: Women's Masturbation as Self-Discovery and Subversion in American Cinema*). The whole is available at https://etd.ohiolink.edu/rws_etd/ document/get/bgsu1300749024/inline. In medias res, Adams presents one of the famous ideas of French feminist Luce Irigaray: "Women's autoeroticism . . . exists even in the simple [and *continuous* — AS] contact between the two lips of a woman's genitals." (It seems to me that by titling her thesis *Flicking the Bean*, Adams has trivialized that which brings about significant "self-discovery" and gender "subversion.")

18. Robert T. Francoeur, Timothy Perper, Norman A. Scherzer, George P. Sellmer, and Martha Cornog, *A Descriptive Dictionary and Atlas of Sexology* (New York: Greenwood, 1991), 381.

19. Lester Dearborn, "Autoerotism," in *The Encyclopedia of Sexual Behavior*, edited by Albert Ellis and Albert Abarbanel (New York: Jason Aronson, 1973), 204–15.

20. Sexual performance artist Annie Sprinkle believes that orgasm is "possible from breathing alone, without any touching." See "Beyond Bisexual," in *Living with Contradictions: Controversies in Feminist Social Ethics*, edited by Alison M. Jaggar (Boulder, Colo.: Westview, 1994), 510–12. Breathing is not touching at a distance? A subtle, nearly insensible low-frequency vibration? And men can ejaculate solely by the power of their internal muscular twitching apparatus.

21. Dearborn, "Autoerotism," 211.

22. Dearborn includes, in solo "oral masturbation," women sucking on their own nipples and men's self-fellatio ("Autoerotism," 212).

23. St. Thomas Aquinas, *Summa Theologiae*, 2a2ae, question 154, articles 1–12.

24. Consult my *The Philosophy of Sex and Love*, 2nd edition (St. Paul, Minn.: Paragon House, 2008), chapter 4, and *Sexual Investigations*, chapter 1.

25. Kant, *Lectures on Ethics*, trans. Louis Infield (Indianapolis, Ind.: Hackett, 1963), 170. My discomfort with Kant's philosophy of sex, including masturbation, is expressed in my "Kant and Sexual Perversion," *The Monist* 86:1 (2003), 57–92, and in "Sexual Use," this volume.

26. Keith Ward, *The Development of Kant's View of Ethics* (Oxford: Basil Blackwell, 1972), 109.

27. Kant, *Education*, trans. Annette Churton (Ann Arbor: University of Michigan Press, 1960), 117–18.

28. See my "Kant and Sexual Perversion" and "Sexual Use."

29. Arthur Schopenhauer, *On the Basis of Morality*, trans. E. F. J. Payne (Indianapolis, Ind.: Hackett, 1995), 60.

30. Consult Thomas Szasz, "The New Product — Masturbatory Insanity," in his *The Manufacture of Madness: A Comparative Study of the Inquisition and the Mental Health Movement* (New York: Harper and Row, 1970), 180–206; Chip Rowe, "Is This Man Crazy? Psychiatrists Say Deviants Deserve Another Look," *Playboy* (August 2005), 56; Peter Conrad and Joseph Schneider, *Deviance and Medicalization: From Badness to Sickness* (St. Louis, Mo.: Mosby, 1980). Plato noticed two thousand years ago the possible move from ethics to medicine; see my *Sexual Investigations*, 146–49.

31. Bernard Mandeville, *A Modest Defence of Publick Stews*, edited by Richard I. Cook (Los Angeles, Calif.: Augustan Reprint Society, Publication 162, 1973), 30.

32. Mandeville, *Defence*, 31. Does anyone hear a faint implication that indiscriminate manufriction may lead a young boy into inversion? Regardless, note Mandeville's "onanism," which is wrong (see Genesis 38:8–10). Freud, too, often used "onanie," the German word, in the title of his essay "Contributions to a Discussion on Masturbation," trans. James Strachey, in *The Standard Edition of the Complete Psychological Works of Sigmund Freud*, vol. 12 (London: Hogarth Press, 1953–1974), 243–54.

33. Freud, "Contributions to a Discussion," 252.

34. Mandeville, *Defence*, 31.

35. M. Joycelyn Elders, "The Dreaded 'M' Word," *Nerve* (26 June 1997), www.nerve.com/dispatches/elders/mword.

36. The Latin says that sexual intercourse is a remedy against (for) masturbation; the phrase is modeled on *"ad remedium concupiscentiae,"* which describes St. Paul's view (1 Corinthians 7:2–5) that marriage, particularly sexual activity in marriage, is the remedy for soul-destroying promiscuous fornication.

37. See Augustine's *Confessions*, 2.7–2.8, any edition, translated by R. S. Pine-Coffin (New York: Penguin, 1961).

38. Freud, "Contributions to a Discussion," 251–52.

39. A notable exception is Russell Vannoy, *Sex without Love: A Philosophical Exploration* (Buffalo, N.Y.: Prometheus Books, 1980), 111–17.

40. Alan Goldman, "Plain Sex," in this volume, 56.

41. Thomas Nagel, "Sexual Perversion," in this volume, 47.

42. Robert Solomon, "Sex and Perversion," in *Philosophy and Sex*, 1st ed., edited by Robert B. Baker and Frederick A. Elliston (Buffalo, N.Y.: Prometheus Books, 1975), 268–87, at 283. Once again, see Luke Roelofs, "Philosophy and Masturbation: Anatomy of a Metaphor" (note 2) (https://majesticequality.wordpress.com/2011/08/04/philosophy-and-masturbation-anatomy-of-a-metaphor/).

43. James Giles, "A Theory of Love and Sexual Desire," *Journal for the Theory of Social Behaviour* 24:4 (1994), 339–57, at 353.

44. Throughout *The Philosophy of Sex and Love*, 2nd edition, *Sexual Investigations*, and the various versions of my masturbation essays (note 1).

45. In Michael Thomsett and Jean Thomsett, *Sex and Love Quotations* (Jefferson, N.C.: McFarland, 1995), 87, entry 1404.

46. David Sue, "Erotic Fantasies of College Students during Coitus," *Journal of Sex Research* 15:4 (1979), 299–305.

STUDY QUESTIONS

1. In criticizing the *OED*'s definition of "masturbation," Soble claims that none of its three features is necessary for an act to be one of masturbation: "other body parts may be stimulated; the stimulation need not be manual, digital, or comprehensible; and the goal need not be sexual pleasure." Why does Soble say, about the second feature, that the stimulation "need not be comprehensible"? What does he mean? And can you think of other (non-genital) body parts that would, when stimulated, make an act masturbatory?

2. Recapitulate Soble's argument as to why he thinks that there is a double standard for men and women when it comes to masturbation. Is the argument successful? Might women's masturbation be (as or more strongly) condemned but for social and cultural reasons different from those that condemn men's masturbation?

3. Try to define "solitary masturbation," "mutual masturbation," and "dual masturbation" (add to the mix also "group masturbation"), making sure to avoid the type of objections raised by Soble in the essay.

4. Do you agree that "mutual masturbation" is a confused misnomer? Can you provide a plausible definition of it that avoids Soble's objections?

5. Can you think of any moral grounds on which to criticize masturbation in any of its types or under certain circumstances (inclusive "or")? If masturbation is morally in the clear, at least generally, are there any good reasons to define it (beyond that defining it is a philosophically interesting task on its own)?

6. Consider the analyses of sexual desire and sexual activity given by Alan Goldman, Thomas Nagel, Robert Gray, and others in this volume. Do they short-change or even completely neglect masturbation? And if yes, at what philosophical price? Would bringing in masturbation reveal defects in these analyses? Why or why not? (For help in thinking through these issues, read Alan Soble's "On Jacking Off, Yet Again," in *The Philosophy of Sex: Contemporary Readings*, 6th ed., edited by Nicholas Power, Raja Halwani, and Alan Soble [Lanham, Md.: Rowman & Littlefield, 2013], 77–99.)

7. After making the point that masturbation is primary to paired sex (in that masturbation occurs more frequently and that people start masturbating way before they have paired sex), Soble states, "If so, we should understand paired sex in terms of masturbation instead of concocting miserable understandings of masturbation in terms of paired sex." Flesh out this idea more. Keep in mind as you do so the distinction between masturbation being primary as a concept and its being primary temporally and in terms of frequency (maybe even in terms of the intensity of its sexual pleasures).

EIGHT

Trans 101

Talia Mae Bettcher

As its title indicates, this essay by **Talia Mae Bettcher** *introduces some of the crucial issues in philosophical reflections about trans people. After explaining some basic concepts, such as "gender identity," "gender expression," and "gender presentation" and the connections between them, Bettcher discusses the history of the terms used to refer to trans people, and how choosing to use certain terms can be morally important (e.g., in the phenomenon of misgendering). She discusses some linguistic analyses of the meanings of terms such as "woman" and "man" to see whether any of them are more inclusive of trans people, arguing that none seem promising enough. She argues that a better account starts with how the terms are used by trans people and within trans communities. She then explores accounts of why trans people transition to begin with, and finds them all lacking. The essay concludes with a discussion of some of the issues regarding the spaces (e.g., restrooms) that trans people may legally use, including decency and privacy, which might underlie the prevalent linguistic practices surrounding the use of gender terms.*

Talia Mae Bettcher is a professor of philosophy at California State University, Los Angeles. Some of her articles include "Evil Deceivers and Make-Believers: Transphobic Violence and the Politics of Illusion" (*Hypatia* 2007), "Trapped in the Wrong Theory: Re-Thinking Trans Oppression and Resistance (*Signs* 2014), and "When Selves Have Sex: What the Phenomenology of Trans Sexuality Can Teach about Sexual Orientation" (*Journal of Homosexuality* 2014). With Susan Stryker, she coedited the *Transgender Studies Quarterly* special double issue "Trans/Feminisms" (2016). She is currently at work on the monograph *Personhood as Intimacy: A Trans Feminist Philosophy* (under contract with Minnesota University Press). © 2017, Talia Mae Bettcher, who kindly gave permission for her new essay to be included in this volume.

The goal of this essay is to introduce some trans issues from a philosophical perspective. It is divided into seven parts: (1) basic concepts, (2) terminology, (3) misgendering and transphobia, (4) the philosophical analysis of gender terms, (5) the nature and basis of gender identity, (6) transgender, sexuality, and sexual orientation, and finally, (7) ethical issues concerning sex segregation.

BASIC CONCEPTS

Let's call the categories *male* and *female* "sex categories" and the categories *man* and *woman* "gender categories." While the former apply more broadly to sexually reproducing animals and plants, the latter are restricted to human beings. (Actually, this isn't quite clear. Insofar as we allow fictional characters such as Superman, an alien being from Krypton, to count as a man, it may be that membership within the species *Homo sapiens* is not a necessary condition for being a man or a woman.) At least in a pre-theoretical way, it seems that sex and gender categories are interrelated insofar as being female is often taken as a necessary condition for being a woman and being male is often taken as a necessary condition for being a man.

For now, *sexual orientation* can be understood as a man or a woman's stable sexual attraction to either men or women; we can speak of same-gender attractions (men to men, women to women) and opposite-gender attractions (men to women, women to men). By *sexual identity* I mean how a person conceives of themselves with respect to their sexual orientation. So sexual orientation and sexual identity are not the same thing. A man could be sexually oriented to men, but he might not have come out to himself yet; he might not yet (or ever) *self-identity* as gay. His sexual identity would be "straight" while his sexual orientation would not.

By *gender expression* I mean ways of feeling, thinking, speaking, behaving, and expressing oneself characterized as either masculine or feminine. While it is sometimes said that women are feminine and men are masculine, this is scarcely always the case. And although it is sometimes affirmed (as a stereotype) that gay men are feminine and lesbians are masculine, it is obvious that many gay men are masculine, and many lesbians are feminine. Moreover, some straight men are feminine and some straight women are masculine. People tend to exhibit complex ways of being that include both masculinity and femininity within them.

By *gender identity* I mean how one conceives of oneself, or feels oneself to be with respect to sex and/or gender categories (so the fact that it is called *gender identity* and not *sex/gender identity* is somewhat misleading). *Gender identity* is a central concept with regard to trans issues. Many trans people do not self-identify with the sex and gender categories assigned to them at birth. Consequently, they may wish to change various things about themselves and their lives. They may decide to *transition* from one sex/gender category to another. What this transition could amount to will be discussed in due course.

Note, first, that gender identity is distinct from both sexual orientation and sexual identity. A trans person assigned to the categories *male* and *man* but who has the gender identity of *female/woman* and has transitioned accordingly could very well be exclusively attracted to women. If so, she would have a lesbian sexual orientation and would, if she so identifies, have the sexual identity of lesbian as well. Distinguishing gender identity from sexual orientation and sexual identity is important in combating the harmful misconception that trans people transition because of their sexual orientation. On the contrary, trans people who transition do so to bring their material and social realities in alignment with their sense of who they are with respect to the sex/gender categories. It is worth noting, however, that some sexual identities such as being a lesbian and a gay man *are* partially gender identities or at least include gender identifications within them since to see oneself as a lesbian is presumably to see oneself as a woman.[1]

Second, note that gender identity is distinct from gender expression. There are some trans women who not only self-identify as lesbians but also identify as *butch* lesbians, expressing themselves in highly masculine ways. Similarly, there are some trans men who express themselves in highly feminine ways. Again, it is not one's gender expression that motivates transition; rather, it is one's gender identity and its incongruence with the material and social realities.

That said, what typically *does* change in transition is one's gender *presentation*. While gender presentation and expression are often conflated, they are worth distinguishing. Gender presentation concerns one's gendered sensory appearance to others. Does one look like a woman? Does one sound like a woman? Does one "read" as a woman? While gendered clothing and grooming are obviously relevant, presentation also includes mannerism and comportment. So there is an overlap with gender expression. But it is one thing to read as masculine, and quite another to read as a man. And it is entirely possible to read as a masculine woman or a feminine man. Typically having a gender presentation that more or less reflects one's gender identity is an important component in transitioning—in bringing social and material reality into conformity with one's sense of self with respect to the sex/gender categories.

To this component, several others may be added: changes in gendered name (informal or legal), legal changes in sex designation on various records (driver's license, birth certificate, passport), bodily changes effected through hormone replacement therapy, silicon injections, surgical interventions such as breast augmentation or breast removal, genital reconstruction surgery (of which there are different kinds), hysterectomy, orchiectomy, as well as facial reconstruction surgery. Trans people effect their transitions differently—some avail themselves of medical interventions, some don't. In general, however, trans men and women effect transitions from assigned sex and gender categories toward socially recognized sex and gender categories that conform better to their gender identities.

TRANS/TRANSGENDER/TRANS* TERMINOLOGY

Thus far I have used only the expressions *trans men* and *trans women* because they are easy to understand and they are often used by trans people themselves. But the terminology used to refer to trans people is actually quite complicated and sometimes frustrating. The reason is twofold. First, terminology changes over time. Second, terminology is usually highly contested by trans people at any given point in time: We use terms differently, sometimes in opposition to each other. Consequently, it is impossible to provide neat definitions of the terms. The best one can do is to explain how the terms have evolved over time and how they continue to be contested. With regard to any given trans person, one will need to get to know them to better understand what categories they use to self-identify and what those labels mean to them. The following is a brief account of trans terminological developments in the United States. Obviously, terminology differs widely across the globe.

By the mid 1950s, the term *transsexual* was separated from the term *transvestite*. It was used to refer to individuals whose gender identities were incongruent with the sex-gender categories assigned to them at birth. The identity was thought impervious to change, consequently the only solution was to change the body to conform to the identity. Initially, *transsexual* was a medical term connected to ways of diagnosing transsexualism and curing it through surgical intervention. There was an emphasis on the importance of passing as a member of the gender category one had transitioned into and fading into the mainstream as a non-transsexual person.

The 1990s, however, saw the emergence of the transgender political movement in the United States. While *transgenderist* had been earlier used to refer to individuals who transitioned but who did not avail themselves of medical technologies, it came to be used as an umbrella term that included transsexuals, drag queens and drag kings, and cross-dressers (which had replaced the stigmatizing term *transvestite*). This movement saw transgender people as oppressed by an insistence on sharp binaries between masculine/feminine, man/woman, and male/female. In the transgender framework, the term *transsexual* was broadened to include trans men and women who did not avail themselves of any medical technologies at all.

But not everybody was happy. Some transsexuals rejected transgender politics, refusing to identify as transgender, using *transsexual* in the older sense. Meanwhile, other trans men and women chose not to identify as *transsexual* on the grounds that it was too associated with a pathologizing medical model. They preferred *transgender* or just plain *trans*. Notably, while drag queens and kings, cross-dressers, and some butch lesbians were thought to be included under the umbrella, some did not want to be included; some did, however, but they did not always feel included. *Transgender* was starting to be equated with trans men and women only. There is an irony here in that while the term was supported by a politic celebrating disruptions of binaries, it came to be associated mostly with those trans people who identified *within* a binary category.

By the early 2010s, *trans** began to gain popularity as a replacement umbrella term. One of the concerns driving this shift was that individuals who did not identify within binary gender categories—genderqueer individuals (who position themselves outside the categories), genderfluid individuals (who can move in and out of categories), and agender individuals (who do not identify with gender categories at all) did not feel they were included under the transgender umbrella. *Trans** was thought to be more inclusive. Even now, however, concerns about this terminology are emerging. One concern is that this new terminology will only serve to replicate the problem that motivated its introduction in the first place. For example, if we start to use expressions like *trans** *men* and *trans** *women*, the binary will once again move to the foreground!

Finally, around the time that *trans** came into vogue, the term *cis* (which roughly means *non-trans*) was also adopted. One of the difficulties is that it is not always clear whether the term is supposed to contrast with *transsexual*, *transgender*, or *trans**. Sometimes this is made clear through expressions such as *cissexual*, *cisgender*, and *cis**. But this is not always the case. And, as we have seen, the meanings of the former are themselves contested. There are other difficulties, however, that I will not discuss because the issues are complex and would take us too far off course.[2] For the purposes of this chapter, I will simply use *non-trans*.

TRANSPHOBIA AND MISGENDERING

Trans people are subject to various forms of discrimination, harassment, and even violence. One of the most basic forms of transphobia is often called "misgendering." Misgendering involves using gender pronouns, terms, and names to refer to trans people that are at odds with their gender identity. For example, to refer to a trans woman as a man and to use the pronouns *he* and *him* or male-gendered names is to misgender the trans woman. According to Stephanie Kapusta, misgendering may also include analyses of gender terms which *marginalize* trans people in the gender category within which they identify.[3] Some of these analyses will be discussed in the following sections. I will also add that since many trans people's identifications refer to sex categories (trans women may also identify as female), we should likewise speak of "missexing" or else we should include this phenomenon in the general notion of misgendering (which, for simplicity's sake, I will do).

Stephanie Kapusta outlines some specific harms inflicted by misgendering.[4] It can undermine self-respect (the worth one recognizes in one's one agency and life-plans) insofar as gender identity deeply informs a trans person's life-struggle: To be regarded as "really a man" at every turn can undermine a trans woman's sense of worth as an agent attempting to set forth her conception of what it is to live her life on her own terms, as a woman. Moreover, many misgenderings can be viewed as "microaggressions" (verbal and non-verbal slights and insults that communicate negative messages based on group membership).[5] Pervasive subjection to microaggressions, such as being constantly "sir-ed," mispronouned, and so on, can have an impact on one's psychological well-being, leading, for example, to "anxiety, fatigue, stress, hypervigilance, anger, fear, depression, shame, and a sense of loneliness."[6] Constant misgendering can prevent trans people from participating in descriptions of who and what they are, leading to what Miranda Fricker calls "hermeneutic injustice" (the injustice of having some significant area of one's social experience obscured from collective understanding owing to hermeneutical marginalization).[7] To see a trans woman's experience through a framework that positions her as "a man living as a woman" is to simply fail to adequately represent her experience at all. Finally, misgendering can lead to political oppression and domination (institutional constraints on self-development and self-determination). For example, by being denied the ability to alter sex designation on a birth certificate, a trans person may be subject to constant abuse and harassment as well as the burden of having to explain themselves to various officials.

These ethical and political considerations can be distinguished from metaphysical questions such as "What is a woman?" "What is a man?" "Are trans women women?" and "Are trans men men?" These types of questions are answered by philosophers through conceptual analysis of the relevant concepts or, relatedly, through an analysis of what terms such as "man" and "woman" mean (for the purposes of this chapter I will treat these approaches as equivalent). Yet these conceptual and semantic questions are also importantly related to the ethical and political issues discussed above. In particular, semantic and conceptual questions are often advanced in the service of the ethical ones.

One position claims to prioritize the conceptual: It says that getting "the facts" right is more important than the ethical considerations mentioned above. One might say, "If somebody is really male, then it is appropriate to refer to them that way, regardless of how they feel about it." While versions of such a position are espoused by some anti-trans feminists,[8] the position is also implied by individuals who deliberately misgender trans people, knowing full well how these trans would *like* to be treated. Such a position is implausible, however, in light of the seriousness of the harms cited above. A more palatable position separates the conceptual from the ethical: Regardless of the conceptual facts of the matter, it is still ethically required to treat trans men and women *as if* they were men and women.[9] Such a position, however, entails that trans men and women are ultimately confused about who and what they are and may likewise perpetuate the harm of hermeneutic injustice, because it undermines trans people as reliable (unconfused) describers of their experiences.

Finally, Kapusta has argued for a priority of the ethical over the conceptual: Prevalent linguistic practices can themselves be contested on ethical and political grounds. A physician may identify a trans woman as a man when she is undergoing a screening for prostate cancer by appealing to the view that prostates are relevant to the categorizing of individuals as men or women within a medical context. However, such linguistic practices may be contested—regardless of the physician's competence with them. After all, the medical issues themselves merely concern the health issues and so on that arise for *individuals* with prostates. Categorizing someone as a man or a woman seems of little importance. Indeed, categorizing all individuals with prostates as men may obscure possible issues that some trans women face specifically. While it might be common practice in the medical domain to use gender terms in that way, and while the physician themselves may be an expert in those common linguistic practices, such practices can be contested on ethical grounds.

CONCEPTUAL ANALYSIS

The positions above presuppose the existence of prevalent linguistic practices that yield the phenomenon of misgendering. Another view is that once a proper analysis of the concepts as they are deployed in such practices is made manifest, it will become clear that trans women are women and trans men are men according to those very practices. The problem, on this view, is not with the linguistic practices themselves but, rather, with the fact that some practitioners are confused about those practices or misuse them in harmful, misgendering ways. But such an account seems, on the face of it, to be implausible. How could so many speakers be that confused?

Certainly, the analysis of gender terms by appeal to biological sex looks like a non-starter. Trans women who have not availed themselves of medical technologies to alter their bodies but who gender-present in ways that reflect their identities do not appear to have changed biological sex (at least as sex concepts are usually applied). However, there are other possible strategies for the analysis of gender terms: While gender terms might seem related to biological sex terms, one can argue that they contain significant social content and, indeed, name social positions or roles as *fashion model*, *banker*, and *baseball player* name roles or positions that depend on social practices. That gender terms often seem to include cultural norms and expectations bolsters this view. Consider the expressions "Man up!" and "Act like a man!" Such injunctions appear to include cultural content—that is, they seem to include notions about how individuals who possess such features ought to act. Perhaps, then, analyses that include such cultural content can fare better in the inclusion of trans people. And perhaps it is the case that many people who deploy these terms are, upon closer inspection, simply confused about how they really work.

There are two analytic strategies for thinking of gender concepts as inclusive of cultural content. First, according to a family-resemblance analysis, there are no necessary or sufficient conditions for category membership.[10] Instead, there's only a set of overlapping specifiable features that some members of the category share and others do not. This allows for the inclusion of various cultural features (gender presentation, gender expression, and gender identity) in addition to biological features (genitalia, gonads, chromosomes, and so forth). The problem, however, is that, at a minimum, such an analysis will marginalize trans people, since they will lack some of the biological features still included in the list while most non-trans women will not lack those features. After all, it is difficult to deny that features such as chromosomes and genitalia are *very heavily* weighted in the prevailing gender concepts. And this means that trans people who don't have those central features, if admitted into the relevant categories, can only be admitted marginally at best. Indeed, some may be in between the concepts *man* and *woman* and therefore more properly viewed as "intergendered."[11]

To be clear, the problem here is not with the family-resemblance approach to conceptual analysis per se (although there may be problems beyond the scope of this chapter). The problem is that, given the way the concepts work according to prevailing linguistic practices, there is only so much that a family-resemblance analysis can do in securing trans membership in the relevant categories. As an analysis, then, it does not support the claim that trans men and women are men and women—at least not in a non-marginalizing way—per prevalent linguistic practices.

Second, a semantic contextual analysis maintains that gender terms operate like indexicals: Their extensions vary by context according to a semantic rule. Cultural content will likewise be allowed in this analysis since in some contexts features like "sincere self-identification as a woman" will determine membership rather than biological sex.[12] Consequently, in some contexts trans women will count as men and in others they will count as women. Again, such an account appears to run afoul of marginalization (most non-trans women will count as women in *any* context) and of the worry that at least in some contexts trans people will be misgendered.

It seems likely, then, that no account of our prevalent linguistic practices is going to reveal them to be entirely validating of trans people.[13] That is, the view that the practitioners of common linguistic practices are simply confused about how those practices operate, that upon proper analysis validates trans men and women, is a view that seems rather dubious. On the contrary, dominant linguistic practices are not likely to be friendly to trans people. At worst, they can undermine the self-identities of trans people altogether, at best they allow for a validation that is nonetheless marginalizing.

I have elsewhere argued, however, that such prevalent linguistic practices are not the only practices.[14] As the meanings of trans terminology are politically contested by trans people themselves (discussed in the preceding section), the meanings of gender terms themselves are likewise subject to contestation. In particular, there are also linguistic practices adopted in trans subcultural spaces through which trans women *do* count paradigmatically as women and trans men *do* count paradigmatically as men.

While the way in which the meanings are contested can vary, it often works like this: Being a trans woman is taken as a sufficient condition for being a woman while being a trans man is taken as a sufficient condition for being a man.[15] That is, trans women and men are viewed respectively, simply, as one type of woman and man, among many.[16] One of the consequences of the logic of these practices is that features such as the presence of a penis and XY chromosomes go no distance in undermining or marginalizing a trans woman's claim to womanhood: Given that trans women are paradigmatic women, it follows that some women do possess such features and that such features are irrelevant to the application of the concept "woman." This case is clearer with regard to sex categories. Insofar as trans women typically identify as female (regardless of whether they have had any surgical interventions), it becomes plain that the use and meaning of sex terms have been contested in trans subcultures. Consequently, I argue that there are at least two sets of gender (and sex) concepts at stake—those that marginalize or invalidate trans people and those that do not.

However, perhaps this contrast between dominant and subcultural practices is too strong. It may be that now even within mainstream cultural practices, particularly as transgender politics become increasingly prominent, there are multiple linguistic practices contesting the meanings and deployments of gender terms and their usages. Such contestation, no doubt, concerns the ethical and political ramifications of these practices. This would not be surprising if gender terms should turn out to change over time, often through contestation, every bit as much as the transgender terminology we considered in the early section. This may be what is happening now.

WHAT IS THE SOURCE OF TRANS GENDER DISCONTENT
AND THE MOTIVATION TO TRANSITION?

A natural question one might ask is *why* trans people transition. One of the things to observe, however, is that this question is probably already problematic. One might worry that such a question reflects a bias analogous to the question "What causes homosexuality?"—a question that seems to presuppose that heterosexuality is not in need of explanation. That said, more general questions *can* be asked about how sexuality orientation (hetero, homo, bi) arises. Similarly, questions can be asked about the basis of gender discontent and the motivation to transition. In a common view, the origin of trans gender discontent and the motivation to transition emerges from an incongruence between gender identity and material/social features that appear to conflict with that identity. Transition is motivated by the desire to alleviate the discontent by bringing those material/social features into alignment with identity. This notion of gender identity allows for perfectly general questions about it. Where does gender identity come from? Are we born with it? If not, how does it arise?

The issues are tricky, however. We have to think more deeply about the nature of gender identity. If we understand it merely as a conscious self-identification of oneself or as the belief that one is a man or a woman, then it turns out that it cannot be used as a complete explanation of trans gender discontent. Contrary to traditional accounts, many trans people do not know who they are right away. For many trans people, there is a process of discovering that one is trans. Such a process typically involves undoing one conscious self-conception and adopting a new one (as when one is raised to see oneself as male, but then comes to recognize that one is really female). But if gender identity, in this sense, is one of the things that changes, it cannot be the complete source of trans gender discontent. For while a trans person may undergo a change in conscious gender identity, they may also report gender discontent *prior* to the identity change—a discontent that was finally illuminated in the recognition of their being trans, a discontent partially alleviated by the development of this gender identity. What is the basis for the trans gender discontent that underlies the change in conscious self-conception in the first place?

One standard move is to appeal to some deeper, abiding feeling, a bodily sense of self that does not always show up on the conscious radar. For example, Julia Serano speaks of "subconscious sex," writing, "It seems as if on some level, my brain expects my body to be female."[17] One way to get a handle on this is to consider the phenomenon of phantom limb experiences (i.e., the internal experience of body parts that are no longer present) and bodily agnosia (the failure to experience or register a body part as belonging to oneself). The idea here is that we all have an internal bodily scheme that, in the case of trans people, is incongruent with their physical bodies. So trans gender discontent, in this view, is explained by appeal to this incongruence.

There are different accounts about the basis and origin of this internal body scheme. In what I call the nativist view, we all have an inborn sense of our bodily sex.[18] In what I call the constructionist view, such a notion is not feasible.[19] One main reason for this rejection is that gender and sex are socially constructed. The gender part is fairly easy to understand. As has already been suggested, one might argue that *woman* and *man* name social roles assigned on the basis of sex. If true, one's sense of being a woman or a man could be no more innate than one's sense of being a fashion model or banker: The latter are roles that are sustained by social practices relative to a given society, and certain societies may not even recognize models and bankers. How, then, could one have an inborn sense of being a model or banker, a man or a woman?

The second part of the constructionist claim, that sex itself is socially constructed, is not as intuitive. However, there are other concerns that point to difficulties with the nativist account. As I mentioned earlier, transitions are not uniform. Some trans people undergo phalloplasty or vaginoplasty. But others do not. Some trans women take hormones and develop breasts and some trans men have their breasts removed. Some do not. Does this mean that there is a plethora of body schemes, rather than just two? Are they all innate? Never mind, because there is a deeper problem: Consider a trans woman who is comfortable with her body — she has breasts and a penis. On what basis should we say that this is a *female* body scheme? It could just as well be a male body scheme for a trans man. Or it could be a non-binary body-scheme for a person who identifies as gender queer. If so, such an innate body scheme would not provide a basis for trans discontent at being located within given sex categories. This is because the latter involves the *interpretation* of a given sex category, particularly as it relates to bodily morphology. And there are other, related problems that concern the very restriction of trans gender content to the body alone.

Consider trans men and women who are content to change only their public gender presentation. It is implausible to believe that one could have an innate sense of one's gender presentation since gender presentation is clearly cultural. In order to maintain a nativist thesis, one would have to draw a distinction between trans people who want to change their bodies and those who do not. While the former would have their gender identities grounded in an innate body scheme, the latter would not. But this is a questionable distinction to draw, particularly given the patent idiosyncrasies of transition, including ones that involve bodily alterations.

Unfortunately, a social constructionist position may not fare any better. After proclaiming sex and gender categories socially constructed, one will still need to provide an account of how this bodily sense *does* arise. In light of the arguments above, this account may also have to include one's experience of gender presentation and its relationship to one's body. One possibility is that such a scheme is formed in interaction with the environment over time.[20] One of the interesting features about such a view is that this scheme need not correspond with one's actual body given the important role that body memory may play. For example, one might acquire a sense of possessing a certain body part over time, lose that body part, and then continue to experience it as present because of the considerable role that memory plays in helping constitute a stable sense of body. The problem, however, is that such an account appears to fare badly in accommodating trans experience. Consider a trans woman, raised as a boy, and expected to engage with the world in a particular way (in compliance with gender norms, say). Then it is difficult to see how she could develop a female body scheme over time, given that she will not have had the environmental engagements in which it would be apt to arise.

The other aspect to which one might appeal is our affective investments in our body.[21] Our experiences of our bodies do not merely involve representing them internally, but involve feelings (e.g., comfort and discomfort). And our affective investments in our body need not cleave so closely to our environmental engagements. While this is a good starting point, however, the problem is that by itself, it does not amount to an account as much as the absence of one. One wants to know what types of investments arise and, more crucially, how and why they arise *in opposition* to the bodily scheme that would be predicted to develop through environmental engagements.

One way in which a negative investment in certain body parts could certainly arise is through the effects of misgendering. To the extent that possession of a penis is taken to count against her sense of womanhood, a trans woman may feel intense discomfort with it. This may be because of the views of other people about what a woman is. It may also be because she herself takes possession of a penis as threatening to her sense of womanhood. In such a view, however, it is conscious gender identity (under the pressure of misgendering) that yields bodily discomfort, rather than bodily discomfort yielding conscious gender identity. But what would remain unexplained is the original discomfort that yields the transformation in gender identity in the first place. With regard to this more fundamental question, it seems to me, there is yet no well-developed account.

SEXUALITY AND SEXUAL AND AFFECTIONAL ORIENTATION

At the outset of this chapter, I drew a distinction between gender identity and sexual orientation. While this distinction is important, it is also the case, as I mentioned earlier, that trans people do have sexual orientations and do in fact have sex. This points to interesting issues concerning sexual orientation and sexual identity.[22] First, it is worth noting that the phenomenon of misgendering can "spill over" onto sexual identities. Consider a non-trans woman in a relationship with a trans woman. If the latter is viewed as "really a man" then the relationship will be viewed as a heterosexual one. Not only is the trans woman's gender identity invalidated, but her sexual identity is also invalidated. And the sexual identity of her non-trans partner is invalidated as well! The issues we considered earlier—namely, the ethical and political harms associated with such invalidation, the conceptual analysis of gender and sex concepts, and the relation between the ethical and political, on the one hand, and the conceptual and semantic dimensions, on the other—will mediate what we decide to say about this.

More deeply, the complexity of trans bodies and presentations raises questions about the very meaning of sexual orientation. On the face of it, the notion of a sexual orientation to men seems straightforward. But now, one might ask: How does such an orientation operate in the case of trans men? Does an orientation to men revolve around attraction to a body type? Is attraction to a penis, for example, central? If so, such an attraction would appear broad enough to include trans women who have penises. Or does the orientation revolve around attraction to a particular sort of gender presentation and gender expression? No doubt, it is going to depend upon the individual. So does this mean that there are different types of orientation at stake? What should we make of specific attractions to bodies that might be represented as "in between"? Is that a distinct orientation? And what of specific attractions to trans women or trans men? Are these distinct orientations? It turns out that sexual orientation is not nearly as simple as it seemed.[23] And such complexities obviously intersect with concerns about misgendering. Does identifying as a gay man on the basis of an attraction to penises not effectively involve a kind of misgendering when trans women with penises fall within the scope of that attraction? That is, are some orientations harmful to trans people?

But this is only the tip of the iceberg. It is notable that some of the body parts with which trans people might experience discomfort are body parts (penises, vaginas, breasts) that are only used in select contexts such as sexual relations (touching/fondling, oral sex, penetrative sex). For example, a trans woman may feel uncomfortable with having her genitals touched during sexual relations owing to the identity-related discomfort that she feels with it. How do trans people navigate such discomfort? Sometimes trans people engage in the practice of "recoding." That is, private body parts are renamed. For example, what might be regarded in the mainstream as a penis might be regarded a "trans clit," and what might be regarded as a vagina is reinterpreted as a "hole."[24] Sometimes such body parts (or at least certain activities involving those body parts) might be excluded from one's sexual scripts and repertoires altogether. This points to the idea that what might be important in a sexual encounter is not a given body part per se, but the moral and sexual interpretation of that body part within the contexts of various forms of sexual engagement. And this, in turn, has interesting consequences with respect to the *content* of sexual orientation. It also has consequences with respect to various forms of social sex segregation that I discuss in the concluding section.

SEX SEGREGATION

Recently, debates about trans people using public restrooms in accord with their gender identities have gained increasing prominence with laws being passed in various states that ground the use of sex-segregated restrooms in terms of original (unaltered) birth certificates so as to prevent trans women from using the women's restroom and trans men from using the men's restroom. From a trans political perspective, such moves can be viewed as institutionalized forms of misgendering: By requiring trans women to use the men's restroom, trans women are institutionally considered men. The rationalizations for doing this seem extraordinarily weak. Consider, for example, the charge that trans women will engage in sexual predatory behavior to non-trans women while in the restroom. Such a claim is easily falsifiable as trans women typically use the restroom to pee, rather than to harass other women.[25] Indeed, such a claim rests on the view that trans women are actually men (who want to harm women). By contrast, if trans women are recognized as women, then the same rationale of protecting (non-trans) women ought to apply to trans women as well.

The position also leads to consequences clearly not intended by the advocates of such laws, that is, when the position insists that trans women use men's restrooms and trans men use women's. Consider a trans woman who passes as a (non-trans) woman. What will men think when she enters the men's restroom? At best, they may worry about their own privacy; at worst, the trans woman may be at risk for harassment and even violence. And consider a trans man who passes as a (non-trans) man. What will women think when he enters the women's restroom? Won't they have the very concerns that are supposed to have motivated the exclusion of trans women in the first place? What is being obscured here are the risks that some trans and non-gender conforming people face when it comes to restroom use. A trans or gender non-conforming person who does not pass consistently in one gender (i.e., whether she "passes" is variable, depending on context) may find that no restroom is free from possible scrutiny and harassment. This suggests, at least in a society that continues to sex segregate restrooms, that gender neutral restrooms be made readily available.

On the face of it, then, debates about trans people using sex-segregating restrooms raise very little philosophical interest: The arguments against trans people using the restrooms that reflect their gender identities seem very poor. However, sex-segregated restrooms are really only the beginning. Once we start looking at other forms of institutional sex segregation (e.g., change rooms, domestic and homeless shelters, prison housing, invasive strip searches), particularly those that involve individuals seeing and being seen or touching and being touched, some interesting philosophical questions and insights can come to the fore.

Consider a specific example. I was part of a working group that designed and attempted to have implemented procedures and policies for the Los Angeles Police Department's interaction with transgender individuals. We proposed that with regard to invasive strip searches trans people be allowed to determine the sex of the officers who searched them. Our reasoning was that because trans people's bodies are often complex and because they understand and sometimes "recode" their bodies in different ways, it would be best to leave it up to the individual trans person.

Some of the LAPD's concerns with this proposal concerned possible litigation from female officers being expected to search bodies with penises. Underlying worries about litigation were moral concerns. Initially those concerns were expressed in terms of implausible fears of female officers being raped by trans women. The idea at play, of course, was that trans women (with penises) are "really men" who may be disposed to subject women to sexual violence. Curiously, however, the dividing line (whether the person has a penis or not) seems to have little to do with the attributed psychological disposition. Why should an individual who no longer has a penis possess a disposition to commit rape? Such an individual is still capable of committing acts of sexual violence, even without a penis; nothing else in terms of physical capacity (e.g., physical strength) has been at all altered.

It appeared, then, that what was largely at stake were concerns about privacy and decency. These concerns also arose in our discussion around sex-segregated jail housing. Basically, the worries were that trans women might be in a position to invade the privacy of (non-trans) females and, moreover, that trans women might be in a position to commit indecency offenses against females. Thus, concerns about strip-searches seemed to turn on the possible harms of female officers coming into contact with penises (i.e., concerns about indecency).

This points to the ways in which body parts are interpreted socially in sex-differentiated ways—particularly with respect to moral boundaries that govern privacy and decency. Indeed, it is suggestive of the respect in which nakedness itself may be socially constituted. Nakedness as a morally laden phenomenon certainly presupposed the standardization of clothedness in most social contexts and is to that extent entirely cultural. Such concerns also highlight ways in which trans people *contest* these boundaries by interpreting their bodies in different ways.

If this is right, what is at stake in sex segregation is actually something quite philosophically rich—namely, the social interpretation of sex-differentiated body parts in terms of moral boundaries. It is certainly not a trivial affair, as such moral interpretations run very deep in our understandings of the distinction between the male and female categories, at least in regard to human beings.[26] Such moral boundaries may underlie the linguistic practices which involve categorizing trans men as really women and trans women as really men. Indeed, they may lay the basis for crucial affective investments in our bodies as well as our public gender presentation—investments such as a sense of public gendered dignity, experiences of vulnerability and invulnerability, even experiences of violation and offense. In other words, perhaps this is a good place to start looking for an account of some of the affective investments that ground gender identity.

NOTES

1. For a more complex discussion, see C. Jacob Hale, "Are Lesbians Women?" *Hypatia: A Journal of Feminist Philosophy* 11:2 (1996), 94–121. See also Robin Dembroff's essay "What Is Sexual Orientation?" in this volume.

2. For further discussion, see A. Finn Enke, "The Education of Little Cis: Cisgender and the Discipline of Opposing Bodies," in *The Transgender Studies Reader 2*, edited by Susan Stryker and Aren Aizura (Routledge: New York, 2013), 234–47.

3. Stephanie Kapusta, "Misgendering and Its Moral Contestability," *Hypatia: A Journal of Feminist Philosophy*, forthcoming.

4. Kapusta, "Misgendering and Its Moral Contestability."

5. For a more developed definition, see Derald Wing Sue, *Microaggressions and Marginality: Manifestation, Dynamics, and Impact* (Hoboken, N.J.: Wiley and Sons, 2010), cited in Kapusta, "Misgendering and Its Moral Contestability," 504.

6. Kapusta, "Misgendering and Its Moral Contestability." See also Sonny Nordmarken, "Microaggressions," *Transgender Studies Quarterly* 1:1–2 (2014), 129–34.

7. Miranda Fricker, "Powerlessness and Interpretation," *Episteme* 3:1/2 (2006), 96–108.

8. For example, Janice Raymond, *The Transsexual Empire: The Making of the She-Male* (Boston: Beacon Press, 1979).

9. John Corvino, "Analyzing Gender," *Southwest Philosophy Review* 17:1 (2000), 173–80.

10. There are many examples of this type of account. For example, see Hale, "Are Lesbians Women?" and Corvino, "Analyzing Gender."

11. See Corvino, "Analyzing Gender." For more critiques of the family resemblance strategy, see Kapusta, "Misgendering and Its Moral Contestability," and Talia Mae Bettcher, "Trans Women and the Meaning of 'Woman,'" in *The Philosophy of Sex: Contemporary Readings*, 6th ed., edited by Nicholas Power, Raja Halwani, and Alan Soble (Lanham, Md.: Rowman & Littlefield, 2013), 233–50.

12. See Jennifer Saul, "Politically Significant Terms and the Philosophy of Language: Methodological Issues," in *Out from the Shadows: Analytical Feminist Contribu-*

tions to Traditional Philosophy, 1st ed., edited by Sharon L. Crasnow and Anita M. Superson (Oxford: Oxford University Press, 2012), and Esa Diaz-Leon, "'Woman' as a Politically Significant Term: A Solution to the Puzzle," *Hypatia: A Journal of Feminist Philosophy* (forthcoming).

13. For a more thorough discussion, see Talia Mae Bettcher, "Trans Women and the Meaning of 'Woman.'"

14. Bettcher, "Trans Women and 'Interpretive Intimacy.'"

15. While it is difficult to provide an analysis of expressions such as *trans woman* within the various subcultures, roughly one can say that gender-presenting as a woman or at least wanting to so present along with self-identifying as either a woman or a trans woman are typically taken as sufficient conditions.

16. This is actually more complex. Some trans women don't self-identify as women per se. Instead they might self-identify as "beyond the binary." So, more accurately, being a trans woman and self-identifying as a woman are taken as jointly sufficient for category membership.

17. Julia Serano, *Whipping Girl: A Transsexual Woman on Sexism and the Scapegoating of Femininity* (Emeryville, Calif.: Seal Press, 2007), 80.

18. Jay Prosser, *Second Skins: The Body Narratives of Transsexuality* (New York: Columbia University Press, 1998), and Serano, *Whipping Girl*.

19. For example, Gayle Salamon, *Assuming a Body: Transgender and Rhetorics of Materiality* (New York: Columbia University Press, 2010).

20. For a detailed discussion, see Paul Schilder, *The Image and Appearance of the Human Body* (New York: John Wiley and Sons, 1950), and Salamon, *Assuming a Body*.

21. Schilder, *The Image and Appearance of the Human Body*, and Salamon, *Assuming a Body*.

22. For a detailed discussion of the issues that follow, see Talia Mae Bettcher, "Trans Women and 'Interpretive Intimacy': Some Initial Reflections," in *The Essential Handbook of Women's Sexuality Volume 2*, edited by Donna Marie Casteñada (Santa Barbara, Calif.: Praeger, 2013), 51–68.

23. For more on sexual orientation, see William S. Wilkerson, "What Is 'Sexual Orientation'?" in *The Philosophy of Sex: Contemporary Readings*, 6th ed., edited by Nicholas Power, Raja Halwani, and Alan Soble (Lanham, Md.: Rowman & Littlefield, 2013), 195–214, and Dembroff, "What Is Sexual Orientation?" in this volume.

24. See C. Jacob Hale, "Leatherdyke Boys and Their Daddies: How to Have Sex Without Women or Men," *Social Text*, 52/53 15:3&4 (1997), 223–36.

25. For related discussion, see Rachel McKinnon, "The Epistemology of Propaganda," *Philosophy and Phenomenological Research* (forthcoming).

26. For a detailed discussion of these ideas, see Talia Mae Bettcher, "Full-Frontal-Morality: The Naked Truth about Gender," *Hypatia: A Journal of Feminist Philosophy*, 27:2 (2012), 319–37.

STUDY QUESTIONS

1. Bettcher states, "Distinguishing gender identity from sexual orientation and sexual identity is important in combating the harmful misconception that trans people transition because of their sexual orientation." How and why is the misconception that trans people transition because of their sexual orientation harmful?

2. Can one argue that while it is easy to see why someone would not be born with an innate sense of being a banker or fashion model, being born with an innate sense of being a man or a woman is different and makes more sense?

3. "Male," "female," "man," "woman," "sexual orientation," "sexual identity," "gender identity," "gender expression," and "gender presentation" are different, yet connected, concepts that Bettcher uses in her essay. Try to be clear on how they connect to each other. Do so by coming up with examples of (hypothetical) individuals, each of whom has a different combination of the properties to which the above concepts refer.

4. Explain Bettcher's argument that the desire of some trans people to transition is explained by the fact that their conscious gender identity leads to discomfort with their bodily configuration but that this still leaves a puzzle about the cause of "the original discomfort that yields the transformation in gender identity in the first place."

5. Bettcher, in discussing the history of the terms used to refer to trans people, briefly notes, "There was an emphasis on the importance of passing as a member of the gender category one had transitioned into and fading into the mainstream as a non-transsexual person." Is passing nowadays not as important as it was in the old days? And what connections do you see between the terms (including pronouns, which Bettcher does not discuss at length) used to refer to trans people and issues having to do with passing?

6. After mentioning the view that if someone is really male then they should be addressed as a man, Bettcher states, "While versions of such a position are espoused by some anti-trans feminists, the position is also implied by individuals who deliberately misgender trans people, knowing full well how these trans would *like* to be treated. Such a position is implausible, however, in light of the seriousness of the harms cited above." Assuming that the view leads to harms, does the harm render the view implausible, as Bettcher states?

7. In arguing that the meanings of gender terms such as "man" and "woman" are contested in trans communities, Bettcher claims that one main way that such contestation occurs is by starting with the claim that being a trans woman is a sufficient condition for being a woman. However, one might ask: How is it decided that such a condition is sufficient? And might this question take us back to the very conceptual analyses that Bettcher claims are not likely to help?

8. Bettcher argues that body parts as such are not the cause of the comfort or discomfort that some trans people might feel toward them, but how these parts are interpreted in specific contexts. She suggests that "recoding" or renaming them might help. Would such a strategy work in sexual encounters between trans people who know about and use recoding and people (trans and non-trans) who do not?

9. Consider the example of the Los Angeles Police Department and strip searches, in which Bettcher suggests that because each trans person might recode their body differently, it should be up to them to decide on the gender of the police officer to search them. Might there be reasons for a police officer to be legitimately troubled by this suggestion (that is, not because the officer thinks that a trans woman is "really" a man or that a trans man is "really a woman")?

NINE

The Negotiative Theory of Gender Identity and the Limits of First-Person Authority

Burkay Ozturk

In this essay, **Burkay Ozturk** *assesses the first-person authority view about gender, according to which X's self-identification of what X's gender is is the final say on what X's gender is, such that if others disagree with X regarding what X's gender is, the others are mistaken. One main reason is that overriding X's identification amounts to denying X's autonomy—it amounts to wrongful paternalism. Ozturk, however, criticizes this view using religious and patriotic self-identifications as analogies: if in some cases Y can permissibly claim that X is not a true Muslim or a real patriot, then such rejections can be permissible in some cases, which implies that there might also be cases of permissible rejection of gender self-identification. Ozturk offers instead the negotiative theory of identity, according to which it is permissible to reject a self-identification if and only if the three constraints of no-harm (to the self-identifier), (their) privacy, and (their) dignity are not violated. If Ozturk's negotiative theory is correct, it would be relevant to all types of self-identifications.*

Burkay Ozturk received his BA from Bilkent University in 2007 and his PhD from the University of Illinois at Chicago in 2014. He does research in ethics, philosophies of science, logic, mathematics, and religion. He has several publications, including "Of German Tanks and Scientific Theories" in *Southwest Philosophy Review* (2015) and "Facsimiles of Flesh" in *Journal of Applied Philosophy* (2016, coauthored with Robert W. Fischer). He teaches at Texas State University. © 2017, Burkay Ozturk, who kindly gave permission for his new essay to be included in this volume.

139

The first-person authority view (FPA) is the current dominant view about what someone's gender is. According to FPA, the person has authority over her own gender identity; her sincere self-identification trumps the opinions of others. There are two versions of FPA, epistemic and ethical. Both versions try to explain why a person has authority over her own gender identity. But both have problems. Epistemic FPA attributes to the self-identifier an unrealistic degree of doxastic reliability. Ethical FPA implies the existence of an unreasonably strong and unqualified obligation on the part of others not to reject the person's identification. This essay offers an alternative: the negotiative theory of identity. Unlike epistemic FPA, the negotiative theory doesn't presume the reliability of self-directed beliefs. Unlike ethical FPA, the negotiative theory doesn't imply an obligation not to reject. Instead, it contends that an act of rejection is morally permissible if and only if it respects three ethical and epistemic constraints. In doing so, the negotiative theory combines the strengths and avoids the weaknesses of both versions of FPA, and gives us substantive insight into how far first-person authority reaches in terms of grounding rights and obligating others.

The Story of Susan and Joe

Susan is a self-identified woman who works in an office. Susan makes it clear to her coworkers that she wants them to call her "Susan" and abandon her given name, "Edward." She also asks them to use female pronouns when they refer to her in the third person.

Joe, a coworker of Susan, sees several reasons for complying with Susan's requests. Some of these reasons are prudential, such as maintaining a positive professional relationship and avoiding being identified as a bigot. Some are moral,[1] as Joe worries that not complying can cause Susan to suffer. However, Joe thinks that he has reasons against complying as well. According to Joe, Susan is mistaken about her gender identity. Complying with her requests would amount to participating in deception and enabling a delusion. It would also be insincere and dishonest because, according to Joe, Susan is not really a woman. Joe thinks he ought not participate in deception, enable a delusion, or be dishonest.

Would Joe be doing anything wrong in rejecting Susan's self-identification? If yes, why would he be wrong? Would he be wrong regardless of how he rejects? Or are there modes of rejection that wouldn't be wrong?

We must first clarify what "acceptance" and "rejection" mean. I understand acceptance of Susan's self-identification at least as assent to the proposition expressed by the sentence "Susan is a woman" where "woman" is meant literally and without contextualization or qualification,[2] or anything that implies such assent. Rejection is explicit or implied dissent. It is also possible to have a neutral position that is neither acceptance nor rejection.

Both acceptance and rejection often involve more than mere assent or dissent. For instance, if lawmakers accept Susan's self-identification, then Susan will also be able to legally marry a man even in places where same-sex marriages aren't recognized by law. Some implied rejections are delivered in the form of harassment, refusal to accommodate, discrimination, and even physical violence. But at the core of acceptance and rejection there is implied or explicit assent and dissent. Respectively, assent and dissent are the minimally necessary and sufficient conditions for acceptance and rejection, and can be thought of separately from their social and political associations, and modes of delivery.

When acceptance and rejection are understood in this way, one might think it obvious that Joe is doing something wrong by rejecting Susan's self-identification regardless of how he does it. One might think that Joe is wrong to reject because Susan being a woman, a man, neither, or both is not something that Joe gets to decide for Susan. Only one person gets to decide Susan's gender—or lack thereof—and that person is Susan. That's why, rejecting a sincere gender self-identification like Susan's is *always* wrong. Following Talia Mae Bettcher,[3] I will call this view "the first-person authority view of gender identity (FPA)."[4]

EPISTEMIC AND ETHICAL FPA

Epistemic FPA, whose roots can be traced back to Donald Davidson,[5] is the view that the gendered person has the ultimate say over her gender because of her unique epistemic position. Gender, on this view, is *constituted by* the contents of the gendered person's mind, such as beliefs and desires, and one has privileged and reliable access to the contents of his or her own mind.

Crispin Wright, Krista Lawlor, and Bettcher identify several difficulties with epistemic FPA, including the possibility of stable but unintentionally erroneous self-directed beliefs.[6] If the authority Susan has over her gender has merely epistemic roots, then Joe's refusal to accept Susan as a woman is not necessarily a factual mistake. Anybody might have erroneous beliefs about themselves, who or what they are, and even about the content of their own minds. So epistemic FPA fails to show that it is *always* wrong to reject.

The *ethical* version of FPA characterizes the authority Susan has over her gender identity as ethical, *not* epistemic. On this view, being mistaken in one's beliefs is irrelevant:

> When one person reports one's attitudes and emotions, one's authority rests not on being right, but on being responsible. Evidence of one's fallibility . . . has no bearing on one's *authorial status*. Social psychology's unrelenting skepticism about our self-knowledge is apparently defanged [emphasis added].[7]

Bettcher, the most prominent defender of ethical FPA, appeals to this "authorship account" to formulate an argument from autonomy, which justifies ethical FPA and tries to explain why it is always wrong to reject:

> [C]onsider a case in which a second person simply tells the first person with certitude what her attitudes are. For example, even if it is clear one wants to go home (one looks at the clock, taps one's foot), it is odd for one's date to announce, unprompted, "You want to go home now." To be sure, he might ask, "Do you want to go home? Because it seems like you do." He might even say, "It seems to me you want to go home." What seems problematic is the attempt to avow somebody else's mental attitudes on their own behalf, and there is the sense that if "You want to go home now" is not meant humorously, *it is an attempt to control*. Again, there is something that feels "ungrammatical." More important, *there is an infringement on the first person's autonomy*. The second person is inappropriately treating his own interpretive assessment as authoritative [emphasis added].[8]

In other words, making avowals on someone else's behalf (and by implication, responding to self-directed avowals with rejection) is a denial of that person's autonomy and is an attempt at control, both of which are wrong.

According to the argument from autonomy, rejecting is not wrong just because and when it is a factual mistake, or causes Susan to suffer. Rejecting is wrong because rejection is essentially paternalistic. That's why Joe's rejection of Susan's self-identification is morally wrong regardless of how he rejects. As an autonomous being, Susan is in charge of herself and ought to be recognized as such. No one rejecting Susan's gender self-identification can avoid denying Susan's autonomy, whether explicitly or implicitly.

As the obligation not to reject is grounded in Susan's autonomy, it is arguably overriding. It trumps most other moral considerations Joe might have for rejecting, such as the obligations not to participate in deception, enable a delusion, or be dishonest. Therefore, what Joe does to Susan is wrong regardless of the consequences or the mode of his rejection. Ethical FPA and the argument from autonomy that grounds it imply that Joe has an unqualified moral obligation not to reject Susan's gender self-identification.

WHY ETHICAL FPA IS IMPLAUSIBLE

Since the argument from autonomy concerns not just gender-related self-identifications but all self-directed avowals, it implies that rejecting any sincere self-identification would amount to moral wrongdoing. However, here are two scenarios in which it is pro tanto permissible to meet a sincere self-identification with resistance and even outright rejection.[9]

Sam sincerely believes that he is a Muslim, lives his life as a Muslim, and sees this as an important part of his identity. Offended by some visual depictions of the prophet Muhammad published by a French magazine, Sam and his two friends drive over to the magazine and kill several staff members. Muslims all over the world, including Zahra, condemn Sam and his friends' actions and denounce them as "incompatible with Islam." They declare that Sam, contrary to his sincere and public self-identification, isn't a real Muslim.

Andy sincerely believes that he is a patriotic American, lives his life as one, and sees this as an important part of his identity. He publicly supports political candidates and policies which he perceives as patriotic, raises his children with what he considers patriotic values and actively encourages his peers to be patriotic. However, it comes to Robert's attention that whenever Andy is summoned for jury duty, he concocts a lie to avoid having to serve. The next time he catches Andy touting his patriotism in public, Robert retorts, "Andy, you aren't a real patriot."

Now consider the following argument:

1. If Joe had an unqualified obligation not to reject Susan's self-identification as a woman, then Zahra would have had an unqualified obligation not to reject Sam's self-identification as Muslim.
2. Zahra doesn't have an unqualified obligation not to reject Sam's self-identification as Muslim.
3. Therefore, Joe doesn't have an unqualified obligation not to reject Susan's self-identification as a woman.

The argument above hinges on the strength of the purported analogy between Susan's self-identification as a woman, on the one hand, and Sam's self-identification as a Muslim, on the other. Its counterpart involving Andy likewise hinges on the strength of the purported analogy between Susan and Andy. So, just how strong are those two analogies?

The analogies might appear weak because gender identity could be seen as a special kind of identity that is very much *unlike* religious and political identities. If that's the case, the scenarios involving Sam and Andy might not be sufficiently similar to the one involving Susan to draw any conclusions about Susan's rights and Joe's obligations. While one can reject Sam's and Andy's self-identifications without denying their autonomy, only gender and transgender self-identifications would command the authority which makes rejecting always wrong.

This, however, requires that there is a principled distinction between gender identity, on the one hand, and other kinds of identity, including religious and political identities, on the other.[10] What could this principled distinction be?

I can think of two answers. First, one might claim that being gendered is so important to all of us that gender self-identification is more important than any other self-identification. Perhaps gender identity is so existentially and morally significant to all individuals that self-avowals over gender identity *alone* command an overriding ethical authority. Second, one might point at the phenomena of political and religious conversions, and contrast how society reacts to them differently than gender transitions. If Thomas More had recanted his Catholicism and converted to Anglicanism, his peers would not have rejected his new identity on the grounds that you just can't recant your Catholicism. In fact, even religions that punish conversions with death (such as certain strains of Sunni and Shi'a Islam) do so *because* they recognize those conversions as *successful changes in one's religious identity*. In contrast, when someone like Private Manning publicly states that she is a woman, some folks (including CNN's Jake Tapper) take it as a duty upon themselves to publicly deny that Manning is, ever was, or ever will be a woman.[11]

Let's first consider the idea that gender identity has a unique degree of existential and moral significance that sets it apart from all others. People like Sam, however, will disagree that gender identity is more important than religious identity. For Sam, being Muslim is likely to be at least as important as being a man, if not more. It is conceivable that Andy should say something similar about himself in his patriotic fervor. The same is arguably the case for many people who hold strong religious or political convictions. That is why thinking of gender identity as more significant would be underappreciating the existential and moral significance of religious and political identities for the people who profess to have them. After all, some people die for their faith, for their ideology, for their nation. Some, such as Sam, even kill. It is not clear how self-identification can get more existentially and morally significant than that.

I am not defending the claim that gender identity is less important than other identities. Although being a woman might have the utmost existential and moral import for some people, for many others religious or political identities are at least as important. So if it's always wrong to reject Susan's self-identification, it would also be always wrong to reject Sam's. But Zahra rejecting Sam's self-identification is pro tanto permissible. Therefore, Joe has no unqualified obligation not to reject Susan's self-identification.

It might be objected that I am taking the point of view of the self-identifier (e.g., Sam's and Andy's). Shouldn't we instead focus on whether it is important *objectively*? If gender has more *objective* existential and moral significance than other identities, the analogy between Susan's and Sam's self-identifications would break down and we would have no reason to accept the first premise of the argument above.

I don't see how this line could be pursued cogently. Part of the issue is "*objective* existential significance" is an oxymoron. Perhaps more important, the disagreement between Sam and those who consider gender identity to be more important than Muslim identity seems intractable, which is a pro tanto reason to disfavor any meta-theory valuing one over the other.

The second proposed principled distinction—that the success of religious and political conversions are universally recognized, while gender transitions are often met with serious resistance by some—is at odds with facts of the sociology of religion and politics. In particular, some religious individuals don't recognize conversions to (or, in some cases, away from) their religions, just as some cisgendered people do not recognize gender transitions. These religions include the vast majority of Anatolian Alevites and Syrian Alawites, a substantial number of Hindus, and some conservative Jews. Also like gender conversions, some political conversions are met with strong resistance (e.g., Albert Speer's recanting of his Nazism at the Nuremberg trials and Hillary Clinton's embrace of same-sex marriage). If anything, this supposedly principled distinction between religious and political identities, on the one hand, and gender identity, on the other, further highlights the strength of the analogies between them.

However, we shouldn't overstate the point of these analogies and the objection they raise against ethical FPA. I do not deny that there are ethical (or epistemic) grounds for accepting a self-identification. Nor am I arguing that it is always permissible to reject a self-identification. I am arguing that it is not always morally wrong to reject; sometimes it is permissible to challenge a self-identification by subjecting it to some form of external scrutiny and reject those self-identifications that fail to withstand scrutiny. The important task here is to identify the instances and forms of rejection that are permissible and distinguish them from those that are not. The negotiative theory of identity aims to do precisely this.

THE NEGOTIATIVE THEORY OF IDENTITY AND THE CONSTRAINTS ON PERMISSIBLE REJECTION

I have so far concluded, contrary to what ethical FPA entails, that there is no unqualified obligation to not reject. This does not mean, however, that self-identifiers have no rights to any form of social recognition.

There are morally permissible and impermissible modes of rejection. Whether rejection is morally permissible depends on compatibility with three ethical and epistemic constraints of the framework in which negotiations of identity take place. The constraints are those of harm, privacy, and dignity. They jointly determine when and how the rejection of someone's self-identification is permissible.

The constraints of harm and of privacy require that an act of rejection not cause unjustifiable harm or constitute a morally impermissible violation of privacy. The constraint of dignity is both ethical and epistemic; it requires that an act of rejection not deny the dignity of the person professing a certain identity if that person is in possession of adequate defenses of self, which are reasonable responses to the attempted defeaters against her self-identification. Individually, each of these three constraints is a necessary condition for permissible rejection. That is, if the rejecter fails either, the rejection is impermissible. They are also collectively sufficient: If the rejecter satisfies all, then the rejection is permissible. The negotiative theory of identity claims that *rejection of a self-identification is permissible if and only if none of these three constraints is violated.*

Let's examine each constraint individually.

1. The Harm Constraint

Gender is often said to be "policed" by society. The ethics of gender must pay close attention to the actual and potential harms associated with various forms of coercive and non-coercive gender policing. Sometimes the policing is more than metaphorical. Many adolescent and adult gender non-conformists are coerced into accepting traditional roles. This coercion relies on the threat of violence and sometimes even on actual violence. When rejection is coercive, it undeniably causes harm.

Other forms of policing are subtler, and not all are coercive. For instance, a softer kind of gender policing starts early with most parents giving their children unambiguously gendered names matching the gender assigned to them at birth. They also verbally correct their behavior whenever it clashes with traditional gender roles. If and when these corrections clash with a child's own deeply felt gender identity, they could cause harm to the child's psyche.[12]

In some exceptional cases, potential and even actual harm can be justified. For instance, if someone made such a strong emotional investment in an identity that *any* rejection would cause that person emotional injury, the person in question is liable to harm. Consider again Sam and Zahra. If Zahra's rejection of Sam's self-identification as Muslim will cause Sam emotional suffering regardless of how gingerly Zahra rejects, the harms Sam suffers are justifiable harms, unless Sam suffers from a mental issue that prevents him from constructing an emotionally stable self-image that is not so vulnerable to the judgments of semi-strangers.

Here, one might argue that trans people can't help being so vulnerable due to the systemic injustices and the history of discrimination they have been putting up with. This line of reasoning, however, is a form of infantilization that is not only in tension with the argument from autonomy for ethical FPA but also something that many trans individuals might find repugnant.

The upshot here is that *rejection ought not cause unjustifiable harms.* This constitutes a constraint both on when it is permissible to reject, and in what mode a rejection can be permissibly delivered.

Due to their incomplete psychological development, and because they are developmentally not ready to cope with rejection, children are not in a position to articulate adequate defenses of self and might be unjustifiably harmed by *any* act of rejection. Studies indicate that childhood rejection is associated with negative long-term effects on the child's general psychiatric health and academic success as well as problems in internalization and externalization.[13] This is also true of psychologically vulnerable adults; they are likely to be harmed by rejection regardless of its mode. Since it is impossible to justify such harms, we have an unqualified obligation not to reject when it comes to children and other psychologically vulnerable persons. Obviously, this is not a reason to abandon the negotiative theory of identity as applying to psychologically healthy adults.

2. The Privacy Constraint

Gender is often characterized as a private matter, which is sometimes presented as an argument for an obligation to accept all gender self-identifications and preferred gender pronouns. Although the argument is not convincing, examining it closely will help us identify an important ethical constraint on the permissibility of rejection: rejection is permissible only if it doesn't violate prohibitive or consensual privacy. However, we need to first understand the claim that gender is private.

We can distinguish between three senses in which a matter can be private: prohibitive, consensual, and prudential. When something is prohibitively private, revealing it to the public is *always* morally impermissible, even when the person it concerns directly consents to revealing it. Penis size, for example, is prohibitively private in most communities. Consensual privacy, on the other hand, makes it morally impermissible to reveal to the public *unless* the relevant person consents. Age, in many (but not all) contexts, is considered a consensually private matter. Some consensually private things are also prudentially private, which obtains when making the matter public would be imprudent, even if it is ethically permissible (when the person consents), such as posting pictures of yourself drunk on social media.

Clearly, for the rejection of gender self-identification to be wrong it has to be a violation of prohibitive or consensual privacy. Sometimes the rejection of gender self-identification is wrong because it *is* a violation of prohibitive privacy. For instance, if Joe insists on referring to Susan as "Edward" while conversing with others, he might mean that "that person has (or used to have) a penis." Most would agree, however, that the current state and the history of someone's genitalia are prohibitively private. That implies that Joe should not refer to Susan as "Edward" with that intention, even if Joe thinks that trans women aren't really women.[14] Similarly, if Joe was privately told by Susan that she used to identify as a man, telling everyone in the office that Susan is "not a real woman" would be a violation of consensual privacy and therefore wrong.

However, not all rejections are violations of prohibitive or consensual privacy. First, rejections need not be made in public. Suppose Susan reveals to Joe that she used to identify as a man. Then Joe responds to her and her alone, "then you aren't a real woman." Although such a response could be disappointing for Susan, it is not a violation of privacy. More important, there are ways of rejecting gender self-identification in public but on *public* grounds. To do so, it is sufficient to commit to the claim that gender is determined at least partly by things that are independent of the gendered person's own beliefs and desires. This is a strikingly weak commitment.

The weakness in question allows for significant diversity among what we can call the "externalist theories of gender identity." Although all externalist theories are orthogonal to the existence of an overriding first-person authority, they come from very different places in the political spectrum. Some, such as the *social conservative* worldview, identify gender with the history and current status of one's genitalia and deny that trans women (and men) are real women (and men).

Nevertheless, there are other externalist theories of gender identity that neither identify gender with genital status nor deny the possibility of transgenderism. For instance, the received view of the metaphysics of gender is that gender is socially constructed and is therefore constituted by social recognition of some sort, at least in part. Unlike the social conservative, the proponent of the received view does not have to subscribe to any form of biological determinism or essentialist views about genital status or history, and can and would acknowledge a significant degree of fluidity in gender identity.[15] A social constructivist could accept or reject a trans identity depending on the congruence or lack thereof between it and the social norms that determine the person's gender.

Likewise, when Joe publicly refers to Susan as "Edward," he could mean that the way Susan looks or behaves is not congruent with the social construct that we call "woman." Saying and meaning such a thing is entirely consistent with acknowledging that Susan can later become a woman with or without genital alteration, or that there are other real women who were assigned to the male sex at birth without presupposing that the assignment had been a medical mistake.

Equally important, Joe saying such a thing doesn't have to infringe Susan's right to privacy. Susan's looks and behavior are directly accessible to the people Susan interacts with, which makes them public. If what grounds Joe's rejection of Susan's gender self-identification is her looks and behavior rather than her genitalia, then, though Joe might still be guilty of something, it can't be disseminating information about Susan's genitals or forcing her to disclose such information. The fact that *some people* use gender terms as code for "genitalia" and the rejections they express are violations of prohibitive privacy does not imply that rejecting gender self-identification is *always* gossiping about someone's genitalia. Susan's gender self-identification *could be* rejected on public grounds without necessarily violating her right to privacy.

To be clear, I am not saying that rejection never violates privacy. There are times when people use "man" and "woman" to harass, shame, indignify, and oppress people like Susan by violating their prohibitive or consensual privacy. Those cases, which could even be the majority of all cases, are wrong; *rejection ought not violate prohibitive or consensual privacy.* My claim instead is that the argument from privacy doesn't apply to all those who reject a gender self-identification, and therefore cannot explain why rejection as such is morally wrong.

3. The Dignity Constraint

A rejection of gender self-identification is also wrong when it denies the earned *negotiative dignity* of the self-identifier.

Negotiative dignity is a special kind of recognition that the parties engaged in an argument, a dispute, or any other negotiation might earn. What gives a person the right to negotiative dignity is their epistemic position in the dialectic of the negotiation. In particular, if a person possesses reasonable responses to all available attempted defeaters against their position in the negotiation, he deserves that his position be treated as a moral equal to that of his interlocutors, even if he doesn't have a right to their agreement.

Court opinions are often illustrations of negotiative dignity. For instance, when the Supreme Court justices argue about the law and fail to reach unanimous agreement, minority opinions are written as dissents. These dissents are not mere formalities: they command respect from even their critics, and they inform and inspire later legal reasoning, which sometimes culminates in a change in the law. Dissents have this prospective moral influence because they include reasonable responses to all the decisive concerns and objections of the majority. That's why any lawyer who comments on Murphy's dissent in *Korematsu v. United States* ought to do so with an explicit recognition that it is a respectable and reasonable piece of moral and legal reasoning, even if he disagrees with it.

Similarly, who and what we are is also a matter of negotiation, because who and what we are is always a conceptualization of a moral ideal. When Susan says that she is a woman, when Sam says that he is a Muslim, and when Andy says that he is patriotic, they express judgments about what is worth being and living for.

Thus, when in a dispute over self-identification a party possesses reasonable responses to all the criticisms raised against their position, that party deserves recognition of the dignity of their position. In other words, if the self-identifier possesses an adequate defense of self against the

defeaters they encounter, then others ought to either refrain from rejecting or reject with dignity.

In other words, a person S has the right to negotiative dignity with
regards to a certain self-identification X if

a. S currently lives his or her life as an X, and sincerely identifies as
an X, and

b. S (or someone else on behalf of S) delivers an adequate defense of
self against all reasons made available in good faith to S for rejecting S's self-identification.

Consider Sam's case again. Sam's self-identification as Muslim clearly
satisfies (a). To see how (b) might be satisfied, we should first identify
what reasons someone like Zahra might have to reject Sam's self-identification. Zahra, like Mohammad Ali,[16] might argue from the core tenets of
the Muslim faith that killing someone because of cartoons is a behavior so
far removed from those tenets that the killer cannot be a Muslim or—at
least—a good Muslim. In this case, whether Zahra's rejection is morally
wrong depends on the following. Suppose Sam gets a chance to defend
himself against the rejection and explains why his actions are consistent
with Islam's core tenets. For instance, he discredits some of the Hadith,
on which Zahra relied, as false reports. He also offers excerpts from the
Quran that appear to not only excuse but also justify or even glorify his
actions. Sam's defense might not suffice to convince Zahra that Sam is a
Muslim, but it might constitute an adequate defense of self by casting
serious doubt on the authoritativeness of Zahra's arguments in the eyes
of disinterested observers. This would obligate Zahra to treat Sam with
the respect and dignity other self-identifying Muslims get from her merely by virtue of being Muslims.

If Zahra persists in denouncing Sam's self-identification *in an irrever-
ent mode* without displaying recognition of Sam's negotiative dignity, she
would be guilty of a moral failure. However, Zahra could remain unconvinced and reject Sam's identity without doing anything morally wrong.
But she now ought to treat him with a non-trivial degree of dignity.

The same is true of Andy and Robert. Suppose after Robert's rebuke,
Andy responds with an explanation of why he lies to get out of jury duty:
he thinks that as it is practiced today, the jury system is a far cry from the
patriotic ideal of citizen-governance it once represented. Actually, Andy
reasons, it would be unpatriotic to play any part in it, since that would
provide false legitimacy to a judicial regime that is fundamentally incompatible with his patriotic values.

If Robert presses on with his public accusations, ridicule, and disrespect without responding to Andy's defense, he is also guilty of moral
failure. If he keeps parroting his "you aren't a real patriot" line as if Andy
had not just explained why he does what he does, Robert would be in the
wrong. Even if he is not convinced by Andy's defense of self, Robert

ought to *change the mode of his rejection* by limiting himself to a mode of rejection that recognizes Andy's negotiative dignity as someone who can think for himself on political issues. Robert can still dispute Andy's claim, even publicly, but because Andy possesses an adequate defense of it, Andy cannot anymore be reasonably characterized *as someone who is simply delusional about who he is, as someone who cannot take charge of his own identity*. Unlike the now-notorious Rachel Dolezal's convoluted responses to her critics,[17] Andy's defense of self earns him the right to this dignity.

Likewise, Susan would have access to a defense of self that grounds her negotiative dignity. When someone like Joe rejects her womanhood, Susan (or someone on her behalf) will be able to mount that defense of Susan's self against Joe's defeaters. Suppose that Joe asks Susan a number of rhetorical questions, such as "If you are really a woman, why don't you have a uterus?" Susan could reply by pointing out the existence of millions of cisgendered women who do not have uteri, whom Joe recognizes as women without hesitation. Once Susan (or someone else on behalf of Susan) mounts an adequate defense of self against all of Joe's defeaters, Joe can no more see Susan *as someone who is simply delusional about who she is, as someone who cannot take charge of her own identity*. He might remain unconvinced that Susan is a woman but now owes Susan the social recognition that he used to withhold from her, which must entail the dignity any other self-identifying woman gets from Joe.[18]

The dignity in question is not a mere abstract matter. It has practical implications. It renders morally wrong legislative attempts, public policies, or private actions that are designed to deprive her of the rights and privileges other women are granted qua women.

The upshot of this is the third and final constraint on identity negotiation, the dignity constraint: *rejection ought not deny the negotiative dignity of the self-identifier.*

OBJECTIONS AND REPLIES

I anticipate two objections. The first objection raises the worry that the harm constraint and the dignity constraint are too narrowly construed because they focus on harms caused or dignities denied *by the rejecter* while ignoring the rejecter's moral complicity in harms caused or dignities denied *by others*. The second objection is that the asymmetry in the way the negotiative theory treats trans and cisgendered persons is unfair.

1. The Objection from Moral Complicity

My claim is that *rejection with dignity* is morally permissible if it doesn't cause unjustifiable harm or constitute any morally impermissible violation of privacy. "But how can this be?" one might object. Susan is already deeply wronged by society's prejudice, discrimination, and bigotry. She can't expect to find work in most areas, can't hope to get elected for public office, and she might even be harassed and victimized every day. Given this pervasive social injustice, doesn't rejecting Susan's self-identification make Joe complicit in the harms as well as indignity that Susan has to suffer even if Joe doesn't cause any harm or indignity by actively participating in those acts of prejudice, discrimination, and bigotry?

As this objection recognizes, moral complicity is possible even in the absence of active participation in the wrongdoing. Suppose that Nathan sells a shotgun to Bob even though he suspects that Bob intends to use it to commit armed robbery. Then the fact that Nathan does not participate in the robbery would not absolve him of moral responsibility for it.[19] This is true even if Nathan does not intend the robbery to take place. As long as Nathan knows that he will be facilitating a morally impermissible act by selling the weapon, he ought not to sell it even if he doesn't intend it to be used for that purpose.

The same could be said about Joe's rejection. Perhaps Joe doesn't actively participate in any acts aiming to harm Susan or undermine Susan's dignity, and doesn't even intend Susan to be harmed or be denied dignity. But he might nonetheless be complicit in the harms or indignity she has to suffer at the hands of others.

Joe's and Nathan's situations are morally different, however. One reason for Nathan's complicity in the robbery is that Nathan's selling of the weapon is counterfactually necessary for the robbery. We might be presupposing that "if the sale hadn't occurred, no crime would have taken place."[20] But Joe's rejection is not counterfactually necessary for harming Susan or denying her dignity.

In the absence of counterfactual necessitation, taking partial ideological agreement as sufficient grounds for moral complicity would lead to absurd results: all anti-abortion folks would be complicit in abortion clinic bombings, all socialists would be complicit in the horrors of the Soviet gulags, and all Muslims would be complicit in the *Charlie Hebdo* attacks. Setting up counterfactual necessitation as a necessary condition for complicity is one way a theory of moral complicity could block such absurd results.[21]

Still, commonsense morality tells us that Joe doesn't get off the hook merely by not *actively* participating. He might be obligated to do more than just stand idly by as Susan gets treated without dignity. Unless Joe clarifies his position and publicly states his opposition to denying Susan dignity, his public act of rejection can be seen as participation. By saying "Susan is not a real woman" in public, for instance, he might encourage the bigots who harass Susan, as they might find courage in what they perceive to be Joe's approval of their bigotry. In this regard, Joe should speak out against those who harm Susan or treat her with indignity, even as he rejects Susan's self-identification himself.

2. The Objection from Fairness

According to the negotiative theory of identity, Susan (or someone else on her behalf) has to find an adequate defense of self against all good faith defeaters she knows of. Otherwise, she doesn't get to earn the negotiative dignity that guarantees moral and social equality, and constrains the modes of permissible rejections. But Mary, a cisgendered woman, faces no such requirement. This asymmetry in the way the theory treats cis and transgendered people indicates that the negotiative theory unfairly discriminates against Susan on the basis of her trans identity.

The objection sees any asymmetry in the epistemic duties between cis and transgender women as an indication of surrendering too much ground to "the dominant understanding of gender categories."[22] Therefore, we should avoid characterizing

> the inclusion of trans women in the category of "woman" [as] something in need of defense (unlike the taken-for-granted inclusion of non-trans women). Notably, this asymmetry, which places the womanhood of trans women in jeopardy, arises only if we assume the dominant understanding of "woman." If we assume a resistant understanding of "woman," no question arises since trans women are exemplars of womanhood.[23]

It is true that the negotiative theory of identity often puts a heavier epistemic burden on people like Susan.[24] But this inconvenient and frustrating asymmetry is not unfair discrimination. After all, Sam and Andy face the same asymmetry when we compare them to Muslims who don't kill French cartoonists and patriots who don't perjure themselves.

Moreover, the asymmetry does not assume the dominant understanding of "woman," "Muslim" or "patriot." On the contrary, it stems from a basic fact about the epistemic and ethical framework in which negotiations of identity must take place—namely, in order to negotiate any identity claim, we have to deal with real societies which are populated by agents who make sense of the world through comprehensive doctrines. Even if we disqualified the unreasonable comprehensive doctrines (after all, their defenders either negotiate in bad faith or don't negotiate at all), there still would remain a large number of individuals who would take good faith objections against Susan's self-identification as sufficient grounds to deny her the rights they grant to Mary with ease.

To secure Susan's rights within this framework, the disbelief of the majority must be countered with defenses of self. Otherwise, self-identifications of trans people will continue to be met with acts designed to undermine their dignity. More important, we can't occupy the moral high ground against indignity unless the associated epistemic burden is met. Here is why: Comprehensive doctrines do not just tell people who is and who isn't a woman, a Muslim, or a patriot. They—especially the dominant ones—also inform the actions of individuals and thereby help maintain public order and a semblance of a moral community without requiring them to justify their every choice. That's why a comprehensive doctrine that is shared by the majority has a degree of moral and epistemic authoritativeness that the members of the society are entitled to take for granted. If your parents, teachers, and most peers believe certain things that you also believe, you have every right to expect the dissident to carry a heavier epistemic burden than the conformer. This is true for the vegetarian in a community of meat-eaters as it is true for the vegetarian in a community of vegans as it is true for the dissenting justices of the Supreme Court.

None of this indicates unfair discrimination. Wherever there is a majority, the minority has to earn the majority's respect by showing it that the members of the minority are not simply delusional. This basic fact gives moral and ethical authority to the majority view. That's why Susan—and those who agree with her self-identification—have the burden of mounting an adequate defense of self to earn negotiative dignity that has currency outside the trans community. The bar, of course, should not be set unreasonably high, but this does not mean that none at all should be set.

Some proponents of FPA and pro-LGBT organizations such as GLAAD consciously abandon the painstaking and open-ended moral theorizing that the negotiative theory requires and attempt to replace it with a revolutionary ethic. Their solution to Susan's peril is to replace the dominant understanding of gender with the resistant subculture's understanding. This strategy could indeed achieve the desired goal if and when it succeeds. However, its proponents make it sound as if the dominant and the trans subculture's understanding of gender cannot coexist in a society in which trans people are treated with dignity and respect.

But there exists an alternative missed out by this revolutionary ethic, supplied by the negotiative theory. Thus it is not true that Susan and the people on her side can either "assume the dominant understanding of gender" or "reject, on philosophical grounds, the entire system of gender that dominant cultures circulate."[25] Such wholesale rejections and attempted revolutions are not necessary to protect trans people from unjustifiable harms, privacy violations, or indignities. Indeed, if they fail, they might encourage a closing of the ranks among the members of the dominant culture and further marginalize Susan. What Susan should do is carry her epistemic burden. She should show that she is a dissenter who is neither out of her mind nor convinced that everyone else must be out of theirs.

I firmly believe that this epistemic burden has already been met by and for many trans people. That's why treating them without dignity is morally wrong even when it doesn't harm them or violate their privacy. The burden might have also been met for the majority of trans people. In the latter case, negotiative dignity might be seen as a given. However, from the wrongness of those modes of rejection that deprive people of the dignified treatment they deserve we cannot infer the wrongness of all rejections in all modes and manners. Rejecting with dignity is morally permissible if it doesn't cause unjustifiable harms or violate privacy.

CONCLUDING REMARKS

I identified some problems with both epistemic and ethical FPA. Epistemic FPA attributes to the beliefs of the self-identifier an unrealistic degree of reliability. Ethical FPA implies the existence of an obligation—an unqualified obligation not to reject—which is too strong to be plausible.

I offered a third way of explaining why a person has authority over her own identity and how far that authority reaches in terms of grounding her rights and obligating others. I called this third alternative the "negotiative theory of identity." According to the negotiative theory, *rejection of a self-identification is permissible if and only if rejection doesn't cause unjustifiable harm, doesn't impermissibly violate privacy, and doesn't deny negotiative dignity.*

The negotiative theory avoids the objections which the epistemic and ethical versions of FPA run into. It also gives a better explanation for why Joe might be doing something morally wrong by rejecting Susan's self-identification. The explanation has to do with *the mode of* Joe's rejection. If Joe's rejection causes Susan unjustifiable harm, violates her privacy, or denies her negotiative dignity, Joe would be doing something morally wrong. Moreover, the authority the negotiative theory attributes to the self-identifier and the epistemic burden it demands apply to all cases of self-identification, involving gender and non-gender, with agents who can deploy an adequate defense of self.

NOTES

1. In his "Analyzing Gender," *Southwest Philosophy Review* 17:1 (2000), 173–80, at 179, where he recognizes such reasons in Brandon's story from *Boys Don't Cry*, John Corvino distinguishes between the *conceptual* and *ethical* issues of gender identity: "There is also an *ethical* matter at hand. . . . Perhaps we should call Brandon by whatever pronouns with which he felt comfortable. Given the great power of gender (in our society), there may be a strong case for respecting people's self-conception in the matter of gender, notwithstanding the other important defining characteristics.

While accuracy is paramount in conceptual analysis, ethics requires sensitivity as well."

2. For an articulation and defense of contextualizing gender pronouns, see Jennifer Mather Saul's "Politically Significant Terms and the Philosophy of Language: Methodological Issues," in *Out from the Shadows: Analytical Feminist Contributions to Traditional Philosophy*, edited by Sharon L. Crasnow and Anita M. Superson (Oxford: Oxford University Press, 2012), 195–216.

3. Talia Mae Bettcher, "Trans Identities and First-Person Authority," in *You've Changed: Sex Reassignment and Personal Identity*, edited by Laurie Shrage (Oxford: Oxford University Press, 2009), 98–120; Talia Mae Bettcher, "Trans Women and the Meaning of 'Woman,'" in *The Philosophy of Sex: Contemporary Readings*, 6th ed., edited by Nicholas Power, Raja Halwani, and Alan Soble (Lanham, Md.: Rowman & Littlefield, 2013), 233–50.

4. Henceforth, I will use "FPA" to refer to the view that gender identity is settled by first-person authority. I will use "first-person authority" to refer, not to the view or versions thereof, but to first-person authority itself.

5. Donald Davidson, "First Person Authority," *Dialectica* 38:2–3 (1984), 101–12.

6. Crispin Wright, "Self-Knowledge: The Wittgensteinian Legacy," *Royal Institute of Philosophy* 43 (1998), 101–22; Krista Lawlor, "Elusive Reasons: A Problem for First-Person Authority," *Philosophical Psychology* 16:4 (2003), 549–64; Bettcher, "Trans Identities and First-Person Authority."

7. Lawlor, "Elusive Reasons," 550.

8. Bettcher, "Trans Identities and First-Person Authority," 102. The origins of the authorship account can be traced to Charles Taylor, *Human Agency and Language: Philosophical Papers, Vol. 1* (Cambridge: Cambridge University Press, 1985); Richard Moran, "Interpretation Theory and the First-Person," *Philosophical Quarterly* 44: 175 (1994), 154–73; Richard Moran, "Making Up Your Mind: Self-Interpretation and Self-Constitution," *Ratio* 1:2 (1988), 135–51; Richard Moran, "The Authority of Self-Consciousness," *Philosophical Topics* 26:1&2 (1999): 179–200; Richard Moran, *Authority and Estrangement: An Essay on Self-Knowledge* (Princeton: Princeton University Press, 2001); Victoria McGeer, "Is 'Self-Knowledge' An Empirical Problem? Renegotiating the Space of Philosophical Explanation," *Journal of Philosophy* 93:10 (1996), 483–515.

9. It would be uncharitable to formulate eccentric scenarios (such as a person believing that he is Napoléon Bonaparte) as counterexamples to the general logic of ethical FPA. As Bettcher notes in "Trans Identities and First-Person Authority," when we think about the scope of the first-person authority about which ethical FPA talks, we should focus on contexts where "words have relatively fixed meanings: Persons may not declare themselves teapots and thereby make it so. Nor may they, through sheer force of will, alter the meaning of words within determining cultural contexts. In advocating FPA over gender, I am discussing an already regulated cultural interaction rather than an 'anything goes' or 'because I say I am' doctrine" (98–99). So, for an overriding authority and unqualified obligation not to reject to arise, the self-identification must be made in a linguistic community regulating the application of the terms picking out that identity.

10. This path is not open to some defenders of ethical FPA because they themselves rely on analogies between gender self-identifications and other public avowals. For instance, Bettcher uses examples of ordinary avowals (such as "I do not want to go home") from everyday life to explain why rejection of gender self-identification is wrong. So this commits them to an ethical principle that addresses all self-directed avowals, not just those concerning gender.

11. http://www.cnn.com/videos/bestoftv/2013/08/22/lead-intv-mcnamara-friend-wikileaks-bradley-manning.cnn; date of access January 23, 2017.

12. There are worries in the other direction too. Conservative critics of non-traditional parenting, for instance, argue that the *absence* of non-coercive gender policing during childhood could also lead to harm: this absence deprives the child of the tools and skills necessary to "fit in"—which might not seem valuable until you *don't* fit in.

However, because there is no solid evidence for this, I will disregard them in this paper. If future evidence reveals otherwise, the negotiative theory should be amended to account for it.

13. Patricia McDougall et al., "The Consequences of Childhood Peer Rejection," in *Interpersonal Rejection*, edited by Mark. R. Leary (Oxford: Oxford University Press, 2001), 213–49.

14. See Bettcher, "Trans Identities and First-Person Authority" (108–9), for an eloquent defense of the view that all rejections are violations of prohibitive privacy. Bettcher's considered view, however, is that her argument from privacy is not meant to show that rejections of gender self-identification are *always* violations of privacy but to expose and illustrate a particular form of oppression and harassment trans people generally suffer (personal communication).

15. See Jacob Hale, "Are Lesbians Women?" (*Hypatia*, 11:2 [1996]: 94–121), where Hale argues that the concept of "gender" cannot be analyzed into a set of necessary and sufficient conditions but should be thought of in terms of family resemblance: that there are a number of factors that work in tandem to determine gender, some of which are external but not biological, such as having a "womanly" occupation or demeanor. Internal factors such as self-identification are also included in the gender-determining cluster of factors. Importantly, however, none of these factors are individually necessary or sufficient to be a woman. Therefore, a Halean externalist doesn't have to rely on genital status or history to reject a person's gender self-identification.

16. David Mencer, "Muhammad Ali was a 'Champion of Islam' Who Wanted to Distinguish the Religion from Isis, Says Muslim Leader," *The Guardian* (June 5, 2016). Retrieved from http://www.independent.co.uk/news/people/muhammad-ali-dead-muslim-islam-champion-distinguish-religion-from-isis-a7065941.html; date of access: January 23, 2017.

17. See *Moore v Howard University*, CA-7193-02, District of Columbia Court of Appeals, June 14, 2005.

18. The epistemic burden the negotiative theory associates with self-identification doesn't have to be carried alone. A colleague, a family member, a religious figure, a philosopher, or a social scientist can articulate defenses of self with or on behalf of Susan, depending on the case. Thus it is possible that the burden has already been met as far as most transgender individuals are concerned. If a defense of self fitting Susan's self-identification has already been made public and widely circulated by others, Susan cannot be reasonably required to reiterate the defense herself on every occasion. So, it is likely that Susan's burden might have already been met and Joe already has an obligation to treat her with dignity with regards to her gender identity.

19. Christopher Kutz, *Complicity: Ethics and Law for a Collective Age* (Cambridge: Cambridge University Press, 2000), 168.

20. Kutz, *Complicity*, 169.

21. Although there are good reasons to think that counterfactual necessitation is required for complicity (Kutz, *Complicity*, 120, 130), this subtlety doesn't matter for our purposes because the counterfactual necessitation requirement is waived *only when there is participation*.

22. Bettcher, "Trans Women and the Meaning of 'Woman,'" 245.

23. Bettcher, "Trans Women and the Meaning of 'Woman,'" 245.

24. But not always. For example, a cisgendered woman might face a greater number of attempted defeaters if her behavior and appearance are sufficiently at odds with the society's standards and expectations. See Hale's "Are Lesbians Women?"

25. Bettcher, "Trans Women and the Meaning of 'Woman,'" 245 and 243, respectively.

STUDY QUESTIONS

1. Explain fully the First Person Authority theory in both its epistemic and ethical versions, and explain one problem with the epistemic version and Ozturk's main objection to the ethical version.

2. Is Ozturk correct to use religion and patriotic self-identifications as a way to assess gender self-identification? If yes, why? If no, is it because gender is unique or is it because these two types just happen to be different enough from gender to sink the analogy? Are there other types of self-identifications that Ozturk could have used instead or in addition?

3. Explain and evaluate (1) the two reasons one might give in defense of the claim that gender self-identification is unique and (2) Ozturk's replies to these two reasons. Which is the more plausible position?

4. Is the significance of self-identification an issue to be decided by each person, or is there a fact of the matter as to which self-identifications are significant and which are not (and degrees in between—for example, "somewhat significant")? Might some be a matter of objective decision while others subjective? (What does Ozturk mean by the claim that "part of the issue is '*objective* existential significance' is an oxymoron"? And why does he make this claim?) In answering these questions, use a large sample of examples of self-identifications, from being a woman (or a man) to being an artist, to being a fan of *Star Wars*, to being an American, to being the brother (or sister, or son, etc.) of X.

5. Explain fully the harm constraint on rejecting someone's self-identification. How feasible is it to heed this constraint in practice?

6. Explain the privacy constraint on rejection, making sure to explain what it means to permissibly reject on public grounds. Give an example or two of such permissible, public rejections.

7. According to Ozturk, when a self-identifier has a proper defense of self, the rejecters of the identification should either refrain from rejecting or reject with dignity. Explain this claim fully, making sure to give one or two examples of rejecting with dignity. Crucially, must the self-identifier (or someone on their behalf) have epistemic access to this proper defense, or is its mere existence enough to obligate the rejecter to reject with dignity? What would rejection with dignity mean in those cases in which agents lack epistemic access to the proper defense?

8. Think of the differences (in the consequences to the self-identifier) between rejecting someone's identity as, say, a woman and rejecting someone's identity as, say, a true fan of *Star Wars*. Not much socially, politically, and legally hinges on the latter self-identification, while much hinges on the former. Does the rejecter-with-dig-

nity thereby have additional moral obligations were they to persist in their public rejection? What would such obligations be? Read what Ozturk has to say on this in his reply to the first objection in the penultimate section of his essay.

9. What does Ozturk mean by a "comprehensive, dominant doctrine"? Why is it authoritative, and in what sense? And what implications does it have for uneven burdens in terms of defending one's self-identification? Are these uneven burdens unfair? Why or why not? In answering these questions, use and elaborate on the examples of the vegetarians who live in a community of meat-eaters and those who live in a community of vegans.

TEN

Bisexuality and Bisexual Marriage

Kayley Vernallis

Kayley Vernallis *distinguishes between two types of bisexuals: (1) gender-specific bisexuals, who are attracted to people based on their gender, and for that reason are attracted to both males/men and females/women, and (2) gender-nonspecific bisexuals, who are attracted to people based on their personality and character, regardless of their gender. She further distinguishes between bisexuals who prefer to maintain concurrent but separate relationships (X is in a relationship with Y and Z but Y and Z are not in a relationship with each other) and those who prefer simultaneous relationships (X, Y, and Z are in a triadic relationship). Vernallis argues that neither the availability of opposite-sex marriage nor that of same-sex marriage guarantees the equal treatment of gender-specific bisexuals who desire to maintain concurrent or simultaneous relationships. If two central ideals of marriage are to allow the full expression of the sexuality of the spouses and to maintain sexual fidelity, then perhaps either foursome marriages—of two female bisexuals and two male bisexuals, all married to each other, what Vernallis specifically calls "bi-marriage"—or two concurrent-yet-separate marriages would allow such bisexuals to uphold both of these ideals of marriage. Vernallis concludes with some remarks about how various sorts of plural marriages might benefit society.*

Kayley Vernallis is a professor in and associate chair of the Philosophy Department at California State University, Los Angeles. Her publications include "Queer Portraiture and the Politics of Representation" in *Queer Philosophy: Presentations of the Society of Lesbian and Gay Philosophy* (2012); "Tedium, Aesthetic Form, and Moral Insight in *Silverlake Life*," *Film and Philosophy* (2008); "Bisexuality" in *Sex from Plato to Paglia: A Philosophical Encyclopedia* (2006), and "Bisexual Monogamy: Twice the Temptation but Half the Fun?" *Journal of Social Philosophy* (1999). This essay originally appeared under the title "Bisexual Marriage," in *The Philosophy of Sex: Contemporary Readings*, 6th ed., edited by Nicholas Power, Raja Halwani, and Alan Soble (Lanham, Md.: Rowman & Littlefield, 2013), 215–32. It is reprinted here, revised and under a new title, with the permission of Kayley Vernallis.

> Changing traditional attitudes toward homosexuality is in itself a
> mind-expanding experience for most people. But we shall not really
> succeed in discarding the straitjacket of our cultural beliefs about sexu-
> al choice if we fail to come to terms with the well-documented, normal
> human capacity to love members of both sexes.[1]
>
> —Margaret Mead

Bisexuality is a form of sexual orientation that should be distinguished
from biological sex (female, male, intersexed), gender (attitudes and behaviors identified as feminine, masculine, or androgynous), and gender
identity (self-identification as a woman or man, including transwoman or
transman). Although the categories of gender identity in public discourse
have recently expanded to include such variations as "gender queer,"
"gender fluid," and "intergender," my focus in this essay will be on
bisexual individuals who identify as women or men.

I begin by explaining bisexuality and by exploring the distinction between gender-specific bisexual attraction, which is attraction *on the basis
of gender*, and gender-nonspecific attraction, which is *independent of gender*. I then briefly discuss a new way of looking at sexual orientation,
before turning to bisexual marriage and argue that bisexuals have a right
to a form of marriage that I call "bi-marriage"—a marriage of four bisexuals, two women and two men—only if (1) bisexual attraction is gender-
specific and (2) the members to the marriage wish to be in simultaneous
bisexual relationships (which I will explain). I end the essay by suggesting that bi-marriage may benefit not just bisexuals but also society as a
whole.

BISEXUALITY AND ITS TWO FORMS

1. Bisexual Orientation

Bisexuality, like heterosexuality and homosexuality, is a sexual orientation. Sexual orientation is usually defined in terms of one or more of the
following criteria: *behavior*—the gender of the people with whom one *has*
sex; *sexual desire*—the gender of the people to whom one is *attracted* or
finds arousing; *fantasy*—the content of one's sexual *imaginings*; and *self-
identification*—the *label* one uses to describe or think of oneself.

We cannot rely only on behavior to characterize sexual orientation
because people can engage in transient sexual behaviors that don't reflect
their stable desires or their sense of themselves. For instance, men and
women in prison may have same-sex encounters that serve as sexual
outlets rather than expressions of their identities; some lesbians work as
prostitutes for a male clientele because it pays them more than they can
earn in other jobs; many young people who have both male and female
sexual partners may merely be experimenting with their sexuality. A

desire (or dispositional) model handles these sorts of complications and also captures our sense that sexual orientation is a personality trait that can be central to an individual's sense of identity. It is like other personality traits, such as compassion, religiosity, and intelligence, that we expect to show up in behavior. A dispositional approach can accommodate such facts as that celibate nuns have sexual orientations and that an individual can be bisexual even if he or she is in a long-term monogamous relationship with a gender-stable individual. So, on this dispositional view, a person can be regarded as bisexual if he or she is sexually attracted to both women and men and might be disposed to engage in sexual interactions with women or men, given common and appropriate circumstances. We can even accommodate the possibility that one can be bisexual while not consciously aware of their sexual orientation. Thus, while homosexuals and heterosexuals are oriented toward partners belonging to one gender, bisexuals are oriented toward partners belonging to both genders.

It is important to identify temporal variations in bisexual relationships. For instance, we should distinguish between bisexual relationships which are simultaneous, in which at least three individuals are all in a relationship with each other; concurrent bisexual relationships, in which an individual has two *distinct* relationships, one with a man and one with a woman, during the same period of his or her life; and serial bisexual relationships, in which an individual practices serial monogamy, alternating between same-sex and opposite-sex relationships.[2]

A further distinction is between gender-specific bisexual attraction and gender-nonspecific sexual attraction. According to the gender-specific attraction model, bisexuals are sexually attracted to members of both genders *on the basis of their gender*. Thus, X might be attracted to Y partly in virtue of Y's having a penis and expectations about having sex with a man. On the second model of bisexuality, bisexuals are sexually attracted to members of both genders *independently of gender*. Note that when I first introduced bisexuality as one form of sexual orientation, I described bisexuals as *being attracted to both genders*. Although this characterization provides a simple way of distinguishing bisexuals from heterosexuals and homosexuals, it is important to see that it is ambiguous because there is more than one kind of attraction: some bisexuals are attracted to both genders and some are attracted to individuals irrespective of gender. So we need to clarify the differences between these models of bisexual attraction.[3]

2. Gender-Specific Bisexuality

Bisexuals who experience gender-specific attraction say that being able to sexually express themselves in gay *and* straight sexual relationships is crucial to their sense of sexual identity.[4] They are attracted to women as women, with their range of bodily traits (breasts, vagina, capacity to bear children, larger hip-to-waist ratio, etc.) and, often, with the character traits (warmth, empathy, etc.) associated with women. They are attracted to men as men, with the range of bodily traits (penis, facial and chest hair, physical strength, larger shoulder-to-waist ratio, etc.) and, often, the character traits (competitiveness, assertiveness, etc.) associated with men. They accept the duality of their attractions and feel richer in having both kinds of attraction. Sexual desire for both genders does not mean that one has the same number of male and female partners in a lifetime, or even that one's attractions to men and women are equally strong, but it does mean that being attracted to *both* men and women is a defining feature of this form of bisexuality.

Gender-specific bisexuals desire both men and women as potential sexual partners.[5] Indeed, if they are forbidden to actualize their desires for one gender, they lose their opportunity to express their full sexual selves, thereby experiencing a loss of identity. The depth of that loss depends on how much their bisexual attraction is part of their identities. Sexual attraction might simply be the inducement of physiological arousal in one's sexual organs, but in gender-specific bisexuals, the object-directedness of their desires is important to who they are. Their satisfaction in sexual relationships is important in a way that goes beyond pleasure; they are integral to an individual's personality. In satisfying these desires one is, somehow, more authentic. After all, the satisfaction of desires is not peripheral to who someone is, but is a form of self-cultivation and self-expression because it shapes the self and generates new desires whose character is conditioned by this dynamic process.

On this view (often called "expressivism"), the self is not given a fixed set of desires and character traits that one unveils or discovers. Instead, the intertwining of desire, action, and self-reflection constitute one's identity. This self-shaping is not done alone, but with other people, socially (whether that relation is antagonistic or supportive). Of course, sometimes one's desires are not very important, as when one desires vanilla instead of chocolate ice cream. In contrast, sexuality and sexual object choice are more central to our identity and self-expression than ice cream preferences. As Freud writes, "The sexual behavior of a human being often *lays down the pattern* for all his other modes of reacting to life."[6]

But what is a person's identity? It is a dynamic but predictable structure for action and self-interpretation made up of a collection of traits, such as psychological dispositions, desires, habits, physiological tendencies, beliefs, commitments, and values. A trait is identity-constituting if other traits depend on it—if it is manifested across several life spheres (e.g., work, leisure); it is resistant to conscious change; it can lead to the production of new traits through self-reflection and self-understanding; it leads others to label one as possessing that trait; it is dominant over other traits; and it tends to be dominant in stressful situations.[7] Typical traits that may be identity-constituting include bodily traits such as weight, attractiveness, athleticism; psychological traits such as self-doubt, shame, narcissism, competitiveness; social-role traits such as being a prankster, leader, enabler; social-group traits generated by in-group and out-group expectations about ethnicity, race, gender, class, religion, sexual orientation. Note that such traits need not be acknowledged or affirmed by the person who possesses them. Note also that most of us identify some traits as ideals, and that these idealized traits often play a complex role in relation to the traits we actually have. For instance, one may have as an ideal the capacity to forgive, and commitment to this ideal may help dampen other more censorious tendencies, such as being judgmental. On the other hand, some ideals, such as being perfect, may contribute to strengthening the trait of shame—which can be particularly activated when one inevitably falls short of the ideal of perfection.

To say that sexuality and sexual orientation are central to our identities, then, is to say that our sexual desires, dispositions, activities, judgments, and ideals possess at least some of the structural and causal powers listed above. If one questions the legitimacy of one's desires, or if others characterize them as, for instance, sexually perverted, one may experience an "identity crisis" which involves some loss of one's individuality or "me-ness." Alternatively, if one is prevented from manifesting one's sexual orientation, or even if one chooses to make a painful tradeoff in the satisfaction of one's sexual object choice, one may experience a loss of self.[8]

Above, I characterized gender-specific bisexuals as desiring both men and women as sexual partners. In order to understand why it would be a loss of sexual flourishing for a gender-specific bisexual to be forbidden or to forego making love with members of one gender, we need to know how that person experiences herself differently in same-gender, as opposed to opposite-gender, sexual interactions (or vice versa). It can't simply be reduced to having sex with different objects. If one's experience is the same, the objects are substitutable. To put it simply, if there is no difference between having sex with members of one gender than the other, how could discontinuing sex with members of one gender constitute a real loss? But for gender-specific bisexuals, sex with male and female partners satisfies qualitatively different desires, and hence they incur a loss if they don't satisfy one of these types of desire. In contrast, the sexual desires of heterosexuals and homosexuals are confined to one gender, so they suffer no such loss.

This expressivist picture can explain the nature and significance of the gender-specific bisexual's loss. For, according to expressivism, in satisfying her sexual desires for women, the gender-specific bisexual experiences herself in a certain way. And in satisfying her sexual desires for men, the gender-specific bisexual experiences herself in yet another way.

For example, consider a woman who feels that she is more dominant or masculine when making love with women and more passive and feminine when making love with men. Furthermore, she may feel proud that she can play both dominant and receptive roles. Playing both these roles in her sexual life may be central to her sexual identity and hence her personhood. When she cannot satisfy her desires for sex with the alternate gender, it is not just that she has lost a sexual object; it is as though one half of her sexual self has gone to a nunnery, given how non-substitutable her self-expression is in these kinds of experiences.

3. Gender-Nonspecific Bisexuality

Gender-nonspecific bisexuals consider gender to be *irrelevant* to their sexual object choice, although their pattern of bisexual activity (simultaneous, concurrent, serial) may be just the same as for gender-specific bisexuals. The two forms of bisexuality are distinguished in terms of impulse, desire, and self-understanding. So both the ground of attraction and self-reflection play important roles in differentiating the two from each other. A bisexual woman's gender-nonspecific sexuality may be an important identity-constituting feature of who she is; however, it won't be essential to her identity that she expresses her sexuality with both men and women.

Gender-nonspecific bisexuals are likely to say that they are attracted to an individual's personality or that they "fall in love with the person." There is something very appealing about this form of bisexuality. It is more admirable to be drawn to a person on the basis of character (which we tend to regard as deep and as being under a person's control) rather than on the basis of bodily attractiveness (which we regard as superficial and as being less under a person's control). It also seems that gender-nonspecific bisexuals are not prejudiced. Unlike heterosexuals, homosexuals, and gender-specific bisexuals, they can see past not only people's bodily attractiveness and unattractiveness but also their gendered features. The best phrase to describe gender-nonspecific bisexual attraction is "character-based attraction."

I have two concerns about this form of bisexuality. First, it is unclear to what degree bodies are relevant to character-based attraction. If bodies are not relevant, then it cannot be characterized as a form of *sexual attraction*. Second, character is, at least to some degree, manifested in bodies, and societal expectations about character and gender make our sexual attractions more gender-laden than we think. This makes character-based attraction no longer what it claims to be. For what does it mean to say that sexual attraction is falling in love with a person, period, rather than a person as gendered?

Consider Erin, a gender-nonspecific bisexual, who describes her sexual attraction this way: "I fell in love with my college roommate Terry after spending so much time with her and seeing how caring and special she is. I didn't expect to become romantically involved with her. Sexual intimacy is just one aspect of our shared love and concern. It wouldn't matter to me whether Terry was a man or a woman. I love Terry as a person." This example relegates sexual attraction to being a byproduct of character attraction. X's love for Y's character is such that it eventually generates sexual desire for Y regardless of Y's gender. The *only* thing that matters for generating sexual desire is the beloved's personality. Perhaps she hopes to enjoy her lover's body only as the body of her lover.

But is such a neutral description possible? I don't think so. If she doesn't eventually celebrate her lover's body as a gendered body that can give and receive sexual pleasure, then we cannot say that her connection to her lover's body is a sexual one at all.[9] The reason is that all of us, at least in our culture, have, to varying degrees, gendered body-specific attractions, which are also specific to the body's age, race, height, and other such physical features. One phenomenon that makes this apparent is how many of us experience being sexually attracted to "ideal sexual types." A slender but large-breasted woman with a pretty face is a common preferred sexual type for heterosexual men. A short, bald, pudgy man is not a typical sexual type for a heterosexual or bisexual woman.

I do not wish to deny that our sexual responsiveness is, to varying degrees, conditioned by our experience of a person's character. But a gender-neutral attitude is practically impossible to attain because *our sexual attractions are predominantly, if not always, gender-inflected*. For instance, we culturally project far more sexual attractiveness onto male novelists than female novelists.[10] What looks like commanding presence in a man often looks like overly aggressive—indeed, "ball-breaking"—behavior in a woman. Forthright sexiness in a man looks like slutty behavior in a woman. In a female Terri, caring may be attractive; in a male Terry, it may not be.

Gender-nonspecific bisexuals might accept these points. But they might point out that, unlike heterosexuals, homosexuals, and gender-specific bisexuals, primary sexual organs (e.g., penis, vagina) and secondary sexual ones (e.g., beard hair) are *not* the *determining* features in their sexual partner preference. Instead, they might note that their sexual attractions are robust but independent of gender-marked bodily features. Such a bisexual might say, "I don't care what my partners' primary and secondary sexual traits are, but I do care about whether they are small-bodied or graceful or athletic or youthful. Unlike penises and vaginas, these aren't gender-linked traits."

But this is wrong. A man is often considered to be in his prime at age fifty, but a woman almost never is. Physical grace in a man often translates to ponderous movement in a woman.[11] A small-bodied woman is petite, but a small-bodied man is . . . what? It is hard to think of a positive description. Gender cannot be *irrelevant* to sexual attraction if it is diffi-

cult to identify any gender-neutral bodily traits. There can be no genuinely gender-nonspecific sexual attraction that truly acknowledges the reality of bodies, at least as they are constituted by our current social world.[12]
Gender-nonspecific bisexuals, then, have desires that, at best, can be seen
as gender-semi-specific. Their preference for partners with athletic grace
is best understood as a preference, generally implicit (if not unconscious),
for, say, fine athletic grace that is to some degree indexed to men, and for
fine athletic grace that is to some degree indexed to women.

So gender-nonspecific bisexuals' preferences are not likely to be truly
gender-free, even if they think they are. This should not surprise us.[13] We
still live in a world dominated by gender dualisms. However, even if the
world were to change such that there are more and more nongendered
bodies to which more and more people are attracted, the claim that the
latter are bisexuals is still problematic. This is so for a conceptual reason,
which is that the way we understand "bisexual" is in contrast to "heterosexual" and "homosexual." In many ways, a bisexual is understood as
someone who is attracted to both genders, which implies that a bisexual's
sexual orientation is two-pronged, for men and for women, in which case
gender-nonspecific bisexuals are not so much bisexuals as they are people with an altogether different sexual orientation.

4. A Different Way of Looking at Sexual Orientation?

It is possible that we have drawn our sexual orientation distinctions in
the wrong way. Under the current way of understanding sexual orientation, for example, lesbians and heterosexual men have different sexual
orientations. Yet why should this be so? James Weinrich interestingly
suggests that we should regard lesbians and heterosexual men as having
the same sexual orientation because they are *both attracted to members of
the same gender*: *women*. And we should regard gay men and heterosexual
women as having the same sexual orientation because they are both attracted to men.[14] In this way of categorizing bisexuals, the gender of the
person whose orientation is under discussion is irrelevant: what matters
is only the gender of their object choice. If X is attracted to men, then both
male and female X's have one form of sexual orientation; perhaps they
are "men-phile." If X is attracted to women, regardless of whether X is
male or female, X would be a "women-phile."

This is an interesting idea. It is reasonable that people who are attracted to the same gender have much more in common than the two
groups of people we currently lump into the same category (homosexual)—namely, gay men and lesbians. Moreover, while this new way of
looking at sexual orientation threatens to erode the categories of homosexuals and heterosexuals, it simply renames gender-specific bisexuals as
something else ("m+w-philes," say), while assigning gender-nonspecific
bisexuals an orientation of their own (much like it would assign people

attracted to inter-sex people another orientation). Moreover, this might be politically good for bisexuals: given how in the past they have been seen as existing outside the two sexual orientations, which has led to suspicions about their very existence, this new way of looking at sexual orientation might help in establishing their credentials as people with a genuine orientation.[15]

Because we are not accustomed to this way of thinking about sexual orientation, in the discussion that follows I will continue to speak of "bisexuality" and "bisexuals," and to understand them under the common way of understanding sexual orientation.

BISEXUALITY AND MARRIAGE

One reason why we have not heard much of bisexual marriage is because it is still commonly thought that bisexuality is not a real sexual orientation, that bisexuals are merely confused individuals or cowards, so marriage laws need not accommodate them.[16] Gays and lesbians might not advocate for bisexual marriage perhaps because they believe that between straight and gay marriages, bisexuals would be covered.[17] Some feminists, such as myself, support bisexuals' right to form plural marriages, but they worry that they would then have no legal ground on which to exclude sexist polygamous practices. Others have not thought about bisexual marriage much, but insofar as they have, they dismiss it as inherently unstable and hence not deserving of legal recognition. At the very least, I hope to show that bisexual marriage is a topic we should take quite seriously.

1. Gender-Nonspecific Bisexual Attraction and the Ground for Marriage

Given that both heterosexual and homosexual marriages are legal, *there would be no need for bisexual marriage if all bisexuals' attractions were gender-nonspecific*, because gender-nonspecific bisexuals do not choose their partners on the basis of gender. The extension of marriage to include same-sex couples would provide a gender-nonspecific bisexual with all the legal protection necessary for the full expression of her sexual orientation. Laws that permit two individuals to marry without regard for gender will protect a gender-nonspecific bisexual no matter what the gender of the other marriage partner is.

2. Gender-Specific Bisexual Attraction and Marriage

Will heterosexual and homosexual marriage laws fully protect gender-specific bisexuals? Recall that a gender-specific bisexual is attracted to both men and women. He desires women as women—for the distinctive character and bodily traits they possess. He also desires men as men—for *their* distinctive traits. For these bisexuals, their sexual identity is only expressed if they have sexual relationships with both men and women. If so, then neither option of heterosexual or homosexual marriage enables a gender-specific bisexual to fully realize his sexual identity, because, as I argued above, one's experience of oneself is qualitatively different depending on whether one is in a relationship with a man or a woman. One may express different aspects not just of one's sexual identity but also of one's gender identity in these relationships. A loss of either homosexual or heterosexual relationships is potentially a partial loss of identity. This is the basis of my argument for forms of marriage for bisexuals that would allow them to express fully their sexual and gender identities. Specifically, what I call "bi-marriage" applies to bisexuals whose desires are gender-specific and who wish to be in simultaneous relationships. Those who wish to be in concurrent relationships would have to enter multiple marriages. So from this point on I use "bisexual" to refer to gender-specific bisexuals.

If a bisexual's orientation is expressed in serial relationships, her right to marry can be accommodated by legal heterosexual and homosexual marriage. For instance, she can marry a man for several years and then divorce him; she can then marry a woman for several years and then divorce her. And so on for the rest of her life. She may be happy with these serial marriages, but her spouses are not likely to be unless (1) they are happy to commit to a short-term marriage, or (2) they are bisexuals whose preferred timing of serial relationships matches hers. Besides, it is a rare thing—not to mention a bad idea—for anyone to enter a marriage while anticipating divorce. Indeed, it is one thing for people to fail to live up to the ideal of "till death do us part," but it is another thing to abandon that ideal from the get-go.[18]

However, for bisexuals in concurrent or simultaneous relationships things are different. Given that we understand marriage as an expression of love and sexual fidelity, gender-specific bisexuals are presently denied the opportunity to jointly (1) fulfill their sexual identities and (2) participate in the fundamental ideal of fidelity in marriage.[19] It is not fair that bisexuals have to give up the full expression of their sexual orientation in order to be in a sexually exclusive marriage. This suggests that we ought to explore a rational grounding for other forms of marriage for bisexuals.

3. Contemporary Marriage Ideals

The following are contemporary marriage ideals that our current conception of marriage includes:

Choice

Marriage unions are the product of adult partners' rational choice, reflecting their individual desires, not dictated by the parents, the larger community, or, generally, people other than the partners to the marriage.

Mutuality

Marriage is based upon mutual love, affection, and respect between spouses. If X is married to Y, then they love and respect each other mutually. It is not ideal for one partner to marry for love while the other for money or status.

Commitment

Marriage involves a serious commitment to long-term shared duties and responsibilities, including significant financial, medical, social, and legal ones.

Sexual Self-Expression

Marriage supports forms of individual sexual expression and sexual intimacy that promote the stability of the marital relationship and the love, affection, and respect between the spouses. Although not all one's sexual desires need to be met in marriage, certainly basic forms of sexual self-expression should be realized.

Exclusivity or Fidelity

It is expected that partners to a marriage remain sexually and emotionally faithful to each other—they are not supposed to have sex with anyone outside the marriage (if the marriage is plural, then everyone in the marriage has one sexual outlet with at least one of the partners to the marriage).

Family Stability

Although marriage does not require parenthood, if spouses choose to be parents, they should aim for emotional and financial stability that promotes social development in children. Even in the absence of children, stability is still a central feature of families that grows out of the first four ideals. When achieved, family members are readied to withstand adversity, support one another in old age, and so on.

The legalization of homosexual marriage rests on the claim that homosexuals should not be excluded from the institution of marriage simply because their sexual object choice differs from heterosexuals, and that homosexual relationships, like heterosexual relationships, can attain the ideals identified above. Can bisexual relationships attain the above ideals? Certainly bisexuals are capable of making autonomous, rational choices about whom they want to marry, and they can be as committed to carrying out the financial, legal, and social duties associated with marriage as any other individuals. But if we do not accept different marital arrangements, including "bi-marriage," then bisexuals cannot meet the ideals of sexual self-expression, fidelity, and perhaps stability, under the available models of marriage—married to only one other person at a time. This is because each partner to the marriage would have no access to someone of the opposite gender of their spouse without violating sexual fidelity or exclusivity. We need something different.

4. Marriage and Gender-Specific Bisexuals in Concurrent and Simultaneous Relationships

If a bisexual's orientation is expressed in *concurrent* sexual relationships with men and women, her orientation will be fully accommodated only by being in more than one marriage: X, a bisexual woman, marries a man and a woman, but such that the man and the woman are not married to each other. In this way, X can maintain her bisexuality in her favored manner, by maintaining two distinct relationships. What the sexual orientation of the man and the woman is can be left up to the parties, unless it is a requirement of our current concept of marriage that all parties to it be of the same sexual orientation (I do not think that this is a requirement, though it might be desirable).

If a bisexual's orientation is expressed in *simultaneous* sexual relationships with men and women, her orientation will also not be fully accommodated by heterosexual and homosexual marriage. It will also not be fully accommodated by multiple, concurrent marriages, such as the ones that X is in (per the previous paragraph). Even a triad marriage won't do: it is not possible to simultaneously satisfy the requirement of sexual self-expression with the requirement of sexual exclusivity. The individual who is the only man or woman in the triad cannot both fully satisfy his or her bisexual desires while also being sexually exclusive. If X is a woman, and both Y and Z are men, X cannot fully satisfy her bisexual *desires* after she marries unless she violates the requirement of sexual exclusivity by finding a female lover.

We can preserve sexual exclusivity and full sexual self-expression by making X a heterosexual woman. Now she has two bisexual male sexual partners, each of whom has both a female and a male partner. However, it would be odd for bisexual marriage to logically require that at least one of its members be heterosexual. For one thing, this goes against the spirit of bisexual marriage, which is to extend to one group (bisexuals) the entitlements available to heterosexuals and homosexuals. For another, a heterosexual woman in such triadic arrangements receives an additional entitlement that she wouldn't receive under traditional two-person monogamous marriages—namely, having two husbands with whom she has heterosexual sex. A parallel entitlement would be available for X, were X the sole heterosexual man in a bi-marriage.

Problems also arise if we change the original case by making Z a heterosexual male and Y a bisexual female (X is still a heterosexual female). Z then has mutual relationships with X and Y, but X and Y do not have a relationship with each other. A similar problem arises if X is a homosexual female, Z is a heterosexual male, and Y is a bisexual female: now Y has mutual relationships with X and Z, but X and Z do not have relations with each other. Although sexual exclusivity can be maintained in these cases, we unfortunately give up mutuality, the idea that each member loves, and is sexually intimate with, every other member.

Another solution is if the gender-minority member of the triad (say, X, a bisexual woman, in a marriage with Y and Z, two bisexual men) is willing to forego sexual and love relations with members of her own sex in order to be in the marriage. The loss of her sexual flourishing might be offset by other gains. Still, she makes a sacrifice that heterosexual and homosexual individuals do not have to make when they choose to be sexually exclusive. In any case, though some bisexuals might be willing to make such sacrifices, marriage for bisexuals should not be such that they are required to make these sacrifices. This is significant, because the moral justification for extending marriage to gays and then to bisexuals depends, at least in part, on the idea of a right to the forms of sexual flourishing that are distinctive to each kind of sexual orientation.

The only way to guarantee the fulfillment of the above ideals while maintaining the desirability of having all the partners to the marriage be of the same sexual orientation is by expanding the marriage to four persons, with two partners from each gender. Thus we have the following form of marriage: W and X, two bisexual men, and Y and Z, two bisexual women.[20]

The advantage of this proposal is that no member will need to sacrifice his or her bisexual identity, and hence all members will be theoretically equal to one another in their choices. On the other hand, this four-person model dictates that each member has two alternate-gender partners but only one same-gender partner. Although this ratio may not reflect some bisexuals' preferences, a foursome model doesn't deny any individual's capacity for sexual flourishing. In traditional polygamous marriages, stability is achieved through male power.[21] In bi-marriage, mutual love and sexual relationships among equals provide stability. Because all spouses love one another and are in sexually mutual relationships with one another, jealousy can be readily diffused; one can receive affirmation from more than one spouse, which can lead to better self-reflection and a more realistic understanding of oneself. Bi-marriages of foursomes will, at least in principle, make it possible for all members of the marriage to be bisexual, sexually flourish through sexual intimacy with members of both genders, have mutual sexual and love relationships, and be sexually exclusive. Of course, bi-marriage will face challenges. For instance, the more spouses there are, the harder it may be to come to consensus about what movie to see, which house to buy, and so on. This poses challenges to stability, which makes good communication skills even more important.

Marriage is of course a legal matter, an institution backed, honored, and regulated by the state. Given that for those bisexuals who wish to be with both genders at the same time can do so in concurrent or in simultaneous relationships, should the state allow both to be reflected in marriage or just one—should the state allow marriages of four people, all married to each other, *and* multiple marriages involving one person separately married to two others? If just one form of marriage should be permitted, which one? I am not sure how to answer this question. One way is to decide which desire is more basic to bisexuality and use that as the basis for the decision: if being in simultaneous relationships is a more basic bisexual desire, then the state should honor only bi-marriage, not multiple marriages. But I see no way of convincingly arguing which desire is more basic. Perhaps a better approach is to argue that since the state usually honors the choices of the parties to a relationship who decide to marry, then the state should honor both models. After all, once the state admits one of these two models, why not admit both? If so, then we ought to argue that bisexuals have a right to bi-marriage (plural marriage) or to plural marriages, depending on the choices of the parties to the relationship.[22]

THE SOCIAL CONTRIBUTIONS OF BISEXUALITY AND BI-MARRIAGE

Heterosexual marriage traditionally embodies false dualisms: (1) men and women are opposites; (2) these opposites complement one another in traditional marriage roles; and (3) homosexuality is the opposite of heterosexuality and is, at worst, a perversion, and at best, an exception to proper sexual relations. According to religious conservatives, God created gender, heterosexuality, and patriarchy. God made men physically strong and rational, as well as driven toward autonomy, competition, and leadership. God made women physically weak, emotional, nurturing, and in need of protection and guidance. Gender-based traits complement each other in the traditional heterosexual marriage and are necessary to raising children. This conservative religious view is represented in the Danvers Statement (1988) published by the Council on Biblical Manhood and Womanhood.[23] A slightly more moderate view that does not mention religious values is expressed by David Blankenhorn, president of the Institute of American Values: "Ultimately, the division of parental labor is the consequence of our biological embodiment as sexual beings and of the inherent requirements of effective parenthood. . . . Historically, the good father protects his family, provides for its material needs, devotes himself to the education of his children, and represents his family's interests in the larger world."[24]

Feminists and gay theorists have successfully challenged these traditional gender norms. In some heterosexual families, fathers now engage in childcare and mothers work outside the home. Among gay couples, both spouses often share work and family roles equally. As Susan Moller Okin notes, "Gay marriage has the potential to do more for gender equality than almost any other social change because it demonstrates that there aren't natural gender roles and a natural gendered division of labor within the family."[25] Bi-marriage can also contribute to gender equality. One spouse may stay home to care for children while the other spouses go to work. These roles may change year to year, thereby exhibiting the fluidity of such complex marriages of equal partners. Bi-marriage, even more than same-sex marriage, makes it harder to believe that there must be one spouse who truly "wears the pants" in the family.

The acceptance of homosexuality has made it far easier for straight-identified young men to give voice to and appreciate their emotional connection to other men, as Eric Anderson and Adi Adams show in a recent study of American male college athletes. One college soccer player says of his friend, "I love Dom . . . I mean I really love him. Call it a bromance if you want, but he's my boy. . . . There's nothing I can't talk to him about."[26] Many of the young men said things like "we are all a little gay," but they did not refer to themselves or others as bisexual. I think that Margaret Mead is right that acknowledging same-sex love is an additional step in the acknowledgment of a rich capacity to love individuals of both sexes. This may be because far more of us have this capacity than we would like to admit.[27] Bi-marriage is a way for our culture to acknowledge the truth that emotional attachment, love, and commitment are just as integral to bisexuality as to other sexual orientations.

Obviously, the greatest challenge of bi-marriage—stable mutuality—is not made any easier by discrimination. We have few models or conventions to guide us in maintaining such marriages.[28] But as I suggested earlier, there are advantages to having more than one spouse or life-partner. One can better see oneself through the eyes of more than one other person because of the greater possibilities to correct distortions about oneself and others. The task of defining and delineating oneself in threesome or foursome marriages requires communication skills and sensitivities that might be instructive for all of us. Practical benefits for children in bi-marriages include greater financial stability from three or four parent incomes; better basic care for infants, as each adult has more time to sleep; and more adult attention for young children, which is linked to better school performance.[29]

I have argued that the main reason for extending marriage rights to bisexuals is the same reason why heterosexuals and homosexuals have the right to marry—namely, that marriage expresses a person's desires for love and sexual intimacy. However, the best way for marriage to fully express bisexuals' identities, especially the identities of gender-specific bisexuals, is in the form of marriage of four individuals that includes two from each gender. Thus, bisexual marriage is both an extension of marriage and a radical reconceptualization of it.[30]

NOTES

1. Margaret Mead, "Bisexuality: A New Awareness," in *Aspects of the Present*, edited by Margaret Mead and Rhoda Metraux (New York: William Morrow and Company, in conjunction with Redbook Magazine, 1980), 269–75, at 271.

2. This threefold temporal distinction is introduced by Gary Zinik, "Identity Conflict or Adaptive Flexibility? Bisexuality Reconsidered," *Journal of Homosexuality* 11:1–2 (1985), 7–20.

3. A few psychological studies distinguish between gender-linked and nongender-linked attraction. See, for instance, Michael W. Ross and Jay P. Paul, "Beyond Gender: The Basis of Sexual Attraction in Bisexual Men and Women," *Psychological Reports* 71:3 (1992), 1283–90.

4. Note that sexual attraction (desire, fantasy, and their related physiological and psychological constituents) does not tell the whole story of sexual orientation and identity. But, as we go along, I attempt to show the various connections sexual attraction can have to broader psychological identity and selfhood. For a discussion of sexual orientation, see John Corvino, "Orientation, Sexual," in *Sex from Plato to Paglia: A Philosophical Encyclopedia*, edited by Alan Soble (Westport, Conn.: Greenwood Press, 2006), 728–34, and Robin Dembroff's essay, "What Is Sexual Orientation?" in this volume.

5. I do not wish to exclude love relationships from this discussion, but since sexual orientation is basically about sexual attraction, I will mostly speak in terms of this type of attraction, with the understanding that love relationships often start with and build on it.

6. Sigmund Freud, "'Civilized' Sexual Morality and Modern Nervous Illness," in *The Standard Edition of the Complete Psychological Works of Sigmund Freud*, vol. 9. Translated by James Strachey (London: Hogarth, 1959), 181–204, at 198 (italics in original).

7. The last three traits come from Amelie Rorty and David Wong, "Aspects of Identity and Agency," in *Identity, Character, and Morality: Essays in Moral Psychology*, edited by Owen Flanagan and Amelie Oksenberg Rorty (Cambridge, Mass.: MIT Press, 1990), 19–36. These structural and functional characteristics of traits (for instance, predominance of a trait in stressful situations, strong causal effect on other traits, etc.) do not provide necessary and sufficient conditions for the constitution of identity. For instance, even if one's identity is centrally tied to one's physical appearance, thoughts about ruining one's hairdo will not be predominant in the stressful situation of saving a child from drowning. For some individuals, a sexual fetish for shoes might be a central yet compartmentalized trait. At best, we can identify a fairly loose set of conditions for identifying which traits can be said to contribute to identity.

8. I defend this claim in more detail in "Bisexual Monogamy: Twice the Temptation but Half the Fun?" *Journal of Social Philosophy* 30:3 (1999), 347–68.

9. In short, given how our society is presently structured, there are no gender-neutral personality traits and no gender-neutral bodies. A transgender individual will possess inflections of both, and those multiple inflections may be very sexually attractive to many individuals, including some gender-specific bisexuals. Individuals whose

attractions seem especially close to being gender-nonspecific are, perhaps, pedophiles attracted to both very young girls and very young boys. Small body size, smooth skin, and lack of body odor may be the features that are most attractive in their eyes.

10. I owe this point to the novelist Michelle Huneven. Some female writers, such as Anaïs Nin and Erica Jong, are read as sexually attractive, but they can't compete with the "sexually potent" great writers such as Ernest Hemingway.

11. In fact, context matters quite a bit. A professional male ballet dancer will look incredibly graceful in the company of moderately trained female dancers.

12. Gender-nonspecific attraction may be even more difficult to attain if one's potential sexual partners are extremely unattractive. For some, sagging breasts in a man may be more disgusting than in a woman. I owe the general point to Raja Halwani.

13. It is similar to the case of those who espouse anti-racist views, yet unconsciously harbor racial prejudice. For a substantial list of articles on implicit attitudes, see http://projectimplicit.net/articles.php (accessed March 12, 2012). A typical article on race at the site is A. S. Baron and M. R. Banaji, "The Development of Implicit Attitudes: Evidence of Race Evaluations from Ages 6 to 10 and Adulthood," *Psychological Science* 17:1 (2006), 53–58. If you would like to take the implicit attitudes test, see https://implicit.harvard.edu/implicit (accessed March 20, 2012). Can we devise an implicit-attitudes test for gender-nonspecific sexual attraction?

14. James Weinrich, "Personality and Sexual Orientation Factors as Determinants of Interpersonal Attraction" (master's thesis, Department of Psychology, San Diego State University, 2008). For a defense of a similar view of sexual orientation, see Dembroff, "What Is Sexual Orientation?"

15. For some of the advantages, political or other, of seeing sexual orientation in this new light, see Dembroff, "What Is Sexual Orientation?"

16. It is very common to think that men who identify as bisexual are closeted gays. Women in lesbian communities frequently deny the existence of bisexual women, "It just strikes me as . . . I just don't think bisexuality exists. There! As a legitimate category." Or they regard them as promiscuous, "When I think of 'bisexual' I think of bedhopping" (quoted by Amber Ault, "Hegemonic Discourse in an Oppositional Community: Lesbian Feminists and Bisexuality," *Critical Sociology* 20:3 [1994], 106–22, at 112, 117).

17. It is also true that gay and lesbian groups aren't rushing to defend bisexual marriage in the face of some social conservatives' claims that gay marriage will lead to something much worse: polygamy. For the conservative view, see Stanley Kurtz, "Beyond Gay Marriage: The Road to Polyamory," *Weekly Standard* 8:45 (August 4–11, 2003), reprinted in *The Philosophy of Sex: Contemporary Readings*, 6th ed., edited by Nicholas Power, Raja Halwani, and Alan Soble (Lanham, Md.: Rowman & Littlefield, 2013), 143–59.

18. On the other hand, serial bisexuals are not likely to do worse than other Americans in terms of the longevity of their marriages. The average length of marriages that end in divorce is about eight years; see http://www.census.gov/prod/2005pubs/p70-97.pdf (accessed March 4, 2012). Measuring the overall divorce rate is tricky, but the highest it has ever been is 41 percent as a measurement of all those ever married or ever divorced. Also see Dan Hurley's "Divorce Rate: It's Not as High as You Think," *New York Times* (April 19, 2005). For a defense of temporary marriages (for everyone, not just bisexuals), see Daniel Nolan, "Temporary Marriage," in *After Marriage: Rethinking Marital Relationships*, edited by Elizabeth Brake (New York: Oxford University Press, 2016), 180–203.

19. Bisexuals can engage in "open marriages" in which both partners agree that one or both of them will have sexual and love relationships outside the marriage, and their sexual identities can be fulfilled in this way. However, because heterosexuals and homosexuals do not need to resort to open marriages in order to fully express their sexual orientations, bisexuals are not being treated equally to heterosexuals and homosexuals.

20. Will bisexuals most naturally express themselves and find solidarity best in relationships with other bisexuals? I don't know. Only the future will tell.

21. In traditional polygamous marriage, girls are commonly forced into marriage and many boys are ejected from the community. But it would be unfair, surely, to outlaw all marriages between more than two individuals simply in order to eliminate sexist polygamist practices; otherwise we ought to have already abandoned marriage altogether given its history of oppressing women in monogamous male-female marriages.

22. For more on polyamorous relationships, see the essay by Elizabeth Brake, "Is 'Loving More' Better? The Values of Polyamory," in this volume.

23. See http://www.cbmw.org/Resources/Articles/The-Danvers-Statement (accessed March 4, 2012). Only a few selected quotations from the Bible are included in the Danvers statement, but among them is Timothy 2:12–14 (English Standard Version): "I do not permit a woman to teach or to exercise authority over a man; rather she is to remain quiet."

24. David Blankenhorn, "The Unnecessary Father," excerpted from *Fatherless America*, The Institute for American Values (New York: Basic Books, 1995), reprinted in *Applied Ethics: A Multicultural Approach*, 4th ed., edited by Larry May, Shari Collins-Chobanian, and Kai Wong (Upper Saddle River, N.J.: Pearson Prentice Hall, 2006), 380–88, at 385. Blankenhorn characterizes himself as a liberal Democrat. At a recent federal trial, Blankenhorn was an expert witness in support of Proposition 8, the California proposition that made gay marriage illegal. Judge Walker ruled against the constitutionality of Proposition 8. See http://www.newyorker.com/news/news-desk/judge-vaughn-walkers-opinion (accessed June 9, 2017).

25. Susan Moller Okin, "Sexual Orientation, Gender, and Families: Dichotomizing Differences," *Hypatia* 11:1 (1996), 30–48, at 43. We can extend Okin's point. Because bisexual marriage involves bisexuals whose identities are, in some ways, "and" or "in-between" identities, it may lead to greater acceptance of transgender, intersex, multiracial, and multiethnic individuals. We all gain from a social world where there is more room for "in-between," open, and evolving identities.

26. Eric Anderson and Adi Adams, "Aren't We All a Little Bisexual? The Recognition of Bisexuality in an Unlikely Place," *Journal of Bisexuality* 11:1 (2011), 3–22, at 13.

27. In 1948 Alfred Kinsey noted, "Nearly half (46%) of the population engages in both heterosexual and homosexual activities, or reacts to persons of both sexes, in the course of their adult lives." Alfred Kinsey, W. B. Pomeroy, and C. E. Martin, *Sexual Behavior in the Human Male* (Philadelphia: W. B. Saunders, 1948), 656.

28. The Bloomsbury group in 1920s Britain provides perhaps the closest illustration.

29. See John McMurtry, "Monogamy: A Critique," *The Monist* 56:4 (1972), 587–99, for arguments in support of expanding the members of families.

30. Special thanks to Randal Parker and Nicholas Power. Raja Halwani provided extraordinary assistance and support in revising the essay for the seventh edition.

STUDY QUESTIONS

1. Explain Vernallis's central argument to the effect of what shape should bisexual marriage take. Do you agree with the argument?

2. Is Vernallis correct to claim that "our sexual attractions are predominantly, if not always, gender-inflected"? What about those people who are attracted to transgendered people and to transsexuals?

3. How might Vernallis reply to the following objection? "Allowing foursome bisexual marriages would require major economic costs. Think of health insurance, resources devoted to divorces, wed-

dings, and all the other things that come with marriage. It's not worth it."

4. How might Vernallis reply to the following objection? "Why is the sexual orientation of gender-specific bisexuals so fundamental as to entitle bisexuals to a foursome marriage? What about people—straight and gay—who desire multiple spouses? Replying that it is fundamental to bisexuals' identity might not be enough, because someone can argue that having multiple spouses is also fundamental to who they are."

5. Consider the argument that because (or if) sexual fidelity is not always a good thing in ordinary two-person heterosexual marriage, it should not be an ideal of marriage. What implications would this have for Vernallis's conclusions about bi-marriage and multiple marriages?

6. Would the fact that marriage—at least these days—is based mostly on (romantic) love undermine Vernallis's view as to what bi-marriage is? Explore the answer to this question, keeping in mind the issue of whether love is exclusive. That is, if romantic love is exclusive (if X loves Y during t, then X loves Y and only Y during t), bisexuals would have the same reason as anyone else to enter marriages with only one other partner. See the discussion of this issue in Elizabeth Brake's essay on polyamory in this volume.

7. Is there a principled reason as to why bi-marriages cannot or should not involve more than four people? If there is no such reason, what implications would this have for Vernallis's view?

8. Read the essay "Gay Divorce" by Claudia Card (*The Philosophy of Sex: Contemporary Readings*, 6th ed., edited by Nicholas Power, Raja Halwani, and Alan Soble [Lanham, Md.: Rowman & Littlefield, 2013], 177–93), in which Card argues against marriage (partly) on the basis of the messiness of divorce. What implications would her argument have for Vernallis's bi-marriage?

9. Consider the following triadic arrangement: X, a bisexual woman, marries Y, a heterosexual man, and Z, a bisexual woman. None of the partners to the triad seem to be denied sexual fulfillment, and the arrangement seems to fulfill the ideals of marriage listed by Vernallis. Yet she objects to such triads on the ground that "it would be odd for bisexual marriage to logically require that at least one of its members be heterosexual," since this "goes against the spirit of bisexual marriage, which is to extend to one group (bisexuals) the entitlements available to heterosexuals and homosexuals." Would bisexual marriage *require* that one member be a heterosexual, or would this be just one option for some bisexuals? More important, *if* triads such as the above can satisfy the ideals that Vernallis lists, on what other grounds can bisexuals demand that, *as a group*, they are *entitled* to have a marriage of *four* partners, *all* of

whom are bisexuals? Or should Vernallis add to the list of ideals of marriage an ideal to the effect that all the marital partners should be of the same sexual orientation? Would the addition of this ideal run afoul of Robin Dembroff's account of sexual orientation in the essay (in this volume) "What Is Sexual Orientation?"

ELEVEN

Racial Sexual Desires

Raja Halwani

Raja Halwani *addresses the issue of whether there is something morally defective with someone who sexually prefers or desires only members of a particular race or ethnic group (or someone who does not sexually desire or prefer members of a particular race or ethnic group). People with such "racial desires" are often viewed as racists, but virtually no sustained arguments have been given in support of this view. In this essay, Halwani constructs three possible arguments—those based in discrimination, exclusion, and stereotypes—that might support the charge of racism. He argues that none is convincing. He further argues that only in some cases are people with racial desires racist, but that in those cases their racism is not because of their sexual desires.*

People who sexually desire or do not sexually desire members of a racial or ethnic group have, let's call them, "racial sexual desires" or "preferences"—for example, men who are into Asian women or women who are into Latino men. I will call such people PRSDs ("people with racial sexual desires"). I have had many discussions of racial sexual desires with friends, colleagues, students, and others, and in almost all of them, PRSDs come out looking bad; they are always considered, because of their sexual desires, ethically defective people—usually racist.

There is no focused discussion of this issue in the philosophical literature.[1] One finds mention of it here and there in cultural studies, yet they tend to be superficial and lacking in argumentation. Here are two examples.

In her essay, "Eating the Other: Desire and Resistance," bell hooks, speaking of white men who are not racist in the traditional sense, writes,

> These young men see themselves as non-racists, who choose to transgress racial boundaries within the sexual realm not to dominate the Other, but rather so that they can be acted upon, so that they can be changed utterly. Not at all attuned to those aspects of their sexual fantasies that irrevocably link them to collective white racist domination, they believe their desire for contact represents a progressive change in white attitudes towards non-whites. They do not see themselves as perpetuating racism.[2]

There are two sweeping claims in this passage: that white men's fantasies are "irrevocably" linked to "collective white racist domination," and that their actions perpetuate white racism. Even though hooks allows for interracial romantic encounters that are not tainted by racism as long as there is "mutual recognition of racism" (a condition I find neither necessary nor sufficient for non-racism), what is troubling about hooks's claims is their lack of supporting reasons or arguments.

The second example comes from Daniel Tsang, who, commenting on white men who are attracted to Asian men, writes, "He views Asians as a class lumping Chinese, Japanese, Koreans, Vietnamese, etc., into one amorphous group. He is attracted to Asians for our youthfulness, our lack of body hair, and our perceived submissiveness, dependence, and dependability."[3] Note Tsang's reasons behind white men's attraction to Asian men: the latter's youthfulness, lack of body hair, and perceived submissiveness, dependence, and dependability—"rice queens" are attracted to Asian men because of stereotypes. Yet Tsang gives no argument as to why desiring Asian men for these reasons is a problem.

My direct aim in this essay is to evaluate some possible reasons for why PRSDs might be racists. Because, as I mentioned, there is no sustained discussion of this issue in the literature, I construct what I think are the three strongest arguments in support of the idea that PRSDs are racist. I will argue that none is convincing. I conclude that though some PRSDs might be racists, they are not so *because* of their sexual desires.

My indirect aim is that this essay be a starting point for more sustained discussions of these issues. I hope that the points I raise and address are taken up in future discussions so that the topic of racial sexual desires receives more attention.

PRELIMINARIES

1. PRSDs fall into at least five conceptual categories. If G is the racial group whose members are (or are not) the objects of desire, then the categories are: those who *exclusively* sexually desire members of G;[4] those who sexually *prefer* members of G; those who have

weak sexual desires for members of *G* (they find them attractive but only infrequently or faintly); those who do not sexually desire members of *G*; and those who feel sexual aversion to members of *G*, perhaps feeling nausea or some similar reaction at the thought of having sex with them.

To keep the discussion manageable, I will discuss PRSDs who have exclusive sexual desires for members of a racial or ethnic group, and those who feel revulsion at the thought of having sex with these members (the PRSDs I discuss are also not members of these groups). These two types seem to adequately represent what people have in mind when they think of PRSDs as racist.[5]

2. Preferences admit of degrees, so those with non-exclusive preferences admit of variations depending on the strength or weakness of the preference.[6]

3. PRSDs fall into four types as far as their attitudes toward their sexual desires are concerned: rejection or unhappiness, indifference, acceptance or happiness, or no attitude. For example, the person who has weak desires for members of a particular group might have no thoughts or attitudes about his state of sexual desires, might be unhappy about it, might be happy, or might be indifferent.

4. To claim that *X* prefers Latinos does not mean that *X* finds every Latino sexually attractive. *X* might not find particular Latinos attractive simply because they happen to be not to *X*'s taste (e.g., too skinny, too short). Thus, to claim that *X* sexually prefers *G*s, where "*G*" refers to a racial or ethnic group, is to claim that *X* prefers (or does not prefer) *G*s only in regards to *X*'s racial preferences.[7]

5. Finally, it is important to bear in mind that my discussion is solely about sexual desire, not about love, relationships, marriage, or even sexual acts. It is about what people *sexually desire* as far as race and ethnicity are concerned. Though sexual desire is often connected to these other phenomena, it need not be, and my discussion is only about it.

THE FIRST ARGUMENT FOR WHY PRSDs ARE RACIST

The first argument revolves around the idea of unfair discrimination. It goes as follows. Suppose that *X* sexually desires only members of group *G*, which is other than *X*'s own. Given *X*'s sexual desires, *X* sexually discriminates against members of some groups and in favor of others. When *X* desires only members of *G*, *X* discriminates against members of other groups. Because such discrimination is pernicious, *X* is racist. Thus, PRSDs are racist because of pernicious discrimination.[8]

For example, if John is white and sexually desires only Asians, then John discriminates against, say, blacks in not sexually desiring them. This type of reasoning is easiest seen in employment: Suppose that Mark hires only Asians to work in his company, even though an employee's race or ethnic group is irrelevant to the job performance. In this type of case, Mark unfairly discriminates against non-Asians.

There is no doubt that John, in sexually preferring Asians, engages in some sort of discrimination: his sexual taste is discriminatory in targeting Asians. The question is whether this discrimination is bad (pernicious, unfair, or unjust). The argument under discussion does assume that the discrimination is bad. But is it?

In most cases, one's racial and ethnic background is irrelevant to one's proper performance of a job or task.[9] For example, hiring a good accountant should not depend on the candidate's racial or ethnic background. His or her accounting qualifications should suffice. But this is different when it comes to sexual desire. How someone looks can, and usually is, relevant to sexual desire. This is because one crucial goal of sexual desire is sexual satisfaction or pleasure.[10] And for X to attain sexual pleasure or sexual satisfaction it is usually necessary that X be sexually attracted to X's object of sexual desire.[11] If Juan is not attracted to skinny people, for example, it is hard for him to attain sexual pleasure by having sex with them. Being non-skinny is a property that Juan's sexual partners need to usually have if Juan is to enjoy his sexual acts with them.

PRSDs are similar in this respect. Their sexual partners must usually have (or lack) a property related to their race or ethnicity for PRSDs to find them attractive. Because racial or ethnic looks are normally part of physical looks, and because physical looks are normally necessary for satisfying the goal of sexual pleasure or satisfaction, PRSDs choose their sexual partners (partly) on the basis of racial or ethnic looks. Such looks determine whether the PRSD finds his or her sexual partner attractive. This means that, just as in the case of Juan we have no good reason to claim that he unfairly discriminates against skinny people, we also have no good reason to claim in the case of John that he unfairly discriminates against non-Asians.

To see this argument better, compare it to the following argument about employment: If P is necessary for the proper performance of a task, then in hiring Y's who are P, X is not unfairly discriminating against people who are not P. Similarly, if P is necessary for the proper satisfaction of sexual desire, then in choosing Y's who are P, X is not unfairly discriminating against people who are not P. It just so happens that in this case P is a racial or ethnic property.

One might object that although in employment some properties (e.g., accounting skills) are necessary for the proper performance of a task, racial and ethnic properties are not necessary for attaining sexual pleasure. After all, John might sexually enjoy having sex with a non-Asian if he were to give it a try (provided that the non-Asian meets John's other sexual preferences—for example, he or she is not too skinny). So in not having sex with non-Asians, John does discriminate; he could, after all, try having sex with non-Asians and see what happens.

It is true that John might enjoy sex with a non-Asian, but unless he, for some reason, insists on not having sex with non-Asians, this would not show that he is discriminating. All it would show is that he prefers to act on his sexual desires because acting on them has the best chance of yielding sexual pleasure. Moreover, sexual pleasure is somewhat peculiar in that attaining it is usually desired through the satisfaction of sexual desire, not through some substitute that can yield the same or similar pleasures. That is, sexual pleasure partly consists in acting on one's desires. Consider a machine that would simulate the sexual pleasures one would feel if one were to have sex with Mario Lopez. [12] One would not normally consider the option of hooking up into the machine to be equal to having sex with Lopez. Far from it. [13]

This means that in wanting to act on his sexual desires John is not wrongfully discriminating against anyone, much like in wanting to act on her preference for hairy men Anna is not wrongly discriminating against non-hairy ones. It is only if John insists on not having sex with non-Asians that problems might arise ("might" because a lot depends on why John refuses to have sex with non-Asians; see below for more discussion).

What if unfair discrimination is not tied to tasks and performance? What if it is tied, simply, to exclusionary practices? That is, what if PRSDs engage in unfair discrimination because they arbitrarily exclude entire groups from their sexual practices? John, in desiring only Asians, arbitrarily excludes blacks, Latinos, and other groups as potential sexual partners. In doing so, he unfairly discriminates against them.

To see this, suppose that the government of country *C*, which has two ethnic groups, decides, for no reason whatsoever, that only members of *C1* can use the country's highways, whereas members of *C2* can use only the back roads. This decision is arbitrary and thus unfairly excludes members of *C2* from the use of the *C*'s highway system.

The issue now is whether John's exclusion of non-Asians is arbitrary. To see whether it is, consider Rafael, who is gay. He excludes women as sexual partners. Is he unfair to them because he arbitrarily excludes them? Rafael can (plausibly) argue, "I don't know why I am attracted only to men, but I am. And being gay means that I am not sexually attracted to women. It is not as if I am sexually attracted to them, but I decide, somehow, that I want to have nothing sexually to do with them. This is just the way that I am."

And John can say the same when it comes to race: "I don't know why I am attracted only to Asians, but I am. And being attracted only to Asians means that I am not sexually attracted to non-Asians. It is not as if I am sexually attracted to non-Asians, but I decide, somehow, that I want to have nothing sexually to do with them. This is just the way that I am." If Rafael does not sexually arbitrarily exclude women, then neither does John arbitrarily exclude non-Asians. So PRSDs are not engaged in arbitrary and thus unfair discrimination.

It might be that John can try to change. He might try to find ways to get himself to feel attraction to non-Asians (and here the parallel with sexual orientation might break down), but until that happens, John is right that his exclusion is not arbitrary. Because, again, if one crucial goal of sexual desire is pleasure and satisfaction, excluding non-Asians is not arbitrary given that having sex with them will not normally yield for John sexual pleasure or satisfaction. Hence, we cannot sustain the claim that PRSDs are racist on the grounds that they engage in arbitrary exclusionary practices.

We can conclude that PRSDs are not racists *if* the accusation of racism is based on wrongful discrimination against others. If they are racist, it has to be because of some other consideration, to which I now turn.

THE SECOND ARGUMENT FOR WHY PRSDs ARE RACIST

According to the second argument, PRSDs are racist because they are defective individuals. And they are defective individuals because their desires are narrow and are not as encompassing as they can be. A morally healthy individual, on this argument, is someone who sexually desires other people regardless of their racial or ethnic membership. He finds people sexually desirable not because of their race or ethnicity, but because of their own individual (albeit often physical) attractive properties, according to how these properties match his own tastes. Thus, an ethically non-defective person, as far as sexual desire is concerned, is someone who finds others attractive by virtue of their individual looks, as these looks cut across ethnic or racial lines. Someone who does not is defective. Since in this type of case we are discussing racial preferences, the defect is that of racism.[14]

But this argument faces a dilemma. Either it is an exercise in overkill or it arbitrarily targets racial and ethnic preferences for moral condemnation. To see this, consider that if this argument is sound, then we are *all* morally defective individuals, because we all have sexual preferences of some sort or other. By this argument, a gay man is sexist for not preferring women, a straight woman is (also?) sexist for not preferring women, and, to add a third example, a straight man would be anti-averagist and anti-shortist for preferring tall women. We can agree that the individuals in question have sexual preferences, but these preferences seem to be morally neutral. Thus, if the argument under consideration insists that we must have democratic desires across the board, we would all be morally defective given that our sexual preferences are bound to exclude some groups of people. This is an absurd conclusion, and it constitutes the first horn of the dilemma.

Thus the argument must select some sexual preferences and not others as morally objectionable—in this case, racial or ethnic ones. But why select race and ethnicity? What is it about them that make PRSDs racists? The argument needs to address this point, for otherwise it would be arbitrary in its insistence on race, thus facing the second horn of the dilemma.

An advocate of the argument might claim that in a purely natural state people would have no racial preferences whatsoever, though they would still have sex or gender-based preferences. So in a "state of nature" type of existence, we would expect men to desire women and women to desire men. But because all human beings, regardless of their race, belong to the same species, we should expect them to sexually desire each other on the basis of individual looks, not on the basis of race. So when racial preferences exist, this is not an expected thing and is an aberration of sorts.

The problem with the above reasoning is that even if in a state of nature people do not have racial preferences (actually, there is no reason to believe that they would not), it is not clear why this would be a morally good thing as opposed to simply being a biological or natural norm. That is, the above argument derives a moral judgment from a biological or social claim (depending on how we describe the state of nature). Even if things should naturally be a certain way, this does not entail anything moral. For example, we are biologically set up to eat the flesh of other animals. But it does not follow that being a vegetarian makes one morally defective. Indeed, one might argue that eating meat, despite its "naturalness," is the morally wrong thing to do. Not conforming to nature *might be* a defect,[15] maybe even a moral defect, but not simply because of non-conformance to nature. If it is a moral defect, which is what an accusation of racism is, it would have to be for other reasons. Thus, for this reasoning to succeed, it needs to show why not conforming to our sexual nature means that we are racist. I suspect that this is a difficult task.

The advocate of the argument can change the strategy and argue that we do not need to discuss nature in order to see that PRSDs are morally defective. She can argue that it is precisely because we do *not* live in a state of nature—it is precisely because we live in a world where races and ethnic groups have access to each other—we should expect people to sexually desire each other on the basis of individual looks rather than racial types. When someone is a PRSD, this indicates that something has gone wrong with his process of growing up. Instead of growing up with sexual desires for people based on their individual looks, something has interfered with this process to skew his sexual desires. Perhaps he grew up in a racist society that made him not sexually desire members of the race considered inferior. Thus, owing to a skewed causal process, he ends up with racial desires. He thus has a defective character.

However, this reasoning confuses the causal history of a person's sexual desires with what his sexual desires ethically tell us about him. It might be that X's sexual desires were caused by a pernicious causal history, but it is not clear why X is racist because of that. After all, X might have no bad beliefs, feelings, or values toward members of G, as he finds himself sexually (or not sexually) preferring them (see below for more discussion on how intricate judgments of racism are). At best, what this reasoning shows is that it is the society and the way individuals are formed that are morally defective, not the individuals themselves.

Moreover, we must avoid a simplistic picture of how sexual preferences are caused. Consider for example homosexuality (and heterosexuality). We still have no idea of how homosexuals come to be. There are even cases of identical twins growing up in the same family but such that one is gay and the other straight.[16] The formation of racial preferences is more complex than twins raised in the same family—it is about different individuals raised in different contexts (even if they are raised in the same society during the same time period). The formation of sexual preferences can go in all directions, such that X might find X's-self attracted to members of G, while Y, growing up in the same society as X and belonging to the same race as X, might not. So even if we ignore the first mistake in this argument and claim that someone is morally defective because of the way he or she were "made," it is not obvious that the processes that result in PRSDs are really pernicious.

Thus, the second argument does not provide a good reason why racial preferences are pernicious. It then faces the second horn of the dilemma, which is that it arbitrarily targets racial preferences for moral condemnation. The argument then fails.

THE THIRD ARGUMENT FOR WHY PRSDs ARE RACIST

The third argument is probably the most popular among people who think that PRSDs are racist. On this argument, X is racist because X's desires for members of G are, per the Tsang quotation above, based on or because of stereotypes about them. Such stereotypes either are sexualized to begin with or become sexualized.[17] The argument goes as follows: If X sexually prefers members of G because of sexual stereotypes, X is racist, since one understanding of a racist person is someone who has stereotypes about members of the group against which he is a racist. If, however, X is sexually averse to having sex with members of G, then X is racist for the same reasons, except that the stereotypes operate more blatantly. For example, in a 2010 *Playboy* interview, the (white) pop star John Mayer replied to the question, "Do black women throw themselves at you?" by saying, "I don't think I open myself to it. My dick is sort of like a white supremacist. I've got a Benetton heart and a fuckin' David Duke cock."[18] Discussing this quotation, Nathaniel Adam Tobias Coleman takes Mayer to have evinced sexual aversion to black women (to be sexually averse to a property, according to Coleman, is to be frightened or repulsed by it). Coleman claims that this is due to Mayer's belief in stigmatizing narratives about black women that see them fit for work, not sex or marriage.[19]

Before we evaluate this argument, it is good to say something about stereotypes. There is no generally accepted definition of "stereotype." Beyond the common claim that stereotypes are beliefs containing generalizations, there is no agreement that stereotypes are necessarily bad, though the word "stereotype" has come to have a negative connotation.[20] The popular understanding of a stereotype is that it is a belief containing generalizations that are *false*.[21] Thus, the belief that "Russians drink vodka" is not a false generalization because it is, well, true, while the belief that "Latinos eat beans" is false.

However, just because a generalization is false need not mean that believing it is morally objectionable. For example, "Arabs wear turbans" is a false generalization, but believing it is not necessarily morally objectionable, and for two reasons. First, its content is non-moral: the property being attributed to Arabs is not a moral one (cf. "Arabs are terrorists"). Second, one need not believe it on morally objectionable grounds. For example, if a young adult believes it because her teacher said it in class, the young adult need not be culpable (unless we are to hold her culpable for looking up every claim her teachers make in class). But if an adult believes it on the grounds that Arabs are backward people (or so he thinks) and backward people wear turbans, then he is morally culpable for adopting a claim that he should have known better than to adopt.[22]

Note then that stereotypes can be morally objectionable in at least two ways. The first has to do with their content: "Arabs want to kill Jews," "Mexicans are lazy," "Jews are treacherous people," and "Black men are dangerous" are all examples of beliefs that falsely attribute immoral properties to their subjects. Second, stereotypes can be morally objectionable in the way they come to be accepted. Consider: "Asians are excellent at math" is a false generalization, though the property it attributes to its subjects is not morally problematic. However, accepting this claim is objectionable because one ought to know better.

I will assume, to strengthen the argument that PRSDs are racist, that *accepting* these stereotypes is sufficient for being a racist: even if the stereotypes attribute non-moral properties to the people, and even if nothing else is going on in the PRSD's psychology other than accepting the stereotypes, the PRSD is racist. So someone who accepts the belief that Asian men have hairless bodies is racist, even if the property being attributed to Asians is non-moral and even if the person in question does not, say, *feel* anything toward Asians because of this belief.[23] Note here that *believing* a stereotype might not be enough to make one racist because one might struggle against one's beliefs, believing them despite one's better judgment. It is agreeing with them, accepting them, endorsing them, or having a pro-attitude toward them, that makes one racist. [24]

A second assumption I will make to further strengthen the arguments that PRSDs are racist is that all stereotypes about races and ethnic groups have morally objectionable content. This way we do not get sidetracked by whether someone is racist for accepting a stereotype that attributes a non-moral property to the group in question.

In sum then, I assume that (1) all stereotypes about races and ethnic groups are morally objectionable, and that (2) accepting them is enough to make someone racist. Thus, to be racist because of stereotypes means that one is racist because one accepts these stereotypes.

Let us now evaluate the argument. Suppose that all we know about someone is that he is sexually attracted to members of G. On its own this does not tell us anything morally substantive about him, because, with the possible exception of sexual aversion, sexual preferences on their own still tell us little about their possessor's overall moral character. To know whether he is racist, we need to know what he believes about members of G, because, according to the view of racism we are adopting, he would be racist if he were to accept stereotypes about G. (Or if he is repulsed by members of G—if he negatively viscerally reacts to them; this is the possible exception, which I discuss below.)

Let's flesh out this thought. Suppose that John is a white straight male who desires Asian women. Obviously, it is possible that he sexually desires them based simply on their looks, *because* they are Asian-looking. But is this possible with no stereotypes about them? It *seems* to be. It is not necessary that John *must*, somehow, have stereotypes about Asian women. It is this claim that constitutes the reply to the third argument that PRSDs are racist—namely, that it is *possible* that people have racial sexual desires in morally non-defective ways. And we know this claim is true because it is easy to imagine such cases. In such cases, what causes or constitutes someone's attraction to the group in question are not stereotypes, but features, mostly physical but perhaps also non-physical, that members of the group tend to have. To see this better, imagine a case in which John is sexually attracted to a woman who has Asian physical features but who is actually not Asian. Upon finding this out, he continues to sexually desire her, precisely because of her physical features.

Because such cases are obviously possible, someone who wishes to defend the third argument must deny their possibility—a difficult, if not impossible, task. Of course, it is possible that someone likes Asian women because of stereotypes. But it is also possible that he likes Asian-looking women simply based on their looks, not on anything else, and this is the point.

However, even in cases of PRSDs with stereotypes, we cannot simply infer, without further information, that X is racist. Such cases come in at least three types: (i) the stereotypes are part of the sexual desires; (ii) they cause the desires; and (iii) they are the agent's reasons for the desires.

(i) Abstractly, it is easy to see how stereotypes are part of sexual desires. Sexual desires usually have content; they have intentionality, focusing on specific individuals (or acts) and accompanied by particular beliefs: X sexually desires Y because X finds Y good-looking or believes that Y is good in bed, and so forth.[25] Because stereotypes can be beliefs, we can see how they can be part of sexual desires. Consider Seiriol Morgan's example of a man whose sexual arousal is enhanced by the thought that the woman with whom he has sex is a police officer, "to the extent that he found himself repeating the inner mantra 'I'm fucking the Police! I'm fucking the Police!,' as he was penetrating her."[26]

Something similar can happen in the case of stereotypes. As X has sex with an Asian man, X repeats a stereotypic mantra, such as, to use the Tsang quotation, "His body is so smooth and hairless!" or "I'm fucking such a smooth and hairless man." In such ways, stereotypes can be part of an agent's sexual desires. So wouldn't having these stereotypes make X racist?

Not necessarily. This is because the stereotypes need not operate outside the sexual context. When it comes to sexual desire, which is often intimately connected with fantasy, people are able to compartmentalize: they can have sexual desires containing weird or immoral beliefs, yet not have these beliefs across the board. A man might find it sexually exciting to masturbate while watching (e.g., in a pornographic film) a woman having sex with three or four men, and might entertain the thought that women "just love to have this kind of sex" as he masturbates, but not actually accept it outside a sexual context (even outside the particular sexual context of masturbation). Because of the way sexual desire operates, it is not necessary for someone with immoral desires to maintain the immoral thoughts (that belong to the desires) outside the desires.

Similarly, someone's (call him "Paul") sexual desires might contain the belief that Asian men are smooth and hairless; yet Paul might not have this belief in general, let alone accept it. Thus, we cannot simply infer from the fact that people with racial stereotypes as part of their sexual desires have these stereotypes across the board, let alone accept them. It is not obvious, then, that someone like Paul is racist.

How do we decide whether people like Paul are racist? Are they racist because the content of their sexual desires is enough to make them racists? Or are they not racist because this content does not extend beyond their sexual desires? One answer is that it partly depends on which beliefs are "deeper" in the person's psyche. But it is not obvious that not-so-deep beliefs take a back seat to sub- or unconscious ("deeper") ones as far as the "real truth" about someone is concerned. Another answer is that since X's sexual desires, on the one hand, and beliefs and attitudes, on the other, reflect his values, perhaps we ought to check and see which reflect his true values. Here, much depends on the person's higher-level attitudes toward his sexual desires. So a third answer is that if he ensures that they do not pervade his belief system, he seems to be morally in the clear. But if he, somehow, bemoans the fact that they are confined to his sexual desires, he certainly smacks of racism.[27]

Even if the stereotypes are not confined to the agent's sexual desires, we still cannot simply infer that the agent is racist, because the agent might not accept them and might even struggle against them. If he does not accept them, judging him racist becomes tricky at best.

Obviously, the issues here are complex. But the complexity is instructive. It shows, first, that the inference that someone is racist from the fact that his sexual desires contain stereotypes is not (obviously) valid, given that the stereotypes need not be part of the agent's general belief system. It shows, second, that even the inference that someone is racist from the fact that stereotypes are part of his general belief system is not (obviously) valid, given that he might not accept these beliefs.

Now consider someone, Peter, who does accept the stereotypes: not only are they part of his sexual desires and general belief system, but he also endorses them. On my assumption, Peter is racist because accepting stereotypes is enough to make someone racist. But then note something important: the indictment of racism is based not on the content of Peter's sexual desires but on his attitude and his value system in general; it comes from his *acceptance* of stereotypes. His sexual desires play no role in the indictment of racism; they might play an epistemological role, alerting us to the possibility that Peter is racist, but they are not necessary (or sufficient) for the moral claim that Peter is racist.[28]

(ii) The second possibility is that stereotypes *cause* the agent to have racial sexual desires, which need not contain these stereotypes (for simplicity's sake, let's assume that they don't). For example, the belief that broccoli is good for me causes me to desire to eat it. Similarly, the belief that Latinos are passionate lovers might get Belinda to form a sexual preference for Latinos, even if this belief is not part of her sexual desires for them. The belief causes the desire to exist, but it need not be part of the desire.

Still, Belinda is not necessarily racist. First, the stereotypes need not exist anymore; they might have caused the desires to exist but then they ceased to exist. If so, she *has no* stereotypes on which to indict her of racism. Second, we need to check her attitude toward these stereotypes. If she rejects them or is indifferent to them, it is not clear that she is racist. If she accepts them, she is racist, but then, again, her sexual desires play no role in forming this judgment. Thus, again, there is no direct inference from having racial sexual desires to a judgment of racism.

(iii) The third possibility is that the stereotypes are the agent's *reasons* for having racial sexual desires. The best sense to make of this idea is that the agent *accepts* his sexual desires. It is as if Belinda says, "Yes. I do like Latino men, and I like them *because* they are passionate lovers." Whether in such a case the stereotypes have to continue to *cause* Belinda to have the sexual desires she has is unclear. But they are certainly her *reasons* for having these sexual desires. It is, I think, such cases that animate the defenders of the third argument for the racism of PRSDs: it is because the PRSDs endorse the stereotypes.

Still, it is crucial again to note that the agents' sexual desires play no role in supporting the judgment of racism. That is, for us to claim that Belinda is racist, we do not need her sexual desires. All we need is the fact that she accepts the belief that Latinos are passionate lovers.

To conclude the discussion so far: the inference that X is racist is very far from the fact that X has racial sexual desires. First, we must check whether the sexual desires contain stereotypes. If they don't, X is not racist. If they do, then, second, we must check whether the stereotypes are confined to X's sexual desires. If they are, then our confidence in X's non-racism remains intact, especially if X does not believe the stereotypes in general, let alone accept them. If the stereotypes are not confined to X's sexual desires, then, third, we must check X's higher-level attitudes. If X does not accept these beliefs, our judgment that X is not racist, though shaken, is not undermined. So we cannot infer, simply on the basis of having racial sexual desires, that their possessor is overall racist.

Only in the case in which X somehow accepts these stereotypes, whether they are confined to his sexual desires or not, is the judgment that X is racist true. But, again, in such a case it is not X's racial desires that imply the racism but X's acceptance of them.

Consider now PRSDs with sexual aversion, and let's use the above three possibilities. Suppose that Mabel believes that Arabs are, literally, dirty people, and it is because of this belief that Mabel has a sexual aversion to Arabs. Now, because Mabel lacks sexual desires for Arabs, stereotypes won't be part of her desires, so possibility (i) is not relevant. Getting (iii) out of the way next, if Mabel accepts her belief about Arabs, she is racist, though, again, her sexual desires play no role in this judgment.

This leaves us with (ii). If Mabel's stereotypes not only causally blocked her sexual desires but also instilled nausea in her at the thought of having sex with Arabs, we still need to check whether the stereotypes exist. If they don't, then whether Mabel is racist would depend on how much weight we want to give her aversion (see the next paragraph). If the stereotypes do still exist, we need to check her attitude toward them; Mabel might not be racist if she does not accept them. Similarly, John Mayer might fit this type of PRSD but still not be racist because his "Benetton heart" rejects whatever beliefs cause his aversion, which might force us to issue a mixed judgment about his racism or to withhold such judgment.[29]

Still, what complicates things with such PRSDs is their gut reaction of aversion, because this might reveal much about the person. Indeed, perhaps such PRSDs are racist because their visceral reaction reveals quite a bit about their value system, indicating that the agent, at some level, harbors negative values about members of the group in question.

But we need to be careful. Consider a straight man who sincerely says, "I find the idea of having sex with men disgusting. If I have to go down on a guy I will throw up." (Consider a gay man who says similar things about having sex with women.) Is the straight man homophobic? A "yes" is hasty. After all, the man need not have any negative values, beliefs, thoughts, emotions, and so on about gay men (or women). He might be honestly reporting his physical reactions. Why not say the same about racial sexual desires?

Perhaps sexual orientations are more natural or basic to us than racial sexual desires, so that such reactions do not indicate anything bad. But this is not always true. The straight man's reaction might exist because of his homophobia; two straight men might say the exact same thing about fellating another man yet one of them is merely reporting his physical reaction while another is doing more; he is expressing his disgust at gay men. This point is the same as the one about what warrants accusations of racism: they are not warranted simply because of the content of the sexual desires but because of the agent's attitude toward that content, whether there is endorsement of them or not.

A WRONG VIEW OF RACISM?

Perhaps one potential problem with the discussion so far is the view of racism that I have adopted. Maybe stereotypes or beliefs are not the crucial factor when characterizing racism, but something else, such that were we to adopt this something-else view of racism, we would have a convincing picture of how PRSDs are racist.

J. L. A. Garcia's famous view of racism denies the necessity or sufficiency of beliefs (including stereotypes) for someone being a racist. According to Garcia, racism is a "vicious kind of racially based disregard for the welfare of certain people. In its central and most vicious form, it is hatred, ill-will, directed against a person or persons on account of their assigned race."[30] Racism on this view is essentially not about beliefs but about wants, intentions, and vices; its core is constituted by vicious attitudes toward members of the hated race.

It is hard to think of wants, desires, or vices as devoid of beliefs. Indeed, we need beliefs to be able to distinguish between different cases or types of, say, hatred or contempt.[31] For example, suppose that Mabel hates Ziad, who is Arab. To find out whether her hatred is racist, we need to know what she believes about Arabs and about Ziad; after all, she could hate Ziad for all sorts of reasons. And it is not just hate: Mabel could have contempt for Ziad, she could dislike him, she could scorn him, and she could be repulsed by him. But none of these on its own shows that Mabel is racist. To know whether she is, we need to know what beliefs animate or constitute her emotions.

So beliefs are unavoidable in a characterization of racism (certainly in individuals, as opposed to institutions). But let us assume that an account such as Garcia's is basically correct. Would that help the case that PRSDs are racist?

No. If all we know about Belinda is that she is sexually attracted to Latinos, or if all we know about Mabel is that she is sexually repulsed by Arabs, this tells us nothing about their other emotional or desirous states: we know nothing about whether they hate Latinos and Arabs, feel contempt for them, or, generally, have vicious attitudes toward them. Belinda's sexual attraction for Latinos is compatible with three states of her character: vicious emotions toward Latinos, virtuous ones, or neither.[32] Thus, a vice-based or an emotion-based account of racism is neutral as far the issue of PRSDs is concerned. The only way it could entail that PRSDs are racist is if it were to assume, from the start, that racial sexual preferences are forms of hatred or viciousness. But this assumption would beg the very issue under discussion.

CONCLUSION

I have argued that we cannot justify accusations of racism against PRSDs because none of the arguments I have reconstructed on behalf of such a view succeeds. Thus, either better arguments need to be offered or we have to agree that some PRSDs are racist (in which case their racism stems from their overall beliefs, not their sexual desires) while others are like people with other sexual preferences—warranting at most a "Who cares?" attitude.[33]

NOTES

1. Some philosophical essays discuss related issues—for example, Charles W. Mills, "Do Black Men Have a Moral Duty to Marry Black Women?" *Journal of Social Philosophy*, 25th Anniversary Special Issue (1994), 131–53; Lewis R. Gordon, *Bad Faith and Antiblack Racism* (Atlantic Highlands, N.J.: Humanities Books, 1995), chapter 16; Laurence M. Thomas, "Split-Level Equality: Mixing Love and Equality," in *Racism and Philosophy*, edited by Susan E. Babbitt and Sue Campbell (Ithaca, N.Y.: Cornell University Press, 1999), 189–201; Robert Gooding-Williams, "Black Cupids, White Desires," in *Look, A Negro! Philosophical Essays on Race, Culture, and Politics* (New York: Routledge, 2006); and Ronald R. Sundstrom, *The Browning of America and the Evasion of Social Justice* (Albany, N.Y.: SUNY Press, 2008), chapter 4. Recently Robin Zheng has

addressed this issue head-on in her essay "Why Yellow Fever Isn't Flattering: A Case Against Racial Fetishes" (*Journal of the American Philosophical Association* 2:3 [2016], 400–419). The focus of her paper is different from mine: hers is about the effects of racial desires, not the character of the person who has them. She argues that such desires subject Asian/American women to disproportionate harms. However, I think that her essay is deeply marred because of three mistakes. First, Zheng does not take seriously the distinction among love, relationships, and sex; she collapses the three together for the purposes of her essay. Given that many of the data on which she relies are about relationships and love, as opposed to mere sexual desire, and given that racial sexual desires are, basically, *sexual* desires, this leaves her with the unanswered question of what effects racial sexual desires have on their own, outside the context of love and relationships (e.g., many of the doubts that the women express in the studies have to do with the status of their relationships). Second, Zheng does not take seriously the distinction between the *reasons* (or bases) for sexually desiring someone (or loving someone, if love is the issue) and the *object* of someone's sexual desire (or love). Not accounting for this distinction undermines Zheng's claim that racial desires "depersonalize" and "otherize" people.

Third, and most crucially, Zheng distinguishes neither between hurts and harms nor between subjective harms and objective harms. She relies (almost) unquestioningly on what Asian/American women have to say about this issue. Assuming (heftily) that there are no problems with the studies on which Zheng relies, not making these distinctions is problematic because it assumes that the doubts and anxieties that the sampled women go through constitute morally objectionable harm, whereas *this is precisely* the issue, especially given that not all psychological pain is a form of morally objectionable harm, given that Zheng does not hold the men with racial desires culpable for their desires (at least not directly), and given that she does not assume that all racial desires are permeated by stereotypes. That is, *if* racial desires are morally problematic because they lead to harm, Zheng needs to make the case that the harm in question is morally objectionable in order to show that the racial desires are morally problematic. Consider: suppose that I am very sensitive to noise, and that when I'm home any noise made by my neighbors causes me severe anxiety. We cannot infer from the fact that the noise makes me anxious that when my neighbors move around they are doing something wrong, because my anxieties, as miserable as they make me, are my own issue to cope with, and so are not a form of morally objectionable harm. I am not arguing that all mental anguish is like this, only that by itself mental anguish does not constitute objectionable harm. (It is interesting, in this connection, to compare the doubts that some minority members entertain on being hired to, say, an academic position ["Was I hired because of my ethnicity?"] to the doubts that some Asian/American women feel when they are pursued by a white man ["Does he want me because I am Asian?"].)

There's more written on this issue in cultural studies; in addition to the citations below, see, for example, Laurel C. Schneider, "What Race Is Your Sex?" in *Disrupting White Supremacy from Within: White People on What We Need to Do*, ed. Jennifer Harvey, Karin A. Case, and Robin Hawley Gorsline (Cleveland, Ohio: The Pilgrim Press, 2004), 142–62; and Abdul R. JanMohamed, "Sexuality on/of the Racial Border: Foucault, Wright, and the Articulation of 'Racialized Sexuality,'" in *Discourses of Sexuality: From Aristotle to AIDS*, edited by Domna C. Stanton (Ann Arbor, Mich.: The University of Michigan Press, 1992), 94–116.

2. bell hooks, "Eating the Other: Desire and Resistance," in *Feminist Approaches to Theory and Methodology: An Interdisciplinary Reader*, edited by Sharlene Hesse-Biber, Christina Gilmartin, and Robyn Lyndenberg (New York: Oxford University Press, 1999), 179–94, at 182.

3. Quoted in Laurie Shrage, *Moral Dilemmas of Feminism: Prostitution, Adultery, and Abortion* (New York: Routledge, 1994), 151.

4. I speak here of members of racial or ethnic groups as being the *objects* of sexual desires or attraction, not as the reasons why they are desired or as the causes of the desire—I discuss the reasons and causes below.

5. Future discussions of this issue might have to amend what we have to say about them to apply to other types of PRSDs.

6. Moreover, a person's sexual preferences usually change over time. Thus, in referring to PRSDs, we are actually referring to time-slices of such people. Even if someone's preferences never change, we are still referring to a time-slice, in this case the person's whole life (or the years of his life that mark the beginning and the end of his non-changing sexual preferences). I use "PRSD" to refer to whatever time-slice is necessary.

7. This is no different than saying that someone prefers blondes; it does not mean that he prefers *every* blonde.

8. Strictly, discrimination occurs through actions, not desires, but I gloss over this point and assume, for the sake of the argument, that one can discriminate through one's desires.

9. This is, however, a complicated discussion, and a lot depends on, for example, how we describe the task in question. See Alan Soble, "Physical Attractiveness and Unfair Discrimination," *International Journal of Applied Philosophy*, 1:1 (1982), 37–64, and *Sexual Investigations* (New York: New York University Press, 1996), chapter 5.

10. Alan Goldman defines "sexual desire" as "desire for contact with another person's body and for the pleasure which such conduct produces" ("Plain Sex," in this volume, 54), and Igor Primoratz defines it as "the desire for certain bodily pleasures, period" (*Ethics and Sex* [London and New York: Routledge, 1999], 46).

11. I say "usually" because many prostitutes can perform the sexual act even if they are not sexually attracted to a client, though here things can get complicated depending on what sexual act they perform, since some acts, such as oral sex, are easier to perform without sexual attraction. And I say "necessary" because despite the sexual attraction, the sexual act might not end up being satisfactory for many types of reasons.

12. You can substitute your favorite example of an object of sexual desire.

13. Goldman (see note 10 above) goes on to say about the desire for bodily contact, "It is not a desire for a particular sensation detachable from its causal context, a sensation which can be derived in other ways" ("Plain Sex," in this volume, 54).

14. Note that this argument is not about what members of other groups are sexually entitled to, but about what the defect in a PRSD is. That is, even if a PRSD is entitled to his sexual preferences and has no obligations to have sex with members of groups he does not desire, the argument insists that he is defective because of the narrowness of his desires.

15. The defect might be biological, related to health, or to proper functioning (as opposed to moral). But since PRSDs seem to evince no such defects, it will be hard to argue for one or more of them. The case would be easier if we knew that racial preferences are defects, but, of course, this is the point under debate.

16. A famous study in 2000 seemed to show that under 50 percent of male and female identical twins with the same sets of genes are both gay. This indicates how crucial the environment is in forming sexual orientation. We would expect things to be even more complicated with the formation of racial desires. See J. M. Bailey, M. P. Dunn, and N. G. Martin, "Genetic and Environmental Influences on Sexual Orientation and Its Correlates in an Australian Twin Sample," *Journal of Personality and Social Psychology* 78:3 (2000), 524–36.

17. For example, the stereotype that Asian women are demure is not as such a sexual one. But it might become sexualized by playing a causal role in how some men sexually desire Asian women or by becoming part of the very sexual desire itself.

18. Quoted in Nathaniel Adam Tobias Coleman, "The John Mayer Interview, or How to Start Dating Separately from Your Dick" (unpublished paper; I thank Cole-

man for sharing it with me). Benetton is a clothes retailer known for its racially and ethnically inclusive advertisements. David Duke is a notorious white supremacist.

19. Coleman, "The John Mayer Interview." There are a number of problems, however, with Coleman's claim, some of which emerge below.

20. For some discussion of stereotypes and racism, see Lawrence Blum, *"I'm Not a Racist, But . . .": The Moral Quandary of Race* (Ithaca, N.Y.: Cornell University Press, 2002); Sally Haslanger, *Resisting Reality: Social Construction and Social Critique* (New York: Oxford University Press, 2012); and Erin Beeghly, "What Is a Stereotype? What Is Stereotyping?" *Hypatia* 30:4 (2015), 675–91.

21. And these are *generalizations*. No one ever says, "*Every* A is P"; instead, it is more like "As tend to be Ps."

22. See Blum, *"I'm Not a Racist, But . . ."*, chapter 1, for a discussion of believing non-racist beliefs on racist grounds.

23. This goes against some major definitions of "racist," such as Blum's (*"I'm Not a Racist But . . ."*, chapter 1), according to which a racist is someone whose motives and attitudes are deeply embedded in his or her psyche.

24. These have different strengths: agreeing with a belief might not be as strong as endorsing it. Still, I will treat them interchangeably.

25. See Seiriol Morgan, "Sex in the Head," *Journal of Applied Philosophy* 20:1 (2003), 1–16, reprinted in *The Philosophy of Sex*, 6th ed., edited by Nicholas Power, Raja Halwani, and Alan Soble (Lanham, Md.: Rowman & Littlefield, 2013), 99–121.

26. "Sex in the Head," 7. The man, "Johnny Drugs," is a drug dealer or user, thus making "fucking the police" even more sexually exciting for him.

27. A fourth answer is that our judgment of people like X is mixed: X is racist in certain aspects but not in others.

28. Even if we assume that merely believing the stereotypes is enough to make someone racist—that is, the person does not have to accept them to be racist—the indictment of racism still comes from outside the person's sexual desires.

29. It is actually not clear that Mayer is averse to black women—that he is frightened and repulsed by them, to use Coleman's understanding of "averse" —as opposed to not sexually desiring them (his use of racist imagery might have been an attempt, albeit a stupid, thoughtless one, at humor).

30. J. L. A. Garcia, "The Heart of Racism," in *Race and Racism*, edited by Bernard Boxill (New York: Oxford University Press, 2001), 257–96, at 259.

31. Thus, I think that even a view such as Garcia's cannot escape the essentiality of beliefs; see Tommie Shelby's criticism to this effect in "Is Racism in the 'Heart'?" *Journal of Social Philosophy* 33:2 (2002), 411–20.

32. A nice example is the novel *Season of Migration to the North* by the Sudanese writer Tayyeb Saleh. Its protagonist was sexually attracted to white women, but what motivated him was his hatred of white people because of their colonization of Arab lands.

33. I thank Linda Martín Alcoff, Elliot Layda, Patricia Marino, and Kunitoshi Sakai for extremely helpful comments and discussion on earlier drafts of this paper. Special thanks go to Sarah Hoffman, David Haekwon Kim, and Alan Soble for extensive and insightful comments.

STUDY QUESTIONS

1. Can you think of examples of (sexually relevant) properties or traits that are found among members of only one race or ethnic group, and not others? Suppose that such traits do not exist. Would then PRSDs exist? How?

2. Halwani tackles what he considers to be the three strongest arguments in support of the idea that PRSDs are racist. Can you think of additional arguments in support of this idea?

3. Halwani claims that from the fact that someone's sexual desires contain stereotypes we cannot infer that he is racist. But can we infer that he is morally defective in *some* way? Consider a man whose sexual fantasies consist of raping women; even if these fantasies are confined to the man's sexual desires, is there not something ethically defective about him as a person? And if we assume, along with Halwani, that all stereotypes are morally objectionable, why not say the same about people whose sexual desires have stereotypes?

4. What happens to the view that PRSDs are racist if we argue that not all stereotypes are morally objectionable? Can you think of examples of stereotypes that are morally neutral or even benign?

5. Is Halwani right to compare racial sexual preferences to other types of sexual preferences? Are there important and relevant differences between them that Halwani is overlooking?

6. Suppose that John strongly prefers Asian women, but he can, by taking certain steps, change his sexual desires over time to come to equally desire non-Asian women. *Should* John do so? Why? Would this "should" apply to other sexual preferences that people have— for skinny people, for full-bodied people, for redheads? And what type of "should" is it—moral, aesthetic, prudential, something else?

7. What role, if any, does the race of the PRSD play in this discussion? What if a black man sexually prefers white women? What if he prefers black women?

8. What role, if any, does the history (or lack thereof) between the two racial or ethnic groups play in the discussion about PRSDs? Suppose that X, who belongs to group $G1$, sexually prefers members of $G2$, but such that there is (or was) no bad blood between $G1$ and $G2$. What would that tell us about X? And if there were bad blood—would it matter whether X belonged to the oppressed group or to the oppressing one? What if neither group oppressed the other, but there was still bad blood?

9. Halwani never mentions in his essay the issue of fetishism, even though many people might think of racial sexual desires as some sort of fetish. What connections do you see between fetishism and racial sexual desires? Are some of the latter fetishes while others are not? Why? Try to define as clearly as possible the concept of "fetish" as, or even before, you answer these questions.

TWELVE

Is "Loving More" Better?
The Values of Polyamory

Elizabeth Brake

Elizabeth Brake *begins by offering a rough definition of the practice of polyamory—that it includes multiple sexual or romantic partners, and that some sort of commitment to polyamorous ideals must be held by the partners to the relationship. She then turns her attention to moral objections to polyamory—from the Kantian one that sex should be confined to a two-party monogamous marriage, to the objection that polyamorous relationships have less value than monogamous ones (because they lack—or have less of—something crucial, such as intimacy, love, or specialness), to the objection that it has harmful effects. Brake argues that they all fail to be convincing. In addition, she argues that polyamory can be shown to be superior to monogamy (in some respects, at least): its practitioners espouse ideals such as radical honesty, non-possessiveness, and a rejection of jealousy. These aspects might make polyamory a morally better practice than monogamy. Moreover, in a society in which polyamory is widespread, people might be happier and lead less psychologically troubled lives, not to mention the existence of communal benefits. Brake ends with some remarks on polyamory and legal marriage.*

Elizabeth Brake is associate professor of philosophy at Arizona State University. Her research is primarily in ethics and political philosophy. She is the author of *Minimizing Marriage: Marriage, Morality, and the Law*, and the editor of *After Marriage: Rethinking Marital Relationships* (both with Oxford University Press). She has held a Murphy Institute Fellowship at Tulane, a Canadian SSHRC Grant, and an ASU Provost's Humanities Fellowship. She is currently working on a project on the state's role in disaster response. © 2017, Elizabeth Brake, who kindly gave permission for her new essay to be included in this volume.

Most people think that love and sex are good. And having more of a good thing is usually better than having less. So why isn't polyamory, which its practitioners claim involves having more love and sex than monogamy, more widely accepted and practiced? (*Loving More* is in fact the name of the major polyamory support organization and magazine.[1]) Indeed, why isn't polyamory the *rational* choice for someone who values love and sex, because it—reportedly—increases those goods?

One common response is that polyamory is immoral, according to an objective standard of morality. Others have argued that polyamory does not truly involve love at all—as romantic or sexual love is necessarily exclusive, for only one person at a time—or that the love it involves is in some way less valuable than exclusive love. Others suggest that, given the prevalence of responses such as jealousy or risks of unfairness, polyamory is likely to be less satisfying than monogamy.

On the other hand, polyamory incorporates ethical values of its own—indeed, a case could be made that it is the *superior* approach to relationships. Some polyamorists claim to value love and sex more than exclusivity and possessiveness—indeed, in other areas of life, exclusivity and possessiveness are not usually good things. It could even be argued that we should all aspire to polyamory. This prompts the deeper question of whether one approach to relationships is better for everyone or whether there are simply different preferences.

This chapter explores the nature, ethics, and, to some extent, the politics of polyamory. I begin with a short discussion of its definition. I then explore arguments that it is impermissible or less valuable than monogamy, before turning to polyamory as an ideal. Finally, I briefly address its status under law.

WHAT IS POLYAMORY?

The etymology of "polyamory" is "many loves." This distinguishes it from "polygamy," which means "many marriages," and its two subsets polyandry (many husbands) and polygyny (many wives). Unlike polygamy, polyamorous relationships are not predicated on a traditional form of marriage (legal or substantive) or spousal roles—thus, they need not involve the gendered spousal roles often associated with polygamy, in which husbands and wives take on very different sets of responsibilities and powers.

Polyamory, in the simplest definition, involves multiple love and sex relationships. Polyamorous relationships can be same-sex or different-sex, and polyamorists can be straight, gay, bisexual, or, more generally, queer. Polyamory is not defined by a particular form of relationship (as the monogamous dyad is). For example, it could involve an individual pursuing more than one simultaneous sexual relationship, in an open and forthright way, with varying degrees of love or commitment. Polyamory can also be practiced by a dyadic couple in an open relationship, in which partners agree to pursue independent romantic and sexual relationships. Some such different-sex dyads adopt a "one-penis" or "one-vagina" policy, meaning that partners' independent relationships are only same-sex. Polyamory can also take the form of a group relationship of more than two people.

Group relationships also take multiple forms. A group of three is referred to as a triad, and four as a quad. If group members only have sexual relationships within the group, it is "polyfidelity" (polyfidelity could in fact be seen as multiple monogamy, as opposed to an open and fluid relationship). A group could consist of three or more people who all have sex with each other, but each member in a polyamorous group need not have sex with every other member. For example, Elizabeth Emens describes "the woman with two husbands" who cohabited with and had sexual relationships with two men, who did not have sexual relationships with each other.[2]

Because polyamory is not defined by its formal structure, polyamorous units can evolve into different formations. For example, a network of people can grow out of a polyamorous marriage as partners enter longer-term, more intimate relationships with people who in turn have other connections. Emens describes such a case, in which the bisexual male partner of a male-female couple entered a relationship with another man; the three formed a close relationship (of over fifteen years) and eventually included in their "family" a third man. In this way, an open relationship transitioned to a group relationship, in which not all the parties interact with one another sexually, but all consider themselves part of a family.[3]

Polyamory is not defined by the formal structure of its relationships, nor is it best defined as a sexual orientation.[4] While it may be that some people find monogamy more onerous than others, and so could perhaps be said to have a polyamorous orientation, this does not seem essential to being polyamorous. Rather, polyamory is best characterized as adopting, and consequently practicing, a certain set of attitudes toward monogamy, exclusivity, love, and sex. In my view, a core constituent of being polyamorous, or in a polyamorous relationship, is commitment to some of the values of polyamory. Being poly or identifying as poly, or having a polyamorous relationship, is not just a set of behaviors: it also requires adopting a core set of polyamorous beliefs or attitudes, as articulated in texts such as Dossie Easton and Catherine Liszt's *The Ethical Slut* and Deborah Anapol's *Polyamory in the 21st Century*.[5]

Thus, someone openly having multiple sexual relationships is not necessarily polyamorous. Polyamorous dating can be distinguished from simply dating multiple partners in that polyamorists are not aiming at eventually "settling down" in a monogamous relationship; polyamory typically involves intentionally living without exclusive, monogamous commitment. Likewise, polyamorous open relationships can be distin-

guished from "swinging," in which couples swap partners or seek out
extra partners for sexual excitement and variety; by contrast, polyamory
focuses on emotional relationships as well as sex (there is some dispute
over this classification).[6]

Polyamorous values center on non-possessiveness, communication,
honesty, and critical reflection on the norms of monogamy, as well as
love and sex. Polyamory is typically a choice made *against* marriage,
possessiveness, and gendered spousal roles.[7] Polyamorists claim that,
unlike many married couples, they are deeply honest with their partners
regarding their sexual desires and experiences outside the marriage. Such
honesty is part of the consciously adopted ethical rules of polyamorists.
While they can cheat on one another, polyamorists typically agree on
rules of engagement, such as whether they will tell their partner(s) about
every lover, what means of contraception and protection against STDs
they will take, whether one partner has priority, and what that priority
entails. Cheating within polyamory would consist of breaking these
rules.

Polyamory is not an organized and monolithic movement, and hence
there are disputes among polyamorists about the core tenets of polyamorous practice. One issue is whether polyamory primarily involves sex,
love, or both. It seems that polyamory must involve sex, as otherwise
polyamorous relationships would simply be affectionate relationships
like friendships. (But complications arise, such as when group relationships involve sexual relationships between some, but not all, group members, and when the parties to the relationships are romantic asexuals.)
They must also involve romantic love, otherwise polyamory would simply be promiscuous or "swinging" relationships. In general, then, polyamorous relationships involve sex and romantic love or affection.

Before turning to ethical issues, it is worthwhile addressing one objection to the claim that polyamory involves multiple romantic love relationships. Numerous philosophers of love have argued against the very
possibility of polyamorous love, arguing that we cannot love more than
one person at a time, at least in the sense of romantic or sexual love (for
clearly we can love more than one parent, sibling, child, or friend at a
time). If we cannot love more than one person at a time, then polyamory
cannot involve multiple love relationships. Carrie Jenkins has called the
view that it is conceptually impossible to love more than one person at a
time "modal monogamy."[8]

As Jenkins points out, many philosophers of love have defended modal monogamy, taking exclusivity to be a defining feature of romantic
love relationships. That is, they assume that romantic love necessarily
focuses exclusively on one other person.[9] But Jenkins offers reasons
against modal monogamy. First, many people report loving more than
one person at a time—not only polyamorists but also people who are torn
between two lovers. Jenkins writes, "Unless all such people are either

confused or lying, Modal Monogamy is false. And I know of no reason to suppose that all such people are either confused or lying." Second, other forms of love, such as love for friends or children, are not exclusive; why should romantic love be uniquely exclusive?

Additionally, Jenkins warns that conceptual analysis of the nature of love may conflate culturally dominant norms with what is true *by definition* of the concept under examination. Given that monogamous romantic love is indeed a dominant cultural conception, there is reason to think that cultural paradigms have shaped the intuitions of philosophers undertaking conceptual analysis of love. In other words, while it may seem as if exclusivity is essential to romantic love, this may simply reflect the cultural practice of our society—and it might be mentioned here that many societies have practiced polygamy or some form of institutionalized extramarital sex.[10]

But precisely because of these cultural paradigms, it might be *psychologically* (as opposed to conceptually) impossible to love more than one person at a time. Just as our philosophical intuitions have been shaped culturally, our psychology has also been shaped culturally. Indeed, many people report that when in love with someone, they cannot be in love with someone else, at least during the initial passionate stages of love. The early stages of romantic love can bring an overwhelming and narrow focus on the love object which Sigmund Freud compared to "a neurotic compulsion"![11] However, it is clearly possible to love multiple people at one time *in different ways*: so while one might be in a state of limerence (early love) with one person, they might also love another person in a companionate way—just as we do not cease loving friends and family when we fall into romantic love. An underlying assumption of modal monogamy is that romantic love involves being in love in the same way at the same time with one's love objects, but even within monogamy, the nature of romantic love for a single object can change over time—from limerence to companionate pair bonding.

THE ETHICS

While honesty and non-possessiveness are central to the "ethics" of polyamory, is polyamory really ethical? To those who see monogamy as the only permissible form of sexual relationships, it cannot be ethical. But what is the reason for such judgments?

Perhaps it is best to start with the following question: What is the ethical status of polyamorous relationships? We can distinguish worries about wrongs, harms, or deficiencies intrinsic to the practice (those which cannot be separated from it) from concerns about side effects likely to accompany polyamory. To take a parallel example, some people argue that assisted suicide is inherently wrong, because it violates human dignity; it is wrong in itself. Others argue that it is not inherently wrong, but that permitting it would likely have bad side effects, such as leading hospitals or families to pressure elderly members to agree to be euthanized. If such side effects are sufficiently serious and widespread, they provide reason against a practice. But if such side effects are contingent on the social context, this would allow the practice to be ethical in some contexts or societies but not in others.

I will first look at the concerns that polyamory is inherently wrong. Then I will look at arguments that the practice of polyamory risks harmful side effects. I conclude by looking at the ethical values of polyamory and asking whether polyamory may be ethically *preferable* to monogamy.

1. Is Polyamory Inherently Wrong?

A first set of possible concerns about the nature of polyamory should be set aside. This is the assumption that polyamory—like many instances of extramarital sex—involves deception and promise-breaking. Extramarital sex (or sex outside committed relationships) may involve lies about the sex itself, as well as smaller lies concerning where spouses or partners have been, with whom, and so on. When spouses (or partners) have promised sexual exclusivity, sex outside the relationship also involves promise-breaking. However, such promise-breaking can be found in all types of relationships, not just in polyamorous ones (indeed, they might be less frequent in polyamorous than in monogamous relationships given that each partner has access to more than one sexual partner). Moreover, as we have seen, polyamorists aspire to avoid dishonesty and promise-breaking by engaging in radical honesty and only promising to obey rules which they believe they can keep.

More subtly, it might be suggested that because many people expect and want romantic love to be monogamous, offering non-monogamous love disappoints their expectations.[12] This, however, could be guarded against through honest disclosure. People can have many expectations about their romantic partners (that they be employed, or healthy, etc.); generally, disappointing such expectations is wrong only when there is an intention to deceive or when the expectations involve reasonable assumptions.

Thus, although polyamorists can be dishonest or break their promises, monogamists can do so also. The point is that these moral wrongs are not *intrinsic* to polyamory. They are moral failures by many polyamorists' own lights. We can then set aside concerns about cheating, deception, and promise-breaking because they are no more inherent to polyamory than to monogamy.

This cautions against idealizing or demonizing either monogamy or polyamory. Such overgeneralizations make fair comparisons impossible. Claims such as "monogamy is stable, loyal, and loving," "polyamory involves radical honesty and openness," or "monogamy leads to deceptive extramarital sex" all involve overgeneralizations, to the extent that they are not true in all cases. To assess either practice, we should keep in mind both the ideals to which it aspires and the reality of human beings imperfectly practicing such ideals. The fact that some polyamorists do not live up to their ideals of honesty and openness does not show that polyamory is inherently flawed, just as the fact that some monogamists do not live up to their ideals of exclusivity and loyalty does not show that monogamy is inherently flawed.

Some sexual ethicists, though, argue that even in its ideal form polyamory is inherently wrong, because sex outside a monogamous relationship (even stronger: outside *marriage*) is immoral. The philosopher Immanuel Kant, for example, held that sex involved giving oneself up to another, to be used for their pleasure, and this could be avoided only when the sex is between a couple who are in a monogamous (legal) marriage.

On Kant's view, respect for humanity requires always treating others as valuable in themselves, and not as a mere means for one's own purposes. Treating someone as a mere means to one's purposes is thus a grave wrong, violating their moral rights.[13] Kant found many moral problems with sex. Indeed, he thought that in sex or masturbation we use our own bodies as mere means for pleasure. But he focused on the concern that sexual use of another treats them as a mere means for the purpose of sexual pleasure. Kant thought that our bodies are an essential part of our personhood, which morally demands respect as "beyond all price." Hence, respect for our personhood must extend to any use of our bodies. Even selling our hair or teeth, according to Kant, contravenes the respect we owe ourselves. When we offer up our bodies to another person for their pleasure, it is not like allowing them to use a tool that we own but rather allowing them to use as a mere means what must always be treated with respect. Kant's solution to this involved both parties reciprocally giving themselves up to each other in marriage: when both give themselves up wholly to each other, each in essence gets themselves back.

Kant's view involves some mysterious metaphysics, but we can attempt a sympathetic reconstruction of his views on polygamy. Kant explained what is wrong with multiple sexual relationships as follows (he focused on polygamy, but his reasoning would also extend to polyamory): when a man is involved with two women (say), each woman gives all of herself, but she receives only half of the man in return. Not only is this unfair and lopsided, but since the solution to the moral problem of sex requires that partners give themselves up to each other wholly and reciprocally, the man in this scenario is using each woman as a mere means to his sexual pleasure (and they are allowing themselves to be used).

There are problems with this account. First, it is difficult to see how Kant's view precludes three people giving themselves to each other wholly and reciprocally in polyfidelity. Members of a small group can give themselves up to the group, and thus get themselves back, just as members of a couple can. Second, it is difficult to see why consensual polyamory would inevitably treat the person as a mere means. In most cases, informed consent is sufficient to render treatment of others respectful; Kant's view that, in sex, both consent and reciprocal exchange of exclusive rights over each other are needed adds an unusual requirement, one found only in the context of sex. But we can use one another's bodies for pleasure in other ways—massage, partner yoga, dancing, cuddling—where consent does seem sufficient for the interaction to be permissible.

The difficulty for Kant's account is to explain why special moral requirements apply to sex.[14] On a less stringent standard of sexual ethics—one requiring only respect, consent, honesty, and affection and concern for the other—it is hard to see how polyamory could be judged inherently wrong. After all, polyamory can involve respect, consent, honesty, affection, and concern for the others.

But it might be thought that although polyamory is not inherently wrong, polyamorous relationships inherently have less value than monogamous relationships—less intimacy or emotional depth, less of whatever makes romantic relationships valuable. For example, Chris Bennett has argued that being the "only one" for someone else confirms a sense of specialness. On his view, exclusive (although not necessarily sexually exclusive) dyadic love relationships uniquely support our autonomy by providing "reassurance about our own value."[15] Bennett writes:

> In conjugal love another person chooses to assume responsibility for you as a whole, because they value the detail of your life. They choose *you*. Furthermore, they choose you *and not anyone else*. The evaluation of you that is expressed in the choice, and in the very form of the relationship and its structures of responsibility, singles you out. You have been chosen over everyone else. This should not make you think that you are more special than everyone else. But it does quite rightly back up your sense that you are special in your own right. Being special for someone else affirms and recognises your sense that the things that make you a particular individual are valuable, because someone has chosen you *for* those things.[16]

Being special for someone else does likely bolster our sense of our own value. But our specialness is not only confirmed in monogamous love relationships. Imagine, for example, a triad in which members pledge mutual fidelity. A member of this triad may feel that the others have chosen her for just who she is and feel confirmed in her specialness by their regard. And polyamorist couples can also commit to one another

above everyone else—for example, they might draw a distinction between partners, who take priority, and companions.

A related objection might be that in polyamory, each partner shares
their partner with another who competes for attention and so receives
less love, affection, intimacy, or even sex than they would in a monogamous relationship. But this assumes that relations of love, affection, intimacy and sex are a zero-sum game—that is, a situation in which there
must be winners and losers, as opposed to a situation in which everyone
can achieve more by cooperating than they could on their own. The argument assumes that if one's partner loves someone else, one therefore
must receive less love. But we don't think this way in relation to parental
love or love for friends. There may well be a point at which someone
simply lacks the time and psychological capacity to love and care for
more children, friends, or partners equally, so each additional person will
detract from what the others receive. But there is no reason to think that
this point is reached at "more than one," and it plausibly differs from
person to person.

Another problem with arguing that polyamorous relationships have
less value than monogamous relationships—that they have "second-rate"
love and sex—is that not everyone seeks the same qualities in a relationship. Some prize stability over spontaneity, closeness over independence,
while others do not. So even if polyamory falls short of some monogamous ideal of priority or intimacy, polyamorists might respond, "Yes, but
it's more important to me to have love and sex with more people than
more exclusive or intimate love and sex if 'exclusivity' and 'intimacy'
mean 'between only two people.'" At this point, to respond to the polyamorist's claim that relationships might involve multiple values requiring trade-offs and that such trade-offs are a matter of subjective preference, the critic must show that polyamory lacks something of objective
value, such as something crucial to human flourishing or welfare. That is,
the argument must show that polyamory falls short of an objective standard of value that the polyamorist cannot or should not opt out of. But
this is a high argumentative standard to meet, especially given the diversity of people's emotional needs and capacities.

Indeed, even if most people do prefer monogamy, the polyamorist can
go on the offensive and claim that polyamory is the ideal that most of us
are unable to meet. After all, "one and only," "exclusive," and other
language surrounding romantic love suggests selfishness and possessiveness. Before examining this point, I'll consider harms which are "side
effects" of the practice, not inherent to it.

2. Is It Harmful?

The foregoing concerns are about the alleged inherent wrongness of
polyamory. But many objections to polyamory are about its likely side

effects given contingent facts about society or facts of human psychology and biology. These concerns hold that even if polyamory is permissible in principle, it is likely to be harmful, and this generates reasons to refrain from it.

One concern often voiced regarding polyamory is the side effects on children of polyamorous parents. Critics worry that children will be confused, or, in the case of the judge cited by Emens, that polyamorous parents will serve as poor moral role models.[17] There is little research on such children to make a strong empirical case either way. Literature concerning polygamous families (such as that cited in Thom Brooks's "The Problem with Polygamy"[18]) is unlikely to be representative due to demographic differences between typical polygamists and typical polyamorists. While polygamy in the United States and Canada tends to be practiced in small, isolated religious communities where access to education is restricted, polyamorists tend to be well-educated urban professionals.[19]

In fact, there may be little research on polyamorous families because they tend to be closeted. Polyamorists have no legal protections against employment and housing discrimination and, in the case cited by Emens, a child was removed from the custody of otherwise fit parents simply because those parents were polyamorous. Polyamorists fearing loss of jobs, homes, or children have reason to be closeted.

Elizabeth Sheff has recently published the first study on polyamorous families, "a fifteen-year longitudinal, ethnographic study of polyamorous people and their children," which includes interviews with twenty-two children.[20] Sheff's analysis of the data focuses on two themes: first, having multiple, biologically unrelated parties in parental roles is not distinctive of polyamory. Both serial monogamy and some assisted reproductive technologies (involving gamete donation or contract pregnancy) create families with more than two parents, not all of whom are biologically related to the child. So the challenges of polyamorous families—in particular, identifying the adults responsible for a child—are already posed by other family forms.

Second, polyamorists argue that "multiple parenting" benefits children, and Sheff's data appear to suggest that benefits, as well as disadvantages, exist for children of polyamorous parents. The benefits include practical benefits such as more rides and more money, as well as the love and supervision of more parents, and a greater variety of parenting styles (due to the multiplicity of adults involved in a parental way with the child). While these benefits might also accrue to children in stepfamilies, some benefits are unique to polyamory: an emphasis on honesty and choice regarding sexual experience, and on maintaining friendly relations among former partners when sexual relationships end. These must be balanced with disadvantages such as the loss of parents' partners when relationships end (again, also found in monogamous divorce) and overcrowding in the home. Other disadvantages arise from social stigma and the unfamiliarity of such family forms.[21]

A different objection concerns the gender politics of polyamory. Thus, Brooks suggests that polyamory, while potentially egalitarian, mainly takes the form of gender-structured polygyny-like relationships—one male and multiple females.[22] Given significant gender inequality in income, wealth, and social power, it is reasonable to worry that women who are financially dependent on their male partners may be pressured into polyamory. Of course, the concern that structural inequality between men and women may result in unequal decision-making power, even subtle coercion, also applies to monogamy.[23] But critics could suggest that, within polyamory, competition between women might increase the opportunity for exploitation. On the other hand, some polyamorists are explicitly feminist, rejecting monogamous norms that they see as patriarchal, and advocates of polyamory argue that it allows the division of household work and childcare between more people—benefiting women, who typically take on a greater share of such work.[24]

It might also be objected that the practical challenges of polyamory introduce risks and potential unfairness. One set of risks is sexual: possible transmission of STDs or unplanned pregnancy. These risks suggest the importance for polyamorists of creating explicit agreements regarding their practices, such as using protection and regularly taking STD tests (as, in fact, monogamists might be less likely to do). But polyamorists might point out that because their relationships are more open and involve access to multiple sexual partners, there is less temptation to cheat (by breaking the rules) and partners are aware of the risks, as they are not in a monogamous relationship in which one partner secretly cheats.

Another risk is that of unfair treatment. Polyamorists may experience sexual or romantic jealousy, and while partners may agree on prioritizing a primary relationship, with the expectation that secondary companions respect the primary relationship, this might not work in practice. One of the biggest reported challenges for polyamorists is simply making time for multiple relationships. The potential conflict between different partners, particularly in time spent together, might lead to forms of unequal treatment. Polyamorists, however, might respond that because communication is a core tenet of polyamorist practice, discussions of fairness and priority will be central to polyamorist practice—and monogamists might also benefit from embracing such discussions. While polyamorists might create hierarchies—between, for instance, a primary partner and a secondary companion—these hierarchies are both acknowledged and, to some extent, dynamic. Explicit attention to the hierarchies in relationships and openness to their fluidity could be better conditions for identifying and changing unfair hierarchies than the static hierarchies which emerge without discussion in some monogamous relationships. Finally, unfair treatment and jealousy are possible in monogamous relationships in which a partner might devote time or attention to non-romantic passions such as work, hobbies, friendships, or addictions.

Polyamorists, whether in open or in group relationships, can define their own rules, and doing so is essential given the risks and logistical challenges of polyamory. For example, an open couple might limit their contact with third parties to anonymous sexual encounters, or they might permit the formation of independent emotional relationships. A triad might agree to polyfidelity or agree to practice only safe sex with non-group members. Partners may find it important to establish rules setting out the priority of their relationship. For example, a couple in an open relationship might agree that partners have veto power over each other's lovers, or that partners will limit the time spent with secondary companions. Once again, polyamory does not mean that anything goes—infidelity can exist in an open relationship as much as in a closed one, if one partner breaks the agreed-upon rules.[25]

3. The Values of Polyamory

As Luke Brunning writes in a recent essay, some polyamorists have tended to defend polyamory by comparing it to monogamy, focusing on similarities between the practices. But Brunning suggests a full understanding of the value of polyamory lies in its distinctiveness. Because of the potential for conflict it involves, it requires partners to practice communication, self- and other-awareness, and emotional work, thus making it, he argues, more emotionally challenging but also more emotionally rich than monogamy.[26] Indeed, critical reflection on the norms of monogamy is partly constitutive of polyamory, suggesting a crucial distance between the practices.

Polyamorists have articulated a range of values according to which polyamory could be seen as an improvement on monogamy. Honest communication is a foundational rule for polyamorous relationships.[27] The ideal of "radical honesty," or openness about sexual desires, feelings, and encounters that monogamists typically conceal from their partners, could create greater intimacy and prompt partners to confront and work through negative feelings of jealousy. Not all polyamorists espouse the extreme of radical honesty; they may prefer a "don't ask, don't tell" policy, for example. But such a choice is still based on honest communication, rather than deception.

The ideal of non-possessiveness rejects relationship norms that treat partners as possessions who can be controlled. Monogamist norms resemble property norms (particularly when we examine the historical law of coverture in marriage): partners exclude all others from their holdings. The critic of capitalism John McMurtry, for instance, saw monogamy as an ideological tool of capitalism, disposing individuals to see the world—

including their sexual partners—in terms of ownership and exclusion.[28] And of course such possessiveness has, historically, been gendered: thus the rejection of possessiveness is sometimes an explicitly feminist repudiation of traditional marriage norms which treated wives as tantamount to their husbands' property and limited women's value to their status as wives and mothers. Dossie Easton, the self-described "ethical slut," became a principled polyamorist after escaping an abusive relationship with a sexually possessive man. In part, she rejected monogamy so that she would gain self-knowledge, as opposed to losing her identity and independence in a relationship: "I resented those cultural values that said that my sense of security and self-worth were contingent on the status of whatever man I managed to attract to me, as if I had no status of my own. So I vowed to discover a security in myself, the stable ground of my very own being, something to do . . . with self-respect and self-acceptance."[29]

But polyamorists also aspire to a positive emotional ideal of non-possessiveness, taking delight in their partner's sexual and romantic experiences. Deborah Anapol describes the emotion of "compersion," which is "the opposite of jealousy," as feeling "joy and delight when one's beloved loves or is being loved by another."[30] This expands empathy to one's sexual partner, against cultural norms and feelings of sexual jealousy. From a polyamorous standpoint, such jealousy is irrational (though challenging): love and sex are good, and we should wish for our loved ones to have good things. For similar reasons, new partners are generally expected to respect the autonomy of existing relationships.

We can consider polyamory as an ideal by asking what it would be like if we lived in a society where polyamory (with its ideals of honesty, communication, and non-possessiveness) was the norm. We can imagine, as Easton suggests, that marital status would no longer be a marker to determine one's value or a symbol of adulthood. Marriage or being "coupled" is one of the primary means we now use to categorize ourselves and others socially. But in a polyamorous world these markers would be less clear-cut. Relationships would be more fluid, so the distinction between being in and out of a relationship would no longer be so important. This would allow romantic asexuals and friendships to flourish without being marginalized by cultural norms of coupledom; if being in a relationship of a certain form became less culturally important, it could become more acceptable to choose to opt out of romantic or sexual relationships altogether. A polyamorous society would be a post-monogamous society, in a way parallel to ideals of post-racial or post-gender societies: different sexual identities would not carry arbitrary penalties, and sexual identity itself might become more fluid.[31]

A polyamorous hegemony might also have wider social, economic, and environmental effects. Communal living might become more common, with environmental benefits, and all the time spent on communication and pursuing relationships might lead toward a less consumerist society where people were more entranced by relationships—and conversations about how to conduct them—than the latest consumer items or celebrity gossip. It might even be a more fun society, in which flirtation and sexual possibility were more widespread, without the threat of disrupting existing relationships or requiring messy deceptions. At the same time, because sexuality was more open and polyamorous desires allowed open expression, popular culture might become less sexualized. People might come to better knowledge of themselves and others through the "emotional work" of polyamory. And as sex wouldn't carry the burden of uniting oneself with one monogamous partner, people who are currently disadvantaged on "mating markets"—perhaps those with less income, worse social skills, or unconventional looks—might have more access to sexual and romantic relationships.

There is also the tempting, albeit somewhat controversial, thought—which I will not pursue here—that polyamory is more suited to human nature (let's set aside doubts about the existence of such a thing as human nature): at least as far as sex is concerned, we might not be sexually monogamous by nature, and human sexual desire might target multiple sexual partners. (In a society that values monogamy, this could be one important reason why cheating is rampant and why polyamorists value honesty.) If so, polyamory might be truer to who we are than sexual monogamy.

For all these reasons, people might be more sexually and romantically fulfilled in a polyamorous world.

LAW AND POLITICS

While some forms of plural marriage or bigamy are illegal, polyamory as such is not criminalized in Western countries. In a liberal society, sexual freedom protects one's right to have sex with multiple partners (and freedom of association grants a right to interact with those whom one chooses, so long as they consent). But (at least in the United States) polyamorists have no protections against discrimination in housing and employment. In fact, a survey of polyamorists found that "employment nondiscrimination was one of their three highest priority legal issues."[32]

Polyamorists have not—yet—sought marriage equality. This may be because many reject the possessiveness and gender norms associated with traditional marriage. Moreover, legislating group marriage poses challenges not associated with recognizing same-sex marriage: How will marital rights and responsibilities be divided among three people, for example? And whose legal consent would be required to add another party to the relationship?[33] But some form of legal recognition for groups or network relationships might be possible—and perhaps required for equal treatment.[34]

Some legal theorists have considered whether being polyamorous should be construed as a minority sexual orientation such as being gay or lesbian, and hence arguably eligible for legal protection against discrimination. One concern with such a strategy is that almost everyone who is not asexual can be considered polyamorous in orientation, if that simply means desiring more than one person sexually. But it might be argued that polyamory is sufficiently embedded—deeply entwined with identity and pursued in the face of significant risks—to be legally classified as an orientation.[35] Perhaps one minority can claim a more profound polyamorous orientation: bisexuals. For bisexuals, Kayley Vernallis argues, expressing their sexual identity fully might require polyamory, thus giving rise to a claim, perhaps even a right, to what she calls "bi-marriage," a group of (at least) four individuals, all of whom are bisexuals and two of whom are men and two women.[36]

In a tolerant, liberal society, the state has no reason to discriminate among its citizens' different approaches to love, sex, and intimacy, as long as their choices do not harm unconsenting or incompetent others. The vibrant coexistence of polyamory alongside monogamy could benefit monogamists too, by encouraging the adoption of values such as radical honesty, communication, and more attention to needs for love and sex.[37]

NOTES

1. This can be found online at www.lovemore.com; accessed December 28, 2016.

2. Elizabeth F. Emens, "Monogamy's Law: Compulsory Monogamy and Polyamorous Existence," *New York University Review of Law and Social Change* 29:2 (2004), 277–376; see especially 310–12.

3. Emens, "Monogamy's Law," 312–14.

4. See the essay "What Is Sexual Orientation?" by Robin Dembroff in this volume, where the account of sexual orientation defended implies that polyamory is not a sexual orientation.

5. See Dossie Easton and Catherine Liszt, *The Ethical Slut: A Guide to Infinite Sexual Possibilities* (Emeryville, Calif.: Greenery Press, 1997), and Deborah Anapol, *Polyamory in the 21st Century: Love and Intimacy with Many Partners* (Lanham, Md.: Rowman & Littlefield, 2010).

6. See Anapol, *Polyamory in the 21st Century*, 13–14. Anapol suggests that the clearest difference is that whereas swinging centers around couples, polyamory does not.

7. But see Kayley Vernallis, "Bisexuality and Bisexual Marriage" (in this volume) and "Bisexual Marriage" (in *The Philosophy of Sex: Contemporary Readings*, 6th edition, edited by Nicholas Power, Raja Halwani, and Alan Soble [Lanham, Md.: Rowman & Littlefield, 2013], 215–32), where she argues that the optimal form of bisexual marriage would have to be polyamorous.

8. Carrie Jenkins, "Modal Monogamy," *Ergo* 2:8 (2015). Online at http://dx.doi.org/10.3998/ergo.12405314.0002.008; accessed December 28, 2016.

9. She cites S. Matthew Liao, "The Idea of a Duty to Love," *Journal of Value Inquiry* 40:1 (2006), 1–22, at 16; Alan Soble, "The Unity of Romantic Love," in *Philosophy and Theology* 1:4 (1987), 374–97, at 389; and Robert Solomon, *About Love: Reinventing Romance for Our Times* (New York: Simon & Schuster, 1988), 197.

10. Stephanie Coontz, *Marriage: A History* (London: Penguin, 2006), 20–31.

11. Sigmund Freud, *On Narcissism: An Introduction*, in *The Philosophy of (Erotic) Love*, edited by Robert Solomon and Kathleen Higgins (Lawrence, Kans.: University Press of Kansas, 1991), 165.

12. Richard Wasserstrom, "Is Adultery Immoral?" *Philosophical Forum* 5:4 (1974), 513–28. Wasserstrom critically discusses such expectations as well as promise-breaking in the context of extramarital sex.

13. Immanuel Kant, *Groundwork of the Metaphysics of Morals* and *The Metaphysics of Morals*, in *Practical Philosophy*, translated and edited by Mary Gregor (Cambridge: Cambridge University Press, 1996), 37–108 and 353–603, esp. 426–29, and 546–50.

14. But see the essays "Sexual Use" by Alan Soble and "Dark Desires" by Seiriol Morgan in this volume.

15. Christopher Bennett, "Liberalism, Autonomy, and Conjugal Love," *Res Publica* 9:3 (2003), 285–301, at 291.

16. Bennett, "Liberalism, Autonomy, and Conjugal Love," 297–98.

17. Emens, "Monogamy's Law," 311.

18. Thom Brooks, "The Problem with Polygamy," *Philosophical Topics* 37:2 (2009), 109–22. See also British Columbia Supreme Court, *Reference re: Section 293 of the Criminal Code of Canada*, 2011 BCSC 1588. Retrieved from http://www.courts.gov.bc.ca/jdb-txt/SC/11/15/2011BCSC1588.htm; accessed December 28, 2016.

19. For discussion of the demographics of polygamists, see British Columbia Supreme Court, *Reference re: Section 293 of the Criminal Code of Canada*. On polyamorists, see Mark Goldfeder and Elisabeth Sheff, "Children of Polyamorous Families: A First Empirical Look," *Journal of Law and Social Deviance* 5 (2013), 150–243, at 193.

20. Goldfeder and Sheff, "Children of Polyamorous Families," 189, 172–6.

21. Goldfeder and Sheff, "Children of Polyamorous Families," 186, 208–36.

22. Brooks, "The Problem with Polygamy," 117.

23. Laurie Shrage, "Polygamy, Privacy, and Equality," in *After Marriage: Rethinking Marital Relationships*, edited by Elizabeth Brake (New York: Oxford University Press, 2016), 160–79.

24. Goldfeder and Sheff, "Children of Polyamorous Families," 165; Emens, "Monogamy's Law," 314–17.

25. See Anapol, *Polyamory in the 21st Century*, ch. 11, and Easton and Liszt, *The Ethical Slut*, on the logistical and emotional complexities of such arrangements.

26. Luke Brunning, "The Distinctiveness of Polyamory," *Journal of Applied Philosophy* Online First (2016): DOI: 10.1111/japp.12240; accessed December 28, 2016.

27. See Anapol, *Polyamory in the 21st Century*, 62–63; Emens, "Monogamy's Law," 322–24.

28. John McMurtry, "Monogamy: A Critique," *The Monist* 56:4 (1972), 587–99.

29. Easton and Liszt, *The Ethical Slut*, 11–12, cited at Emens, "Monogamy's Law," 319.

30. Anapol, *Polyamory in the 21st Century*, 22, 121.

31. Here, one might object that just as strong social norms with corresponding social exclusions develop under monogamy, so too a polyamorous society could stigmatize or marginalize monogamists. However, because polyamory involves negotiation and fluidity, it might be more difficult for stark discriminations of this kind to emerge.

32. Emens, "Monogamy's Law," 331, fn. 316; and see Ann Tweedy, "Polyamory as a Sexual Orientation," *University of Cincinnati Law Review* 79:4 (2011), 1461–1515, at 1489–90.

33. Brooks ("The Problem with Polygamy") raises such questions regarding polygamy; for responses, see Laurie Shrage and Gregg Strauss, "Is Polygamy Inherently Unequal?" *Ethics* 122:3 (2012), 516–44.

34. See Elizabeth Brake, *Minimizing Marriage: Marriage, Morality, and The Law* (New York: Oxford University Press, 2012), 156–85, and "Recognizing Care: The Case for Friendship and Polyamory," *Syracuse Law and Civic Engagement Journal* 1 (2013). On-

line at http://slace.syr.edu/issue-1-2013-14-on-equality/recognizing-care-the-case-for-friendship-and-polyamory/; accessed December 28, 2016.

35. Tweedy, "Polyamory as a Sexual Orientation," 1482–98.

36. Vernallis, "Bisexual Marriage," *passim*. See also Vernallis, "Bisexuality and Bisexual Marriage," in this volume.

37. Thanks to Raja Halwani for extensive comments, some of which have been incorporated into the current essay, and to Jason Butco Sams and Cynthia Stark for discussion.

STUDY QUESTIONS

1. Brake states, "Polyamory, in the simplest definition, involves multiple love and sex relationships." Can you provide a more robust or substantive definition of "polyamory," one that involves individually necessary conditions and jointly sufficient ones? In undertaking this task, think carefully about whether polyamory necessarily involves romantic love, sex, or both.

2. Brake states, "In my view, a core constituent of being polyamorous, or in a polyamorous relationship, is commitment to some of the values of polyamory." This suggests, to continue with the above question, that such a commitment is a necessary condition of any adequate definition of "polyamory." Is this correct? Can you think of counter-examples (cases of polyamory such that one or more members do not have the commitment that Brake has in mind)? Suppose you come up with such counter-examples, why and how might Brake's claim still be correct?

3. Make the case, especially after reading Robin Dembroff's essay in this volume ("What Is Sexual Orientation?") as to whether being polyamorous is a sexual orientation. Keep in mind what Brake has to say about this issue as you answer this question.

4. If romantic love is by its nature exclusive to one person at a time, then if X loves Y during t, then X can love Y and only Y during t, and if X claims to love both Y and Z, then X loves Y or Z during t (but not both) or neither. Is the exclusivity of romantic love a plausible view? In thinking about this, how helpful is it to rely on the idea that in other types of love (e.g., friendship, parent-child, and sibling love), a person can love more than one other person simultaneously? And is the following common (though perhaps false) psychological belief relevant to this issue—"To be able to love someone, you must love yourself first"? That is, does loving oneself count as an additional person in this discussion?

5. As Brake explains, one objection to polyamory is that because many people expect and want romantic love to be monogamous, offering non-monogamous love disappoints their expectations. Brake replies, "People can have many expectations about their romantic partners (that they be employed, or healthy, etc.); generally,

disappointing such expectations is wrong only when there is an intention to deceive or when the expectations involve reasonable assumptions." Give an example in which an honest polyamorist wrongly disappoints their potential partner when the latter's expectations involve "reasonable assumptions." Think of analogous cases not related to love or sex.

6. In replying to Kant's proposal that only in a two-party monogamous marriage is sex permissible, Brake claims that "members of a small group can give themselves up to the group." What does this mean exactly? Is Brake suggesting that in such a group each person gives him- or herself to *each other person* or to the *group* as a whole? And which of the two options is needed to defend polyamory against the Kantian objection? (Kant thought that if X and Y marry each other, X gives X's self to Y, and Y gives Y's self to X. Because in giving X's self to Y, Y now "has" X, then in Y giving Y's self to X, X gets back X's self. So both X and Y would have rights over the other [by "owning" each other], yet, somehow, be non-owned by the other. How would this would work in, say, a group of three or four people?)

7. Is being special to someone "likely" to bolster our own sense of value? Is the mere fact that X loves Y likely to bolster Y's sense of value—even if X is a bad person? That is, does the identity of the person loving me matter, or is merely being loved enough? Would being in a polyamorous relationship help, given that one can say to oneself, "If that many people love me, then I must have *some* value!" Does it matter if the value came from being loved romantically or in some other type of love? (Do you get a sense of value knowing that your parents love you?)

8. Read the essay "Gay Divorce" by the philosopher Claudia Card (reprinted in *The Philosophy of Sex: Contemporary Readings*, 6th ed., edited by Nicholas Power, Raja Halwani, and Alan Soble [Lanham, Md.: Rowman & Littlefield, 2013], 177–93), in which she argues that (legal) marriage—gay, straight, or any other form—should be opposed because divorce can be hell to go through. Trace the implications of Card's argument to polyamorous groupings, especially with the last section of Brake's essay in mind.

9. Think about the ideal of "radical honesty," whereby one is expected to be radically honest about one's sexual desires and romantic feelings, especially in the context of polyamory but also perhaps outside it. Is it a good ideal? Should we be honest always about these things? Can you think of cases in which such honesty would be unethical? Or would such cases not be cases of genuine honesty?

10. Do you think that polyamory is more suited to human nature than monogamy? Why or why not? In answering this question, keep in

mind that polyamory might involve both sexual desire and romantic love.

THIRTEEN

What Is Sexual Orientation?

Robin Dembroff

Ordinary discourse is filled with discussions about sexual orientation. This discourse might suggest a common understanding of what sexual orientation is. But even a cursory search turns up vastly differing, conflicting, and sometimes ethically troubling characterizations of this concept. **Robin Dembroff** *lays the groundwork for philosophical exploration of "sexual orientation." Dembroff offers an account of sexual orientation—"Bidimensional Dispositionalism"—according to which sexual orientation concerns what sex(es) and gender(s) of persons one is disposed to sexually engage, and makes no reference to one's own sex and gender. This account improves upon preexisting conceptions of sexual orientations while avoiding their shortcomings, and it meets crucial theoretical, social, and legal goals.*

Robin Dembroff is a PhD candidate in philosophy at Princeton University, having transferred from the University of Notre Dame after completing an MA in philosophy in August 2014. Dembroff's current research is in metaphysics, in particular topics related to social ontology, such as the nature of race, gender, sexual orientation, and social identities. Dembroff's dissertation focuses on the relationship between social ontology and social justice. An earlier, lengthier version of this essay, "What Is Sexual Orientation?" is published in *Philosophers' Imprint* (2016). © 2017, Robin Dembroff, who kindly gave permission for this revised version of the essay to be included in this volume.

Ordinary discourse is filled with discussions about "sexual orientation." Everyone seems to have opinions about it—whether it should be a legally protected class, whether it is apt for moral judgment, and whether Lady Gaga is right that, whatever our sexual orientations, we were "born that way."[1]

This discourse suggests a common understanding of what "sexual orientation" is. But even a cursory search turns up vastly differing, conflicting, and sometimes ethically troubling characterizations of sexual or-

ientation. Consider the following, taken from (respectively) a professional scientific association, an LGBTQ advocacy organization, a neuroscien-
tist and a philosopher:

1. Sexual orientation refers to an enduring pattern of emotional, romantic, and/or sexual attractions to men, women, or both sexes.[2]
2. "Sexual orientation" is the preferred term used when referring to
   an individual's physical and/or emotional attraction to the same
   and/or opposite gender.[3]
3. Sexual orientation . . . is the trait that predisposes us to experience
   sexual attraction to people of the same sex as ourselves (homosexual, gay, or lesbian), to persons of the other sex (heterosexual or
   straight), or to both sexes (bisexual).[4]
4. A person's sexual orientation is based on his or her sexual desires
   and fantasies and the sexual behaviors he or she is disposed to
   engage in under ideal conditions.[5]

To name just a few of the worries that might be raised for these characterizations: (1), (2), and (3) assume binary categories of sex or gender (i.e.,
male/female or men/women);[6] (2) and (3) disagree on whether sexual
orientation concerns gender attraction (attraction to individuals with certain genders) or sex attraction (attraction to individuals with certain sexes); and (4) appeals to the opaque notion of "ideal conditions" for acting
on one's sexual desires (more on these conditions later).

Characterizations like these—assuming they are attempts to elucidate
a shared, preexisting concept of sexual orientation—reveal that we have
an extremely poor grasp of this concept. Moreover, we have good reason
to resist adopting many of these characterizations. Inadequate understandings of sexual orientation can reinforce heteronormative assumptions (i.e., assumptions that heterosexuality should be privileged within
society) by maintaining a majority/minority divide between heterosexuality and other sexual orientations that historically has been normatively
loaded and policed. They also can reinforce cisnormative assumptions
(i.e., assumptions that all persons are cisgender—that all persons' genders are the ones assigned to them at birth on the basis of their anatomy)
by failing to provide recognition or clarity for persons who are not cisgender or who are attracted to persons who are not cisgender within the
sexual orientation taxonomy. (Often this cisnormative assumption is
paired with the views that gender is biologically determined by one's
anatomy, and that gender is essentially a biological, rather than social,
category.)[7]

The conceptual jumble surrounding sexual orientation suggests that
the topic is overripe for analytical philosophical exploration.[8] This essay
lays the groundwork for one such in-depth exploration and, in so doing,
encourages further analytic philosophical discussion of sexual orientation. Its target is twofold: (i) the everyday concept of sexual orientation,

and (ii) the corresponding concepts associated with the taxonomy of sexual orientation (e.g., gay, straight).[9] In particular, my project sets out to *elucidate* and *improve* our everyday concepts of sexual orientation in light of particular theoretical and sociopolitical purposes.[10]

On my proposed account of sexual orientation, Bidimensional Dispositionalism, sexual orientation is based on someone's dispositions to engage in sexual behaviors under "ordinary" conditions (more in section 3).[11] Importantly, this account implies that categories of sexual orientation do *not* refer to the subject's own sex or gender.[12]

In what follows, I assume that sex and gender are real features of persons. I use the terms "male" and "female" to refer to sex categories, though I do not assume that these terms exhaust or refer to discrete sex categories. Similarly, I use the terms "man" and "woman" to refer to gender categories, though I do not assume that these terms exhaust or refer to discrete gender categories.

METHODOLOGY AND FRAMEWORK

In her work on gender, Sally Haslanger points out the importance of distinguishing between three projects that ask a question of the form, What is *x*? One project is conceptual: it asks only about the content of our ordinary concept of *x*. Another is naturalistic: it asks which natural kind (if any) our ordinary concept of *x* tracks. The last project, and the one that best categorizes the methodology of this paper, is what I will call the "engineering project": it asks about the purposes of our concept of *x* and (if necessary) improves or replaces the existing concept to better realize the purposes we want this concept to fulfill.[13] This project takes seriously that, as Alexis Burgess and David Plunkett put it, "our conceptual repertoire determines not only what we can think and say but also, as a result, what we can do and who we can be."[14] Given this important feature of our conceptual repertoire, we can think of the engineering project as one that sets out to elucidate and possibly revise or replace our everyday concepts in light of the impact we would like them to have.

Given that this is an engineering project, we should begin by asking what purposes are ideally served by a concept of sexual orientation. I suggest that an account of sexual orientation should aim toward satisfying the following theoretical needs:

a. Clarifies the criteria for ascribing sexual orientation, as well as how these criteria translate into a taxonomic schema of sexual orientation.

b. Is consistent with relevant social scientific research—in particular, research concerning sex and gender.

    c. Reduces or eliminates the presumption that cisheterosexuality[15] is
       the normatively standard sexual orientation and all queer sexual
       orientations are normatively deviant.[16]
    d. Is conducive for establishing legal and social protections for per-
       sons who have queer sexual orientations.

These purposes are not merely stipulative; someone could disagree
with me concerning whether these purposes should guide our concept of
sexual orientation. I take each of them, though, to be rooted in everyday
political and social realities.

My reasons for adopting (a)–(b) are both theoretical and practical. As
I've shown, sexual orientation is understood in a variety of conflicting
ways—there is disagreement about how to articulate the criteria for ascribing sexual orientation (e.g., in terms of gender or sex attraction), as
well as corresponding disagreement about the taxonomy of sexual orientation. There also are regular confusions between sex and gender, which
suggests that these understandings are not informed by recent research
on the distinction between sex and gender. This alone immediately reveals a need for an elucidation of the concept and taxonomy of sexual
orientation, and possibly a revision ensuring their consistency with relevant research on sex and gender.

More practically, clarifying the criteria for ascribing sexual orientation
(and how they translate into a taxonomic schema of sexual orientation) is
a key ingredient in developing a concept that serves the social and political purposes stated in (c)–(d). Confusions between sex and gender—especially with regard to sexual orientation—regularly create difficulties for
queer, gender non-conforming, and intersex persons, as well as their
partners. How should a gender non-conforming, transgender, or intersex
person (or their partners) describe their sexual orientations? How can or
should non-discrimination laws address these sexual orientations? The
current categories of sexual orientation offer little to no flexibility or clarity for these individuals. For these reasons, the current categories reinforce cisnormativity as well as heteronormativity. That is, because the
current categories place queer orientations in a vast minority and have no
place at all for many transgender or intersex individuals (or persons attracted to these individuals), they perpetuate prejudices that sexual orientations and gender identities that do not meet standard binaries of
homosexual/heterosexual and cisgender man/cisgender woman are
somehow deviant, dysfunctional, or even nonexistent.[17] Ideally, our concept of sexual orientation would rid or at least diminish these harms by
achieving purposes (c)–(d) above, and do so (at least in part) by employing the tools articulated in purposes (a)–(b).

In addition, purposes (c)–(d) constrain my project to construct a concept of sexual orientation that is feasible for public uptake. So, rather than
rebuilding the concept of sexual orientation from scratch, I restrict myself

to engineer a concept that clarifies and improves upon the *preexisting* structure of our everyday concept and—on the basis of this clarification and improvement—rebuilds and expands the taxonomy of sexual orientation.

Given my project's constrained scope, it is important to get a sense of the everyday concept's extension. To this end, I will now argue that we should distinguish the everyday concept of sexual orientation from three other, closely related concepts.

The first is *sexual identity,* which I understand to refer to an individual's self-identification with regard to sexual orientation. Because sexual identity concerns sexual orientation in this way, the concept of sexual identity is sensitive to the concept of sexual orientation. But we also acknowledge that someone can be self-deceived or in denial about their sexual orientation (or even lack the concepts necessary for self-identification) but still be truly said to have the sexual orientation that they fail to recognize. Given this, I will not address sexual identity in what follows.

The second is merely *romantic or emotional attraction.* Some accounts of sexual orientation—for example, that of the American Psychological Association—define sexual orientation in terms of "emotional, romantic, and/or sexual attractions."[18] However, I am not concerned with merely emotional or romantic attraction—with emotional or romantic attractions that have no effect upon one's dispositions toward sexual behavior, and only indirectly concerned with those that do. Should, for example, someone's romantic attractions significantly influence these dispositions, her romantic attractions will be part of what forms her sexual orientation under my account insofar as they have this influence. Any concern with attraction in the sequel will focus upon sexual (and I mean *sexual!*) attraction regardless of whether other forms of attraction accompany it. To clarify this distinction, I will generally forego talk of attraction and instead focus upon dispositions to engage in sexual behaviors.[19]

The third concept to distinguish from sexual orientation is what I call *sexual druthers,* which refers to specific preferences of sexual partners within potential partners according to one's sexual orientation. This is often referred to as someone's "type." Height, hair color, body structure and voice quality are all examples of traits about which people may have sexual druthers. I do not include sexual druthers in my account of sexual orientation, instead focusing upon preferences of sexual partners with regard to sex and gender categories.

Admittedly, the cultural distinction we make between sexual orientation and sexual druthers seems somewhat arbitrary. It is not clear why attraction to certain sexes or genders is considered relevant to one's sexual orientation but not attraction to a certain hair color, race or economic status. But sex and gender are, for better or worse, particularly salient social categories with respect to sexual orientation. As a result, we find ourselves in the position of classifying persons' sexual orientations on the basis of their sex and gender attractions, and not on the basis of other sexual attractions. And this makes persons with particular sex and gender attractions more vulnerable to discrimination than persons with attractions to persons with a certain hair color or economic status. No one is interested in creating nondiscrimination laws to protect people attracted to blondes or baritones. We are, though, interested in creating legal and social protections for queer, transgender and gender non-conforming persons. I will therefore retain these boundaries and separate sexual orientation from sexual druthers.

BIDIMENSIONAL DISPOSITIONALISM

In what follows, I propose a concept of sexual orientation that is designed to satisfy purposes (a)–(d). However, I first address two issues that constrain and shape my concept of sexual orientation: the distinctions between sex and gender and between behaviorism and dispositionalism.

1. Preliminary Issues

1.a. Sex and Gender

As mentioned, previous accounts of sexual orientation typically make the mistake of equating and assuming binary categories of sex and gender. They often also analyze sexual orientation in terms of either sex attraction to the exclusion of gender attraction or vice versa. The first of these mistakes assumes cisnormativity.[20] The second assumes that sexual orientation is unidimensional—that sexual attraction tracks either sex or gender, but never both.

The cisnormative assumption was famously challenged by Simone de Beauvoir, who marked sex as a biological category and gender as a cultural construction.[21] While the details of de Beauvoir's ideas have been challenged and adapted in contemporary discussions, her distinction is standardly recognized in psychology, sociology, and queer and women's studies, as well as in philosophical work on gender.[22] Not only is the distinction theoretically useful, dividing what are clearly distinct phenomena, but it is also politically and socially advantageous. For one, it provides a helpful framework through which to understand the gender identity of, for example, gender nonconforming, androgynous, and transgender individuals. It also creates an avenue for addressing the ways in which gender categories can be altered to combat patriarchal social structures.[23] For all (but certainly not only) these reasons, I place the following constraint on my account of sexual orientation:

> (i) The account must be compatible with the distinction between sex and gender.

Once the cisnormative assumption is dismissed, the unidimensional assumption also should be. The distinction between sex and gender allows for various combinations of sex and gender across individuals, making it clear that an account of sexual orientation should be sensitive to the fact that individuals may be sexually attracted to a variety of these sex/gender combinations.[24] For example, someone may be attracted only to transgender men who have not had gender-confirmation surgery, or only to cisgender men and women. Given this, I place a further constraint on my account of sexual orientation:

> (ii) The account must allow individuals' sexual orientations to involve both gender attraction and sex attraction.

Someone can accept (i), yet resist (ii), arguing that sex attraction (or gender attraction) should be taken as a mere sexual druther, allowing sexual orientation to remain unidimensional. Consider, for example, someone who is attracted to women and not men, but is only attracted to cisgender women. Why think that this latter attraction is anything more than a sexual druther? That is, why should we think that someone attracted only to cisgender women has a different *sexual orientation* than someone attracted to both transgender and cisgender women? This line of argument might suggest that, while we preserve the extension of our ordinary sexual orientation concept, we should make the relevant criteria for ascribing sexual orientation only gender attraction (or only sex attraction) and also categorize sexual orientations along only one of these dimensions.

There are a number of considerations against thinking of sex attractions (or gender attractions) as mere sexual druthers. The two most weighty (and related) considerations are: (i) the frequency with which people experience sexual attraction not only to individuals with particular gendered features but also to individuals with particular primary and secondary sex characteristics, and (ii) the need to recognize the community of persons who are exclusively (or strongly) attracted to transgender individuals, or who are themselves transgender and seeking persons with these attractions.[25] Only by allowing our concept of sexual orientation to include both gender and sex attraction will we be able to locate these persons in our sexual orientation taxonomy.

That aside, (i) and (ii) do not resolve the issue of whether sex or gender (and therefore sexual orientation) should be understood as containing discrete or continuous categories. But this neutrality is, I think, appropriate for a general account of sexual orientation. Understanding sexual orientations as discrete or continuous should piggyback on, and not decide, understanding sex and gender categories as discrete or continuous. And, unlike distinguishing between sex and gender, the debate over this issue has not reached a clear consensus.[26]

1.b. Behaviorism and Dispositionalism

The previous subsection argued that we should take sexual orientation to involve both sex and gender attraction. But it is not clear how to assess these attractions in order to determine someone's sexual orientation. The following discussion compares two main approaches to this task: *behaviorism* and *dispositionalism*.

Behaviorism: One way of understanding sexual orientation is as nothing over and above (i.e., reducible to) one's *observable* behaviors—as something solely concerning behavior and not at all concerning psychological states, except perhaps states that can be in turn reduced to behavior. We can understand this view—behaviorism—as the following claim:

> A person's sexual orientation is determined solely by their observable sexual behavior.[27]

In other words, under a behaviorist account, an individual's sexual orientation is decided simply by looking at their sexual behaviors, and seeing what sex(es) and gender(s) of persons they sexually engage with. For example, if they only sexually engage with cisgender men, their sexual orientation is ascribed accordingly.

An immediate difficulty for behaviorism is determining what behaviors and span of time are relevant to someone's sexual orientation. Even setting this aside, though, three more egregious problems remain.[28] First, behaviorism doesn't allow that individuals can behaviorally repress their sexual orientation. Consider, for example, the case of Episcopal Bishop Gene Robinson, a cisgender man who, after privately identifying himself as gay during seminary, was married and faithful to a cisgender woman for fifteen years.[29] Cases like these are extremely common within the LGBTQ community—under extreme social pressure to conform to cisheteronormativity, many individuals enter so-called straight relationships and so behaviorally (if not also psychologically) repress their sexual desires. Additionally, homeless LGBTQ persons are often forced into prostitution, thereby sexually engaging with individuals of sexes and genders that these persons do not find sexually desirable.[30]

But by behaviorist lights, it is correct to categorize these individuals' sexual orientations according to their coerced behaviors, rather than according to their (freely or forcibly) behaviorally repressed desires. This is a bad result. Because sexual behavior can be—and for LGBTQ persons, frequently is—coerced by societal pressures, we must understand sexual orientation as something "deeper" than observable behavior. Even if influenced by social pressures, sexual orientation cannot be explicitly forced upon someone by these pressures.[31] To deny this is to do an injustice to a large number of LBGTQ persons, especially in countries where queer sexual behavior can result in prison or even death.

Two other, related problems for behaviorism regard its implications for voluntary celibates and persons who are not sexually active, as well as sexually active persons in situations lacking a variety of potential sexual partners (e.g., prisons and boarding schools). Behaviorism wrongly dictates that persons in the first situation either lack a sexual orientation or ought to be classified as asexual, and that the sexual orientation of persons in the second situation should be determined with no regard to the extremity of their circumstances. These, too, are bad results, and ones that blatantly conflict with the general extension of our everyday concept of sexual orientation.

Dispositionalism: A plausible account of sexual orientation should account for situationally specific sexual behaviors. Behaviorism fails to do this. And yet behaviorism admittedly captures something important about sexual orientation: our concept of sexual orientation tracks (with qualifications) sexual behavior, and not self- or other-identification, emotions, or *purely* psychological states. But insisting that it concerns only *actual* behavior is, as we have seen, riddled with problems. For this reason, I propose that analyses of sexual orientation should move toward dispositional accounts—that is, accounts that define sexual orientation in terms of individuals' *dispositions* to engage in sexual behaviors with a certain class of persons (rather than their actual sexual behaviors), and that concern psychological states only insofar as they influence individuals' behavioral dispositions.

After assuming this shift to talk of dispositions, though, significant questions remain. A standard account of dispositions tells us that:

> Something X has the disposition to do A in response to being in conditions C just in case, if X were to be in C, it/they would do A.[32]

For example, a match is disposed to light in response to being struck if and only if, were the match to be struck, it would light. Applying this to sexual orientation, we can let X stand for a person, and let A stand for engagement in sexual behavior (broadly construed) with persons of a certain sex and gender. But locating C is a much more complicated task. And without specifying C, dispositionalism gives us:

> A person's sexual orientation is determined solely by what sex(es) and gender(s) of persons S is disposed to sexually engage under *some* conditions.

This claim is enough to get us to the idea that there is *some* particular basis of sexual orientation—namely, relevant sexual behavioral dispositions. Without specifying the conditions under which these relevant dispositions manifest, though, we have not made much headway beyond behaviorism. To assign *actual* conditions to C would make the view indistinguishable from behaviorism—if the manifesting conditions are actual conditions, then the relevant dispositions should be those dispositions manifested in actual conditions—that is, actual behaviors. And this is what we wanted to avoid. To capture the general extension of our everyday concept, we will need a different theory of what circumstances manifest these dispositions—one less narrow than "actual conditions," and more informative than, say, "all the physical facts."

We can identify these conditions by looking at the purpose of the disposition. Because, for example, we apply the term "flammable" to matches when we want to determine whether it will light when it is struck in normal temperatures, when dry, and so on, we know that these conditions are the ordinary manifesting conditions for the disposition. In the case of sexual orientation, then, the manifesting conditions for the behavioral dispositions relevant to determining sexual orientation must be understood within the framework of the purpose behind the operative concept of sexual orientation—finding potential partners, establishing laws (be they protective or discriminatory), predicting behavior, scientific research of sexual attraction, and so on.[33] These purposes determine the "ordinary" conditions under which the term is applied.

More needs to be said about what these ordinary conditions are: What *is* the operative concept of "sexual orientation"? What conditions lie behind our ascriptions of sexual orientation?

Similarly to the discussion of sexual druthers, I will not pretend to give necessary and sufficient conditions for the operative concept of "sexual orientation"—nor do I maintain that such conditions exist. The conditions determining our ascriptions of sexual orientation admit, no doubt, of borderline and vague cases. Still, a number of things can be said. I propose the following as conditions constraining our ascriptions of sexual orientation—as elements of the operative concepts—reminding the reader to think of these as generalities that admit of exception and vagueness, rather than as strict rules of use.

(I) *The operative concept assumes attraction to persons of a certain sex or gender (at least partially) because they are that sex and/or gender.* For example, say that Elijah has strong sexual druthers for persons with long hair but no preference between men or women as sexual partners. Elijah lives in a town where the only people with long hair happen to be women. As a result, it is true to say that Elijah is attracted only to women. But because he is not attracted to them *because* they are women, we would not say that Elijah has the sexual orientation corresponding to exclusive attraction to women.[34] This sort of case illustrates that we expect an explanatory relation to hold between one's sexual orientation and the sex or gender of the persons they are attracted to.

(II) *The operative concept assumes attraction to certain persons while having a reasonable diversity of potential sexual partners.* This generalization is intended to capture why we do not consider behaviors in outlying circumstances where potential partners are extremely limited or homogenous (e.g., prisons, boarding schools, deserted islands) as reliable indicators of one's sexual orientation.

(III) *The operative concept assumes that one is willing and able to sexually engage with other persons.* We refuse to ascribe sexual orientations to someone on the basis of their actual sexual behaviors if, for example, they are voluntarily celibate, subject to sexual contact without consent, or possess a prohibitive medical condition. These scenarios indicate that it is also important to the operative concept of "sexual orientation" that the behaviors relevant to ascribing sexual orientation are ones that are engaged in willingly and with the physical and psychological ability to engage or not engage in the behavior.[35] It might also explain why we judge abnormal sexual behavior under the influence of alcohol or narcotics (and therefore, nonconsensual) to be an unreliable indicator of sexual orientation.

Again, (I)–(III) are generalizations of the conditions that I think are built into the operative concept of sexual orientation, and will therefore admit of occasional exceptions or borderline cases. They remain, though, useful guidelines explaining why we consider extreme circumstances poor guides to determining sexual orientation, and how we can reliably ascribe sexual orientation to persons.

2. Bidimensional Dispositionalism

Putting together the previous discussions of gender/sex and behaviorism/dispositionalism, we arrive at my positive proposal:

> *Bidimensional Dispositionalism (BD)*: A person S's sexual orientation is grounded[36] in S's dispositions to engage in sexual behaviors under the ordinary condition(s) for these dispositions,[37] and which sexual orientation S has is grounded in what sex(es) and gender(s) of persons S is disposed to sexually engage under these conditions.[38]

In other words, I propose that—whatever the categories we place within "sexual orientation"—their ascription should be based on the sex and gender of the persons someone is disposed to sexually engage with under ordinary conditions for ascribing sexual orientation.[39]

This analysis recasts sexual orientation as pertaining to bidimensional attraction—as pertaining to both sex *and* gender attraction. But, importantly, BD does not require that, in order to be ascribed a sexual orientation, someone must have a certain sex attraction or gender attraction. One could be neutral as to one or both, or one can be attracted to neither (i.e., be asexual with regard to sex and gender). All of this would be revealed by their dispositions to engage (which could be dispositions to never engage) in sexual behavior with certain persons (at least partially) on the basis of their sex and gender.[40]

By emphasizing only these dispositions, BD understands sexual orientation *solely in terms of the sex and gender of the persons one is disposed to*

sexually engage, without reference to the sex or gender of the person so disposed.
Under this framework, for example, a cisgender man and transgender
woman disposed to sexually engage only with cisgender women have
the same sexual orientation, and so too for a cisgender man and gender-
nonconforming female disposed to engage only with men. In emphasizing this shift in our categories of sexual orientation, BD rejects the idea
that sexual orientation can be classified in terms of a relation between
persons of the "same" or "opposite" sex or gender.

This taxonomical shift is important to the fulfillment of purposes
(c)–(d). Recall that these purposes stated that an analysis of sexual orientation should "reduce or eliminate the presumption that cisheterosexuality is the normatively standard sexual orientation and all queer sexual
orientations are normatively deviant," and be "conducive for establishing
legal and social protections for non-cisheterosexual persons." The categorization shift proposed by BD moves us closer to accomplishing both
of these tasks.

First, BD promotes the aims of purpose (c) because BD *eliminates the
distinction between cisheterosexuality and queer sexual orientations* and *provides a taxonomic schema capable of recognizing persons outside the gender or
sex binaries.* On the former point, on BD, there are no such sexual orientations as "homosexual" or "heterosexual." And there is no distinction between the sexual orientations of, for example, a cisgender man and a
transgender woman who both are exclusively attracted to women. The
statistical divide between cisheterosexuality and queer sexual orientations simply disappears because these categories disappear, and their
members are reorganized into new categories. While this will not of itself
eliminate discriminatory attitudes, it does change the concept of "sexual
orientation" such that it does not simply fall out of the concept that cisheterosexuality is statistically standard, and all else is deviant. It also re-
moves the connotation that "sexual orientation" is what distinguishes,
for example, the so-called straight and queer communities. This is a socially and politically beneficial result, encouraging dismantling the divide between these communities.

On the latter point, BD does not build in either discrete or binary
gender or sex categories, and so has the flexibility to adopt a variety of
sex and gender taxonomies. With this flexibility, it is capable of providing
taxonomic recognition for persons outside the sex or gender binaries
(e.g., gender queer or intersex persons), as well as their sexual partners.

Second, BD achieves (or at least moves toward achieving) purpose (d)
by providing the conceptual tools for lawmakers to secure protections for
sexual orientation under preexisting protections against gender and sex
discrimination. That is, because sexual orientation makes no reference to
one's *own* sex and gender on BD, any discrimination against someone in
response to their sexual orientation can be redescribed as discrimination
on the basis of their gender or sex.

This conceptual shift is, in fact, ripe for public uptake. Supreme Court Chief Justice John Roberts recently articulated a similar shift in thought during oral argument in *Henry v. Hodges*, a case concerning the legalization of same-sex marriage. Justice Roberts redescribed the same-sex marriage question in terms of sex discrimination, and (perhaps rhetorically) asked why the issue could not be decided on the basis of preexisting protections against sex discrimination: "I'm not sure it's necessary to get into sexual orientation to resolve this case. . . . I mean, if Sue loves Joe and Tom loves Joe, Sue can marry him and Tom can't. And the difference is based on their different sex. Why isn't that a straightforward question of sexual discrimination?"[41]

As Justice Roberts here notes, cases of sexual orientation discrimination can be easily redescribed in terms of gender or sex discrimination by holding fixed that multiple individuals share the same sex or gender attractions, and yet some are discriminated against simply because they have a particular sex or gender in addition to those attractions. BD goes a step further by saying that the sex and gender attractions—again, understanding these attractions in terms of behavioral dispositions under ordinary conditions—are all that matter for sexual orientation. My own sex and gender, for example, do not matter for my sexual orientation. And so, if I am discriminated against for having the attractions constituting sexual orientation X and a man who has sexual orientation X is not discriminated against, I can recast this discrimination as gender discrimination and appeal to preexisting laws prohibiting this discrimination as the basis for my legal protection.

One worry about BD is that it does not give us enough epistemic access to our own sexual orientations. How will we know our sexual orientation if it would require being placed under circumstances that we are not actually in? How could, say, a lifelong celibate priest *know* that they would take certain actions if they were under these "ordinary circumstances"? It might seem as though any compelling account of sexual orientation will make it possible for someone to know their own sexual orientation, and BD does not do this.[42]

This objection, though, makes a substantive assumption: that the correct metaphysical analysis of sexual orientation must bend to a demand for (something close to) epistemological transparency. I see no reason to think this. In fact, we have good reason to deny it, given the many examples of repression and self-deception of sexual orientation under social, religious, or familial expectations, for example.[43] But this does not mean that we have no idea what our sexual orientations are—in general, people seem to have a "good enough" idea of their sexual attractions and how they do or would act under certain circumstances that they also have a "good enough" idea of the sexual orientation to seek out specific (or no) sexual partners. Insofar, too, as we think that persons have some manner of epistemic privilege in self-assessments of desire, attraction, and so on—features that inform and direct their behavioral dispositions—we can maintain that persons also have some manner of epistemic privilege in self-ascribing sexual orientation.

Another worry for BD concerns the relation between sexual dispositions and sexual desires. Why, someone might ask, should we go to the trouble of analyzing sexual orientation in terms of dispositions and all their metaphysical baggage, when we can much more simply analyze it in terms of sexual desire, understood as an occurrent mental state?

My central response to this is to point out that, currently, we have little scientific evidence that suggests that a single mental state is the basis of sexual orientation. That is, regardless of what mental state someone thinks is picked out by the term "desire," I see no reason why we should think that this mental state (or even states) is always the basis for sexual orientation. Unlike a sexual desire view of sexual orientation, then, BD allows sexual behavioral dispositions to result from a range of categorical psychological bases (or no categorical basis), and certainly does not restrict the relevant dispositions to ones grounded in the mental states that we would call "sexual desire." For example, if someone is attracted to women on the basis of, say, a constant curiosity about what it is like to have sex with women, but not because of desire-like attitudes typically considered sexual attraction, my account does not rule out that this person can be classified as sexually women-oriented.

CONCLUSION AND IMPLICATIONS

I consider BD only the beginning of a full analytic account of sexual orientation. This does not mean, however, that BD is an uncontroversial thesis. To clarify this, I will briefly state its central implications.

First, to adopt BD is to reject our current taxonomy of sexual orientation. The assumptions that sexual orientation is always one-dimensional—concerning either sex attraction or gender attraction, but never a combination of the two—and that sexual orientation concerns the sex or gender of *both* potential partners are deeply embedded within the concepts associated with these categories. For this reason, the current concepts of "homosexual" and "heterosexual" do not pick out sexual orientations under BD. These terms inherently refer to a relation between the sexes (or genders) of sexual partners, whereas BD focuses exclusively on the sex and gender of the persons one is attracted to.

Second, BD implies—but does not necessitate—that we should reject biological essentialism about sexual orientation. This again comes on the heels of BD's incorporation of both sex and gender attraction in its analysis of sexual orientation. Third, and also for this reason, BD implies that the categories of sexual orientation ought to be continuous, rather than discrete. Contemporary research suggests that the categories of gender (and perhaps sex) are continuous, and so any dispositions related to gender (including the ones at issue in BD) must be sensitive to this continuous scale. This has political and social implications, as it raises questions about how to understand sexual orientation as a protected class or legal decisions concerning sexual orientation, and it puts pressure on the idea that cisheterosexuality (or any sexual orientation) is normative or non-deviant.

Fourth, because BD appeals to the "ordinary conditions" for ascribing sexual orientation, it requires that we hesitate in ascribing any category of sexual orientation to an individual on the basis of their behavior without first carefully considering their social context. This hesitation is particularly required when considering persons under such contexts as religious, situational, or familial pressures to partner with someone of a certain sex or gender, as well as any cross-cultural applications of our categories of sexual orientation.

Though not directly tied to BD, I also hope to have shown that the issues surrounding sexual orientation need further philosophical analysis. A vast number of questions about essentialism, dispositions, choice, reduction, social kinds, and properties—not to mention the political and ethical implications of our answers—remain unexplored. BD only scratches the surface of this promising philosophical landscape.[44]

NOTES

1. Lady Gaga, "Born This Way," *Born This Way*, Abbey Road Studios, 2011.
2. The American Psychological Association, *Answers to Your Questions: For a Better Understanding of Sexual Orientation and Homosexuality* (Washington, DC, 2008), www. apa.org/topics/sorientation.pdf; accessed December 4, 2016.
3. Human Rights Campaign, *Sexual Orientation and Gender Identity: Terminology and Definitions*, 2014, http://www.hrc.org/resources/entry/sexual-orientation-and-gender-identity-terminology-and-definitions; accessed December 4, 2016.
4. Simon LeVay, *Gay, Straight, and the Reason Why: The Science of Sexual Orientation* (Oxford: Oxford University Press, 2011), 1.
5. Edward Stein, *The Mismeasure of Desire: The Science, Theory, and Ethics of Sexual Orientation* (Oxford: Oxford University Press, 1999), 45.
6. I am here understanding sex as a classification solely on the basis of biological characteristics, and gender as a classification (at least in part) on the basis of social situatedness. For more on this distinction, see the section "Bidimensional Dispositionalism." Also, I acknowledge that gender identity (the gender one self-attributes) and gender expression (the external characteristics and behaviors that are socially interpreted as communicating that one belongs to a certain gender category) can come apart. In this chapter, talk of gender attraction is most easily understood as attraction to certain gender expressions, but I leave open that persons' gender identities can also play a role in gender attraction.
7. Throughout this chapter, I will use "their" as a gender-neutral singular pronoun. If you take grammatical issue with this, I encourage you with all good will to incorporate a gender-neutral singular pronoun of your own choosing into ordinary English discourse.

8. While sexual orientation has received little attention in the analytical tradition, the continental tradition has a rich history of thinking about sexual orientation. See, for example, Michel Foucault, *The History of Sexuality. Volume 1: An Introduction*, trans. Robert Hurley (New York: Vintage Books, 1990), and David Halperin, *One Hundred Years of Homosexuality and Other Essays on Greek Love* (New York: Routledge, 1990), and *How to Do the History of Homosexuality* (Chicago: University of Chicago Press, 2002).

9. These concepts are highly interwoven, since the concept of "sexual orientation" constrains the taxonomy. For example, a concept of "sexual orientation" that centrally concerns a relation between a subject's own sex (or gender) and the sex (or gender) of the persons to whom they are attracted will imply a taxonomy containing correspondingly relational concepts.

10. For this reason, my project also is limited in scope: the proposed concept and taxonomy of sexual orientation are not meant to apply across any cultural context. Instead, my project constructs a concept that is both responsive to and critical of our everyday thinking in contemporary Western society about sexual orientation.

11. Acknowledging that some people wholly lack dispositions to sexually engage with other persons on the basis of sex or gender attractions will include asexuality with regard to sex and gender among the class of sexual orientations.

12. On this view, for example, a man and a woman who both are attracted to cisgender women have the same sexual orientation.

13. See Sally Haslanger, "Gender and Race: (What) Are They? (What) Do We Want Them to Be?" *Noûs* 34:1 (2000), 31–55, at 32–33. Haslanger calls this the "analytic project." However, in order to distinguish it from "conceptual analysis," which is more akin to the "conceptual project," I will refer to it throughout as the "engineering project." In addition, though I do not want to take a strong stance on the nature of concepts, I loosely understand concepts here as ways of representing the world. I mean this, though, in a deflationary sense that remains neutral on the issue of whether concepts can carry non-descriptive, expressive content.

14. Alexis Burgess and David Plunkett, "Conceptual Ethics I," *Philosophy Compass* 8:12 (2013), 1091–1101, at 1091.

15. As will become clear in the subsequent section, because I understand sexual orientation as concerning both sex and gender, I reject the idea that heterosexuality picks out a specific sexual orientation. I believe that talk about "heterosexuality" in ordinary discourse is usually talk about "cisheterosexuality"—that is, the attraction of a cisgender woman to a cisgender man or vice versa.

16. I use the term "queer" to mean something like "not cisheterosexual." For reasons that hopefully become clear, I intentionally avoid terms such as "same-sex," "homosexual," and so forth.

17. Consider, for example, the well-recognized phenomenon known as "bisexual erasure" (a tendency to explain away or simply deny evidence that persons are attracted to both men and women, or on alternative accounts, females and males). See, for example, Heron Greenesmith, "Drawing Bisexuality Back into the Picture: How Bisexuality Fits into the LGBT Strategy Ten Years After Bisexual Erasure," *Cardozo Journal of Law and Gender* 17:1 (2010), 65–80, and Stein's critiques of the binary operationalization of sexual orientation in scientific studies in *The Mismeasure of Desire*.

18. The American Psychological Association, *Answers to Your Questions*.

19. Michael Rea raises the interesting question of what this distinction (between emotional/romantic attraction and sexual orientation) implies for someone who lacks dispositions to engage in sexual behaviors (perhaps, e.g., due to chronic deficiency of sex hormones), but who has higher-order desire for sexual intimacy. Does having only this higher-order desire preclude such persons from having a sexual orientation? I would answer "no"—not so long as we consider asexuality a sexual orientation. Asexuality is generally understood as the lack of sexual attraction, or lack of first-order desire to have sexual content with someone else (see, e.g., the Asexual Visibility & Education Network *General FAQ*, 2012, http://www.asexuality.org/?q=general.html, accessed June 20, 2017). Asexuals can and often do experience romantic or emotional

attractions, though. And they might have higher-order desire to experience first-order sexual desire or sexual intimacy. A person in the situation that Rea describes seems, for these reasons, to be best categorized as asexual.

20. See note 2 for a rough definition of "cisnormativity."

21. See Ásta Kristjana Sveinsdóttir, "The Metaphysics of Sex and Gender." In *Feminist Metaphysics: Explorations in the Ontology of Sex, Gender and the Self*, edited by Charlotte Witt (Dordrecht, the Netherlands: Springer, 2011), 48. As de Beauvoir famously said, "One is not born, but rather becomes, a woman."

22. For an overview of recent philosophical approaches to sex and gender, as well as the interaction between philosophical approaches and other (e.g., psychology, political) approaches to sex and gender, see Mari Mikkola, "Feminist Perspectives on Sex and Gender," *The Stanford Encyclopedia of Philosophy*, edited by Edward N. Zalta, 2012 (http://plato.stanford.edu/archives/fall2012/entries/feminism-gender/; accessed December 4, 2016).

23. See, for example, Haslanger, "Gender and Race."

24. I take it to be a fairly uncontroversial assumption that we can experience sexual attraction to purely physical characteristics as well as gendered characteristics. Given this, we can begin to see how sexual orientation is significantly dependent upon both biological traits and particular social contexts. For example, if we hold that sexual orientation concerns (at least in part) gender attraction, and that gender is merely a social construct, sexual orientation will be dependent on placement in that context that has the same gender constructs.

25. Of course, some transgender people are able and elect to undergo hormone therapy and gender confirmation surgery in order to have physical features stereotypically associated with their gender—my focus here is on attraction to persons for whom this is not the case.

26. Conditions (i) and (ii) are also intended to be neutral with regard to whether we can in the future adopt *further* dimensions of sexual orientation, and subsequently expand our concept of sexual orientation.

27. Alternatively, Edward Stein describes this as the view that "a person's sexual orientation is indexed to his or her sexual behavior" (*The Mismeasure of Desire*, 42).

28. For further discussion of the merits and demerits of behaviorism, see Stein, *The Mismeasure of Desire*.

29. Gene Robinson, *God Believes in Love: Straight Talk about Gay Marriage* (New York: Knopf, 2012).

30. See Nicholas Ray, "Lesbian, Gay, Bisexual and Transgender: An Epidemic of Homelessness" (New York: National Gay and Lesbian Task Force Policy Institute and the National Coalition for the Homeless, 2006), http://www.thetaskforce.org/downloads/HomelessYouth.pdf; accessed December 4, 2016.

31. See, for example, the near-universal recognition of the total failure of so-called reparative therapy.

32. Sungho Choi, "Dispositional Properties and Counterfactual Conditionals," *Mind* 117:468 (2008), 795–841, at 796. For simplicity, I have removed the variable ranging across times.

33. While these purposes at bottom will result in the same behaviors as the purposes behind the manifest concept of sexual orientation, they importantly differ in the interpretation of those behaviors. Whereas those applying the term "sexual orientation" may take themselves to be, for example, identifying moral failing or categorizing psychological defects, this is simply using fictions as a mask for what Sally Haslanger calls the "explicitly social content of the operative concept" (*Resisting Reality: Social Construction and Social Critique* [Oxford: Oxford University Press, 2012], 92). So, too, those applying the term may take the manifesting conditions relevant to sexual orientation to be anything from "having certain genetics" to "being cursed by God," but these cannot be the conditions we are concerned with. We are instead concerned with the conditions that *actually* determine application of the term "sexual orientation," regardless of what someone thinks they are doing when applying it.

34. Or because Elijah *thinks* they are women. This would leave room for cases in which, for example, someone attracted to cisgender men is attracted to someone they take to be a cisgender man, but who is in fact female.

35. Of course, some (and perhaps all) asexual persons will never be in a situation in which they are willing to engage in sexual behavior. In that case, we can determine that, because it is impossible for them to meet condition III, they do not have any sexual behavioral dispositions that would be manifested under the ordinary conditions; that is, they are asexual. This distinguishes asexuals from, for example, voluntary celibates.

36. I use the term "grounding" here in the loose sense of "is dependent on" or "is derivative of." One may also be able to understand it in terms of "is built on," which (roughly) means "is less fundamental than" or "is accounted for in terms of" (see Karen Bennett, *Making Things Up* [Oxford University Press, forthcoming]).

37. I remain neutral on the debate over whether properties can have dispositional essences or if all dispositions reduce to categorical properties. For my purposes here, I don't have a dog in that fight.

38. As Shamik Dasgupta pointed out (in person), someone might be concerned that BD, as stated, does not ensure that the dispositions relevant to sexual orientation are particularly "deep" or "self-disclosing." Sexual orientation, one might think, deserves protection *because* it is deep and in this way outside (or mostly outside) a person's control. While I acknowledge this worry, I disagree with the idea that sexual orientation must be particularly "deep" to merit special protections. Whether or not sexual orientation has these features is orthogonal to its merit for protection. Even if we shifted sexual orientation every week (and even if we could do so by choice), I would insist that sexual orientation deserves protections. However, one might worry that even apart from questions of protections, an account of sexual orientation should ensure that sexual orientation is a "deep" and unchangeable (or nearly unchangeable) feature of who someone is. I want to remain neutral on this question, and so the formulation of BD allows but does not require someone's sexual orientation to undergo frequent shifts.

It is important to note that by "sex(es) and gender(s) of persons . . ." I do not mean to imply that there must be any particular persons of this sex and gender, or particular persons with whom S is disposed to sexually engage. That is, S can be disposed to engage with persons who are cisgender women even if there were no cisgender women, or even if there were no particular cisgender women with whom S is disposed to engage.

39. While I will not address this issue here, we arguably should also acknowledge that these dispositions themselves come in a range of strengths, which would add a third dimension to sexual orientation. (Thanks to Justin Christy for this suggestion.)

40. I expect that we are often attracted to certain persons because they have characteristics that are associated with particular genders, and not because of the totality of their gender expression. For my purposes, this sort of connection is sufficient to allow for the explanatory connection between gender and attraction, though it leaves many open questions regarding what (if anything) is essential to particular gender expressions, and more generally, how we should think about the constitution of gender expressions. I leave these questions to persons working in the metaphysics of gender.

41. Quoted in Adam Liptak, "Gender Bias Issue Could Tip Chief Justice Roberts into Ruling for Gay Marriage," *New York Times*, 2015 (http://nyti.ms/1OD08RL; accessed December 4, 2016). This argument in favor of legalizing same-sex marriage on the basis of preexisting laws against sex discrimination was also the central argument of an *amicus curiae* brief filed by a number of legal scholars in *Henry v. Hodges*, Supreme Court Case No. 14-556.

42. Thanks to Peter Finnochiaro for raising this objection.

43. Indeed, the testimony of many queer persons suggests that discovery of one's own sexual orientation can be a long and difficult process.

44. Many thanks to David Black, Judith Card, Justin Christy, Shamik Dasgupta, Esa Diaz-Leon, Peter Finnochiaro, Vera Flocke, Sarah-Jane Leslie, David Plunkett, Michael Rauschenbach, Michael Rea, Cat Saint Croix, Father Raphael Mary Salzillo, O.P., Sami Sumpter, Elizabeth Victor, Ted Warfield, and audiences at Princeton University, Notre Dame, UC Irvine's Perspectives on Gender Conference, the New York Society for Women in Philosophy, the 2015 Central APA and the Berkeley Social Ontology Group for helpful feedback and conversation during the development of this chapter. Special thanks as well to two anonymous referees at *Philosophers' Imprint* for insightful comments. As is the case with most philosophy papers, to call this paper "single-authored" does not do justice to the vast amounts of time and energy that others have generously donated to help me develop these ideas.

STUDY QUESTIONS

1. What are the cisnormative and the unidimensional assumptions that underlie some existing conceptions of sexual orientation? Why does Dembroff wish to dispose of these assumptions?
2. Clearly explain the "Bidimensional Dispositionalism" account of sexual orientation, making sure to explain its central concepts and how the view is, according to Dembroff, an improvement over existing views of sexual orientation.
3. Explain in what ways the bidimensional dispositionalist account of sexual orientation meets the four aims that Dembroff lists early in the essay.
4. Explain what the differences are among sexual orientation, romantic attraction, sexual identity, and sexual druthers, according to Dembroff. Focus on sexual druthers: Can you think of examples of objects of attraction that Dembroff would include under "druthers" that you would not? What would such examples be? What effects, if any, would this have on the account of bidimensional dispositionalism?
5. In fleshing out dispositionalism, and in attempting to distinguish it from behaviorism, Dembroff states, "To assign *actual* conditions to C [the conditions under which one engages in sexual behavior] would make the view indistinguishable from behaviorism." Explain why this is so.
6. What is the difference between a sexual desire-based account of sexual orientation and the bidimensional dispositionalist account of sexual orientation? In answering this question, keep in mind Dembroff's example of someone who is attracted to women because of being curious about what it is like to have sex with women. Is the example convincing in what it says about the person's sexual orientation, especially given Dembroff's earlier claim, stated in the example of Elijah who is attracted to people with long hair, that "we expect an explanatory relation to hold between one's sex-

ual orientation and the sex or gender of the persons they are attracted to"?

7. On the ordinary concept of sexual orientation that Dembroff rejects, there is a reference to the person's own sex or gender, and this partly explains why we have two (or three) types of sexual orientations, which, to some, might be a neat way of classifying the world. On bidimensional dispositionalism, how many sexual orientations do we end up with? (Try to list as many as you can.) Is this a benefit or a problem for the account?

8. Dembroff states, "My project sets out to *elucidate* and *improve* our everyday concepts of sexual orientation in light of particular theoretical and sociopolitical purposes" (emphases in the original). For this reason, Dembroff warns us in note 10 that the project is "limited in scope: the proposed concept and taxonomy of sexual orientation are not meant to apply across any cultural context. Instead, my project constructs a concept that is both responsive to and critical of our everyday thinking in contemporary Western society about sexual orientation." Can you imagine or think of another cultural context with different sociopolitical purposes that would necessitate a different account of sexual orientation? More crucially, might culturally limiting the project, as Dembroff desires, threaten to undermine it?

FOURTEEN

Thinking Queerly about Sex and Sexuality

Kim Q. Hall

Kim Q. Hall *explains in this essay some crucial aspects of queer theory, especially in relation to sex and sexuality. Beginning with Michel Foucault's genealogical method and its insights into how sexuality has always been a "site" for the operation of power and the production of "truths" about sex, queer theory has come to be both a critical platform (e.g., criticizing homonormative politics that aim to show that gay people are just like straight people by excluding undesirable members of the diverse sexual community) and an inclusive one, stressing the importance of including, in theory and in practice, those who are socially and politically marginalized. In this vein, queer theory points out that sexual identities are not as fixed as we think they are, that sex and gender are not as tightly linked as we believe, and that we need a new conception of sexual agency that goes beyond the capacity to make sexual choices to involve a sense, on the part of oneself and of society, that one is a sexual being. All these claims have important implications for how we think of a large number of issues, including sex and disability, asexualism, and our connections to the nonhuman animal world.*

Kim Q. Hall is professor of philosophy and Director of Gender, Women's, and Sexuality Studies at Appalachian State University. She is the guest editor of *New Conversations in Feminist Disability Studies*, a special issue of *Hypatia: Journal of Feminist Philosophy*, and she is the editor of *Feminist Disability Studies* (Indiana University Press). Her recent articles include "Cripping Sustainability, Realizing Food Justice" (in *Disability Studies and the Environmental Humanities: Toward an Eco-Crip Theory*, edited by Sarah Jaquette Ray and J. C. Sibara) and "Toward a Queer Crip Feminist Politics of Food" (in *philoSOPHIA: A Journal of Continental Feminism*). © 2017, Kim Q. Hall, who kindly gave permission for her new essay to be included in this volume.

Ever since its emergence as an interdisciplinary academic field in the United States in the early 1990s, queer theory has challenged normalizing

Queer theory ≠ LGBT studies

assumptions about the relationship between sex, gender, sexuality, identity, and embodiment. Queer theory is indebted to analyses of gender and sexuality in feminist, and lesbian, gay, bisexual, and transgender (LGBT) studies, and it offers a critique of identity that challenges the assumption that gender and sexual identities refer in consistent, reliable, and non-contingent ways to a person's experience, inner self, or biology. But despite areas of mutual influence and overlap, LGBT studies and queer theory have somewhat different orientations. While LGBT people, experiences, histories, and cultural productions are the objects of study in LGBT studies, queer theory is critically attuned to the relations of power and knowledge that create the conditions for the emergence of identity categories and the experiences that are presumed to inevitably follow from them—that is, the relations of power and knowledge that make possible gender and sexual subjectivity.[1]

Queer theory's critique of identity has many implications for thinking about sex, sexuality, and erotic justice. In particular, it raises questions about the nature and meaning of sex and sexuality, and the possibility of a "counter-erotics."[2] In this chapter I discuss some of the main themes of queer theory and its contributions to thinking about sex, sexuality, and erotic justice, and I explain how thinking queerly about sex and sexuality is influenced by queer theory's critique of identity, nature, and normalization. The chapter is organized into the following parts: (1) the significance of queer theory's genealogical approach to sexuality; (2) the meaning of queer; (3) queering sex and gender; (4) queerness, disability, and sexual ableism; and (5) queer ecological critiques of human exceptionalism and the nature of sex.

THINKING GENEALOGICALLY ABOUT SEXUALITY

In *The History of Sexuality, Volume 1*, Michel Foucault puts forward a genealogical approach to sexuality that has been foundational for queer theory. Foucault challenged the prevailing assumption that power is repressive, a view he characterized as the "repressive hypothesis" that the history of sexuality is a story of silence and invisibility. The repressive hypothesis implies that speaking about sexuality and making it visible are liberatory acts. Foucault contended that power is not only or even primarily repressive; it is also productive.[3] In other words, rather than silence sexuality and regard it as taboo, Foucault described a "regime of power-knowledge-pleasure" that produced sexuality as an object of scientific knowledge, a target of individual and population management, and a site of self-knowledge. The conception of sexuality as an innate, determined, and determining characteristic of individuals is, Foucault pointed out, historical and, thus, not an inevitable consequence of nature. That is, following Foucault, the categorization of erotic acts and desires into discrete sexualities that form the foundation of sexual identities is an historical occurrence rather than an innate (and thus inevitable) characteristic of human nature.

For Foucault, power produces sexuality as an internal truth that must be known. He writes, "The nineteenth-century homosexual became a personage, a past, a case history, and a childhood, in addition to being a type of life, a life form, and a morphology, with an indiscreet anatomy and possibly a mysterious physiology. Nothing that went into his total composition was unaffected by his sexuality."[4] Thus, contrary to the widespread assumption shared by homophobes and many who advocate for the rights of sexual minorities, Foucault argues that sexuality is not a fixed, determining truth of innate desire. Furthermore, the idea that one's erotic desires and practices make one a certain kind of person, a person who *has* a sexuality, is an effect of power, not an inevitability. Foucault explains how sexuality emerged as a truth about individuals in Western societies. Individuals, he proclaims, do not simply have a sexuality that is either repressed or expressed (or liberated); instead, individuals are compelled to have a sexuality. According to Foucault, power not only produced "the homosexual" as a "type of species"[5] but also made possible a "reverse discourse" in which "homosexuality began to speak in its own behalf, to demand that its legitimacy or 'neutrality' be acknowledged, often in the same vocabulary, using the same categories by which it was medically disqualified."[6]

Foucault's genealogical approach to sexuality made the case for the reconceptualization of sexuality as primarily an epistemic rather than an erotic space.[7] The relations of power and knowledge that inform the desire to know the truth of sexuality produce the very truths about sexuality they purport to merely make visible and describe. As a result, knowing the truth of one's sexuality does not empower and liberate; it is instead a site for the operation of power.[8] As Ladelle McWhorter explains, sexual categorization is neither biologically determined nor neutral.[9] The truth of sexuality must be known, and one must be made to know the truth of one's sexuality.[10]

Foucault's insights about sexual subjectivity have profound implications for queer politics. For example, in an effort to combat homophobic pathologization of same-sex desire, some activists have advanced a "born gay" position: the claim that being gay or lesbian, for instance, is not a choice, and that one is born with particular erotic desires and the sexual identities that are assumed to correspond to them. In other words, the "born gay" view claims that same-sex desire is just as natural as heterosexual desire. However, from a perspective informed by queer theory, people are not born gay any more than one is born a woman or a man.[11] Queer theory denaturalizes gender and sexual subjectivity. If gender and sexuality aren't reflections of an innate nature, there is nothing inevitable about their meaning and relationship. It is certainly understandable why, at least in Western societies, the born-that-way argument is seductive; sexuality is often lived as a feeling that one did not choose and that could not have been otherwise. Nonetheless, even our felt sense of our bodies, identities, and sexual preferences does not exist in a vacuum. As Gayle Salamon explains, "Social construction must not be construed oppositionally to a 'felt sense' of bodily being, for one can contend both that a body [or desire] is socially constructed and that its felt sense is undeniable. . . . Claiming that the body [or desire] *feels* natural is not the same as claiming that it is natural."[12] Instead, our felt sense of our bodies and desires is forged in a sedimented historical context in which gender, sex, and sexuality come to have meaning and intelligibility.[13]

While Foucault's influence in the development of queer theory is undeniable, it is important to not universalize his account of sexuality. Foucault offers a specifically Western genealogy of sexuality, and many theorists question whether it applies to the meaning and experience of sexuality in non-Western societies.[14] In his account of being an Africa-based queer scholar, Keguro Macharia proclaims, "I am a queer scholar. By which I mean to say, I am trained in and identify with a field that does not exist in my present geography."[15] Macharia's point is to make visible and critique how mainstream queer theory ignores its geohistorical locatedness even as it aims to destabilize identity. Macharia elaborates using an example of a Kenyan scholar who says that *tala* is a word used by the Akamba people to describe what he is and a word for which the Western word "queer" is an inadequate translation.[16] He asks, "What would queer studies have to unlearn about its geohistories to encounter *tala* on shared ground? What fluencies would queer studies have to give up to enter into conversation with *tala*?"[17] One of these fluencies concerns queer theory's archive, an archive in which Foucault is a central figure. As Macharia contends, it is only by building on an archive peopled with African writers and theorists that one can begin to develop a theory of intimacy in which blackness "is not an afterthought."[18] U.S.-based theorists of color have also critiqued the white-centeredness of mainstream queer theory and its archive and have sought to rethink sexuality and sexual identity building on histories and experiences of communities of color in the U.S. and on figures such as Gloria Anzaldúa and Audre Lorde.[19] These critiques raise important questions about the meaning of the word "queer" that has shaped mainstream queer theory.

WHAT IS QUEER?

In the early part of the twenty-first century the word "queer" is often used an as an umbrella term to refer to lesbian, gay, bisexual, transgender, and other gender and sexual minorities. When used in this way, queer is intended to encompass all non-dominantly situated gender identities and sexualities (that is, gender identities and sexualities that fall outside heterosexual and binary gender norms). However, "queer" is more than another non-heterosexual sexual identity category. David Halperin writes that "queer" operates "oppositionally and relationally, but not necessarily substantively, not as a positivity but as a positionality, not as a thing, but as a resistance to the norm."[20] In the context of queer erotic politics this understanding of queer has generated trenchant critiques of both heteronormativity and the homonormativity of the mainstream LGBT rights movement in the United States.

Homonormative politics aims for the recognition of sexual minorities as "normal" (meaning not significantly different from heterosexual people) and, thus, as deserving of the rights of full citizenship. In the context of sexual politics, homonormativity posits sexual minorities as deserving of rights because they are good, which means that they participate in "normal," and thus, "good" sex. Gayle Rubin's classic conception of the "charmed circle of sexuality"[21] offers an excellent description of erotophobia in the United States. Sexual desires and practices that count as natural, normal, and good are located inside the charmed circle and are characterized as, among other things, private, monogamous, coupled, and non-commercial, whereas sex that is perverse, abnormal, and unnatural is located outside the charmed circle and includes sadomasochism, nonmonogamy, public sex, and any other practice or desire that falls outside sexual norms. Those whose desires and practices place them outside the charmed circle are stigmatized as deviant and immoral. The charmed circle of sexuality is also racialized and classed. For example, people whose economic survival includes sex work or whose precarious access to stable housing does not provide privacy for sexual encounters are cast out of the charmed circle.[22] Because the homonormative movement has argued that same-sex desires belong to this charmed circle, the discourse of homonormative politics reflects the perspective of the most privileged members of sexual minority communities and advocates for rights, recognition, and inclusion at the expense of members of queer communities whose identities and erotic practices place them outside the charmed circle.[23]

Michael Warner argues that the mainstream LGBT movement's preoccupation with being recognized as normal results in a "desexualized identity politics."[24] Rather than work to transform society based on queer values, assimilationism further stigmatizes queer people who either cannot or will not assimilate to the sex negative norms that characterize homo- and heteronormativity. Warner argues for a queer politics and ethics informed by a repudiation of sexual shame and by queer-affirming ways of being and relating that have emerged in queer sexual cultures.

Warner critiques the mainstream LGBT movement in which "dignity and sex are incompatible."[25] In an effort to change the hearts and minds of homophobic people, the mainstream movement strives to remove the

taint of sex from sexual identities like gay and lesbian. This move produces a desexualized politics that distances itself from queer politics that
have developed in queer communities. One example of queer sexual politics is the critique of efforts to scapegoat and eliminate queer public sex
culture in purported efforts to prevent HIV/AIDS. As Warner argues,
efforts at HIV/AIDS prevention are enhanced when public sex culture is
utilized as a resource rather than demonized.[26] Another example is the
queer critique of efforts to control the conduct of HIV positive people in
ways that demonize and criminalize them and deny them access to sexual experiences.[27]

A queer erotic politics is forged in the sexual and gender diversity of
queer communities and resists the sexual stigma and shame that have
characterized heteronormative responses to desires, identities, and practices labeled "perverse." Warner writes, "When you begin interacting
with people in queer culture . . . [y]ou learn that everyone deviates from
the norm in some context or other, and that the statistical norm has no
moral value. . . . To seek out queer culture, to interact with it and learn
from it, is a kind of public activity. It is a way of transforming oneself,
and at the same time helping to elaborate a commonly accessible
world."[28] Participating in queer cultures is crucial for queer political
movements that resist the privatizing conception of sexuality as mere
lifestyle or a marginal, negligible part of experience.

Regarding identity, the queer in queer theory signals a critical stance
toward representational accounts of identity that assume identity's stability. In a patriarchal and heteronormative society, sex, gender, and sexuality are assumed to follow linearly from each other. That is, biological sex
is assumed to be binary and to determine gender, which is assumed to be
binary and to determine sexuality. So, for example, if one's assigned sex
is male, one is assumed to be, and is assigned, the gender man, and one is
assumed to be heterosexual and to thus desire the opposite sex and gender. This is the presumed normal relationship between sex, gender, and
sexuality, and erotic practices and sexual identities that deviate from that
presumed normal relationship are considered abnormal within a patriarchal and heteronormative society. Queer theorists critique this presumed
natural and determining relationship between sex, gender, and sexuality.

"Queer" is a controversial, fraught term, and Judith Butler stresses the
unresolvable nature of the tension between those who want to reclaim
"queer" and those for whom the term remains a source of injury.[29] For an
older generation of lesbians and gay men in the United States (especially
those who were adolescents in the 1960s or earlier), "queer" was a stigmatizing term of insult and hate, and for many of them the term cannot
be reclaimed. Yet in the early 1990s some (mostly younger) people began
to reclaim the term, and for many activists during that time (such as the
members of Queer Nation), the term stood for an anti-assimilationist, in-
your-face politics. For Butler, "queer" is not a term that unproblematical-

ly refers to a mode of being. What are the borders between those who are included and those who are excluded by the term, and how are those borders maintained?

Contestations over the usefulness, applicability, and legitimacy of identity categories point to the contingencies and instabilities of identity, including sexual and gender identity. Given this, "queer," according to Butler, must be understood and used critically. To be critically queer, Butler asserts, is to understand "queer" as "a site of collective contestation, the point of departure for a set of historical reflections and futural imaginings."[30] "Queer," she continues, is "never fully owned, but always and only redeployed, twisted, queered from a prior usage and in the direction of urgent and expanding political purposes."[31] Butler points out that even terms like "queer" that are meant to be inclusive are informed by exclusions, whereas a democratized politics requires critical awareness of and responsiveness to both the exclusions and inclusions of identity categories.[32] Thus understood, to be critically queer is to be cognizant that terms deemed useful at present will be most likely replaced by other, as-yet-unknown terms in the future.[33] Given its critical stance toward identity, many queer theorists argue that "queer" is best understood as a verb rather than a noun and, as such, queer theorists focus more on what categories of sexuality and gender do rather than on the innate identities and erotic desires they are assumed to represent.[34]

SEX AND GENDER

Queer theory's critique of norms and normalization aims to denaturalize and destabilize the presumed connection between sex and gender.[35] According to Butler, gender is not something that one has as an inevitable result of the body's sexed characteristics. Instead, gender is something one does, and there are more than two ways of doing one's gender.[36] Butler's claim that gender is performative is a claim that there is no reality of gender independent of the acts that materialize it. Binary assumptions about gender fail to attend to the rich multiplicity of genders that have emerged in queer communities.

In *Assuming a Body*, Gayle Salamon builds on Butler and Maurice Merleau-Ponty to propose a phenomenology of transgender men's embodied experiences that challenges assumptions about transgender, sex, and the body.[37] Salamon's analysis aims to undermine the transphobic assumption that the sex one is assigned at birth establishes one's real gender, an assumption that presents transgender people as in denial about their real sex and gender.

Queer theory's denaturalization of sex and gender binaries provides a theoretical ground from which to understand the difference between assigned sex and gender and gender identity and lived embodiment. In

denaturalizing sex and gender, queer feminist theory offers an explanation of what gender and the sexed body are: their lived reality. Furthermore, the meaning of body parts, especially those parts that are taken as
signs of sex, are not unmediated.[38] This insight presents a queer critique
of claims to a true sex and gender, whether those claims are articulated
by transgender or cisgender people.

DISABILITY AND SEXUAL ABLEISM

Michael Warner's conception of a queer politics that aims at destigmat-
ization and accessibility resonates with disability justice movements.[39]
As disability studies scholar Tania Titchkosky argues, access alone is not
synonymous with justice; rather access is a point of departure for critical
questioning that is transformative.[40] Reconceiving access as a "site for
critical questioning" opens public space to transformation through participation of diverse bodies and minds. Within a queer crip feminist politics, erotic justice for disabled people requires access to sex, access that
itself critically questions and transforms ableist, patriarchal, and heteronormative conceptions of sex and desirability.[41]

Crip theory builds on insights in both disability studies and queer
theory to question ableism in queer theory and the uncritical adoption of
a neoliberal paradigm of rights and inclusion on some disability analyses.[42] Crip theorists are interested in the entanglements of compulsory
heterosexuality, compulsory able-bodiedness, and compulsory able-
mindedness—systems of power and knowledge that seek to categorize,
manage, and rehabilitate queer and disabled bodies, minds, and lives. As
Robert McRuer puts it, "Compulsory heterosexuality is intertwined with
compulsory able-bodiedness: both systems work to (re)produce the able
body and heterosexuality. But precisely because these systems depend on
a queer/disabled existence that can never quite be contained, able-bodied
heterosexuality's hegemony is always in danger of collapse."[43] The en-
tanglement of compulsory heterosexuality and compulsory able-bodiedness also makes possible coalitions between queer and disability justice
movements that can potentially expand the meaning of "disability" and
"queer."[44]

Disability studies offers a critique of the medical model of disability,
which conceives of disability as a fact of body-mind impairment in need
of rehabilitation and cure. By contrast, disability studies offer a social
model of disability that conceives of disability as an effect of built envi-
ronments and sociocultural norms. While the medical model understands disability as an individual problem requiring medical intervention, the social model conceives of disability as a justice issue requiring
political movements and social, political, and economic change.

Queerness and disability share a history of medicalization, and both disability studies and queer theory advance critiques of the pathologization of queer and disabled bodies and lives. Nonetheless, many disabled people critique the social model for its failure to attend to the lived realities of limitation and pain that characterize some impairments.[45] Alison Kafer proposes a political and relational model of disability that critiques the medical model's depolitization of disability, rather than medical intervention or medicine per se, and seeks coalitional expansions of the meaning of "disability" that challenge the centrality of diagnosis in definitions of disability and disability identity.[46] Building on Butler's notion of critically queer, crip theory posits the meaning of disability as a site of contestation.[47]

Crip theory's critique of normativity entails a critique of sexual ableism. Sexual ableism is a system of erotic injustice that conceives of disability as incompatible with sex and sexiness and, as a result, desexualizes and denies the sexual agency of disabled people.[48] There are many ways in which sexual access is denied to disabled people in heteronormative, patriarchal, and ableist contexts. For example, disabled people are stereotyped as sexually undesirable, and desire for disabled people is marked as perverse, a pathological deviation from erotic norms.[49] As a result, disabled people are sexually marginalized and denied adequate information about sex and opportunities to exercise sexual agency (especially in institutions), and they can experience sexual shame.[50] Furthermore, as a result of stereotypes that either infantilize or cast them as hypersexual, people with intellectual disabilities are denied sexual agency.[51] Abby Wilkerson defines sexual agency as more than "the capacity to choose, engage in, or refuse sex acts, but a more profound good that is in many ways socially based, involving not only a sense of oneself as a sexual being but also a larger social dimension in which others recognize and respect one's identity."[52] Sexual agency is a crucial component of sexual access.

In resistance to the desexualization of disabled people and denial of their sexual agency, queer crip feminist scholars and activists reconceive disability as desirable and a site for the development of a counter-erotics that challenges narrow, genitally focused understandings of sex in heteronormative, patriarchal, and ableist contexts and expands erotic possibilities. As Wilkerson points out, contrary to hetero- and phallocentric understandings of sex, many people with spinal cord injuries report "a diffuse sexuality, including orgasms centered in the earlobes, nipples, sensitive areas of the neck, and elsewhere."[53] Far from reflecting an absence of sex, these erotic experiences help to enhance awareness of the body's erotic possibilities and in the process challenge heteropatriarchal and ableist norms about what counts as sexy or a sexual act. Sexual access for disabled people also involves understanding the role of surrogates in enabling sexual experience for some disabled people.[54]

For the most part, queer crip analyses posit desexualization and denial of sexual agency as examples of erotic injustice, and posit access to sexual practice and recognition of disabled people as desirable and sexual as examples of erotic justice. However, such conceptions of erotic justice risk further marginalizing and pathologizing disabled people who identify as asexual. It also offers a conception of erotic justice that fails to reckon with the fact that some impairments occasion a loss of the body's capacity to experience the same sexual pleasures one once enjoyed. Such loss can be the occasion of grief. The challenge for queer crip approaches to erotic justice is to critique desexualization without naturalizing and normalizing sexual desire as a necessary part of personhood[55] and to expand awareness of the body's erotic possibilities while acknowledging some disabled people's sexual grief at a loss of capacity for forms of sexual activity and pleasure that were once a source of joy.[56]

In relation to Western norms of sexuality, disabled people are presumed asexual, and asexuality itself is pathologized.[57] Using a queer crip approach to sexuality can reveal connections between the sexual marginalization and possibilities for sexual agency of both disabled and asexual people, as well as disabled people who are asexual. On the banner of its homepage the Asexual Visibility and Education Network (AVEN) defines "an asexual person" as "a person who does not experience sexual attraction."[58] Eunjung Kim offers a broader definition of "asexuality" as "a relative absence or insufficiency of sexual interest, biologically and socially described function, and interpersonal sexual engagement."[59] There is a great deal of diversity among asexual people. For instance, not all asexuals are sex-repulsed, and some are romantic (open to intimacy with one or more people), while others are aromantic. AVEN's participation in the 2009 San Francisco LGBT Pride Parade sparked controversy among some queer people, raising questions about what it means to consider sex as central to being queer.[60] However, as Kim points out, asexuality shares with queerness and disability a history of marginalization and pathologization.[61] Both queerness and disability are marked as abnormal in relation to the norm that establishes sexual desire as part of human nature, what it means to be human. Kim argues that erotic justice must distinguish between "[a]sexuality as embodied identity and asexuality as imposed stigma."[62] Sexual agency is not only about choices regarding whether to participate or refrain from participating in sexual activity; a queer crip approach to sexual agency also expands its scope to include expressions of no interest in sexual activity with another person.

HUMAN EXCEPTIONALISM AND THE NATURE OF SEX

Assumptions about the natural have long been used against queer people. As Foucault noted, the "incorporation of perversions" that solidified categories of "peripheral" sexuality, including homosexuality, established the contours of the normal and natural in the domain of sexuality.[63] According to Foucault, the concept of sexual perversion that emerged in the late eighteenth century was and continues to be a concept of "nature gone awry."[64] In response to homophobic claims that "homosexuality" is wrong because it is unnatural, some LGBT people point to the plethora of scientific evidence that documents sexual and gender variance among nonhuman animals.[65] According to Bruce Bagemihl, if nonhuman animal behavior provides evidence for what is natural, "the 'birds and the bees,' literally, are queer."[66] Nonetheless, Stacy Alaimo cautions against presenting the nonhuman natural world as a resource or backdrop for human self-definition.[67] Such an approach reinforces rather than challenges the human-animal, nature-culture binaries that queer theory seeks to destabilize. Instead of striving to find a reflection of existing categories of human sexual and gender identity in nature, Alaimo contends that nonhuman animals present a stunning array of diverse behavior that unsettles and exceeds the definitional scope of existing categories of sexuality and gender. For Alaimo, the queerness of animals isn't contained by the presence of same-sex sexual activity or same-sex pair bonding. Instead, the queerness of nature can inspire a sense of awe at the possibilities of desire.[68]

A queer conception of the nonhuman natural world also questions prevailing frameworks in which we make sense of bonds between humans and other animals. For example, Kathy Rudy extends the scope of "queer" to what she believes is a radical or revolutionary love for animals.[69] Rudy writes, "In keeping with queer theory, I am asking the reader . . . to imagine the possibility that certain kinds of relationships can undo even the strongest and most trenchant categories."[70] At least two of the categories Rudy has in mind are Western conceptions of the human-animal binary that inform human exceptionalism. In the context of human exceptionalism, love for animals is permissible provided that it stays within the recognizable, acceptable boundaries of pet love, a love that conceives of animals as property.[71] Human love for animals that exceeds pet love in conceiving of relationships with animals as equally or more important than one's intimate bonds with other human beings is not considered acceptable. Rudy thus bemoans the paucity of imagination that marks the boundary of the permissible within the pathologizing discourse of bestiality and zoophilia. Here, it is important to note that Rudy does not defend bestiality. Instead, she critiques the extent to which the language of bestiality remains tied to the framework of human exceptionalism and thus does not reflect what Rudy means by the revolutionary potential of queer love for animals. According to Rudy, love for animals is radical to the extent that it is a site for undoing human exceptionalism and becoming otherwise.[72]

In describing her sense of her identity as an animal lover, Rudy writes, "It is not so much that I'm no longer a lesbian . . . it's that the binary of gay and straight no longer has anything to do with me. My preference these days is canine."[73] For Rudy, there is a connection between love and bringing into being new worlds, and love for animals can constitute a form of queer kinship that can inform new modes of animal advocacy.[74] Rudy's analysis of animal love builds on queer theory's critique of identity, gender, and sexuality and challenges norms of sexual desire and assumptions about what sex is.

Rudy is surely right that queer theory presents important challenges to our understanding of sex and intimacy in ways that challenge human exceptionalism. Nonetheless, a critically queer position also questions the notion that the problem of human exceptionalism is necessarily overthrown by radical love for animals. After all, what is "the animal" without "the human"?[75] Borrowing from Foucault, a declaration of one's preference as canine could be said to constitute a reverse discourse that is made possible by and, thus, must grapple with the human-animal binary one critiques. As Christopher Peterson observes, "To privilege the animal and marginalize the human is to reverse rather than displace the human/animal opposition."[76] In general, queer ecology cautions against a denaturalization of gender, sex, and sexuality that leaves unquestioned assumptions about human-animal, nature-culture binaries, binaries that also frame the meaning of sex and sexuality in heteronormative contexts.

CONCLUDING REMARKS

Queer theory challenges assumptions about the relationship between sex, gender, and desire that inform identities, experiences, and relationships. Its persistent critique of naturalization and normalization points to the possibility of new meanings, transformed worlds, and lives lived otherwise.

NOTES

1. Michel Foucault, *The History of Sexuality Volume 1: An Introduction*, translated by Robert Hurley (New York: Vintage, 1990).
2. See Abby Wilkerson, "Normate Sex and Its Discontents," in *Sex and Disability*, edited by Robert McRuer and Anna Mollow, 183–207, at 186 (Durham, N.C.: Duke University Press, 2012).
3. See Foucault, *The History of Sexuality*, 6.
4. Foucault, *The History of Sexuality*, 43.
5. Foucault, *The History of Sexuality*, 43.
6. Foucault, *The History of Sexuality*, 101.
7. Ladelle McWhorter, *Bodies and Pleasures: Foucault and the Politics of Sexual Normalization* (Bloomington, Ind.: Indiana University Press, 1999), 40–41. For more about sexuality as an epistemic space, see also Eve Kosofsky Sedgwick, *The Epistemology of*

the Closet (Berkeley, Calif.: University of California Press, 1990); Kim Q. Hall, "Queer Epistemologies and Epistemic Injustice," in *The Routledge Handbook on Epistemic Injustice*, edited by Gaile Pohlhaus, Ian Kidd, and José Medina (New York: Routledge, forthcoming 2017).

8. McWhorter, *Bodies and Pleasures*, 35.

9. McWhorter, *Bodies and Pleasures*, 35.

10. Foucault, *The History of Sexuality*; Sedgwick, *Epistemology of the Closet*; McWhorter, *Bodies and Pleasures*.

11. See Simone de Beauvoir, *The Second Sex*, translated by Constance Borde and Sheila Malovany-Chevallier (New York: Vintage, 2011), especially her famous assertion, "One is not born, but rather becomes, a woman," 283.

12. Gayle Salamon, *Assuming a Body: Transgender and Rhetorics of Materiality* (New York: Columbia University Press, 2010), 77.

13. Salamon, *Assuming a Body*, 76–78.

14. See for example Ann Laura Stoler, *Race and the Education of Desire: Foucault's History of Sexuality and the Colonial Order of Things* (Durham, N.C.: Duke University Press, 1995).

15. Keguro Macharia, "On Being Area-Studied: A Litany of Complaint." *GLQ: A Journal of Lesbian and Gay Studies* 22:1 (2016), 183–90, at 183.

16. Macharia, "On Being Area-Studied," 184.

17. Macharia, "On Being Area-Studied," 184.

18. Macharia, "On Being Area-Studied," 186.

19. See for example José Esteban Muñoz, *Disidentifications: Queers of Color and the Performance of Politics* (Minneapolis: University of Minnesota Press, 1999) and E. Patrick Johnson, "'Quare' Studies, or (Almost) Everything I Know about Queer Studies I Learned from my Grandmother," *Text and Performance Quarterly* 21:1 (2001), 1–25.

20. David Halperin, *Saint Foucault: Towards a Gay Hagiography* (New York: Oxford University Press, 1997), 66.

21. Gayle Rubin, "Thinking Sex: Notes for a Radical Theory of the Politics of Sexuality," in *The Lesbian and Gay Studies Reader*, edited by Henry Abelove, Michele Aina Barale, and David M. Halperin (New York: Routledge, 1993), 3–44.

22. See Samuel R. Delaney, *Times Square Red, Times Square Blue* (New York: New York University Press, 1999); Michelle A. Gibson, Jonathan Alexander, and Deborah T. Meem, eds., *Finding Out: An Introduction to LGBT Studies*, 2nd ed. (Thousand Oaks, Calif.: Sage, 2014); Michael Warner, *The Trouble with Normal: Sex, Politics, and the Ethics of Queer Life* (Cambridge, Mass.: Harvard University Press, 1999), 172–93.

23. Warner, *The Trouble with Normal*.

24. Warner, *The Trouble with Normal*, 24.

25. Warner, *The Trouble with Normal*, 40.

26. Warner, *The Trouble with Normal*, 170.

27. Chris Bell, "I'm Not the Man I Used to Be: Sex, HIV, and Cultural 'Responsibility,'" in *Sex and Disability*, edited by Robert McRuer and Anna Mollow (Durham, N.C.: Duke University Press, 2012), 208–28, at 212 and 226.

28. Warner, *The Trouble with Normal*, 70–71.

29. Judith Butler, *Bodies That Matter: On the Discursive Limits of 'Sex'* (New York: Routledge, 1993), 227–28.

30. Butler, *Bodies That Matter*, 228.

31. Butler, *Bodies That Matter*, 228.

32. Butler, *Bodies That Matter*, 229.

33. Butler, *Bodies That Matter*, 228.

34. Nikki Sullivan, *A Critical Introduction to Queer Theory* (New York: New York University Press, 2003), 49.

35. Judith Butler, *Gender Trouble: Feminism and the Subversion of Identity* (New York: Routledge, 1990), 5.

36. Butler, *Gender Trouble*.

37. Salamon, *Assuming a Body*.

38. See Salamon, *Assuming a Body*; Kim Q. Hall, "Queerness, Disability, and the Vagina Monologues," *Hypatia: Journal of Feminist Philosophy* 20:1 (2005), 99–119; Kim Q. Hall, "Queer Breasted Experience," in *"You've Changed": Sex Reassignment and Personal Identity*, edited by Laurie J. Shrage (New York and Oxford: Oxford University Press, 2009), 121–34.

39. Robert McRuer, *Crip Theory: Cultural Signs of Queerness and Disability* (New York: New York University Press, 2006), 198 and 211n9.

40. Tania Titchkosky, "'To Pee or Not to Pee?' Ordinary Talk about Extraordinary Exclusions in a University Environment," *Canadian Journal of Sociology/Cahiers Canadiens de Sociologie* 33:1 (2008), 37–60, at 39.

41. Carrie Sandahl first proposed "crip" as a critical term that builds connections between queerness and disability ("Queering the Crip or Cripping the Queer? Intersections of Queer and Crip Identities in Solo Autobiographical Performance," *GLQ: A Journal of Lesbian and Gay Studies* 9:1–2 [2003], 25–56). "Crip" names a critical approach to normalizing assumptions of identity within disability studies. (Sandahl, "Queering the Crip or Cripping the Queer?"; McRuer, *Crip Theory*; and Alison Kafer, *Feminist Queer Crip* [Bloomington: Indiana University Press, 2013]). The term "crip" within crip theory is understood and deployed critically in ways that are influenced by Judith Butler's understanding of the meaning of "critically queer" (McRuer, *Crip Theory*, 40–41; Kafer, *Feminist Queer Crip*, 13–17).

42. McRuer, *Crip Theory*.

43. McRuer, *Crip Theory*, 31.

44. Kafer, *Feminist Queer Crip*, 10–12, 15–16.

45. See Susan Wendell, "Unhealthy Disabled: Treating Chronic Illnesses as Disabilities," *Hypatia: Journal of Feminist Philosophy* 16:4 (2001), 17–33; Tobin Siebers, *Disability Theory* (Ann Arbor, Mich.: University of Michigan Press, 2008); Kafer, *Feminist Queer Crip*.

46. Kafer, *Feminist Queer Crip*, 13–14.

47. Kafer, *Feminist Queer Crip*, 10–11.

48. Michael Gill, *Already Doing It: Intellectual Disability and Sexual Agency* (Minneapolis, Minn.: University of Minnesota Press, 2015); Wilkerson, "Normate Sex and Its Discontents"; Robert McRuer and Anna Mollow, "Introduction," in *Sex and Disability*, edited by Robert McRuer and Anna Mollow (Durham, N.C.: Duke University Press, 2012), 1–34.

49. Alison Kafer, "Desire and Disgust: My Ambivalent Adventures in Devoteeism." In *Sex and Disability*, edited by Robert McRuer and Anna Mollow (Durham, N.C.: Duke University Press, 2012), 331–54, at 333–34.

50. Gill, *Already Doing It*; Abby Wilkerson, "Disability, Sex Radicalism, and Political Agency," in *Feminist Disability Studies*, edited by Kim Q. Hall (Bloomington, Ind.: Indiana University Press, 2011), 193–217.

51. Gill, *Already Doing It*.

52. Wilkerson, "Disability, Sex Radicalism, and Political Agency," 195.

53. Wilkerson, "Disability, Sex Radicalism, and Political Agency," 209.

54. Tracy DeBoer, "Disability and Sexual Inclusion," *Hypatia: Journal of Feminist Philosophy* 30:1 (2015), 66–81, at 73.

55. Eunjung Kim, "Asexuality in Disability Narratives," *Sexualities* 14:4 (2011), 479–93.

56. Christina Crosby, *A Body Undone: Living On After Great Pain* (New York: New York University Press, 2016), 118.

57. See Kim, "Asexuality in Disability Narratives"; and Karli June Cerankowski and Megan Milks, "New Orientations: Asexuality and Its Implications for Theory and Practice," *Feminist Studies* 36:3 (2010), 650–64.

58. AVEN, "Asexual Visibility and Education Network," www.asexuality.org; date of access February 12, 2017.

59. Kim, "Asexuality in Disability Narratives," 481.

60. Karli June Cerankowski and Megan Milks, "New Orientations." See also Angela Tucker, dir., *(A)Sexual*, IMDbPro (2011), DVD.

61. Kim, "Asexuality in Disability Narratives."

62. Kim, "Asexuality in Disability Narratives," 490.

63. Foucault, *The History of Sexuality*, 39.

64. Foucault, *The History of Sexuality*, 39.

65. Bruce Bagemihl, *Biological Exuberance: Animal Homosexuality and Natural Diversity* (New York: St. Martin's Press, 1999); Joan Roughgarden, *Evolution's Rainbow: Diversity, Gender, and Sexuality in Nature and People* (Berkeley, Calif.: University of California Press, 2004).

66. Bagemihl, *Biological Exuberance*, 9.

67. Stacy Alaimo, "Eluding Capture: The Science, Culture, and Pleasure of 'Queer' Animals," in *Queer Ecologies: Sex, Nature, Politics, Desire*, edited by Catriona Mortimer-Sandilands and Bruce Erickson (Bloomington, Ind.: Indiana University Press, 2010), 51–72, at 67.

68. Alaimo, "Eluding Capture," 67.

69. Kathy Rudy, "LGBTQ . . . Z?" *Hypatia: Journal of Feminist Philosophy* 27:3 (2012), 601–15, at 611 (reprinted in this volume).

70. Rudy, "LGBTQ . . . Z?" 610.

71. Rudy, "LGBTQ . . . Z?" 605.

72. Rudy, "LGBTQ . . . Z?" 611.

73. Rudy, "LGBTQ . . . Z?" 610.

74. Rudy, "LGBTQ . . . Z?" 601.

75. Christopher Peterson, *Bestial Traces: Race, Sexuality, Animality* (New York: Fordham University Press, 2013), 2 and 9; Jacques Derrida, *The Animal That Therefore I Am*, edited by Marie-Louise Mallet, translated by David Wills (New York: Fordham University Press), 34.

76. Peterson, *Bestial Traces*, 9.

STUDY QUESTIONS

1. Explain what Michel Foucault means by the claim that power produces sexuality, and how understanding how power works implies denying the view that sexuality is an innate and identifying feature of who one is. In answering this question, make sure to also explain Hall's connected claim that "The relations of power and knowledge that inform the desire to know the truth of sexuality produce the very truths about sexuality they purport to merely make visible and describe." Can you use examples from other, non-Western cultures (past or present) to support Foucault's view?

2. Suppose that being gay and being straight, as they are commonly understood, are not innate features of who we are and are not found across all (or most) cultures and times. Might the "born this way" movement nonetheless be asserting true claims, especially in light of the many personal accounts given by people that they have "always felt this way"? How? In addition, might changing the way we commonly understand sexual orientation render Foucault's claims false? Read the essay "What Is Sexual Orientation?" by Robin Dembroff in this volume before you answer this question.

3. About homonormative politics, Hall states, "In the context of sexual politics, homonormativity posits sexual minorities as deserving of rights because they are good, which means that they participate in 'normal,' and thus, 'good' sex." In doing so, it ends up excluding (whether intentionally or not is unclear) many queer people, according to Hall. Who is excluded and why? Should everyone be included simply on the basis of being queer? Are all sexual desires and activities deserving of rights? Think of these issues in light of Hall's discussion of Michael Warner's arguments.

4. In discussing the denaturalization of sex and gender, Hall states that "the meaning of body parts, especially those parts that are taken as signs of sex, are not unmediated." Explain this claim, especially in light of Talia Mae Bettcher's essay, "Trans 101," in this volume.

5. If the insights of queer theory are correct, one consequence might be that there is very little that is natural about our sexual desires — it might be that they are almost fully formed and given content by the social and political culture to which we are born. Evaluate this claim (is it plausible?) and trace how, if true, it would explain why disabled bodies are thought of as undesirable (would it imply that they are, under certain conditions, also found to be desirable?). What other bodies could, in principle, be excluded by such cultural and social power relations?

6. What is sexual agency? What abilities does it include in addition to the ability to make sexual choices and to be sexually assertive? In answering this question, consider Abby Wilkerson's claim, which Hall quotes, that sexual agency involves "a larger social dimension in which others recognize and respect one's identity." What connections do you see between sexual agency and sexual justice?

7. About disability, Hall states, "While the medical model understands disability as an individual problem requiring medical intervention, the social model conceives of disability as a justice issue requiring political movements and social, political, and economic change." Explain each of these two models. Are they incompatible with each other, as Hall seems to imply?

8. Try to articulate, in a few (crisp) sentences, how queer theory changes our (common?) views of sex and sexuality were we to think queerly about them. After going through queer theory's screening process (so to speak), what happens to some types of identities that are commonly held — that one is straight, disabled, asexual, or a zoophile, for example?

9. Is queer theory a theory about concepts and their meanings, or is it about social and political issues (facts, relationships, identities, etc.)? If you take the cheap way out and answer "both," explain how queer theory connects these two themes together.

FIFTEEN

LGBTQ . . . Z?

Kathy Rudy

In this essay, **Kathy Rudy** *uses queer theory in general, and the thought of Eve Kosofsky Sedgwick in particular, to rethink our attitudes toward, and conceptions of, having sex with animals. Rudy's general argument is that our prohibition on having sex with animals depends on a more or less firm notion of what sex is. But, according to queer theory, we have no such firm notion because sex and sexuality are much more diffuse and pervasive than such firm notions have us believe (this is, of course, in line with queer theory's general questioning of all fixed concepts, conceptions, and definitions—see Kim Q. Hall's essay in this volume, "Thinking Queerly about Sex and Sexuality"). Thus, we have reason to question the prohibition on having sex with animals. More positively, Rudy also argues that our deep connections with animals (she uses her relationship with her dogs as an example) has the potential to change both parties to the relationship: the human being is no longer only human and the animal is no longer only animal. With such changes, Rudy seems to suggest, the big divide between human beings and animals might be somewhat bridged, with crucial implications for our beliefs about the wrongness and rightness of having sex with animals. Her conclusion seems to be not so much that sex with animals is sometimes not morally wrong but that it is no simple matter to divide our relationships with animals into "sexual" and "nonsexual," and that loving animals teaches us new ways to advocate for animals and to think of human exceptionalism.*

Kathy Rudy is professor of women's studies at Duke University. She is the author of *Loving Animals: Toward a New Animal Advocacy* (Minnesota, 2011), along with earlier books and articles on ethics, sexuality, abortion, reproduction, natural birth and death, other animals, and on how these subjects trace each other in the frame of biopolitics. This essay was first published in *Hypatia*, vol. 27, no. 3 (2012), 601–15. It is reprinted here with the permission of Kathy Rudy and *Hypatia*.

> I think many adults (and I am among them) are trying, in our work, to keep faith with vividly remembered promises made to ourselves in childhood: promises to make invisible possibilities and desires visible; to make the tacit things explicit; to smuggle queer representation in where it must be smuggled and, with the relative freedom of adulthood, to challenge queer eradicating impulses frontally.[1]

I start my thinking with two conflicting and competing realities. The first is the pervasive social taboo against bestiality and zoophilia; the act of sex with animals is so prohibited in contemporary American culture that it is often difficult to speak of such things in public. This is interesting. Humans can kill animals, force them to breed with each other, eat them, surround them, train them, hunt them, nail them down, and cut them open for science, and, for the most part, the humans who perform those acts can be thought of as normal, functioning members of society. Yet having sex with animals remains an almost unspeakable anathema. Indeed, it was Peter Singer who first proposed in his 2001 essay "Heavy Petting" that, from the animals' point of view, having sex with them wasn't nearly as harmful as killing or torturing them.[2] Although he condemned all sex acts where animals were killed, he brought up the interesting point that in many cases, animals appear to initiate sex, to have erections, to seek out genital intimacy, and so on. Why, then, in this most intimate domain, is our use of animals most vociferously condemned?

The second reality that needs to be taken into consideration for this essay is the burgeoning pet culture in America of the last thirty or so years. Humans have never been closer to their pets, or spent more time or money on them.[3] Part of me would like to see these new developments as seeds of transgression, or early markers of the demise of human exceptionalism. That is, in one sense the intense relationships some of us have with pets could itself be disruptive of the human-oriented world most of us inherited. Although I completely recognize that the vast majority of humans who participate in relationships with their pets don't recognize those relationships as transgressive, part of me would like to claim that for them anyway. It's not that the family dog is himself a paradigm-shifting entity, but the massive scale of pet culture could signal a shift that many of us humans have indeed fallen in love with someone besides ourselves.

But we don't think of pet culture that way at all. For the most part, pet animals are add-ons to postmodern, consumption-based, globalized life, not paradigm shifters. The easiest answer, and one that I will circle around and around in this essay, is that pets are not really threatening to twenty-first-century American life precisely because of the deeply ingrained taboos against bestiality. After all, we may love them, but we don't really love them, right? We don't ever view our love of animals as transgressive simply because the activities of bestiality and zoophilia seem so unthinkable. Loving animals is safe, for most of us, because it is not "that." As Midas Dekkers aptly expresses it, "the high regard in which love for animals is held is matched only by the fierceness of the taboo on having sex with them."[4]

Enter queer theory. At the most cursory level, queer theory persuasively teaches us that sex itself is difficult to define; sexuality pervades many different levels of many different relationships; and sexual identity is famously unstable. Sex is an energy that can be tapped into but never nailed down. So in relation to bestiality, queer theory points out that the "that" that is performed between humans and animals by necessity must remain unnamed. Stated differently, the widespread social ban on bestiality rests on a solid notion of what sex is, and queer theory persuasively argues that we simply don't have such a thing. The interdict against bestiality can only be maintained if we think we always/already know what sex is. And, according to queer theory, we don't.

To tell this part of the story well, I need to reveal the event that prompted me — in the middle of writing a book about animals and ethics — to return to queer theory as a central organizing theme: that event was the death of Eve Sedgwick in the spring of 2009. Eve was a mentor to me when I was a grad student at Duke, and a wise senior colleague when I joined the faculty there. I found myself rereading some of her books after her death as a way to invite her to be more present in my life, as a way for me to remember her well. To my knowledge, although Eve mentions bestiality and zoophilia in passing, she never turns her wise and clever gaze completely on the subject. The rest of this essay, then, is something of a thought experiment connecting Eve's insights about queerness and sexuality with my own obsessions about animals. It has been exceedingly fun to write this for her.

Studying with Eve Sedgwick as a young scholar was like adding a new and different dimension to the feminist theory I brought with me to grad school. Before Eve, I rummaged through liberal, radical, and socialist theories of gender to make arguments about the importance and value of women in the world. Before Eve, gender was pretty much an unchecked constant in my intellectual landscape; it was the thing I worried over all the time in every context but never really saw because it loomed so large. In looking back on that time, I lived in a very two-dimensional world where the things that "made" gender (and feminism) went more or less unstudied.

Exploring feminist theory with Eve was like stepping into an IMAX 3D movie for the first time. I wasn't just watching the movie of gender anymore; I was in it and could see behind and beneath the structures that before had been utterly flat. Eve was a different kind of feminist; she cared about all the regular things the rest of us cared about, but she also cared about how gender itself was made. In watching the world through her eyes, I got to see a differently inflected reality; it wasn't the case, as I had previously thought, that gender came first and then sexual preference flowed from there. Rather, all of our identities stemmed, in part, out of our desires. To be sure, lots of feminists before Sedgwick noted that gender was "socially constructed." From de Beauvoir to Barrett and many others, we already knew that gender was made, but from those perspectives it mostly looked like society or culture or language or something outside us pressed down on us like cookie-cutters and made us into men and women. With Eve, the thing that made us gendered also came from inside of us. It came in the way we identified outside ourselves, it came in the way we desired an other and made ourselves into a person who could be in relation to that particular other; it came in the ways we loved. Our realities are made for us through the worlds and meanings available to us, but they are also made by the connections in the affective realm. Whom we loved mattered, not just as a point of feminist justice but also because that process of love contained the seeds of world-making.

I was a lesbian when I knew Eve at Duke back in the 1990s. I had "come out" in my early twenties, and it was an identity that almost fit for a long time. Well into my thirties I tried very hard to make that description of myself work for me. For ten years I "settled down" with one partner, focused on family life, "owned" only two dogs and one cat (with no fenced yard). I tried very hard to be reasonable about the animals; I would put them in kennels when we traveled and lock them in bedrooms when we entertained. But when I wasn't with them I was miserable. It was like they carried a piece of my heart, and when they were not involved in some function or activity, a part of me wasn't present, either. Eve knew of these predilections and always encouraged me to think about them in a positive frame. Claiming a solid "gay" identity never felt right to Eve, and she filled the world with feminist queer theory to explain why "being woman" or "being gay," although certainly not wrong, wasn't quite right, either. Nor was "being lesbian" quite right for me, mostly because my mind was always on the dogs. From as far back as I can remember, dogs have been the most vibrant, colorful, and important players in the landscape of my life. When I was a child, they were my very best friends. Soon after Eve left Duke, I found myself single, and in part due to her influence, I decided to pay serious attention to these intense feelings I had toward animals. Like the epigraph that opens this essay, I wanted to return to a childhood promise to make my relationships with them more visible and explicit.[5]

For me, paying attention to that childhood first love of animals was possible only as a result of Eve's formulation of theory. In her world, gender and sexuality were terribly messy and unwieldy constructs, and she was absolutely delighted when they could be rendered even messier and more unwieldy. Had she lived, reaching outside the boundaries of the human would have been the next logical step in her feminism. Following Eve, I filled my new house with six rescues of various shapes and sizes, and multitudes of fosters looking for new homes. People think I am crazy. But I have never ever been happier.

So here I sit with my six dogs, wondering, from the theory-world Eve bequeathed to me, what could it mean to love animals? What does it mean to make myself in relation to the love I have for these dogs? How do they help me construct my gender, my class, my race, the inward, internal topography of identities and desires that connect me to the world? How does living inside this 3D, big-screen movie with dogs all around me look to the rest of the world? How does it feel to the dogs themselves? And how does it look to me, inside it?

There is not an adequate name for the kind of life I lead, the way my desires organize themselves around animals. In the first half of the twentieth century, the heterosexual public either detested or felt sorry for women who were named by the then emerging category "lesbian." They thought that the only women who would ever choose lesbianism were ugly, or unfeminine, or somehow lacking in the ability to capture a man. Now, on the other side of gay rights, feminism, and queer theory, such ideas seem silly or quaint, almost forgotten. But can people like me even hope for such liberation, when choosing animals as partners or companions doesn't really even have an adequate name? At best, we fall under the radar of identity and are named (wrongly) as gay or straight, single or married, parents or childless. Our most important relationships, though, are never recognized. At worst, we are pitied. Like those early lesbians, people "feel sorry" for us because we can't seem to sustain "real" relationships with "real" people.[6] I came out as a lesbian nearly twenty-five years ago, and although that was hard on friends and family who were homophobic, the task of coming out as a lesbian was a piece of cake compared to coming out as—what?

I know I love my dogs with all my heart, but I can't figure out if that love is sexually motivated. Queer theory has schooled me in ways that make the question of what counts as sex seem rather unintelligible. How do we cordon off sexual desire from all the other desires that move our lives? What does sex mean? Do I think I am having sex with my dogs when they kiss my face? How do we know beforehand what sex is? I get more affection from my dogs than I ever did from any girlfriend. We all always sleep together, sometimes under the same blankets when it's cold. When I was gay, was I gay because of a narrowly defined genital act that I performed with a person who happened to be another woman? Those words don't make any sense to me. I was gay then, I believe, because I chose to share my emotional, financial, and daily life with a person of the same gender. Now I choose to share that same life with six dogs.

Although I am not arguing that living with pets is necessarily a life-shifting paradigm, I am suggesting that the number of people who find community and communion with domesticated animals has both risen recently and become more visible. In a queer frame, this phenomenon is extremely interesting, as it—loving animals—could constitute a new way of being with another species. Put differently, queer theory teaches us that it's not really a question of whether we have "sex" with animals; rather, it's about recognizing and honoring the affective bonds many of us share with other creatures. Those intense connections between humans and animals could be seen as revolutionary, in a queer frame. But, instead, pet love is sanitized and rendered harmless by the presence of the interdict against bestiality. The discourses of bestiality and zoophilia form the identity boundary that we cannot pass through if we want our love of animals to be seen as acceptable.

In American public culture today, conversations about bestiality and zoophilia exist in four different locations.[7] I want to look briefly at those positions, and then move to analyze them through the lens of queer theory. Ultimately, of course, my argument is not *for* or *against* humans having sex with animals, but is a meditation on both the elusive nature of sex itself and the subjectivities of human versus nonhuman animals. The line policed by the fear of bestiality is about more than just what we can or can't do with our pets. As we shall see, it helps to form the very architecture of human exceptionalism.

The first two sites I speak about are (1) "bestiality" and (2) "zoophilia"; both exist mostly on the Internet, where sex with animals is portrayed more or less as a form of pornography. Acts are performed either by objectifying animals to the point where they are treated as props for certain sexual encounters (bestiality) or, conversely, by endowing animals with human characteristics, such as the desire to express love for their humans through sexual intimacy (zoophilia). The third site is closely associated with (3) "animal rights," where sex with animals is strongly condemned because animals are seen as needing protection from human manipulation in general, and sex with them can never be anything but a misuse of human power. Finally, sex with animals is discussed in (4) "mental health" literature, where the context is almost always therapeutic intervention; these therapy-based works reflect a dominant cultural notion that sex with animals needs to be "cured" because it's simply not normal. Attitudes and arguments from these four venues gives us unique vantage points to think about what sex is and what animals are.

On many bestiality websites (1), the dominant orientation toward animals really supports and adheres to the idea that animals are nothing more than forms of property. On these private, for-pay websites, animals are dressed up, stimulated, filmed from angles that don't show their faces or their expressions. They are, in short, props or tools to aid the human-centered sexual experience.[8] In the logic of these practices, sex with these "things" is no more wrong than sex with other "things," such as dildos, blow-up dolls, and so on. In these settings, sex acts don't happen "between" humans and animals; rather, humans are simply using animals for their own pleasure and fantasy. For these bestialists, it doesn't matter if the animal lives or dies as a result of this activity; the goal here is human pleasure. Examples of using animals as things include inserting rodents into a human rectum for pleasure, or beheading chickens and other birds at the point of orgasm to intensify the convulsions of the sphincter, or withholding food and fluids from dogs for long periods of time so they will lick and swallow various human secretions and excretions. From this point of view, such bestial practices aren't wrong because animals have no subjectivity, no self-interest. After all, we kill them to eat them or because we don't want them infesting our homes, why not use them for a little sexual pleasure first? Here, humans occupy a place in the world that is unrivaled.

A counterdiscourse emerges within the realm of pornography that portrays sex between humans and animals differently. Self-described zoophiles (2) argue that humans involved in loving relationships with animals are distinct from bestials; for zoophiles, animals are not "things," rather they are full and equal partners in sexual discovery. Zoophilia, they say, does not involve animal cruelty; it's not about hurting animals for human pleasure but about loving animals to pleasure both the human and the animal. In this frame, animals are not only not "things" but also capable of entering into something like a partnership with humans, for love and for sex. Indeed, in loving relationships, zoophilists suggest, animals can experience such a robust subjectivity that they not only give consent to sexual acts but also can initiate those acts, communicate desires for specific kinds of pleasure, and even opt out of sex if they so choose. In this perspective, animals aren't less-than-human pieces of property; they become something very close to human. From a zoophile's perspective, although nonhuman animals don't use spoken or written language, they can communicate their sexual desires in a myriad of ways. Here, nonhuman animals are elevated to the level of human subjectivity and granted the kinds of characteristics usually reserved only for humans.

On the other side of the debate, the taboo against sex with animals is secured and reinforced by two unlikely bedfellows. Possibly the strongest admonition against bestiality and/or zoophilia comes from the discourse of animal rights (3). For theorists committed to a platform that releases animals from "enslavement" by humans, humans and animals having sex is always and unconditionally wrong simply because animals cannot give consent. Much like children, prisoners, or slaves, they say, animals are subject to such coercion that they cannot participate in meaningful sexual encounters. It's not a question of pain or pleasure, but simply that by the very nature of their lack of agency, they cannot give consent to such acts. Partly it's a question of lacking a common language, but according to many animal rights theorists, even if we suddenly were able to communicate with nonhuman animals, sex between humans and animals would be wrong because animals are not authors of their own worlds. Piers Beirne calls all sex between human and non-human animals "interspecies sexual assault" and argues "animals are beings without an effective voice."[9] Essentially, most people in the animal rights movement think that because animals are powerless and voiceless, sex between humans and animals is always wrong.[10]

Finally, most material addressing both bestiality and zoophilia from psychological perspectives (4) reflects disgust at the idea of human/animal sex. In these essays and books, the desire to have sex with animals is seen as abnormal and in need of cure. The most liberal approaches try to explain how someone came to develop a predilection for bestiality, but I found no therapeutically based literature that advocated for acceptance of these practices. In each essay, there is the unquestioned perception that such behavior needs to be corrected. There seems to be a general sense of disgrace in wider American culture that fuels and reinforces the need for therapeutic resolution. This taboo on sex with animals is a powerful force that also functions, I suggest, to help us differentiate ourselves from animals very well. In the interdict against sex with animals, animals emerge as figures over which we define our superiority. In other words, maintaining the ontological boundary between humans and animals requires us to feel disgusted by breaches of that boundary, most especially around the issue of sex. Our psychological approaches operationalize this boundary by "curing" those who cross it.

I've mapped the four sites as a "pro and con" diagram above (two in favor of sex with animals, but from different positions, two opposed to sex with animals, but also from different positions). But in an interesting way, the pro and con sides of the argument also act as mirrors for each other's ontologies. That is, bestialists (1) and therapists (4) both see animals as "less than human"; whereas bestials use this less-than status as the reason to accept sex practices with animals ("who cares what happens to them, they are just things"), many therapists see sex with animals as degrading to the humans because animals are less than us ("we belittle humanity to engage in sex with unworthy creatures"). Similarly, zoophiles (2) see animals as equal or equivalent to humans, and therefore think sex with animals is fine as long as it's not abusive, painful, or degrading; animal rights activists (3) also see animals as equal or equivalent to humans, but because animals are so highly regarded, many activists believe that animals need protection from human domination (much the way children or mentally handicapped people need protection from those who would abuse them).

If Eve Sedgwick had written about sex with animals, I bet she wouldn't be interested in validating any of the four orientations. She would want to know how the four views compete with one another, and on what grounds they share in their common definitions about subjects and practices. She would want to know how we ended up in a world where these frameworks constructed our only options. She would want to know how the categories themselves came into being, how they rub up against one another, how they overlook and obscure many aspects of life filled with animals. Eve would ask how we organized ourselves such that animals have to be either just like us or not like us at all, and thus have no value. She would want to know how it was possible that all animals can exist in one category. She would want to examine how our perceptions about the gender of animals both construct and reflect our perceptions about the gender of our selves. Are there other ways to think about animals other than "equal to us" or "less than us"? Are there ways to think about sex with animals other than in terms of right or wrong? What is it that can't be said? What other realities do these four positions obscure?

It's worth noting just how much slippage exists among positions that try to define themselves against one another. What looks different on the surface may be similar underneath (and vice versa). Eve addresses the way the subject positions of gay men and lesbians do or do not relate: "There can't be an a priori decision about how far it will make sense to conceptualize lesbian and gay male identities together. Or separately." [11] The same is true, for example, for the distinction between bestiality (1) and zoophilia (2). Although zoophiles try to distance themselves from bestials, the two occupy similar domains on the Internet, and I suspect many viewers care little about the affective relationships zoophiles advocate. They are lumped together in the therapeutic literature, and also by the condemnatory discourses of animal rights. A whole series of questions emerges to blur the distinction: How can we be certain about what kind of bond exists behind the sex? How does one know beforehand the difference between bestiality and zoophilia? Is a woman who becomes sexually aroused riding a horse a bestial or a zoophile? What if she gets aroused only on the back of one particular horse? Can emotional bonds exist, say, between a farmer and the livestock he is about to slaughter for meat? Although killing animals in the act of sex is more associated with bestiality, what if the sex and the killing are separated by periods of days or weeks or years? Can you love someone and still kill her?

Slippage and condensation occur on the other side of the divide as well. Although animal rights activists intend only to protect animals from human abuse, in their interdicts against human/animal sex, they also shore up the psychosocial position that human sex with animals is somehow abnormal. Both positions oppose sex with animals, and in doing so they perform a kind of violence on animals by lumping them all together into one seamless identity.

Here is Eve on the question of human identity categories: "People are different from each other. It is astonishing how few respectable conceptual tools we have for dealing with this self-evident fact. A tiny number of inconceivably coarse axes of categorization have been painstakingly inscribed in current critical and political thought: gender, race, class, nationality, sexual orientation are pretty much the available distinctions."[12] With these words, Sedgwick opened up not only the study of sexuality but also the study of human identity to attend to complexity and messiness. I want now to extend this insight to nonhuman animals. If, as she argues, the available tools to categorize humans are paltry, the labels associated with animals are downright crude. Although the discourse of species recognizes certain biological differences between animals, most humans categorize animals only in the broadest strokes: as pets, livestock, or wild animals. These categorizations are slippery: a given species can occupy multiple categories (for example, feral cats, wild horses, and pet pigs all come to mind). Our method of categorizing animals is not only blunt but also famously unstable. Thus, mostly we refer to all of them as "animals."

The problem with both the animal rights and the psychotherapeutic positions is that they want to make universal rules for all animals, and in so doing sacrifice the richness of particularity. They advance an agenda that produces the human/animal duality as firmly and narrowly as the homo/hetero binary. They crowd all animals into one categorical way of thinking and tell us, even if subconsciously, that humans and animals occupy different ontological realms, that one is EITHER human OR animal—never neither, never both. It's precisely the same logic that forces us to conform to the homo/hetero binary.

What I am trying to introduce here is the possibility that as human and nonhuman, animals share an intensely bonded life together, we are all becoming something new, something part human, part animal, a part of one another. Both antisex positions rest on the idea that all humans are different from all other animals, and the wall between them can never be breached. Like the way we used to think of race and gender "identity," these positions contend that one's species rests on physical markers that are immutable, that belonging to the categories of "animal" or "human" is grounded in a biological essence untouched by culture. Positions that universalize all animals—even if allegedly to improve their lives—are unable to explore heterogeneity and fragmentation within each category.

Put differently, both animal rights (3) and psychosocial perspectives (4) do not believe that borders can be crossed. Queer theory, on the other hand, tells us that few of us have stable identities anymore, that borders are always crossed. We're all changing, shifting, splitting ourselves up this way and that. It labels these processes "hailing," "suturing," and "interpolation"; where once we saw ourselves affiliated in a certain way, a new interpretive community emerges to capture our passions and move us differently. I am asking the reader to entertain the possibility that the same kinds of shifts and disruptions happen with categories like "human," "rabbit," "ape," or "dog." As the result of our relationships, interpolations occur; my dogs and I have changed each other such that I am no longer human and they are no longer only canine. For these particular dogs and this particular person, something rather magical has happened to alter not only the way we perceive but also the way we live in the world.

In keeping with queer theory, I am asking the reader here to imagine the possibility that certain kinds of relationships can undo even the strongest and most trenchant categories. No one would deny that, as a result of their physical differences, my dogs experience the world differently than I do (for example, they hear better and smell better, but they can't read or write, and so on). But using only those experiences to invoke a unitary and stable world with unbridgeable boundaries for them (what we call species) completely discounts the other experiences they have had as a result of living with me, of us being a family together.[13] They know what my words mean, even if they can't write or speak. I've learned to be much more attuned to smell and sound and other shifts of energy that are hard to put into words. These experiences matter because they change us all.

Detractors of pet keeping might call this kind of life sad. We are investing in these creatures, they think, because we cannot "find" a human person to love. But from my perspective, it looks completely different. These majestic, wonderful beings are not empty ciphers; they have needs and desires that they communicate to me in a myriad of ways, and in listening and responding to them, I am not only changed but also fulfilled. They help me carry my burdens and increase my joys. I know I am content when they rest soundly at my feet. It's not so much that I am not a lesbian, then—it's that the binary of gay and straight no longer has anything to do with me. My preference these days is canine.

Collectively, the four positions tell us that it's perfectly fine to love animals, to sleep with them, to cuddle with them, to enjoy their bodies in a myriad of ways, but if we have "sex" with them, we immediately locate ourselves in the dangerous territory of bestiality. As Dekkers notes:

> If you drop the requirement that for sexual contact something has to be inserted somewhere and that something has to be fiddled with, and it is sufficient simply to cuddle, to derive a warm feeling from each other, to kiss perhaps at times, in brief to love, then bestiality is not a deviation but a general rule, not even something shameful but the done thing. After all, who does not wish to be called an animal lover?[14]

But without a coherent and agreed-upon definition of sex (which queer theory persuasively argues is impossible), the line between "animal lover" and zoophile is not only thin but also nonexistent. How do we know beforehand whether loving them constitutes "sex," and how can sex be so dangerous if it is so nebulous and undefined? In other words, the sense of danger associated with human/animal sex emerges as a result of a cultural anxiety about our own animality. That is, if we do "that" (leaving "that" unnamed and unrepresented), we will lose something about what it means to be human, to be superior.

Indeed, Dekkers, along with Alphonso Lingus, argues that sex itself turns us humans into animals, that in orgasm, animality saturates every pore and gene and bone of our being. As Dekkers claims, "Every sexual encounter is a breaking of bounds, an intrusion into an alien realm, every sexual encounter retains a whiff of bestiality."[15] Both of these authors argue for the pervasiveness of bestiality by insisting that it underlies all acts of love; in making love even to a fellow human, we are always encountering an animal or animalized other. Although this is clearly an interesting idea, my claim is slightly different. I'm not so much arguing that through sex we all become animals, but more that in deep connection, we all—humans and animals alike—become something different. The very contours of stable identities shift under the revolutionary power of love.

My point, then, is not to make something called bestiality more visible but, by using animal love in various permutations, to disrupt the stability and superiority of human identity. Convincing love stories between humans and animals—such as J. R. Ackerley's *My Dog Tulip* or Mark Doty's *Dog Years*[16]—do just this; that is, they don't tell us of an identity called bestiality but show us a world transformed by human/animal love. Such love destabilizes what we think we know about sex, what we think we know about gender, and what we think we know about being human. It can lead to what Margaret Grebowicz calls "an inscription of a wholly new imaginary of animality and the condition for the possibility of new imaginaries of gender."[17] It can also lead, I think, to a different imaginary of what it means to be human. As Kalpana Seshadri-Crooks articulates it, "The ethical questions that follow [bestiality] entail an intervention at the level of the fundamental fantasy of being human."[18]

Animals are emerging in the academy as a newly legitimized subject matter, and it's not a moment too soon. At no point in history have humans used animals like we're using them in America today. Factory farms crank out three pounds of meat per person per day from twenty billion food animals who function literally as flesh machines; thousands of breeders offer inbred, often aggressive, damaged pets for sale on the Internet and in pet stores every day; millions upon millions of homeless pets are killed every year in shelters across America simply because they lack homes, and we humans don't want to deal with them in our communities; the black market in exotic animals from chimps to tigers to wolves crosses through zoos, laboratories, and collectors of all sorts; and the numbers of animals maimed and killed for the testing of products and pharmaceuticals is almost double what it was twenty years ago. In terms of sheer numbers alone, the situation for animals in America today has never been more dire. Something Eve wrote reflects the urgency that I now feel toward these questions. She was writing, of course, about the homo/hetero boundary, but I take the liberty here of inserting my own agenda (and I hope wherever she is, she won't mind): "An understanding of virtually any aspect of modern Western culture must be, not merely incomplete, but damaged in its central substance to the degree that it does not incorporate a critical analysis of modern [human/animal definitions]."[19]

Thinking about bestiality/zoophilia and the human/animal boundary is a good way into a larger discussion of these urgent problems, but only if we subject bestiality/zoophilia to the scrutiny of feminist queer theory. That is, we need to ask a set of questions that problematizes the limited subject positions we allow animals to occupy, and opens the conversation about sex itself onto a wider territory: What do we mean by sex? What kinds of ideologies accompany a worldview that separates all human animals from every other living thing on earth? How can we bridge this gap sexually, metaphorically, and literally? How can we deploy a discourse of sexuality that grants animals agency and fulfillment? How can we make a more fulfilling world for ourselves and for other animals? What do sex, animals, and sex with animals contribute to this worldmaking? Perhaps a preliminary answer to some of these questions lies in a refiguring of my title: L, G, B, T, Z, and, overarching all of them, Q?

In Loving Memory of Eve Sedgwick

NOTES

1. Eve Kosofsky Sedgwick, *Tendencies* (Durham, N.C.: Duke University Press, 1993), 3.

2. Peter Singer, "Heavy Petting." *Nerve.* February 14, 2009. http://www.utilitarian.net/singer/by/2001----.htm (accessed January 2, 2012).

3. Much has been written on the recent rise of pet culture in America; a full survey of that material is beyond the scope of this essay. See Donna Jeanne Haraway, *The Companion Species Manifesto: Dogs, People, and Significant Otherness* (Chicago: Prickly Paradigm Press, 2003); Katherine C. Grier, *Pets in America: A History* (Chapel Hill, N.C.: University of North Carolina Press, 2006); and Heidi Nast, "Critical Pet Studies?" *Antipode* 38:5 (2006), 894–906.

4. Midas Dekkers, *Dearest Pet: On Bestiality* (London: Verso, 1994), 149.

5. Of note here is a delightful chapter titled "Why the (Lesbian) Child Requires an Interval of Animal: The Family Dog as a Time Machine," in Kathryn Stockton's *The Queer Child, or Growing Sideways in the Twentieth Century* (Durham, N.C.: Duke University Press, 2009). She writes, for example, "The family dog is not just a pet. It is a metaphor for all that is loyal, familial, and family-photogenic" (90). Although I like the ways Stockton talks about the importance of animals in the life of a queer child, my goal in this essay is to make the family dog into something much more present than a metaphor.

6. See, for example, Heidi Nast, "Loving Whatever: Alienation, Neoliberalism, and Pet-love in the Twenty-first Century," *ACME: An International E-Journal for Critical Geographies* 5:2 (2006), 300–327.

7. Throughout human history, of course, the vast majority of discussions around bestiality existed in the twinned realms of moral theology and juridical practices.

Interdicts against bestiality go as far back as the book of Leviticus, or farther, and are brought forward in court cases involving bestiality up through the Western seventeenth century. In most of these cases, events, and rules, bestiality is used as an attempt to regulate sexuality more generally, and all formed the foundation of the long-standing taboo we have inherited. In claiming that bestiality today resides in four locations, I do not mean to diminish the historical record at all. Rather, my point is that the taboo against bestiality is so widely accepted today that neither the church nor the courts need to involve themselves in policing it. Iterations of popular culture manage to accomplish this policing just fine on their own. For historical works on bestiality, see John Canup, *Out of the Wilderness: The Emergence of an American Identity in Colonial New England* (Middletown, Conn.: Wesleyan University Press, 1990); Jonas Liliequist, "Presents against Nature: Crossing the Boundaries between Man and Animal in Seventeenth- and Eighteenth-Century Sweden," *Journal of the History of Sexuality* 1:3 (1991), 393–423; Richard Godbeer, *Sexual Revolution in Early America: Gender Relations in the American Experience* (Baltimore: Johns Hopkins University Press, 2002); and Jens Rydstrom, *Sinners and Citizens: Bestiality and Homosexuality in Sweden, 1880–1950* (Chicago: University of Chicago Press, 2003).

8. For an excellent feminist analysis of bestiality pornography, see Margaret Grebowicz, "When Species Meat: Confronting Bestiality Pornography," *Humanalia: A Journal of Human/Animal Interface Studies* 1:2 (2010), 1–17.

9. Piers Beirne, "Rethinking Bestiality: Towards a Concept of Interspecies Sexual Assault," *Theoretical Criminology* 1:3 (1997), 317–40, at 323.

10. It's interesting to note that many formulations of animal rights secure their arguments based on the similarity of humans to nonhuman animals. As Tom Regan writes, "We understand their behavior because we understand ourselves and our behavior. . . . There is somebody there behind those canine eyes, somebody with wants and needs" (*Empty Cages: Facing the Challenge of Animal Rights* [Lanham, Md.: Rowman & Littlefield, 2004], 55). One might ask animal rights advocates why we couldn't also know their wants and needs in relation to sex.

11. Eve Sedgwick, *Epistemology of the Closet* (Berkeley, Calif.: University of California Press, 1990), 36.

12. Sedgwick, *Epistemology of the Closet*, 22.

13. Eve wrote extensively on this question of family, and as a result I am somewhat hesitant to insert it here, unproblematized. The term sets up a hierarchy where heteronormative coupling resulting in human children is "natural," and every other social arrangement gains legitimacy only insofar as it can argue its likeness to "the family." Nevertheless, recuperation may be possible. As Eve writes, "It's been a ruling intuition for me to disengage the bonds of blood, of law, of habitation, of privacy, of companionship and succor, from the lockstep of their unanimity in the system called 'family'" (*Tendencies*, 6). I take her to mean that her familial affections were not ruled by blood ties or marital contracts, that they floated outside these domains in ways that were unpredictable and queer. It's only in this sense that I want to make family with my dogs.

14. Dekkers, *Dearest Pet*, 149.

15. Dekkers, *Dearest Pet*, 3. For a similar analysis, see Alphonso Lingus, "Bestiality," in *Animal Others: On Ethics, Ontology, and Animal Life*, edited by Peter H. Steeves (Albany, N.Y.: State University of New York Press, 1999), 37–54.

16. J. R. Ackerley, *My Dog Tulip* (London: Secker & Warburg, 1956); Mark Doty, *Dog Years: A Memoir* (New York: HarperCollins, 2007).

17. Grebowicz, "When Species Meat," 14. Of course, I do not mean to suggest that feminist theory in general, or even in its queer inflections, embraces or should embrace bestiality. Many feminists would disagree. See Carol Adams, "Bestiality: The Unmentioned Abuse," *The Animal's Agenda* 15:6 (1995), 30–31; Carol Adams and Josephine Donovan, eds., *The Feminist Care Tradition in Animal Ethics: A Reader* (New York: Columbia University Press), 2007; and Colleen Glenney Boggs, "American Bestiality: Sex, Animals, and the Construction of Subjectivity," *Cultural Critique* 76 (2010), 98–125.

18. Kalpana Seshadri-Crooks, "Being Human: Bestiality, Anthropology, and Law," *UMBR(a)* 1:1 (2003), 97–115, at 112.
19. Sedgwick, *Epistemology of the Closet*, 1.

STUDY QUESTIONS

1. Try to clearly state the main claim(s) that Rudy is arguing for in her essay, and the main reasons she provides in its support. What, exactly, does queer theory contribute to the claim and the argument? (In answering these questions, read the essay in this volume by Kim Q. Hall, "Thinking Queerly about Sex and Sexuality.")

2. Is it true that the ban on bestiality depends on a clear notion of what sex is? Why can't one argue, "We don't know what sex is, but we don't need to know what it is to know that some sexual activities are wrong, including sex with animals"? Would a comparison to other sexual acts considered wrong help Rudy's argument or undermine it? Moreover, why does Rudy frequently write that it is impossible to define sex "beforehand"? Why "beforehand"? Might there be confusion here between conceptual issues and causal ones? (See Study Question 9 for Kim Q. Hall's essay in this volume, "Thinking Queerly about Sex and Sexuality.")

3. Take seriously people's attitude of feeling sorry for those who have relationships only with animals. On what beliefs is such an attitude based? (Consider the uniqueness of human/human relationships, emotional bonds, reciprocity and recognition, empathy, etc.) Can this attitude—or one similar to it—be justified? Can it be justified despite everything that Rudy says to counteract it?

4. Can animals consent to sexual acts with human beings? (In answering this question, make sure to read the other essays in this volume on consent, especially the one by Alan Wertheimer.) If they can consent to other activities with human beings (can they?), why not to sex?

5. Rudy maps out two axes reflecting our attitudes toward sex with animals, one axis supporting sex with animals, the other prohibiting it. Each axis, however, contains opposite reasons for the support and for the prohibition (thereby leaving us with four "sites" of such attitudes). Explain the two axes fully and what role they play in Rudy's overall argument. And, in the spirit of what Eve Kosofsky Sedgwick would have thought, are there ways to combine two or more of these four sites of the axes? Are there options additional to them?

6. Try to make sense of the following two sentences by Rudy: "It's not so much that I am not a lesbian, then [when she is in a relationship with her dogs]—it's that the binary of gay and straight no longer has anything to do with me. My preference these days is canine."

In connection with this, read the brief criticism of Rudy's claim given by Kim Q. Hall in her essay "Thinking Queerly about Sex and Sexuality" in this volume.

7. Rudy states, "The sense of danger associated with human/animal sex emerges as a result of a cultural anxiety about our own animality. That is, if we do 'that' (leaving 'that' unnamed and unrepresented), we will lose something about what it means to be human, to be superior." Is this true? Might there be better (or simply other) explanations for this taboo on sex with animals? (Consider: Many human groups have believed that they were superior to other human groups, even that they were more human than them [or just that the other group was not human, period], without ceasing to have sex with them. Indeed, having sex with them was often a way to assert their superiority.)

8. Rudy states that "my dogs and I have changed each other such that I am no longer human and they are no longer only canine." Indeed, her main claim is that "in deep connection, we all—humans and animals alike—become something different"; our "stable identities shift" because of the love connections. What does she mean by this claim? Is Rudy here making an ontological claim about what it means to be human and animal? If yes, would this take the teeth out of her daring (albeit never fully explicit) suggestion that sometimes human-animal sex might not be wrong? (Does she suggest this, even if implicitly?) If in such deep relationships the boundaries of being human and being animal changes, would the boldness of her suggestion diminish?

9. There seem to be two argumentative strategies in Rudy's essay. The first is to keep fixed the categories of being human and of being (a nonhuman) animal, and then argue that because, according to queer theory, we have no firm definition or concept of sex or of sexual identity, we cannot convincingly maintain the prohibition on sex between human beings and animals. The second strategy is to start with the idea that love or deep connection between human beings and animals has the potential to change both parties to the relationship (so she does not keep fixed the two just-mentioned categories), and then argue that we must think of our intimate relationships with animals more fluidly, not as either sexual or nonsexual. Can you find textual evidence for these two strategies in her essay? More important, are these two strategies compatible with each other or in tension with each other? If the former, how so? If the latter, why and which strategy is more convincing or successful?

SIXTEEN

Sexual Morality and the Concept of Using Another Person

Thomas A. Mappes

The Second Formulation of Immanuel Kant's famous Categorical Imperative (also called the "Formula of Humanity")—"always treat humanity, whether in your own person or in the person of any other, never simply as a means, but always at the same time as an end"—continues to frame philosophical discussions of the moral value of rational autonomy and our contemporary thoughts about the moral power of consent. Its proper application to sexual relations is the nexus of many essays in this volume, including the contribution of **Thomas A. Mappes**, *who sees Kant's views on objectification and using others for one's own goals as suggesting both necessary and sufficient conditions for morally licit sexual activity. On Mappes's (perhaps "libertarian") reading of the Second Formulation, sexual relations are morally permissible just in case they occur with the free and informed consent of the participants (a view not dissimilar from that of the utilitarian John Stuart Mill). Mappes examines different ways in which misinformation or deception (outright lies) as well as pressure or coercion (as in rape, for example) can poison sexual relations, and describes for our consideration a number of difficult or borderline cases. Mappes's remarks on the wrongness of sexual exploitation at the end of his essay are an interesting extension of his Kantian perspective.*

In order to do competent exegetical work in this area one must study Kant's writings, especially his Lectures on Ethics *(trans. Peter Heath, ed. Peter Heath and J. B. Schneewind [Cambridge: Cambridge University Press, 1997]) and* The Metaphysics of Morals *(trans. Mary Gregor [Cambridge: Cambridge University Press, 1991, 1996]). Other editions of these works are available, but these are undoubtedly currently the best.*

Thomas Mappes is professor emeritus of philosophy at Frostburg State University in Maryland. He is the editor, with David DeGrazia, of *Biomedical Ethics*, 6th edition (McGraw-Hill, 2006), and the editor, with Jane S. Zembaty, of *Social Ethics: Morality and Social Policy*, 7th edition (McGraw-Hill, 2007). This essay is reprinted with the permission of the author from *Social Ethics: Morality and Social Policy*, 3rd edition (McGraw-Hill, 1987), 248–62, edited by Thomas A. Mappes and Jane S. Zembaty. © 1985, Thomas A. Mappes.

The central tenet of *conventional* sexual morality is that nonmarital sex is immoral. A somewhat less restrictive sexual ethic holds that *sex without love* is immoral. If neither of these positions is philosophically defensible, and I would contend that neither is, it does not follow that there are no substantive moral restrictions on human sexual interaction. Any human interaction, including sexual interaction, may be judged morally objectionable to the extent that it transgresses a justified moral rule or principle. The way to construct a detailed account of sexual morality, it would seem, is simply to work out the implications of relevant moral rules or principles in the area of human sexual interaction.

As one important step in the direction of such an account, I will attempt to work out the implications of an especially relevant moral principle, the principle that it is wrong for one person to use another person. However ambiguous the expression "using another person" may seem to be, there is a determinate and clearly specifiable sense according to which using another person is morally objectionable. Once this morally significant sense of "using another person" is identified and explicated, the concept of using another person can play an important role in the articulation of a defensible account of sexual morality.

I. THE MORALLY SIGNIFICANT SENSE OF "USING ANOTHER PERSON"

Historically, the concept of using another person is associated with the ethical system of Immanuel Kant. According to a fundamental Kantian principle, it is morally wrong for A to use B *merely as a means* (to achieve A's ends). Kant's principle does not rule out A using B as a means, only A using B *merely* as a means—that is, in a way incompatible with respect for B as a person. In the ordinary course of life, it is surely unavoidable (and morally unproblematic) that each of us in numerous ways uses others as a means to achieve our various ends. A college teacher uses students as a means to achieve his or her livelihood. A college student uses instructors as a means of gaining knowledge and skills. Such human interactions, presumably based on the voluntary participation of the respective parties, are quite compatible with the idea of respect for persons. But respect for persons entails that each of us recognize the rightful authority of other persons (as rational beings) to conduct their individual lives as they see fit. We may legitimately recruit others to participate in the satisfaction of our personal ends, but they are used merely as a means whenever we

undermine the voluntary or informed character of their consent to interact with us in some desired way. A coerces B at knifepoint to hand over
$200. A uses B merely as means. If A had requested of B a gift of $200,
leaving B free to determine whether to make the gift, A would have
proceeded in a manner compatible with respect for B as a person. C
deceptively rolls back the odometer of a car and thereby manipulates D's
decision to buy the car. C uses D merely as a means.

On the basis of these considerations, I would suggest that the morally
significant sense of "using another person" is best understood by reference to the notion of *voluntary informed consent*. More specifically, A immorally uses B if and only if A intentionally acts in a way that violates the
requirement that B's involvement with A's ends be based on B's voluntary informed consent. If this account is correct, using another person (in
the morally significant sense) can arise in at least two important ways: via
coercion, which is antithetical to voluntary consent, and via *deception*,
which undermines the informed character of voluntary consent.

The notion of voluntary informed consent is very prominent in the
literature of biomedical ethics and is systematically related to the much-
emphasized notion of (patient) autonomy. We find in the famous words
of Supreme Court justice Cardozo a ringing affirmation of patient autonomy: "Every human being of adult years and sound mind has a right to
determine what shall be done with his own body." Because respect for
individual autonomy is an essential part of respect for persons, if medical
professionals (and biomedical researchers) are to interact with their patients (and research subjects) in an acceptable way, they must respect
individual autonomy. That is, they must respect the self-determination of
the patient/subject, the individual's right to determine what shall be done
with his or her body. This means that they must not act in a way that
violates the requirement of voluntary informed consent. Medical procedures must not be performed without the consent of competent patients;
research on human subjects must not be carried out without the consent
of the subjects involved. Moreover, consent must be voluntary; coercion
undermines individual autonomy. Consent must also be informed; lying
or withholding relevant information undercuts rational decision making
and thereby undermines individual autonomy.

To further illuminate the concept of using that has been proposed, I
will consider in greater detail the matter of research involving human
subjects. In the sphere of researcher-subject interaction, just as in the
sphere of human sexual interaction, there is ample opportunity for immorally using another person. If a researcher is engaged in a study that
involves human subjects, we may presume that the "end" of the researcher is the successful completion of the study. (The researcher may desire
this particular end for any number of reasons: the speculative understanding it will provide, the technology it will make possible, the eventu-
al benefit of humankind, increased status in the scientific community,

a raise in pay, etc.) The work, let us presume, strictly requires the use (employment) of human research subjects. The researcher, however, immorally uses other people only if he or she intentionally acts in a way that violates the requirement that the participation of research subjects be based on their voluntary informed consent.

Let us assume that in a particular case, participation as a research subject involves some rather significant risks. Accordingly, the researcher finds that potential subjects are reluctant to volunteer. At this point, if an unscrupulous researcher is willing to resort to the immoral using of other people (to achieve his or her own ends), two manifest options are available—deception and coercion. By way of deception, the researcher might choose to lie about the risks involved. For example, potential subjects could be explicitly told that there are no significant risks associated with research participation. On the other hand, the researcher could simply withhold a full disclosure of risks. Whether pumped full of false information or simply deprived of relevant information, the potential subject is intentionally deceived in such a way as to be led to a decision that furthers the researcher's ends. In manipulating the decision-making process of the potential subject in this way, the researcher is guilty of immorally using another person.

To explain how an unscrupulous researcher might immorally use another person via coercion, it is helpful to distinguish two basic forms of coercion.[1] "Occurrent" coercion involves the use of physical force. "Dispositional" coercion involves the threat of harm. If I am forcibly thrown out of my office by an intruder, I am the victim of occurrent coercion. If, on the other hand, I leave my office because an intruder has threatened to shoot me if I do not leave, I am the victim of dispositional coercion. The victim of occurrent coercion literally has no choice in what happens. The victim of dispositional coercion, in contrast, does intentionally choose a certain course of action. However, one's choice, in the face of the threat of harm, is less than fully voluntary.

It is perhaps unlikely that even an unscrupulous researcher would resort to any very explicit measure of coercion. Deception, it seems, is less risky. Still, it is well known that Nazi medical experimenters ruthlessly employed coercion. By way of occurrent coercion, the Nazis literally forced great numbers of concentration camp victims to participate in experiments that entailed their own death or dismemberment. And if some concentration camp victims "volunteered" to participate in Nazi research to avoid even more unspeakable horrors, clearly we must consider them victims of dispositional coercion. The Nazi researchers, employing coercion, immorally used other human beings with a vengeance.

II. DECEPTION AND SEXUAL MORALITY

To this point, I have been concerned to identify and explicate the morally significant sense of "using another person." On the view proposed, A immorally uses B if and only if A intentionally acts in a way that violates the requirement that B's involvement with A's ends be based on B's voluntary informed consent. I will now apply this account to the area of human sexual interaction and explore its implications. For economy of expression in what follows, "using" (and its cognates) is to be understood as referring only to the morally significant sense.

If we presume a state of affairs in which A desires some form of sexual interaction with B, we can say that this desired form of sexual interaction with B is A's end. Thus A sexually uses B if and only if A intentionally acts in a way that violates the requirement that B's sexual interaction with A be based on B's voluntary informed consent. It seems clear then that A may sexually use B in at least two distinctive ways, (1) via coercion and (2) via deception. However, before proceeding to discuss deception and then the more problematic case of coercion, one important point must be made. In emphasizing the centrality of coercion and deception as mechanisms for the sexual using of another person, I have in mind sexual interaction with a fully competent adult partner. We should also want to say, I think, that sexual interaction with a child inescapably involves the sexual using of another person. Even if a child "consents" to sexual interaction, he or she is, strictly speaking, incapable of *informed* consent. It's a matter of being *incompetent* to give consent. Similarly, to the extent that a mentally retarded person is rightly considered incompetent, sexual interaction with such a person amounts to the sexual using of that person, unless someone empowered to give "proxy consent" has done so. (In certain circumstances, sexual involvement might be in the best interests of a mentally retarded person.) We can also visualize the case of an otherwise fully competent adult temporarily disordered by drugs or alcohol. To the extent that such a person is rightly regarded as temporarily incompetent, winning his or her "consent" to sexual interaction could culminate in the sexual using of that person.

There are a host of clear cases in which one person sexually uses another precisely because the former employs deception in a way that undermines the informed character of the latter's consent to sexual interaction. Consider this example. One person, A, has decided, as a matter of personal prudence based on past experience, not to become sexually involved outside the confines of a loving relationship. Another person, B, strongly desires a sexual relationship with A but does not love A. B, aware of A's unwillingness to engage in sex without love, professes love for A, thereby hoping to win A's consent to a sexual relationship. B's ploy is successful; A consents. When the smoke clears and A becomes aware of

B's deception, it would be both appropriate and natural for A to complain, "I've been used."

In the same vein, here are some other examples: (1) Mr. A is aware that Ms. B will consent to sexual involvement only on the understanding that in time the two will be married. Mr. A has no intention of marrying Ms. B but says that he will. (2) Ms. C has herpes and is well aware that Mr. D will never consent to sex if he knows of her condition. When asked by Mr. D, Ms. C denies that she has herpes. (3) Mr. E knows that Ms. F will not consent to sexual intercourse in the absence of responsible birth control measures. Mr. E tells Ms. F that he has had a vasectomy, which is not the case. (4) Ms. G knows that Mr. H would not consent to sexual involvement with a married woman. Ms. G is married but tells Mr. H that she is single. (5) Ms. I is well aware that Ms. J is interested in a stable lesbian relationship and will not consent to become sexually involved with someone who is bisexual. Ms. I tells Ms. J that she is exclusively homosexual, whereas the truth is that she is bisexual.

If one person's consent to sex is predicated on false beliefs that have been intentionally and deceptively inculcated by one's sexual partner in an effort to win the former's consent, the resulting sexual interaction involves one person sexually using another. In each of the above cases, one person explicitly *lies* to another. False information is intentionally conveyed to win consent to sexual interaction, and the end result is the sexual using of another person.

As noted earlier, however, lying is not the only form of deception. Under certain circumstances, the simple withholding of information can be considered a form of deception. Accordingly, it is possible to sexually use another person not only by (deceptively) lying about relevant facts but also by (deceptively) not disclosing relevant facts. If A has good reason to believe that B would refuse to consent to sexual interaction should B become aware of certain factual information, and if A withholds disclosure of this information in order to enhance the possibility of gaining B's consent, then, if B does consent, A sexually uses B via deception. One example will suffice. Suppose that Mr. A meets Ms. B in a singles bar. Mr. A realizes immediately that Ms. B is the sister of Ms. C, a woman that Mr. A has been sexually involved with for a long time. Mr. A, knowing that it is very unlikely that Ms. B will consent to sexual interaction if she becomes aware of Mr. A's involvement with her sister, decides not to disclose this information. If Ms. B eventually consents to sexual interaction, since her consent is the product of Mr. A's deception, it is rightly thought that she has been sexually used by him.

III. COERCION AND SEXUAL MORALITY

We have considered the case of deception. The present task is to consider the more difficult case of coercion. Whereas deception functions to undermine the *informed* character of voluntary consent (to sexual interaction), coercion either obliterates consent entirely (the case of occurrent coercion) or undermines the voluntariness of consent (the case of dispositional coercion).

Forcible rape is the most conspicuous, and most brutal, way of sexually using another person via coercion.[2] Forcible rape may involve either occurrent coercion or dispositional coercion. A man who rapes a woman through the employment of sheer physical force, by simply overpowering her, employs occurrent coercion. There is literally no sexual *interaction* in such a case; only the rapist performs an action. In no sense does the woman consent to or participate in sexual activity. She has no choice in what takes place, or, rather, physical force results in her choice being simply beside the point. The employment of occurrent coercion for the purpose of rape "objectifies" the victim in the strongest sense of that term. She is treated like a physical object. One does not interact with physical objects; one acts upon them. In a perfectly ordinary (not the morally significant) sense of the term, we "use" physical objects. But when the victim of rape is treated as if she were a physical object, there we have one of the most vivid examples of the immoral using of another person.

Frequently, forcible rape involves not occurrent coercion (or not *only* occurrent coercion) but dispositional coercion.[3] In dispositional coercion, the relevant factor is not physical force but the threat of harm. The rapist threatens his victim with immediate and serious bodily harm. For example, a man threatens to kill or beat a woman if she resists his sexual demands. She "consents"—that is, she submits to his demands. He may demand only passive participation (simply not struggling against him) or he may demand some measure of active participation. Rape that employs dispositional coercion is surely just as wrong as rape that employs occurrent coercion, but there is a notable difference in the mechanism by which the rapist uses his victim in the two cases. With occurrent coercion, the victim's consent is entirely bypassed. With dispositional coercion, the victim's consent is not bypassed. It is coerced. Dispositional coercion undermines the *voluntariness* of consent. The rapist, by employing the threat of immediate and serious bodily harm, may succeed in bending the victim's will. He may gain the victim's "consent." But he uses another person precisely because consent is coerced.

The relevance of occurrent coercion is limited to the case of forcible rape. Dispositional coercion, a notion that also plays an indispensable role in an overall account of forcible rape, now becomes our central concern. Although the threat of immediate and serious bodily harm stands out as the most brutal way of coercing consent to sexual interaction, we must not neglect the employment of other kinds of threats to this same end. There are numerous ways in which one person can effectively harm, and thus effectively threaten, another. Accordingly, for example, consent to sexual interaction might be coerced by threatening to damage someone's reputation. If a person consents to sexual interaction to avoid a threatened harm, then that person has been sexually used (via dispositional coercion). In the face of a threat, of course, it remains possible that a person will refuse to comply with another's sexual demands. It is probably best to describe this sort of situation as a case not of coercion, which entails the *successful* use of threats to gain compliance, but of *attempted* coercion. Of course, the moral fault of an individual emerges with the *attempt* to coerce. A person who attempts murder is morally blameworthy even if the attempt fails. The same is true for someone who fails in an effort to coerce consent to sexual interaction.

Consider now each of the following cases:

Case 1: Mr. Supervisor makes a series of increasingly less subtle sexual overtures to Ms. Employee. These advances are consistently and firmly rejected by Ms. Employee. Eventually, Mr. Supervisor makes it clear that the granting of "sexual favors" is a condition of her continued employment.

Case 2: Ms. Debtor borrowed a substantial sum of money from Mr. Creditor, on the understanding that she would pay it back within one year. In the meantime, Ms. Debtor has become sexually attracted to Mr. Creditor, but he does not share her interest. At the end of the one-year period, Mr. Creditor asks Ms. Debtor to return the money. She says she will be happy to return the money so long as he consents to sexual interaction with her.

Case 3: Mr. Theatregoer has two tickets to the most talked-about play of the season. He is introduced to a woman whom he finds sexually attractive and who shares his interest in the theater. In the course of their conversation, she expresses disappointment that the play everyone is talking about is sold out; she would love to see it. At this point, Mr. Theatregoer suggests that she be his guest at the theater. "Oh, by the way," he says, "I always expect sex from my dates."

Case 4: Ms. Jetsetter is planning a trip to Europe. She has been trying for some time to develop a sexual relationship with a man who has shown little interest in her. She knows, however, that he has always wanted to go to Europe and that it is only lack of money that has deterred him. Ms. Jetsetter proposes that he come along as her traveling companion, all expenses paid, on the express understanding that sex is part of the arrangement.

Cases 1 and 2 involve attempts to sexually use another person, whereas cases 3 and 4 do not. To see why this is so, it is essential to introduce a distinction between two kinds of proposals, viz., the distinction between *threats* and *offers*.[4] The logical form of a threat differs from the logical form of an offer in the following way. Threat: "If you *do not* do what I am proposing you do, I will bring about an *undesirable consequence* for you." Offer: "If you *do* what I am proposing you do, I will bring about a *desirable consequence* for you." The person who makes a threat attempts to gain compliance by attaching an undesirable consequence to the alternative of noncompliance. This person attempts to *coerce* consent. The person who makes an offer attempts to gain compliance by attaching a desirable consequence to the alternative of compliance. This person attempts not to coerce but to *induce* consent.

Since threats are morally problematic in a way that offers are not, it is not uncommon for threats to be advanced in the language of offers. Threats are represented as if they were offers. An armed assailant might say, "I'm going to make you an *offer*. If you give me your money, I will allow you to go on living." Though this proposal on the surface has the logical form of an offer, it is in reality a threat. The underlying sense of the proposal is this: "If you do not give me your money, I will kill you." If, in a given case, it is initially unclear whether a certain proposal is to count as a threat or an offer, ask the following question. Does the proposal in question have the effect of making a person *worse off upon noncompliance*? The recipient of an offer, upon noncompliance, is *not worse off* than he or she was before the offer. In contrast, the recipient of a threat, upon noncompliance, is *worse off* than he or she was before the threat. Since the "offer" of our armed assailant has the effect, upon noncompliance, of rendering its recipient worse off (relative to the preproposal situation of the recipient), the recipient is faced with a threat, not an offer.

The most obvious way for a coercer to attach an undesirable consequence to the path of noncompliance is by threatening to render the victim of coercion materially worse off than he or she has theretofore been. Thus a person is threatened with loss of life, bodily injury, damage to property, damage to reputation, etc. It is important to realize, however, that a person can also be effectively coerced by being threatened with the withholding of something (in some cases, what we would call a "benefit") to which the person is entitled. Suppose that A is mired in quicksand and is slowly but surely approaching death. When B happens along, A cries out to B for assistance. All B needs to do is throw A a rope. B is quite willing to accommodate A, "provided you pay me $100,000 over the next ten years." Is B making A an offer? Hardly! B, we must presume, stands under a moral obligation to come to the aid of a person in serious distress, at least whenever such assistance entails no significant risk, sacrifice of time, and so forth. A is entitled to B's assistance. Thus, in reality, B attaches an undesirable consequence to A's noncompliance with the proposal that A pay B $100,000. A is undoubtedly better off that B has happened along, but A is not rendered better off by B's proposal. Before B's *proposal*, A legitimately expected assistance from B, "no strings attached." In attaching a very unwelcome string, B's proposal effectively renders A worse off. What B proposes, then, is not an offer of assistance. Rather, B threatens A with the withholding of something (assistance) that A is entitled to have from B.

Since threats have the effect of rendering a person worse off upon noncompliance, it is ordinarily the case that a person does not welcome (indeed, despises) them. Offers, on the other hand, are ordinarily welcome to a person. Since an offer provides no penalty for noncompliance with a proposal but only an inducement for compliance, there is *in principle* only potential advantage in being confronted with an offer. In real life, of course, there are numerous reasons why a person may be less than enthusiastic about being presented with an offer. Enduring the presentation of trivial offers does not warrant the necessary time and energy expenditures. Offers can be both annoying and offensive; certainly this is true of some sexual offers. A person might also be unsettled by an offer that confronts him or her with a difficult decision. All this, however, is compatible with the fact that an offer is fundamentally welcome to a rational person in the sense that the *content* of an offer necessarily widens the field of opportunity and thus provides, in principle, only potential advantage.

With the distinction between threats and offers clearly in view, it now becomes clear why cases 1 and 2 do indeed involve attempts to sexually use another person whereas cases 3 and 4 do not. Cases 1 and 2 embody threats, whereas cases 3 and 4 embody offers. In case 1, Mr. Supervisor proposes sexual interaction with Ms. Employee and, in an effort to gain compliance, threatens her with the loss of her job. Mr. Supervisor thereby attaches an undesirable consequence to one of Ms. Employee's alternatives, the path of noncompliance. Typical of the threat situation, Mr. Supervisor's proposal has the effect of rendering Ms. Employee worse off upon noncompliance. Mr. Supervisor is attempting via (dispositional) coercion to sexually use Ms. Employee. The situation in case 2 is similar. Ms. Debtor, as *she* might be inclined to say, "offers" to pay Mr. Creditor the money she owes him *if* he consents to sexual interaction with her. In reality, Mrs. Debtor is threatening Mr. Creditor, attempting to coerce his consent to sexual interaction, attempting to sexually use him. Though Mr. Creditor is not now in possession of the money Ms. Debtor owes him, he is *entitled* to receive it from her at this time. She threatens to deprive him of something to which he is entitled. Clearly, her proposal has the effect of rendering him worse off upon noncompliance. Before her proposal, he had the legitimate expectation, "no strings attached," of receiving the money in question.

Cases 3 and 4 embody offers; neither involves an attempt to sexually use another person. Mr. Theatregoer simply provides an inducement for the woman he has just met to accept his proposal of sexual interaction. He offers her the opportunity to see the play that everyone is talking about. In attaching a desirable consequence to the alternative of compliance, Mr. Theatregoer in no way threatens or attempts to coerce his potential companion. Typical of the offer situation, his proposal does not have the effect of rendering her worse off upon noncompliance. She now has a new opportunity; if she chooses to forgo this opportunity, she is no worse off. The situation in case 4 is similar. Ms. Jetsetter provides an inducement for a man whom she is interested in to accept her proposal of sexual involvement. She offers him the opportunity to see Europe, without expense, as her traveling companion. Before Ms. Jetsetter's proposal, he had no prospect of a European trip. If he chooses to reject her proposal, he is no worse off than he has theretofore been. Ms. Jetsetter's proposal embodies an offer, not a threat. She cannot be accused of attempting to sexually use her potential traveling companion.

Consider now two further cases, 5 and 6, each of which develops in the following way. Professor Highstatus, a man of high academic accomplishment, is sexually attracted to a student in one of his classes. He is very anxious to secure her consent to sexual interaction. Ms. Student, confused and unsettled by his sexual advances, has begun to practice "avoidance behavior." To the extent that it is possible, she goes out of her way to avoid him.

Case 5: Professor Highstatus tells Ms. Student that, though her work is such as to entitle her to a grade of B in the class, she will be assigned a D unless she consents to sexual interaction.

Case 6: Professor Highstatus tells Ms. Student that, though her work is such as to entitle her to a grade of B, she will be assigned an A if she consents to sexual interaction.

It is clear that case 5 involves an attempt to sexually use another person. Case 6, however, at least at face value, does not. In case 5, Professor Highstatus *threatens* to deprive Ms. Student of the grade she deserves. In case 6, he *offers* to assign her a grade that is higher than she deserves. In case 5, Ms. Student would be worse off upon noncompliance with Professor Highstatus's proposal. In case 6, she would not be worse off upon noncompliance with his proposal. In saying that case 6 does not involve an attempt to sexually use another person, it is not being asserted that Professor Highstatus is acting in a morally legitimate fashion. In offering a student a higher grade than she deserves, he is guilty of abusing his institutional authority. He is under an obligation to assign the grades that students earn, as defined by the relevant course standards. In case 6, Professor Highstatus is undoubtedly acting in a morally reprehensible way, but, in contrast to case 5, where it is fair to say that he both abuses his institutional authority and attempts to sexually use another person, we can plausibly say that in case 6 his moral failure is limited to abuse of his institutional authority.

There remains, however, a suspicion that case 6 might after all embody an attempt to sexually use another person. There is no question that the literal content of what Professor Highstatus conveys to Ms. Student has the logical form of an offer and not a threat. Still, is it not the case that Ms. Student may very well feel threatened? Professor Highstatus, in an effort to secure consent to sexual interaction, has announced that he will assign Ms. Student a higher grade than she deserves. Can she really turn him down without substantial risk? Is he not likely to retaliate? If she spurns him, will he not lower her grade or otherwise make it harder for her to succeed in her academic program? He does, after all, have power over her. Will he use it to her detriment? Surely he is not above abusing his institutional authority to achieve his ends; this much is abundantly clear from his willingness to assign a grade higher than a student deserves.

Is Professor Highstatus naive to the threat that Ms. Student may find implicit in the situation? Perhaps. In such a case, if Ms. Student reluctantly consents to sexual interaction, we may be inclined to say that he has *unwittingly* used her. More likely, Professor Highstatus is well aware of the way in which Ms. Student will perceive his proposal. He knows that threats need not be verbally expressed. Indeed, it may even be the case that he consciously exploits his underground reputation: "Everyone knows what happens to the women who reject Professor Highstatus's little offers." To the extent, then, that Professor Highstatus intends to convey a threat in case 6, he is attempting via coercion to sexually use another person.

Many researchers "have pointed out the fact that the possibility of sanctions for noncooperation is implicit in all sexual advances across authority lines, as between teacher and student."[5] I do not think that this consideration should lead us to the conclusion that a person with an academic appointment is obliged in all circumstances to refrain from attempting to initiate sexual involvement with one of his or her students. Still, since even "good faith" sexual advances may be ambiguous in the eyes of a student, it is an interesting question what precautions an instructor must take to avoid unwittingly coercing a student to consent to sexual interaction.

Much of what has been said about the professor/student relationship in an academic setting can be applied as well to the supervisor/subordinate relationship in an employment setting. A manager who functions within an organizational structure is required to evaluate fairly his or her subordinates according to relevant corporate or institutional standards. An unscrupulous manager, willing to abuse his or her institutional authority in an effort to win the consent of a subordinate to sexual interaction, can advance threats and/or offers related to the managerial task of employee evaluation. An employee whose job performance is entirely satisfactory can be threatened with an unsatisfactory performance rating, perhaps leading to termination. An employee whose job performance is excellent can be threatened with an unfair evaluation, designed to bar the employee from recognition, merit pay, consideration for promotion, and so on. Such threats, when made in an effort to coerce employee consent to sexual interaction, clearly embody the attempt to sexually use another person. On the other hand, the manager who (abusing his or her institutional authority) offers to provide an employee with an inflated evaluation as an inducement for consent to sexual interaction does not, at face value, attempt to sexually use another person. Of course, all of the qualifications introduced in the discussion of case 6 above are applicable here as well.

IV. THE IDEA OF A COERCIVE OFFER

In section III, I have sketched an overall account of sexually using another person *via coercion*. In this section, I will consider the need for modifications or extensions of the suggested account. As before, certain case studies will serve as points of departure.

Case 7: Ms. Starlet, a glamorous, wealthy, and highly successful model, wants nothing more than to become a movie superstar. Mr. Moviemogul, a famous producer, is very taken with Ms. Starlet's beauty. He invites her to come to his office for a screen test. After the screen test, Mr. Moviemogul tells Ms. Starlet that he is prepared to make her a star, on the condition that she agree to sexual involvement with him. Ms. Starlet finds Mr. Moviemogul personally repugnant; she is not at all sexually attracted to him. With great reluctance, she agrees to his proposal.

Has Mr. Moviemogul sexually used Ms. Starlet? No. He has made her an offer that she has accepted, however reluctantly. The situation would be quite different if it were plausible to believe that she was, before acceptance of his proposal, *entitled* to his efforts to make her a star. Then we could read case 7 as amounting to his threatening to deprive her of something to which she was entitled. But what conceivable grounds could be found for the claim that Mr. Moviemogul, before Ms. Starlet's acceptance of his proposal, is under an obligation to make her a star? He does not threaten her; he makes her an offer. Even if there are other good grounds for morally condemning his action, it is a mistake to think that he is guilty of coercing consent.

But some would assert that Mr. Moviemogul's offer, on the grounds that it confronts Ms. Starlet with an overwhelming inducement, is simply an example of a *coercive offer*. The more general claim at issue is that offers are coercive precisely inasmuch as they are extremely enticing or seductive. Though there is an important reality associated with the notion of a coercive offer, a reality that must shortly be confronted, we ought not embrace the view that an offer is coercive merely because it is extremely enticing or seductive. Virginia Held is a leading proponent of the view under attack here. She writes:

> A person unable to spurn an offer may act as unwillingly as a person unable to resist a threat. Consider the distinction between rape and seduction. In one case constraint and threat are operative, in the other inducement and offer. If the degree of inducement is set high enough in the case of seduction, there may seem to be little difference in the extent of coercion involved. In both cases, persons may act against their own wills.[6]

Certainly a rape victim who acquiesces at knifepoint is forced to act *against her will*. Does Ms. Starlet, however, act against her will? We have said that she consents "with great reluctance" to sexual involvement, but she does not act against her will. She *wants* very much to be a movie star. I might want very much to be thin. She regrets having to become sexually involved with Mr. Moviemogul as a means of achieving what she wants. I might regret very much having to go on a diet to lose weight. If we say that Ms. Starlet acts against her will in case 7, then we must say that I am acting against my will in embracing "with great reluctance" the diet I despise.

A more important line of argument against Held's view can be advanced on the basis of the widely accepted notion that there is a moral presumption against coercion. Held herself embraces this notion and very effectively clarifies it:

> Although coercion is not always wrong (quite obviously: one coerces the small child not to run across the highway, or the murderer to drop his weapon), there is a presumption against it. . . . This has the standing of a fundamental moral principle. . . .
>
> What can be concluded at the moral level is that we have a *prima facie* obligation not to employ coercion.[7] [all italics hers]

But it would seem that acceptance of the moral presumption against coercion is not compatible with the view that offers become coercive precisely inasmuch as they become extremely enticing or seductive. Suppose you are my neighbor and regularly spend your Saturday afternoon on the golf course. Suppose also that you are a skilled gardener. I am anxious to convince you to do some gardening work for me and it must be done this Saturday. I offer you $100, $200, $300 . . . in an effort to make it worth your while to sacrifice your recreation and undertake my gardening. At some point, my proposal becomes very enticing. Yet, at the same time, in no sense is my proposal becoming morally problematic. If my proposal were becoming coercive, surely our moral sense would be aroused.

Though it is surely not true that the extremely enticing character of an offer is sufficient to make it coercive, we need not reach the conclusion that no sense can be made out of the notion of a coercive offer. Indeed, there is an important social reality that the notion of a coercive offer appears to capture, and insight into this reality can be gained by simply taking note of the sort of case that most draws us to the language of "coercive offer." Is it not a case in which the recipient of an offer is in circumstances of genuine need, and acceptance of the offer seems to present the only realistic possibility for alleviating the need? Assuming that this sort of case is the heart of the matter, it seems that we cannot avoid introducing some sort of distinction between *genuine needs* and *mere wants*. Though the philosophical difficulties involved in drawing this distinction are not insignificant, I nevertheless claim that we will not achieve any clarity about the notion of a coercive offer, at least in this context, except in reference to it. Whatever puzzlement we may feel with regard to the host of borderline cases that can be advanced, it is nevertheless true, for example, that I *genuinely need* food and that I *merely want* a backyard tennis court. In the same spirit, I think it can be acknowledged by all that Ms. Starlet, though she *wants* very much to be a star, does not in any relevant sense *need* to be a star. Accordingly, there is little plausibility in thinking that Mr. Moviemogul makes her a coercive offer. The following case, in contrast, can more plausibly be thought to embody a coercive offer.

Case 8: Mr. Troubled is a young widower who is raising his three children. He lives in a small town and believes that it is important for him to stay there so that his children continue to have the emotional support of other family members. But economic times are tough. Mr. Troubled has been laid off from his job and has not been able to find another. His unemployment benefits have ceased and his relatives are in no position to help him financially. If he is unable to come up with the money for his mortgage payments, he will lose his rather modest house. Ms. Opportunistic lives in the same town. Since shortly after the death of Mr. Troubled's wife, she has consistently made sexual overtures in his direction. Mr. Troubled, for his part, does not care for Ms. Opportunistic and has made it clear to her that he is not interested in sexual involvement with her. She, however, is well aware of his present difficulties. To win his consent to a sexual affair, Ms. Opportunistic offers to make mortgage payments for Mr. Troubled on a continuing basis.

Is Ms. Opportunistic attempting to sexually use Mr. Troubled? The correct answer is yes, even though we must first accept the conclusion that her proposal embodies an offer and not a threat. If Ms. Opportunistic were threatening Mr. Troubled, her proposal would have the effect of rendering him worse off upon noncompliance. But this is not the case. If he rejects her proposal, his situation will not worsen; he will simply remain, as before, in circumstances of extreme need. It might be objected at this point that Ms. Opportunistic does in fact threaten Mr. Troubled. She threatens to deprive him of something to which he is entitled—namely, the alleviation of a genuine need. But this approach is defensible only if, before acceptance of her proposal, he is entitled to have his needs alleviated *by her*. And whatever Mr. Troubled and his children are entitled to expect from their society as a whole—they are perhaps slipping through the "social safety net"—it cannot be plausibly maintained that Mr. Troubled is entitled to have his mortgage payments made *by Ms. Opportunistic*.

Yet, though she does not threaten him, she is attempting to sexually use him. How can this conclusion be reconciled with our overall account of sexually using another person? First of all, I want to suggest that nothing hangs on whether we decide to call Ms. Opportunistic's offer "coercive." More important than the label "coercive offer" is an appreciation of the social reality that inclines us to consider the label appropriate. The label most forcefully asserts itself when we reflect on what Mr. Troubled is likely to say after accepting the offer. "I really had no choice." "I didn't want to accept her offer but what could I do? I have my children to think about." Both Mr. Troubled and Ms. Starlet (in our previous case) *reluctantly* consented to sexual interaction, but I think it can be agreed that Ms. Starlet had a choice in a way that Mr. Troubled did not. Mr. Troubled's choice was *severely constrained by his needs*, whereas Ms. Starlet's was not. As for Ms. Opportunistic, it seems that we might describe her approach as in some sense exploiting or taking advantage of Mr. Troubled's desperate situation. It is not so much, as we would say in the case of threats, that she coerces him or his consent, but rather that she achieves her aim of winning consent by taking advantage of the fact that he is already "under coercion," that is, his choice is severely constrained by his need. If we choose to describe what has taken place as a "coercive offer," we should remember that Mr. Troubled is "coerced" (constrained) by his own need or perhaps by preexisting factors in his situation rather than by Ms. Opportunistic or her offer.

Since it is not quite right to say that Ms. Opportunistic is attempting to coerce Mr. Troubled, even if we are prepared to embrace the label "coercive offer," we cannot simply say, as we would say in the case of threats, that she is attempting to sexually use him via coercion. The proper account of the way in which Ms. Opportunistic attempts to sexually use Mr. Troubled is somewhat different. Let us say simply that she attempts to sexually use him *by taking advantage of his desperate situation*. The sense behind this distinctive way of sexually using someone is that a person's choice situation can sometimes be subject to such severe prior constraints that the possibility of *voluntary* consent to sexual interaction is precluded.

A advances an offer calculated to gain B's reluctant consent to sexual interaction by confronting B, who has no apparent way of alleviating a genuine need, with an opportunity to do so, but makes this opportunity contingent upon consent to sexual interaction. In such a case, should we not say simply that B's need, when coupled with a lack of viable alternatives, results in B being incapable of *voluntarily* accepting A's offer? Thus A, in making an offer which B "cannot refuse," although not coercing B, nevertheless does intentionally act in a way that violates the requirement that B's sexual interaction with A be based upon B's voluntary informed consent. Thus A sexually uses B.

The central claim of this chapter is that A sexually uses B if and only if A intentionally acts in a way that violates the requirement that B's sexual interaction with A be based on B's voluntary informed consent. Clearly, deception and coercion are important mechanisms whereby sexual use takes place. But consideration of case 8 has led us to the identification of yet another mechanism. In summary, then, limiting attention to cases of sexual interaction with a fully competent adult partner, A can sexually use B not only (1) by deceiving B or (2) by coercing B but also (3) by taking advantage of B's desperate situation.

NOTES

1. I follow here an account of coercion developed by Michael D. Bayles in "A Concept of Coercion," in *Coercion: Nomos XIV*, edited by J. Roland Pennock and John W. Chapman (Chicago: Aldine-Atherton, 1972), 16–29.

2. Statutory rape, sexual relations with a person under the legal age of consent, can also be construed as the sexual using of another person. In contrast to forcible rape, however, statutory rape need not involve coercion. The victim of statutory rape may freely "consent" to sexual interaction but, at least in the eyes of the law, is deemed incompetent to consent.

3. A man wrestles a woman to the ground. She is the victim of occurrent coercion. He threatens to beat her unless she submits to his sexual demands. Now she becomes the victim of dispositional coercion.

4. My account of this distinction largely derives from Robert Nozick, "Coercion," in *Philosophy, Science, and Method*, edited by Sidney Morgenbesser, Patrick Suppes, and Morton White (New York: St. Martin's Press, 1969), 440–72, and from Michael D. Bayles, "Coercive Offers and Public Benefits," *The Personalist* 55:2 (Spring 1974), 139–44.

5. The National Advisory Council on Women's Educational Programs, *Sexual Harassment: A Report on the Sexual Harassment of Students* (August 1980), 12.

6. Virginia Held, "Coercion and Coercive Offers," in *Coercion: Nomos XIV*, edited by J. Roland Pennock and John W. Chapman (Chicago: Aldine-Atherton, 1972), 49–62, at 58.

7. *Ibid.*, 61, 62.

STUDY QUESTIONS

1. Some philosophers take the principle of free and informed consent so seriously that they apply it to all human activities. Thus, the moral considerations relevant to having sex with another person are no different from those that govern, say, playing tennis. (A version of this thesis can be found in Alan Goldman's "Plain Sex," in this volume.) But suppose someone says, "Any comparison between the informed consent I give in a hospital setting to that I give for sexual relations must be flawed, because sexual relations are significantly different in nature from medical procedures." Do you agree? How is sex different—if it is different—from the other ways we allow our bodies to be touched by others?

2. Mappes says that one person could immorally sexually use another person by failing to disclose relevant facts to the other person prior to engaging in sexual activity. What specific facts are relevant? One possibility is Mappes's suggestion, that if I know that for you fact F would be relevant, would have an effect on your decision and consent, then I must not deceive you (by commission or omission) about F. Is this account adequate? Am I committed to disclosing anything about me that you might find relevant?

3. Suppose that X and Y are two gay men who meet in a venue where gay men have casual sexual encounters. Suppose also that X is HIV positive. Should X disclose his HIV status to Y if Y does not ask? What about if Y does ask? Does the fact that they are in a place where casual sex regularly occurs, and in which certain conventions are in place, have any bearing on this case? Think about how this issue might affect Mappes's principle.

4. In the movie *Indecent Proposal*, actors Woody Harrelson ("David") and Demi Moore ("Diana") play a young married couple who gamble away all their savings in Las Vegas. They then encounter a billionaire, John Gage (played by Robert Redford). John sexually desires Diana and offers David one million dollars to allow John to spend an evening with Diana. David and Diana eventually accept the offer. Who, if anyone, used whom here, according to Mappes? Who, if anyone, was morally culpable in this scenario? Would you take part in such an arrangement—as David, John, or Diana?

5. On Mappes's view, should a client of a prostitute feel less guilt about hiring her, if he knows her to be hungry, than about hiring a prostitute he knows to be a drug addict? Try to get clear about Mappes's notion of "exploitation" and how it fits, logically, with the rest of his Kantian sexual ethics.

6. Suppose that Romeo brags to his friends about his sexual adventures with Juliet. (This case is from Howard Klepper, "Sexual Exploitation and the Value of Persons," in *The Philosophy of Sex: Con-*

temporary Readings, 6th ed., edited by Nicholas Power, Raja Halwani, and Alan Soble [Lanham, Md.: Rowman & Littlefield, 2013], 291–300.) By Mappes's lights, does Romeo dispositionally coerce Juliet into having sex, or does he simply disrespect her? Is this a case of (impermissible) sexual use at all?

7. Which of Mappes's cases do you think are realistic? Do you think some of them are far-fetched? If so, why? And what implications would your answer have for Mappes's thesis?

8. Suppose that Mr. Dark Desires offers Mr. Adventurous $1,000 to have sex with him and indulge him sexually, by allowing Mr. Dark Desires to act out his dark desires on Mr. Adventurous (you can come up with your own example of the former's dark desires). Mr. Adventurous agrees. Would this be a morally permissible act? (Keep in mind Seiriol Morgan's essay "Dark Desires" in this volume as you answer this question.) What would Mappes say? Does (or would) he make room for sexual acts that are morally impermissible not because they involve immoral sexual use but for other reasons?

SEVENTEEN

Sexual Use

Alan Soble

If sexual desire is by its nature directed from one person toward another person as an object; if experiencing sexual desire and sexual arousal diminishes a person's rationality and autonomy; and if while engaging in sexual activity, people are essentially making use of each other as instruments of their own pleasure — then human sexual activity seems morally suspicious or, worse, morally wrong, in the absence of special overriding reasons that yield justifiable exceptions. This is what **Alan Soble** *calls the "Kantian Sex Problem." The philosophical task is not to sidestep the problem by denying the Kantian account of the nature of sexual desire and sexual activity, or by denying the validity of the Second Formulation of Kant's Categorical Imperative, or by denying Kant's claim that we are rationally autonomous and have inherent worth or dignity. Rather, the task is to fashion a sexual ethics consistent with Kant's views. It must entail that sexuality is not as morally pernicious as Kantian considerations suggest. While examining the literature on Kant and sex, Soble offers a typology of the various proposed solutions, critically discusses each type, and finds them lacking in some way or another. Soble also scrutinizes the writing of Kant, trying to make sense of the passages in which Kant himself tries to solve the problem he created. Kant's restriction of sex to marriage, Soble concludes, derives from the duty to protect one's own personhood from the noxious objectifying nature of sexual desire, rather than that of those one sexually desires.*

piece is a corrected revision of the *POS6e* (2012) essay, which I am not embarrassed to confess contained more than a few howlers. An early, short paper on the same topics ("Kant on Sex") was presented at a meeting of the Society for the Philosophy of Sex and Love, New Orleans, May 8, 1999. Another early paper was presented at Washburn University (Topeka, KS) as the Keynote Lecture of the 54th Mountain-Plains Philosophy Conference, October 13, 2000. The original article was reprinted, unchanged, in Robert Baker and Kathleen Wininger, eds., *Philosophy and Sex*, 4th edition (Prometheus, 2009), 268–301; and in Adrianne McEvoy, ed., *Sex, Love, and Friendship*, vol. 2 (Rodopi, 2011), 263–94. The original was also reprinted in *Comprendre: Review de philosophie et de sciences sociales*, No. 5 (2005), 3–29, titled "L'instrumentalisation sexuelle d'autrui et ce qu'on doit en penser. Éthiques sexuelles internalistes et externalistes," translated (hence probably changed, for the better) by Kora Andrieu.

Human sexuality is hideous. Critter sexuality is no better (you gotta love cannibalistic female bugs), but at least they know not what they do. We know what we do, we know it is hideous, and we do it anyway. Human sexual desire and the sexual activity to which it leads can easily be, and often are, foolish, feeble, foul, fetid, filthy, freaky, fatal, and, as a result, spiritually and morally destructive. Given these anthropological, sociobiological, or metaphysical considerations about the Human Sexual Condition, an application of Immanuel Kant's Second Formulation of the Categorical Imperative yields the conclusion that human sexuality is absolutely condemnable.[1]

KANT ON SEX

Sex robs people of autonomy

A person who sexually desires another person engages in objectification both before and during sexual activity. Manipulation and mild deception (primping, padding, breath freshening, making a good first impression) are so common, from Paris to Patagonia and Stonewall to Shanghai, as to seem a natural component of human sexual mating rituals.[2] The other's body features, her eyes, lips, nose, hands, fingers, thighs, buttocks, and toes, which are distinct from the (whole) person, are exquisitely alluring, painfully enticing, overwhelmingly entrancing and exciting. They become in themselves objects of desire, the focus (or target) of desire.[3]

Both the body and the compliant or complicit actions of the other person are tools or means that one relies on, uses, for one's pleasure. The body parts, the bodily movements, and the person are treated as things. Sexual arousal brings about a yearning to dominate or consume the other's body. Sexual desire is thus a threat to the other's personhood, but the one under the spell of desire also loses hold of his personhood, for a desiring person depends on the consent of another person for satisfaction, thereby (in the absence of rape or deceptive seduction) becoming vulnerable to the other's demands and machinations.[4] As a result of flirting and other sexual cues and triggers, a person feels unwilled flashes of arousal and involuntary bodily reflexes. Being sexually aroused by another person can be experienced as coercive; similarly, someone who proposes an irresistible sexual offer may be coercing (or exploiting) another who has been made weak by sexual desire.[5] The power of the

→ Hunchback Hellfire song!!

sexual urge shows itself in these situations and makes us aware of the danger it poses. Sexual desire is inelastic, relentless, capable of challenging and destroying reason. It seeks satisfaction ubiquitously, whether the acts are partly undressed dark-alley gropings or occur after slithering slinkings around carpeted professional hallways. Sexually motivated acts are known to undermine self-respect—if, contemplating a bath of infectious fluids with lascivious anticipation, we have any to begin with.

That's not the end of it. A person who willingly complies with another's request for sexual activity voluntarily makes an object of himself. As Kant puts it, "For the natural use that one sex makes of the other's sexual organs is *enjoyment*, for which one gives oneself up to the other. In this act a human being m<u>akes himself into a thing</u>."[6] Because a person engaging in sex with another acquiesces in that person's treating her as the source and means of pleasure, she allows the other to treat her as an object.

> When a man wishes to satisfy his desire, and a woman hers, they stimulate each other's desire; their inclinations meet, but their object is not human nature but sex, and each of them dishonours the human nature of the other. They make of humanity an instrument for the satisfaction of their lusts and inclinations, and dishonour it by placing it on a level with animal nature.[7]

The hideousness of human sexuality led Kant, as it much earlier led St. Augustine (and as it much later led me), to think that humans would be delighted to be free of sexual impulses:

> Inclinations . . . as sources of needs, are so far from having an absolute value to make them desirable for their own sake that it must rather be the universal wish of every rational being to be wholly free from them.[8]

Amen.

[handwritten: Sex only good when married & can demean another w/o repercussion since you "own" another]

THE SECOND FORMULATION

Having examined the nature of sexuality, let's review the Second Formulation: "Act in such a way that you always treat humanity, whether in your own person or in the person of any other, never simply as a means, but always at the same time as an end." Or "man . . . *exists* as an end in himself, *not merely as a means* for arbitrary use by this or that will: he must in all his actions, whether they are directed to himself or to other rational beings, always be viewed *at the same time as an end*."[9] The questions arise: Can sexual desire be satisfied by actions that avoid merely using the other or the self as an object? Can sexual activity be carried out while "at the same time" treating the other and the self as persons, treating their *humanity* as an end and confirming their autonomy and rationality? The

[handwritten: treat someone as an end of themselves, not an ends mean]

Second Formulation directs us not to treat ourselves and others *merely* as means. Permissible, then, is treating another and ourselves as objects if *at the same time* we are also treated as persons. Can this be done?

In general, for Kant, a person's providing free and informed consent to interactions with other persons is a necessary but not sufficient condition for satisfying the Second Formulation. Treating someone as a person also includes taking on the other's ends as if they were one's own ends: "the ends of a subject who is an end in himself must, if this conception is to have its *full* effect in me, be also, as far as possible, *my* ends."[10] I take on the other's ends for their *own* sake, not because doing so is effective in advancing my goals. Of course, taking on the other's ends assumes that their ends are permissible. It is further required—this is an example of the moral importance of reciprocity for Kant—that the other takes on my ends.[11]

Even though Kant proposes additional conditions beyond free and informed consent, for some situations Kant relaxes the standard. In these, I must, beyond obtaining consent, make sure that the other person *retains* his or her personhood and I do *not interfere* with his personhood, even if I do not actively take on his goals. This weaker test may be important in Kant's view of the morality of work-for-hire and sexual relations.[12] There are a variety of ways to argue that sexual activity can (or cannot) satisfy the modified (or unmodified) Second Formulation.

In what follows, I examine a number of different approaches. What I call *Internalist* approaches to the Kantian sex problem advise us to modify the character of sexual activity so that the participants satisfy the Second Formulation. For internalists, restraints on how sexual acts are carried out, or restraints on the expression of the sexual impulse, are required. Consent, then, is necessary but not sufficient for the morality of sexual acts. Note that one may fix a sexual act internally so that qua sex act it is unobjectionable, but it still might be wrong for other reasons (e.g., adultery). There are two versions of internalism: *behavioral* internalism, according to which the physical components of sexual acts make the moral difference, and *psychological* internalism, according to which certain attitudes must be present during sexual activity.

BEHAVIORAL INTERNALISM

Alan Goldman defines "sexual desire" as the "desire for contact with another person's body and for the pleasure which such contact produces. . . . The desire for another's body is . . . the desire for the pleasure that physical contact brings" (he defines "sexual activity" as activity which tends to fulfill sexual desire).[13] Because sexual desire is a desire for one's own pleasure, it is understandable that Goldman senses a Kantian problem. Thus Goldman writes that sexual activities "invariably involve at different stages the manipulation of one's partner for one's own pleasure" and thereby, he notes, seem to violate the Second Formulation—which, on Goldman's truncated rendition, "holds that one ought not to treat another as a means to such private ends." (Kant would have said "subjective," "discretionary," or "arbitrary," instead of "private" ends.) Goldman suggests that from a Kantian perspective, "using other individuals for personal benefit," in sex or other interactions, is wrong "only when [the acts] are one-sided, when the benefits are not mutual." So,

> Even in an act which by its nature "objectifies" the other, one recognizes a partner as a subject with demands and desires by yielding to those desires, by allowing oneself to be a sexual object as well, by giving pleasure or ensuring that the pleasures of the act are mutual. [14]

This sexual moral principle—make sure to provide sexual pleasure for your partner—seems plausible and at least in spirit consistent with the Second Formulation. [15]

Pleasing the other person sexually can be done, as Goldman knows, by actively touching the other, *or* by allowing the other to touch us, to treat us as an object who passively acquiesces. But *why* might one sexually please the other (in either way)? One answer comes from sexual egoism or hedonism: pleasing the other is *necessary for or contributes to one's own pleasure.* How so? By inducing the other, through the other's arousal or gratitude, to furnish pleasure to oneself; or because sexually pleasing the other satisfies one's desire to exert power over the other; or because, in providing pleasure to the other we get pleasure by witnessing the effects of our exertions;[16] or because while giving pleasure to the other we identify with their arousal and pleasure, which increases our own arousal and pleasure. [17] Or . . .

Another answer is that providing pleasure to the other should be done for the sake of pleasing the other, just because you know the other person has sexual needs and desires and hopes for their satisfaction. The sexual satisfaction of the other is an end in itself, is valuable in its own right, is not merely instrumentally valuable. It follows that in some circumstances you must be willing to please the other person sexually when doing so does not contribute to your own satisfaction or even runs counter to it. Kant likes to focus on this sort of scenario in the *Groundwork*, cases that separate genuine dutiful benevolence from inclination.

Goldman is a behavioral internalist because all he asks for, in order to make sexual activity morally permissible through the Second Formulation, is the *behavior* of providing, or trying to provide, pleasure for the other person. Goldman never claims that providing pleasure be done with a benevolent *motive* or purity of purpose. But this feature of his proposal is exactly why it fails. If providing pleasure to the other is a mechanism for attaining or improving one's own pleasure, providing pleasure to the other continues, does not negate, treating the other merely as a means. Since giving pleasure to the other is instrumental in obtaining pleasure, giving pleasure has not succeeded in internally *fixing* the nature of the sexual act. Providing pleasure can be a genuine internalist solution, by changing the nature of the sexual act, only if providing pleasure is an unconditional giving. Goldman's proposal thus fails to accommodate his own Kantian commitment. When Kant claims that we must treat the other as a person by taking on her ends as our own—by providing sexual pleasure, if that is her end—Kant does not intend that as a hypothetical imperative, as if taking on the other's ends were a mechanism for getting the other to allow us to treat her as a means. We must take on the other's ends as our own, but not because doing so generates our own pleasure or achieves our sexual goals; sharing the ends of the other person means viewing those ends as valuable in themselves.

Further, for Kant, we may take on the ends of the other as our own only if the other's ends are morally permissible: I may "make the other's ends my ends provided only that these are not immoral."[18] Given the objectification involved in sexual activity, as conceded by Goldman, the moral permissibility of the end of seeking sexual pleasure by means of another person has not yet been established for *either* party. We are not to make the other's ends our ends if the other's ends are not already morally permissible, and whether the sexual ends of the other *are* permissible is precisely the question at issue. Goldman's view that it is permissible for one person to objectify another in sexual activity if the other also objec-tifies the first, with the first's allowance, does not solve the problem. Goldman's internalist solution attempts to change the nature of the sexu-al act, from what it is essentially to what it would be were we to behave *slightly* better in the bedroom, by avoiding raw selfishness. This doesn't go far enough to improve the nature of sexual activity, which by nature remains self-centered. Finally, Goldman ignores, in the Second Formula-tion, that we must also respect the humanity *in one's own person*. Making oneself an object for the sake of the other person's pleasure doesn't re-duce but multiplies the use.

Sexual activity is morally wrong, for Goldman, if only one person experiences pleasure and only one bears the burden of providing it, or the giving and getting is lopsided; "one-sided" sexual activity is immoral. Sex is fine, then, if the benefit of receiving pleasure, and the burden of the restraint on seeking pleasure to give some to the other, are followed by everyone. This is accomplished by the reciprocity of using and being used. Suppose, though, that Goldman's externalism works only if the giving is unconditional; both parties should inject unconditional giving into an act that is essentially self-centered. They must buckle down more formidably in order to restrain impulses for their own pleasure. If altruis-tic giving were easily done, given our sexual natures, there would be less reason for thinking, to begin with, that sexual desire tends to use the other in a self-interested way. Hence to the extent that the sexual urge is self-interested, as in Goldman's view, it is implausible that we could be induced by morality to provide pleasure unconditionally. Such a duty, assuming Kant's view of sexuality, may be impossible to fulfill.

PSYCHOLOGICAL INTERNALISM

If we want to fix the sexual act internally, we must insist not merely on performing acts that produce pleasure for the other but also on producing that pleasure for a certain reason. In this way, we move from behavioral to psychological internalism, which claims that to ensure the satisfaction of the Second Formulation sexual acts must be accompanied by specific attitudes.

In her essay "Defining Wrong and Defining Rape," Jean Hampton lays out a view similar to Goldman's, in which mutual pleasure alone solves the Kantian problem:

> [W]hen sex is as much about pleasing another as it is about pleasing oneself, it certainly doesn't involve using another as a means and actually incorporates the idea of respect and concern for another's needs.[19]

Providing sexual pleasure to the other person seems to make sexual activity fine for Hampton. However, as we have seen, providing pleasure does not, by itself, solve the Kantian problem. Hampton, though, goes beyond Goldman in her perception of the depth of sexual experiences:

> [O]ne's *humanity* is perhaps never more engaged than in the sexual act. But it is not only present in the experience; more important, it is "at stake" in the sense that each partner puts him/herself in a position where the behavior of the other can either confirm it or threaten it, celebrate it or abuse it.[20]

Yes, sexual interactions are metaphysically and psychologically dangerous. She continues:

> If this is right, then I do not see how, for most normal human beings, sexual passion is heightened if one's sexual partner behaves in a way that one finds personally humiliating or that induces in one shame or self-hatred or that makes one feel like a "thing." . . . Whatever sexual passion is, such emotions seem antithetical to it, and such emotions are markers of the disrespect that destroys the morality of the experience. . . . [W]hat makes a sexual act morally right is also what provides the groundwork for the experience of emotions and pleasures that make for "good sex."[21]

> If the wrongness of the act is a function of its diminishing nature, then that wrongness can be present even if, ex ante, each party consented to the sex. So . . . consent is *never by itself* that which makes a sexual act morally right. . . . Lovemaking is a set of experiences . . . which includes

attitudes and behaviors that are different in kind from the attitudes and behaviors involved in morally wrongful sex.[22]

Hampton's thesis is that sexual activity must be accompanied by humanity-affirming attitudes or emotions that are manifested in sexual activity itself.[23] Attitudes and emotions that repudiate humanity or are behaviorally disrespectful—"behaves in a way that one finds personally humiliating"—are both morally wrong *and* prevent mutual pleasure, while morally right sexual acts promote mutual pleasure.[24] Hampton's internalism thus satisfies the Second Formulation. Consent to sex may be necessary but is not sufficient for behaving respectfully; giving pleasure to the other, taking on their sexual ends, is required; why the persons produce pleasure for each other is morally relevant; and humiliating attitudes expressed sexually must be absent while attitudes that celebrate humanity are present.

Hampton's view entails that some casual sex, in which both parties aim to satisfy their own horniness, is morally wrong, along with prostitution, because these sexual acts are not likely to be robustly humanity-affirming. Sadomasochism is also wrong; it involves what Hampton perceives as humanity-denying attitudes. Yet casual sex and prostitution, as objectifying and instrumental as they can be, and sadomasochism, as humiliating to one's partner or oneself as it can be, nevertheless produce tremendous sexual excitement, contrary to Hampton's claim about the biconditional correlation between the moral and the pleasurable. She believes that morally permissible sex involves mutual sexual pleasure; hence, the morality of sexual activity depends in part on its producing well-distributed pleasure; and disrespectful attitudes embodied in sexual acts destroy mutual pleasure. At this point a problem emerges: Are disrespectful attitudes morally wrong because they destroy the other's sexual pleasure or because they are disrespectful? Ask this question while assessing sadomasochism. If her argument is that disrespectful attitudes that occur during sexual events are morally wrong because they are disrespectful, S&M is morally wrong even if they do, contra her intuition, produce pleasure for the participants. (In this case, Hampton may be better understood as what I call an *Externalist*.) But if her argument is that disrespectful attitudes are wrong because they destroy mutual pleasure, S&M does not always rank as wrong.

Perhaps Hampton means that sexual activity is morally permissible only when it is *both* mutually pleasure-producing *and* incorporates humanity-affirming attitudes, where these vary independently. This test for the morality of sexual acts prohibits prostitution, casual sex, and S&M, no matter how sexually felicitous. But I could find in Hampton's essay no definition of "humanity-affirming" other than "provides pleasure." This is why Hampton has trouble denying the permissibility of S&M. Consider what the lesbian sadomasochist Pat Califia says about S&M: "The things that seem beautiful, inspiring, and life-affirming to me seem ugly, hateful, and ludicrous to most other people."[25] Califia, I think, means "provides pleasure" by "life-affirming." If so, not much disagreement exists between Hampton and Califia, if Hampton means "provides pleasure" by being "humanity-affirming." What Hampton does not take seriously is that force and humiliation may make sex mutually pleasurable.[26] That helps me understand why my powdered donuts are high-cholesterol, high-carbohydrate, and high-fat, yet still luscious.

"THIN EXTERNALISM"

According to *Externalism*, morality requires that we place restraints on when sexual acts are engaged in, with whom sexual activity occurs, or on the conditions in which sexual activities are performed. Properly setting the background context in which sexual acts occur enables us to satisfy the Second Formulation. One distinction among externalisms is that between *minimalist* externalism, which claims that morality requires that only the context of sexual activity be set, while the sexual acts may be whatever they turn out to be, and *extended* externalism, which claims that setting the context will also affect the character of the sexual acts. Another distinction among externalisms is between *thin* externalism, according to which free and informed consent is necessary and sufficient for the moral permissibility of sexual acts (with a trivial *ceteris paribus* clause), and *thick* externalism, which claims that something beyond consent is required for the morality of sexual activity. We'll start with thin externalism.

Thomas Mappes argues that only weak contextual constraints are required for satisfying Kantian complaints about sexual activity.[27] The giving of free and informed consent by the persons involved in a sexual encounter is both necessary and sufficient for the morality of their sexual activity, for making permissible the sexual use of one person by another.[28] Consent is not sufficient for the morality of sexual acts *simpliciter*, because even though a sexual act might be morally permissible qua sexual act, it still may be, for example, adulterous. Mappes's position is a thin minimalist externalism. Indeed, thin externalism, defined as making consent necessary and sufficient, must be minimalist. This criterion for the morality of sexual activity is contentless, or fully procedural; it does not evaluate the form or nature of the sexual act (e.g., what body parts are involved) but only the antecedent and concurrent conditions or context in which the act occurs. In principle, the acts engaged in need not even produce sexual pleasure for the agents.

Mappes, while developing his theory of sexual ethics, repeats a point frequently made about Kantian ethics:

> According to a fundamental Kantian principle, it is morally wrong for
> A to use B *merely as a means* (to achieve A's ends). Kant's principle does

not rule out A using B as a means, only A using B *merely* as a means—
that is, in a way incompatible with respect for B as a person.

Then Mappes lays out his central thesis:

A immorally uses B if and only if A intentionally acts in a way that
violates the requirement that B's involvement with A's ends be based
on B's voluntary informed consent.[29]

For Mappes, the presence of free and informed consent—there's no
deception and no coercive force or threats—satisfies the Second Formulation, because each person's providing consent ensures that the persons
involved in sexual activity with each other are not *merely* or *wrongfully*
using each other as means. Mappes intends that this principle be applied
to any activity, whether sexual or otherwise; he believes, along with
Goldman, that sexual activity should be governed by moral principles
that apply in general to human behavior.[30]

Mappes spends almost all his essay discussing various situations that
may (or not) involve violating the free and informed consent criterion. He
discusses which acts are deceptive, coercive (by force or threat), or exploitative; sexual activity made possible by such maneuvers are morally
wrong. Some of these cases are intriguing, as anyone familiar with the
literature on the meaning and application of the free and informed consent criterion in the area of medical ethics knows. But, putting aside for
now the question of the sufficiency of consent, not everyone agrees that
free and informed consent is always necessary. Jeffrie Murphy has raised
some doubts:

"Have sex with me or I will find another girlfriend" strikes me . . . as a
morally permissible threat, and "Have sex with me and I will marry
you" strikes me . . . as a morally permissible offer. . . . We negotiate our
way through most of life with schemes of threats and offers . . . and I
see no reason why the realm of sexuality should be utterly insulated
from this very normal way of being human.[31]

"Have sex with me or I will find another girlfriend" and "Marry me or I
will never, ever sleep with you" seem to be coercive yet permissible.
Sexual activity (or marriage) obtained by means of coercive threats may
violate the "no coercion" clause of Mappes's criterion. In some circumstances the "no deception" clause may be violated without doing something morally wrong (even if we ignore the use of cosmetics and clothing). Mappes says that *withholding* information that would knowingly
influence the other person's decision about engaging in sexual activity is
deception that makes subsequent sexual activity wrong. But if a guy
withholds the fact that he has a huge *or* tiny penis, and withholding that
information plays a role in the other's agreeing to engage in sex, it is not
obvious that obtaining sex by this particular deception-by-omission is
wrong. If so, we cannot rely comprehensively on a principle of consent to

answer all pressing questions about sexual morality.[32] Does the other person have a *right* to know the size of a penis while deliberating about sex? What types of coercive threat are *rightfully* used in achieving our goals? These questions may not be answerable by a free and informed consent criterion. They also imply that free and informed consent by itself may not satisfy the Second Formulation.

Mappes provides slender reasons for blessing his proposal that free and informed consent is sufficient for satisfying the Second Formulation or guarantees moral permissibility. He writes that "respect for persons entails that each of us recognize the rightful authority of other persons (as rational beings) to conduct their individual lives as they see fit,"[33] which suggests the following argument: If the other's consent controls whether the other may be used for my sexual ends, that means I respect that person by seriously taking his autonomy, his ability to make reasonable choices, while not to defer to the choice of the other to make decisions about whether to be used for my sexual ends is disrespectfully paternalistic. If the other's consent is granted sufficiency, that shows that I respect her choice of ends, or that even if I do not think much of her particular choice of ends, at least I show respect for her ends-making capacity or self-determination. Further, taking the other's consent as sufficient may be to take on his sexual ends as my own ends as well as his taking on my sexual ends in accepting my proposal to use him. For this argument, the Second Formulation is nearly libertarianism, or a quasi-libertarianism that also, as Mappes does, pays attention to situations that are ripe for economic or psychological exploitation, cases in which one person takes advantage of another's desperation.[34]

Even if the argument makes Kantian sense, Mappes's criterion misses the point. Kant's problem with sex is not (only) that one person might make false promises, engage in deception, or employ force or threats against another to gain sex. The problem of the objectification of both the self and other arises for Kant even when both persons give free and informed consent. Thin externalism does not get to the heart of *this* problem. Perhaps no liberal philosophy that borders on libertarianism could sense it as a problem; at any rate, no minimalist externalism could. The only sexual objectification that Mappes considers is that which arises with manipulation by lies or compulsion, most dramatically in rape. He ignores what Kant discerns as the intrinsically objectifying nature of sexuality. As does Goldman, Mappes assimilates sexual activity to other human activities, all of which should be governed by the same moral principles. Hence whether Mappes's proposal succeeds depends on whether sex is not so different from other activities that free and informed consent is not too weak (or irrelevant) a criterion for the morality of sex.

It's a good question why the consent principle does not, for Kant, solve the problem. It seems so obvious to many today (in the West) that

Mappes's consent principle solves the sex problem that we are puzzled about what Kant was up to. Kant's rejection of the consent criterion fits well with his perceiving deeper troubles in sexuality than Mappes and Goldman recognize. In *Lectures on Ethics*, Kant accepts a consent principle for work-for-hire but rejects it for sex:

> Man can, of course, use another human being as an instrument for his services; he can use his hands, his feet, and even all his powers; he can use him for his own purposes with the other's consent. But there is no way in which a human being can be made an Object of indulgence for another except through sexual impulse.[35]

For Kant, it seems that using another person in a work-for-hire situation is permissible, just with free and informed consent (as long as one does not deny the worker's humanity in some other way?). But Kant finds something problematic about sexual interaction that does not exist during, say, a tennis game between two people or in a work-for-hire situation, while Mappes sees no moral difference between playing tennis with someone and playing with their genitals. This disagreement between philosophers who view sexual activity as something uniquely different and those who conflate all human interactions requires further study, for Kant's claim, that only in sexuality is one person "made an Object of indulgence" for another, provides (if true) no clear reason for treating sexuality as a special case.

"THICK EXTERNALISM"

Thick externalism claims that more stringent contextual constraints, beyond free and informed consent, are required for the morality of sexual activity. My central example is Martha Nussbaum's essay "Objectification," in which she submits that the Kantian problem is solved if sexual activity is confined to the context of an abiding, mutually respectful and regarding relationship. However, Nussbaum advances both a thick minimalist externalism and a thick extended externalism. In her long and complex essay, two theses emerge: (1) a background context of an abiding, mutually respectful relationship makes noxious objectification during sexual activity morally *permissible*; and (2) a background context of an abiding, mutually respectful relationship turns what might have been noxious objectification into something *good* or even "wonderful," a valuable objectification in which autonomy is happily abandoned, a thesis she derives from Cass Sunstein and D. H. Lawrence.

In several passages, Nussbaum proposes a thick minimalist externalism, according to which sexual objectification is morally permissible in the context of an abiding, mutually respectful relationship. Consider this modest statement of her first thesis:

> If I am lying around with my lover on the bed, and use his stomach as a pillow, there seems to be nothing at all baneful about this [instrumental objectification], provided that I do so with his consent . . . and without causing him pain, provided, as well, that I do so in the context of a relationship in which he is generally treated as more than a pillow. This suggests that what is problematic is not instrumentalization per se but treating someone *primarily* or *merely* as an instrument [e.g., a pillow]. The overall context of the relationship thus becomes fundamental.[36]

Let's modify the passage so that Nussbaum's point about permissible instrumental objectification is applied directly to sex:

> If I am lying around with my lover on the bed, and use his penis for my sexual satisfaction, there seems to be nothing at all baneful about this instrumental objectification, provided that I do so with his consent . . . and without causing him [unwanted] pain, provided, as well, that I do so in the context of a relationship in which he is generally treated as more than a penis. This suggests that what is problematic is not instrumentalization per se but treating someone *primarily* or *merely* as an instrument [e.g., a penis]. The overall context of the relationship thus becomes fundamental.

Other passages in Nussbaum's essay express thick minimalist externalism: "where there is a loss in subjectivity in the moment of lovemaking, this can be and frequently is accompanied by an intense concern for the subjectivity of the partner *at other moments*."[37] Again: "When there is a loss of autonomy in sex, the context . . . can be . . . one in which, on the whole, autonomy is respected and promoted."[38] And "denial of autonomy and denial of subjectivity are objectionable if they persist throughout an adult relationship, but *as phases* in a relationship characterized by mutual regard they can be all right, or even quite wonderful."[39]

One of Nussbaum's theses, then, is that a loss of autonomy and subjectivity in sex, and the reduction of a person to his sexual body or its parts, in which the person is used as a tool (hence object), are acceptable if they occur within the context of a psychologically healthy and morally sound relationship, a relationship in which one's personhood—one's autonomy and subjectivity—is generally acknowledged and respected. This view seems plausible. It confirms the common (sexually conservative) intuition that one difference between morally permissible sexual acts and those that are wrongful because they are merely mutual use is the difference between sexual acts that occur in the context of a loving, caring, or supportive relationship and those that occur in the absence of love, care, or concern (say, casual sex between strangers). Further, the view appeals to the willingness to tolerate, exculpate, or bless (as the partners' own private business) whatever nastiness that occurs in bed between two people *as long as* the rest, and the larger segment, of their relationship is morally sound. The lovers may sometimes engage in objectifying sexual games, by role-playing boss/secretary, client/prostitute, or teacher/student (phases of their relationship in which autonomy and subjectivity are sacrificed), because *outside* these sexual games, they do display respect for each other and support their humanity.

This position is inconsistent with the Second Formulation; that principle requires that a person be treated as an end *at the same time* he is treated as a means. On Nussbaum's thick minimalist externalism, small sexually vulgar chunks of a couple's relationship, small pieces of noxious sexual objectification, are permissible in virtue of the larger or more frequent heavenly chunks of mutual respect that comprise their relationship. It is not true, however (except for some Utilitarians), that treating you badly today is *justified* or *excusable* if I treated you admirably the whole day yesterday and will treat you superbly tomorrow. As Nussbaum acknowledges, Kant insists that we ought not to treat someone *merely* instrumentally or as an object, but by that qualification Kant does not mean that treating someone instrumentally or as an object at *some* particular time is permissible as long as she is treated as a full, dignified person at *other* times.

That Nussbaum's thick minimalist externalist solution to our problem violates the Second Formulation is not the fault of the details of the background context; the problem arises whether the background context is posited to be abiding mutual respect, love, marriage, or something else. Any version of thick minimalist externalism violates Kant's idea that someone who is treated as a means must be treated *at the same time* as an end. Thick minimalist externalism fails because, unlike internalism, it makes no attempt to improve the nature of sexual activity itself. It leaves sexual activity unchanged, as essentially objectifying or instrumental, although it claims that even when having this character, it is morally permissible.

"THICK EXTENDED" EXTERNALISM

Thick extended externalism tries to have it both ways: to justify sexual activity when it occurs within the proper context *and* to fix the nature of sexual acts. So Nussbaum's second proposal would seem to stand a better chance of conforming with the Second Formulation. In explaining the thesis that sexual objectification can be a wonderful or good thing in the right context, Nussbaum says that in Lawrence's *Lady Chatterley's Lover*,

> both parties put aside their individuality and become identified with their bodily organs. They see one another in terms of those organs. And yet Kant's suggestion that in all such focusing on parts there is denial of humanity seems quite wrong. . . . The intense focusing of attention on the bodily parts seems an *addition*, rather than a subtraction.[40]

Nussbaum means that being reduced to one's body or its parts is an addition to one's personhood, not a subtraction from it, *as long as* the background context of an abiding, mutually respectful relationship exists, as she assumes it did between Constance Chatterley and Oliver Mellors. Nussbaum claims that sexual objectification, the reduction of a person to his flesh, and the loss of individuality and autonomy in sexual activity, can be a wonderful aspect of sexuality and life. Being reduced to one's flesh, to one's genitals, supplements, or is an expansion or extension of, one's humanity, as long as it occurs in a psychologically healthy and morally sound relationship.

Nussbaum goes so far as to make the astonishing assertion that "in Lawrence, being treated as a cunt is a permission to expand the sphere of one's activity and fulfillment." [41] In the ablutionary context of an abiding, respectful relationship, it is permissible and good for persons to descend to the level of their bodies, to become "cock" and "cunt," to become identified with their genitals, as long as in the rest of the relationship they are treated as *whole* persons. Or, more precisely, the addition of being sexually reduced to their flesh *makes* their personhoods whole (it is not a "subtraction"), as if without descending into their flesh each would remain incomplete. This is suggested when Nussbaum writes, "Lawrence shows how a kind of sexual objectification . . . how the very surrender of autonomy in a certain sort of sex act can free energies that can be used to make the self *whole and full*." [42] To be whole and full, must I realize all my potentials? Some of my potential, it is not unreasonable to think, should not be realized, because it would be immoral or stupid to do so. Shall I, a professor of philosophy, fulfill my humanity by standing on street corners in Kensington to lease out my body? No. I may raise the fullness of my humanity only in ways that are moral. But, whether adding to my personhood the identification of myself with my genitals is moral is precisely the question. That reducing myself to my genitals is an "expansion" of myself and of my "sphere of . . . activity" does little to justify it.

In any event, one implication of Nussbaum's requirement of a background context of an abiding, mutually respectful relationship annoys me, whether this background context is part of a thick minimalist or a thick extended externalism: all casual sex is morally wrong. In the sexual activity that transpires between strangers or between those who do not have much or any mutual regard for each other, sexual objectification makes those sexual acts wrong; there is no proper background context that would justify sexual objectification or transform it into something good. Casual sex is a descent to the level of the genitals with nothing for the persons to hang on to, nothing that would allow pulling themselves back up to personhood when their sexual encounter is over. (This is, in effect, what Kant claims about prostitution.) [43] Sounding like Kant, Nussbaum seems not to consider it a defect of her account that casual sex is jettisoned:

> For in the absence of any narrative history with the person, how can
> desire attend to anything else but the incidental, and how can one do
> more than use the body of the other as a tool of one's own states? . . .
> Can one really treat someone with . . . respect and concern . . . if one has
> sex with him in the anonymous spirit? . . . [T]he instrumental treatment
> of human beings, the treatment of human beings as tools of the pur-
> poses of another, is always morally problematic; if it does not take
> place in a larger context of regard for humanity, it is a central form of
> the morally objectionable.[44]

Nussbaum's in trouble. If casual sex is wrong, if objectification is permissible or made into something good only in abiding, mutually respectful relationships, then it is impermissible as well to engage in sexual
activity in getting a relationship *underway*. Two persons may not engage
in sexual activity early in their romance, before they know whether they
will come to have such an abiding, respectful relationship, because the
sexual objectification of that premature sex could not be cleansed; the
requisite background context is missing. It is an idea of Western culture
that engaging in sexual activity, even when the persons do not know each
other well, often reveals to them important information about *whether* to
pursue a relationship, whether to attempt to ascend to the abiding level.
This exploratory sex is ruled out by Nussbaum. Persons must *first* have
an abiding, mutually respectful relationship before engaging in sex.
Nussbaum has replaced the Christian prohibition of premarital sex with
a prohibition of the innovative yet pompous pre-abiding-respectful-rela-
tionship sex. Nussbaum is out of touch with a question that confronts
young people (although they solve it): After how many days/weeks/
months do the panties come off? Or how many days/weeks after the bra
has already been liberated and tossed?

It is unconvincing to argue, in response, that sexual objectification in
the early stages of their relationship is morally permissible, after all, because that sexual activity may contribute to the formation of an abiding,
mutually respectful relationship that succeeds, later, in cleansing the sexual objectification of the couple's earlier sexual activity. This rejoinder
repeats the dubious claim that morally bad segments of a relationship are
justified or excused in virtue of the larger or more frequent morally good
segments of that relationship. Further, in this case the cleansing part of
the relationship occurs *later* and cannot be known in advance to exist. In
response to a Nussbaumian claim that the objectification of casual or
premarital sex can be overcome through a later abiding, respectful relationship, a Kantian would argue that premarital sex is wrong precisely
because we cannot know that the sex will be cleansed by a later relationship.[45] Young people come to steer through this start-and-stop, start-and-
stop routine.

Another problem arises in Nussbaum's discussion of S&M. In response to her question, "Can sadomasochistic sexual acts ever have a

simply Lawrentian character, rather than a more sinister character?" Nussbaum replies:

> There seems to be no . . . reason why the answer . . . cannot be "yes." I have no very clear intuitions on this point . . . but it would seem that some narrative depictions of sadomasochistic activity do plausibly attribute to its consensual form a kind of Lawrentian character in which the willingness to be vulnerable to the infliction of pain . . . manifests a more complete trust and receptivity than could be found in other sexual acts. Pat Califia's . . . short story ["Jessie"] is one example of such a portrayal.[46]

Oh, Martha, give us a break. Califia describes in this lesbian sadomasochistic short story the first sexual encounter between two *strangers,* women who have just met at a party, an encounter about which neither lady knows in advance whether it will lead to a respectful narrative history or an abiding relationship. In the sexual encounter described by Califia, there is no background context of an abiding, let alone mutually respectful, relationship. This means that the nature of their sexual activity *as sadomasochism* is irrelevant; the main point is that each woman, as a stranger to the other, must, on Nussbaum's account, be merely using the other in the "anonymous spirit." Something Califia writes in "Jessie" makes a mockery of Nussbaum's proposal:

> I hardly know you—I don't know if you play piano, I don't know what kind of business it is you run, I don't know your shoe size—but I know you better than anyone else in the world.[47]

Which, of course, is insane nonsense. If Nussbaum wants to justify S&M, she must say that, *in the context of an abiding, mutually respectful relationship,* either (1) S&M is permissible, no matter how humiliating or brutal the acts are to the participants (thick minimalist externalism), or (2) S&M is permissible because, given the background context, it can be a good or wonderful thing, an expansion of the couple's humanity (thick expanded externalism).

KANT ON PERMISSIBLE SEX[48]

Kant asserts in *Lectures* and *Metaphysics* that sexual activity is morally permissible only within a legal, heterosexual, lifelong, and monogamous marriage. Hence Kant advances a thick externalism, replacing Nussbaum's abiding respectful relationship with the not very innovative legal marriage. Kant barely argues in these texts, or argues weakly, that marriage must be lifelong and heterosexual. By contrast, Kant's argument that the only permissible sex occurs in marriage is distinctive. In *Metaphysics*, he writes:

There is only one condition under which this is possible: that while one person is acquired by the other *as if it were a thing*, the one who is acquired acquires the other in turn; for in this way each reclaims itself and restores its personality. But acquiring a member of a human being [i.e., access to or possession of the other's genitals and associated sexual capacities] is at the same time acquiring the whole person, since a person is an absolute unity. Hence it is not only admissible for the sexes to surrender and to accept each other for enjoyment under the condition of marriage, but it is possible for them to do so *only* under this condition.[49]

Sexual activity, with its essential sexual objectification, is morally permissible only in marriage; only in marriage can each person engage in sexual activity *without losing* their personhood or humanity. In a *Kantian* marriage (a special type), each person is "acquired" by the other (along with his or her genitals and sexual capacities) as if she were an object; in being acquired, she loses her humanity (autonomy, subjectivity, individuality, rationality). Because the acquisition in marriage is reciprocal, each person *regains* her personhood (and does not, after all, lose it). When I "surrender" myself to you, and you thereby acquire me, and you also "surrender" yourself to me, and I thereby acquire you, which "you" includes the "me" that you have already acquired, we each surrender and reacquire ourselves. (In a Kantian marriage ceremony, the two "I do" promises must be spoken simultaneously—due to the Second Formulation's "at the same time," or from the threat to personhood created by the phasic progression of mutual acquisition?)

Kant does not state, while laying out his theory of permissible sex in a Kantian marriage, that through the reciprocal surrender and acquisition the persons treat each other as persons or acknowledge each other's humanity as an end, in bed or otherwise. That is, after laying out his relentless criticism of sexuality, Kant never poses the question, "How might two people treat themselves and each other as persons during sexual activity?" In only one place could I find, in a note in *Metaphysics*, Kant using the Second Formulation to speak about marriage:

[I]f I say "my wife," this signifies a special, namely a rightful, relation of the possessor to an object as a *thing* (even though the object is also a person). Possession (*physical* possession), however, is the condition of being able to *manage* . . . something as a thing, even if this must, in another respect, be treated at the same time as a person.[50]

But in neither the footnote nor the text does Kant explain what "in another respect" (sexually or otherwise) being treated as a person amounts to. The language of the Second Formulation is plainly here, including the crucial "at the same time," but not its substance. Further, in the text, Kant refrains from using the language of the Second Formulation:

> What is one's own here does not . . . mean what is one's own in the sense of property in the person of another (for a human being cannot have property in himself, much less in another person), but means what is one's own in the sense of usufruct . . . to make direct use of a person *as of* a thing, as a means to my end, but still *without infringing* upon his personality.[51]

It is permissible in *some* contexts to use another person as a means or treat as an object (with free and informed consent?) as long as one does not violate the humanity of the other in some other way—that is, as long as one allows her to retain her personhood. The reciprocal surrender and acquisition of Kantian marriage, which involves a contractual free and informed agreement to exchange selves, *prevents* this denial or loss of personhood. But this moral principle is far removed from the Second Formulation as Kant usually articulates it.

Kant's externalism, I submit, is minimalist: the objectification and instrumentality that attach to sexuality remain even in marital sexual activity. Hence not even Kant abides by the "at the same time" requirement of the Second Formulation. Nussbaum seems to recognize Kant's minimalism when she writes, "Sexual desire, according to his analysis, drives out every possibility of respect. This is so even in marriage."[52] Raymond Belliotti finds, instead, thick extended externalism:

> Kant suggests that two people can efface the wrongful commodification inherent in sex and thereby redeem their own humanity only by mutually exchanging "rights to their whole person." The *implication* is that a deep, abiding relationship of the requisite sort ensures that sexual activity is not separated from personal interaction which honors individual dignity.[53]

Belliotti illicitly reads the "implication" into Kant's texts. Kant nowhere says that in marriage, which is for him a contractual relationship characterized by mutual acquisition of persons as if they were objects (not a "deep, abiding relationship"), sexual activity "honors individual dignity." When Kant asserts in *Metaphysics* that sexual activity is permissible only in marriage, he speaks about the *acquisition* or *possession* of the other person by each spouse and never mentions benevolence, altruism, or love.

For similar reasons, Robert Baker and Frederick Elliston's view is inadequate. They claim that, for Kant, "marriage transubstantiates immoral sexual intercourse into morally permissible human copulation by transforming a manipulative masturbatory relationship into one of altruistic unity."[54] But Kant never says anything about "altruism" in his account of marriage or sex in marriage; nowhere does he claim that married persons treat each other as ends and respect their humanity in sex by unconditionally providing pleasure for each other. Indeed, Kant writes in the *Metaphysics* that "benevolence . . . deter[s] one from carnal enjoyment."[55]

Further, both these readings of Kant are insensitive to the sharp contrast between Kant's glowing account of male friendship (in *Lectures* and the *Metaphysics*) as a morally exemplary and fulfilling balance of love and respect, and Kant's dry, mechanical account of heterosexual marriage. Kant never says about marriage anything near this: "Friendship . . . is the union of two persons through equal mutual love and respect. . . . [E]ach participat[es] and shar[es] sympathetically in the other's well-being through the morally good will that unites them" (recall Aristotle and Montaigne).[56]

The virtue of Belliotti's reading, and of Baker and Elliston, is that if sexual activity can be imbued with Kantian respect or altruism, then the "at the same time" requirement of the Second Formulation is satisfied. But there is further evidence that Kant's view is minimalist. When Kant writes in the *Lectures*,

> If . . . a man wishes to satisfy his desire, and a woman hers, they stimulate each other's desire; their inclinations meet, but their object is not human nature but sex, and each of them dishonours the human nature of the other. They make of humanity an instrument for the satisfaction of their lusts and inclinations, and dishonour it by placing it on a level with animal nature.[57]

He intends this description to apply to sexual activity even in marriage, not only to casual sex or prostitution. This point is confirmed by Kant's correspondence with C. G. Schütz, who wrote to Kant to complain about Kant's similar treatment of sexuality in the *Metaphysics*. Schütz makes the point that "married people do not become *res fungibiles* just by sleeping together," to which Kant replies, "An enjoyment of this sort involves at once the thought of this person as merely *functional*, and that in fact is what the reciprocal use of each other's sexual organs by two people *is*."[58] Marriage does not change the nature of the sexual act.

Further, that marriage for Kant is only about having access to the other person's sexual capacities and body parts — for pleasure, not necessarily for reproduction — also suggests minimalism. Consider Kant's definition of marriage in the *Metaphysics*: "Sexual union in accordance with principle is *marriage* (*matrimonium*), that is, the union of two persons of different sexes for lifelong possession of each other's sexual attributes."[59] There is no hint in this definition that Belliottian human, individual dignity will make its way into marital sexual activity (quite the contrary). Howard Williams tartly comments that "sex, for Kant, seems simply to be a form of mutual exploitation for which one must pay the price of marriage. He represents sex as a commodity which ought only to be bought and sold for life in the marriage contract."[60] If sexual activity in marriage is, for Kant, a commodity, its objectifying qualities remain. Kant's view of marriage has much in common with St. Paul's, in which each person has power over the body of the other spouse, and each spouse has a "conjugal debt" to engage in sexual activity with the other nearly on demand.[61] That marriage is defined by Kant to be about access to sex is a shock, even incomprehensible, to the contemporary Western Enlightenment mind, and may explain why modern philosophers attribute to Kant more congenial views of sex and marriage.

Finally, a frequently neglected aspect of the Second Formulation, that one must *also* treat the humanity in one's own person as an end, must be acknowledged in understanding Kant's sexual morality. Duties to self are important for Kant, a fact overlooked by those philosophers (e.g., Mappes, Goldman) who emphasize the Second Formulation's treat-the-*other*-as-an-end. Notice the prominence of Kant's discussion of duties to self in the *Lectures*. They are elaborately discussed early in the text, well before Kant discusses moral duties to others, and Kant in the *Lectures* launches into his treatment of sexuality immediately after he concludes his account of duties to self and before he finally gets around to duties to others. Allen Wood gets this right:

> [Kant] thinks sexual intercourse is "a degradation of humanity" because it is an act in which "people make themselves into an object of enjoyment, and hence into a thing" (VE 27:346). He regards sex as permissible only within marriage, and even there it is in itself "a merely animal union" (MS 6:425).[62]

Kant makes it clear that a duty to treat the humanity in one's own person as an end is his primary concern in restricting sexual activity to marriage:

> [T]here ar[ises] from one's duty to oneself, that is, to the humanity in one's own person, a right (*ius personale*) of both sexes to acquire each other as persons *in the manner of things* by marriage.[63]

For Kant, then, the argument does not turn on a duty to avoid sexually objectifying the other in marriage, but a duty to avoid the sexual objectification of the self. It would be an ironic reading of Kant to say that he claims that *my right to use you* in sexual activity in marriage arises from *my duty to myself*. What Kant is saying, without irony, is that as a result of the duty to myself, I cannot enter into sexual relations with you unless I preserve my personhood; similarly you cannot enter into sexual relations with me unless you preserve your personhood. We can accomplish that goal only by mutual surrender and acquisition, the exchange of rights to our persons, parts, and sexual capacities that constitute marriage. It is not the right to use you sexually that is my goal, although I do gain that right. My goal is to preserve my personhood in the face of the essentially objectifying nature of sexuality. Preserving my own personhood, as admirable as that might be, is not the same thing as treating you with dignity or altruism during marital sexual activity. Kant has done nothing to accomplish that. Nor was that his intention.[64]

NOTES

1. Kant's views on sexuality are in *Lectures on Ethics* [ca. 1780], translated by Louis Infield (Indianapolis, Ind.: Hackett, 1963), 162–71; and *The Metaphysics of Morals* [1797], translated by Mary Gregor (Cambridge: Cambridge University Press, 1996), 61–64, 126–28, 178–80. The clash between sex and the Second Formulation is noted by Michael Ruse, *Homosexuality: A Philosophical Inquiry* (Oxford: Blackwell, 1988), 185.

2. Bernard Baumrin, "Sexual Immorality Delineated," in *Philosophy and Sex*, 2nd ed., edited by Robert Baker and Frederick Elliston (Buffalo, N.Y.: Prometheus, 1984), 300–302.

3. Kant may have made the claim about the genitals, but this impression may be an artifact of translation: "[S]exuality is not an inclination which one human being has for another as such, but is an inclination for the sex of another. . . . [O]nly her sex is the object of his desires. . . . [A]ll men and women do their best to make not their human nature but their sex more alluring" (*Lectures*, 164). Freud and others did not find much beauty in the genitals. See my *Sexual Investigations* (New York: New York University Press, 1996), 201.

4. "In desire you are compromised in the eyes of the object of desire, since you have displayed that you have designs which are vulnerable to his intentions" (Roger Scruton, *Sexual Desire: A Moral Philosophy of the Erotic* [New York: Free Press, 1986], 82).

5. See Virginia Held, "Coercion and Coercive Offers," in *Coercion: Nomos VIX*, edited by J. Roland Pennock and John W. Chapman (Chicago: Aldine, 1972), 49–62.

6. Kant, *Metaphysics*, 62.

7. Kant, *Lectures*, 164. Kant also claims that sexuality can reduce humans *below* the level of animals, who (unlike humans) do not engage in horrific same-sex sexual activity. See my "Kant and Sexual Perversion," *Monist* 86:1 (2003), 57–92.

8. Immanuel Kant, *Groundwork of the Metaphysic of Morals*, translated by H. J. Paton (New York: Harper Torchbooks, 1964), 95–96 (AK 4:428). For Augustine, see *City of God*, translated by Marcus Dods (New York: Modern Library, 1993), bk. 14, sec. 16, 464–65. For discussion of Kant, see Marcia Baron, *Kantian Ethics (Almost) without Apology* (Ithaca, N.Y.: Cornell University Press, 1995), 199–204, and H. J. Paton, *The Categorical Imperative: A Study in Kant's Moral Philosophy* (New York: Harper and Row, 1967), 55–57.

9. Kant, *Groundwork*, 96 (AK 4:429); 95 (AK 4:428).

10. Kant, *Groundwork*, 98 (AK 4:430); see *Metaphysics*, 199.

11. Kant, *Groundwork*, 97 (AK 4:429). See Christine Korsgaard, "Creating the Kingdom of Ends: Reciprocity and Responsibility in Personal Relations," *Philosophical Perspectives* 6 (1992), 305–32.

12. C. E. Harris Jr. has this weaker version of the Second Formulation in mind when he claims that we are permitted to use another person (post office worker, doctor, professor) as long as we "do nothing to negate [their] status as a moral being," "do not deny him his status as a person," or "do not obstruct [their] humanity," beyond using them for our own purposes. Casual sex is permissible when "neither person is overriding the freedom of the other or diminishing the ability of the other to be an effective goal-pursuing agent" (*Applying Moral Theories*, 4th edition [Belmont, Calif.: Wadsworth, 2002], 153–54, 164).

13. Alan Goldman, "Plain Sex," in this volume, 54.

14. Goldman, "Plain Sex," 65.

15. For a similar view, see David Archard, *Sexual Consent* (Boulder, Colo.: Westview, 1998), 41.

16. "The delight men take in delighting, is not sensual, but a pleasure or joy of the mind consisting in the imagination of the power they have so much to please" (Thomas Hobbes, "Human Nature, or the Fundamental Elements of Policy," in *The English Works of Thomas Hobbes*, vol. IV, ed. Sir William Molesworth [Germany: Scientia Verlag Aalen, 1966], chap. 9, sec. 15, 48). For discussion, see Alan Soble, "Hobbes, Thomas," in

Sex from Plato to Paglia: A Philosophical Encyclopedia, edited by Alan Soble (Westport, Conn.: Greenwood, 2006), vol. 1, 454–60.

17. See Thomas Nagel, "Sexual Perversion," in this volume.

18. Kant, *Metaphysics,* 199.

19. Jean Hampton, "Defining Wrong and Defining Rape," in Keith Burgess-Jackson, ed., *A Most Detestable Crime: New Philosophical Essays on Rape* (New York: Oxford University Press, 1999), 118–56, at 147.

20. Hampton, "Defining Wrong," 147. Emphasis added to "humanity," to which "it" refers throughout.

21. Hampton, "Defining Wrong," 147–48.

22. Hampton, "Defining Wrong," 150.

23. Alan Donagan (*The Theory of Morality* [Chicago: University of Chicago Press, 1977]) similarly praises "life-affirming and nonexploitative" sexuality. By contrast, "sexual acts which are life-denying in their imaginative significance . . . are impermissible" (107; italics omitted). His principle, says Donagan, implies that prostitution, casual sex, and sadomasochism are wrong. Another internalism can be found in Augustine's *On Marriage and Concupiscence*: "A man turns to good use the evil of concupiscence . . . when he bridles and restrains its rage . . . and never relaxes his hold upon it except when intent on offspring, and then controls and applies it to the carnal generation of children . . . not to the subjection of the spirit to the flesh" (bk. 1, chap. 9). The evil of lusty congress is permissible or excusable if a man fights off sexual arousal and focuses attention entirely on procreation.

24. "For most normal human beings" is her claim. I wince.

25. Pat Califia, "Introduction," *Macho Sluts* (Los Angeles: Alyson Books, 1988), 9. Califia was a lesbian sadomasochist when *Macho Sluts* was published. I do not know her sexual self-identification as of 6/13/2016.

26. Why? Hampton's view is that these folk are not members of the set of "most normal humans." Hence, those who enjoy S&M *are* normal but are unlike other normal humans, or they are not normal, or they're not human. In any event, I'd like an explanation of Hampton's "fact," regardless of what spin she puts on it.

27. Thomas Mappes, "Sexual Morality and the Concept of Using Another Person," in this volume.

28. Mappes, "Sexual Morality," 275.

29. Mappes, "Sexual Morality," 274, 275. For another Kantian consent view, see Raymond Belliotti, "A Philosophical Analysis of Sexual Ethics," *Journal of Social Philosophy* 10:3 (1979), 8–11. See also the role of consent in Igor Primoratz, *Ethics and Sex* (London: Routledge, 1999).

30. Seiriol Morgan ("Dark Desires," in this volume) disputes the claim, as proposed by Igor Primoratz ("Sexual Morality: Is Consent Enough?" *Ethical Theory and Moral Practice* 4:3 [2001], 201–18), that consent is sufficient for the morality of sexual acts. Morgan undermines the claim that consent is sufficient by providing a counterexample, a case in which there is consent, yet the sexual events are still morally corrupt. I do not mean that I'm overall convinced that consent is sufficient, but Morgan's argument against Primoratz fails, because in Morgan's counterexample the informed clause of the consent principle has not been satisfied.

Within the field of medical ethics, *genuine consent* is understood as having two components, a "free" consent feature (voluntary, uncoerced) and an "informed" consent feature (knowledgeable, understanding the consequences, absence of lies, fraud, and deception); putting them together yields "the principle of free and informed consent." For example, see Nir Eyal, "Informed Consent," in *The Stanford Encyclopedia of Philosophy* (Fall 2012), edited by Edward Zalta, http://plato.stanford.edu/archives/fall2012/entries/informed-consent/. Eyal writes early in the entry, "Informed consent is shorthand for informed, voluntary, and decisionally-capacitated consent," and proceeds to examine each feature in great detail. Looking at writings about consent in sexual contexts—for example, Thomas Mappes's essay in this volume, the book by Alan Wertheimer (*Consent to Sexual Relations*), Wertheimer's essay in this volume, and the essays in philosophy or law (Google searchable) that suggest that rape may be accomplished by lies and deception—leads to the conclusion that the principle is the "free and informed consent" principle, not a principle of "free consent" to which "adequately informed" is merely welded on as an afterthought and plays no role in whether consent is genuine. In any event, that fraud and deception *invalidate* or *negate* or *block* or *disempower* consent is hardly controversial.

A crucial question in evaluating whether Morgan's counterexample demonstrates that Primoratz's "consent is sufficient" moral principle is false is: What does "consent" mean in *his* principle? The three philosophies of sex that Primoratz criticizes in defending the sufficiency of consent (Catholic, or Geachian, Natural Law; Scruton's "Individuating Intentionality"; Feminist theories of Patriarchy) do not establish, in his view, that factors beyond consent are necessary to invoke in developing a comprehensive morality of sex. Rejecting these philosophies of sex occupies almost all of Primoratz's paper; defining "consent" does not receive much attention. However, what Primoratz writes makes it imperative that a counterexample to his "consent is sufficient" proposal be a case in which consent, *both* informed and free, occurs, yet the sexual activity resulting from this full-bodied consent, or made possible by it, is morally wrong. Primoratz's thesis is that genuine consent, understood as free and informed, is sufficient for the moral permissibility of sexual encounters (of course with the Millian proviso that no third parties are harmed).

Morgan presents an elaborate example in "Dark Desires," the details of which I am not going to repeat. We need for now only his summary of what the example has accomplished, in his view: "All in all, then, the Vicomte presents us with a clear-cut case of sexual behaviour which is consensual and yet contrary to the Kantian conception of duty."[23] (The note number is in the original.) Hence, according to Morgan, Primoratz's "consent is sufficient" is false. However, anyone who reads Morgan's intricately detailed description of the Vicomte (based on Pierre Choderlos de Laclos, *Les Liaisons dangereuses*) will notice the stack of lies carried out by the Vicomte in his seduction of Madame de Tourvel. The point is that the example fails against Primoratz; his principle is that free *and* informed consent is sufficient for the morality of sex. Morgan's counterexample has the wrong logical form.

I found something mysterious, yet revealing, in Morgan's paper. The only significant place he brings up the conceptual or moral role of deception in sexual encounters is note 23, where Morgan speaks about "someone holding the infringement of freedom to be the only possible thing wrong with sexually motivated behavior." This "someone" is a straw person; no such person exists who claims that "free" alone is sufficient for the morality of sex. This someone is surely not Primoratz. Morgan claims that this "someone" could argue that the Vicomte's actions are wrong on the grounds that "he repeatedly lies," when lying behavior is morally wrong, for the "someone," because it is an infringement of *freedom*—that is, it violates *autonomy* and is already wrong by the principle that consent must be free. Morgan does not admit, or even bring up the possibility, that "informed" is part of genuine consent or that the presence of deception negates consent. Has he never heard that "informed" can be an independent piece of the consent doctrine? Morgan fails to acknowledge that deception undermines consent and, as a result, that his counterexample misses the mark. To refute Primoratz, one must describe a case in which the free *and* informed consent principle is satisfied, yet the sexual activity is immoral. "Dark Desires" may have a slew of philosophical virtues. One of them is not that Morgan has delivered even a slight blow to Primoratzian sexual morality.

Morgan should have known this. In my 1986 *Sexual Investigations* (33–34), I had reason to mention (in contrasting Primoratz with Bertrand Russell on prostitution) that Primoratz's principle was "free and informed consent." A decade later, in the third edition of *Philosophy of Sex* (1997), I pointed readers in the direction of the discussion of Primoratz in *Sexual Investigations* (xivn10). Much more important, though, is that the 3rd edition includes the entire text of Primoratz's "What's Wrong with Prostitution?" (339–61), in which the author speaks explicitly of free and informed consent.

(The essay appears again in *POSe4*, 251–73.) By the way, a new textbook in the philosophy of sex, by Laurie Shrage and Robert Stewart, *Philosophizing About Sex* (Peterborough, Can.: Broadview Press, 2015), uses a couple of pages (35–37) on this topic, presenting Morgan's case against the sufficiency thesis in a favorable (i.e., disappointingly uncritical) light. All that Shrage-Stewart and Morgan get is the uninteresting conclusion that the "free" feature of consent is not sufficient.

31. Jeffrie Murphy, "Some Ruminations on Women, Violence, and the Criminal Law," in *In Harm's Way: Essays in Honor of Joel Feinberg*, edited by Jules Coleman and Allen Buchanan (Cambridge: Cambridge University Press, 1994), 218.

32. This thesis is exquisitely proposed and defended by Alan Wertheimer in *Consent to Sexual Relations* (Cambridge: Cambridge University Press, 2003). Portions of the book are reprinted in *Philosophy of Sex* 4th edition, 5th edition, and 6th edition.

33. Mappes, "Sexual Morality," 274.

34. Mappes's principle implies that prostitution is permissible if and only if the prostitute is not coerced, is not deceived, and is not taken advantage of (e.g., in virtue of her economic needs). The implications of Goldman's internalism are less clear. He does not advance a simple free and informed consent criterion, but adds that each person must make a sexual object of himself for the sake of the pleasure of the other, or must give sexual pleasure to the other so that their activity is mutually pleasurable. That rule seems to condemn prostitution, unless the client provides sexual pleasure for the prostitute (and the prostitute allows it). On the other hand, perhaps the mutual benefits need not reflect an "exchange in kind"; the prostitute's benefit is receiving an amount of money that makes their encounter sufficiently mutual. If, as Goldman claims, sexuality is governable by moral principles that apply generally in other areas of life, conceiving of prostitution as both a sexual and an economic activity is not odd, and the sex-money exchange may be justifiable by a variant of the principle of informed consent. For confirmation, see a more recent essay by Goldman, "Sexual Ethics," in *A Companion to Applied Ethics*, edited by R. G. Frey and C. H. Wellman (Oxford: Blackwell, 2003), 188–91.

These conclusions may be reached by another route. Let's investigate the implications of Goldman's definitions for prostitution (ideas I have expressed in a number of places: *Sexual Investigations*, 1996, 70–71; *POS3e*, 1997, 73–75; *Philosophy of Sex and Love*, 1st ed., 1998, 12–13; *Philosophy of Sex and Love*, 2nd ed., 2008, 56–57; and *POS6e*, 2013, 83, 85). Sex workers engage in acts with clients; for the clients, the acts are sexual because they (tend to) satisfy the client's Goldmanian sexual desire, but for the sex workers, the acts cannot be sexual acts—because these workers have no Goldmanian sexual desire to begin with. Their motive is to get money. The outward form of their acts is sexual, and they *are* sexual, for the client, but for the sex worker they are purely economic acts, like putting together toys on an assembly line. Shrage and Stewart give a persuasive account of sex work conceived as work and not as sex: "a sex worker typically remains emotionally and erotically detached while performing her job and manipulating her client's body, using at times sexual parts of her own body. For her, this is a simulation of sex and not the real thing" (*Philosophizing About Sexuality*, 3). I don't know why they don't refer to a provocative article by Shrage herself that supports the passage: "Do Lesbian Prostitutes Have Sex with Their Clients? A Clintonesque Reply," *Sexualities* 2:2 (1999), 259–61.

Shrage and Stewart, however, take one step too many in criticizing Goldman's definitions of sexual activity and desire. After mentioning (*Philosophizing*, 12) the well-known problem that Goldman has with masturbation, they proceed to write, "Goldman's definition of 'sex' marginalizes the sexual desires and tastes of people who practice 'BDSM' (bondage, discipline, domination, submission, and sadomasochism). Sexual desire in a BDSM encounter involves desires to dominate or submit to another, which can be accomplished with language, or other forms of play involving ropes, paddles, whips, boots, and so on. Although bodies are involved in acts of sexual domination and submission, BDSM activities do not necessarily involve or aim at contact with the body of another." The argument is that BDSM activities, like masturbation, do not fit comfortably with Goldman's definitions of sexual activity and desire; and so much the worse for his definitions. To complain, however, that Goldman's definitions are wrong because they "marginalize" BDSM is perverse. How can a definition (wrongly) marginalize that which is *already marginal*? BDSM is a set of practices that only a small percent of people engage in on a regular basis, to enough of an extent that it becomes part of their sexual identities. If Shrage and Stewart want to argue that no sexual acts should be marginalized by any definition, because all sexual acts, identities, and lifestyles are on a par with each other, no matter that some are preferred by 95 percent of the population and the others are preferred by only 1 percent or 7 percent, and no matter that some are bizarre, let them offer *the argument*. Necrophilia is performed by a very small percent of the world's population; it is also "marginalized" by Goldman's definitions. That seems to be exactly right. It is not on par with nonmarginal loving, heterosexual, mutual oral sex that ends with simultaneous orgasm.

35. Kant, *Lectures*, 163.

36. Martha Nussbaum, "Objectification," *Philosophy and Public Affairs* 24:4 (1995), 249–91, reprinted in *Philosophy of Sex*, 4th ed., 381–419 (the passage is on p. 394; references to the essay are to *POS4*). In an updated version of "Objectification" (*Sex and Social Justice* [New York: Oxford University Press, 1999]), Nussbaum changed "without causing him pain" to "without causing him unwanted pain" (223). An essay that splices Rae Langton's ideas about objectification to Nussbaum's is Evangelia Papadaki, "Feminist Perspectives on Objectification" (December 2015), in *Stanford Encyclopedia of Philosophy*, edited by Edward Zalta, at https://plato.stanford.edu/entries/feminism-objectification/.

37. Nussbaum, "Objectification," 401, italics added.

38. Nussbaum, "Objectification," 401.

39. Nussbaum, "Objectification," 411, italics added.

40. Nussbaum, "Objectification," 400–401, italics added.

41. Nussbaum, "Objectification," 405.

42. Nussbaum, "Objectification," 402, italics added.

43. Kant, *Lectures*, 165–66.

44. Nussbaum, "Objectification," 409, 410, 411. Note the tension between Nussbaum's rejecting sex in the "anonymous spirit" and her legal and moral defense of prostitution ("'Whether from Reason or Prejudice': Taking Money for Bodily Services," *Sex and Social Justice*, 276–98). On Nussbaum, see my *Pornography, Sex, and Feminism* (Amherst, N.Y.: Prometheus, 2002), 72–78, 163–74, and "Concealment and Exposure," in *Sex and Ethics: Essays on Sexuality, Virtue, and the Good Life*, edited by Raja Halwani (Basingstoke, U.K.: Palgrave Macmillan, 2007), 248–51.

45. See my *Sexual Investigations*, 55.

46. Nussbaum, "Objectification," 404. Nussbaum mistakenly calls Califia's short story "Jenny."

47. Pat Califia, "Jessie," in *Macho Sluts*, 28–62, at 60. This sweet speech was uttered by the top, Jessie, to the bottom, Liz, the morning after their sexual encounter.

48. For Kant on sex, see Vincent Cooke, "Kant, Teleology, and Sexual Ethics," *International Philosophical Quarterly* 31:1 (1991), 3–13; Onora O'Neill, "Between Consenting Adults," in *Constructions of Reason* (Cambridge: Cambridge University Press, 1989), 105–25; Susan Meld Shell, *The Embodiment of Reason* (Chicago: University of Chicago Press, 1996) and *The Rights of Reason* (Toronto: University of Toronto Press, 1980); Irving Singer, *The Nature of Love, vol. 2: Courtly and Romantic* (Chicago: University of Chicago Press, 1984); and Keith Ward, *The Development of Kant's View of Ethics* (Oxford: Blackwell, 1972).

49. Kant, *Metaphysics*, 62; see *Lectures*, 167.

50. Kant, *Metaphysics*, 126*n*.

51. Kant, *Metaphysics*, 127; italics added.

52. Nussbaum, "Objectification," 415*n*30.

53. Raymond Belliotti, *Good Sex: Perspectives on Sexual Ethics* (Lawrence, Kans.: University Press of Kansas, 1993), 100; italics added. Belliotti reads Kant as if Kant were Nussbaum.

54. Baker and Elliston, "Introduction," *Philosophy and Sex*, 1st ed. (Buffalo, N.Y.: Prometheus, 1975), 8–9; 2nd ed. (1984), 17–18, or the "Introduction" in *Philosophy and Sex*, 3rd ed., edited by Robert B. Baker, Kathleen J. Wininger, and Frederick A. Elliston (Amherst, N.Y.: Prometheus, 1998), 23. These passages are missing from *Philosophy and Sex*, 4th ed., edited by Robert B. Baker and Kathleen J. Wininger (Amherst, N.Y.: Prometheus, 2009), which includes my original "Sexual Use" essay.

55. Kant, *Metaphysics*, 180.

56. Kant, *Metaphysics*, 215. For Aristotle and Montaigne, see Soble, ed., *Eros, Agape, and Philia* (New York: Paragon House, 1989), 57–70, 299–301.

57. Kant, *Lectures*, 164.

58. Immanuel Kant, *Philosophical Correspondence: 1759–99*, translated by Arnulf Zweig (Chicago: University of Chicago Press, 1967), letter dated 7/10/1797, 235–36; italics added to "is."

59. Kant, *Metaphysics*, 62.

60. Howard Williams, *Kant's Political Philosophy* (New York: St. Martin's Press, 1983), 117.

61. 1 Corinthians 7:1–9; see Kant, *Metaphysics*, 179–80.

62. Allen Wood, *Kant's Ethical Thought* (Cambridge: Cambridge University Press, 1999), 2. Here's the line in the *Metaphysics* to which Wood refers: "Even the permitted bodily union of the sexes in marriage . . . [is] a union which is in itself merely an animal union" (179). This is Kantian minimalism.

63. Kant, *Metaphysics*, 64.

64. This version of "Sexual Use" is lacking "Section IX. Metaphilosophical Finale." See *Philosophy of Sex*, 6th edition.

STUDY QUESTIONS

1. About sexual desire Soble writes, "Sexual arousal brings about a yearning to dominate or consume the other's body. Sexual desire is thus a threat to the other's personhood." Is it true that sexual desire brings about this yearning? And what does it mean to yearn to dominate and consume another's body? If true, how would this be (one) reason why sexual desire threatens another's personhood?

2. Explain Kantian doubts about the morality of sexuality. Focus on the role that each of sexual desire and sexual activity plays in these doubts.

3. Define as carefully as possible the different types of solutions to the Kantian sex problem. Are there more beyond the types provided by Soble?

4. Suppose that Kant is right that only in sexuality is one person "made an Object of indulgence" for another. How might this provide a good reason for treating sexuality as a special case, and as a special case in the Kantian sense—that it threatens the personhood of both (or all the) parties to the sexual act?

5. Interestingly, none of the proposed solutions to the Kantian sexual problem mention love. Explore the possibility of whether two (or more?) people having sex with each other as an expression of love

(for each other) fixes the Kantian sexual problem. Would such an attempted solution be internalist or externalist? Why? (The answer to this question will reveal much about how you view the connections between love and sexual desire.) If this solution fails, why does it fail? (In this regard, Kant says something curious on page 163 in the *Lectures*: "Sexual love can, of course, be combined with human love and so carry with it the characteristics of the latter, but taken by itself and for itself, it is nothing more than appetite.")

6. Take seriously the joke, "Is sex an autonomy-killing, mind-numbing, subhuman passion? Yes, but only when it's good." Work out its personal, social, and ethical implications.

7. If Kant is correct that marriage is necessary for the moral permissibility of sex, what implications would this have for other forms of marriage, such as plural marriage and same-sex marriage? Could Kant's view be used to support these forms of marriage? Read what Kant has to say in the *Lectures* about non-heterosexual, one-man-one-woman sexual acts to help you decide.

EIGHTEEN

Consent and Sexual Relations

Alan Wertheimer

It is often thought that moral questions about behavior, including sexual activity, can be appreciably if not finally answered by determining whether the participants consented. Although in this essay **Alan Wertheimer** *does not reject the moral power of consent or deny that consent can be "morally transformative," he does raise fascinating questions about consent: its nature, when it is present and absent, and its ultimate moral force. Wertheimer argues that it is too simple to deal with all sexual moral questions by referring to consent alone, that other moral factors and deliberations play an essential role. He presents a number of conundrums about the use of fraud or deception in sexual interactions as well as about the use of coercion and other sorts of pressures. In an intriguing section of his essay, Wertheimer suggests that whether and when "yes" means "yes" is a more important question than whether and when "no" means "no." He also discusses the novel idea that persons might, in some circumstances, have a moral duty to give consent to sexual relations. The very wording of this inquiry shows that other factors, beyond consent, must be brought to bear on questions in sexual ethics.*

Alan Wertheimer (1942–2015) was a professor at the University of Vermont and senior research scholar in the Department of Bioethics at the National Institutes of Health. He is the author of *Coercion* (Princeton University Press, 1987), *Exploitation* (Princeton University Press, 1996), and *Consent to Sexual Relations* (Cambridge University Press, 2003). This essay is reprinted with the permission of Alan Wertheimer and Cambridge University Press, from *Legal Theory* 2:2 (1996): 89–112. © 1996, Cambridge University Press.

I. INTRODUCTION

This essay has two broad purposes. First, as a political philosopher who has been interested in the concepts of coercion and exploitation, I want to consider just what the analysis of the concept of consent can bring to the question, what sexually motivated behavior should be prohibited through the criminal law?[1] Put simply, I shall argue that conceptual analysis will be of little help. Second, and with somewhat fewer professional credentials, I shall offer some thoughts about the substantive question itself. Among other things, I will argue that it is a mistake to think that sexual crimes are about violence rather than sex and that we need to understand just why the violation of sexual autonomy is a serious wrong. I shall also argue that the principle that "no means no" does not tell us when "yes means yes," and that it is the latter question that poses the most interesting theoretical difficulties about coercion, misrepresentation, and competence. In addition, I shall make some brief remarks concerning two questions about consent and sexual relations that lie beyond the criminal law: What "consent compromising behaviors" should be regarded as indecent, although not criminal? When *should* someone consent to sexual relations within an enduring relationship? (A word about notation: In what follows, A will represent a person who attacks B or makes a proposal to B, and it is B's consent that is at issue. A will always be male and B will always be female.)

II. CONSENT AND CONCEPTUAL ANALYSIS

A standard picture about this topic goes something like this. We start with the principle that the criminal law should prohibit behavior that seeks to obtain sexual relations without valid consent. To determine which specific behaviors should be prohibited by the criminal law, we must engage in a detailed philosophical analysis of the concept of consent (and related concepts). If such an analysis can yield the criteria of valid consent, we are then in a better position to identify the behaviors that should be prohibited.

I believe that this picture is mistaken. My central point in this section is that the questions (and their facsimiles)—What is consent? What is valid or meaningful consent?—are less important than they first seem. The concept of consent provides a useful template to organize many of the moral issues in which we are interested, but it cannot do much more than that. The question as to what behavior should be prohibited through the criminal law will be settled by moral argument informed by empirical investigation. Any attempt to resolve that question through an inquiry into the "essence" of consent or the conditions under which we can use the word "consent" will prove to be of only limited help.

A. Consent as Morally Transformative

Let us begin by noting that we are not interested in consent as a freestanding concept. Rather, we are interested in consent because consent *is morally transformative*—that is, it changes the moral relationship between A and B and between them and others.[2] B's consent may *legitimate* an action by A that would not be legitimate without B's consent, as when B's consent to surgery transforms A's act from a battery to a permissible medical procedure. B's consent to a transaction with A provides a reason for others not to interfere with that transaction, as when B's consent to let A put a tattoo on her arm gives C a reason to let them be. And B's consent may give rise to an *obligation*. If B consents to do X for A, B acquires an obligation to do X for A.

To say that B's consent is morally transformative is not to say that B's consent is either necessary or sufficient to change an "all things considered" moral judgment about A's or B's action. It may be legitimate for A to perform surgery on a delusional B without B's consent. It may be wrong for A to perform surgery on B with B's consent if the procedure is not medically indicated.[3] Similarly, we may believe that exchanging money for sexual relations is wrong even if the prostitute consents to the exchange. But this does not show that the prostitute's consent is not morally transformative. After all, the prostitute's consent to sexual relations with A eliminates one very important reason for regarding A's behavior as wrong—namely, that A had sexual relations with B without her consent. B's consent is morally transformative because it provides a reason, although not a conclusive reason, for thinking that A's behavior is legitimate.

B. The Logic of Consent Arguments

To put the point of the previous section schematically, we are interested in the following sort of argument.

Major Premise: If B consents to A's doing X to B, then it is legitimate for A to do X to B.
Minor Premise: B has (has not) consented to A's doing X to B.
Conclusion: It is (is not) legitimate for A to do X to B.

Given the major premise, it seems that we must determine when the *minor premise* is true if we are going to know when the conclusion is warranted. For that reason, we may be tempted to think that an analysis of the concept of consent will identify the *criteria* or necessary and sufficient conditions of valid consent, and that empirical investigation can then (in principle) determine if those criteria are met. If the criteria are met, then the minor premise is true and the conclusion follows. If not, then the minor premise is false and the conclusion does not follow.

If things were only so simple. It is a mistake to think that we will be able to make much progress toward resolving the substantive moral and legal issues in which we are interested by philosophical resources internal to the concept of consent. In the final analysis, we are always going to have to ask: Given the facts that relate to issues of consent, how should we think about the moral and legal status of a transaction or relationship? In that sense, I am squarely in the camp that maintains that the concept of consent is fundamentally normative.

In suggesting that consent is essentially normative, I do not deny that it is possible to produce a morally neutral account of consent that would allow us to say when B consents by reference to specific empirical criteria. I do maintain that if we were to operate with a morally neutral account of consent, we would then have to go on to ask whether B's consent legitimates A's action, and that we will be unable to answer that question without introducing substantive moral arguments. A morally neutral account of consent would do little work in our moral argument. If we want consent to do more work in our moral argument, we must build some of our substantive moral principles into the account of consent that we deploy. We could say that B "really" consents only when B's consent token is morally transformative. In the final analysis, it does not matter much whether we adopt a thin, morally neutral account of consent or a thick, morally laden account of consent. Either way, the point remains that we will not be able to go from a morally neutral or empirical account of consent to moral or legal conclusions without introducing substantive moral arguments.

C. The Fallacy of Equivocation

Precisely because we can pack a lot or a little into our account of consent, it is all too easy for a "consent argument" to commit the fallacy of equivocation, in which the meaning of consent assumed by the major premise is not identical to the meaning of consent in the minor premise, and, thus, the conclusion does not follow even though both the major premise and minor premise may be true (given different meanings of consent). Consider a classic problem of political philosophy: Do citizens have a general (prima facie) obligation to obey the law? A standard argument goes like this:

Major Premise: One is obligated to obey the laws if one consents to do so.

Minor Premise: (Version 1): One who remains in his society rather than leaving thereby gives his consent to that society (Plato).[4]

Minor Premise: (Version 2): One who benefits from living in a society gives his consent to that society (Locke).[5]

Conclusion: One who does not leave his society or benefits from living in a society has an obligation to obey its laws.

Is either version of the minor premise true? The problem is this: There may be a linguistically plausible sense in which one who accepts the benefits of one's government has consented to that government or in which one who remains in one's society has consented to remain in that society. But, even if that were so, that will not resolve the problem of political obligation. We will have to determine if the type or strength of consent that figures in the major premise has been met in the minor premise. And it may not. Thus, we could agree with Plato that there is a sense in which one who does not leave his society gives his consent, while also agreeing with Hume that it is not the sort of *free* consent that would justify the ascription of a strong obligation to obey the law.[6] We can make a similar point about Locke's view.

The danger of equivocation arises with respect to two other concepts that will figure in our analysis: coercion and harm. Let us assume that one who is coerced into consenting does not give valid or morally transformative consent. When is consent coerced? Consider Harry Frankfurt's example:

> The courts may refuse to admit in evidence, on the grounds that it was coerced, a confession which the police have obtained from a prisoner by threatening to beat him. But the prisoner's accomplices, who are compromised by his confession, are less likely to agree that he was genuinely coerced into confession.[7]

Was the prisoner's confession coerced? There is no reason to think that there must be a single acceptable answer to this question. The answer to this question will depend on the sort of moral transformation that consent is meant to trigger. The sort of pressure to which the prisoner was subject may be sufficient to deprive his confession of legal validity. At the same time, and if there is anything like honor among thieves, the very same pressures may not be sufficient to excuse his betrayal of his accomplices. It will do no good to ask what appears to be a conceptual and empirical question: Was his confession coerced? Rather, we need to answer two moral questions: What sorts of pressures on prisoners to confess are sufficient to bar the introduction of the confession as evidence? What sorts of pressures on prisoners are sufficient to excuse the ascription of blame by those to whom the prisoner has obligations of silence?

A similar point can be made about the concept of harm. Suppose we start from the Millian principle that the state can justifiably prohibit only conduct that causes harm to others. The following questions arise: Does the psychic distress caused by offensive speech count as harmful? Does trespass that causes no physical damage to one's property constitute a harm? Does a Peeping Tom harm his target? Does he harm his target if she is unaware of his voyeurism? Clearly there is a sense in which psychic distress caused by offensive speech is harmful. As a matter of empirical psychology, it is simply untrue that "sticks and stones will break your bones, but names will never hurt you." And there is clearly a sense in which one has not been harmed by trespass that causes no physical damage, or by the Peeping Tom, particularly if the target is unaware of his voyeurism. But these observations will not tell us which activities can be legitimately prohibited by the state under the Millian principle.[8]

Once again, we have two choices. We could opt for a morally neutral or neurological account of harm, but then we will have to go on to ask whether harm so defined should or should not be prohibited, and whether some acts excluded by that definition can be legitimately prohibited. On the other hand, we could opt for a moralized account of harm, say, one in which one is harmed if one's rights are violated. On this view, we can maintain that the psychic distress caused by offensive speech does not count as a harm because it does not violate one's rights, whereas trespassing and voyeurism do count as harm because they violate one's rights to property and privacy. From this perspective, sexual offenses may cause a particularly serious harm because they violate an important right of the subject, not (solely) because they are physically or psychologically more damaging than nonsexual violence (although that may also be true).

III. A (BRIEF) THEORY OF CONSENT

With these anti-essentialist ruminations behind us, I shall sketch an account of consent in two stages. First, I shall consider the ontology of consent, the phenomena to which the template of consent calls our attention. Second, I shall consider what I shall call the "principles of consent," the conditions under which these phenomena are morally transformative.

A. The Ontology of Consent

First, morally transformative consent always involves a verbal or nonverbal action, some token of consent. Consent is performative rather than attitudinal. It might be objected that there is a plausible understanding of the word consent, in which mental agreement is sufficient to establish consent. I do not want to quibble over words. If one wants to insist that mental agreement is sufficient to establish consent, then I shall say that B's mental agreement to allow A to do X does not *authorize* or *legitimate* A's doing X in the absence of B's communication. If B has decided to accept A's business proposal and was about to communicate that decision to A when their call was disconnected, it would not be legitimate for A to proceed as if B had agreed. Similarly, that B actually desires sexual relations with A does not authorize A to have sexual relations with B if B has said "no."

Second, and to cover well-trod ground, B's consent token can be explicit or tacit, verbal or nonverbal. B gives verbal explicit agreement to A's proposal when B says "yes" or some equivalent. B may give nonverbal but explicit consent to A's proposal that they have sexual relations if B smiles and leads A into her bedroom. One gives tacit consent when silence or inaction is understood to constitute agreement. Thus if my department chair says, "Unless I hear from you, I'll assume that you can advise students at orientation," my silence is an indication that I am available. In general, it is of no fundamental importance whether consent is explicit or tacit, if it is understood that silence or inaction indicates consent, if there is a genuine opportunity for B to dissent, and if B's dissent will have moral force.

And that brings me to the third consideration. Consent will be valid or morally transformative only when certain conditions are met or, perhaps more helpfully, only in the absence of certain background defects. Those conditions will include, among other things, that B is competent to give consent, the absence of coercion, and also perhaps the absence of misrepresentation and concealment of important information. We could say that one who signs a contract at the point of a gun has not consented at all, or that her consent isn't sufficiently free to give rise to an obligation. Either way, her consent token will not be morally transformative.

B. The Principles of Consent

To put the argument in somewhat different terms, we do not start from the assumption that B's consent is morally transformative, in which case the question for philosophical analysis becomes whether B has or has not consented to A's action. Rather, the determination as to when consent is morally transformative is an *output* of moral theorizing rather than an *input*. Let us call the principles that define when a consent token is morally transformative the *principles of consent*.

The principles of consent may vary from context to context. To see this, consider four cases: (1) A physician tells his patient that she has breast cancer and that she should immediately undergo a mastectomy. He does not explain the risks of the procedure or other options. Because the patient trusts her physician, she signs a consent form. (2) A patient's leg is gangrenous and she must choose between amputation and death. She understands the alternatives, and, because she does not want to die, she signs the consent form. (3) A dance studio gets an elderly woman to contract to pay $20,000 for dance lessons by "a constant and continuous barrage of flattery, false praise, excessive compliments, and panegyric encomiums."[9] (4) A psychotherapist proposes that he and the patient have sexual relations. Because the patient has become sexually attracted to the psychotherapist, she enthusiastically agrees.

We might think that the woman's consent in (1) is not valid because the principles of consent for medical procedures require that the physician explain the risks and alternatives. In this case, valid or morally transformative consent must be *informed* consent. Yet the principles of consent may also entail that the consent given in (2) is valid even though the patient reasonably believed that she had no choice but to agree, say, because the very real constraints on her decision were not the result of *illegitimate* pressures on her decision-making process. By contrast, the principles of consent might hold that the consent given in (3) is not valid or morally transformative because the dance studio acted illegitimately in procuring the woman's consent, even though she had more "choice" than in (2). And the principles of consent might hold that the consent given in (4) does not render it legitimate for the psychotherapist to have sexual relations with his patient because he has a fiduciary obligation to refrain from sexual relations with his patient. Period.[10] These are just intuitions. How do we determine the correct principles of consent for one context or another? At one level, the answer to these questions will ultimately turn on what is the best account of morality in general or the sorts of moral considerations relevant to this sort of problem. Somehow, I think we are unlikely to resolve that here. Suppose that the best account of the principles of consent reflect a commitment to impartiality, and that this commitment will be cashed out along consequentialist or contractarian lines. If we adopt a consequentialist outlook, we will want to examine the costs and benefits of different principles of consent and will adopt those principles that generate the best consequences—all things considered. From a contractarian perspective, we can think of the principles of consent as the outcome of a choice made under conditions of impartiality, perhaps as modeled by a Rawlsian veil of ignorance, although here, too, we will want to consider the costs and benefits of different principles (which is not to say that a contractarian will consider them in the way in which a consequentialist would). But the crucial and present point is that, from either perspective, the point of moral theorizing is not to determine when one consents, per se. The task is to determine the principles for morally transformative consent.

IV. CRIMINAL OFFENSES

In this section, I want to bring the previous analysis to bear on the central question of this symposium: What sexually motivated behaviors should be regarded as criminal offenses? In considering this question, I shall bracket several related issues. First, I have nothing to say about the history of the law of rape. Second, I shall have little to say about problems of proof that arise because sexual offenses involve behavior that is frequently consensual, and because we operate in a legal context in which we are especially concerned to avoid the conviction of the innocent. Third, I shall not be concerned with questions as to the best interpretations of existing statutes. The question here is not, for example, whether Rusk was guilty under an existing statute if he caused his victim to fear being stranded in an unknown part of the city unless she engaged in sexual acts with him, but whether legislation should be designed so as to regard such behavior as a criminal offense.[11] Finally, I shall have little to say about questions of culpability, the sorts of issues raised in the (in)famous case of *Regina v. Morgan*, in which several men claimed to believe that the wife of a friend consented to sexual relations with them even though she strongly objected at the time.[12] I am concerned with the question as to what conduct should be criminal, and not the conditions under which one might be justifiably excused from liability for such conduct.

A. Criminal Elements

In considering the question so posed, it will be useful to disaggregate some of the ways in which sexually motivated behavior might be seriously wrong.

First, a sexual offense involves a nonconsensual touching or bodily contact—that is, the elements of a standard battery. Nonconsensual touchings need not be violent or painful or involve the penetration of a bodily orifice.

Second, a sexual offense may involve a violent assault or battery—that is, physical contact that involves overpowering restraint of movement or physical pain or harm to the victim's body that lasts beyond the duration of the incident.

Third, a sexual offense may involve *threats* of violence. The perpetrator puts the victim in fear of harm to her life or body, and then uses that fear to obtain sexual relations. As the victim in *Rusk* put it, "If I do what you want, will you let me go?"

Fourth, sexual offenses may often involve harm or the fear of harms that *flow from* penetration as distinguished from the penetration itself, for example, unwanted pregnancy and sexually transmitted diseases.

Fifth, and of greatest relevance to this essay, is the moral and psychological harm associated with the fact that a sexual offense involves unwanted and nonconsensual penetration, that it "violates the interest in exclusive control of one's body for sexual purposes."[13]

B. Seriousness

The seriousness of a sexual offense may vary with the way in which these elements are combined. We can distinguish at least five sorts of sexual offense. Although reasonable people may disagree about the precise ranking, one view of their relative seriousness, in descending order of seriousness, looks like this: (1) sexually motivated assault with penetration and where violence is actually used to inflict harm or overcome resistance; (2) sexually motivated assault with penetration where violence is threatened but not used; (3) sexually motivated assault (where violence is used or threatened) where penetration does not occur ("attempted rape"); (4) penetration of the victim in the face of the victim's refusal to have sexual relations or her inability to consent to sexual relations, but without the use or threat of violence; (5) sexual battery or sexual harassment, where the victim is touched without her consent, but where penetration does not occur.

Before going further, let me make several points about this list. First, this list makes no distinction between cases in which the penetrator and victim are strangers and those in which they are acquaintances (or married). Second, this ordering does not draw a fundamental distinction between the *use* and *threat* of violence, an important departure from the traditional law of rape, in which actual violence and resistance to that violence were sometimes required. It is clearly a mistake to minimize the importance of threats. Consider a case in which A says something like this (perhaps using cruder language):

> You and I are going to play a game. We are going to have sex and I want you to act like you want it and are enjoying it. If you play the game, you won't be hurt. Indeed, I will do everything I know how to do to make the sex as pleasurable as possible. Otherwise, I will kill you with this gun.

Because B regards A's threat as credible, B goes along with A's game. This example indicates that the mere utterance of a phrase that would constitute valid consent if uttered in the absence of such threats ("Please do it!") does not constitute any kind of valid consent in the presence of such threats.[14]

For the purposes of this essay, the most interesting questions concern cases (3) and (4). A sexual offense may involve assault without what Dripps calls the "expropriation" of the victim's body (as in (3)) and may involve expropriation without the use or threat of violence (as in (4)). It might be argued that (4) is a more serious offense than (3) because nonconsensual sexual penetration is a greater harm than the use or threat of violence that does not result in penetration. If this is a plausible view, even if not the most widely held or correct view, we need to ask why nonconsensual penetration is such a serious wrong. Second, if it should be criminal to have sexual relations with someone who has refused sexual relations, if "no means no," we still need to ask when "yes means yes." We have already described a case in which a consent token ("Please do it!") does *not* mean yes. Other cases are more difficult.

A currently fashionable view maintains that rape is about violence, not sex. That view might be resisted in two ways. It might be argued that rape is about sex because sex itself is about violence (or domination).[15] I have little to say about that view, except to note that even if there is a violent dimension to "ordinary" sex, there is still a distinction between the violence intrinsic to ordinary sex and the violence peculiar to what we have traditionally regarded as sexual crimes.

But I want to suggest that, for both empirical and moral reasons, it is crucial to see that sexual offense is at least partly about sex. First, there is considerable evidence that nonconsensual sexual relations are "a substitute for consensual sexual intercourse rather than a manifestation of male hostility toward women or a method of establishing or maintaining male domination."[16] Second, we cannot explain why the use or threat of violence to accomplish sexual penetration is more traumatic and a graver wrong than the use or threat of violence per se, except on the assumption that invasion of one's sexual being is a special sort of violation. Third, if women experience *non*violent but nonconsensual sex as a serious violation, this, too, can be explained only in the view that violation of a woman's sexual being is special. Consider, for example, the case in which A has sexual relations with an unconscious B. Some of the elements associated with a violent sexual assault would be lacking. There would be no fear, no overpowering of the will or experience of being coerced, and no experience of pain. Yet, even if B never discovers that A had sexual relations with her while she was unconscious, we might well think that B has been harmed or violated by A.[17]

The view that nonconsensual but nonviolent sex is a serious violation has been previously defended by several [authors]. Stephen Schulhofer argues that it should be a criminal offense to violate a person's sexual autonomy.[18] On Donald Dripps's "commodity" theory of sexual crime, the "expropriation" of another person's body for purposes of sexual gratification violates that person's interest in exclusive control over her body for sexual purposes.[19] Joan McGregor connects nonconsensual sexual relations to the invasion of privacy and the control of information about ourselves. She argues that nonconsensual sexual relations can be understood as violating an individual's right to control the "borders" of her relations with others.[20]

For present purposes, there is not much difference among these views. Although Dripps uses the avowedly "unromantic" language of commodity and expropriation, whereas Schulhofer and McGregor use the more philosophically respectable language of autonomy and control, these views are virtually extensionally equivalent.[21] They all maintain that it should be a criminal offense for A to engage in sexual penetration of B if B objects, whether or not A uses or threatens physical harm. It is true that Dripps would criminalize only the disregard of another's refusal to engage in sexual acts (except in cases in which the victim is unable to refuse) whereas Schulhofer and McGregor require a verbal or nonverbal yes. But this is of little practical import. If the law clearly states that B need only say "no" to render A liable to a criminal offense, then B's passivity will not be misunderstood.

Let us assume that this general view is correct. But why is it correct? Jeffrie Murphy suggests that it is not self-evident why the nonconsensual "penetration of a bodily orifice" is such a grave offense. He maintains that there is nothing that makes sexual assault "objectively" more serious than nonsexual assault, that the importance attached to penetration "is essentially cultural," and that if we did not "surround sexuality with complex symbolic and moral baggage," then nonconsensual sex would not be viewed as a particularly grave wrong.[22]

Murphy's science is probably wrong. A woman's abhorrence of nonconsensual sex may be at least partially hard-wired. Evolutionary psychologists have argued that because reproductive opportunities for women are relatively scarce, it is genetically costly for a woman to have sex with a man whose attributes she could not choose and who shows "no evident inclination to stick around and help provide for the offspring."[23] Thus, evolution would favor those women who were most disposed to abhor such sexual encounters. This is not to deny that there is great individual and cultural variability in the way in which people experience nonconsensual sexual relations. It is only to say that there is no reason to assume that culture is writing on a blank slate.

Yet, for our purposes, it does not really matter whether the best explanation for a woman's aversion to nonconsensual penetration is cultural or biological. The important question for moral and legal theory is whether the seriousness of a violation should be understood as *experience-dependent* or (at least partially) *experience-independent*. Although Murphy contrasts a "cultural" explanation of the wrongness of sexual crime with an "objective" explanation, what would an "objective" explanation look like? Murphy thinks that we need to explain why the penetration of an orifice is objectively more harmful than a punch in the nose. Fair enough. But then we also need to explain why physical injury is "objectively" worse than harm to our property or reputations or feelings or character. If the objective seriousness of harm is experience-*dependent*, there is nothing inherently special about physical injury, which Murphy takes to be the paradigm case of objective harm. After all, we could experience insults to our reputations as worse than physical injury and harm to our souls or character as a fate worse than death. On the other hand, if an objective account of harm is experience-*independent*, we would also need to explain why violations of sexuality are more serious than a punch in the nose. But here, once again, sexual harm is on a par with physical harm, for we would need to explain why harm to one's body is objectively more harmful than harm to one's property or reputation or soul.

I cannot produce an adequate account of the objective seriousness of sexual offense in this essay (and not just for lack of space), although the truth about that matter will affect the criminal penalties we are prepared to apply.[24] Although I am inclined to think that the character of this harm is at least partially experience-independent (that is, it would be a serious wrong even if it is not experienced that way), it should be noted that, even if it is experience-dependent, the criminal law is not designed to respond to the harm to the individual victim. Suppose, for example, that A rapes B, who, unbeknownst to A, actually embodies the alleged male fantasy: B wants to be raped. If the wrongness of a crime depends on the harm to the particular victim, then we might regard the rape of B as a lesser wrong. But, while the harm to a specific victim may affect the compensation owed to the victim in a civil action, the criminal law concerns harms to society and can be triggered even when there is no harm to a specific victim, as in an attempted crime in which no one is hurt. Similarly, even if the rape of a prostitute is a less serious offense because it does not involve the forcible taking of something that she regards as a "sacred and mysterious aspect of her self-identity" but merely the theft of a commodity that she normally trades for monetary gain, it does not follow that the criminal law should treat this rape as a less serious wrong.[25]

C. Defective Consent: When Does Yes Mean Yes?

Let us assume that the criminal law regards the disregard of a "no" (or the absence of a verbal or nonverbal "yes") as a basis for criminal liability. As we have seen, that would not resolve all of the problems. We have already seen that when B says "yes" in response to a threat of violence, her consent has no morally transformative power. The question arises, however, as to what other consent-eliciting behavior should be criminal. In this section, I want to focus on three ways in which B's consent token might be considered defective: (1) coercion; (2) misrepresentation or concealment; and (3) incompetence.

1. Coercion

Let us say that A coerces B to consent to engage in a sexual act when (a) A threatens to make B worse off if she does not perform that act and (b) it is reasonable to expect B to succumb to the threat rather than suffer the consequences.

It can be ambiguous as to whether condition (a) is met for two reasons. First, it can be ambiguous as to whether A threatens B at all. We do not say that a panhandler threatens B if he says, "Do you have any money to spare?" But does a large and tough-looking A threaten B when he says, "I would appreciate it if you would give me your wallet," but issues no threat as to what he will do if B refuses? We are inclined to think that some nonverbal behaviors are reasonably understood as proposing to make B worse off if B refuses, and that it is also reasonable to expect A to understand this.

Let us assume that there is no misunderstanding as to the likely consequences of refusal. It can be ambiguous as to whether condition (a) is met because we must ask, "Worse off than what?" I have argued elsewhere that the crucial element in coercive proposals is that A proposes to make B worse off than she has a *right* to be vis-à-vis A or that A proposes to violate B's right, and not (as it might seem) that A proposes to make B worse off than her status quo.[26] Whereas the gunman's proposal—"Sign this contract or I will shoot you"—proposes to make B worse off than both her status quo baseline and her right-defined baseline, those baselines can diverge. If a drowning B has a right to be rescued by A, then A's proposal to rescue B only if she pays him $10,000 is a coercive proposal on this view because A proposes to make B worse off than her right-defined baseline, even though he proposes to make her better off than her status quo–defined baseline. On the other hand, A's proposal is not coercive on this view if A proposes to make B worse off than her status quo–defined baseline, but not worse off than her right-defined baseline ("Plead guilty to a lesser offense or I will prosecute you on the charge of which we both know you are guilty").

Consider six cases:

1. A says to B, "Have sex with me or I won't return your car keys and you will be left stranded in a dangerous area."
2. A says, "Have sexual relations with me or I will dissolve our dating relationship."
3. A, a professor, says, "Have sexual relations with me or I will give you a grade two grades lower than you deserve."
4. A, a professor, says, "Have sexual relations with me and I will give you a grade two grades higher than you deserve."
5. A, who owes B money, says, "Have sexual relations with me and I will repay the money that I owe you. Otherwise, ciao."
6. A, a jailer, says, "Have sexual relations with me and I will arrange your escape; otherwise you and I know that you will be executed by the state."[27]

On my view, A makes a coercive proposal in cases (1), (3), and (5), but not in cases (2), (4), and (6). In cases (1), (3), and (5), A proposes to make B worse off than she has a right to be if she refuses—to have her car keys returned, to receive the grade she deserves, to have her loan repaid. By contrast, in cases (2), (4), and (6), A does not propose to make B worse off than she has a right to be if she refuses. B has no right that A continue their dating relationship or a right to a higher grade than she deserves or not to be executed by the state (bracketing general objections to capital *punishment*).

To anticipate objections, I do not deny that it is wrong for A to make his proposal in (4) and (6) or (sometimes) in (2). A jailer violates his obligation to society if he helps a prisoner escape and commits an additional wrong if he trades that favor for sexual services. It is wrong for a professor to use his control over grades to obtain sexual favors. He violates his responsibility to his institution and to other students. Moreover, and perhaps unlike (6), A's proposal in (4) may entice B into accepting an arrangement that she will subsequently regret. In general, it is often wrong for A to make a "seductive offer" to B—that is, where A has reason to believe it is likely that B will mistakenly perceive the (short-term) benefits of accepting the offer as greater than the (long-term) costs.

In any case, I do not say that A's proposals are coercive in (4) and (6) simply because, like (3), they create a choice situation in which B decides that having sexual relations with A is the lesser of two evils. After all, we could imagine that B, not A, initiates the proposals in (4) and (6) or is delighted to receive them, and it would be strange to maintain that B is coerced by a proposal that she initiates or is delighted to receive.

Now, consider (2) once again. B may regard the consequences of refusing A's proposal as devastating, as worse, for example, than receiving a lower grade than she deserves. It is also true that B's situation will be worse than her status quo if she refuses. Still, B cannot reasonably claim that she is the victim of "status coercion" or, more important, that her consent is not morally transformative.[28] And this [is] because A does not propose to violate B's rights if she refuses, for B has no right that A continue his relationship with B on her preferred terms.

The general point exemplified by (2) is that people make many decisions that they would not make if more attractive options were available to them. If I were independently wealthy, I might not choose to teach political philosophy for a living. If I were not at risk of losing my teeth, I would not consent to painful dental work. But it does not follow that I have been coerced into teaching or agreeing to have dental work performed. In principle, sex is no different. If B were wealthier or more attractive or more famous, she might not have to agree to have sexual relations with A in order to keep him in the relationship. Things being what they are, however, B might well decide that what she wants to do—all things considered—is to have sexual relations with A. It may be regrettable that people bargain with their sexuality, but there is no reason to regard bargaining *within the framework of one's rights* as compromising consent, at least in any way that should be recognized by the criminal law.

Let us now consider condition (b), which states that A coerces B only when it is reasonable to expect B to succumb to A's (admittedly coercive) threat rather than suffer the consequences or pursue a different course of action. Suppose that A proposes to tickle B's feet if she does not have sexual relations with him. I believe that A has made a coercive proposal to B, because A proposes to make B worse off than both her status quo baseline and her right-defined baseline. Still, if B decides to have sexual relations to avoid being tickled, I doubt that we would want to charge A with a criminal offense (unless, perhaps, A believed that B had an extreme aversion to being tickled). Here, we expect B to endure the consequences of A's coercive proposal rather than succumb to it.

Now, recall case (5). In my view, A has made a coercive proposal because A has proposed to violate B's right to be repaid if B refuses. But we might also say that B should sue A for breach of contract, and that we should not regard A's proposal as so compromising B's consent (because she has other legal options) that it should render A subject to a criminal charge.[29] We might disagree about this case. There are resources internal to the notion of coerced consent that allow us to go the other way. But it is moral argument, and not conceptual analysis, that will determine whether this is the sort of sexually motivated behavior that should be punished through the criminal law.

2. Fraud and Concealment

Suppose that A does not threaten B or propose to violate B's rights if she refuses to have sexual relations with A, but that B agrees to sexual relations with A only because B has certain beliefs about A that result from things that A has or has not said.
Consider:

7. A falsely declares that A loves B.
8. A falsely declares that he intends to marry B.
9. A falsely declares that he intends to dissolve the relationship if B does not consent (unlike (2), A is bluffing).
10. A fails to disclose that he has a sexually transmitted disease.
11. A fails to disclose that he has been having sexual relations with B's sister.

Has B given "valid" consent in these cases? We know that A has misrepresented or concealed important information in all of these cases. That is not at issue. The question is whether we should regard A's conduct as criminal.

There are several possibilities. If we were to extend the principle of *caveat emptor* to sexual relations, then there is arguably no problem in any of these cases. On the other hand, if we were to extend principles of criminal fraud or anything like the well-known medical principle of informed consent to the arena of sexual relations, then we could conclude that many representations that are now part and parcel of courtship should be illegal. I do not have anything close to a firm view about this matter. I think it entirely possible that, from either a contractualist or a consequentialist perspective, we would choose a legal regime in which we treat the failure to disclose information about sexually transmitted diseases as criminal, but that we would not want to treat misrepresentation or failure to disclose information about one's feelings or marital intentions or other relationships as criminal offenses.[30] But that is only a guess. For now, I want only to stress that the question as to whether A should be criminally liable in any of these cases will be resolved by moral argument as to what parties who engage in sexual relations owe each other by way of intentional falsehood and disclosure of information, and not by an analysis of the concept of consent.

3. Competence

B can give valid or "morally transformative" consent to sexual relations with A only if B is sufficiently competent to do so. It is uncontroversial that B cannot consent to sexual relations with A if she is unconscious.[31] It is also relatively uncontroversial that B cannot give valid or morally transformative consent if she does not possess the appropriate mental capacities, say, because B is below an appropriate age or severely retarded.

The most interesting *theoretical* questions about competence arise with respect to (otherwise) competent adults who consent to sexual relations because they are under the influence of voluntarily consumed alcohol or some other judgment-distorting substance. Consider two possible positions about this issue. It might be argued that if a competent adult allows herself to become intoxicated, her initial competence flows through to any decisions she makes while less than fully competent. In a second view, A should be liable for a criminal offense if he engages in sexual relations with B when B's first indication of consent is given while intoxicated, even if B is responsible for having put herself in that position.[32]

I do not have a firm view as to what position we should adopt about this matter. But we should not say that A should not be held liable just because B has acted imprudently, or even wrongly, in allowing herself to become intoxicated. Although B's behavior may put her on the moral hook, it does not take A off the moral hook. Although B acts imprudently if she leaves her keys in an unlocked car, A still commits a theft if he takes it. We could adopt a similar view about sexual relations with an intoxicated B.

D. Benefits and Costs

I have argued that the principle that society should make it criminal for individuals to engage in sexual acts without the consent of the other party is highly indeterminate, that we must decide under what conditions consent is morally transformative. Suppose that we were to consider a choice between what I shall call a *permissive legal regime* (LR$_P$), under which A commits a sexual crime only when he uses violence or the threat of violence against B, and a *rigorous legal regime* (LR$_R$), say, one in which it is a criminal offense (1) to engage in sexual acts without the express consent of the other party, (2) to obtain that consent by proposing to violate a legal right of the other party, (3) to misrepresent or fail to disclose information about sexually transmitted diseases, (4) to engage in a sexual act with a party whose consent was first given when severely intoxicated, and so on. It is not important to define the precise contours of these two legal regimes. The point is that we are considering a choice between a (relatively) permissive and a (relatively) rigorous regime.

Which regime should we choose? I have suggested that we could model the choice along consequentialist lines, where we would calculate the costs and benefits associated with different sets of rules, or we could model the choice along contractualist lines, in which people would choose from behind a Rawlsian veil of ignorance. Suppose that we adopt the Rawlsian approach. To make progress on this issue, we must relax the veil. The contractors must know what life would be like for people under different sets of laws and norms, including the full range of information about the trade-offs between the costs and benefits of the two regimes. Here, as elsewhere, the contractors would know that there is no free and equal lunch. At the same time, the veil would be sufficiently thick to deprive them of information regarding their personal characteristics. They would not know whether they were male or female, a potential perpetrator or victim, or, say, their attitude toward sexual relations. They would not know whether *their* sexual lives would go better under one set of rules or another. I don't think we can say with any confidence what rules would be chosen under any of these models, but we might be able to say something about the sorts of benefits and costs they would have to consider.

On the assumption that LR$_R$ would actually affect behavior in the desired direction, it would provide greater protection to the sexual autonomy of women and would promote an environment in which men come to consider "a woman's consent to sex significant enough to merit [their] reasoned attention and respect."[33] These are clear benefits. But there would be costs. Some of these costs would be endogenous to the legal system. LR$_R$ may consume legal resources that would be better spent elsewhere. It may result in the prosecution or conviction of more innocent persons. LR$_R$ may also generate some negative effects on the general structure of sexual and social relations. It may cause a decline in spontaneity and excitement in sexual relations. In addition, just as some persons enjoy the process of haggling over consumer transactions, some may enjoy the game of sexual negotiation, the haggling, bluffing, and concealment that have been a standard fixture of courtship. After all, whether coyness is biologically hard-wired or culturally driven, many women have long thought that it is better to (first) consent to sex after an initial indication of reluctance, lest they be viewed as too "easy" or "loose."[34] So B may suffer if A is too respectful of her initial reluctance. Finally, it is distinctly possible that some persons choose to become intoxicated precisely to render themselves less inhibited—the reverse of a standard Ulysses situation in which one acts ex ante to inhibit one's actions ex post.[35] So, if A were to comply with LR_R by refusing to have sexual relations with an intoxicated B, A would prevent B from doing precisely what B wanted to do.

Of course, to say that there is no free lunch does not mean that lunch isn't worth buying: the gains may be worth the costs. Whether that is so will depend, in part, on the way in which we aggregate the gains and costs. From a contractarian perspective, it is distinctly possible that we should give some priority to the interests of the worse off—that is, the potential victims of sexual offenses—rather than simply try to maximize the sum total of preference satisfaction or happiness or whatever. The weight of that priority will depend on the gravity of that violation, an issue that has not been settled. But I do not think we should be indifferent to numbers. If LR_R would work to the detriment of many and help but a few, that would make a difference. Still, here as elsewhere, we should be prepared to trade off considerable positive benefits to some persons in order to provide greater protection to those who would otherwise be harmed.

V. DECENT SEXUAL RELATIONS

Even if we were to expand the range of sexually motivated behaviors subject to criminal sanctions, the criminal law is a blunt instrument to be used relatively sparingly. There remains the question of what sort of behaviors should be regarded as indecent or seriously wrong. Is it seriously wrong for A to obtain B's consent to sexual relations by threatening to end a dating relationship? Is it less wrong if A is *warning* but not *threatening* B—that is, if A is not trying to manipulate B's behavior but is stating the truth, that he would not want to continue the relationship without sexual relations? Is it seriously wrong for A to falsely declare love in order to secure B's consent to sexual relations or to secure her consent while she is intoxicated?

I have no intention of trying to answer these questions in this essay. I do want to make a few remarks about the issues they present. First, there is no reason to think that the justified legal demands on our behavior are coextensive with the moral demands on our behavior. Just as we may have a (morally justified) legal right to engage in behavior that is morally wrong (for example, to give a lecture that the Holocaust is a hoax), we may have a morally justified legal right to produce another's consent to sexual acts in ways that are seriously wrong. Second, just as we might regard the principles of consent for the criminal law as the output of moral theorizing, we can regard the principles of consent for acting decently as the output of moral theorizing, although there would be a different mixture of benefits and costs. Third, this is not an issue without practical consequences. When millions of students are enrolled in sex education courses, it is a genuine question as to what principles we should teach them.

I think it fair to say that, at present, there is no consensus as to what constitutes immoral behavior in this arena. I believe that many people view the pursuit of sexual gratification in dating relationships along the lines of a "capitalist" model, in which all parties are entitled to try to press for the best deal they can get. On a standard (predominantly male) view of dating relationships, it is legitimate for A to seek B's consent to sexual relations, even if A believes B will come to regret that decision. Moreover, just as it is thought legitimate to misrepresent one's reservation price in a business negotiation (there is no assumption that one is speaking the truth when one says, "I won't pay more than $15,000 for that car"), one is entitled to misrepresent one's feelings or intentions. By contrast, in a fiduciary relationship, such as between physicians and patients, A has an obligation to act in the interests of his client rather than his own interests. A should not seek B's consent to a transaction if A believes it is not in B's interest to consent to that transaction.

It would probably be a mistake to apply a strong fiduciary model to sexual relations among competent adults. It might be argued that a paternalistic attitude toward another's sexual life would be rightly rejected as failing to respect the autonomy of the parties "to act freely on their own unconstrained conception of what their bodies and their sexual capacities are for."[36] This is all well and good as far as it goes, but it begs the question of how to understand autonomy, the pressures that it is reasonable for one to bring to bear on another's decision and whether one fails to respect another's autonomy when one fails to tell the truth and nothing but the truth about one's feelings, intentions, and other relationships. It may well turn out that some hybrid of these two models best captures A's moral responsibilities. Unlike the capitalist model, A must give considerable weight to B's interests, as well as his own. Unlike the fiduciary model, B's decision as to what serves her interests is in the driver's seat.

VI. WHEN SHOULD ONE CONSENT TO SEXUAL RELATIONS?

In this section, I want to open up a question that is frequently discussed among parties in enduring relationships but rarely mentioned in the academic literature: How should a couple deal with an asymmetrical desire for sexual relations? Let us assume that A desires sexual relations more frequently than B. Let us also assume that A and B agree that it is not permissible for A to have sexual relations with B when B does not consent. Their question—indeed, it is B's question—is whether she should consent to sexual relations when, other things being equal, she would prefer not to consent. In particular, they want to know if they could reasonably view the frequency of sexual relations or the distribution of satisfaction with their sexual lives as a matter to be governed by a principle of distributive justice. If, as Susan Moller Okin has argued, justice applies to some intra-familial issues, such as the control of economic resources and the distribution of household labor, does justice also apply to sex?[37]

It might be thought that it is wrong to think that B should ever consent to sexual relations when she does not want sex. But this simply begs the question, for people's "wants" are complex and multifaceted. Consider the problem that has come to be known as the "battle of the sexes." In one version of the problem, A and B both prefer to go to the movies together than to go alone, but each prefers to go to different types of movies. Their problem is to determine what movie they should see.[38] Although the "battle of the sexes" is usually used to exemplify a bargaining problem, I want to use the example to make a point about the character of one's "wants." We can well imagine that A may not "want" to see B's preferred movie, other things being equal. Still, given that B really wants to see the movie and given that they most recently went to the movie that A preferred, A may genuinely want to see the movie that B prefers—all things considered.

It might be objected that "I want to do what you want to do" is fine for movies, but not sex. In this view, there are some "not wants" that are legitimate candidates for "all things considered wants," but the lack of a desire for sexual relations is not among them. In one variant of this view, sexual relations are radically different from other activities in which partners engage together because it would be self-defeating for partners to think that they are having sexual relations on this basis. A can enjoy the movie that he sees with B, although he knows that B would (otherwise) prefer to see something else, but A would not get satisfaction from sexual relations with B if A knows that B wants to have sexual relations only to satisfy or placate A's desire for sexual relations.

With some trepidation, I want to suggest that to think of sexual relations between partners in an enduring relationship as radically different from all other activities in which they engage "wildly misdescribes" their experience.[39] Sexual relations among such partners are simply not always viewed as sacred or endowed with greater mystery. But my point is not solely negative or deflationary. After all, to say that the most desirable form of sexual relations occurs within a loving relationship is also to say that sexual relations are a way of expressing affection and commitment, and not simply to express or satisfy erotic desire. It is, for example, entirely plausible that parties who have been fighting might engage in sexual relations as a way of demonstrating to themselves that the disagreement is relatively minor in the context of their relationship, that their love for each other is unshaken. In general, I see no reason to tightly constrain what count as legitimate reasons to want to engage in sexual relations—all things considered.

But what about distributive justice? Assume that A and B both understand that it is frustrating for A to forgo sexual relations when B does not desire sexual relations, whereas it is erotically unsatisfying for B to engage in sexual relations when she does not desire sexual relations—not awful or abhorrent, just unsatisfying. On some occasions, A would rather have sex than go to sleep, whereas B's utility function is the reverse. Given this situation, there are three possibilities: (1) A can absorb the burden of the asymmetry by forgoing sexual relations when B is not otherwise motivated to have sex; (2) B can absorb the burden of the asymmetry by consenting to have sexual relations whenever A desires to do so; or (3) A and B can share the burden of the asymmetry by agreeing that they will have sexual relations less often than A would (otherwise) prefer and more often than B would (otherwise) prefer. And B is trying to decide if she should choose (3). Note, once again, that the question is not whether B should consent to sexual relations that she does not want. Rather, she is trying to decide if she should want to have sexual relations—all things considered—when the things to be considered involve a commitment to fairness.

It might be objected that even if we do not tightly constrain the reasons that might legitimately motivate B to "want" to have sex with A, sexual relations lie beyond reasons based on justice or fairness. It might be maintained that a concern with fairness or justice arises only when interests conflict. As Hume remarked, justice has no place among married people who are "unacquainted with the *mine* and *thine*, which are so necessary and yet cause such disturbance in human society."[40] From this perspective, a conscious preoccupation with fairness in a marriage can be a symptom that the parties have failed to achieve the identity of interests that characterize a good marriage and may (causally) inhibit the formation of a maximally intimate relationship.[41] Love precludes a concern with justice, what Hume described as "the cautious, jealous virtue."[42]

I want to make several replies to this line of argument. First, and least important, there is obviously a limit to the identity of interests it is logically possible to achieve. If each party has an overall want to do what the other has a primary want to do, they will achieve an altruistic draw ("I want to do what you want to do." "But I want to do what you want to do."). And if each has an overall want to do what the other has an overall want to do, there will be no wants for the overall wants to get hold of.

Second, if we think that a good marriage is characterized by an identity of interests, this still leaves open the question as to how married partners should respond to the asymmetry of desire for sexual relations. Just as A might say, "I wouldn't want to have sexual relations if B doesn't want to," B might say, "If A wants to have sexual relations, then I want to have sexual relations." So if we reject the argument from distributive justice because it assumes that the interests of the parties conflict, there is no reason to think that the parties will settle on (1) rather than (2) or (3).

Third, I think it both unrealistic and undesirable to expect that the desires or interests of persons in the most successful intimate relationships will fully coincide. It is relatively, although not absolutely, easy for married partners not to distinguish between "mine" and "thine" with respect to property. It is much more difficult to achieve a communal view with respect to activities. Do loving spouses not care at all how many diapers they change? To which movies they go? Where they locate? Are they no longer loving if they do care? Indeed, it is not clear that it is even desirable for people to strive for a relationship in which their interests are so completely merged. It might be thought that a good marriage represents a "union" of autonomous individuals who do and should have goals and aspirations that are independent of their relationship.

From this perspective, a couple's concern with fairness simply reflects the fact that their desires are not identical, that they do not see why this fact should be denied or regretted, and that they want to resolve these differences in a fair way. As Susan Moller Okin puts it (albeit in a different context), "Why should we suppose that harmonious affection, indeed deep and long-lasting love, cannot co-exist with ongoing standards of justice?"[43] Indeed, I would go further. It might be argued that it is not merely that love can coexist with justice, but that to love another person is to want to be fair to them, or, more precisely, to want not to be unfair to them, for to love someone is typically to want to be more than fair to them, to be generous.

I have not actually argued that the distribution of satisfaction with one's sexual life in an enduring relationship is an appropriate topic for distributive justice. Although I have argued against several objections to the view that sexual relations are beyond the scope of justice, it is possible that other arguments would work. Moreover, even if the distribution of satisfaction with one's sexual life is an appropriate topic for a principle of justice, I make no suggestions here as to what the substance of a theory of justice in sexual relations would look like. It is entirely possible that such a theory would dictate that the parties choose something like (1) rather than (3) (I take it that (2) is a nonstarter). I only want to suggest that the topic may belong on the table.

NOTES

1. See Alan Wertheimer, *Coercion* (Princeton, N.J.: Princeton University Press, 1987) and *Exploitation* (Princeton, N.J.: Princeton University Press, 1996).

2. I borrow this phrase from Heidi Hurd's remarks at the conference at the University of San Diego Law School, which gave rise to this symposium.

3. For example, it may be wrong for a physician to accede to a beggar's request to have his leg amputated so that he can enhance his success as a beggar.

4. "You have never left the city, even to see a festival, nor for any other reason except military service; you have never gone to stay in any other city, as people do; you have had no desire to know another city or other laws; we and our city satisfied you. So decisively did you choose us and agree to be a citizen under us." Plato, *Crito*, in *The Trial and Death of Socrates*, translated by G. M. A. Grube (Indianapolis, Ind.: Hackett, 1975).

5. "[E]very man that hath any possession or enjoyment of any part of the dominions of any government doth thereby give his tacit consent, and is as far forth obliged to obedience to the laws of that government, during such enjoyment, whether this his possession be of land to him and his heirs for ever, or a lodging only for a week; or whether it be barely travelling freely on the highway." John Locke, *Second Treatise of Government*, chap. 8 (1690).

6. "Can we seriously say, that a poor person or artisan has a free choice to leave his country, when he knows no foreign language or manners, and lives, from day to day, by the small wages which he acquires? We may as well assert that a man, by remaining in a vessel, freely consents to the dominion of the master; though he was carried on board while asleep, and must leap into the ocean and perish, the moment he leaves her." David Hume, *Of the Original Contract* (1777).

7. Harry Frankfurt, "Coercion and Moral Responsibility," in *Essays on Freedom of Action*, edited by Ted Honderich (London: Routledge & Kegan Paul, 1973), 65.

8. As Jeremy Waldron has put it, "[T]he question is . . . not what 'harm' really means, but what reasons of principle there are for preferring one conception to another . . . the question is not simply which is the better conception of harm, but which conception answers more adequately to the purposes for which the concept is deployed" (*Liberal Rights: Collected Papers 1981–91* [Cambridge: Cambridge University Press, 1993]). For a somewhat different view, see Frederick Schauer, "The Phenomenology of Speech and Harm," *Ethics* 103: 4 (1993), 635–53.

9. *Vokes v. Arthur Murray, Inc.*, 212 So. 2d 906 (1968), at 907.

10. See "Sexual Exploitation in Psychotherapy," chapter 6 in Wertheimer, *Exploitation*.

11. See *State v. Rusk*, 289 Md. 230, 424 A. 2d 720 (1981). The defendant had also intimidated the prosecutor by taking the keys to her car, disregarded her statement that she did not want to have sexual relations with him, and was said to have "lightly choked" her.

12. *Director of Public Prosecutions v. Morgan* (1975), 2 All E.R. 347.

13. Donald A. Dripps, "Beyond Rape: An Essay on the Difference between the Presence of Force and the Absence of Consent," *Columbia Law Review* 92: 7 (November 1992), 1780–1809, esp. 1797.

14. Indeed, it might be thought that this case is, in one way, more serious than those in which force is used to overcome the victim's resistance—namely, that it requires the victim to act inauthentically.

15. See Catharine MacKinnon, *Feminism Unmodified* (Cambridge, Mass.: Harvard University Press, 1987), 5–6.

16. See Richard A. Posner, *Sex and Reason* (Cambridge, Mass.: Harvard University Press, 1992), 384.

17. For a discussion of nonexperiential harm, see Joel Feinberg, *Harm to Others: The Moral Limits of the Criminal Law* (New York: Oxford University Press, 1984), chapter 2.

18. Stephen J. Schulhofer, "Taking Sexual Autonomy Seriously: Rape Law and Beyond," *Law and Philosophy* 11:1–2 (1992), 35–94, esp. 70.

19. Dripps, "Beyond Rape," 1796n3.

20. Joan McGregor, "Force, Consent, and the Reasonable Woman," in *In Harm's Way: Essays in Honor of Joel Feinberg*, edited by J. L. Coleman and A. Buchanan (Cambridge: Cambridge University Press, 1994), 231–54, esp. 235. McGregor says that she borrows the notion of "border crossings" from Robert Nozick's *Anarchy, State and Utopia* (New York: Basic Books, 1974).

21. I think it no objection to the commodity (or any other) view of the law of sexual crimes that it "wildly misdescribes" the victim's experience. Robin West, "Legitimating the Illegitimate: A Comment on *Beyond Rape*," *Columbia Law Review* 93 (April 1993), 1442–1448, esp. 1448. The question is whether a view provides a coherent framework for protecting the rights or interests that we believe ought to be protected. Indeed, it is an advantage of a "property" theory that it provides a basis for critiquing the traditional law of rape. That A takes B's property without B's consent is sufficient to show that A steals B's property. Force or resistance is not required.

22. See Jeffrie G. Murphy, "Some Ruminations on Women, Violence, and the Criminal Law," in *In Harm's Way: Essays in Honor of Joel Feinberg*, edited by J. L. Coleman and A. Buchanan (Cambridge: Cambridge University Press, 1994), 214.

23. Robin Wright, "Feminists, Meet Mr. Darwin," *New Republic* (November 1994), 37. The evolutionary logic of nonconsensual sex is different for men. It is physically difficult to accomplish, and "the worst likely outcome for the man (in genetic terms) is that pregnancy would not ensue . . . hardly a major Darwinian disaster."

24. This is obviously true on a retributive theory of punishment, in which the level of punishment is related to the seriousness of the offense. But it is also true on a utilitarian theory, for the more serious the harm to the victim, the greater "expense" (in punishment) it makes sense to employ to deter such harms.

25. Murphy, "Some Ruminations on Women," 216n22.

26. Wertheimer, *Coercion*.

27. This is derived from a case introduced by Schulhofer, "Taking Sexual Autonomy Seriously," 70n18.

28. C. L. Muehlenhard and J. L. Schrag, "Nonviolent Sexual Coercion," in *Acquaintance Rape: The Hidden Crime*, edited by A. Parrot and L. Bechhofer (New York: Wiley, 1991), 115–28, esp. 119.

29. Don Dripps has suggested to me that case (5) is a variant on prostitution. In the standard case of prostitution, A proposes to pay B with A's money. In this case, A proposes to pay B with B's money.

30. As Stephen Schulhofer says, because there are "few pervasively shared intuitions" with regard to what constitutes serious misrepresentation as distinct from puffing or "story telling," the decisions as to "whether to believe, whether to rely and whether to assume the risk of deception . . . are often seen as matters to be left to the individual." "Taking Sexual Autonomy Seriously," 92n18.

31. It is less clear—and informal intuition (and pumping of friends) has done little to help—whether women would regard sexual relations while unconscious as worse than or not as bad as forcible sexual relations. One might think that it is worse to consciously experience an assault on one's bodily and sexual integrity, but it might also be thought that it is better to know what is happening to oneself than not to know.

32. I say "first" indication, because B could consent while sober to what she subsequently consents to while intoxicated.

33. Susan Estrich, *Real Rape* (Cambridge, Mass.: Harvard University Press, 1987), 98.

34. See the discussion of coyness in Robert Wright, *The Moral Animal* (Gloucester, Mass.: Peter Smith, 1994).

35. "Here are the keys to my car; don't let met drive home if I'm drunk." See, e.g., Thomas C. Schelling, "The Intimate Contest for Self-Command," in *Choice and Consequence* (Cambridge, Mass.: Harvard University Press, 1984), chapter 3.

36. Schulhofer, "Taking Sexual Autonomy Seriously," 70n18.

37. Susan Moller Okin, *Justice, Gender, and the Family* (New York: Basic Books, 1989).

38. See Brian Barry, *Theories of Justice* (Berkeley, Calif.: University of California Press, 1989), 116–17.

39. With apologies to Robin West.

40. David Hume, *A Treatise of Human Nature*, bk. III, sect. II.

41. I thank Pat Neal and Bob Taylor for pressing me on this point.

42. David Hume, *An Enquiry Concerning the Principles of Morals*, sect. III, pt. I, par. 3.

43. Okin, *Justice, Gender, and the Family*, 32n37.

STUDY QUESTIONS

1. What does Wertheimer mean when he calls consent "morally transformative"? Why does he claim that consent will *be* morally transformative, all things considered, only when certain conditions are met? What are these conditions?

2. Wertheimer discusses both sayings: "no means no" and "yes means yes." What do these expressions literally mean? What do they mean when particular people use them in particular contexts?

3. The legal philosopher Jeffrie Murphy believes that women's abhorrence for being raped is due to cultural conditioning and that, as a result, if we did not teach women certain things about sexuality, they would not experience being raped as such a grave harm. (A similar position is held by H. E. Baber in "How Bad Is Rape? — II," in *The Philosophy of Sex: Contemporary Readings*, 6th ed., edited by Nicholas Power, Raja Halwani, and Alan Soble [Lanham, Md.: Rowman & Littlefield, 2013], 485–501.) On the contrary, Wertheimer claims, women's abhorrence is "hard-wired" — that is, is due to women's biology as molded by natural and sexual selection. Who do you think is right here, and why? And what difference does it make, philosophically, legally, or politically? Is the spiritual and psychological repugnance of a strict Orthodox Jew or a religious Muslim for pork biological or cultural? Does it matter if someone shoves a piece of bacon, the forbidden meat, into his or her mouth?

4. Is it morally wrong for a person A to say falsely to another person B "I love you" just so A can induce B to engage in sex? Should it be legally culpable fraud or deception? Is it morally wrong for a person A to say truly to another person B, "Have sex with me or find yourself some other boyfriend [girlfriend]" just so A can induce B to engage in sex? Should it be legally culpable coercion? Might that threat be, in some circumstances, morally suspicious exploitation? When? (See Thomas Mappes, "Sexual Morality and the Concept of Using Another Person," in this volume.)

5. In many marriages and relationships between two people, one person desires sexual activity from or with the other person more frequently than the second desires it with the first. Also, in many marriages and relationships one person desires a specific type of

sexual activity that the second person finds distasteful or even immoral and prefers not to do. How would you propose to solve such conflicts—without suggesting that the two people get divorced or split up? What helpful suggestions does Wertheimer make in his essay? What solution does he reject, and why?

NINETEEN

Dark Desires

Seiriol Morgan

Although many philosophers (especially liberal ones) believe in the sufficiency (and necessity) of consent for the moral permissibility of a sexual act, not all do. In this essay **Seiriol Morgan** *argues that the complex and frequently dark nature of sexual desire makes the consent of the parties to a sexual act insufficient for its moral permissibility. This is because some sexual desires should not be gratified, even if they were consented to. He illustrates this with a discussion of a famous literary character, the Vicomte de Valmont, and draws on Immanuel Kant's anthropology to illuminate the nature of such desires, before offering an account of their psychological roots.*

Seiriol Morgan is senior lecturer in philosophy at the University of Bristol. He works mainly on moral philosophy and the history of philosophy, particularly on Kant. This essay originally appeared in *Ethical Theory and Moral Practice* vol. 6 (2003), 377–410. It is reprinted here (edited for length) with the permission of Seiriol Morgan, *Ethical Theory and Moral Practice*, and Springer Publishing.

1

My aim in this chapter is to advance a line of criticism against an influential contemporary view of sexual morality. The view is that universal participant consent is sufficient for the moral permissibility of any sexual act. From this standpoint, then, if sexual activity is consented to by everyone involved, and there is no one involved who is unable to give genuine consent for any reason, then engaging in the activity is not morally wrong. An advocate of this position has no difficulty in identifying sexual behavior that is morally wrong, of course. For instance, rape and child abuse are always morally wrong on this view, as they are on any plausible view of sexual morality, since they are both coercive by nature. But in general this is obviously a very liberal and permissive sexual morality, advanced in conscious contrast to the conservative positions which have dominated Western thinking about sex for most of the last two thousand years or more. The view has recently been defended in detail by Igor Primoratz in a book and a series of articles, which I am going to take as representative,[1] and is widely held among the populations of much of Europe and America.

Nevertheless, I think it is mistaken. Of course, all sensible people agree that consent is necessary for the moral permissibility of a sexual act, so the question of consent remains a central one for sexual morality. I am going to argue that it is insufficient, however. Yet I will not be defending a conservative sexual morality which aims to identify and proscribe sexual practices which fail to live up to some alleged purpose or special status sex possesses—for instance, by being essentially non-reproductive. I fully agree that the bulk of stipulations that emerge from traditional sexual morality, for example those condemning homosexuality and pre-marital sex, are without rational foundation. Rather, I will be arguing that the complex and frequently dark nature of human sexual desire requires a certain kind of ethical sensitivity from us, and also gives us reason not to act on certain sexual impulses we might have, even if there is no one who fails to consent to their gratification. I think that Primoratz fails to see this for two reasons. First, his view of sexual morality rests on an impoverished view of the nature of sexual desire, a view which conceals the true nature of certain phenomena of human sexuality. Second, he has an inadequate understanding of the resources of moral theory and the corresponding variety of normative claims that can be made. The claims I wish to make will not fit into his limited taxonomy of the normative without distortion, a distortion which prevents him from fully appreciating their force.

2

The account of sexual desire to which Primoratz subscribes is known as the "hedonistic" account, and also the "plain sex" account, after Alan Goldman's chapter of that name.[2] On this view sexual desire is simply the desire to experience a very particular kind of essentially bodily pleasure, a kind of pleasure usually though not essentially achieved by physical contact with the body of another human being.[3] The main opponents of the "plain sex" view are a number of views which take sexual desire to be essentially bound up with the interpersonal intentional relations between the participants in a sexual act. According to Thomas Nagel, for example, normal human sexual desire aims at a state of arousal which can only be achieved through the mutual perception by each lover of her partner's deepening pleasure in response to her own.[4] And Roger Scruton takes sexual desire to be "individually intentionalising," that is, dependent for its satisfaction upon the thought that one's partner is the very particular person she is.[5]

The "plain sex" view is superficially plausible, but nevertheless profoundly mistaken. Since I have argued for this claim elsewhere I will restrict myself to simply stating what I take to be wrong with it.[6] Its apparent plausibility rests on the numerous examples of human beings engaging in activity which is obviously sexual and yet appears not to be motivated by intentionalized desires—for instance, solo masturbation, sex with prostitutes, random one-night stands, routine mechanical sex between long-term partners and the like. Since sexual desire in these instances is clearly desire for an essentially physical pleasure, the essence of sexual desire must therefore be desire for an essentially bodily sensation unconnected with any complicated considerations of intentionality, *contra* the intentionalists. Or so the advocates of the "plain sex" view argue. The mistake they make is to generalize the nature of the pleasure which is aimed at in the most basic sexual encounters across the entire range of human sexual activity. Goldman and Primoratz rightly see that some forms of sexual activity can only be understood as motivated by an animal appetite for an essentially physical pleasure, unmediated by considerations of intentionality. They subsequently conclude that sexual desire as such essentially has the character it has in these very basic sexual scenarios.

But the assumption underlying this, that sexual pleasure has a uniform nature, is unargued for, and in fact it is false. It is false because in a self-conscious being the character of the appetites which are a function of its animal body can be transformed both in intensity and in nature by its mental operations, both conscious and unconscious. Consequently, self-conscious and social beings such as ourselves can end up with a host of desires with contents and objects which significantly differentiate them from the appetites out of which they've evolved. Further, the character of the pleasure we take in their satisfaction may be different for those desires in which our mentality is implicated than for those in which it is not, though this difference can be very subtle. Sometimes a broad class of desires contains both untransformed appetites and more complex desires presupposing self-consciousness and immersion in society, which nevertheless share a clear family resemblance. Human sexual desire forms just such a class.

In the case of sexual desire, then, our bodies generate a brute animal appetite for the pleasure produced by sexual contact with other human beings. Sometimes when we act to gratify sexual desire we act to gratify it in this animalistic form. But because we are self-conscious and things have significance for us, we can come to experience sexual pleasure *at* or *in* some feature of the situation in which intercourse occurs, and although this pleasure has a vital physical component, the nature of the experience is not exhausted by its physical intensity. For an individual experienced in these kind of pleasures, sexual desire can become desire not simply for appetitive gratification but for pleasures of these more complex kinds, although in their absence perhaps non-intentional physical pleasure might go some way toward providing the person with satisfaction. Most commonly of course the element of the sexual situation which is meaningful and gives the experience its particular quality is the identity of one's partner, and one's beliefs about her mental states. One experiences in such a case not just (say) intense and exciting sensations in various parts of one's body, perhaps culminating in orgasm; rather, one experiences pleasure at [the] dynamic bodily interaction, and so pleasure is taken in an act experienced as being pleasurable for both [partners]. One only needs to consider how perception of someone's rising excitement can intensify one's own experiences, pulling one's own level of arousal up toward theirs, to see that our sexual desire is oriented toward the experiences of our partners as well as our own. Physical sensation is still obviously central, but sensation is interpreted, saturated with meaning, and so is experienced very differently from uninterpreted sensation.

It might be helpful to raise an example here, one which in itself will take us a considerable distance toward understanding the moral implications of a rejection of the "plain sex" account of sexual desire. The example also shows that the range and variety of sexual intentionality is much greater than any intentionalist account has so far allowed. Consider the Vicomte de Valmont, from Laclos's famous novel *Les Liaisons Dange-reuses*.[7] The novel concerns the plot concocted between two jaded eighteenth century French aristocrats, the Vicomte and his accomplice the Marquise de Merteuil, to effect the Vicomte's seduction and ruin of the virtuous Madame de Tourvel. What is interesting about the Vicomte from our point of view is that what motivates his pursuit of Madame de Tourvel is precisely her virtue, the quality which on the face of things should most discourage it. It is nothing about her physical appearance that excites him, nor even her personality as such, but the sheer difficulty of seducing her. What he wants is for this woman *to give in to him*, and give in after a struggle, since her acquiescence in an act that morally appalls her would be the ultimate affirmation of his sexual power in his own eyes. The Vicomte has become so jaded that appetite for a purely physical pleasure no longer interests him. To attract his interest sex must be highly significant, and what makes sex significant for him is its being an act of conquest.

Central to his anticipated pleasure is Madame de Tourvel's mental state. He needs to have made her want him in order to experience the kind of pleasure he craves through intercourse with her, a pleasure different and vastly superior in quality to the "insipid" pleasure of gratified bodily appetite. Nor is it only her wanting him, of course; what is so jaded about the Vicomte is that what he desires is for her to want him in spite of herself, for her to be unable to resist the desire he has made her feel, despite her identification with chastity and virtue.[8] So the pleasure he anticipates is clearly an essentially intentional one, and not just the pleasure of sensation, though it will be in part experienced through his sexual sensations. After all, should he seduce her, one would expect his physical sensations to be intense, and his orgasms violent. This is because the physical experiences of a lover can be intensified by the meaningful nature of a sexual encounter, with its mental aspects feeding into and enhancing the physical aspects. But it would be totally wrong to describe a non-intentional physical intensity as his aim, and the significance of his seduction of the virtuous Madame de Tourvel as the independent means to that end. If one were to offer the Vicomte some eighteenth-century equivalent of ecstasy or Viagra, which would allow him to achieve physical sensations of similar intensity with willing prostitutes, he would not be interested at all. It is the quality of the experience and not its physical intensity he is interested in, although its intensity is part of its quality. We cannot understand the character of the Vicomte's pleasure at all unless we see it as essentially pleasure *in* or *at* her downfall.

3

This phenomenon whereby our animal sexual appetite is transformed through a context of intentional significance is the phenomenon of *eroticization*, and from the "plain sex" perspective it is a phenomenon distorted at best, and invisible at worst. Human sexual desire is pretty diverse, and all manner of different things are eroticized by different people. Very frequently, of course, what we eroticize is the pleasure of our sexual partners and our emotional connections with them. This is why intentionalist writers on sex have taken interpersonal reciprocal arousal to lie at the heart of sexual desire. But the nature of the intentionality possessed by the Vicomte's desires is very unlike the intentionality ascribed to sexual desire by standard intentionalist accounts like those of Nagel and Scruton. Whereas their accounts focus on normal people who find erotic significance in the pleasure and love of their partners, the Vicomte is a thoroughly evil man who eroticizes thoroughly unwholesome things. The nature of his desire is not captured by standard intentionalist accounts, which is one reason why they are too narrow.

It is probably clear where I will eventually be taking this line of argument. But at this point I want to investigate further how a person might come to eroticize such dark significances as these.

According to Kant the ability that rational beings possess to choose to set ourselves ends brings a natural desire for freedom. This desire can express itself in more than one way. One way it can always express itself is in the development of a natural passion for freedom (that is, we have a "propensity" to develop an inclination of this nature).[9] This passion is the yearning of the free being to express his or her will as he or she wills, and to accept no limitation on that will.

Kant uses the term "passion" (*Leidenschaft*) to refer to a very particular kind of inclination. All passions run very deep, and are extremely difficult for reason to control, but it is by their source and objects that passions are identified. Passions arise from the interaction of two essential elements of our natures, our freedom and our sociability. The will has a natural propensity to affirm its own choices as of supreme importance, and to chafe when those choices are thwarted by others.[10] But we live (since we have a natural instinct toward sociability, being unable to achieve our potential except in society with others[11]) in proximity to any number of other free beings like ourselves, many of whom will similarly take their own choices to be supremely important, choices which will inevitably come into conflict with our own. This combination generates a kind of primal conflict in human society, and in response to this conflict individuals very easily develop the habit of striving to impose their wills upon others, and subordinating the interests of those others to their own, that is, treating them as mere means to their own ends. A desire which has become habitual is an inclination,[12] and an inclination, arising from the awareness and resentment of external constraints on the will, to subordinate the wills of others to our own in this way is a passion.

Kant calls this tendency to take our ends to have objective priority simply because they are ours "self-conceit" (*arrogantia*). Self-conceit is a combination of benevolence toward self combined with an attitude of "well-pleasedness" (*complacientia*), in which the individual falsely takes his supposedly greater personal worth to license the subjugation of the wills of others to his own.[13] For Kant, who takes all rational beings to possess absolute worth, such self-conceit is an inherently self-deceptive attitude, since there is nothing one could do or be that could license this kind of relative elevation. It is also an inherently competitive one, of course, and for that reason inherently unstable. The person who grounds his sense of self-worth through a comparison with others exposes that self-conception to the threat of being diminished or even entirely overwhelmed by the achievements, qualities, and resources of his competitors.[14] Since the passion for natural freedom is so strong, this antagonism easily generates some very unsociable motives, the "acquired passions"[15] of ambition, lust for power and avarice,[16] the lust for vengeance,[17] and the "diabolical vices" of envy, ingratitude, and malice.[18] All these motives provide us with incentive to endorse as ends maxims which run counter to morality.

I am much inclined to agree with [Kant]. We clearly sometimes are motivated by ambition, malice, envy, and the like, and when we are we actively will the misery, inferiority, and exploitation of others. Human beings take pleasure in imposing their wills on others. We take pleasure in feeling ourselves superior to others, and we can enormously enjoy their humiliation. We are indeed perfectly capable of enjoying inflicting pain upon and even killing other people. Corresponding fantasies of violence, revenge, and domination can play a prominent role in our mental lives. We can also equally perversely take pleasure in our own abjection.[19] Since human beings eroticize factors of interpersonal significance, and a great deal of what we find interpersonally significant is our superiority and power over others and our ability to make them suffer, it should be entirely unsurprising that human beings eroticize some very unsociable significances, which in turn generate very dark desires and fantasies.

4

[T]here is clearly something of a natural hierarchy of sexual desirability among human beings. Some human beings are simply more sexually attractive than others. Other things being equal, more attractive individuals attract more and better-looking potential sexual partners, and generate greater intensity of desire and arousal in other people than less attractive people do. This hierarchy is not fully determinate, of course. We have idiosyncratic tastes regarding the physical features of our sexual partners, so that an individual thought very attractive by one person may not be found particularly attractive by another. But despite this there seems to be enough agreement for such a hierarchy to be clearly visible, and for generally accepted comparative judgments between individuals to be made. Of course, other things are frequently not equal. Other factors about a person can enhance or diminish his or her attractiveness significantly, in general or to a particular individual—money, power, intelligence, personality, even sheer decency, or the lack of these things. Nevertheless the hierarchy provides a measure by which people can compare themselves and others, and a ground for self-conceited judgments of superiority over others, both regarding one's own perceived sexual desirability and the desirability of the partners one is able to attract. Since sexual desire is so central to human life a strong sense of sexual worth and success can contribute immensely to self-conceit. Hence sexual "success" or "failure" can become central to a person's sense of self-worth, which can fluctuate considerably according to whether, how frequently and with whom one is having sex. Just as the vices of perceived superiority can easily emerge from a person's sexual life, so can the vices of failed ambition in those dissatisfied with it.

We now need to ask how these unsociable inclinations are eroticized. Let me try to provide an example, a broadly Kantian natural history of the eroticization of misogynist contempt.[20] Consider a cultural context in which female sexual expression and liberty is curtailed by familiar social mores, which, for instance, license viewing women who have had a number of sexual partners with contempt. Obviously the hangover from such unenlightened attitudes is to some extent still with us in modern Western society, despite the moral and intellectual successes of feminism, though thankfully it seems to be on the wane. It is not difficult to see how collective male self-conceit can in various ways have played a major role in generating these cultural mores in the first place. Men raised in such a cultural context will have been socialized to view sexually active women with contempt, and will probably have learnt to use and think in terms of a vocabulary which expresses this. But upon reaching sexual maturity this will rather ironically give rise to a problem, since they will find that the social mores to which they themselves contribute provide women with a strong incentive to resist their own sexual advances. As we saw, in the self-conceited, resistance and frustration of this kind frequently generate bitterness and its corresponding ill will. Since it is the behavior of women as a class that frustrates such men, women as a class become the target of their antipathy. Further, an individual who is in the process of forming a misogynist worldview is likely to find the vocabulary of female denigration all the more congenial, since its use expresses and mildly gratifies the resentment and corresponding malice he feels toward women. So he uses it with increased fervor, and a vicious circle begins to form. Nevertheless, he still sexually desires women, and so finds himself strangely wanting them and disliking them at the same time.

This unstable combination of conflict and desire is likely to loom large in his psyche. One obvious psychological strategy to deal with this instability is for him to adopt a disturbingly instrumentalized attitude to women. If he does so, he will come to see his relations with women as a kind of battle, in which his goal is to manipulate them through techniques of seduction into gratifying his sexual desire. Meanwhile he retains the attitude that women who consent to sexual intercourse outside of certain strictly defined parameters are contemptible. What he wants to do, then, is to persuade women to collude in what he sees as their own degradation. Conceiving of the sexual act as he does, he will find it tremendously reinforcing of his conceited sense of self. If he sleeps with her, he has defeated her, her resistance having been overcome by his attractiveness, his intelligence, his social standing, his mastery of the techniques of seduction. Or so he tells himself. Meanwhile, he consolidates his sexual status in the masculine community, massaging his vanity and fueling his desire for further esteem. Such significances will be partly constitutive of the sexual pleasure he experiences. In his head he is not making love to her, he is *fucking* her, and part of what is pleasurable about it for him is that through this sexual act he makes it the case that *he has had her*. This is not just something he thinks about the event afterward; he experiences himself as triumphing over her in the act of intercourse, and that triumph is part of its quality. For some men this self-conceited contemptuous delight can become the central psychological focus of their sexual desire and erotic pleasure.

Such an attitude is manifested in its most extreme form in someone like the Vicomte, who is clearly replete with the kind of highly unsociable incentives Kant discusses. He takes pleasure in engineering the misfortune of others;[21] is moved to seek vengeance against any who cross him, even trivially, and is entirely lacking in sympathy for their perfectly understandable motives in doing so;[22] is quite prepared to dominate others to achieve his ends;[23] and begrudges and disparages the success of any who might compete with him.[24] Most important, his entire sense of self rests on self-conceit. What he craves as a condition of his own self-respect is to be in his own eyes and that of others superior to other people, in particular those he betrays and ruins. And from his fundamentally competitive perspective upon the world what that superiority consists in is his power over other people, and his success in manipulating them in ways that hurt and degrade them. It should be no surprise, then, that the Vicomte desires sexual gratification in circumstances which are maximally affirmative of his self-conceited sense of self, and he aims to experience his sexual pleasure within this intentional context. Conquest has become the central psychological focus of his sexual desire. And it is precisely Madame de Tourvel's sense of propriety and virtue which makes her the ultimate conquest, and hence the most desirable object of his concupiscence. Having such ostensibly high standards, she has such a deliciously long distance to fall.

5

So far much of the paper has been rather gloomy, to say the least. I now want to try to cheer things up a bit. [A]lthough it seems clear that human beings are motivated by the passions that Kant identifies, and that we can eroticize such passions, we need not agree with him about the prevalence or power of such motives within human psychology, eroticized or otherwise. The narrative of the development of eroticized contempt I outlined above is very simple, but that is because its purpose is merely to illustrate how this can occur. It would be entirely simplistic if it was intended as a blanket claim about the psychological development of all men in such a social context. There are numerous factors that might prevent the evolution of such attitudes or combat them once they appear, most centrally the ability of women to elicit and foster affection and love, and to command esteem. Even in a social milieu replete with misogyny individual men will reject the socially mandated judgments of their peers, which they know to be refuted by their own experience of the women in their own lives. In addition, those men whose attitudes have been shaped by sexism can easily find themselves unable to sustain them in the face of their growing genuine affection for particular sexual partners, so that even if they once conceived of intercourse as conquest and experienced it accordingly, they will cease to do so. It seems to me that although when we think about it we know that sex can be a dark and disturbing affair, we are also pretty confident that most of it isn't, that most of it takes place between persons who like if not love one another, wish each other well and for whom the pleasure of their partners is important and indeed frequently a constituent part of their own sexual pleasure. This is why intentionalist accounts of sexual desire such as Scruton's and Nagel's are so prominent and so plausible.

And there is also a conceptual reason why there is never anything inevitable about the psychological processes I have been describing. There is nothing inevitable about them precisely because they emerge from our freedom. Since they presuppose freedom, their existence presupposes our ability to step back from them and assess them from the point of view of reason.[25] Even the most jaded and self-conceited among us have the ability to ask ourselves whether we have reason to pursue a life in competition with others for power, wealth, and esteem, and whether an excess of these is really grounds for an ascription of superiority. Anyone who does properly so reflect will discover that these attitudes are abjectly irrational.[26] Nevertheless . . . the Kantian account does suggest that unsociable eroticization will be an ever-present danger. Some social milieus will encourage the growth of unsociable motives, others may discourage it, but since they spring so naturally and directly from the fundamental elements of our humanity, it will be difficult if not impossible to eradicate them altogether.

6

How then do these observations relate to the issue of sexual morality and consent? . . . I'll approach the question from a Kantian perspective, partly because I've drawn significantly on Kant's moral philosophy already, and partly because I don't want to base my rejection of Primoratz's view on a partisan moral theory he clearly doesn't accept, whereas his normative position has recognizable affinities with Kant's, most critically because they both stress the moral centrality of the rational agent and her free choices. For Primoratz, normative considerations in general divide into two categories, "norms" and "ideals." According to him all norms enjoin in one way or another that no one's freedom of choice is ignored or flouted in pursuit of some other person's end, and their normative force is that of moral obligation. Any normative consideration which is not a norm has the status of an ideal. Ideals are genuine values, but there is no requirement upon agents, moral or otherwise, to attempt to live up to them. The decision about whether and to what extent to guide one's behavior by any ideal is a matter of personal choice. Successfully living up to the requirements of a genuine ideal is an achievement for which an agent can be praised, but no one is appropriately censured for failing to live up to any ideal. On this view, then, any normative consideration which extends beyond the interpersonal requirements of respect for autonomous choice has the same status as, say, an aspiration to write a great novel. Should I succeed in writing a great novel this is highly laudable, but I am in no way appropriately subject to criticism if I fail, or fail even to try. Hence for Primoratz consent is the central moral issue. The only moral requirements are that one does not do anything to anyone to which they do not consent, except under special circumstances stemming from their own actions, as in the case of legitimate punishment. If they meaningfully consent, then the behavior is morally permissible.[27]

But despite the immediately evident similarities, even in the *Groundwork* the concept of moral duty in Kant's moral theory encompasses much more than Primoratz's notion of a norm, and in the later ethical writings Kant spends a great deal of time expounding specific duties to which he insists we are subject, which nevertheless do not stem from the choices of others. The most important text here is the *Metaphysics of Morals*.

According to Kant we are bound by the requirements of virtue, which are the duties of "inner freedom." These duties of virtue are ends which it is our duty to adopt.[28] His claim is that the Categorical Imperative requires us to incorporate certain goals into the system of ends we pursue as practical reasoners. Therefore he must think both that a maxim of failure to adopt these ends or one incompatible with their adoption cannot be universalized, and that not doing so in some way fails to treat humanity as the end in itself it is. The classic example is the duty of mutual aid first mentioned in the *Groundwork*.[29] Attempting to univeralize a maxim of failure to help others in need brings about a contradiction in will, since one might find oneself in need of such aid and in such a situation would certainly will that one received it. Similarly, adopting it would be to fail to treat humanity as an end in itself. It is clear that Kant holds us to have moral duties in addition to those that the free choices of others impose upon us.

Returning to the question of sexual morality, then, I think that Kant's discussion of the specific duties of virtue casts considerable light on exactly what it is that is wrong with the Vicomte's behavior (and much of what is said about him goes equally for his less glamorous imitation, the self-conceited contemporary misogynist described above). I'll focus my discussion on our duties to others, since these are the most important. Taking first the duties we owe to others with regard to the respect due to them as human beings, what Kant usually means by respect (*Achtung*) is simply treating them as ends in themselves, as required by the Formula of Humanity. Hence the vast majority of specific duties we have toward others because of the respect due to them are duties not to infringe upon their free choices by doing something to them to which they don't or can't consent. But Kant also uses the term in a narrower sense, closer to the ordinary use of the word, to mean holding "the maxim of limiting our self-esteem by the dignity of humanity in another person."[30] Failure to do so is a failure of respect generally because it fails to treat the humanity of others in a manner appropriate to its real value. Understood in this sense it is possible to flout the respect that is owed to others without directly undermining their choices, by possessing attitudes which denigrate the worth of other human beings and by acting in ways which express them. So a person who possesses a sense of superiority to other people demonstrates self-conceit[31] and in taking himself to be higher than them he shows a contempt for their humanity which is always contrary to duty.[32] The practical manifestation of this contempt is arrogance, behavior through which one insinuates that others should hold themselves of lesser worth to oneself. [T]he arrogant person fails to express the respect for others they deserve, and hence his behavior is unjust.[33] In addition, Kant mentions a number of other ways in which we can fail to respect the humanity of others without hindering their free choices, including defaming and ridiculing them,[34] and, interestingly, scandalizing them, in the old sense of the term, that is imperiling their virtue by tempting them to wrongdoing, either by counsel or by example.[35] Kant is quite clear that we cannot have duties to produce virtue in other people, since no quality could be a virtue unless its possessor were herself responsible for producing it.[36] But in tempting people to denigrate their own humanity by acting in immoral ways we are endeavoring to bring about a degrading of human dignity, and so act wrongly. Of course, in tempting someone to do wrong we are inviting someone to make a free choice rather than taking away their choice, so this is a very clear example of how respect for humanity for Kant goes beyond simply not infringing external freedom. Respect for humanity is not only for what we choose but also for the rational nature we are.

As we might expect, the Vicomte's conduct fails to live up to Kant's benchmark in this area in a number of ways. Superiority to Madame de Tourvel is precisely what the Vicomte is trying to achieve via his seduction attempt. Its success is life-affirming for him because it demonstrates that his attractiveness and powers of persuasion are such as to defeat her virtue, making him superior to her in his own twisted scheme of values. Taking another human being to lack equivalent worth to oneself implies that one takes them to have less than the absolute worth they in fact have, which as contempt is contrary to duty. And because his sexual pleasure is partially constituted by the experience of it being a defeat of the woman he takes himself to be conquering, he has eroticized self-conceit and placed it at the centre of his psychology and sexual life. What he sexually desires is sexual victory through the degradation of some other human being, experienced through the intentionalized physical sensations of intercourse. Since it is this intentionalized experience he desires, he cannot satisfy the sexual desire he feels outside of a context in which he experiences himself through his actions as defeating another. Indeed, since this is so central to his erotic experience he cannot fully experience sexual satisfaction at all without this massaging of his vanity. Since feeling oneself as superior to another and particularly taking pleasure in this are always contrary to the duty of respect we have for others, we see in the Vicomte a species of sexual desire which of its nature should not be gratified, whether its gratification is consented to or not.

Similarly with our duties of love. The most basic duty we have in this area is that of benevolence, enjoining us to value the happiness of others.[37] According to Kant it is impermissible to fail to adopt the permissible happiness of other human beings in general as an end. At its most basic, this requires us to abstractly view the good fortune of others in achieving their ends as something to be celebrated,[38] and consequently identifies as vice delight taken in its opposite, such as envy or spite.[39] But benevolence also needs to take the form of "practical love," as beneficence, the adoption of a maxim in which we aim through our actions to make others happy.[40] This is required because, as I mentioned, the failure to adopt a maxim of assisting others in need cannot be universalized. Because the maxim of refusing to provide aid fails the universalization test through a contradiction in will and not conception, the duty of beneficence is a wide duty.[41] However, whatever latitude we have in performing beneficent acts, we may never adopt ends that are contrary to the general requirement of benevolence, and the duty not to do so is a strict one.[42]

I think it is obvious that the Vicomte fails to comply with his obligations of practical love for Madame de Tourvel, since he has so clearly failed to make her happiness any part of his end. Never mind that he fails to carry out any beneficent actions, at most hypocritically effecting the appearance of it in pursuit of his own goals. His practical reasoning clearly takes absolutely no account of her long-term well-being, thinking nothing of how his plans might affect her relationship with her husband, her place in society and so on. And things are even worse than this. The basest of the three vices opposed to the duty to love others is malice, the delighting in their misfortune and unhappiness.[43] Simply the inner feeling of joy at another's misery is a manifestation of the vice and hence a demonstration of the agent's failure to adopt the morally required end, according to Kant. But even worse is active malice, in which the agent attempts to engineer the unhappiness of the other in which he revels. But this is precisely what the Vicomte does. As his letter to the Marquise amply demonstrates, he wants her to experience torments, fears and the pains of remorse. Indeed, it is central to his sexual pleasure that Madame de Tourvel's acquiescence is a source of anguish to her. Consequently, he has adopted an end which is contrary to beneficence, which is a violation of a strict duty.[44] All in all, then, the Vicomte provides us with a clear-cut case of sexual behavior which is consensual and yet contrary to the Kantian conception of duty.[45]

7

Primoratz's emphasis on the importance of consent has deep roots in the Kantian insistence on respect for the autonomous choices of rational agents. And he is of course quite right to see this as central to any adequate account of morality. But giving a concept a central place in morality and making it the whole of morality are very different things, and consequently his view of the contours of morality is much more attenuated than the Kantian position which is in large part its ancestor.[46] In my view this diminishing of the moral sphere is not to its credit. Primoratz appears to think that his way of carving up the normative ground is obviously the right way. The most we see by way of argument for it is an appeal to an allegedly unavoidable hard and fast distinction between prudential and moral reasons.[47] By contrast, I think it is significantly revisionary and leaves no conceptual space for many of our common-sense categories of wrongdoing. As we have seen, it is much narrower than Kant's Formula of Humanity,[48] which it superficially resembles, much narrower even than "It's OK to do whatever you want as long as you're not hurting anyone else," the immediate answer most citizens of liberal democracies tend to give when asked what makes actions morally permissible. I have not of course conclusively *demonstrated* that Primoratz is wrong about this. What I have shown is that the moral philosopher who most clearly places respect for human autonomy at the heart of his moral theory holds that we have duties that extend well beyond avoiding actions which are not consented to, and that these are of a kind that rule out the expression of certain sexual desires *simpliciter*. [I]n broad outline his account is compelling, and in particular the claims about our duties of benevolence and respect. In addition, all this is very much in accord with our everyday intuitions. We do think that active concern for others is an important part of morality, and that taking pleasure in the abasement or suffering of others is wrong. Common sense does not hold someone who simply doesn't take the happiness of others as in itself giving him any reason for action as having non-culpably failed to live up to a praiseworthy ideal. Common sense holds that person's moral standing in contempt.

Why is [Primoratz] so insistent that the sphere of moral obligation cannot extend beyond that of external freedom? One possibility is a general fear of paternalism. The thought perhaps is that if we insist that people have duties to refrain from certain actions for the good of another, when that other consents to or wants those very actions to be performed, we ourselves are somehow interfering with the other person's choices in a morally objectionable way. Surely, one might think, it is a short step from here to some form of benign autocracy in which people are ordered about by others who supposedly know better what is good for them. My appeal to Kant's duties of love might be thought particularly worrying in this context. Among the Vicomte's many failings was his disregard of his duty of benevolence to Madame de Tourvel. But suppose someone pursues "plain sex" with someone else in a manner which does not fail to respect his humanity, but pays no attention to the question of whether the encounter is something that would undermine his happiness. Is this wrong? Surely it happens all the time.

There is a genuine issue here, but much of the concern is misplaced. Paternalism is a danger that Kant himself recognized, insisting that in our duty to promote the happiness of others it is their own conception of happiness that we are supposed to be promoting, as well as emphasizing the great range of idiosyncratic conceptions of happiness that exist.[49] He seems to be well aware that obstructing or refusing to assist people in realizing their chosen way of life on the alleged grounds that this is for their own good is frequently a form of oppression, and indeed a particularly troublesome one, partly due to the mask it wears and partly because it is peculiarly prevalent in those personal relationships of our lives in which we are most vulnerable.[50] But he does explicitly say that one may refuse something which another thinks will make him happy if one disagrees that it will do so, as long as it isn't something he is entitled to.[51] Since the duty of beneficence is imperfect and consequently no particular act of beneficence is ever a duty, we must first of all interpret such a refusal as an exercise of beneficence in its own right. Second, since the claim is conjoined with the insistence that we are to make the happiness of others according to their conception of it our end, Kant must mean that in our reasoning about how to attain the end of another's happiness we are entitled to take into account beliefs that the other does not share about the best way to realize their conception of happiness. So Kant draws a distinction between an offensive paternalism in which an agent attempts to force her choice of ends onto another person, and a permissible moderate paternalism in which an agent who disagrees with another about the best or appropriate means to the other's end does not demonstrate a failure of benevolence in refusing to adopt the proposed course of action (indeed, benevolence sometimes requires such a refusal).

I think this is eminently sensible, and immediately puts paid to the worries about the path to coercion. Benevolence can never require or entitle one to deprive another of his freedom or what belongs to him. Nor may anyone act against someone who acts to make another miserable, as long as her actions do not in doing so infringe his freedom. But what of the thought that in taking ourselves to have obligations not to act as others want us to because we know better than them what will make them happy we are affronting their agency in some way? This issue is difficult, but consider the following scenario. Suppose you were the object of another's desperate unrequited love. Knowing that person's state of mind and temporarily desiring sex with him for whatever reason (a fleeting appetitive whim, the need for temporary companionship, an attempt to bolster self-esteem or to put another "notch in the bedpost") you offer yourself to him, knowing you will shortly abandon him. Perhaps the other person is a former partner, crushed by or now remorseful about the break-up. In such a case consent is not the issue. We know he will consent. Indeed, his acquiescence might have the power of a near-compulsion. But it is entirely foreseeable that such a liaison will be significantly detrimental to his happiness in the long run, and it may be quite devastating. The fervent memories of recent intimacy, the raised then dashed hopes, the bitter self-loathing that can come from being the object of sexual rejection or perceived betrayal—all these factors accentuate the pain of estrangement from a loved person, significantly outweighing the brief if intense pleasures of intercourse.

I bite the bullet here. I think that in this situation sleeping with the person is morally wrong, his consent and prior enthusiasm notwithstanding, precisely because such knowing self-centeredness runs counter to our duty of benevolence. "Don't play around with people's emotions" doesn't seem to me an offensively intrusive moral principle. (Consider how one feels when someone does something like this to one of our friends. We don't think they've merely failed to live up to a praiseworthy ideal. We think they're bastards.) To anyone who thinks this is paternalist arrogance, I say this in an attempt to sweeten the pill. First, the duty of beneficence does not require that we actively pursue the happiness of any particular person, so we are not obliged to be confident that someone's happiness will be furthered by the encounter before having sex with them. We only need to be confident that it will not bring them substantial unhappiness. Since sex in general is a pleasurable affair, we don't even need to think about the happiness of the other person unless we have some special reason for thinking that sex will turn out to be to their detriment. Second, such considerations of benevolence will not ground any hard and fast rules of sexual conduct (e.g., "Never sleep with anyone who is in love with you if you don't love them"). The relevant rule is that you must adopt a maxim of pursuit of the happiness of others. Beyond that it takes judgment to see how to achieve that end in practice;[52] sometimes even the most sensitive and experienced of us will find this very difficult to discern. This is partly because of the enormous variation in individuals' desires, and consequently in the kind of actions and situations that make people happy and unhappy, and partly because since the desires of others are directly inaccessible to us it is often difficult to know what people really want. So behavior that would make one person very unhappy can leave another entirely unconcerned, and it is hard to tell what will upset who. As a result, the most we have in this area are rules of thumb, and any example has its force only *ceteris paribus*. Adding or subtracting an element can significantly affect the nature of the whole situation, and consequently the morality of the action.

So liberals need not be afraid that my appeal to benevolence is intended to reintroduce a set of specific sexual proscriptions, since the kind of generalization required to ground such rules would be fundamentally unsafe. Furthermore, one factor that is very likely to be relevant is that people tend to be made unhappy by an inability to realize their chosen projects. Adding to this the observation that people have intimate (though not infallible) acquaintance with their own desires, we get a very strong presumption that what will make people happy is what they say will make them happy. But this isn't always the case. Sometimes it can be perfectly obvious that someone's ignorance or inexperience or emotion is leading them to ruin, and that aiding them in their self-destructive project is not the kind thing to do. And certain sexual scenarios are good examples of the unusual cases where one person knows better than another whether a course of action will make him happy. Consider the unrequited love example. The lover does not want sex as such, but a sexual relationship, so will likely be motivated by the hope that this sexual encounter will be the beginning of it. The object of the unrequited love is in a very good position to know that this hope will be dashed, since he is aware of his current feelings and intentions for the future. Since the other's imagined happiness depends on him, he knows as the other does not that this is not the route to it.

All in all as far as Primoratz's normative claims are concerned, I suspect that the sexual morality tail is wagging the moral philosophical dog. People are strongly motivated to embrace certain philosophical positions by fears of various kinds, and what those who insist on consent as the only relevant factor in sexual ethics tend to fear most is the repressive sexual agenda associated with various conservative social and political viewpoints. And clearly this conservative agenda is alive and well in various quarters of modern Western societies, particularly in the United States. I am entirely at one with Primoratz and others over the need to resist the kind of putative sexual ethics which denigrates homosexuality, insists on confining sex to certain institutionally sanctioned relationships, problematizes contraception, and so on. It may seem surprising, considering the tone of much of my argument so far, but I really do agree with what I take to be Primoratz's guiding thought, which, to be blunt, is this: He thinks that you can have a nice friendly fuck with someone you hardly know, with no intention of forming any kind of long-standing relationship or even repeating the encounter, and that there's nothing whatever wrong about this. Not only is there nothing wrong with it, but such an experience can also be extremely pleasurable and life-affirming for everyone involved, and a thoroughly good thing all round. This view is quite right. Human sexuality may not be essentially innocent, but it certainly isn't essentially threatening or guilty or something to be ashamed of either.

Let me conclude then by suggesting that something of a rapprochement between us may be possible. The view I have outlined may be more conservative than that of Primoratz, but it is nothing like the reactionary accounts of sexual morality which he takes to be his primary targets. I do not appeal in any way to a dressed-up premodern metaphysics or teleology, nor to theology, nor to a claim about the "proper place" of sex in human life, nor to any contentious conception of what an ideal sexual relationship looks like. I appeal to the Kantian Formula of Humanity with its emphasis on respect for others and concern for their well-being, combined with the observations that sex can be a vehicle for vicious self-conceit which denies the object of desire the respect she deserves, and that sexual desire can motivate people to behave in ways that will foreseeably bring about unhappiness for other people. This appeal puts me squarely in the liberal camp on sexual morality. Consequently no one need worry that I am in the business of producing lists of sexual practices or relationships which are validly consensual but allegedly wrong per se, as conservatives often are, since I don't think that this is the way to capture the morally problematic elements of human sexual desire. Instead I'm happy to produce a (nonexhaustive) list of consensual practices and relationships which are not in my view intrinsically wrong, to demonstrate my liberal credentials: homosexuality, masturbation, oral sex, anal sex, troilism, ménages a trois (or *quatre* or *cinq*), anonymous sex, casual sex, bondage, janus, adultery, sadomasochistic sex, open relationships, transvestism, prostitution, the use of contraception, appearing in pornography, inserting objects into orifices, role play, having sex while watching a video of yourselves having sex last week, ejaculating or even urinating on each others' bodies, and so on.[53] Whatever turns you on. Just so long, that is, as what turns you on is not an eroticized contempt or hatred for other people which demeans human dignity, and does not involve ignoring whether or how one's gratification acts to the detriment of someone else's happiness. Despite the olive branch, then, I still think that Primoratz's optimistic sexual morality is misplaced, ignoring the way that sexuality can be bound up with some of the darkest elements of our nature. The Vicomte shows us this. His desire is as dark as it comes, but it is precisely not a desire to infringe the autonomy of Madame de Tourvel, since it can only be gratified if she consents to sleep with him. This is why there is much more to sexual morality than just consent, and not because sex has a goal or purpose which is in some mysterious sense sacred, and vulnerable to being profaned.[54]

NOTES

1. Igor Primoratz, especially *Ethics and Sex* (London: Routledge, 1999) and "Sexual Morality: Is Consent Enough?" *Ethical Theory and Moral Practice* 4:3 (2001), 201–18.

2. Alan Goldman, "Plain Sex," *Philosophy and Public Affairs* 6:3 (1977), 267–87 [reprinted in this volume—eds.]. Primoratz endorses the essentials of this view in chapter 5 of *Ethics and Sex*, making minor modifications to produce a "plainer" account.

3. Primoratz describes sex as "simply a bodily activity intensely pleasurable in itself" (*Ethics and Sex*, 42), describes his notion of sexuality as "essentially physical . . . reducing sex to bodily activity" (42), claims that sexual desire is "sufficiently defined as the desire for certain bodily pleasures, period" (46) and describes sexual pleasure as "*a* distinctive type of pleasure" (41, my emphasis), "basically physical" (43), "the sort of bodily pleasure experienced in the sexual parts of the body" (46).

4. Thomas Nagel, "Sexual Perversion," in *Mortal Questions* (Cambridge: Cambridge University Press, 1979), 39–52, at 43–47 [reprinted in this volume—eds.]

5. Roger Scruton, *Sexual Desire* (London: Weidenfeld and Nicolson, 1986), 20–21.

6. Seiriol Morgan, "Sex in the Head," *Journal of Applied Philosophy* 20:1 (2003), 1–16, reprinted in *The Philosophy of Sex*, 6th ed., edited by Nicholas Power, Raja, and Alan Soble (Lanham, Md.: Rowman & Littlefield, 2013), 99–121.

7. Pierre Ambroise Choderlos de Laclos, *Les Liaisons Dangereuses*, translated as *Dangerous Acquaintances* by Richard Aldington (London: Routledge, 1924).

8. "Ah! Let her yield herself, but let her struggle! Let her have the strength to resist without having enough to conquer; let her fully taste the feeling of her weakness and be forced to admit her defeat" (*Dangerous Acquaintances*, letter 23, the Vicomte to the Marquise).

9. A 7: 265 I refer to Kant's works [by] citing the volume and page number of the Prussian Academy edition of Kant's complete works and using the standard abbreviations. The texts are the *Groundwork of the Metaphysics of Morals*, trans. Mary Gregor, in *The Cambridge Edition of the Works of Immanuel Kant: Practical Philosophy*, edited by Mary Gregor (Cambridge: Cambridge University Press, 1996), abbr. as G; *The Critique of Pure Reason*, trans. Paul Guyer and Allen Wood, in *The Cambridge Edition of the Works of Immanuel Kant: The Critique of Pure Reason* (Cambridge: Cambridge University Press, 1998), abbr. as KrV; *Critique of Practical Reason*, trans. Mary Gregor, in *The Cambridge Edition of the Works of Immanuel Kant: Practical Philosophy*, edited by Mary Gregor (Cambridge: Cambridge University Press, 1996), abbr. as KpV; *Lectures on Ethics*, Peter Heath, in *The Cambridge Edition of the Works of Immanuel Kant: Lectures on Ethics*, edited by Peter Heath and Jerome Schneewind (Cambridge: Cambridge University Press, 1997), abbr. as VE; *The Metaphysics of Morals*, trans. Mary Gregor, in *The Cambridge Edition of the Works of Immanuel Kant: Practical Philosophy*, edited by Mary Gregor (Cambridge: Cambridge University Press, 1996), abbr. as MS; *Religion Within the Bounds of Mere Reason*, trans. George di Giovanni, in *The Cambridge Edition of the Works of Immanuel Kant: Religion and Rational Theology*, edited by George di Giovanni and Allen Wood (Cambridge: Cambridge University Press, 1996), abbr. as R; *Idea for a Universal History with a Cosmopolitan Intent*, trans. Ted Humphrey, in *Perpetual Peace and Other Essays* (Indianapolis, Ind.: Hackett, 1983), abbr. as I; and *Anthropology from a Pragmatic Point of View*, trans. Victor Lyle Dowdell, revised and edited by Hans Rudnick (Carbondale, Ill.: Southern Illinois University Press, 1978), abbr. as A. The best secondary source is part II of Alan Wood's *Kant's Ethical Thought* (Cambridge: Cambridge University Press, 1999), to which I am indebted in what follows.

10. A 7: 268.

11. I 8: 18–21.

12. MS 6: 212.

13. KpV 5: 73.

14. A 7: 273.

15. A 7: 267.

16. A 7: 272–74; VE 27: 399–405.

17. A 7: 270–71.

18. R 6: 27.

19. In Kant's view this is the other side of the coin of self-conceit. The source of self-hatred, servility and the like is failed ambition. Feelings of personal worthlessness stem from the thought that others are better than oneself, and only someone who views the social world in the competitive way of the self-conceited can come to see themselves as standing in such a relation to others (MS 6: 434–36).

20. Throughout the chapter my examples are largely of the dark desires of men, but this should not be taken to imply that I think that this is an exclusively male phenomenon. Women are perfectly capable of eroticizing some very unhealthy things as well.

21. *Dangerous Acquaintances*, letter 47.

22. *Dangerous Acquaintances*, letter 44.

23. *Dangerous Acquaintances*, letter 44.

24. *Dangerous Acquaintances*, letter 71.

25. G 4: 448.

26. KpV 5: 75–76.

27. Primoratz, *Ethics and Sex*, 168–72, 2001, 215–16. In this and the final section I spend some time addressing some specific arguments advanced by Primoratz that will probably not be endorsed by all defenders of the view that consent is sufficient for the moral permissibility of a sexual act. I think my choice of target is appropriate because Primoratz seems to me to be much the most prominent contemporary moral philosopher defending the view, and I have come across no philosophically stronger example of such a defense in the literature. But in any case throughout the chapter (including the following two sections) I put forward a general argument for the view that we have obligations in the sexual sphere beyond those the free choices of others place upon us. Hence every defender of the contrary position is engaged by this and faces the burden of undermining or refuting it, whether or not her argument relies on those particular elements present in that of Primoratz which I will presently be attacking.

28. MS 6: 383.

29. G 4: 423.

30. MS 6: 449–50.

31. MS 6: 462.

32. MS 6: 463.

33. MS 6: 465.

34. MS 6: 466–67.

35. MS 6: 464.

36. MS 6: 386.

37. MS 6: 393.

38. MS 6: 452.

39. MS 6: 458.

40. MS 6: 452.

41. G 4: 424.

42. MS 6: 390.

43. MS 6: 460.

44. Kant would think that a number of other duties are also broken by the Vicomte. Since he is trying to persuade her to do something that they both see as detrimental to her virtue, his actions constitute a scandal, which is contrary both to our duty of respect to others and also the duty of benevolence, since it potentially exposes the other to the painful ravages of conscience (MS 6: 394). He also breaks various duties to himself, including his duties to know and properly judge himself, since he has an inflated and entirely erroneous conception of his own worth (MS 6: 437–42).

45. Actually, someone holding the infringement of freedom to be the only possible thing wrong with sexually motivated behavior wouldn't have much trouble producing an argument that what the Vicomte did to Madame de Tourvel was wrong. For one thing, he repeatedly lies to her, breaks promises, intimidates and threatens her; indeed, the entire novel is the story of what we would describe as an extended cam-

paign of sexual harassment. But to locate the badness of the Vicomte simply in the fact that he does these things is to rather miss the point. The very nature of the desire he feels and the pleasure he anticipates shows the corruption of his character. It would be contrary to his duty of virtue for him to gratify it, even if he cunningly succeeded in doing so without violating her autonomy in this way.

46. Kant would think that Primoratz only partially grasps what it is to hold humanity as an end in itself, since he understands the end only "negatively" and not "positively" (G 4: 430).

47. Primoratz, *Ethics and Sex*, 168–69.

48. G 4: 429.

49. MS 6: 388, 215–16.

50. MS 6: 454.

51. MS 6: 388.

52. KrV A 133–34/ B 172–73.

53. My claim is that none of these activities or relationships is intrinsically wrong, not that they are all on the face of it morally unproblematic, of course. The social context in which a practice standardly takes place may be such that any instance of it should be presumed prima facie exploitative, and social meanings that become associated with certain activities may make them especially likely to be a vehicle for eroticized contempt.

54. I am grateful to Matthew Kieran, Nafsika Athanassoulis and two anonymous referees for this journal for some very helpful comments, and to Peter Simons and George Macdonald Ross for advice over issues of translation.

STUDY QUESTIONS

1. Morgan draws on Kant's moral anthropology to make the case that some sexual desires are "dark." Can a similar case be made without relying on Kant's philosophy (or any other philosopher's views)? Why is Kant's view important to use in Morgan's essay?

2. The central example that Morgan uses is the (fairly complex) sexual desire of the Vicomte. Can you think of other, perhaps less complex, examples of dark sexual desires? Connected to this, do *all types* of sexual activities possibly admit of underlying dark desires? Do some sexual activities always have benign underlying desires while others always have dark ones?

3. As part of his desire to prove his "liberal credentials," Morgan produces a list of sexual activities that he thinks are not "intrinsically wrong," a list that includes bondage, adultery, sadomasochistic sex, and "water sports" —activities of which even many liberal-minded people might be suspicious, perhaps because of the activities' underlying dark desires. In connection to Study Question 2, think of examples of these activities. For each type of activity, give two examples, one with an underlying dark desire and one without.

4. Morgan accuses philosophers such as Alan Goldman and Igor Primoratz of assuming that "sexual pleasure has a uniform nature," on the grounds that they think it is essentially animalistic in nature. Must such philosophers assume that sexual desire has a

uniform nature to claim that it is *essentially* animalistic? That is, can they claim that sexual desire has an essential core though it can take additional layers, depending on the context? Offer an argument for such a claim on their behalf.

5. Morgan agrees that in sexual desire "physical sensation is still obviously central," but he adds that the "sensation is interpreted, saturated with meaning, and so is experienced very differently from uninterpreted sensation." Can you think of a few convincing examples of adult human sexual desires that are *un*interpreted, that do not have—let alone are saturated with—meaning? (Incidentally, think about whether "uninterpreted sexual desire" means the same thing as "sexual desire that does not have meaning.") If such examples are hard to come by, what does this say about the philosophical disagreement between the views of Morgan and Primoratz?

6. Morgan aims to show that although universal participant consent to a sexual act is necessary for the act's moral permissibility, it need not be sufficient. Can we claim that there is universal consent in the central example that Morgan uses? To what, exactly, does Madame de Tourvel consent? Morgan states (at the end of his essay) that she consents to sleep with the Vicomte, but is this consent genuine, given her ignorance of the Vicomte's intentions? If there is no universal participant consent in this example, what would this show about Morgan's central thesis? One way to think about this is as follows: Come up with an example of a sexual act such that (1) at least one of the parties to the act has a dark desire, (2) all the parties to the sexual act know about this dark desire (and they know that it is motivating its possessor to have the sexual act), and (3) they all genuinely consent to the sexual act. Is this act morally impermissible still? And is it impermissible *because* of the presence of the dark desires? For further discussion, see note 30 in Alan Soble's "Sexual Use" in this volume.

7. In the unrequited love example, Morgan states, "In such a case consent is not the issue. We know he [the lover] will consent . . . Indeed, his acquiescence might have the power of a near-compulsion." If sexual desire has the power of "near-compulsion," to what extent can we meaningfully speak of consent when people agree to have sex out of sexual desire (as opposed to out of the desire, say, to make money)? And if agreeing to have sex because one succumbs to sexual desire instead of consenting to it, what implications would this have for Morgan's main thesis and for Primoratz-like views?

TWENTY

The Harms of Consensual Sex

Robin West

There are several lines of thought that oppose consent as the central moral stan-dard of sexual activity. Some Kantians, for example, argue that consent is not sufficient because consent does not prevent the participants from still treating each other as mere means. The conservative Thomistic Natural Law view is that marriage and openness-to-procreation are also required for sexual activity to be morally permissible. In this essay, legal scholar **Robin West** *finds fault with the consent criterion from a different perspective. She argues that consensual—but unwanted—sex often harms a woman in subtler ways than do rape, assault, and harassment. West provides a compelling picture of the often unhappy circum-stances under which much (not all) everyday heterosexual activity occurs. Even when a woman employs her freedom and rationality in agreeing to sexual activ-ity with a husband or boyfriend, if she consents to sexual contact that she does not genuinely desire, she may undermine that same freedom and rationality. A lone, stringent consent standard, on West's view, is thereby an arrow in patriar-chy's quiver. West concludes by suggesting that feminist-liberal reforms of rape laws might have the unintended consequence of masking (by "legitimating") these subtle kinds of damage. She also wonders whether the radical feminist mantra that all heterosexual penetration perpetrates illicit sex trivializes the subtle harms done to the autonomy of women who consent to unwanted sexual activity.*

Robin West is professor of law at Georgetown University Law Center, where she teaches jurisprudence, torts, law and literature, and feminist legal theory. She is the author of *Narrative, Authority, and Law* (University of Michigan Press, 1994), *Progressive Constitutionalism* (Duke University Press, 1995), *Caring for Justice* (New York University Press, 1997), *Re-Imagining Justice: Progressive Interpretations of Formal Equality, Rights, and the Rule of Law* (Ashgate/Dartmouth, 2003), *Marriage, Sexuality, and Gender* (Paradigm Press, 2007), *Norma-tive Jurisprudence: An Introduction* (Cambridge University Press, 2011), and *Teaching Law* (Cambridge University Press, 2014). She is the coeditor, with Justin Murray, of *In Search of Common Ground on Abortion*

(Ashgate, 2014). This essay originally appeared in *The American Philosophical Association Newsletters* vol. 94, no. 2 (1995), 52–55. It is reprinted here with the permission of Robin West and the American Philosophical Association.

Are consensual, non-coercive, non-criminal, and even non-tortious, heterosexual transactions ever harmful to women? I want to argue briefly that many (not all) consensual sexual transactions are, and that accordingly we should open a dialogue about what those harms might be. Then I want to suggest some reasons those harms may be difficult to discern, even by the women sustaining them, and lastly two ways in which the logic of feminist legal theory and practice itself might undermine their recognition.

Let me assume what many women who are or have been heterosexually active surely know to be true from their own experience, and that is that some women occasionally, and many women quite frequently, consent to sex even when they do not desire the sex itself, and accordingly have a good deal of sex that, although consensual, is in no way pleasurable. Why might a woman consent to sex she does not desire? There are, of course, many reasons. A woman might consent to sex she does not want because she or her children are dependent upon her male partner for economic sustenance, and she must accordingly remain in his good graces. A woman might consent to sex she does not want because she rightly fears that if she does not her partner will be put into a foul humor, and she simply decides that tolerating the undesired sex is less burdensome than tolerating the foul humor. A woman might consent to sex she does not want because she has been taught and has come to believe that it is her lot in life to do so, and that she has no reasonable expectation of attaining her own pleasure through sex. A woman might consent to sex she does not want because she rightly fears that her refusal to do so will lead to an outburst of violent behavior some time following—only if the violence or overt threat of violence is very close to the sexual act will this arguably constitute a rape. A woman may consent to sex she does not desire because she *does* desire a friendly man's protection against the very real threat of nonconsensual violent rape by other more dangerous men, and she correctly perceives, or intuits, that to gain the friendly man's protection, she needs to give him, in exchange for that protection, the means to his own sexual pleasure. A woman, particularly a young woman or teenager, may consent to sex she does not want because of peer expectations that she be sexually active, or because she cannot bring herself to hurt her partner's pride, or because she is uncomfortable with the prospect of the argument that might ensue, should she refuse.

These transactions may well be rational—indeed in some sense they all are. The women involved all trade sex for something they value more than they value what they have given up. But that doesn't mean that they are not harmed. Women who engage in unpleasurable, undesired, but consensual sex may sustain real injuries to their sense of selfhood, in at least four distinct ways. First, they may sustain injuries to their capacities for self-assertion: the "psychic connection," so to speak, between pleasure, desire, motivation, and action is weakened or severed. *Acting* on the basis of our own felt pleasures and pains is an important component of forging our own way in the world—of "asserting" our "selves." Consenting to *un*pleasurable sex—acting in spite of displeasure—threatens that means of self-assertion. Second, women who consent to undesired sex may injure their sense of self-*possession*. When we consent to undesired penetration of our physical bodies we have in a quite literal way constituted ourselves as what I have elsewhere called "giving selves"—selves who cannot be violated, because they have been defined as (and define themselves as) being "for others." Our bodies to that extent no longer belong to ourselves. Third, when women consent to undesired and unpleasurable sex because of their felt or actual dependency upon a partner's affection or economic status, they injure their sense of autonomy: they have thereby neglected to take whatever steps would be requisite to achieving the self-sustenance necessary to their independence. And fourth, to the extent that these unpleasurable and undesired sexual acts are followed by contrary to fact claims that they enjoyed the whole thing—what might be called "hedonic lies"—women who engage in them do considerable damage to their sense of integrity.

These harms—particularly if multiplied over years or indeed over an entire adulthood—may be quite profound, and they certainly may be serious enough to outweigh the momentary or day-to-day benefits garnered by each individual transaction. Most debilitating, though, is their circular, self-reinforcing character: the more thorough the harm—the deeper the injury to self-assertiveness, self-possession, autonomy, and integrity—the greater the likelihood that the woman involved will indeed *not* experience these harms as harmful, or as painful. A woman utterly lacking in self-assertiveness, self-possession, a sense of autonomy, or integrity will not experience the activities in which she engages that reinforce or constitute those qualities *as harmful*, because she, to that degree, lacks a self-asserting, self-possessed self who *could* experience those activities as a threat to her selfhood. But the fact that she does not experience these activities as harms certainly does not mean that they are not harmful. Indeed, that they are not felt as harmful is a consequence of the harm they have already caused. This phenomenon, of course, renders the "rationality" of these transactions tremendously and even tragically misleading. Although these women may be making rational calculations in the context of the particular decision facing them, they are, by making those calculations, sustaining deeper and to some degree unfelt harms that undermine the very qualities that constitute the capacity for rationality being exercised.

Let me quickly suggest some reasons that these harms go so frequently unnoticed—or are simply not taken seriously—and then suggest in slightly more detail some ways that feminist legal theory and practice may have undermined their recognition. The first reason is cultural. There is a deep-seated U.S. cultural tendency to equate the legal with the good, or harmless: we are, for better or worse, an anti-moralistic, anti-authoritarian, and anti-communitarian people. When combined with the sexual revolution of the 1960s, this provides a powerful cultural explanation for our tendency to shy away from a sustained critique of the harms of consensual sex. Any suggestion that legal transactions to which individuals freely consent may be harmful, and hence *bad*, will invariably be met with skepticism—*particularly* where those transactions are sexual in nature. This tendency is even further underscored by more contemporary post-mortem skeptical responses to claims asserting the pernicious consequences of false consciousness.

Second, at least our legal-academic discourses, and no doubt academic-political discourses as well, have been deeply transformed by the "exchange theory of value," according to which, if I exchange A for B voluntarily, then I simply must be better off after the exchange than before, having, after all, agreed to it. If these exchanges *are* the source of value, then it is of course impossible to ground a *value* judgment that some voluntary exchanges are harmful. Although stated baldly this theory of value surely has more critics than believers, it nevertheless in some way perfectly captures the modern zeitgeist. It is certainly, for example, the starting and ending point of normative analysis for many, and perhaps most, law students. Obviously, given an exchange theory of value, the harms caused by consensual sexual transactions simply fade away into definitional oblivion.

Third, the exchange theory of value is underscored, rather than significantly challenged, by the continuing significance of liberal theory and ideology in academic life. To the degree that liberalism still rules the day, we continue to valorize individual choice against virtually anything with which it might seem to be in conflict, from communitarian dialogue to political critique, and continue to perceive these challenges to individual primacy as somehow on a par with threats posed by totalitarian statist regimes.

Fourth, and perhaps most obvious, the considerable harms women sustain from consensual but undesired sex must be downplayed if the considerable pleasure men reap from heterosexual transactions is morally justified—*whatever* the relevant moral theory. Men do have a psychosexual stake in insisting that voluntariness alone ought be sufficient to ward off serious moral or political inquiry into the value of consensual sexual transactions.

Let me comment in a bit more detail on a further reason why these harms seem to be underacknowledged, and that has to do with the logic of feminist legal theory, and the efforts of feminist practitioners, in the area of rape law reform. My claim is that the theoretical conceptualizations of sex, rape, force, and violence that underscore both liberal and radical legal feminism undermine the effort to articulate the harms that might be caused by consensual sexuality. I will begin with liberal feminism and then turn to radical feminism.

First, and entirely to their credit, liberal feminist rape law reformers have been on the forefront of efforts to stiffen enforcement of the existing criminal sanction against rape, and to extend that sanction to include nonconsensual sex, which presently is not cognizable legally as rape but surely should be. This effort is to be applauded, but it has the almost inevitable consequence of valorizing, celebrating, or, to use the critical term, "legitimating" consensual sexual transactions. If rape is bad *because* it is nonconsensual—which is increasingly the dominant liberal-feminist position on the badness of rape—then it seems to follow that *consensual* sex must be good because it is consensual. But appearances can be misleading, and this one certainly is. That nonconsensual transactions—rape, theft, slavery—are bad because nonconsensual does *not* imply the value, worth or goodness of their consensual counterparts—sex, property, or work. It only follows that consensual sex, property, or work are not bad in the ways that nonconsensual transactions are bad; they surely may be bad for some other reason. We need to explore, in the case of sex (as well as property and work), what those other reasons might be. Nonconsensuality does not exhaust the types of harm we inflict on each other in social interactions, nor does consensuality exhaust the list of benefits.

That the liberal-feminist argument for extending the criminal sanction against rape to include nonconsensual sex *seems* to imply the positive value of consensual sex is no doubt in part simply a reflection of the powers of the forces enumerated above—the cultural, economic, and liberal valorization of individualism against communal and authoritarian controls. Liberal feminists can obviously not be faulted for that phenomenon. What I want to caution against is simply the ever-present temptation to *trade* on those cultural and academic forces in putting forward arguments for reform of rape law. We need not trumpet the glories of consensual sex *in order* to make out a case for strengthening the criminal sanction against coercive sex. Coercion, violence, and the fear under which women live because of the threat of rape are sufficient evils to sustain the case for strengthening and extending the criminal law against those harms. We need not and should not supplement the argument with the unnecessary and unwarranted celebration of consensual sex—which, whatever the harms caused by coercion, does indeed carry its own harms.

Ironically, radical feminist rhetoric—which *is* aimed at highlighting the damage and harm done to women by ordinary, "normal" heterosexual transactions—*also* indirectly burdens the attempt to articulate the harms done to women by consensual heterosexual transactions, although it does so in a very different way. Consider the claim, implicit in a good deal of radical feminist writing, explicit in some, that "all sex is rape," and compare it for a moment with the rhetorical Marxist claim that "all property is theft." Both claims are intended to push the reader or listener to a reexamination of the ordinary, and both do so by blurring the distinction between consent and coercion. Both seem to share the underlying premise that that which is coerced—and perhaps only that which is coerced—is bad, or as a strategic matter, is going to be perceived as bad. Both want us to reexamine the value of that which we normally think of as good or at least unproblematic because of its apparent consensuality—heterosexual transactions in the first case, property transactions in the second—and both do so by putting into doubt the reality of that apparent consensuality.

But there is a very real difference in the historical context and hence the practical consequences of these two rhetorical claims. More specifically, there are two pernicious, or at least counterproductive, consequences of the feminist claim which are not shared, at least to the same degree, by the Marxist. First, and as any number of liberal feminists have noted, the radical feminist equation of sex and rape runs the risk of undermining parallel feminist efforts in a way not shared by the Marxist equation of property and theft. Marxists are for the most part not engaged in the project of attempting to extend the existing laws against *theft* so as to embrace nonconsensual market transactions that are currently not covered by the laws against larceny and embezzlement. Feminists, however, *are* engaged in a parallel effort to extend the existing laws against rape to include all nonconsensual sex, and, as a result, the radical feminist equation of rape and sex is indeed undermining. The claim that all sex is in effect nonconsensual runs the real risk of "trivializing," or at least confusing, the feminist effort at rape reform so as to include all truly nonconsensual sexual transactions.

There is, though, a second cost to the radical feminist rhetorical claim, which I hope these comments have by now made clear. The radical feminist equation of rape and sex, no less than the liberal rape reform movement, gets its rhetorical force by trading on the liberal, normative-economic, and cultural assumptions that whatever is coercive is bad, and whatever is non-coercive is morally non-problematic. It has the effect, then, of further burdening the articulation of harms caused by consensual sex by forcing the characterization of those harms into a sort of "descriptive funnel" of nonconsensuality. It requires us to say, in other words, that consensual sex is harmful, if it is, only because or to the extent that it shares in the attributes of nonconsensual sex. But this might not be true—the harms caused by consensual sex might be just as important, just as serious, but nevertheless *different* from the harms caused by nonconsensual sex. If so, then women are disserved, rather than served, by the equation of rape and sex, even were that equation to have the rhetorical effect its espousers clearly desire.

Liberal feminist rape reform efforts and radical feminist theory both, then, in different ways, undermine the effort to articulate the distinctive harms of consensual sex; the first by indirectly celebrating the value of consensual sex, and the latter by at least rhetorically denying the existence of the category. Both, then, in different ways, underscore the legitimation of consensual sex effectuated by non-feminist cultural and academic forces. My conclusion is simply that feminists could counter these trends in part by focusing attention on the harms caused women by consensual sexuality. Minimally, a thoroughgoing philosophical treatment of these issues might clear up some of the confusions on both sides of the "rape/sex" divide, and on the many sides of what have now come to be called the intra-feminist "sex wars," which continue to drain so much of our time and energy.

STUDY QUESTIONS

1. In arguing that a liberal consent criterion of morally permissible sexual activity does not adequately protect women, is West's position ultimately paternalistic, and in this way itself injurious to women's autonomy? In claiming that more than a woman's agreement must be in place to allow her to avoid unwanted sex, are we not robbing her of the freedom to consent to sex on her own terms? Compare West's position with the possibly paternalistic Antioch University "Sexual Offense Policy" (see, for example, Leslie Francis's anthology *Date Rape* [University Park: Penn State University Press, 1996]), which has also been criticized for reducing autonomy even as it aims at promoting autonomy.

2. It is known that some women apply various kinds of strong or weak pressures on men (and women) to engage in sexual activity, without that pressure necessarily amounting to force or coercion that would make these sexual acts rape or nonconsensual. (See, for example, Peter Anderson and Cindy Struckman-Johnson, eds., *Sexually Aggressive Women: Current Perspectives and Controversies* [New York: Guilford, 1998].) Does this consensual but unwanted sexual activity harm men or reduce their autonomy? When and how? Might there be a difference between men and women in their ability to withstand the consequences of unwanted but consensual sex?

3. What if one partner in a couple desires to engage in sexual activity more than the other partner, but both desire sex in general? In many partnerships, this scenario seems to be the rule rather than the exception. What are the implications of this imbalance for

West's position? Contrast the arguments and conclusions reached by Alan Wertheimer about this scenario ("Consent and Sexual Relations," in this volume) to those advanced by West.

4. Is the presence of genuine sexual desire a more reliable moral criterion than consent to sexual activity? Granted, there are difficulties specifying what the consent criterion demands (here, learn to apply Wertheimer's vocabulary of "consent token" vs. "consent"), but what, in practice, does West's no-harm standard mean? Are there any conceptual or normative differences between West's view and that of Robin Morgan, who focuses on desire? "Rape exists any time sexual intercourse occurs when it has not been initiated by the woman, out of her own genuine affection and desire. . . . How many millions of times have women had sex 'willingly' with men they didn't want to have sex with? . . . How many times have women wished just to sleep instead or read or watch the *Late Show*? . . . Most of the decently married bedrooms across America are settings for nightly rape" ("Theory and Practice: Pornography and Rape," in *Going Too Far: The Personal Chronicle of a Feminist* [New York: Random House, 1977], 163–69, at 165–66).

5. Would a genuine form of communication between the sexual partners alleviate any or all the harms that West associates with women's consensual but unwanted sex? If yes, how? (For help with thinking about genuine communication and sexual consent, see Lois Pineau's account of the ideal Kantian imperative regarding consent in "Date Rape: A Feminist Analysis," in *The Philosophy of Sex: Contemporary Readings*, 6th ed., edited by Nicholas Power, Raja Halwani, and Alan Soble [Lanham, Md.: Rowman & Littlefield, 2013], 461–83.)

6. Is it possible that West's examples of consensual sexual activity are cases in which the woman does not really consent? Go through her examples and ask whether she has convincingly claimed or shown that the woman did consent. What are the implications for her thesis if in some of these cases the woman plausibly did not fully consent?

7. It is a well-known fact that sex workers do not desire much of the sexual activity—especially that which involves direct physical contact—that they have with their clients. Do sex workers continuously sustain the harms that West speaks of? Are they therefore deeply harmed beings? If West claims that they do not consent, would she not then have to say the same about the women in the cases she gives?

8. Given the way that West understands harm and its different variations, how easy is it for the women (and their partners) to know that the women are being harmed by the consensual sex that they

are having? In other words, does West's view face epistemological problems?

TWENTY-ONE

Sexual Objectification

Lina Papadaki

In this essay, **Lina Papadaki** *goes over some important accounts of objectification that have been offered in the philosophical literature, using prostitution and pornography to illustrate some of them (she finds each lacking in some respect). Along the way she addresses many issues, such as whether objectification must involve treatment (or whether it can be mere regard), the role of harm, and whether there is such a thing as positive objectification. Papadaki settles on a view of objectification that essentially involves treating someone as an object by denying their humanity.*

Lina Papadaki is assistant professor of philosophy at the Department of Philosophy and Social Studies, University of Crete (Greece). Lina's research interests are in moral philosophy, bioethics, and feminist philosophy, focusing on women's sexual objectification and on Kant's moral philosophy. Her publications include "Women's Objectification and the Norm of Assumed Objectivity" (2008), "What Is Objectification?" (2010), "Kantian Marriage and Beyond: Why It Is Worth Thinking about Kant on Marriage" (2010), "What Is Wrong about Objectification?" (2015), and "Treating Others Merely as a Means: A Reply to Kerstein" (2016). "Sexual Objectification" is printed here for the first time. © 2017, Lina Papadaki, who kindly gave permission for her new essay to be included in this volume.

THE WRONGNESS OF SEXUAL OBJECTIFICATION

1. Kant, Objectification, and the Case of Prostitution

Perhaps the most influential account of objectification was offered by the philosopher Immanuel Kant. Kant thought that sexuality can be extremely problematic. In exercising it, people run the risk of being reduced to mere tools for others' enjoyment. Exercise of sexuality, then, is seen as a threat to people's *humanity*, their rational nature and capacity for rational choice.

As beings with humanity, people have the capacity for rationally setting and pursuing their own ends. That is, they are capable of setting goals and values, as well as finding the means that are necessary to achieve and promote them. Humanity is an objective end. It holds for all rational beings, independently of their particular goals and desires in life. Furthermore, humanity has unconditional and incomparable worth. Because it has *dignity* (an inner worth, as opposed to a price or a relative worth), humanity is not something that can be exchanged with something else. Humanity, therefore, is an "object of respect."[1] We can use objects (even animals) as mere tools for our purposes because they only have conditional worth. But we ought to honor and respect the value of humanity in our person, as well as in the person of any other, and never treat it merely as a means.[2]

Kant thought that when people exercise their sexuality outside the context of monogamous marriage they "degrade" and "dishonor" humanity. Sexual activity can even lead to the "sacrifice" of humanity.[3] The following passage speaks for itself:

> In loving from sexual inclination, they make the person into an object of their appetite. As soon as the person is possessed, and the appetite sated, they are thrown away, as one throws away a lemon after sucking the juice from it . . . as object of the other's appetite, that person is in fact a thing, whereby the other's appetite is sated, and can be misused as such a thing by anybody.[4]

Objectification, for Kant, involves the lowering of a person (*someone* with humanity) to an object (*something* that exists in order to be used by others).

Unfortunately, it is not clear how exactly sexual use can bring about this sacrifice of humanity. Perhaps, we can assume, since Kant thought that others see and treat the loved individual as an object, they can prevent her from exercising her rational capacities. People, then, might force her to act as nothing more than a thing to be used by others. This can lead her to start regarding herself as an object and refrain from exercising her rational capacities. Yet Kant's claim about the loved person *becoming* a thing still sounds like an exaggeration. Even though we might be willing to accept that the sexually used individual's humanity is in some way impeded as a consequence of her being regarded as an object by others as well as by herself, it is hard to see how this individual's humanity can be utterly destructed. There might be reason, therefore, to take Kant's claims about the objectified individual's being *made into* an object with a grain of salt: as an object of appetite, the individual's humanity might be impeded, even though, most likely, not completely eliminated as Kant himself feared.

A characteristic context in which objectification inevitably occurs, for Kant, is prostitution. Kant defines it as the offer for profit of one's person for another's sexual gratification.[5] The prostitute, for Kant, is inevitably objectified. He writes:

> But now if a person allows himself to be used, for profit, as an object to satisfy the sexual impulse of another, if he makes himself an object of another's desire, then he is disposing over himself, as if over a thing, and thereby makes himself into a thing by which the other satisfies his appetite, just as his hunger is satisfied on a roast of pork. . . . Human beings have no right, therefore, to hand themselves over for profit, as things for another's use in satisfying the sexual impulse; for in that case their humanity is in danger of being used by anyone as a thing, an instrument for the satisfaction of inclination.[6]
>
> [M]an is not his own property, and cannot do as he pleases with his body; for since the body belongs to the self, it constitutes, in conjunction with that, a person; but now one cannot make one's person a thing, though this is what happens in *vaga libido*.[7]

It is not possible for the prostitute to offer *just her body* to other people for sexual use. She inevitably offers her *whole person* in exchange for money. In so doing, her person is reduced to a thing.

It is important to note that Kant does not take the prostitute's *consent* to be sexually used by the clients as making this use morally permissible. What the prostitute consents to is to be reduced to an object. Since she ought to respect humanity in her own person, however, she must not allow others to objectify her. This is the reason why Kant blames the prostitute for her objectification and degradation. It seems that there are, for Kant, two wrongs involved in prostitution: what the prostitute does (voluntarily allowing others to use her sexually in exchange for profit), and what the clients do (sexually using and so reducing her to an object of appetite: to a thing).[8]

The view that prostitution involves objectification is shared by a number of contemporary thinkers.[9] However, Kant took it that objectification occurs not only in prostitution but also whenever people exercise their sexuality outside the context of monogamous marriage. In order to avoid sexual objectification people must confine their sexuality to marriage. Kant thought that in monogamous marriage people surrender their persons to one another, giving each other rights of disposal over their persons (including rights to use each other sexually). Monogamy is required because a monogamous relationship is characterized by equality and reciprocity in the surrender and use of the spouses' persons. Furthermore, marriage as a legal institution ensures that this surrender of persons is maintained and secured. Sexual use within the "safe" context of marriage does not lead to the reduction of the spouses to objects because both spouses, for Kant, are committed by their marital contract to regard each other as persons and not as mere instruments for sexual gratification.[10]

Of course, there have been worries regarding Kant's suggested solution to the problem of sexual objectification. To begin with, the view that only marital sex is morally unproblematic sounds too conservative to our sexually liberated ears. Furthermore, feminist thinkers have expressed the concern that marriage is in fact a dangerous context, in which women are often objectified.[11] Kant's more general idea that equality and reciprocity can beat objectification, however, is an appealing one, and it has influenced contemporary views on sexual objectification, as we will see in the following sections.

2. Pornography and Objectification

Radical anti-pornography feminists' views of sexual objectification have striking similarities to Kant's account of objectification. Catharine MacKinnon and Andrea Dworkin emphasize that we live in a world of *gender inequality*. A person's *gender* is, for MacKinnon, distinguished from a person's *sex*. Gender, being a man or a woman, is socially constructed, whereas sex, being male or female, is biologically defined. In our patriarchal societies, men and women have clearly defined roles: *all women* are objectified, whereas *all men* are their objectifiers.[12]

This situation of gender inequality that is so tightly linked to the objectification of women is, MacKinnon and Dworkin believe, created and sustained by men's consumption of pornography. These feminists define "pornography" as "the graphic sexually explicit subordination of women through pictures or words."[13] According to this definition, pornography does not merely cause the subordination of women but also *constitutes* it. Pornography *is* the subordination of women. According to MacKinnon:

> Pornography *participates* in its audience's eroticism through creating an accessible sexual object, the possession and consumption of which *is* male sexuality, as socially constructed; to be consumed and possessed as which, *is* female sexuality, as socially constructed. . . . Pornography defines women by how we look according to how we can be sexually used.[14]

Like Kant, MacKinnon and Dworkin take objectification to involve treating a person (a woman, in particular) as an object of merely instrumental worth. For all these thinkers, furthermore, the objectified individual is made into an object, in the sense of being reduced to a mere tool for others' sexual purposes. Objectification, therefore, constitutes a serious harm to a person's humanity. Sharing Kant's pessimism, Dworkin describes the phenomenon of sexual objectification:

> When objectification occurs, a person is depersonalized, so that no individuality or integrity is available socially or in what is an extremely circumscribed privacy . . . those who can be used as if they are not fully

human are no longer fully human in social terms; their humanity is hurt by being diminished.[15]

MacKinnon too describes the phenomenon of sexual objectification in Kantian terms: "A person, in one Kantian view, is a free and rational agent whose existence is an end in itself, as opposed to instrumental. In pornography women exist to the *end* of male pleasure."[16] What is worse, for MacKinnon, is that use can easily be followed by violence and abuse. Since women are things (as opposed to human beings), it is difficult, if not impossible, for men to see anything problematic in using and, at times, abusing women.[17]

Like Kant, MacKinnon and Dworkin are confident that giving one's consent to be sexually used by others does not make such use permissible. They believe that women consent to be sexually used as objects by men, simply because they cannot, in our societies, do differently. Their consent, therefore, is not *true consent*. MacKinnon writes about pornography and prostitution, "The sex is not chosen for the sex. Money is the medium of force and provides the cover of consent."[18]

Dworkin and MacKinnon, unlike Kant, believe that women are not truly blameworthy for their reduction to things of merely instrumental value. The objectification of women, according to these feminists, is demanded and inflicted by men in our societies. It is men who want (and also, as Dworkin claims, need) to use women as objects and demand women to be object-like.[19] Furthermore, MacKinnon and Dworkin do not share Kant's optimism about the power of marriage to eliminate objectification. For them, marriage too is a relationship plagued by objectification. To use Dworkin's pessimistic language, "Wife beating and marital rape are predicated on the conviction that a man's ownership of his wife licenses whatever he wishes to do to her: her body belongs to him to use for his own release, to beat, to impregnate."[20]

MacKinnon and Dworkin believe that objectification has its roots in gender inequality, which is constructed and sustained by men's consumption of pornography. In order to end gender inequality, then, we must first and foremost eliminate pornography. A worry one might have, here, is whether pornography is special with respect to creating and sustaining gender inequality and women's objectification. In patriarchal societies, the idea that women are object-like is repeatedly expressed in various ways throughout the media. Numerous non-pornographic magazines and popular advertisements, for instance, sustain and reinforce women's object-like status. The elimination of pornography alone, it appears, is a rather ineffective strategy for fighting women's objectification.

Furthermore, some people believe that pornography deserves protection as free speech. An alternative way to fight pornography would be to educate people not to consume pornography, or at least not to uncritically accept its messages. MacKinnon and Dworkin, however, believe that protecting the speech of pornographers is at odds with protecting the speech of women. Pornography, as MacKinnon has famously argued, has the power of *silencing* women, which means that women cannot fight pornography with speech. As MacKinnon puts it, "Pornography and its protection have deprived women *of* speech."[21]

Even if convinced by MacKinnon and Dworkin's argument that pornography ought to be eliminated, however, the way these feminists describe reality is so pessimistic that it is highly doubtful that people will act in order to achieve this goal. Men benefit from being the objectifiers, and women have the status of mere objects for men's use and are completely powerless and victimized. Given MacKinnon and Dworkin's description of reality, then, their goal of eliminating pornography and objectification seems utopic.

IS OBJECTIFICATION QUITE AS BAD?

1. But People Are Objects: Alan Soble and Leslie Green

The argument put forward by Kant and anti-pornography feminists MacKinnon and Dworkin is that objectification is morally wrong because it reduces people to objects. This reduction constitutes harming their status as beings with absolute and incomparable worth: possessors of humanity. According to this line of thought, there is a clear dividing line between objects and persons. While the former are there to be used, exchanged, and even destroyed by us, people's humanity ought to be respected at all times. Therefore, under no circumstances can a person legitimately be treated merely as a means for another's purposes.

All these thinkers take it for granted that people are beings of a higher ontological status, that they are beings with humanity, deserving of respect. But are they really? Alan Soble argues against the view that there is something metaphysically special about human beings. He argues that their elevated status, their dignity, is nothing more than an illusion. As he explains, we have reason to question

> the belief that humans are more than their bodies, more than animals, that, therefore, there is something metaphysically special about humans, their essential dignity, their transcendental value, that makes using them, dehumanizing, objectifying them, morally wrong.[22]

> The claim that we should treat people as "persons" and not dehumanize them is to reify, is to anthropomorphize humans and consider them more than they are. Do not treat people as objects, we are told. Why not? Because, goes the answer, people *qua persons* deserve not to be treated as objects. What a nice bit of illusory chauvinism. People are not as grand as we make them out to be, would like them to be, or hope them to be.[23]

Assuming that Soble is right that it is a mistake to see people as having this higher status, treating people as objects is no longer a morally inappropriate attitude toward them. To objectify a person is not morally wrong because a person is already an object. This means that to objectify a person is to take them to their correct ontological level.

With sexual objectification, Soble admits that pornography does objectify people (both men and women). Yet he believes that there is nothing morally problematic with this objectification:

> To complain that pornography presents women as "fuck objects" is to presuppose that women, as humans or persons, are something substantially more than fuck objects. Whence this piece of illusory optimism? . . . Pornography gives to no one, male or female, the respect that no one, male or female, deserves anyway. It demolishes human pretensions. It objectifies that which does not deserve not to be objectified. It thereby repudiates norms that Christian, Western culture holds dear, that people are not to be used or treated as objects or objectified or dehumanized or degraded.[24]

While Soble shares the view held by MacKinnon and Dworkin that pornography presents women as objects to be sexually used, he believes that there is in fact nothing morally wrong with what pornography does. Since, for Soble, it is a mistake to see people as having an essential dignity, presenting women as objects available for sexual use, and even treating women merely as means for sexual pleasure, is not morally inappropriate.

One problem with this understanding of objectification, however, is that if people *are* objects it is unclear how we can objectify them. If I cannot objectify a table because it is merely an object, I cannot objectify someone if he or she is merely an object. But if I cannot objectify someone, then it is not clear what it would mean to claim that objectification is not wrong (or right).

Leslie Green also argues along the lines that it is permissible to treat people as objects. This is because people are embodied, extended in space, they exist in time, and they are subject to the laws of nature. In other words, people *are* objects. For Green, however, people are more than objects. Unlike Soble, Green is confident that people have dignity, and this is why it is morally wrong to treat people *merely* as objects. It is permissible to treat people as means to our purposes, as long as we refrain from treating them as mere means, and acknowledge and respect the fact that they have their own purposes.[25]

In fact, for Green, we *ought* to treat others instrumentally, "for we need their skills, their company, and their bodies—in fact, there is little that we social creatures can do on our own, and so little that is fulfilling."[26] Treating people merely as subjects can be as equally wrong as treating people merely as objects. Green explains that the elderly, severely disabled, and chronically unemployed, who feel they are of no use to others, "miss . . . their diminished objectivity. . . They become . . . *subjectified*." [27] The correct way to treat people, then, is to treat them as both subjects and objects, respecting both their subjectivity and objectivity.

2. Nussbaum: From Bad to Good Objectification

Nussbaum challenges the idea that objectification should be conceived of as necessarily harmful. Even though she acknowledges that objectification can be harmful, she also argues for the possibility of objectification being benign and even constituting a "wonderful" element of sexual life. [28]

Let us start by looking at Nussbaum's characterizations of objectification:

> Objectification of one person by another [is] the seeing and/or treating of someone as an object.
>
> Objectification [involves] treating one thing as another: One is treating *as an object* what is really not an object, what is, in fact, a human being.
>
> Objectification entails making into a thing, treating *as* a thing, something that is really not a thing. [29]

Objectification, as Nussbaum understands this notion, involves *seeing* as an object, or *treating* as an object, or *seeing and treating* as an object, or *making* into an object, something that is not an object but is, specifically, a human being.

Nussbaum suggests that at least the following seven notions are involved in the idea of objectification:

1. *Instrumentality*: The objectifier treats the object as a tool for his or her purposes.
2. *Denial of autonomy*: The objectifier treats the object as lacking in autonomy and self-determination.
3. *Inertness*: The objectifier treats the object as lacking in agency, and perhaps also in activity.
4. *Fungibility*: The objectifier treats the object as interchangeable (a) with other objects of the same type, and/or (b) with objects of other types.
5. *Violability*: The objectifier treats the object as lacking in boundary-integrity, as something that it is permissible to break up, smash, break into.
6. *Ownership*: The objectifier treats the object as something that is owned by another, can be bought or sold, etc.
7. *Denial of subjectivity*: The objectifier treats the object as something whose experiences and feelings (if any) need not be taken into account. [30]

Each of the above notions is a feature of our treatment of things as objects, even though we do not treat all things in all these ways. In some cases, according to Nussbaum, treating a person in one of these seven ways can be sufficient for objectifying a person, whereas in some other cases it cannot. Usually, however, in a case of objectification more than one of these seven features is at play. [31]

Treating a person as an object, for Nussbaum, is often problematic. For instance, Nussbaum shares MacKinnon and Dworkin's conviction that objectification in pornography is of a negative sort. Nussbaum, however, does not take pornography to be the primary cause of women's objectification. The latter, she believes, is often caused by social inequality, but there is no reason to believe that pornography is the core of such inequality. [32] Moreover, Nussbaum does not appear to share the pessimism of radical anti-pornography feminism that due to pornography women are actually reduced to mere objects for use and abuse. In fact, women's autonomy and subjectivity are to an extent recognized by consumers of pornography, albeit for the wrong reasons: "It is sexier to use a human being as a thing than simply to have a thing, since it manifests greater control, it shows that one can control what is of such a nature as to elude control." [33]

Nussbaum believes that pornography objectifies women in a negative way; yet she does not present women as beings whose humanity has been irretrievably damaged. For Nussbaum, negative objectification occurs when people are seen or treated as objects in a way that involves *denying their humanity*: denying, what Nussbaum herself calls, their "status of being ends in themselves." [34] This denial of humanity, as Nussbaum's own examples suggest, occurs when the objectified individual's humanity is *ignored or not fully acknowledged* or when it is *harmed*. An individual's humanity is not fully acknowledged or is ignored when someone does not take it into consideration. That is, when they do not take into consideration that the individual has rational capacities, and so regard her as not having such capacities. Not acknowledging an individual's humanity, however, does not necessarily mean that her humanity is harmed.

Moreover, Nussbaum suggests that it is indeed possible that "some features of objectification . . . may in fact in some circumstances . . . be even wonderful features of sexual life," and so "the term objectification can also be used . . . in a more positive spirit." [35] *Benign* or *positive objectification* is seeing or treating people as objects in a way that does not involve denying their humanity (either in the sense of harming or in the sense of ignoring or not fully acknowledging their humanity). In cases of positive objectification, people's humanity might even be promoted:

> If I am lying around with my lover on the bed, and use his stomach as a pillow there seems to be nothing at all baneful about this, provided that

> I do so with his consent (or, if he is asleep, with a reasonable belief that
> he would not mind), and without causing him pain, provided as well,
> that I do so in the context of a relationship in which he is generally
> treated as more than a pillow. This suggests that what is problematic is
> not instrumentalization per se, but treating someone *primarily* or *merely*
> as an instrument.[36]

The objectification of my lover, far from posing any risk to his status as a
person, appears to be a beautiful moment in our relationship.

Another example of positive objectification is, for Nussbaum, "Lawrentian objectification," the type of objectification that occurs in D. H.
Lawrence's novel *Lady Chatterley's Lover*.[37] In a context characterized by
equality and mutuality between the two parties, Connie and Mellor identify each other with their body parts, seeing one another in terms of these
organs.[38] Yet, she holds, "The suggestion that they are *reducing* one another to their bodily parts seems quite wrong. . . . The intense focusing of
attention on the bodily parts seems an addition, rather than a subtraction."[39] The two lovers deny each other's autonomy and subjectivity,
when engaging in the sex act, but they overall respect each other's autonomy and subjectivity.[40] Because the relationship is overall one of mutual
respect between its parties of each other's humanity, this, according to
Nussbaum, is a case of positive objectification: the two lovers' humanity
is not in any way denied, even though their autonomy and subjectivity
are denied when they have sex. So, because of the overall respectful
nature of the relationship, the denial of subjectivity and of autonomy,
which occurs only during sex, does not amount to a denial of humanity
in those sexual instances. Hence there is no negative objectification.[41]

Nussbaum's conception of objectification is broader than Kant's,
MacKinnon's, and Dworkin's. First, objectification can be negative even if
it does not involve harming a person's humanity but merely ignoring or
not fully acknowledging their humanity. Second, Nussbaum allows for
the possibility of objectification being benign or positive. That is, objectification can take place, for Nussbaum, even if the objectified individual's
humanity is not in any way denied, and might even be promoted. Third,
objectification (positive and negative) can involve merely *regarding* a person as an object.[42] *Treating* as an object is not, for Nussbaum, necessary
for objectification to take place. So Nussbaum's conception of objectification is quite complex in that (1) it can be positive and negative; (2) when it
is negative it is because of denial of humanity, which can take the form of
harming someone's humanity or ignoring (or not fully acknowledging) it;
(3) it can involve treatment or mere regard; and (4) such that (2) and (3)
cut across each other, and (1) and (3) cut across each other also, harm
need not always come in the form of treatment but can come in the form
of mere regard, and positive objectification can come in the form of treatment or mere regard.

WHAT IS OBJECTIFICATION?

There is disagreement among the above thinkers as to what objectification is, whether it is problematic, and how—if at all—it affects people's humanity. How are we then to understand the concept of "objectification"? In this section, drawing on the conceptions of objectification discussed in the previous sections, my aim is to offer what I take to be a plausible understanding of objectification.

1. A Narrow and a Broad Conception of Objectification

We have discussed two main understandings of objectification, the first put forward by Kant, MacKinnon and Dworkin, and the second by Nussbaum. I will refer to the Kant/MacKinnon/Dworkin conception of objectification as the *narrow conception*. It is narrow in that, first of all, in order for objectification to take place a person must be *treated* as an object. When one is merely regarded as an object, there is no objectification under this conception. Second, it necessarily leads to the *reduction* of a person to the status of a thing (a mere tool for others' use). According to this narrow conception, objectification is a phenomenon inconsistent with respect for humanity, so it is a phenomenon that we ought to eliminate.

The second main conception of objectification we discussed is Nussbaum's *broad conception of objectification*, according to which a person is objectified when he or she is *treated* or merely *regarded* as an object. Objectification is *negative* if it involves denying the objectified person's humanity. This happens when the objectifier harms the objectified individual's humanity by reducing her to the status of a thing of merely instrumental worth or when the objectifier simply fails to acknowledge the objectified individual's humanity. When a person's humanity is harmed through objectification the person is *made into* an object (she is reduced to the level of an object). For example, Kant feared that the objectified individual is turned into a mere thing. MacKinnon and Dworkin, likewise, believe that, when men objectify women, they not only treat them but also *reduce* them to the status of mere things for use. Someone, however, can objectify another without turning her into an object. In some cases, if a person treats his partner as a mere sexual instrument, this does not necessarily mean that he actually reduces her to the status of a mere sexual object, thus harming her humanity. In other words, his treatment might not make it the case that she in fact *becomes* a mere sexual tool. This means that this is a case of ignoring or not fully acknowledging another's humanity, so it is negative objectification but not of the harmful sort.

As we have seen, however, objectification does not necessarily involve denial of humanity, according to Nussbaum. When it does not, it can take *benign* and even *positive* forms.

What seems unintuitive concerning the narrow conception of objectification, in my view, is that, in order for objectification to occur, there must be a *reduction* of a person to the level of an object. We explained in Section I that the Kantian claim about the "sacrifice of humanity" that takes place in sexual objectification sounds exaggerated. This directs us toward Nussbaum's broad conception of objectification. Objectification, for Nussbaum, does not necessarily (or even usually) involve harming an individual's humanity. Negative objectification, for Nussbaum, most commonly involves denying an individual's humanity by ignoring or not fully acknowledging it rather than harming it. Even though this adds appeal to Nussbaum's conception of objectification, it is my belief that we are not better off adopting her conception as it is. This is because, as I will explain, it is overly broad, which creates problems.

Nussbaum's category of benign or positive objectification, as we have seen, includes cases in which a person is regarded or treated as an object in ways such that their humanity is not denied, and might even be promoted. If a person is objectified every time he or she is regarded or treated in one or more of the seven ways Nussbaum mentions even when their humanity is not thereby denied (and may even be promoted), then objectification becomes unreasonably pervasive.

For example, according to Nussbaum's conception, objectification can occur if a person is treated as an instrument for another's purposes, even when she is not treated as a *mere instrument*. In her own example, I objectify my lover in using his stomach as a pillow when we both lie in bed, even though I do not treat him as a mere object. It sounds odd to consider the placing of my head on my partner's stomach as a case of objectification. Furthermore, according to Nussbaum's broad conception, objectification can take place even when there is no treatment at all. This means that I would objectify my lover, even if I merely regarded his stomach as a pillow for a moment but ended up placing my head on my (real) pillow.

Considering the fact that we use or regard each other instrumentally all the time, this would make objectification an inevitable aspect of (nearly) all our interactions with each other. Add to this the fact that a person can be objectified when regarded or treated as an object in one of the other six ways on Nussbaum's list, and it becomes virtually impossible to find an objectification-free interaction. It is impractical and pointless, however, to call all these various ways of seeing and treating one another "objectification."

This point is further supported by the pervasiveness of negative objectification: if ignoring or not fully acknowledging someone's humanity is a form of (negative) objectification, then each of us continuously engages in it, seeing that we, at every moment in our lives, ignore *someone's* humanity *somewhere* on this planet! At this very moment, I am, for example, ignoring or not fully acknowledging the humanity of people passing me by on the street (this is not to mention others: people in their houses, in other countries, etc.). But it is not plausible to claim that we are always negatively objectifying others.[43]

In addition to impracticality and pointlessness, it does not seem correct that people in Nussbaum's positive objectification cases are treated *as objects*, when their humanity is—as Nussbaum herself admits—acknowledged, respected, and even promoted. Take the case of *Lady Chatterley's Lover*, for instance, in which the two lovers occasionally deny each other's autonomy and subjectivity, within the context of a relationship in which their autonomy and subjectivity are deeply acknowledged and valued, and contrast it with our treatment of objects. We treat objects as not having any autonomy or subjectivity whatsoever. We do not treat them as lacking autonomy and subjectivity sometimes but not at other times. Furthermore, since objects clearly do not have humanity, we do not at any time acknowledge, respect or try to promote their humanity. This is not true of human beings, especially in the context of a generally respectful relationship.

It is not accurate, therefore, to say that Connie and Mellor objectify each other. We can simply say that the two lovers occasionally deny each other's autonomy and subjectivity. In fact, this is the best way to accurately describe the situation. It certainly adds more information than simply resorting to calling such treatment "objectification," when the term "objectification" is so broad that it can mean, as we have seen, all sorts of things. Since it is implausible, impractical and inaccurate to call everything "objectification," it seems that we are better off favoring a less inclusive conception than Nussbaum's.[44]

2. Defining "Objectification"

Where do all the above points leave us? What is a plausible understanding of objectification? It appears that there is no reason to accept either the narrow or the broad conception of objectification as they are. However, drawing on these two conceptions and learning from their defects can direct us toward a more plausible conception of objectification.

To begin with, the discussion above indicates that we are better off without the category of benign or positive objectification. In other words, it seems preferable to restrict our conception of objectification to include only those cases in which people's humanity is affected in a negative way. But even if we want to reserve the term "objectification" for the description of the negative, we should not confine ourselves to the claim that objectification necessarily involves harming a person's humanity, because, as we have seen, there are cases of negative, yet harmless, objectification. However, we also want to avoid the consequence that negative, yet harmless, objectification is pervasive.

This leads us back to Nussbaum. According to her, negative objectification is regarding or treating a person as an object in a way that involves denying this person's humanity. A person's humanity can be denied, as we have seen, when it is in some way harmed, or simply when it is ignored or not fully acknowledged. For example, when MacKinnon and Dworkin claim that women are reduced to the status of mere objects for men's use through objectification, they take it that women's humanity is actually harmed. This is because they lose their status as persons and, according to these feminists, become mere sexual tools for men's pleasure. However, we can argue, against MacKinnon and Dworkin, that a man can treat a woman as a mere sexual tool, without her necessarily acquiring the status of an object. In this case, the man in question has not fully acknowledged the woman's humanity, but (maybe because he lacked the power and authority required) he has not reduced her to a thing and thereby harmed her humanity.

Adopting Nussbaum's understanding of negative objectification saves us from committing ourselves to the unreasonable requirement that objectification necessarily involves a serious harm to a person's humanity. What is problematic with objectification, in most of the cases at least, is that it involves ignoring or not fully acknowledging people's humanity. But objectification must also involve some sort of *treatment* (as opposed to mere regard), otherwise we turn objectification into a pervasive feature of our lives, a consequence, we have seen, that we should avoid. For example, if I am walking down the street and do not pay attention to the people walking by me, then this is not objectification, because even though one might argue that I did not acknowledge their humanity, there is no treatment involved. However, if the taxi driver asks to be paid after dropping me at my destination but I laugh in his face and leave without paying, then this would be objectification because my ignoring his humanity involves *treatment*—it involves treating him in a certain way (as a mere tool for my purposes).

The above directs us toward the following definition of objectification:

> *Objectification is treating a person as an object (treating him or her in one or more of these seven ways: as an instrument, inert, fungible, violable, owned, denied autonomy, denied subjectivity), in such a way that denies this person's humanity. A person's humanity is denied when it is ignored or not fully acknowledged, or when it is in some way harmed.* (Inclusive "or" in the whole definition.)

We can, furthermore, distinguish between different forms of objectification:

(a) Reductive–Non-Reductive Objectification: Objectification is *reductive* when the objectified individual's humanity is in some way harmed. When such harm occurs, a person's status as a being with rational capacities is diminished or *reduced*; think of MacKinnon and Dworkin's claim about women losing their humanity and actually acquiring the status of objects. Objectification is *non-reductive* when the objectified individual's humanity is not thus harmed, but merely ignored or not fully acknowledged. For example, even though I ignored the taxi driver's humanity in refusing to pay him for his service, I have nonetheless not made him into an object, damaging his status as a being with humanity.

(b) Intentional–Unintentional Objectification: Objectification is *intentional* when the objectifier, *A*, has the intention of denying (either in the sense of harming or in the sense of merely ignoring or not fully acknowledging) *B*'s humanity, and *A* succeeds in denying *B*'s humanity. Objectification is *unintentional* when *A* does not intend to deny *B*'s humanity, yet *A* does deny it.

The second distinction is very important. Contrary to popular belief, the objectifier is not always a devious being who intentionally adopts a disrespectful attitude toward another's humanity. That is, a person might not *intend* to objectify another, to deny the latter's humanity, and yet do so. For example, assuming pornography has the power to construct reality, as MacKinnon and Dworkin claim, a man who treats a woman as a mere sexual instrument might not have the intention to disrespect her humanity. Pornography passes the message that women exist to be sexually used by men. The man in question, we can say, only intends to gain sexual satisfaction. And he achieves this purpose in using a woman the way it is considered appropriate to do so, not realizing that his behavior is morally problematic.

Given the above, we can see how my conception of objectification does not imply that objectification occurs left and right, and how it is thus narrower than Nussbaum's conception. Like Nussbaum's, my understanding of objectification can involve ignoring or not fully acknowledging a person's humanity (and not necessarily harming a person's humanity). However, my conception of objectification is less inclusive than Nussbaum's because (a) it always involves *treating* a person as an object (as opposed to merely *regarding* her as an object) in ways that lead to the denial of her humanity, in the form of either ignoring or not fully acknowledging humanity or in the form of harming her humanity, and (b) unlike Nussbaum's conception, according to which objectification can occur even if there is no denial of the objectified individual's humanity (positive objectification), my conception leaves no room for positive objectification: if there is no denial of humanity, then there is no objectification. In other words, objectification can only be negative.

According to my suggested conception of objectification, a necessary and sufficient condition for objectification is *denying a person's humanity* in treating them as an object. But when does this denial of humanity occur? For example, in cases where a person is treated merely as a means for another's purposes or as a completely non-autonomous being, there is denial of humanity, thus objectification. But what happens when, for

example, two partners occasionally deny each other's autonomy and subjectivity in their relationship? Do they deny each other's humanity? In
other words, do they objectify each other? Unfortunately, there is not a
straightforward answer to this question. Nussbaum argues that examining the overall context of the relationship can often indicate whether
denial of humanity has occurred.[45] Taking this route, as Nussbaum herself is aware, requires relying largely on our intuitions, and we are to
expect disagreement and confusion. Another option is to claim that in
such cases there is objectification, but its moral wrongness is negligible.[46]
Hopefully, ongoing philosophical research will lead us to a more precise
and coherent understanding of the "slippery" and "multiple" concept of
objectification.[47]

NOTES

1. See Immanuel Kant, *Groundwork of the Metaphysics of Morals*, translated by Mary
Gregor (Cambridge: Cambridge University Press, 1997), 428, 431, 434–36, and Kant,
The Metaphysics of Morals, translated by Mary Gregor (Cambridge: Cambridge University Press, 1996), 4: 434–35, 462.
2. Kant, *Groundwork*, 4: 429.
3. Kant, *Lectures on Ethics*, translated by Peter Heath and edited by Jerome B.
Schneewind (Cambridge: Cambridge University Press, 1997), 27: 384–85.
4. Kant, *Lectures*, 27: 384–85.
5. Kant, *Lectures*, 27: 387.
6. Kant, *Lectures*, 27: 386–87.
7. Kant, *Lectures*, 27: 388.
8. See Alan Soble, "Sexual Use," in this volume on the two wrongs of Kantian
objectification.
9. For example, see Carol Pateman, *The Sexual Contract* (Stanford, Calif: Stanford
University Press, 1988); Laurie Shrage, "Should Feminists Oppose Prostitution?" *Ethics* 99:2 (1989), 347–61; Christine Overall, "What's Wrong with Prostitution? Evaluating Sex Work," *Signs* 17:4 (1992), 705–24; Scott Anderson, "Prostitution and Sexual
Autonomy: Making Sense of the Prohibition and Prostitution," in *Prostitution and Pornography: Philosophical Debate about the Sex Industry*, edited by Jessica Spector (Stanford,
Calif.: Stanford University Press, 2006), 358–93; Patricia Marino, "The Ethics of Sexual
Objectification: Autonomy and Consent," *Inquiry* 51:4 (2008), 345–64.
10. Kant, *Lectures*, 27: 388–89, and Kant, *Metaphysics*, 6: 277–80. For an analysis of
Kant's conception of marriage, see Lina Papadaki, "Kantian Marriage and Beyond:
Why It Is Worth Thinking About Kant on Marriage," *Hypatia* 25:2 (2010), 276–94.
11. See Laurie Shrage, "Exposing the Fallacies of Anti-Porn Feminism," *Feminist
Theory* 6:1 (2005), 45–65, at 49, and Andrea Dworkin, *Men Possessing Women* (New
York: E. P. Dutton, 1989), 19.
12. MacKinnon discusses this distinction between sex and gender in her books:
Feminism Unmodified (Cambridge, Mass.: Harvard University Press, 1987), 6, 32–45, 50,
and *Towards a Feminist Theory of the State* (Cambridge, Mass.: Harvard University
Press, 1989), 113–14, 128, 137–40. For an illuminating analysis of MacKinnon's views
on sex and gender, see Sally Haslanger, "On Being Objective and Being Objectified,"
in *A Mind of One's Own: Feminist Essays on Reason and Objectivity*, edited by Louise M.
Antony and Charlotte Witt (Boulder, Colo.: Westview Press, 1993), 209–53, at 98–101,
and Joan Mason-Grant, *Pornography Embodied: From Speech to Sexual Practice* (Lanham,
Md.: Rowman & Littlefield, 2004).
13. MacKinnon, *Feminism Unmodified*, 196.

14. MacKinnon, *Feminism Unmodified*, 173.

15. Andrea Dworkin, "Against the Male Flood: Censorship, Pornography, and Inequality," in *Oxford Readings in Feminism: Feminism and Pornography*, edited by Drucilla Cornell (Oxford: Oxford University Press, 2000), 19–38, at 30–31.

16. MacKinnon, *Feminism Unmodified*, 158.

17. MacKinnon, *Feminism Unmodified*, 138.

18. MacKinnon, *Only Words* (Cambridge, Mass.: Harvard University Press, 1993), 28.

19. Andrea Dworkin, *Intercourse* (New York: Free Press Paperbacks, 1997), 142–43.

20. Dworkin, *Men Possessing Women*, 19.

21. MacKinnon, *Only Words*, 15. See Rae Langton, "Speech Acts and Unspeakable Acts," *Philosophy and Public Affairs* 22:4 (1993), 293–330, for an illumination of MacKinnon's claim that pornography deprives women of speech.

22. Alan Soble, *Pornography, Sex, and Feminism* (New York: Prometheus Books, 2002), 67.

23. Soble, *Pornography, Sex, and Feminism*, 53–54.

24. Soble, *Pornography, Sex, and Feminism*, 51–52.

25. Leslie Green, "Pornographies," *Journal of Political Philosophy* 8:1 (2000), 27–52, at 44.

26. Green, "Pornographies," 45–46.

27. Green, "Pornographies," 46.

28. Martha Nussbaum, "Objectification," *Philosophy and Public Affairs* 24:4 (1995), 249–91, at 251.

29. Nussbaum, "Objectification," 251, 256–57, 257, respectively.

30. Nussbaum, "Objectification," 257. Rae Langton adds three more features involved in objectification: (8) *reduction to body*: the treatment of a person as identified with their body, or body parts; (9) *reduction to appearance*: the treatment of a person primarily in terms of how they look, or how they appear to the senses; (10) *silencing*: the treatment of a person as if they are silent, lacking the capacity to speak. See "Autonomy–Denial in Objectification," in *Sexual Solipsism: Philosophical Essays on Pornography and Objectification* (Oxford: Oxford University Press, 2009), 223–40, at 22–229.

31. Nussbaum, "Objectification," 258.

32. Nussbaum, "Objectification," 290.

33. Nussbaum, "Objectification," 285.

34. Nussbaum, "Objectification," 265.

35. Nussbaum, "Objectification," 250–51.

36. Nussbaum, "Objectification," 265.

37. Nussbaum, "Objectification," 274.

38. Nussbaum, "Objectification," 274.

39. Nussbaum, "Objectification," 275.

40. Nussbaum, "Objectification," 275–76.

41. For some difficulties (additional to the ones I raise below) with Nussbaum's view, see Soble's "Sexual Use" in this volume.

42. In addition to what she writes on page 251, Nussbaum also writes, "So: we have five examples of conduct that seems to deserve, in some sense, the name of 'objectification.' In each case, a human being is regarded and/or treated as an object in the context of a sexual relationship" (Nussbaum, "Objectification," 254).

43. Whether this also affects past and future people depends on what we mean by "ignoring or not fully acknowledging another's humanity."

44. Raja Halwani also argues that, in Nussbaum's positive objectification cases, there seems to be no objectification to begin with. Taking this line of argument is better than "engaging in mental gymnastics to try to show that there is objectification but that it is okay or good." See Raja Halwani, *Philosophy of Love, Sex, and Marriage: An Introduction* (New York: Routledge, 2010), 197.

45. Nussbaum, "Objectification," 217. According to Nussbaum, if the relationship between the two parties is one characterized by equality and reciprocity, it is less

likely that people's humanity is denied. This is obvious in her discussion of "Lawrentian objectification," where we can see parallels with the ideal of equality and reciprocity in Kant's conception of marriage ("Objectification," 274–75).

46. Raja Halwani takes this approach; see "Casual Sex, Promiscuity, and Objectification," in this volume.

47. Nussbaum, "Objectification," 251. I thank the editors for their helpful suggestions on earlier drafts of this essay.

STUDY QUESTIONS

1. Are human beings mere objects like tables and chairs and so cannot be objectified? If we are different, how are we different? And would this difference (or these differences) be morally relevant? And, finally, depending on your answers, can nonhuman animals be objectified?

2. Is there such a thing as subjectification? What would it be, exactly? Can you give one or two detailed examples? Is subjectification morally problematic for reasons similar to those that make objectification wrong?

3. Papadaki claims that we ought to take Kant's claims about sex reducing someone into a thing with "a grain of salt" because Kant's claims are unclear and might be exaggerated. Is there a way to interpret Kant so that his claims come out plausible? For some help with this, see Raja Halwani, "Casual Sex, Promiscuity, and Objectification," and Alan Soble, "Sexual Use," both in this volume.

4. According to Papadaki's Nussbaum, objectification can involve mere regard, without treatment, and this can be either positive or negative. Provide two detailed examples of objectification as mere regard, one example of positive objectification and the other of negative objectification. Are there examples of objectification involving mere treatment, but no regard?

5. What is the difference between ignoring someone's humanity and not fully acknowledging it? And is there a way to understand these two ideas that would avoid the implication that we are constantly engaging in objectification because we are constantly ignoring or not fully acknowledging someone's humanity, somewhere?

6. Papadaki states about the taxi driver example, "Even though I ignored the taxi driver's humanity in refusing to pay him for his service, I have nonetheless not made him into an object, damaging his status as a being with humanity." Is this correct? *Why* has she not made him into an object by not paying him? To think about this further, consider a variation on the example in which Papadaki *does* pay the driver, but, before she pays him, when he says to her,

"That will be \$35, ma'am," she replies, "You idiot. Of course I will pay you. Here's your stupid money," and she throws it at him.

7. In her concluding paragraph, Papadaki states, "[W]hat happens when, for example, two partners occasionally deny each other's autonomy and subjectivity in their relationship? Do they deny each other's humanity? In other words, do they objectify each other? Unfortunately, there is not a straightforward answer to this question." What do you think? Is there (negative) objectification in such cases? Why or why not?

8. Does pornography objectify women any more than it objectifies men? Is its objectification really bad? What view do you have on this issue, and is it closer to Nussbaum's, Soble's, or Dworkin and MacKinnon's?

9. Papadaki rejects Nussbaum's account of objectification partly because it includes some cases of merely regarding someone as an object (but not subjecting them to any treatment). Given this, can Papadaki consistently also maintain that the women (or men) in pornography are objectified by the viewers of pornography?

TWENTY-TWO

Casual Sex, Promiscuity, and Objectification

Raja Halwani

After discussing the definitions of "casual sex," "promiscuity," and "objectifica-tion" and examining some of their attendant difficulties, **Raja Halwani** *ad-dresses the morality of objectification in connection with casual sex and promis-cuity. He understands casual sex as "no-strings-attached" sex and promiscuity as frequent instances of casual sex (albeit with different partners within a short period of time). Assuming a pessimistic metaphysical view of sexual desire, Hal-wani argues that it is nearly impossible to defend casual sex and promiscuity against the accusation of objectification; even though a case can be made that casual sex and promiscuity do not necessarily involve objectification, they likely do. He concludes by suggesting that the wrongness of the objectification in casual sex and promiscuity might not be very serious and that both types of sexuality might, as a result, be overall morally permissible.*

This essay originally appeared under the title "On Fucking Around," in *The Philosophy of Sex: Contemporary Readings*, 6th ed., edited by Nicholas Power, Raja Halwani, and Alan Soble (Lanham, Md.: Rowman & Littlefield, 2013), 441–60. It is reprinted in our volume, under a new title, with the permission of Raja Halwani.

Many people consider casual sex and promiscuity (CS&P) morally wrong, even if they admit that their practitioners find these activities pleasurable. CS&P are also thought to provide fertile ground for objectifi-cation, a philosophically thorny concept. After discussing issues of defi-nition—philosophically interesting on their own—I discuss the ethics of CS&P as far as objectification is concerned. I argue that, even though the case can be made that they do not necessarily involve objectification, they

401

are likely to objectify, given a particular and plausible view of sexual desire. However, I suggest that the wrongness of objectification can be overcome by other considerations, such that CS&P might in general be morally permissible.

DEFINITIONAL ISSUES

1. Casual Sex

Casual sex is sexual activity that occurs outside the context of a relationship. Often, but not always, the parties who engage in it seek only sexual pleasure. Typical examples include Internet hook-ups, bar hook-ups, sex between pornography actors, and anonymous encounters in gay bathhouses, gay or straight sex clubs, and straight swingers clubs.

However, it is difficult to define "casual sex" in terms of necessary and sufficient conditions; any proposed criterion that distinguishes casual from non-casual sex faces difficulties. Suppose that the criterion is that the intention be only for sexual pleasure. This sounds right, since people who have casual sex usually do it only for sexual pleasure. But people in relationships (e.g., married couples, friends, couples in love) have sex often solely for sexual pleasure, yet the sex between them is not casual. So the criterion won't do as a sufficient condition. It is also not necessary, because some people have casual sex not for sexual pleasure but for other reasons. For example, prostitutes do it for money, stressed individuals do it for release, and vain people do it to maintain their lofty self-image.

Here's a second criterion: that there is no marriage, love relationship, or committed relationship between the parties to the casual sex.[1] If such a relationship exists, the sex is not casual. If there is no such relationship, the sex is casual. Why emphasize marriage, love, and committed relationships, not other types of relationship? Because what matters is the right kind of commitment, whose very nature renders the activities between its parties, whether sexual or non-sexual, non-casual, such as love, marriage, deep friendship (acquaintances and work relationships are not such commitments). Is being in a relationship sufficient for the sex to be non-casual? It seems to be. We have seen above that even if the couple has sex for pleasure, being a couple is enough to make the sex non-casual. Moreover, even if they have a "quickie" before darting off to work, the sex still seems to be non-casual precisely because they are in a relationship. So being in a relationship seems to be sufficient for the sex to be non-casual.

But it does not seem to be necessary. Suppose that Fyodor and Leila meet in a bar, sparks fly (without the help of alcohol), and they go home and have sex with each other, each thinking that they have just met the love of their life, vowing to each other their eternal love. However, come morning, each says to him- and herself, "What was I thinking?" Did

Fyodor and Leila have casual sex? If they did not because they intended the sex to be a prelude to a relationship, then we have an example of non-casual sex outside a committed relationship. So the proposed criterion is not necessary.

Here's a third criterion: that the parties to the sex act intend, hope, or desire (or something along these lines) that the sex act not lead to any commitment. If such an intention (or, more generally, mental state) exists, then the sex is casual. If it doesn't exist, then it is not casual. This criterion is the most plausible one. For if the parties to a sex act have such a mental state it is hard to see how the ensuing sex is not casual. So it seems to be a sufficient condition. Moreover, it seems correct to think that if their sexual activity is casual, then such a mental state exists, so it seems to also be a necessary condition.

The plausible idea behind this criterion is captured by the phrase "no strings attached" (hence the expression "NSA sex"). The idea is that the consent of the parties to the sexual act does not imply a commitment beyond the act—no commitment to love, to marriage, or to even seeing each other again for solely sexual purposes. However, the trick is how to clearly state this idea. Is it (a) that the consent implies no commitment beyond the act? Or is it (b) that the consent does not imply a commitment beyond the act? The first requires an explicit mental state on the part of the parties for no commitment, whereas (b) leaves things open and could be satisfied by the lack of any mental state. Though (b) is probably more common, I adopt (a) because it focuses on clear cases of casual sex, ruling out ambiguous ones (e.g., one or more parties having no clear mental states about the future).

But there are two complications. First, must *each* party to the sex act have such a mental state? Or is it enough that one or some do? What if X does not intend or want a commitment but Y does?[2] Second, *which* mental state should count? Suppose that Leslie and Pat know that they should not be in a committed relationship, so they *intend* the sex between them to not lead to commitment. But suppose they also yearn for love, so they *hope* that it does. Is the ensuing sex between them casual, because of their intention, or not, because of their hope?

Despite these complications, I define "casual sex" as "NSA sex, such that the consent of the parties implies no commitment beyond the act." The definition gives us what we need for our discussion.

2. Promiscuity

Obviously, having sex many times is crucial for understanding promiscuity. But with *whom* one has sex is also crucial. If John has sex twenty times a week with his partner (his marital spouse, the person he loves, or even his friend-with-benefits), we would be happy for him and hope that his partner's sexual drive matches his, but he would not be promiscuous.

A promiscuous person has sex with *different* people, although a precise number is impossible to decide. The period of time is also important: having sex with ten different people during a period of twenty years is not much, but during one month is (again, the precise length of the period is impossible to decide). So the period of time during which one has sex and with whom one has it are crucial to whether someone is promiscuous.

What are the connections, if any, between casual sex and promiscuity? Perhaps promiscuity implies casual sex, but not vice versa: Someone who is promiscuous has, simply in virtue of that fact, casual sex because he has NSA sex (albeit a lot of it), but someone who has casual sex is not, simply in virtue of that fact, promiscuous, because he might have casual sex very few times during his life (maybe even only once). But suppose that Nadia wants to be in a love relationship, but the (or one) way she tries to do so is by having sex with any man she thinks might be Mr. Right, only to be disappointed and to have to start over. Is Nadia promiscuous? Some might say "no" because she intends each sexual act to be the start, or part, of a new love relationship. Some might say "yes" because her intentions are irrelevant and because she has sex with many different men during a brief period of time. Is Nadia having casual sex? Again, some might say "no," because of her intentions, and some "yes," because none of the sex acts leads to, or ends being part of, a love relationship. (On this essay's definition, Nadia is not having casual sex because she desires a commitment beyond the sexual act.) Now, *if* Nadia is promiscuous but is not engaging in casual sex, then promiscuity does not imply casual sex, because someone could be promiscuous and not be having casual sex. Although it depends on the relevance of intentions (and hopes and other such mental states) to promiscuity and casual sex, the Nadia example is strong enough to shake our faith in the idea that promiscuous sex implies casual sex.

However, I set aside cases like Nadia's and focus on cases in which someone intends to engage in casual sex and on cases in which someone intends to be promiscuous (because she, e.g., does not want to be entangled in the complexities of love, who likes sex, and who likes sexual variety). I focus on these cases because, first, if CS&P are morally suspicious, then intentionally engaging in them is worse than unintentionally engaging in them, so we would be in the thick of the moral issues. Second, because as far as *only* objectification is concerned, whatever is morally wrong with someone who intentionally has casual sex would also be wrong with the person who is intentionally promiscuous (thus, the second person might, for non-objectification-related reasons, be ethically defective in ways the first person is not). Any objectification-related differences between them would then be in terms of the number of ethical wrongs committed: a promiscuous person would engage in a lot more objectification than someone who has casual sex only a few times.

One final restriction: I focus on cases of CS&P in which the motive of the parties is to attain sexual pleasure (or to satisfy their sexual desires), not, say, to make money. This keeps the discussion manageable and confined to the type of cases people usually have in mind when they think of CS&P.

3. Objectification

The idea of objectification has its roots in Immanuel Kant's ethics. Kant thought that, because of the very nature of sexual desire, the parties to a sex act use each other and themselves, and then discard each other like "a lemon which has been sucked dry."³ I return to Kant's views below because they are necessary for a discussion of CS&P.

To objectify a person is to treat him only as if an object. For example, Christa treats Tania as an object if she uses Tania as a chair while reading the newspaper. Objectification is a morally charged concept. To accuse someone of objectification is to accuse her of doing wrong. For to objectify someone is to treat him only as an object, thereby bringing him down from the level of being human or a person to the level of an object, thus degrading or dehumanizing him. Why? Because to be a person is to have a special property or quality that other objects (including plants and most, if not all, animals) lack and in virtue of which human beings are to be treated in morally special ways. This property might be dignity, rationality, autonomy, self-consciousness, being created in God's image, or something along these lines. To treat someone merely as an object is to bypass or neglect to treat him in accordance with this property, thereby degrading or dehumanizing him. Thus, it is to treat him in a morally wrong way.

Note three things. First, someone can intentionally *or* unintentionally bypass or neglect this special property, so someone can engage in objectification unintentionally or unawares. This does not mean that no wrong has been done, only that the objectifier is not to be blamed or held responsible (unless he should have known better). So *if* to have casual sex is necessarily to objectify the sexual partner, then one objectifies regardless of whether one intends to objectify (do not confuse intending to have casual sex with intending to objectify).

Second, if human beings are nothing but objects to begin with, albeit with a morally inflated name ("person"), then there is nothing wrong with objectification: we cannot act wrongly in treating an object merely as an object if it is nothing but an object to begin with.⁴ Third, if human beings are not merely objects but are nonetheless *not* loftier than objects, then, again, objectification would not be wrong because by treating human beings as nothing but objects one would not be degrading them or lowering their status. Thus, for objectification to be wrong, we must (and will) assume that human beings are not mere objects (a plausible assumption) *and* that they have a morally higher status than objects (a controversial assumption).[5]

Two crucial questions immediately arise. First, is objectification only an issue of treatment? Can't we objectify someone only by regarding him—purely mentally viewing him—as merely an object?[6] Although it makes sense to speak about objectifying someone merely by regarding him as only an object, if the wrong of objectification is that it dehumanizes and degrades the person who is objectified, it is hard to see how merely regarding someone as only an object actually dehumanizes or degrades him. Mere regard reveals a moral defect or vice in the person who has this attitude, but it does not actually degrade the person so regarded. For actual degradation to occur, some form of treatment must occur. In any case, even if degradation occurs in mere regard, surely its meatiest and most important forms are those that result from treatment, so I shall continue to discuss objectification in terms of treatment.

The second question is: Is the "only" in "to objectify a person is to treat him only as an object" needed to understand the wrong of objectification? Wouldn't X still be objectifying Y, thus doing something wrong, even if X does not treat Y *only* as an object? (Note that if X treats Y with respect and affection most of the time but during sex—or other situations—treats Y only as an object, X still objectifies Y during those times.)[7] To see whether treating someone as an-object-but-not-only-as-an-object is morally problematic, we should ask whether it is possible to treat someone as not an object at all, because if this is possible, then treating them as objects, whether "only" or not, would be morally defective given the better option of not treating them as objects at all.

One way of treating someone as an object is to treat her as an instrument or a tool for our purposes. Yet there seems no escape from this treatment in human interaction. In virtually any example of human interaction—between grocer and shopper, salesperson and client, student and teacher, tenant and landlord, flight attendant and passenger, waiter and diner, and so on—we use people as tools: we use the grocer as a tool to obtain our groceries, the tenant to make an income, and so forth. Even in interactions between friends and loved ones, about which we don't believe that people use each other as tools (e.g., a lover giving his beloved a gift), one might argue that the lover uses his beloved as a tool to attain his goals (of, e.g., giving her a gift: no beloved, no gift-giving).[8] We can then plausibly assume that treating each other as tools is unavoidable. (Perhaps those who believe that not every human interaction involves using people as tools should provide us with uncontroversial cases.) What we should aim for, then, is to treat them *not merely* as tools or objects.

However, one might claim that being used as a tool is only *one* way to be objectified. Are there not other ways in which we *can* avoid using people as objects altogether?

Martha Nussbaum lists seven different ways to objectify someone. Rae Langton adds three. I quote them at length (this is also useful for the discussion in Part II). Nussbaum's list:

1. *Instrumentality*: The objectifier treats the object as a tool of his or her purposes.
2. *Denial of autonomy*: The objectifier treats the object as lacking in autonomy and self-determination.
3. *Inertness*: The objectifier treats the object as lacking in agency, and perhaps also in activity.
4. *Fungibility*: The objectifier treats the object as interchangeable (a) with other objects of the same type and/or (b) with objects of other types.
5. *Violability*: The objectifier treats the object as lacking in boundary integrity, as something that is permissible to break up, smash, break into.
6. *Ownership*: The objectifier treats the object as something owned by another, can be bought and sold, and so on.
7. *Denial of subjectivity*: The objectifier treats the object as something whose experience and feelings (if any) need not be taken into account.[9]

Langton's additional three:

8. *Reduction to body*: One treats [the person] as identified with his or her body, or body parts.
9. *Reduction to appearance*: One treats [the person] primarily in terms of how he or she looks, or how he or she appears to the senses.
10. *Silencing*: One treats [the person] as silent, lacking the capacity to speak.[10]

Other than instrumentality (already addressed), we can treat people as not objects, at all, in any of those ways. We need not treat others as incapable of making decisions (lacking autonomy and self-determination), as lacking in agency (inert), as interchangeable with others (fungible), as permissible to smash up (violable), as owned, as having no feelings and experience, and as reduced to body and appearance. If the above list is a list of ways of treating people as objects, then it is possible to not treat people as objects, at all, in any of these ways.

But note that for each of these ways, the only way to treat someone as an object is by treating her *only* as an object. For example, I cannot treat someone as violable *while at the same time* treating her as inviolable: I cannot treat Omar as something permissible to cut up, lacerate, bounce up and down, and so on, while simultaneously treating him as someone with boundaries that I should not overstep. Similar reasoning applies to the rest (again, excepting instrumentality).[11] Thus, even though we can avoid treating people in any of these ways as objects, if we do treat them as objects, we cannot simultaneously treat them as more than objects. Instrumentality is unique in this respect: as we shall see, it is possible to treat someone as an instrument but not only as an instrument.

Do not confuse "treating X as lacking in A," as the above ways state, with "justifiably overriding X's A." To justifiably override X's A is not to treat X as an object, because the former is morally permissible, even sometimes required. For example, I may override X's inviolability by cutting off X's arm to save X's life. I may override X's capacity to speak to allow others to speak. I may reduce X to mere appearance if I am dressing X for X's role in a play. I may treat X as fungible if I approach X as a grocer, barista, and so on—as someone who agrees to compete with others in offering a service.

Thus, except for instrumentality, none of these eight ways undermines the definition of "objectification" as treating someone *only* as an object. We can then conclude that to objectify someone, one does indeed have to treat her *only* as an object. However, one type of objectification— instrumentality—can be avoided by treating the person as not only an object. Let's now see whether CS&P can avoid objectification.

MORAL ISSUES

1. Why CS&P Might Be Necessarily Objectifying

If objectification is always morally wrong and is a necessary feature of casual sex, casual sex is necessarily wrong. If promiscuity is multiple instances of casual sex with different people, promiscuity is also necessarily wrong. But why believe that objectification is a necessary feature of CS&P? The argument might go as follows. In engaging in CS&P, people have NSA sex for sexual pleasure. They thus use each other—they treat each other as objects, as tools—for the purpose of attaining this pleasure. Even if they provide each other with pleasure, they do so because (i) this gives them pleasure (the man performing oral sex on the woman finds giving oral sex pleasurable), (ii) the receiver's pleasure enhances the provider's own pleasure (the man finds the woman's pleasure from receiving oral sex pleasurable), or (iii) the provider desires that the receiver return the favor. They use each other for their selfish or self-interested (I gloss over the differences between these two categories) sexual pleasure. Thus, CS&P involve objectification: its parties use each other's bodies for the satisfaction of their sexual desires.

Supporting the above argument is a pessimist view of sexual desire according to which:[12] (1) Sexual desire targets people's bodies and body parts, thus coming dangerously close to making us view the people we sexually desire as objects (albeit live ones). (2) To satisfy sexual desire, we engage in all sorts of shenanigans, such as deception and lies ("Yes! I, too, loved *The English Patient!*"), and dressing in ways to conceal our defects and highlight, if any, our assets (which might also be a form of deception). (3) Unless intruded upon by anxieties, worries, or—crucially—moral thoughts, sexual activity can be so pleasurable and consuming that parties to it lose control over themselves and lose "regard for the humanity of the other person."[13] (4) To satisfy sexual desire, we allow our reason to be subverted, and we do irrational, stupid things both to get someone to have sex with us and during the sexual act (e.g., unsafe sex). Finally, (5) when they do attend to each other's desires, they do so, again, either because they find this pleasurable in itself or because they desire to receive sexual attention in return.

CS&P epitomize the above features of sexual desire. Precisely because CS&P are NSA sex whose goal is sexual pleasure, its parties (1) focus on and use the other's body and body parts to attain sexual pleasure; (2) more easily rationalize lies and deception because there is no future commitment to each other; (3) more easily give themselves up to sexual abandon because, again, there is no future commitment; (4) are more willing to put each other at risk for the same reason; and (5) if they do provide pleasure for each other, they do so as a means to attaining their own sexual pleasure. So X attends to Y's pleasure because this gives X pleasure (X enjoys the activity, enjoys Y's pleasure in receiving the activity, or desires that Y return the favor). Indeed, attending to Y's pleasure *for Y's own sake* seems to require that X "snap out" of the grip of X's own sexual desire so that X can focus on Y and on Y's pleasure, which would kill or severely dampen X's sexual desire or pleasure, thereby defeating the very point of X's engaging in CS&P. So CS&P satisfy to the hilt the selfishness or self-interestedness of sexual desire. They are, then, necessarily objectifying.

If pessimism about sexual desire is true, what can the defender of CS&P say in their defense? Obviously, he can reject the pessimist view.[14] But to see whether CS&P objectify, we must accept the worst about sexual desire. If we don't, not only do we take the easy way out, but we also cannot be sure that sexual desire is not objectifying (what if the pessimist about sex is correct?).

Instead, the defender of CS&P can adopt two argumentative strategies. First, he can argue that objectification is not a *necessary* feature of CS&P; whether CS&P objectify depends on whether they fall short of the conditions required to avoid objectification. Second, he can argue that even if CS&P objectify (whether because objectification is a necessary feature of CS&P or because it happens to be present in a particular act), other factors might override it such that the sexual act is not, overall, morally wrong. Let's start with the first strategy.

2. Why CS&P Are Not Necessarily Objectifying: First Attempt

Consider again Nussbaum and Langton's ways in which people can be objectified. Clearly, casual sex need not involve one partner treating the other as lacking in autonomy, as inert, as violable, as owned, and as lacking subjectivity. Indeed, it (usually) involves the exact opposite. For example, in taking into account Clark's sexual desires, Lois considers him to have autonomy, self-determination, and agency. Furthermore, she does not consider him to be violable, because she attributes to him boundaries and integrity in two ways: first, by not treating Clark contrary to his desires and, second, precisely by treating him in accordance with his desires. Lois also, for the same reasons, does not treat Clark as an owned object. Finally, in taking his sexual desires and needs into account, she certainly does not treat him "as something whose experience and feelings . . . need not be taken into account."[15]

Moreover, because partners to casual sex can take each other's desires and wants into account they do not treat each other as mere bodies, even though they usually focus on each other's bodies and even though they probably engage in casual sex *because* they like each other's physical appearance.[16] But it does not follow that objectification is occurring, unless it also follows (which it does not) that in my focusing on a dancer's body or a chef's hands I objectify her.

They also, for similar reasons, don't treat each other as incapable of speaking.[17] And while the focus on each other's body could take the form of treating the other "primarily in terms of how they look," this need not imply objectification. Indeed, in signing up for casual sex, the partners expect and even want to be treated primarily in terms of their appearance: if a woman or a man is proud of their shapely thighs, they might want their partner to pay sexual attention to them. For the same reasons, promiscuity need not involve objectification in any of the above ways.

This leaves us with instrumentality and fungibility. Consider fungibility first. Suppose that X goes to a bar in search of casual sex. In doing so, X treats the people in the bar as fungible, as interchangeable with others of the same type (potential sex partners for X). Yet no one should object that X is somehow treating one wrongly, because, like merchants who compete for people's money, people in a bar often compete for others' sexual attention. They consent to being treated as interchangeable with other people of the same type.

With instrumentality, the argument also relies on consent. So long as the parties consent to the act, they do not treat each other merely as tools. Consent, that is, is sufficient to convert using someone merely as a means into using someone not merely as a means, because in consenting to what Y desires, X respects Y's wishes. Thus, and to return to the grocer example, by, or in, paying him, we respect his wishes to be a seller, not someone to be abused and robbed. This seems to be true of CS&P. Like many non-sexual interactions, the partners respect each other's sexual needs, desires, and wishes. X is willing to perform oral sex on Y if Y desires it (X is even sometimes happy to!). Indeed, even if X uses Y only as a "piece of meat," X would not use Y only as a tool as long as X is complying with Y's desire to "Use me as a piece of meat!" In doing Y's bidding, X seems to not be objectifying Y—that is, treating Y *merely* as an object. If anything, it seems to be a form of respect.

So runs the argument attempting to show why CS&P are not necessarily objectifying. In short, so long as the parties do not treat each other in all the possible ways of objectifying someone, or, if they do, do so with each other's consent, CS&P are not, in those cases, objectifying. Therefore, CS&P are not necessarily objectifying.

3. Why the First Attempt Fails

Given the pessimist view of sexual desire, the above defense of CS&P is problematic because it does not fully appreciate the problem with sexual desire, especially in regard to instrumentality.[18] Consider that while Kant agrees that consent is sufficient to render many human interactions non-objectifying, he disagrees regarding sex. The reason is that sexual desire is pernicious (a pessimist view of sex), since it is the only human "inclination" that "is directed towards other human beings. They themselves, and not their work and services, are its Objects of enjoyment."[19] Sexual desire makes its object exactly that—an *object* of desire. Because by its nature sexual desire pushes human beings to disregard the humanity in each other (and in themselves), consent is *not enough* to make sexual activity non-objectifying. Thus, if X and Y consent to a sexual act, they consent to an immoral activity. Indeed, each consents to two moral wrongs: X consents to objectify Y and to be objectified by Y (ditto for Y).[20]

To Kant, we must never treat people only as a means, but always, at the same time, as an end. It is not fully clear what this means, but one crucial idea is that when dealing with other people we must *respect their morally permissible goals*. Often, this is satisfied simply by not hindering them. But sometimes we must *adopt* them: we must take on others' goals as our own. In Kant's words, "we make others our end" and we have a duty "to make the human being as such as an end."[21] We must help that person promote his goals for his or her sake, not for selfish, self-interested, or other reasons.

Now given the pessimist view of sexual desire, CS&P face two difficulties. First, if sexual desire makes us view our sexual partners as tools for its satisfaction, it is hard to see how partners to CS&P can adopt each other's sexual goals *for their own sakes*. Second, even if this is possible, it is hard to see why they *may*, let alone should, because if sexual desire is by nature objectifying, it is not a morally permissible goal that may be adopted. Thus, the defender of CS&P has her work cut out for her.

But here we should be careful. The reason usually given for why satisfying sexual desire is wrong is that sexual desire is objectifying—X's satisfying Y's sexual desire is wrong because it involves X objectifying Y. So if there were cases in which sexual desire can be satisfied without objectification, satisfying it in those cases would not be wrong. For example, if X can sexually satisfy Y for Y's own sake, then X would not have objectified Y nor would have Y allowed him or herself to be objectified.

So whether sex is wrong hinges on *why* partners sexually satisfy each other's sexual desires—what their motives are. That is, the existence of the second difficulty hinges on the existence of the first. To see this point better, compare it to a non-sexual case. Suppose Y's goal is to murder Z. Can X help Y attain Y's goal for Y's own sake? Yes. Should X do so? No, because murder is wrong regardless of X's motives in helping Y. This is not so with sexual acts. There, if X can help Y attain Y's sexual goals without objectifying Y (or X allowing him or herself to be objectified), the sole (or main) reason for thinking the goal of sexual satisfaction wrong is removed. So whether X's satisfaction of Y's sexual goals is wrong depends on whether X satisfies them for Y's sake.

But the sexual pessimist is still on strong territory. As we have seen, the motives, given the nature of sexual desire, are selfish or self-interested (to attain sexual pleasure). Thus, in CS&P the partners cannot take on each other's goals for their own sakes; they thereby treat each other only as a means. Thus, CS&P are necessarily objectifying.[22]

4. Why CS&P Are Not Necessarily Objectifying: Second Attempt

We can get around this problem by distinguishing between the nature of sexual desire and particular cases of it. The idea is that even if sexual desire is by nature objectifying, this means only that it has to be especially guarded against, not that we must necessarily succumb to its pernicious nature. That is, that something is so-and-so by nature does not mean that its nature cannot be overcome (e.g., lions are by nature dangerous to human beings, but it does not mean that particular lions cannot be tamed). If true, this leaves the door open to cases in which sexual partners do not sexually objectify each other (or themselves).

What cases are these, and could some of them be of CS&P? Could X and Y, partners to a casual sex act, at least at some points during the act, attend to each other's sexual wants and pleasures for their own sake? Yes, because human beings do not always treat each other selfishly or self-interestedly. They can, and sometimes do, show concern for others even when in the grip of sexual desires or other powerful psychological forces. Kant himself gives an example of a man who, though his mind is clouded with sorrow, is able to attend to his duties to his fellow human beings.[23] The power of sexual desire, as overwhelming as it usually is, need not be so thoroughgoing that it blinds us, always, to the sexual needs of our partners. So, for example, realizing that Y enjoys receiving oral sex, X performs oral sex on Y, for the sake of Y, not because X enjoys performing oral sex on Y, not because X sexually enjoys Y's pleasure, and not because X desires Y to reciprocate, but, say, because X is genuinely committed to the happiness of others, including Y's, because X is kind, because X happens to like Y and wants Y to have a good time, because X is fair, believing that because Y gave X pleasure, X should return the favor, or even because X happens to love Y. If X can do so, then X does not objectify Y (nor does Y allow himself to be objectified if Y agrees to allow X to sexually satisfy Y from these motives by X). Thus, because partners to casual sex can satisfy Kant's requirements for treating someone else as an end, and not only as a means, casual sex is not *necessarily* objectifying. And if casual sex is not necessarily objectifying, then neither is promiscuous sex. For if promiscuous sex is frequently-engaged-in casual sex with different partners within a (short) period of time, partners to it could also attend to each other's sexual goals for their own sake; the frequency, variety, and time period of promiscuous sex are irrelevant to this (but see below).

That it is possible for X to attend to Y's sexual needs for the sake of Y says nothing, in and of itself, about X's sexual state of mind. In giving Y oral sex, X might or might not be enjoying it (and keep in mind that just because X enjoys sexually pleasing Y does not imply that X sexually pleases Y *because* X enjoys it), might or might not be disgusted by it, might or might not be indifferent to it. The point is that X performs oral sex on Y *for the sake of* Y. It concerns a type of reason or motive for performing oral sex, not X's sexual mental state. The pessimist about sexual desire (including Kant) claims that when X attends to Y's sexual goals, X does so for selfish or self-interested reasons. The defender of CS&P claims that this is not necessary, that it is possible for X to attend to Y's sexual goals for Y's own sake.[24] And if the Kantian or the pessimist thinks that such cases are impossible, she needs to show us why, given that human beings are capable of overcoming their powerful impulses in some cases.

5. Why the Second Attempt (Probably) Fails

Let's agree that it is possible for X to perform oral sex on Y for Y's own sake, from the motive of wanting to help Y attain sexual satisfaction for Y's sake (and that it is possible for Y to agree to this). Let's also agree that it is even possible that X sexually enjoys the act without thereby making X's motives morally suspect; as noted, we must not confuse X's sexually (or even non-sexually) enjoying something with X's reason for doing that thing. Still, it does not seem possible that X perform oral sex on Y from the motive of *sexual desire* without objectifying Y. That is, *if* what motivates X is sexual desire, as opposed to something else, the case is clinched, for X's sexual desire for Y precludes other motives that might render X's performing oral sex on Y non-objectifying, because to sexually desire Y *is* to desire Y as a body, as an object (on the Kantian pessimist view). Once X attends to Y's sexual needs *from* sexual desire, X objectifies Y. And when X attends to Y's sexual needs for their own sake, X does so *not* from sexual desire (we can tame the lion, but it would no longer be a lion). Indeed, Kant's charitable person who is able to help others despite his sadness does so from the motive of duty, not from sadness or the emotional state he is in. It seems, then, that sexual desire necessarily objectifies, and CS&P are in the thick of it. What needs to be shown to escape this conclusion is that one can act out of sexual desire and simultaneously attend to one's partner's sexual needs for the latter's own sake. I find this task difficult, though I don't deny its possibility (hence the "probably" in this subsection's title). I set it aside.

6. Why Casual Sex and Promiscuity Are Likely Objectifying

Even if it is true that CS&P need not necessarily objectify, this says nothing about how frequently they do and do not. This is an empirical issue, of course, but in all likelihood they *do* objectify. This is for three related reasons. First, human beings tend to be selfish and self-interested. At the very least, people's commitment to morality—if we can speak of commitment at all—is sporadic. This means that whether they act by taking on others' goals as their ends depends on their moods, emotions, what occupies them, and so forth.[25] I have no evidence for this claim in the form of empirical studies (and I'm not sure what form such studies would take), but human history, the complexity of human psychology, and simply looking around give me very little confidence that people have strong moral fiber.

Second, because satisfying sexual desire is so pleasurable (that's what makes the desire so powerful), and because attending to one's partner's sexual goals for their own sake (usually, if not always) requires getting out of the grip of one's desire, the likelihood of people attending to each other's sexual goals for their own sakes decreases. That is, if X is in the grip of sexual desire, paying attention to Y for Y's sake means getting out of the desire's grip, which means not satisfying the desire, which means no pleasure for X. This defeats one of the main purposes of having sex.

Third, because the very point of CS&P is attaining sexual pleasure, and because by definition partners to CS&P lack future commitments to each other, the likelihood that they would act selflessly toward each other is close to zero. In all likelihood, they would use each other so as to satisfy their own sexual desires, including being more willing to deceive each other, to give themselves up to sexual abandon, and to take risks. And if paying more attention to others for their own sake means less sexual pleasure, partners to CS&P are not likely at all to pay sexual attention to each other for each other's sake; otherwise, why engage in CS&P to begin with? Imagine now *both* partners attending to each other's sexual wants for their own respective sakes, and you'll see how the sexual pleasure is entirely sucked out of the act. This is why it is also not likely that the partners would agree to being sexually satisfied by each other out of moral considerations, for this also defeats the point of sexual desire. Knowing that one sexually excites another is a crucial motive for engaging in sex, especially CS&P, because it heightens one's own sexual pleasure.

We must then face the fact that CS&P are likely rife with objectification. Indeed, the promiscuous person carries a very heavy moral burden, because if avoiding objectification requires getting out of the grip of sexual desire to attend to her partner's sexual desires for their own sake, and if getting out of sexual desire's grip is difficult, the chances of one doing so become smaller and smaller the more one engages in casual sex with different people. The promiscuous person is then likely to engage in objectification quite frequently.

7. Two Possible Replies

At this point, defenders of CS&P have two options. The first is familiar: relax Kant's stringent requirements and argue that as long as the parties respect each other's wishes, desires, and boundaries, and as long as they attend to each other's sexual pleasure, even if for selfish or self-interested reasons, the sex is not objectifying. After all, when we pay the grocer we usually do so not for his own sake but for selfish or self-interested reasons (to get the groceries we want) without thereby doing something wrong. Why not, then, apply the same reasoning to sexual interaction? This option, basically, considers sexual desire and activity to be on a par with other human desires and activities. Thus, if consent is sufficient for these other activities, it also is for sexual ones.

This option abandons the pessimistic view of sexual desire, treating sexual desire as benign. For all we know, a benign view might be true, but by assuming it we do not address the worries of the pessimists and we take the easy way out.

The second option is to accept that CS&P are indeed objectifying, but to argue that the immorality of objectification is not so serious as to require the parties to refrain from engaging in sexual activity, including CS&P.

How might one argue for this view? Let's first state the argument loosely. In teaching this issue over the years, my students tended to react as follows: "Okay. Sex has lots of objectification, and objectification is wrong. We get it. But so what? What is so horrible about sexual objectification?" What my students' reaction amounts to is that even though objectification is wrong, it is not so wrong as to require us to refrain from engaging in sex, including CS&P, when sex can be so pleasurable. Putting the argument less loosely, the idea is to first argue that even though sexual objectification is wrong it is not a serious wrong (except in special cases, like rape), and to then argue that other factors compete with objectification's not-so-serious wrong, making sexual activity possibly morally permissible.

How is sexual objectification not a serious wrong? It is usually consensual, attentive, and not harmful. Contrast it with lying or coercion: they are serious moral wrongs because they not only involve using others as mere means but also lack consent, and they can (and often do) harm their victims. Not so with sexual objectification, because, first, X and Y usually consent to the sexual activity, which, second, even though it involves the use of each other, and of themselves, as mere instruments, is not an activity that, especially if they take precautions (against, for example, STDs), harms them (as when they consent to chop off each other's limbs) or harms other beings (as when they agree to rob a bank or to go cow tipping). Third, they are attentive to each other's sexual desires and needs (even if for selfish or self-interested reasons). So the wrong of sexual objectification, as real as it is, is not very serious.[26]

Second, there are good things about sex, including CS&P, that compete with the not-so-serious wrong of objectification, possibly rendering it overall morally permissible. First and most obviously, it is very pleasurable: there is pleasure in the very prospect of having sex, pleasure during the sexual activity itself (including foreplay), and pleasure in attaining orgasms (among other possible pleasures). Indeed, for many people who are not able to experience lofty pleasures (e.g., from reading classical Arabic poetry, contemplating Velázquez paintings, or drowning in the joyous seas of interpreting Wittgenstein), sexual pleasure is one of the few pleasures they have. Second, sexual activity is recreational, often providing (like other activities, such as solving jigsaw puzzles) needed entertainment, release, intense focus, and other forms of distraction from the humdrum or toil of everyday life. Third, for those people who do not desire or have time for monogamy, love, or a relationship, and for those who prefer sexual variety and the lack of love and sexual commitments, CS&P allow them to satisfy their sexual urges without the complications of relationships. Finally, according to some moral views, leading a rich, human life is important for human beings to flourish or live well. If sexual activity, undertaken moderately and in overall morally permissible ways, is part of such a life, then CS&P can contribute to it.[27]

The above four factors need not be the only ones, and they are not all of a moral nature (some are pleasure-related, some pragmatic). But the point is that if we couple the not-so-serious moral wrong of objectification with the above factors, sexual activity, including CS&P, might emerge as overall morally permissible.

CONCLUDING REMARKS

I have argued that on a pessimist view of sexual desire and given the point of CS&P (sexual pleasure), there is a strong case to be made that CS&P *necessarily* objectify, and that even if they do not, they *likely* objectify. I have also suggested an argument that, despite the objectification, CS&P might be overall permissible. However, this does not mean that CS&P are morally in the clear, because they can be wrong for other reasons. For example, casual sex can be wrong because it is adulterous, done from bad motives, or (if conservatives are correct) love-less. It can be wrong because the objectification is not overridden by other factors. Promiscuity might be wrong because it involves the overvaluation of sex. Thus, whether they are wrong in particular cases depends on all the relevant factors.[28]

NOTES

1. This is Albert Ellis's definition, "Casual Sex," *International Journal of Moral and Social Studies* 1:2 (1986), 157–69. For more on CS&P, see G. E. M. Anscombe, "Contraception and Chastity," *The Human World* no. 7 (1972), 9–30 (reprinted, revised, in *Ethics and Population*, edited by Michael Bayles [Cambridge, Mass.: Schenkman, 1976], 134–53); Frederick Elliston, "In Defense of Promiscuity," in *Philosophy and Sex*, 1st ed., edited by Robert Baker and Frederick Elliston (Buffalo, N.Y.: Prometheus, 1975), 223–43; Raja Halwani, *Virtuous Liaisons: Care, Love, Sex, and Virtue Ethics* (Chicago: Open Court, 2003), chapter 3; Raja Halwani, "Casual Sex," in *Sex from Plato to Paglia: A Philosophical Encyclopedia*, edited by Alan Soble (Westport, Conn.: Greenwood Press, 2006), 136–42; Raja Halwani, "Casual Sex, Promiscuity, and Temperance," in *Sex and Ethics: Essays on Sexuality, Virtue, and the Good Life*, edited by Raja Halwani (New York: Palgrave Macmillan, 2007), 215–25; and Kristjan Kristjansson, "Casual Sex Revisited," *Journal of Social Philosophy* 29:2 (1998), 97–108.

2. There are four options, with varying degrees of cogency: (1) X him or *herself* is not having casual sex, though the *sex* X is having is casual (what would this mean?); (2) the sex-that-X-has is not casual, but the sex-that-Y-has is casual; (3) the sex is both casual and non-casual (a contradiction); and (4) there is no single answer because the answer is relative: to X the sex is not casual, to Y it is.

3. Kant, *Lectures on Ethics*, translated by Louis Infield (Indianapolis, Ind.: Hackett, 1963), 163.

4. Of course, human beings are objects in that they are objects of this universe much like any other entity. They are also objects in a physical sense: they are made of the same stuff (the elements) that typical objects are made of. Each of these senses is compatible with human beings having a special property in virtue of which they should not be treated merely as objects are treated.

5. See Alan Soble, *Pornography, Sex, and Feminism* (Amherst, N.Y.: Prometheus, 2002), for an excellent discussion.

6. One philosopher who thinks that mere regard could be objectifying is Martha Nussbaum. See her example of "M" and "F" in "Feminism, Virtue, and Objectification," in *Sex and Ethics*, edited by Halwani, 49–62, at 54–55. See Alan Soble's reply, "Concealment and Exposure: A Mostly Temperate and Courageous Afterword," also in *Sex and Ethics*, 229–52, at 248–51. Another philosopher who thinks that mere regard could be objectifying is Rae Langton ("Autonomy-Denial in Objectification," in *Sexual*

Solipsism: Philosophical Essays on Pornography and Objectification [Oxford: Oxford University Press, 2009], 223–40).

7. Nussbaum argues that objectification is permissible in relationships generally characterized by mutual respect; see "Objectification," *Philosophy and Public Affairs* 24:4 (1995), 249–91 (reprinted in *Philosophy of Sex: Contemporary Readings*, 4th edition, edited by Alan Soble [Lanham, Md.: Rowman & Littlefield, 2002], 381–419). For discussions of her views, see Alan Soble, "Sexual Use" (sections "Thick Externalism" and "Thick Extended Externalism," in this volume); Patricia Marino, "The Ethics of Sexual Objectification: Autonomy and Consent," *Inquiry* 51:4 (2008), 345–64; Rae Langton, "Autonomy-Denial in Objectification"; and Raja Halwani, *Philosophy of Love, Sex, and Marriage: An Introduction* (New York: Routledge, 2010), 194–97.

8. This might stretch the concept of "tool" too much, since we think of tools as things that, though needed to attain goals, are in principle replaceable by other things, so long as the goal is attained, whereas we think that beloveds are not replaceable.

9. Nussbaum, "Objectification," 257. Her seventh way is not well worded. There are cases in which it is permissible to not take someone's feelings and experiences into account. For example, X must set aside Y's fear of syringes in order to inject Y with the needed medicine. What Nussbaum intends, I suppose, is treating someone as if they lack feelings and experiences.

10. Langton, "Autonomy-Denial in Objectification," 228–29. In her three ways (and in her wording of Nussbaum's seventh), Langton changes Nussbaum's "objectifier" to "one" because the latter has a more neutral sense; in cases in which the object is an ordinary object (not a person), one is not being an objectifier (226n7).

11. I would be as confident about the ninth way were it not for the word "primarily"; in some cases—say, at a modeling agency—treating someone primarily in terms of how they look is perfectly appropriate. Then again, it is not clear what Langton means by "primarily."

12. See Alan Soble, "The Analytic Categories of the Philosophy of Sex," in *The Philosophy of Sex: Contemporary Readings*, 6th ed., edited by Nicholas Power, Raja Halwani, and Alan Soble (Lanham, Md.: Rowman & Littlefield, 2013), 1–21, for Soble's discussion—which I freely (and thankfully) borrow and adapt—of the metaphysical sexual pessimists and the metaphysical sexual optimists. I focus on sexual desire and discuss sexual activity insofar as it results from sexual desire. (The essay is reprinted, with additions by Raja Halwani, in this volume. The version in the sixth edition is utilized for ease of reference to Soble's own points.)

13. Soble, "Analytic Categories," 4.

14. There is an optimistic view of sexual desire (which Soble claims to find in the work of Irving Singer), according to which it is a force that can bring people together, bring them pleasure and joy, and is conducive to their well-being ("Analytic Categories," 5–6).

15. Nussbaum, "Objectification," 257.

16. Indeed, beyond paying attention to the quality that purportedly elevates people over objects, few other things can destroy casual sexual activity. (Y: "Why are you suddenly asking me about my hobbies?" X: "I want to treat you as a full person, not as a hobby-less piece of meat." Y: [eyes rolling] "OMG.")

17. The silencing issue is complicated. Langton argues in several essays that sometimes pornography is causally implicated in rendering women silent; she means that their desires, particularly their refusals to engage in sex, are not heard (see *Sexual Solipsism*, especially "Speech Acts as Unspeakable Acts"). It is possible, then, that in casual sex women are not heard and are objectified in this sense. However, the objectification would not occur because the sex is casual, but because women's silence cuts across many social areas.

18. Indeed, those who charge CS&P with necessary objectification should focus on instrumentality, since CS&P need not involve the other objectifications.

19. Kant, *Lectures on Ethics*, 162. On Kant's views, see Thomas Mappes, "Sexual Morality and the Concept of Using Another Person" (in this volume); Lara Denis,

"Kant on the Wrongness of 'Unnatural Sex,'" *History of Philosophy Quarterly* 16:2 (1999), 225–48; Lara Denis, "Sex and the Virtuous Kantian Agent," in *Sex and Ethics*, edited by Raja Halwani, 37–48; Soble, "Sexual Use"; and Halwani, *Philosophy of Love, Sex, and Marriage*, 200–210.

20. For Kant, marriage is the only solution to sexual objectification. I do not discuss his solution because it is problematic; see Lara Denis, "From Friendship to Marriage: Revisiting Kant," *Philosophy and Phenomenological Research* 63:1 (2001), 1–28. Soble, however, thinks that Kant's solution is coherent; see "Sexual Use."

21. Kant, *Metaphysics of Morals* 6:393 and 6:395, trans. and edited by Mary J. Gregor, in *Practical Philosophy*, the Cambridge Edition of the Works of Immanuel Kant (Cambridge: Cambridge University Press, 1996). These remarks by Kant are made in the context of his argument for beneficence as a duty (thanks to Alan Soble for showing me his e-mail exchange with Lara Denis about this issue). See also Onora O'Neill, "Between Consenting Adults," in *Constructions of Reason: Explorations of Kant's Practical Philosophy* (Cambridge: Cambridge University Press, 1989), 105–25.

22. Note an interesting result: sexual acts done *not* from sexual desire need not be morally wrong on this view, because they would not stem from the manipulative, overpowering, and pernicious impulse of sexual desire. Thus, when sex workers have sex with clients from non-sexual desires, when spouses oblige and have sex with their spouses when they do not desire sex, when gorgeous Ahmad has sex with Matt because he wants Matt to have a taste of heaven, and so on—these sexual acts, if wrong, are not wrong on the ground that they are objectifying.

23. *Grounding for the Metaphysics of Morals* 4:398, translated by James W. Ellington (Indianapolis, Ind.: Hackett, 1981).

24. Note that X can attend to Y's sexual goals neither for selfish reasons nor for reasons related to Y's goals: X might believe that God commanded X to do so.

25. This is one reason Kant refused to ground morality in human nature.

26. One might object that (1) the genuineness of consent is problematic because the agreement is warped by the power of sexual desire. This may be true; however, because the consent is usually to a harmless activity, a warped judgment might not be a general serious issue, but serious only in particular cases (e.g., fellatio in the Oval Office). One might object that (2) this argument brings in consequentialist reasons into a non-consequentialist, Kantian framework. But neither Kant himself nor his followers shun consequentialist considerations (their concern is to decide when and to what extent they are morally relevant). Further, Kant or no Kant, harm is an important moral factor that needs to be taken into account in assessing the overall morality of action or types of actions.

27. On temperate and moderate CS&P, see Halwani, *Virtuous Liaisons*, chapter 3; Halwani, "Casual Sex, Promiscuity, and Temperance."

28. Thanks to Patricia Marino and Nicholas Power for comments on an earlier draft. Special thanks to Alan Soble, whose trenchant comments showed me the need to change my arguments and conclusions.

STUDY QUESTIONS

1. Are rape, bestiality, and necrophilia examples of casual sex? And how would you go about answering this question? What are the implications of your answers for understanding "casual sex" as "no-strings-attached" sexual activity?

2. Given Halwani's definition of "objectification," can one objectify animals? Would your answer require a revision in Halwani's definition? In the case of mammals, who are not as linguistically competent as human beings, might their consent rest more on behav-

ioral cues (they seem to enjoy the activity) than on verbal messages?

3. Would adopting different definitions of "casual sex" and "promiscuity" change our (and Halwani's) moral conclusions about them? At the metaphilosophical level, would a "yes" answer imply that the moral evaluations are already (and at least partially) packed into the definitions of "casual sex" and "promiscuity"? Would such definitions be accurate insofar as they are reports about "moral facts"?

4. Suppose we accept a metaphysically optimistic view of sex. Would this strongly support the conclusion that objectification does not occur in CS&P? Or might it, instead, provide equally strong reasons for not engaging in CS&P, because they do not achieve the optimistic model of ideal sexuality?

5. Sex workers engage in casual sex and promiscuity, and their usual motive is to earn money in an exchange for sexual services. Do sex workers (e.g., prostitutes) sexually objectify their clients, both seeing them merely as sources of income and treating them the same way? Do they objectify their clients by manipulating their sexuality and taking advantage of their client's sexual desire and hence sexual vulnerability? Do prostitutes allow themselves to be sexually objectified by their clients, who may be taking advantage of the prostitute's need for money? However, to what extent are these moral faults, when they exist, due to the nature of the sexual interactions as casual and promiscuous?

6. How serious is the wrong of objectification, or on what does the seriousness of objectification rest? Is Halwani right to suggest that in some circumstances objectification is not serious enough to be the overriding or ruling moral consideration? (Martha Nussbaum claims in "Objectification" [n. 7, above] that using a lover's body as a pillow is either not objectification or an innocuous case of objectification.) If sexual desire is as perniciously powerful as the metaphysical pessimists make it out to be, to what extent can a philosopher rely, as Halwani does and as sexual liberals tend to do, on the presence of genuine consent as mitigating, overriding, the wrongfulness of objectification? We are faced here with a perennial and seemingly intractable question: Does it make moral or conceptual sense that a person may consent to be (sexually) used? Start with the essay by Thomas Mappes in this volume, and then consider several others.

TWENTY-THREE

BDSM

Shaun Miller

In this essay, **Shaun Miller** *explains some basic concepts of BDSM (Bondage, Discipline, and Sadomasochism), and responds to two important objections to it—that its practitioners suffer from mental disorders (the medical objection) and that they have morally defective characters because they have morally compromised sexual desires (the ethical objection). Miller argues that BDSM participants suffer from no mental disorders and that their sexual desires for, say, domination or submission are crucially different from such desires in ordinary life, the latter of which are truly morally compromised. Finally, Miller argues that because BDSM desires and practices are looked down upon by society, BDSM participants have to constantly understand them, explore them, and justify them. These activities, he contends, might make for a richer and more interesting life.*

Shaun Miller earned his BA in physics and philosophy at Utah State University and his MA at Texas A&M University. He is currently a PhD student at Marquette University. His dissertation investigates the various moral assumptions in sex education programs throughout the United States and assesses what it means to "take care of the self" in a sexual context. He has published "Quagmire: Virtue and Perversity," in *Family Guy and Philosophy: A Cure for the Petarded,* edited by J. Jeremy Wisnewski (Malden, Mass.: Blackwell, 2007), 27–35. He blogs regularly at shaunmiller.blog. © 2017, Shaun Miller, who kindly gave permission for his new essay to be included in this volume.

Sadomasochism—shortened as BDSM, or "kink"—has gained huge prominence in our cultural imagination. We can see it represented through the media, such as the popular book and movie *Fifty Shades of Grey.* As the stigma has fallen, the participation (or at least the admission of participation) has risen. Still, there is no full acceptance of BDSM for various reasons. Objections focus on whether BDSM is a psychological disorder, and on whether BDSM is ethical. This essay explains and addresses these major issues. I show that BDSM is not a psychological disorder, that having BDSM desires does not reflect badly on one's character, and that BDSM can help one flourish if done in the right way.

WHAT IS BDSM?

BDSM is a multifaceted paraphilia of sexuality. Indeed, it is so multifaceted that it is hard to give a definition of "BDSM," though we can characterize it. The popular representation is that BDSM focuses on pain, but the major component is the consensual exchange of power. For a while, "S&M" was considered the go-to phrase, but now "BDSM" is the umbrella term for any power exchange in sexual relations. The acronym is made of three sets of terms. "BD" stands for "Bondage and Discipline." Acts of bondage include restraining the partner(s) with ropes, handcuffs, or other grapplings that restrict the hands or feet to certain positions. Acts of discipline include spankings or whippings through hands, paddles, or light leather whips. "D/s" stands for "Dominance and Submission." Since the one who dominates has the power, the submissive follows his or her "orders" — hence the "s" is lower case. Dominance is being in control and being the "top." Submission is the one being controlled and being the "bottom." Finally, "SM" stands for "sadomasochism." Sadism is getting pleasure by inflicting pain on a partner. Masochism is getting pleasure by receiving pain from a partner.

BDSM practitioners use two phrases to differentiate BDSM from abuse: "Safe, Sane, and Consensual" (abbreviated as "SSC") and "risk-aware consensual kink" ("RACK"). While both focus on the consent behind the activity, they also emphasize that the activities are essentially risky but the participants are of sound mind ("sane") to understand and consent to the risk.

Finally, BDSM participants "play" various scenarios called "scenes" during which a power exchange occurs. Joanna Zaslow gives a good description:

> In BDSM relationships, all activities and partnerships must be negotiated before they take place. This means that individuals must negotiate what their limitations are, what they are comfortable participating in and what signs or signals they will give when these limits have been crossed (these are known as "safe words"). Most important, the Master/slave relationship requires a contract between individual participants. This contract lays out the requirements and responsibilities for both parties, and also allows room for participants to negotiate how they will end the relationship, if need be.[1]

Participants negotiate what the scene entails and its limits. The scene ends when the activity is over, or when the partner (typically the recipient) says the safeword — a specific word to let the partner know that the intensity must be toned down or the scene must end. Because sometimes "stop" or "no" are part of the play, participants use words irrelevant to the role play to mean "stop" (e.g., "red") and "slow down" or "check in" (e.g., "yellow").

Suppose that a couple agrees that one of them be tied up in bed during sex. Once the scene is over, the power exchange is over. The restrained partner is untied. If, however, the person remains tied up when the scene is over, the power exchange is no longer consensual, so the act is closer to abuse or assault. The scene is set up such that all the participants negotiate it beforehand and consent to and desire it. Therefore, we can say that BDSM is neither assault nor abuse, and we can agree on the following basic claim that grounds the rest of this essay's discussion: BDSM sexual scenes are ones to which the participants consent and desire, no matter whether the scene is taboo, involves pain, or involves the exchange of power.

There have been various objections to BDSM. I will discuss two main ones, the medical objection and the moral objection. I will show that they are not convincing.

THE MEDICAL OBJECTION

BDSM has historically been seen as a neurosis or a mental illness. Consider *Fifty Shades of Grey*, a best-selling book that has helped popularize BDSM and "kink" behavior. The narrator is Anastasia Steele, who asks the title character, Christian Grey, why he does not want to be intimate:

> "Why don't you like to be touched?" I whisper, staring up into soft gray eyes.
> "Because I'm fifty shades of fucked up, Anastasia."[2]

Christian Grey is depicted as carrying a lot of emotional baggage. His mother was a prostitute, and both she and young Christian were abused. After she committed suicide, Christian had to live with a foster family for several months and was later introduced to sex by his mother's female friends. Not only did he lose his virginity, but he was also part of a BDSM relationship in which he played the sub. This background is meant to suggest that these experiences shaped Grey's attitude about relationships and sexuality, and especially his interest in BDSM. The overall message is that BDSM practitioners have psychological and emotional issues.

Is this true? J. Roger Lee gives two reasons in support of this belief, which I will call the "natural function reason" and the "medical reason." Let's start with the natural function reason.

According to Lee, "The administration of pain, its infliction and its enjoyment, have little to no function in" the "natural set of drives called 'human sexuality,'" which, on his view, promotes important goods, such as bonding with one's partner, emotional support, pleasure, and possibly reproduction.[3] Because BDSM often involves the enjoyment of the administration and reception of pain, BDSM does not promote such goods. This is because pain distracts one "from access to desires and tendencies the working through of which is sexuality."[4] To Lee, pain and sexuality are incompatible. This makes superficial sense: if sex is essentially about pleasure, then pain should not be part of it.

However, BDSM, including sadomasochism, can achieve the goods that Lee lists: BDSM can help the participants bond with each other, and it can provide them with emotional support and pleasure.[5] For example, suppose that A and B engage in a flogging scene. Both of them receive pleasure from the activity and feel a strong connection toward each other. Both of them can bond during the experience, especially since the giving and receiving of pleasure (albeit in this case through pain) can bond two people to each other, and especially since sadomasochistic encounters require a lot of trust between the participants, and trust is an agent of human bonding. If sadomasochism can do this, then it and other BDSM activities fulfill the goods that Lee asks for.

Let us now attend to the medical reason. Lee believes that sadomasochistic people have developed Narcissistic Personality Disorder. But this is a problem, according to him, because "[i]f one has developed a personality structure in which the narcissistic, sadomasochistic awareness of pain is central to the sense one has of one's self at its full, intense, most excellent functioning, then the all-consuming intensity of feeling and drive that come with sexuality and sexual activity will feel off, not right, unacceptably disconcerting without a phenomenology of pain as a component part."[6] And if the sex feels off if one does not feel pain, then the "narcissist . . . is made *unable* to make an objective good—knowledge of herself and of her place in the world—be good-for-her."[7] Lee concludes that narcissistic actions, which to him, as we have seen, include some BDSM activities, do not constitute aspects of leading a good and happy life.[8] BDSM practitioners then, or at least those who practice sadomasochism, are not leading as well and as happy lives as they could.

Why believe that sadists and masochists are narcissists? A child may develop Narcissistic Personality Disorder when the child fails to develop its own sense of self from other objects, which can be caused by child abuse or neglect. Thus, the narcissist remains in a state of undeveloped ego and remains in a state of self-centeredness. Masochists believe that the pain they receive is what they deserve, and sadists believe that they teach others the "true" nature of existence, which is painful. The top demands attention to be in charge of the scene to make sure the bottom feels the pain; the bottom is at the center of attention because the scene is based on what the bottom feels. Both the sadist and the masochist thus replay their themes in a sexual and narcissistic encounter where they both give and receive pain, respectively. Lee argues that this is based on a misperception of reality as painful, hence his claim that any of the goods that lead to the "natural set of drives of 'human sexuality'" will "feel off, not right, unacceptably disconcerting" because all forms of sexuality will be distorted through the personality disorder.[9]

Lee's reasoning, however, is mistaken. Laurie Shrage and Robert Scott Stewart argue that "the current definition and description of 'Narcissistic Personality Disorder' (extraordinary sense of self-importance and entitlement, lacking empathy, and so on) does not suggest that people with this disorder would likely be interested in kinky sex, and health professionals claim that they do not fully understand its causes."[10] Moreover, the fifth edition of the *Diagnostic and Statistical Manual of Mental Disorders* (*DSM-5*) distinguishes between paraphilias and paraphilic disorders, meaning that having atypical sexual interests or desires is not a problem unless it causes the person distress or interferes with their ability to function. Alice Dreger makes a nice illustration: "The foot fetishist who keeps getting arrested because he steals shoes, who fondles the feet of unconsenting women strangers, and who can't hold a job because he's too busy obsessing about his next sexual opportunity—he's got a paraphilic disorder. The foot fetishist who is happy, comfortable, and functions fine—he just has a paraphilia."[11]

The *DSM-5* also notes that "[m]ost people with atypical sexual interests do *not* have a mental disorder." To have a paraphilic disorder, the *DSM-5* requires that people feel distress about their interest not resulting solely from society's disapproval, or "have a sexual desire or behavior that involves another person's psychological distress, injury, or death, or a desire for sexual behaviors involving unwilling persons or persons unable to give legal consent."[12] Indeed, there is evidence that BDSM participants have comparable or better mental health than non-participants, most likely because the former have a better understanding of consent and communication.[13] So Lee is mistaken to claim that sadomasochists, let alone other BDSM practitioners, have narcissistic disorders, and that the enjoyment of the affliction and reception of pain leads to a life that is not fully happy or well.

THE ETHICS OF BDSM DESIRES

One way to criticize BDSM is to claim that it is a form of assault, battery, or abuse. After all, some of the scenes look violent and psychologically devastating. However, we can easily assuage this worry by noting that the participants desire and consent to the scene, even if the scene looks violent or involves assault. Consider a boxing match, where the fight can be violent and assaultive, but the fighters desire and consent to the match. Consent converts the boxing match from assault to, well, a boxing match. It seems then that consent is sufficient for the permissibility of the activity.

However, BDSM might be problematic *despite* the consent. The criticism goes as follows. It seems that the desires involved in BDSM are problematic because of the kinds of desires they are. Desiring to inflict pain on someone else, or, worse, desiring to participate in a scene in which one is the master of another or one is the slave of another is surely troubling. This is especially so when those desires take on gender (e.g., a man whipping a woman), racial (e.g., a white person playing the role of a master of a black person who plays the role of the slave), and other roles.[14] This objection has a feminist version. Claudia Card writes,

> My own approach to sadomasochism initially . . . was the liberal, "sexual preference" approach. . . . My present approach perceives sexual sadomasochism as enacting . . . roles of dominance and subordinance that characterize . . . the norms of a patriarchal, misogynist society that is also riddled with homophobia, racism, anti-Semitism, and other forms of oppression. On this understanding, sadomasochistic desires have roots not simply in individual psychologies but in society at large; they are not mysterious givens but social constructions. The direction of my ethical concern has shifted, accordingly, more to the process of their construction than to that of enactment.[15]

In addition, Sandra Bartky claims, "[S]adomasochism is one inevitable expression of women-hating culture. It powerfully reinforces male dominance and female subordination because, by linking these phenomena to our deepest sexual desires—desires defined by an ideologically tainted psychology as instinctual—it makes them appear natural. To participate willingly in this mode of sexuality is to collude in women's subordination."[16]

In a liberal society, each individual chooses how to live their life, based on their view of what the good life is, as long as basic rights are respected. However, the feminist concern is that society is structured such that we *think* that we are living our life based on what we deem good, but the goods are actually not so. Our desires are thus problematic because they contain and reflect unethical values, such as misogyny, homophobia, and racism. BDSM activities are especially worrisome, since the scenes seem to endorse and reinforce patriarchal values. After all, BDSM simulates sexual dominance, which is reflective of patriarchy.

As noted, however, the objection need not be couched in feminist terms or be only about misogyny. Generally speaking, because sexual desires have content (they are object-oriented or intentional), they tend to reflect social and cultural values, which are not always good. BDSM participants seem to represent or duplicate historically oppressive and oppressed positions, such that one person has power over the other in the scene. Thus, according to this objection, in wanting to play such roles,

BDSM participants have unethical desires—to want to play the role of a white master, for example, is to have the desires of white masters, and this is morally unhealthy to say the least. In short, the worry is that BDSM desires reflect patriarchal and other unwholesome values, so are unethical; they indicate that the person who has them is not as good a person as they could be.

To assess this argument, let's use BDSM taboo role play as a case study, as it tends to be the type of BDSM activity of which many are suspicious. In taboo role play the participants play roles such as male dom/female sub (problematic because women submitting to men is paradigmatic of patriarchy); master/slave role play (particularly when the "slave" is of African descent and the "master" is white); Nazi/Jew role play (particularly when the sub is of Jewish descent); and rape fantasies, to give a few examples. The defender of BDSM must show that having and enjoying such desires is not necessarily unethical.

Consider male dom/female sub and white master/black slave role play. If the dom is a closeted racist or secretly wants to rape women and uses BDSM scenes as an outlet for his desires, then his character is vicious. This would make him morally unsound.[17] As for the sub, if she internalizes the racism or misogyny—if she accepts racist or sexist attitudes against her own race or sex—then there is also a problem.

However, BDSM participants' desires are not "real" in the usual sense, and the participants usually understand that even if they are using an injustice as the background to or as part of their play, they do not endorse the actual injustice. For comparison, imagine a U.S. Civil War reenactment. The "play" is set up where the North defeats the South. Imagine a participant who is on the side of the South but who is not a racist and who is against any form of racism. He may still participate and enjoy playing the role for a variety of reasons: he can reenact history, he is playing a part of an ancestor and wants to tell the ancestor's story, or he wants to educate people on exactly how this specific battle went. In short, recognizing an injustice in history and desiring to act it out does not mean that one's desires mirror those of past oppressors, let alone that one endorses the actual injustice.

We can then see how the context of BDSM is different from that of an actual injustice. Imagine a white man and a black woman who have known each other for a long time. They negotiate and discuss a BDSM scene, which she says she has been narrating in her mind for a while. During the scene, the man addresses the black woman using racial and sexual epithets and humiliates and threatens her, even saying that he owns her. The man uses a flogger to beat her. She breaks character a couple of times very briefly and tells her partner that he could go a little harder on the flogging, up to the point where she says "yellow" to signal that he should not go any further. The scene, say, lasts for one hour, after which they snuggle against each other and discuss the intensity and rich-

ness of the scene. After the cuddling, the woman takes a shower while
the man prepares a brief meal so that she can run her errands. When she
gets back from her errands, the man checks in on her to make sure that
she is okay because they had engaged in a physically and psychologically
taxing activity.

Note how the racialized sexual actions do not carry over into the lives
of the partners once the scene is over. This is crucial because it shows that
what the participants experience remains confined to the scene itself,
indicating that the participants' desires do not infect the rest of their
psyches. The scene is just that—a scene; its context is such that the participants trust each other and have ongoing communication before, throughout, and after.

Thus, in addition to consent and communication, there must be what
we might call "good intentions" between the participants. Mollena
Williams-Haas writes that when it comes to these "dark" fantasies, intention is all important: "The *intent* of those participating in taboo role play
is not to harm others. Their intent may vary. It can be a reclamation, a recreation, an exploration—but it is *never* a decimation, an obliteration of
the humanity of the people involved. Intent is all-important when diving
into these dark waters."[18] If the intention is to leave someone broken
without any care afterward or to simply be cruel, there is a problem. The
dom respects the limits of the scene.[19]

The idea that the racialized actions do not carry over into the rest of
the participants' lives is crucial because it indicates an essential dissimi-
larity between racist or sexist desires and desires in the context of BDSM:
the desires are not the same, neither conceptually nor psychologically.
Conceptually, it is possible for someone to desire whipping a black woman but not to desire to whip her in a BDSM context; indeed, such a
context might be weird to the genuine racist. It is possible for someone to
fantasize about raping women but not fantasize about raping women in a
BDSM scene; the BDSM scene might be a turn-off for him. The converse is
true: someone desiring to whip a black woman in a BDSM context may
not desire to whip a black woman in general, and someone fantasizing
about raping women in a BDSM context may not desire to rape women in
general. We can see that, logically, they are not the same. There is no
transference from one desire to the other. What about psychologically? If
Williams-Haas's white partner desires to whip Williams-Haas and he
gets sexual satisfaction from this, he may not be satisfied by whipping
another black woman. He might even be repulsed by it. The same could
be said about rape fantasies in and outside a BDSM context. The desires
are thus not the same, neither conceptually nor psychologically.

The white man who fantasizes about whipping black women will
have "the-desire-to-whip-black-women" and the aim behind that desire
is perhaps power, dominance, or racial superiority. The white man fantasizing about whipping black women in a BDSM context has "the-desire-

to-whip-black-women-in-BDSM-scenes" and the aim is to increase both his and the black woman's pleasure. A real racist has the belief that people of color are inferior, but a BDSM practitioner need not, and only acts during a scene *as if* he does. When the scene is over, he retains the belief that people of all races are equal.[20] Think of actors who prefer and enjoy playing villains: they can embody that character through an intense imaginary state, but it does not mean that they are villains in general. Something similar occurs with BDSM practitioners.

If the objection is correct, then a BDSM scene is not fantasy or simulation of domination—it *is* domination because the desires of the participants make the interaction between them so. The black woman would therefore be complicit in her own oppression because she permitted and relished being dominated by a white man, and the white man is also complicit in the domination. As we have seen, however, the context alerts us that the desires are not really racist or sexist. What we have is a superficial structure of domination. We can then see that changing the context could spell the difference between replicating or endorsing an injustice and merely enjoying its simulation. The context is playful—it is a simulation[21] or make-believe.[22]

BDSM desires are morally permissible as long as they are had in the right way: among other things (e.g., not consuming one's life), the desires must be for "play" rather than real domination, submission. Is it then possible that BDSM practitioners lead a well-lived, flourishing life? I turn to that in the next section.

BDSM AND FLOURISHING

In the previous section, I have considered the moral objection to BDSM that BDSM desires are unethical. However, there is a way to not only defend BDSM from objections but also show that it can be enriching, even helping one lead a flourishing life.

Having kink desires does not automatically make BDSM practitioners vicious people. If the reply to the objection in the previous section is correct, then having BDSM desires is compatible with having a good character. Moreover, acting on BDSM desires is normally confined to specific scenes, which means that BDSM is not a life-consuming activity.[23] Thus, BDSM practitioners are no different in this respect from other people. The BDSM "lifestyle" is no obstacle to having a good character or to other necessary goods in a human life, two things that are necessary, at least on an Aristotelian or neo-Aristotelian view for a good life.

We must also keep in mind that, normally, the inability to satisfy sexual desires, at least on occasion, can render a life frustrating. Satisfying sexual desires is a necessary component for leading a good life. Furthermore, BDSM desires are not mere sexual tastes that can be left unfulfilled without leaving the person frustrated (as long as this is compensated for by the fulfillment of some other sexual desires). Having BDSM desires is akin to having a basic sexual orientation, like being gay or straight, at least in the respect that not being able to act on one's desires leaves one frustrated and unhappy. BDSM desires are experienced as essential to one's identity.[24] Imagine having sexual attractions and desires but not being able to fulfill them. You could survive, but you would live a frustrated and difficult life.

I would, therefore, suggest that there are two different kinds of needs whose fulfillment is crucial for a flourishing life. The first is survival needs. These are the needs that one has to have in order to survive, such as food, water, and shelter. Without these needs, we would die, or be perpetually in pain and deprivation (if they are fulfilled infrequently). The second type of need goes above the minimal standards of survival. These would be "flourishing needs." These include love, having friends, a sense of belonging, being part of a community, and sexual fulfillment. Notice that we can survive without these needs, but we would not live good lives.

So while not satisfying BDSM desires would not render a life impossible to live, it would render it difficult. I now want to further suggest that satisfying BDSM desires may also lead to a feeling of empowerment. In other words, BDSM can *enhance* well-being. The main reason is that because BDSM desires are desires for some sort of power exchange, their possessors will always have to explore and think about them and about what it means to have and act on them. This aspect of BDSM desires allows their possessors to lead non-conventional and thereby richer lives.

Consider friendship as a way to enrich one's life. Friends often make activities more enjoyable than normal. I might enjoy swimming at the beach or watching movies, but doing them with a friend can make them more enjoyable. This is not only because watching the movie with someone else is more enjoyable but also because I enjoy my friend's reactions to the movie, and I enjoy his or her reactions to my own reactions to the movie. Watching a movie with a friend becomes a much more complex and, because of that, much more enjoyable, activity.[25]

Sexual activities are similar. Suppose that Evan and Molly are acquaintances who enjoy having sex with each other. They have sex because it is sex, but also because it is *with each other*. Molly enjoys sex with Evan because it is *Evan's* body, and not just any other person's body. The same is true of how Evan regards Molly. Furthermore, Evan and Molly are comfortable with each other and encourage each other to be open about their sexuality and to pinpoint exactly what they want. Thus, their sex life is enhanced and improved, which in turn rebounds positively to their lives in general.

The above is especially true with respect to BDSM sexual activities. Having BDSM sex with untrustworthy people or, for some reason, unsympathetic ones, leaves the participant's desires unfulfilled. But having BDSM sex with a trusted partner allows the participants to explore their desires, not to mention enjoy acting on them. If Evan and Molly know each other well, they begin to trust and get to know what the other's intentions are. Suppose Molly presents Evan with an opportunity to do a BDSM scene for the first time. She has a fantasy of being tied up and being choked while Evan is penetrating her. She has never done this with anyone, but she feels comfortable enough with Evan to explore this with him. Evan, because he knows Molly well, wants to help her fulfill this desire. They talk through the scene and plan out the details carefully. Although Evan and Molly find the scene fulfilling, Molly thought it was too much; yet she enjoyed it just enough to want to do it again and explore her desires more. Sometime later, they do the scene again. This time, however, Molly asks Evan to ease up on the choking. Evan complies and Molly enjoys the scene even more. After discussing it, it turns out that Molly did not want choking per se but simply some pressure around her neck to simulate choking. They may engage in the scene multiple times with a better understanding of their desires and can fulfill them at a heightened level.

The above example suggests that individuals with taboo desires often have to understand them, think about them, and figure out whether they are justified to act on, and whether the mere having of them reflects badly on their character, including, of course, the importance of consent to what they do. Going back to race play or rape fantasies, the people involved may actually be more self-aware of their desires because they not only know that they are fringe desires but also know that the political backdrop possibly makes those desires troublesome. Thus, they are more in tune with their desires and may have a richer understanding of how problematic they could potentially be. By justifying the permissibility of their desires, and by acting on them in the face of social taboos, BDSM practitioners lead complex lives—intellectually, emotionally, psychologically, and sexually.

Another way to enhance well-being is to be authentic. Much has been written on authenticity, but, roughly, being authentic means that one's actions and thoughts express who one is (in general, not necessarily on every occasion); they flow from and reflect one's character and personality.

Suppose Samantha is gay and desires to be with a woman but decides to be with a man because of social taboos against lesbianism. Although she might feel good because she adheres to social norms, she might feel alienation because of not acting on her genuine desires. Samantha later dates a woman and slowly begins to enjoy it despite the social taboos. She would feel empowered because of acting on her genuine desires. By understanding the truth about herself along with support from others, she develops confidence in her sexual and relationship needs. And by doing what she genuinely wants to do, Samantha feels more in control of her life, more self-directed, and can develop and hone exactly what she desires in relationships, intimacy, and sex. By being sexually and emotionally authentic, her well-being is enhanced.[26]

The same is true were Samantha to have BDSM desires. Fulfilling these desires enhances her well-being because she is being authentic in doing so. This is especially true in societies that consider BDSM activities taboo or perverted. Engaging in BDSM in the face of social disapproval helps one have self-direction, control, power, and confidence in one's self. Thus, engaging in BDSM is empowering and therefore enriching. It helps one live better.

Of course, a time might come when the social disapproval goes away, in which case the taboo aspects of BDSM would cease to be as challenging. But the prospect of social taboos fully going away seems low, because as long as desires are sexual and involve power exchanges, pain, or what is considered bizarre, society will likely always, to some extent at least, frown upon such desires. Thus, practitioners of BDSM are likely to always find themselves in the interesting position of having to struggle with their desires but with the effect of leading richer lives.

To sum up, because BDSM practitioners do not follow the norm, they need to reflect more than usual on their desires, their justification, and the permissibility of acting on them, thereby leading richer and more interesting lives, at least in these aspects. Moreover, acting on their BDSM desires allows them to be in harmony with themselves, to lead an authentic life in the face of social taboos. Leading an authentic life is certainly one way to enhance one's well-being.[27]

CONCLUSION

I aimed to show that BDSM desires need not be ethically or psychologically defective, and that satisfying and acting on them can actually enhance the practitioners' well-being. I argued that when BDSM desires are ethically in the clear, when BDSM practitioners feel sexually empowered, when there is consent, and when the overall lifestyle does not consume their lives, they are doing BDSM "in the right way."

However, although the reader may find nothing philosophically troubling about BDSM, they might still find it unattractive or unappealing. So I want to suggest a notion that has helped me when it comes to others' sexual needs, desires, preferences, and tastes: Don't yuck someone's yum. What you may find sexually desirable, someone else may find abhorrent. Imagine if you wanted to fulfill an ethically permissible sexual desire, but someone else found it unappealing, even disgusting. The response may be judgmental, but the discouragement can cause stress and could stifle someone's sexual curiosity, perhaps even their well-being.

Nowadays, we do not yuck someone's gay orientation, desire to have sex before marriage, or desire to have sexual pleasure for the sake of having pleasure. In the same way, we should not yuck someone's BDSM desires, because shaming someone's sexual desires could not only stifle sexual curiosity but also affect one's well-being.[28]

NOTES

1. Joanna Zaslow, "Control, Power and Pleasure: Relational Autonomy and Female Submission in BDSM," in *Talk About Sex: A Multidisciplinary Discussion*, edited by Robert Scott Stewart (Sydney, Nova Scotia: Cape Breton University Press, 2013), 233–48, at 242.

2. E. L. James, *Fifty Shades of Grey* (New York: Vintage Books, 2011), 269.

3. J. Roger Lee, "Sadomasochism: An Ethical Analysis," in *Philosophical Perspectives on Sex and Love*, edited by Robert M. Stewart (New York: Oxford University Press, 1995), 125–37, at 131.

4. Lee, "Sadomasochism," 131.

5. Sadomasochism does not lead to reproduction, but, as Lee admits, "[p]rogenerative goods will flow from only a small percentage of sexual activities . . . while the other goods that flow from good sexual activity do so at a high level of frequency" (Lee, "Sadomasochism," 131).

6. Lee, "Sadomasochism," 128.

7. Lee, "Sadomasochism," 131.

8. Lee, "Sadomasochism," 131.

9. Lee, "Sadomasochism," 131.

10. Laurie J. Shrage and Robert Scott Stewart, *Philosophizing About Sex* (Broadview Press, 2015), 259. It does seem odd that Lee equates sadomasochism with narcissism; this might be due to the time Lee's essay was written (1994), when sadomasochism was believed to be a mental disorder.

11. Alice Dreger, "Of Kinks, Crimes, and Kinds: The Paraphilias Proposal for the DSM"; http://www.thehastingscenter.org/Bioethicsforum/Post.aspx?id=4494#ixzz47cVXN0q2 (accessed September 18, 2016).

12. American Psychological Association, http://www.dsm5.org/Documents/Paraphilic%20Disorders%20Fact%20Sheet.pdf, my emphasis (accessed May 5, 2016).

13. To cite three studies, Pamela H. Connolly noted that BDSM practitioners had lower levels of depression, anxiety, psychological sadism, psychological masochism, and post-traumatic stress disorder (PTSD) than non-BDSM people. They did, however, show higher levels of narcissism ("Psychological Functioning of Bondage/Domination/Sado-masochism (BDSM) Practitioners," *Journal of Psychology and Human Sexuality* 18:1 [2006], 79–120). Another study from Andreas A. J. Wismeijer and Marcel A. L. M. van Assen showed that BDSM practitioners were more extroverted and less neurotic, and reported subjective well-being, but were less agreeable than those who to do not practice BDSM. Moreover, those who were "tops" reported lower levels of neuroticism and attachment anxiety compared to submissives, who reported higher levels of agreeableness. Also, both the dominant and submissive reported equivalent-to-slightly-better outcomes in most cases, which suggests that neither role is inherently pathological ("Psychological Characteristics of BDSM Practitioners," *Journal of Sexual Medicine* 10:8 [2013], 1943–52).

These studies, however, may not be entirely representative. Connolly's tests were administered to 132 self-identified BDSM practitioners, and Wismeijer and van Assen's study had 902 people, but were based on one website based in the Netherlands. The control group, however, were about six years younger, less educated, and more likely to be female than the BDSM group.

A more representative study concluded that for most BDSM practitioners, "BDSM activities are not a pathological symptom of past abuse or of difficulty with 'normal' sex" (Juliet Richters, Richard O. De Visser, Chris E. Rissel, Andrew E. Grulich, and Anthony Smith, "Demographic and Psychosocial Features of Participants in Bondage and Discipline, 'Sadomasochism' or Dominance and Submission (BDSM): Data from a National Survey," *Journal of Sexual Medicine* 5:7 [2008], 1660–68, at 1667).

14. On how sexual desires can be problematic, see Seiriol Morgan, "Dark Desires," in this volume.

15. Claudia Card, *Lesbian Choices*, http://www.feminist-reprise.org/docs/card.htm (accessed May 7, 2016).

16. Sandra Lee Bartky, *Femininity and Domination: Studies in the Phenomenology of Oppression* (New York and London: Routledge, 1990), 48.

17. However, Patrick Hopkins points out that a dom who has a cruel character but only engages in these scenes in a BDSM context may deserve some praise because he is controlling his immoral impulses ("Simulation and the Reproduction of Injustice: A Reply," *Hypatia* 10:2 [1995], 162–70), at 164). While this may be true, this person clearly does not have a fully good character because of his desires.

18. Mollena Williams, "Digging in the Dirt: The Lure of Taboo Role Play," in *The Ultimate Guide to Kink: BDSM, Role Play, and the Erotic Edge*, edited by Tristan Taorimino (Berkeley, Calif.: Cleis Press, 2012), 366–87, at 370–71 (her emphasis). Willaims-Haas ("Haas" because in 2015 she married the composer Georg Friedrich Haas) is an African American woman who has participated in BDSM for twenty years, including being a sub to white men doms.

19. One must then trust one's partner to know that they are not really a closeted racist. See Williams, http://www.mollena.com/2009/04/race-play-interview-part-iv/ (accessed July 6, 2016).

20. Viola Johnson, a black Jewish female sub who enjoys master/slave and Nazi/Jew play, goes so far as to say that she can ignore the reality of the political backdrop altogether so as to enjoy the fantasy: "We have left reality on the other side of the leather door. In no way have we downplayed the historic bitterness of the past; we have just chosen to keep it in perspective, and outside of the scene. Those who, for personal reasons, can't play slave scenes, just don't play slave scenes." See http://www.leatherweb.com/raceplayh.htm (accessed October 30, 2016). Others such as Goddess Sonya, a black professional dominatrix, does not enjoy race play since she prefers to play the dom and there's nothing racially charged by calling a white man "honky." See Araine Cruz, *The Color of Kink: Black Women, BDSM, and Pornography* (New York: New York University Press, 2016), 68.

21. Hopkins also argues that BDSM is a simulation of injustice, which could make it ethical ("Simulation and the Reproduction of Injustice").

22. Nils-Hennes Stear argues that BDSM is make-believe, which could make it ethical ("Sadomasochism as Make-Believe," *Hypatia* 24:2 [2009], 21–38).

23. There are cases of BDSM engagements that can take over large parts of a life, such as erotic ownership (sometimes referred to as "24/7," "lifestyle BDSM" or "total power exchange"). The dom "owns" the sub, and the sub willingly does what the dom asks, in an arrangement that can last weeks, months, even years. But these are a minority. See Robin Bauer, *Queer BDSM Intimacies: Critical Consent and Pushing Boundaries* (New York: Palgrave Macmillan, 2014), especially chapter 5.

24. On sexual orientation, see the essay by Dembroff in this volume. On comparing BDSM to gayness, see Tess M. Gemberling, Robert Cramer, and Rowland S. Miller, "BDSM as Sexual Orientation: A Comparison to Lesbian, Gay, and Bisexual Sexuality," *Journal of Positive Sexuality* 1 (November 2015), 56–62.

25. We can see these examples in Aristotle's view of friendship in Books VIII and IX in his *Nicomachean Ethics*. My view does not require that the friends be virtuous, but if they are, this ensures that everything they do is good or not bad.

26. On sexual empowerment, see Zoë D. Peterson, "What Is Sexual Empowerment? A Multidimensional and Process-Oriented Approach to Adolescent Girls' Sexual Empowerment," *Sex Roles* 62:5–6 (2010), 307–13.

27. To be clear, I do not claim that BDSM practitioners *are* flourishing. Other conditions, such as being a good person in other aspects of one's life, must be satisfied for them to flourish.

28. Thanks to Alexander Neubauer and Damon Watson for reading sections of this essay and helping me clarify some of the arguments. Special thanks to Raja Halwani for reading drafts, clarifying some of the issues of this essay, and editing the chapter to a manageable length.

STUDY QUESTIONS

1. There are many BDSM scenes in which the participants do not touch each other in any usual sexual sense (e.g., when a dominatrix only whips someone). In what sense, then, can we call BDSM scenes sexual, as Miller does? If we cannot describe all such scenes as sexual, why include an essay on BDSM in this book? (Read Greta Christiana's "Are We Having Sex Now, Or What?" in this volume for some of the complications of what makes an activity sexual.)

2. Miller claims that "the major component [of BDSM activity] is the consensual exchange of power," not pain. Think of examples of BDSM scenes that contain the wielding of power but not pain. Why does Miller use "exchange" in his characterization of BDSM? Is it necessary?

3. Provide a convincing explanation of how the reception of pain (even if pain is not part of every BDSM scene) is also pleasurable. Think of non-BDSM situations that involve physical pain but that are also deeply pleasurable to those who feel the pain.

4. Consent is crucial for the permissibility of many BDSM activities. Miller claims that it is consent that converts a boxing match from being physical assault to being a boxing match. How might he (or you) reply to the following remark? "No. A boxing match is still assault, but one to which the parties consent."

5. Clearly explain Miller's argument as to why BDSM desires, especially those that seem to be racist, misogynist, homophobic, and so forth, are ethically in the clear. Do you find the argument convincing? Why or why not?

6. Think of examples of negative emotions (e.g., fear and sorrow) that are enjoyed or that are pleasurable to experience under certain circumstances (e.g., when on a roller coaster or while watching a sad fictional movie). Might a defender of the ethically suspicious desires of BDSM help themselves to such examples to construct a defense of these desires and how they differ from, say, real racist desires?

7. What does the idea of "good intentions" mean exactly in how Miller uses it? Is it possible for a bad person (e.g., a racist, a misogynist) to use BDSM as a way to act on his desires yet intend no harm to his submissive? What does this tell us about the use of concepts such as "intention," "motive," and "desire" in this discussion?
8. Do BDSM desires have the same place or depth in a person's character as a person's sexual orientation? What reasons do we have for answering this question positively and reasons for answering it negatively?
9. According to Miller, BDSM practitioners lead challenging or authentic lives (inclusive "or") that are also enhanced or flourishing (partly) because of being challenging or authentic. Is this true also of many members of oppressed groups (poor people, some ethnic minorities), who lead complex or authentic (inclusive "or," again) lives? In what ways, if any, are their lives different from those of BDSM practitioners?

TWENTY-FOUR

Two Views of Sexual Ethics

Promiscuity, Pedophilia, and Rape

David Benatar

David Benatar *attempts to construct a disjunctive dilemma arising from two popular philosophical attitudes about sexuality. On one view (the "casual" philosophy of sex), sexual pleasure is a (generally) harmless and basic pleasure, like the pleasure of eating. On the other view (the "significance" philosophy of sex), sexual activity is a serious type of activity that is acceptable only when it "signifies" love or commitment. However, each view faces problems. The casual view implies that pedophilia is not morally wrong and that rape is not as wrong as we thought it to be, because if sexual pleasure is a pleasure like any other, why would sex with children be wrong and rape seriously wrong? On the other hand, if the value of sexual activity lies in its significance (through love or commitment) and not in its pleasure, then rape and pedophilia are wrong, but casual sex and even mild promiscuity are also wrong. Given that the consequents of both conditionals are false (if sexual activity is about pleasure, then rape is in principle justifiable; if sex is about love or commitment, then casual sex is wrong), the "casual" and the "significance" views of sex are unacceptable as stated. The "casual" view has no power to prohibit sexual acts that are immensely pleasurable for one person yet harmful for another, while the "significance" view cannot morally bless what many people both engage in and approve of: sex without love. Benatar proceeds to ask whether there is some hybrid or intermediate philosophical position that is sufficiently permissive to allow casual sex but sufficiently restrictive to condemn rape and pedophilia. Because the child molester is contemporary culture's boogeyman, the embodiment of the darkest fears of many people,*

Benatar's frank discussion of the source of our abhorrence of pedophilia is valuable.

David Benatar is professor of philosophy at the University of Cape Town, South Africa, and the author of *Better Never to Have Been: The Harm of Coming into Existence* (Oxford University Press, 2006), and *The Second Sexism: Discrimination Against Men and Boys* (Wiley-Blackwell, 2012). He has also edited *Life, Death, and Meaning: Key Philosophical Readings on the Big Questions* (Rowman & Littlefield, 2004—now in its 3rd edition, 2016). This essay was first published in *Public Affairs Quarterly*, vol. 16, no. 3 (2002), 191–201. It is reprinted here with the permission of David Benatar and *Public Affairs Quarterly*.

The sexual revolution did not overthrow taboos about sex, but rather only restricted the number of practices regarded as taboo. Some sexual behaviors that were formally condemned are now tolerated or even endorsed. Others continue to be viewed with the opprobrium formerly dispensed to a broader range of sexual conduct. Promiscuity, for example, is widely accepted, but rape and pedophilia continue to be reviled.

On the face of it, this cluster of views—accepting promiscuity but regarding rape and pedophilia as heinous—seems perfectly defensible. I shall argue, however, that the view of sexual ethics that underlies an acceptance of promiscuity is inconsistent with regarding (1) rape as worse than other forms of coercion or assault, or (2) (many) sex acts with willing children as wrong at all. And the view of sexual ethics that would *fully* explain the wrong of rape and pedophilia would also rule out promiscuity. I intend this argument neither as a case against promiscuity nor as a mitigation of rape or a partial defense of pedophilia. My purpose is to highlight an inconsistency in many people's judgments. Whether one avoids the inconsistency by extending or limiting the range of practices one condemns will depend on which underlying view of the ethics of sex one accepts.

There are many views about the ethics of sex, but not all of these bear on the issues at hand. Consider, for instance, the view that a necessary condition of a sexual activity's being morally acceptable is that it carry the possibility of procreation.[1] While this view would be directly relevant to the practice of contraception, it would provide no way of morally judging promiscuity, pedophilia, or rape per se. Under some conditions, all of these practices would have procreative possibility.[2] Under others, none of them would. I shall restrict my attention to two views of sexual ethics that have special relevance to the three sexual practices I am considering.

TWO VIEWS OF SEXUAL ETHICS

The first of these is the view that for sex to be morally acceptable, it must be an expression of (romantic) love. It must, in other words, signify feelings of affection that are commensurate with the intimacy of the sexual activity. On this view a sexual union can be acceptable only if it reflects the reciprocal love and affection of the parties to that union. We might call this the significance view (or, alternatively, the love view) of sex, because it requires sex to signify love in order for it to be permissible.

On an alternative view of sexual ethics—what we might call the *casual view*—sex need not have this significance in order to be morally permissible. Sexual pleasure, according to this view, is morally like any other pleasure and may be enjoyed subject only to the usual sorts of moral constraints. A gastronomic delight, obtained via theft of a culinary delicacy, would be morally impermissible, but where no general moral principle (such as a prohibition on theft) applies, there can be no fault with engaging in gourmet pleasures. Having meals with a string of strangers or mere acquaintances is not condemnable as "casual gastronomy," "eating around," or "culinary promiscuity." Similarly, according to the casual view, erotic pleasures may permissibly be obtained from sex with strangers or mere acquaintances. There need not be any love or affection. (Nor need there always be pleasure. Just as a meal or a theatre performance might not be pleasurable and is not for that reason morally impermissible, so sex is not, nor ought to be, always pleasurable.)

Both the significance view and the casual view are moral claims about when people *may* engage in sex. They are not descriptive claims about when people *do* engage in sex. Clearly both kinds of sex do occur. Sometimes sex does reflect love. Sometimes it does not.

IMPLICATIONS OF THE TWO VIEWS

A sexually promiscuous person is somebody who is casual about sex— somebody for whom sex is not (or need not be) laden with romantic significance. (As promiscuity is obviously a matter of degree, for the most promiscuous people sex need not even be *tinged* with romantic significance.) This is not to say that the sexually promiscuous will have sex with simply anybody. Even the promiscuous can exercise some discretion in their choice of sexual partners just as the gastronomically "promiscuous" may be discriminating in the sort of people with whom they may wish to dine. The sexually promiscuous person is not one who is entirely undiscriminating about sexual partners, but rather somebody for whom romantic attachments are not a relevant consideration in choosing a sexual partner. It is thus clear why promiscuity is frowned upon by advocates of the significance view of sex. The promiscuous person treats as insignificant that which ought to be significant.

The significance view also has an explanation of why pedophilia is wrong. Children, it could be argued, are unable to appreciate the full significance that sexual activity should have.[3] This is not to suggest that children are asexual beings, but rather that they may lack the capacity to understand how sex expresses a certain kind of love. Having sex with a child is thus to treat the child as a mere means to attaining erotic pleasure without consideration of the mental states of which the provision of that pleasure should be an expression. Even if the child is sexually aroused, that arousal is not an expression of the requisite sorts of feelings. If the child is beyond infancy, the experience, in addition to being objectifying, may be deeply bewildering and traumatizing. The significance view of sex also provides an explanation of the special wrong of rape. On this view, raping people—forcing them to have sex—is not like forcing them to engage in other activities, such as going to the opera or to dinner. It is to compel a person to engage in an activity that should be an expression of deep affection. To forcibly strip it of that significance is to treat a vitally important component of sexual activity as though it were a mere trifle. It thus expresses extreme indifference to the deepest aspects of the person whose body is used for the rapist's gratification.

In defending promiscuous or casual sex, it has often been observed that not everybody thinks that sex must be an expression of love or affection. Many people, it is said, take the casual view of sex. For them, as I have said, sex is just another kind of pleasure and is permissible in the absence of love or affection. It is quite clear why this casual view does indeed entail the acceptability of promiscuous sex. What is often not realized, however, is that this view of sexual ethics leaves without adequate support the common judgments that are made about pedophilia and rape. I consider each of these two practices in turn.

If sex is morally just like other (pleasurable) activities and bears no special significance, why may it not be enjoyed with children? One common answer is that sex (with an adult)[4] can be harmful to a child. In the most extreme cases, including those involving physical force or those in which an adult copulates with a very small child, physical damage to the child can result. But clearly not all pedophilic acts are of this kind. Many, perhaps most, pedophilic acts are non-penetrative and do not employ physical force. Psychological harm is probably more common than physical damage. It is not clear, however, as a number of authors writing on this topic have noted, to what extent that harm is the result of the sexual encounter itself and to what extent it is the result of the secrecy and taboo that surrounds that sexual activity.[5] Insofar as a thorough embracing of the casual view of sex would eliminate those harms, the defender of this view cannot appeal to them in forming a principled objection to sexual interaction between adults and children. Because a society in which there were no taboos on pedophilia would avoid harm resulting from taboos on such activities and would simultaneously be inclusive of the pedophile's sexual orientation, it has everything to recommend it for defenders of the casual view.[6] At the most, advocates of this view can say that the current psychological harms impose temporary[7] moral constraints on sex with those children who, given their unfortunate puritanical upbringing or circumstances, would experience psychological trauma. Even such children may not be damaged by every kind of sexual interaction with an adult. For example, there is reason to believe that, where the child is a willing participant, the harm is either significantly attenuated or absent.[8]

Here it might be objected that although a child may sometimes appear to be a willing participant in sexual conduct with an adult, it is impossible for a child to give genuine consent to sexual activity.[9] For this reason, it might be argued, it is always wrong to engage in sexual relations with a child. Now, while this claim is entirely plausible on the significance view of sexual ethics, one is hard-pressed to explain how it is compatible with the casual view. What is it about sex, so understood, that a child is unable to consent to it? On this view, sex need carry no special significance and thus there is nothing that a child needs to understand in order to enter into a permissible sexual encounter. In response, it might be suggested that what a child needs to understand are the possible health risks associated with (casual) sex. That response, however, will not suffice to rule out all that those opposed to pedophilia wish to rule out. First, some sexual activities—most especially the noninvasive ones—do not carry significant health risks. Second, where children themselves are not thought competent to evaluate the risks of an activity, it is usually thought that a parent or guardian may, within certain risk limits, make the assessment on the child's behalf. Thus a parent may decide to give a child a taste of alcohol, allow a child to read certain kinds of books, or permit a child to participate in a sport that carries risks. If sex need be no more significant than other such activities, it is hard to see why its risks (especially when, as a result of safe sex, these are relatively small) and not those of the other activities (even when the latter are greater) constitute grounds for categorically excluding children and invalidating the consent which they or their parents give.

There is another consent-related objection that might be raised against pedophilia.[10] It might be argued that given the differences between adults and children, it is not possible for an adult and a child to understand one another's motives for wanting to have sex. The mutual unintelligibility of their motives makes it impossible for each party to know even roughly what the encounter means to the other, and the absence of this information compromises the validity of the consent. Although this objection, like the previous one, is thoroughly plausible on the significance view, it lacks force on the casual view. Notice that the absence of mutual intelligibility of motives is not thought to be an objection to those activities with children, such as playing a game, that are not thought to carry the significance attributed to sex by the significance view. A child might be quite oblivious that the adult is playing the game only to give the child pleasure and that the adult may even be losing the game on purpose in order to enhance the child's pleasure or to build the child's sense of self-esteem. Yet this is not thought to constitute grounds for invalidating a child's ability to consent to game playing with adults. The need for some mutual intelligibility of motive arises only if sex is significant.

Nor is it evident, on the casual view (unless it is coupled with a child-liberationist position), why children need consent at all. If a parent may pressure or force a child into participating in a sport (on grounds of "character-building"), or into going to the opera (on grounds of "learning to appreciate the arts"), why may a parent not coerce or pressure a child into sex? Perhaps a parent believes that treating sex as one does other aspects of life forestalls neurosis in the child and that gaining sexual experience while young is an advantage. If the evidence were sufficiently inconclusive that reasonable people could disagree about whether children really did benefit from an early sexual start, then those defenders of the casual view who also accept paternalism toward children would have to allow parents to decide for their children.

Whether or not interference with a child's freedom is justified, few people think that it is acceptable to interfere with the freedom of adults by, for example, forcing them to take up sport, go to the opera, or eat something (irrespective of whether it would be good for them). Those who accept this, even if they have the casual view of sexual ethics, have grounds for finding rape (of adults) morally defective. To rape people is to force them to do something that they do not want to do. Rape is an unwarranted interference with a person's body and freedom. The problem, for the defenders of the casual view, is that it need be no more serious an interference than would be forcing somebody to eat something, for example. Thus, although the casual view can explain why rape is wrong, it cannot explain why it is a special kind of wrong. One qualification needs to be added. Perhaps a proponent of the casual view could recognize that rape is especially wrong for those who do not share the casual view—that is, for those who believe (mistakenly, according to the casual view) that sex ought to be significant. A suitable analogy would be that of forcing somebody to eat a pork sausage. The seriousness of such an interference would be much greater if the person on whom one forced this meal were a vegetarian (or a Jew or a Muslim) than if he were not. A particular violation of somebody's freedom can be either more or less significant, depending on that person's attitudes. Although some may be willing to accept that rape is especially wrong only when committed against somebody who holds the significance view of sex, many would not. Many feminists, for example, have argued at length for the irrelevance, in rape trials, of a woman's sexual history. But if the casual view is correct, then her sexual history would be evidence—although not conclusive evidence—of her view of sexual ethics. This in turn would be relevant to determining how great a harm the rape was (but not to *whether* it was rape and thus to whether it was harmful). Raping somebody for whom sex has as little significance (of the sort under consideration) as eating a tomato would be like forcing somebody to eat a tomato. Raping somebody for whom sex is deeply significant would be much worse. Although a significance view of sex might also allow such distinctions between the severity of different rapes, it can at least explain why rape of anybody is more serious than forcing somebody to eat a tomato.

CHOOSING BETWEEN THE VIEWS

Is there any way of choosing between the significance and casual views of sex? Some might take the foregoing reflections to speak in favor of or against one of the views. Those who are convinced that promiscuity is morally permissible may be inclined to think that the casual view must be correct because it supports this judgment. Others, who believe that pedophilia is wrong and that rape is a special kind of evil and is unlike other violations of a person's body or autonomy, may think that the significance view is correct given that it can support these judgments.

There are other factors that are also relevant to evaluating each of these views of sexual ethics. Consider first those who speak in favor of the significance view. This view fits well with judgments most people make about forms of intimacy that, although not sexual practices themselves, are not unrelated to the intimacies of sex: (1) casually sharing news of one's venereal disease (a) with a mere acquaintance, or (b) with one's spouse or other close family member; (2) undressing (a) in the street, or (b) in front of one's spouse in the privacy of one's bedroom. Very few people would feel exactly the same about (a) as about (b) in either of these examples. This would suggest that most people think that intimacies are appropriately shared only with those to whom one is close, even if they disagree about just how close one has to be in order to share a certain level of intimacy. The significance view seems to capture an important psychological feature about humans. Although descriptive psychological claims do not entail normative judgments, any moral view that attempted to deny immutable psychological traits characteristic of all (or almost all) humans would be defective.

But are these psychological traits really universal or are they rather cultural products, found only among some peoples? There are examples of societies that are much less restrictive about sex (including sex with children) than is ours, just as there are societies in which there are many more taboos than in ours pertaining to food and eating. It is too easy to assume that the way we feel about sex and food is the way all people do. If so, and if others are better off for their more open views of sex, then the defender of the casual view may have a message of sexual liberation that would be worth heeding.[11] This is not to say that it would be an easy matter (even for an individual, let alone a whole society) to abandon a significance view and thoroughly embrace the casual view. But if the casual view is the preferable one, then even if it would be difficult to adopt, it would nonetheless be a view to which people ought to strive. One way to do this would be to rear children with the casual view.

Whether viewing sex as significant is characteristic of all humanity or only of certain human cultures is clearly an empirical issue that psychologists, anthropologists, and others would be best suited to determine. This matter cannot be settled here. In the absence of such a determination and of a convincing argument for one or the other view of sexual ethics, the appropriate response is agnosticism (of the theoretical even if not the practical form). Neither form of agnosticism would permit one to follow *both* views—the one for the pedophilia and rape issues and the other for the promiscuity issue. At least at the theoretical level, the choices we make should be consistent if they are to avoid the comfortable acquiescence to whatever happen to be the current mores. Agnosticism about the correct view of sex, like agnosticism on any other issue, is not to be confused with indifference. One may care deeply about an issue while realizing that the available evidence is insufficient to make a judgment on it. Caring deeply, however, should not stand in the way of a dispassionate assessment of the evidence. There is a great danger that in matters pertaining to current sexual taboos, clear thinking will be in short supply.

Hybrids of the two views may be possible. For instance, it may be thought that sex is not quite like other pleasures, but it need not be linked to the deepest forms of romantic love. On one such view, it might be sufficient that one *like*[12] (rather than love) somebody in order to copulate. However, no such mixed view would resolve our problem. Any view that took a sufficiently light view of sex that would justify promiscuity would have difficulty ruling out all pedophilia or classifying rape as the *special* wrong it is usually thought to be.

Nor do I think that a non-hybrid intermediate view will be able to drive a moral wedge between promiscuity, on the one hand, and rape and pedophilia, on the other. Such an intermediate view would (as the casual view does) deny that sex must be an expression of romantic affection but (in common with the significance view) deny that sex is like other pleasures. Although I obviously cannot anticipate every possible way in which such a view might be developed, I find it hard to imagine how any version could distinguish promiscuity from rape and pedophilia. Consider two versions of an allegedly intermediate view that have been put to me.

The first of these[13] is that although sex need not be an expression of romantic affection, it is unlike other pleasures in that it is intimate or private. The latter part of this claim might be understood as being either descriptive or normative. The descriptive claim is that most people prefer to engage in sex (i) with intimates[14] or (ii) away from the view of others. The normative claim is that people *ought* to engage in sex only (i) with intimates or (ii) away from the view of others. If the basis for (some or other of) these claims is that sex is or ought to be a deep expression of a romantic affection, then the view under discussion is either support for or a disguised version of the significance view rather than an alternative intermediate view. I cannot think of other reasons why sex is morally permissible only *between intimates*, but perhaps there is some such reason why sex is or ought to be *private*. If there is, then there would be an intermediate view between the significance and casual views. But what would be wrong, on this intermediate view, with *private* sex between an adult and a willing child? And why would coerced private sex be worse than other kinds of coerced activities in private? I suspect that any plausible answer to these questions would have to appeal to the normative significance of sex as an expression of affection, and any such appeal could not lead to a special condemnation of rape and all pedophilia without also implying a condemnation of promiscuity.

The second version of an allegedly non-hybrid intermediate view that has been suggested to me is that sex is unlike other pleasures because it is "personally involving ([that is,] psycho-dynamically complex)" in ways that other pleasures are not.[15] However, it seems that any interpretation of the view that sex is personally involving would be, or would lend support to, a significance view of sex. It would surely be inappropriate, at least as a moral ideal, to engage in personally involving behaviors with those (such as mere acquaintances) with whom personal involvement (at the relevantly complex or deep level) is not really possible. If that is so, then I cannot see how the second non-hybrid intermediate view can succeed in driving a wedge between promiscuity on the one hand, and rape and pedophilia on the other.

The above conclusions should obviously be extremely troubling to those who approve of promiscuity but who abhor pedophilia and rape. My deliberations show, however, that this should provide little cause for self-satisfaction on the part of those who condemn promiscuity along with rape and all pedophilia. Their moral judgments about these practices may be consistent, but it remains an open question whether they are consistently right or consistently wrong. Which it is will depend on which of the rival views of sexual ethics is better. Until that matter is resolved, adherents of both the significance view and the casual view have cause for unease.[16]

NOTES

1. My own view is that if the possibility of procreation has anything to do with the moral acceptability of sex, then the *absence* rather than the presence of such a possibility is a necessary condition for sex's moral acceptability. The foundation for this admittedly unusual view is my argument that coming into existence is always a harm and therefore to bring somebody into existence is always to inflict a harm. It follows that it is procreative rather than non-procreative sex that bears the burden on moral justification. See my "Why It Is Better Never to Come into Existence," *American Philo-*

sophical Quarterly 34:3 (July 1997), 345–55, and *Better Never to Have Been: The Harm of Coming into Existence* (Oxford: Oxford University Press, 2006).

2. Sexual intercourse with a pre-pubescent child has no procreative possibility. Those opposed to pedophilia, at least in our society, include under the rubric of "pedophilia" not only sex with such children but also with pubescent children, where procreation is a possibility. I assume, then, that the procreative condition is not the grounds on which they oppose pedophilia.

3. Adherents of the significance view need not take all pedophilia to be wrong. They might think that children (beyond a certain age) *can* understand the full significance of sex. I am thus claiming only that the significance view has a way of arguing that pedophilia is wrong, not that it has to argue in that way.

4. It is interesting that many of those who take pedophilia to be harmful do not have the same reprobation for sex between two people both of whom are (in the relevant sense) children.

5. Alfred Kinsey et al., *Sexual Behavior in the Human Female* (Philadelphia: W. B. Saunders Co., 1953), 120–21; Robert Ehman, "Adult-Child Sex," in *Philosophy and Sex* (New Revised [2nd] Edition), edited by Robert Baker and Frederick Elliston (Buffalo, N.Y.: Prometheus Books, 1984), 431–46, at 436; Igor Primoratz, *Ethics and Sex* (London: Routledge, 1999), 138. A commentator on my paper when I presented it at a conference claimed that there is much evidence to suggest that the harm does not result from the taboo. In support of this claim, she cited Anna Luise Kirkengen's *Inscribed Bodies: Health Impact of Childhood Sexual Abuse* (Dordrecht: Kluwer, 2001). I, however, am unable to find any support for her claim in this work. The book does deal with the adverse effects of sexual interactions with children. However, the question of whether it is the sexual interactions themselves or the taboos against them that cause harm is a specialized question that, as far as I can tell, is not addressed in this book. I mention the source in fairness to my commentator and for the benefit of those readers who wish to examine it for themselves.

6. Allen Buchanan has argued, in the context of a different debate, that the "morality of inclusion" requires that cooperative frameworks be made more inclusive where this is possible without unreasonable cost. (See his "The Morality of Inclusion," *Social Philosophy and Policy* 10:2 (June 1996), 233–57.) Notice that even those ways of satisfying pedophilic preferences that do not involve actual children—such as child pornography that is either synthesized (that is, without using real models or actors) or produced by adults being represented as children—are also abhorred, even where adult pornography is not. This suggests that the common abhorrence of pedophilia is not fully explained by the harm it is believed to do to the children involved.

7. That is, until the taboos can be eliminated.

8. T. G. M. Sandfort, "The Argument for Adult-Child Sexual Contact: A Critical Appraisal and New Data," in *The Sexual Abuse of Children: Theory and Research*, vol. 1, edited by William O'Donohue and James H. Geer (Hillsdale, N.J.: Lawrence Erlbaum Associates, 1992), 38–48; Bruce Rind, Philip Tromovitch, and Robert Bauserman, "A Meta-Analytic Examination of Assumed Properties of Child Sexual Abuse Using College Samples," *Psychological Bulletin* 124:1 (1998), 22–53.

9. See, for example, David Finkelhor, "What's Wrong with Sex between Adults and Children: Ethics and the Problem of Sexual Abuse," *American Journal of Orthopsychiatry* 49:4 (1979), 692–97.

10. This objection was raised by an anonymous reviewer for *Public Affairs Quarterly*.

11. Of course, such benefits would have to be offset against the risks of sexually transmitted diseases, or steps would have to be taken within a sexual life governed by the casual view to minimize such risks.

12. In this context, "like" cannot mean "sexually attracted to," because that would be too weak to differentiate it from the pure hedonist view. Instead it would have to mean something like "have psychological affections-less-than-love for."

13. I am grateful to Raja Halwani for putting this to me and for suggesting that I raise and respond to the possibility of a non-hybrid intermediate view.

14. This appears not to be true of the promiscuous unless one stipulates that anybody with whom one has sex is thereby an intimate.

15. This view was suggested to me by an anonymous reviewer for *Public Affairs Quarterly*.

16. An earlier version of this chapter was presented at a meeting of the Society for the Philosophy of Sex and Love at the Eastern Division meeting of the American Philosophical Association on December 30, 2001. The author is grateful to the University of Cape Town's Research Committee, as well as the International Science Liaison of the (South African) National Research Foundation, for providing funding that enabled him to attend and participate in this meeting.

STUDY QUESTIONS

1. Defend the "casual" view against the charge, leveled by Benatar, that it is incompatible with the claim that sexual relations between an adult and a child as a partner are *always* wrong. Try to do so without cutting back on the moral permissibility of sex without love.

2. In laying out the two views, Benatar explains the "casual" view using primarily the concept of "sexual pleasure," but he explains the "significance" view using primarily the concept of "sexual activity." Is there a reason for this discrepancy? (Indeed, *is* it a discrepancy?) Try to explain each view using the same concept—that is, first explain each view using "sexual pleasure," and then explain each view using "sexual activity." Might doing so reveal problems with Benatar's reasoning or, on the contrary, cement it?

3. "Raping a person for whom sexual activity has merely the significance of eating a tomato would be like forcing someone to eat a tomato." Is this analogy psychologically apt or a misleading piece of rhetoric? Explain your answer. Pay attention, in your deliberations, to the issue of the evidentiary status of a claimant's sexual history in a rape trial (e.g., whether she has had a wildly promiscuous lifestyle or has spent many years working as a prostitute).

4. Benatar writes, "Because a society in which there were no taboos on pedophilia would avoid harm resulting from taboos on such activities and would simultaneously be inclusive of the pedophile's sexual orientation, it has everything to recommend it for defenders of the casual view." Is there any rationale for the mention of sexual orientation in this context? How could Benatar's point be made without employing this concept? What is the "sexual orientation" of which he speaks? Furthermore, is his claim true?

5. Benatar dismisses intermediate philosophies of sex that invoke privacy, intimacy, or the "personally involving" nature of sexuality. Relying on views of sexual ethics expressed elsewhere in this volume (for example, Alan Goldman, Alan Wertheimer, Robin West),

try to demarcate some other sort of an intermediate view distinct from these, one that meets his objections.

6. According to Benatar, the "casual" view of sex has difficulty explaining the wrongness of pedophilia and the serious wrongness of rape. But does the "significance" view, according to which sexual activity is morally acceptable only if it expresses reciprocal love, fare any better? Are rape and pedophilia not wrong, or less wrong, if the participants love each other?

7. Benatar closes by posing the question: Which of the rival views is better? What does "better" mean here? Would an explication or definition of "better" depend on which of the rival views one had prior commitments to? Or is there an independent, theory-neutral standard of "better" to which we might appeal in addressing this question?

8. Evaluate the following argument and what Benatar would say in reply to it: "Insignificant pleasures are of two types. Some are significant *enough* that only the agent who would experience them should decide whether to actually experience them, and being forced to experience them would be a serious wrong. Others are not a big deal: being forced to experience them would be wrong but not a serious wrong. An example of the former is the pleasure of rock climbing, and an example of the latter is the pleasure of eating a piece of fruit. Sexual pleasure is more like the pleasure of rock-climbing than the pleasure of eating a tomato: forcing one to undergo the activity that normally gives rise to the pleasure would be a morally serious issue." Would this be a non-intermediate hybrid view? If so, would it succumb already to what Benatar has to say about such views?

TWENTY-FIVE

Gifts and Duties

Alan Soble

*In this essay **Alan Soble** explores the idea of whether there are sexual duties to others—strangers, especially—and what the source of such duties might be. He provides good reasons for thinking that such duties exist (there might even be, ironically, a Christian sexual duty, flowing from the very nature of* agape*). Furthermore, Soble explores whether there are supererogatory sexual actions—sexual actions that go beyond the demands of duty. He begins his essay with a personal example of him having had sex with a woman in graduate school out of moral duty—at least what he thought at the time was moral duty. He ends his essay by addressing numerous factors that can exist in such types of cases, thus reminding us of how intricate and complex our thinking about these issues should be.*

> Never reach out your hand unless you're willing to extend an arm.
> —Pope Paul VI and/or Elizabeth Fuller

> If you go to bed with her, you got to keep seeing her for a month.
> —Carrie Heffernan[1]

I have written on the topic of this essay—the source and morality of preferences, and of acting on preferences, in the personal domain of life (love relationships, marriage, sexual entanglements)—several times, without achieving closure.[2] It continues to plague me, both professionally and in memories of my life. Here I tackle the topic again, except this time the essay will be significantly autobiographical. There's another difference: I accept the failure of closure. In my earlier writings I was overly optimistic to have aimed for definitive answers. This essay, then, is primarily exploratory. If I do not explicitly answer your favorite questions about the matters I deal with, or speak about your favorite sexual scenarios, join the exploration by considering the principles and distinctions that are discussed in this essay in an attempt to tease out for yourself answers to your questions. Good. Philosophy can engage only in enlightening, succinct, open-ended exploration.

GRADUATE SCHOOL

In the early 1970s (then a baby boomer, now geezer), I had a sexual experience about which I wish I had thought more carefully before it took place. The encounter was with another student, a woman in her early twenties, slightly younger than I. Toward the sexual acts that were coming I felt *none* of the excitement of anticipation but, instead and strangely, the pull of powerful *moral* obligation. "Feeling" this pull is compatible with sensing a genuine duty, but it is also compatible with merely imagining that I had a duty. The duty I felt was *to give her sexual pleasure*. The felt duty was made stronger by the nagging thought that I should be faithful to my emerging libertine ideals (a matter of personal integrity, i.e., being honest with myself), about which she knew, and she also knew that I knew that she knew (hence a matter of interpersonal or public integrity as well). I imagined I was a young Bertrand Russell.

This woman had the property "Ψ," often evaluated in our culture as a repulsive physical feature (although preferred by some people). Given my sexual tastes at the time, I felt no sexual desire for her. Nor was I under the confusing irrational spell of indiscriminate appetite (being horny). She approached me tentatively, shyly, and made her request softly. The questions that concern me here are about the morality of taking on and fulfilling this task. Was it morally permissible or was it obviously morally wrong? Did I have, instead of a duty *not* to engage in sex with her, a duty *to* engage in sex with her (my felt sentiment)? Was my behavior, perhaps, even morally exemplary?

You may find relevant the fact that I had been, a year earlier, her exact male counterpart. I had been in her Ψ-physical and social situation and thereby knew (or maybe only surmised or projected) her pains and fears. Sympathy for her arose in me, which was also sympathy for myself—that is, for the self I used to be, for I had undergone, during that year, a miraculous makeover. So, what moved me to accept her plan was sympathy and moral obligation, but also the joy, before any sexual acts occurred, of being able to help someone who needed the same help, or the same gift, that I had needed for years, and so the joy of vicariously helping myself.

MORAL CATEGORIES

Regarding sexuality, as in other areas of life, philosophers distinguish actions that are morally *permissible* (for example, consensual erotic kissing between two adults) from those that are *wrong*, such as rape. Which sexual acts are deemed permissible or wrong (prohibited) varies, depending on the moral perspective or religious allegiance of the persons doing the deeming. Nonetheless, the notion that a sexual act is a moral *duty* usually enters sexual discourse only negatively: people have duties *to refrain* from performing wrong acts. A duty *to* engage in joyous sex seems as incomprehensible as a duty to eat delicious pizza. Nonetheless, I will embrace the intuition that there probably is, in some circumstances, a duty *to perform* sexual acts which prohibits *not* engaging in sex. Further, if the idea of duties to engage in sex is coherent, there is another (and underutilized) moral category: sexual *supererogation*—sexual acts that go "above and beyond" what our duties demand of us and may be exemplary or praiseworthy.[3]

Probably most moral and religious perspectives on human sexuality agree that people have many general and specific duties *to avoid* sexual activity (no rape, no pedophilia, no adultery, no bestiality).[4] It is less frequently acknowledged that people have moral or religious duties *to engage* in sexual activity, that engaging in sex in certain circumstances (e.g., to make better the lives of the sexually deprived, malnourished, or physically disabled) may be morally or religiously required as a duty based on a secular humanist principle of benevolence or on the Judeo-Christian "Love Thy Neighbor." Some sexual acts may be morally or religiously supererogatory, if they are modeled on the behavior of Luke's Good Samaritan (10:25–37). I explore these conceptual and practical possibilities.

It is well-known that the behavior of people is not always consistent with the moral or religious principles that they hold (or think they hold, or pretend to hold). Sometimes acting according to a duty is difficult. A person may be tempted to cut corners for some gain or to avoid a loss of some good thing. People often face such decisions: Should I tell the truth or can I count on getting away with lying? It is also well known that regarding sex, people often violate various prohibitions because they are overwhelmed by the promise of pleasure. If there were duties to engage in sex, despite one's reluctance to do so, people would likely try to find exculpatory reasons, or excuses, for not acting on a duty in those circumstances in which it actually applies. True, *ought* implies *can*. But denying a sexual duty to engage in sex because following it would tax human abilities is a weak consideration; it doesn't, for example, knock out the duty not to commit adultery. Further, the difficulty of acting according to a duty to engage in sex provides a reason for judging that some sexual acts are supererogatory. Hence the difficulty illuminates why it is sometimes unclear whether an act is a duty or supererogatory.

SUPEREROGATION

In teaching courses on ethics over my career of forty-five years, I have introduced the topic of supererogation by laying out the following defining characteristics of a supererogatory act (a particular act-token, not an act-type).[5]

1. The act is not a duty, is not morally required, the agent has no obligation to do it.
2. The act is (or meant to be) beneficial for other people; it benefits others in a significant, not trivial, way. The persons benefited may be individually identifiable or nameable, or not, as when groups of people are benefited. (Maybe there are accidental as well as intentional supererogatory acts. Maybe an interfering event prevents the benefit.)
3. There is (or is likely to be) a significant reduction in the interests or the good of the agent, or the act is risky, significantly, not trivially. The agent knows or believes this feature in advance.
4. The act is morally permissible, the agent has no duty not to do it; there is nothing else about the act that makes it morally wrong.
5. The agent (or the action?) is morally praiseworthy. This feature may not be independent but follows from the satisfaction of the first four features. Note that some agents who perform very difficult duties at great cost may also be deserving of praise.[6]

I ask the class for examples from their own lives in which they were the supererogatory agent or the beneficiary. Sometimes they offer examples spontaneously; other times describing these personal experiences is a homework assignment. I also ask them to explain how each of the conditions is satisfied. The answers are the same, semester after semester: *I took my younger brother to his soccer practice even though I really wanted to hang with my friends.* I reply that this case may not satisfy condition 3—the significance of the loss is unclear. Further, there seems not to be any praise attached for helping a brother. The act is not supererogatory (in addition to its other faults, or instead of them) because siblinghood, being members of the same family, generates duties, in which case condition 1 has not been satisfied. "Take your brother to his practice," yells their mother. "What kind of a brother are you?"[7] *I let the driver of a car pull out of the parking lot into the traffic on the road, in front of me, even though I had the right of way and it meant getting to school a bit later. It wasn't even Christmas week.* Eventually, the class escapes the silly examples and someone proposes, "An old, disheveled, despondent man was sitting on a bench in

Opelousas, outside a donut store, sipping coffee; it turns out that he had fled New Orleans while a hurricane destroyed his home. I had a fifty in my wallet, which I had saved and planned to spend on an infrequent night out with my buds. I took the bill, folded it several times, and slipped it into the dude's jacket pocket. 'Take care of yourself, and good luck,' I said, as I walked away." Loud applause for the student makes me doubt that the story is true.

In a touching and, as always, absurd episode of the animated *Family Guy* ("New Kidney in Town," 2011), Peter Griffin needs a kidney transplant and the only medically satisfactory donor is Brian, the family dog. Because dog kidneys are small, Brian would have to donate both kidneys to save Peter. Still, Peter's friend offers to forfeit his life. "Morally supererogatory" is a description that could be used for Brian's exemplary behavior: it benefits another person through self-sacrifice, going beyond what moral duty demands and is, as a result, praiseworthy. Brian deserves praise even if *he* thinks that his deed flows involuntarily from his virtuous nature. Being good offers no protection against well-intentioned accolade.

Two features of this scenario reduce, however, the quality of Brian's supererogation. First, Brian and Peter are friends and family members. Duties to friends and family members may make an otherwise supererogatory act a duty. Although Brian's gift goes beyond the reach of these duties, his supererogation is not as grand as an unfamiliar dog bestowing both kidneys to save Peter's life. Second, the evening before Brian will lose his kidneys, he asks Lois (Peter's wife, for whom Brian pines) if she would allow him to hump her leg to completion. Because he gains something desirable he otherwise would not have had, the quality of Brian's supererogation is lowered, but not by much; his goal in donating his kidneys was not to hump that leg, and the good of the hump hardly outweighs his loss of life. Lois's gift to Brian is also supererogatory. She offers herself, or her leg, as an object to be used by Brian, which she finds demeaning. Lois also makes a deeper psychological sacrifice, if she is pained by the adulterous nature of this perverted (by her own standards) act. The joke is that Brian ejaculates sooner than the fifteen seconds allotted to him by Lois.

Let's return to sex. Female nurses in Amsterdam have had to insist that providing sexual services to their patients is not required by their job description; it is not one of their professional assignments, and patients should not expect to receive sexual care.[8] But if it is true that providing sexual care is not one of the occupational duties of nurses, logical space exists for it to be, in the particular, right conditions, supererogatory. When I am almost dead, and not even the lure of an easy buck for a noncoital sexual service would convince a seasoned prostitute to try her skills on me, perhaps a Dutch nurse on the staff of my post-retirement home, a sexual Mother Teresa, will take pity on, and be kind to, an old man, using

her hands to go the extra mile beyond the chores the facility has contrac-
tually agreed to pay her to do. I have just provided a paradigm case of a
supererogatory sexual act. To be reasonable, it is not only doing it for free
(no compensation) that makes the nurse's act supererogatory but doing it
at all with someone as repellent as the old man I will be (or already am,
depending on when you read this).[9] The prostitute's supererogation
would be tarnished by a payment that encourages him or her to provide
sexual care but is not erased. The scenario may be closer to an exchange
of gifts than a commercial transaction, or making a contribution to PBS
and receiving a logo apron as a token of appreciation.

SEXUAL DUTIES

The idea that people may have obligations to engage in sex will seem odd
as long as an analogy with a duty to eat pizza is deployed. It will also
seem odd if the philosopher's notion of a duty to *self* is taken seriously; a
slew of philosophers (e.g., Immanuel Kant) and theologians have insisted
that a person has a duty to himself not to pursue *too much* pleasure.[10]
However, if people have obligations to engage in sex, these duties will be
grounded not in an agent's own pleasure (or whatever it is that the agent
would want for herself from sexual activity) but in the value of the act for
the other person or persons (which may be pleasure, but not necessarily;
maybe the intimacy-*cum*-pleasure of sexual activity). Once it is recognized that if there are duties to engage in sex, the goal is to benefit others,
there is a firm basis for asserting that the general duty of benevolence or
beneficence, to which religious and secular moral codes ascribe, applies
in the sexual domain. There are, plausibly, duties to help and to be of
assistance to others, to attend to their pain and suffering, *ceteris paribus*.
These duties might be weak, requiring not much effort or cost on the part
of the agent, and perhaps ignorable in order to fulfill other duties. Some
of these duties might be strong, requiring substantial inconvenience and
effort and not overridden by other duties. Nevertheless, these considerations supply no reason to deny that sexual activity in some particular
circumstances might be obligatory according to a commonly shared general duty of benevolence. Whether the duty is weak or strong is not the
issue; the issue is whether there is *any* obligation to engage in sex, at least
sometimes. I cannot imagine that the duty of benevolence fails altogether
to make some sexual activity mandatory. After all, a humanitarian duty
of benevolence demands that the starving be fed, and there are people
who are sexually malnourished, for lots of reasons. An unimaginative
view resists: "Feeding a starving person is required to save a life, but
people can live without sex." I reply: Beg pardon, you aren't taking the
duty of benevolence seriously enough; nor are you acknowledging the
psychological pain that accompanies sexual deprivation. Medical care is

given to the needy even when it is not a matter of life or death but quality of life. Sexual experiences are required, by most people, for a decent quality of life. "Let them masturbate" or "give them a laptop and Internet access" is as cruel and ridiculous as "Let them eat cake." It also underestimates the richness of sexual experiences.

If a duty to engage in sex is at first glance foreign to the Millennial West, a reminder is fitting, that the idea of an obligation to engage in sex is of ancient origin. One place in scripture is Paul's letter 1 Corinthians 7:1–9, from which theology has extracted two doctrines. First, that marriage is *remedium concupiscentiae*: it provides spouses with sexual satisfaction so that they avoid temptations, felt when single, to fall into promiscuous fornication or opportunistic same-sex encounters. Sex acts and satisfaction in marriage prevent (worse) sins. Paul's second doctrine is the "marriage [conjugal] debt": each spouse has a *duty* to engage in sex with the other spouse pretty much on demand, otherwise marriage could not be *remedium concupiscentiae*. Exceptions include when the spouse is ill or is getting closer to God. "Not tonight, I have a headache" is supplemented with "not right now, I'm praying" but not with "I really want to watch the game." Putting a twentieth-century spin on Paul, Elizabeth Anscombe's version of the marriage debt does not allow a spouse to "insist [on sex] against *serious* reluctance of one's partner."[11] Is *really* wanting to watch the game weighty enough? Or is giving up this entertainment supererogatory? The feminist Robin Morgan once, and famously, claimed (as the feminist Bertrand Russell nearly claimed in 1929) that if a woman gives in to her pestering husband when she prefers to watch *The Late Show* in bed before falling asleep, she's been raped.[12]

Paul's welding the marriage debt to marriage's purpose as a remedy against sin makes sense: if a spouse feels sexual itches and has them dutifully scratched by the other, marriage may succeed as a remedy. Not fulfilling the duty may provoke the spouse, who is left horny, to seek lap dances—a spiritual disaster. As expected, the rationale of the obligation to engage in sex with the other spouse is that doing so benefits the other. If each spouse fulfills the duty, they help each other avoid disaster. The marriage debt also existed, prior to Christianity, in ancient Judaic teachings. A frequently absent-from-home sailor and a hardworking manual laborer owe their wives fewer sexual acts than does a three-classes-a-week professor. I wonder, however, whether engaging in sex as a duty creates a psychological obstacle to mutual pleasure, and hence would not serve as an effective remedy. Indeed, having sex on demand may cause "bedroom death"; here, too, the remedy has been undermined.[13] Of course, there are people for whom sex-as-a-duty is arousing or justifies the otherwise questionable pursuit of sexual pleasure.

Nowadays, Western culture does not advocate the marriage debt, as most of my women students (even Catholic) tell me, perhaps influenced by the announcement by feminism of a woman's inalienable right to control what happens to and in her body. Recent thought about what spouses owe each other sexually is sometimes treated as an issue of distributive justice (through microeconomic domestic welfare functions). "If a woman spends the time and energy to produce someone else's orgasm . . . it is only fair that her partner do the same for her," proposes Janice Moulton.[14] One simple function, then, is "tit for tat." A tit-for-tat policy may imply an equal number of orgasms (as Moulton suggests), or an exchange of cunnilingus and fellatio (or fellatio and fellatio, etc.), or, more generally, that each person gets out of the sexual activity what he or she wants from it: sexual pleasure, or the pleasure of giving pleasure, or intimacy, and so forth.

So a sexual duty, in marriage and other close relationships,[15] persists, even if the dialogue sounds different. Still, talk of sexual acts as a duty in a significant relationship makes me uneasy. A duty implies that things aren't going well, that the partners aren't sufficiently drawn to each other by mutual desire. Where is the joy in pleasing your spouse as if you were performing any other task (washing the dishes)? You, a man or woman, continue licking even though it takes her an hour to come (or she takes the hour to come) and your mouth and jaw are getting sore. The act is not done for your pleasure, and not for mutual pleasure, but because you *must*. Is it a fair exchange, a respectful distribution, if my orgasm occurs in three minutes while your orgasm occurs in thirty? Maybe mine was ten times more intense. Even if I have a duty, as your partner, to keep you sexually satisfied, does that mean I must perform acts for you that I detest? Doing so looks a bit supererogatory.

Women who reject the rhetoric and spiritual rationale of the Pauline marriage debt sometimes admit that it may not be prudent to cash in on feminism's absolute right to say "no." Repeated denials run the risk of alienating the other person, of driving the other person to para-monogamous ways of achieving sexual satisfaction, for example, cybersex.[16] Frequent use of the absolute, non-negotiable, non-compromising, don't-you-dare-beg-or-lay-a-guilt-trip-on-me "no" (or insisting on watching TV in bed) endangers the stability of the relationship. Maybe a spouse doesn't want to have sex here or now but also wants to maintain the relationship, not necessarily for one-sidedly base or economic reasons. The spouse may want to maintain the relationship for the good of both its members. Let's return to this scenario: X does not enjoy a certain sexual act, maybe is disgusted (like Lois) by it. X does it anyway, for the good of the other person Y and to preserve their relationship. Would the intended recipient Y request X to do it, knowing how X feels about the act? (This thoughtfulness did not occur to or dissuade Brian.) The situation is uncomfortably ironic: if Y does not permit X to do the dubious act, Y prevents X from achieving supererogation, prevents X from acting out of love or according to duty, or prevents X's attempt to solidify the relationship. Further, the intended beneficiary of the sexual act refuses to be a beneficiary: if Y cares for and about *X*, *Y* would decline the opportunity, knowing that *X* dislikes the act. The sexual domain is not immune from the paradox of altruism: *Y* out of love and respect for *X* insists that *X* not do it; *X* out of love or respect for *Y* insists that *X* does it. Nor is it immune from the paradox of egoism. *W*: "If you loved me, you would do this," followed by *Z*: "If you loved me, you wouldn't ask me to do this, *and* you wouldn't say I didn't love you if I don't do it." Stubborn *W* continues: "If you loved me, you wouldn't say 'If you loved me, you wouldn't ask me to do this, *and* you wouldn't say I didn't love you if I don't do it.'" At this point, *Z*, instead of embarking on another iteration, tells *W* to fug off.

BROADER SEXUAL DUTIES

If there can be a duty to engage in sex (some sexual activity, not necessarily coitus) for the benefit of a spouse or partner, why not also a similar benefit for a person who is not one's spouse? Søren Kierkegaard once made the astounding and profound claim that your spouse is "first and foremost" your neighbor.[17] His points were that (1) each spouse should behave toward the other spouse with *agape* (as described in 1 Corinthians 13), which is as appropriate for the spouse as it is for any neighbor (domestic *agape* makes "you are so nice to the people next door, why are you so mean to me?" unnecessary), and (2) whatever benefit a spouse would be happy to supply to the other spouse, or has an obligation to supply, should also be happily or obligingly supplied to any neighbor. The idea is that *agape* is universal. There is never a reason to bestow the goodness the flows from *agape* preferentially on one person (or one group) and not another. Christ died for everyone's sins. God loves us all equally. Hence a duty to prevent a spiritual, psychological, medical, social, or personal disaster happening to one's spouse is also a duty to provide sexual activity or pleasure for other people in situations (of which there are many kinds) in which similar disasters are imminent.

If an innocuous version of the marriage debt is acceptable, that is prima facie good reason for not restricting Pauline sexual duties to the narrow realm of the dyad. Why didn't Paul himself, when he had the opportunity in 1 Corinthians, persuade unmarried people to bestow sex benevolently, if not lovingly, on people in general to help them avoid disasters? Paul would have replied that sexual benefactors would be engaging in the same promiscuous fornication that he was attempting to curtail, to which I say: *So what?* A person's promiscuity, done to save others (thousands: Pareto optimality) from promiscuity, abandoning (if necessary) one's salvation to secure salvation for others, is analogous to Jesus's self-sacrifice, which good Judeo-Christians should emulate. Is this a duty or supererogatory? To abandon or risk one's salvation by satisfying the sexual needs of other people, so that they do not fall into soul-destroying promiscuity, may be a "Love Thy Neighbor" duty, or it may be morally exemplary in being contrary to self-interest while going beyond what *agape* requires. Self-sacrificial slutty behavior seems prima facie demanded by the *agape* sponsored by Paul in 1 Corinthians 13. A duty to engage in sex with other people—the sexually deprived, physically disabled, the leper, the enemy, the lonely, the repulsive, old, cranky, humanly unlovable—for *their* good could be a duty of "Love Thy Neighbor" or, perhaps, a secular duty of benevolence. Denying that Christian love includes benefiting other people sexually makes *agape* begrudging or stingy. It doesn't bear all things, believe all things, hope all things, endure all things. But maybe the gifts of a sexual *agape* are actually supererogatory excesses of *agape*. Bearing all things means being kind to an old man or woman, walking the extra mile, giving him sexual pleasure, the last succulent pleasure of his life (better than the delightful last meal of the soon-to-be-executed prisoner), received despite the rotting flesh. By no means would she *want* to be wanted. In view of the spotted, discolored, flabby, cracked, odorous, swollen, oozing, and scabby skin, covering every square centimeter of a surrealistically twisted, arthropathic sack of bony protuberances and bruised organs, being wanted by another person would gross *her* out, would nearly kill her plea for pleasure. This situation is perhaps the only one in which, upon orgasm, "Oh, God!" is perfectly appropriate.

Scholars have debated the meaning of New Testament *agape*.[18] One question is how to limit the demands of *agape*, although if it creates sexual duties (thereby opening logical space for supererogatory sexuality), these duties will not be restricted to marriage or partnerships. In deciding whether giving sexual pleasure to others may be obligatory or supererogatory, let's look at Luke 10:25–37—the parable of the Good Samaritan. Does the presentation of the story in scripture provide any help? I'm not convinced that the Good Samaritan's behavior (as distinct from the Good Samaritan himself) was supererogatory. True, the Samaritan tended to the wounds of a mugged and injured man, a perfect stranger, and paid for a room in an inn where the victim could rest and heal. Modern secular thinking judges these acts to be supererogatory. But in Luke's gospel, before and after the description of the Samaritan's behavior it is explicitly stated that (1) acts of this kind earn people eternal life ("What must I do to inherit eternal life?") *and* (2) people are commanded to do such acts by Jesus ("Go and do likewise"). On the one hand, people are rewarded for following the example of the Samaritan. They are motivated by self-interest (not selfishness) to act in a way that yields eternal life for them and that also, happily, benefits others. On the other hand, taking responsibility for a stranger's life is commanded, it is a duty, it fulfills The Law (Love Thy Neighbor). In either case, the story doesn't suggest supererogation. The Good Samaritan in the parable outshines the surrounding theology.

Maybe the lesson is that there are only two options: either provide, as a duty, sexual pleasure to others as our neighbors (Do Unto Your Neighbor What You Would Have Your Neighbor Do Unto You—put you up at an inn, place a call to an escort agency, leave your American Express card in his pocket) or give sexual pleasure to them out of rational self-interest (Adam Smith's "invisible fingers"). If so, logical space for sexual supererogation may exist only in cases in which others are benefited sexually and the agent gets nothing, not even the pleasure of giving pleasure. Indeed, the *proof* that a person is trying to benefit others sexually for their sake alone is that the agent actually suffers. Kant adored the logic of this idea.[19]

BACK TO GRADUATE SCHOOL

Is it now possible to evaluate my agreeing to provide sex to the Ψ-woman? (It seemed to me to be pity sex, although maybe she intended to give *me* pity sex, knowing that she would be unsuccessful unless she soothed my ego by feigning her need.) My fulfilling her request for sex seems not to be supererogatory. I had nothing to gain, but I also had nothing to lose, except a few hours; we had our tryst in the privacy of her well-kempt, clean bedroom; her personal hygiene was impeccable; we engaged only in safe acts; neither of us was married or committed. Any benefit would be hers, but fulfilling my agreement would not harm me. I did not deserve praise for engaging in sexual acts with her, not even if I was disgusted by Ψ. I was not a hero, a Spider Man. Still, supposing my actions were not supererogatory, did I have a duty toward her? I *felt* that I did, but did I *really*? I like to think that I did, that my moral sense was not faulty, that providing sexual pleasure for others is a weak duty of benevolence or there is a duty to provide sexual acts for those who otherwise would not have (m)any sexual experiences, or who are especially needy. Maybe, though, I felt it to be obligatory in order to justify (to myself) doing it, when *not* doing it was my real obligation. Or I felt it to be a duty because I thought that as soon as the sex was over, my duty would be fulfilled and I would be released, I would be free (again). Feeling it to be a duty, did I fulfill it to avoid nagging guilty thoughts, or did I fulfill it because it was my duty?

In the *Family Guy* episode "Peter-assment" (2010), Angela, Peter's boss, is suicidal and desperately pleads with Peter to have sex with her. Perhaps Peter's having sex with her would be supererogatory, or perhaps, given the circumstances, he had a duty. In any event, what should we make of Peter's duties to other people who might be harmed? In particular, do the obligations of Peter's marriage take precedence, or does he have a more important duty to save this woman (and we hope Lois would agree)? Maybe Angela was lying. If by lying she had been successful in getting Peter to engage in sex with her, she would have been guilty of "fraud in the inducement," a kind of rape. She would have been taking advantage of Peter's generosity or his sense of duty. My Ψ-partner, however, did not lie that she was (or was not) Ψ. Nor did I have a commitment to another person which would have been breached by my sexual acts with the Ψ-woman. Aside from the specter of rationalization, the conclusion that I had a duty which I fulfilled seems fair.

There are two more important details about this encounter. (1) She did not do anything for my pleasure. The lack of reciprocity was obvious. She had an opportunity to attend to my pleasure, but she didn't; for example, she didn't caress my organ. If my actions were a gift to her, or the fulfillment of a duty, I should not expect any reciprocity. But did her failure to touch me amount, anyway, to (mild) ingratitude? Or did she hold back out of inexperience and timidity? That seems likely. Maybe she assumed that a male (or me, in particular, qua libertine male) is adequately pleasured by having access to a proffered female body (guys are dogs). Her manner of lovemaking may have been designed to demonstrate that a male is dog enough to be satisfied by a woman with "Ψ." Part of our exchange—I gave her long and loving oral sex, using my own technique, for which she provided nary a well-aimed touch—exhibited a woman-centric tit-for-tat. This speaks in favor of my behavior with her being slightly supererogatory. How much I wanted to be supererogatory! Wanting to be supererogatory, however, destroyed any supererogation.

(2) Before our sexual activity began, I asked her to promise me that she would abide by a proviso, that we would engage in sexual activity once and only once, to which proviso she smilingly and eagerly consented. Only later was I bothered by the thought that it was wrong for me to have sex with her under the condition I had imposed. The contemporary Western sexual zeitgeist would reply, "Dear Mr. Libertine Philosopher: You laid out the contract clearly; you did not trick or cajole her into accepting the proviso. Her free and informed consent, and your free and informed consent, secure that what you did was morally permissible."[20] I am not convinced by this well-intentioned defense. Extracting the promise was not morally decent. To extricate myself from further obligation toward her, to make sure that our encounter would be casual with no strings attached, I relied on her neediness, which she (perhaps unwisely) had revealed to me. I led her to make a promise that neither she nor I could know, when it mattered, whether, or that, she could keep. If for this reason the proviso is rendered inoperative, I might have created for myself, by agreeing to have sex with her, a duty to do it again ("invisible strings"). The mere uttering of a legalistic proviso did not guarantee that casual sex was casual.

I discovered that accepting her invitation to engage in sex was, due to my naïveté about sexual relationships, a pragmatic blunder. She spent a number of weeks popping up where ever I was, her signal to me that she'd be happy if she received more of the same. I found this stalking oppressive. But she was not wrong to ask for more, if my agreeing once created a duty that I agree again (for a month, says the well-socialized Carrie Heffernan), or if a consent-token that occurs at one time persists into the future. Never mind that this speculation about the longevity of consent has been correctly rejected by contemporary feminist jurisprudence, for in my scenario it is the male, not the female, who succumbs to the expansion of consent.

When I agreed to her proposal, I did not know, and only at most suspected, that certain psychological processes would prevent the Ψ-woman from abiding by the proviso. Maybe this encounter is exactly the one from which I grasped that some people did not know much more about human sexuality than I did. She didn't fully comprehend, although she had a clue, that she could not obey the proviso and accepted it innocently but rashly. Perhaps I learned also that the moral dogma of the sufficiency of consent may lead to shallow decision-making and cruelty.

NOTES

1. Web pages attribute the first epigraph to both (independently) Pope Paul VI and Elizabeth Fuller. Carrie's rule is from the TV sit-com *King of Queens* ("Time Share," 1999). The intended audience would not agree or laugh with this addendum: "or you got to keep seeing *him* for a month."
2. Alan Soble, "Physical Attractiveness and Unfair Discrimination," *International Journal of Applied Philosophy* 1:1 (1982), 37–64 (https://ssrn.com/author=2110669); *The Structure of Love* (New Haven, Conn.: Yale University Press, 1990), 152–53; *Sexual Investigations* (New York: New York University Press, 1996), 198–204.
3. Sexual supererogation was mentioned by Raymond Belliotti, *Good Sex* (Lawrence, Kans.: University Press of Kansas, 1993), 210.
4. Leviticus (18:6–23, 20:10–21) contains a historically (Western) important list of prohibitions.
5. Shooting a gun (period) is an act-type; shooting a gun in particular circumstances is an act-token, one specific occurrence of the act-type.
6. I do not recall the source, decades ago, of this analysis of supererogation. My definition accords in the main with David Heyd's account (plato.stanford.edu/entries/supererogation [2002/2012]). See also the entry on supererogation by Thomas Hill and Adam Cureton (2015), in *International Encyclopedia of Ethics*, http://onlinelibrary.wiley.com/doi/10.1002/9781444367072.wbiee326/full.
7. Are familial duties absolute? If a sibling needs a bone marrow transplant, is a sibling who meets the donor requirements obligated to participate? I think the answer is: the qualified sibling has (only) a prima facie, defeasible duty. Decisions can be made only on a case-by-case basis, taking into account particular circumstances (e.g., the prior relationship between the siblings) that may be morally relevant. The same sensitivity to details is crucial for judgments about the morality of sexual acts.
8. The refusal of Dutch nurses to provide sexual care was noted on 11 March 2010 at www.reuters.com/article/2010/03/11/us-dutch-nurses-idUSTRE62A5A120100311. Pat Califia defends honorable prostitution in "Whoring in Utopia," *Public Sex* (Berkeley, Calif.: Cleis, 1994), 242–48, reprinted in *The Philosophy of Sex*, 4th ed., edited by Alan Soble (Lanham, Md.: Rowman & Littlefield, 2002), 475–81.
9. On old men, I recommend these Philip Roth books: *Patrimony, The Dying Animal, Everyman*, and *Exit Ghost*.

10. Kant's *Lectures on Ethics*, trans. Peter Heath (Cambridge: Cambridge University Press, 1997) comprehensively treats duties to self, with applications to sexuality.

11. G. E. M. Anscombe, "Contraception and Chastity," *Human World*, no. 7 (1972), 28 (widely reprinted; see the entry on Anscombe by K. Burgess-Jackson, in *Sex from Plato to Paglia: A Philosophical Encyclopedia*, edited by Alan Soble [Westport, Conn.: Greenwood, 2006], 55). For more on the marriage debt, see the exchange between Sally Haslanger and Soble, at www.askphilosophers.org/question/1796 (2007). On Judaism, see Berel Dov Lerner, "Judaism, History of," in *Sex from Plato to Paglia*, 525.

12. For discussion of Morgan and Russell, see my entry "Ethics, Sexual," in *Sex from Plato to Paglia*, 273–79.

13. See *Sexual Investigations*, 7–9.

14. Janice Moulton, "Sex and Reference," in *Philosophy and Sex*, edited by Robert Baker and Frederick Elliston (Buffalo, N.Y.: Prometheus Books, 1975), 34–44, at 42. See also Alan Wertheimer, section VI of "Consent to Sexual Relations," in this volume; and Robin West, "A Comment on Consent, Sex, and Rape," *Legal Theory* 2 (1996), 233–51. In my *Sexual Investigations* ("Orgasmic Justice," 53–58), I distinguish between "Catholic" and "Protestant" distributions: every bout of sexual activity must strive for equal pleasure vs. the sexual relationship as a whole must strive for equal pleasure.

15. See Richard Hull (1985), "Have We a Duty to Give Sexual Pleasure to Others?" (www.richard-t-hull.com/publications/intercourse_duty.pdf).

16. If a partner hears "no" from the other too often, the other's "no" may bear some of the blame for the infidelity. Maybe both have a duty to forgive each other for their failures. In other cases, infidelity resists being excused, and forgiveness may be supererogatory.

17. Søren Kierkegaard, *Works of Love*, translated by Howard and Edna Hong (New York: Harper and Row, 1962), 141.

18. Theories of Christian love are presented in *The Love Commandments*, edited by E. Santurri and W. Werpehowski (Washington, D.C.: Georgetown University Press, 1992), and S. Pope, "Love in Contemporary Christian Ethics," *Journal of Religious Ethics* 23 (1995), 165–97, the tip of a huge iceberg. For guidance, see my *Structure of Love* and "Love and Value, Yet *Again*," a review-essay of Harry Frankfurt, *Reasons of Love* (Princeton University Press, 2004), in *Essays in Philosophy* 6:1 (January, 2005), http://commons.pacificu.edu/eip/vol6/iss1/30.

19. See Immanuel Kant, *Groundwork of the Metaphysics of Morals*, trans. Mary Gregor (Cambridge: Cambridge University Press, 1997), AK 4:398–401. For discussion, see Ronald Green, "Kant on Christian Love," in *The Love Commandments*, edited by Santurri and Werpehowski, 261–80.

20. For different views of the moral power of consent, compare Seiriol Morgan, "Dark Desires," in this volume, and Igor Primoratz, "Sexual Morality: Is Consent Enough?" *Ethical Theory and Moral Practice* 4 (2001), 201–18. On the intermingling of consent and promises, see my "Antioch's 'Sexual Offense Policy,'" in *Philosophy of Sex*, 5th ed., edited by Alan Soble and Nicholas Power (Lanham, Md.: Rowman & Littlefield, 2008), 459–77.

STUDY QUESTIONS

1. Can you give a detailed and convincing example of a case in which *X* has an obligation to have sex with *Y*, such that *X* and *Y* are not in a relationship of the type that generates sexual obligations between its parties, and such that *X* has never committed to have sex with *Y*?

2. Should we think of sexual obligations to the sexually needy as a type of obligation of benevolence, similar to the obligation to help

the financially needy? Can you think of differences between the two that would render sexual obligations not a type of obligation of benevolence? Would these differences also make the idea of sexual obligations less plausible?

3. In the third defining characteristic of a supererogatory act, Soble states that "There is (or is likely to be) a significant reduction in the interests or the good of the agent, or the act is risky, significantly, not trivially." Can you think of an example of a supererogatory *sexual* act that plausibly satisfies this characteristic? (Make sure that the example does not violate the fourth characteristic: "there is nothing else about the act that makes it morally wrong.")

4. Soble gives an example of himself (or of the implied author of the essay) in the future, when he is, we are meant to understand, physically repellant due to old age (and to what comes with old age), and a kind nurse in his "post-retirement" home uses her hand to sexually please him. How would the example work if in the place of Soble it were an old woman? And what would any resulting differences, if any, between the two cases say about sexual supererogation and sexual duties?

5. Does a person's sexual orientation matter to his or her sexual duties? Do gay men have sexual obligations only to other (gay?) men? Do straight men have them only to (straight?) women? What about supererogatory acts? Would sexual orientation matter in their case?

6. Given a history of sexism by men against women, including rape and sexual violence, how plausible is the idea of women having sexual obligations to men, especially men who are strangers to the women?

7. In reply to the potential objection that having sex is not a matter of life or death (like being hungry), Soble states, "[Y]ou aren't taking the duty of benevolence seriously enough; nor are you acknowledging the psychological pain that accompanies sexual deprivation. Medical care is given to the needy even when it is not a matter of life or death, but quality of life. Sexual experiences are required, by most people, for a decent quality of life." Is Soble claiming that sexual deprivation is quite dire? Or is he claiming that we have duties of benevolence to not-so-dire situations? Or both? Try to figure out what his reply is and assess whether it is convincing.

8. In moral philosophy, the principle of "ought implies can" is accepted by many philosophers. Its main idea is that if X has a moral obligation to do A, then X can, or is able to, do A (there is no serious impediment to X pulling off the act). If X cannot, for some reason, do A, then X has no moral obligation to do A. Does Soble's view that there are sexual obligations run afoul of this principle? Is there a difference in this regard between men's and women's sexu-

al obligations? If there is, what is it? And what does it tell us about Soble's view?

9. If sexual duties exist, what are they duties to, exactly? If we have duties to others not only when they are in sexually dire need but also to improve their quality of life, would a "handjob" do the trick? What if Y, the moral patient, says to X, the moral agent, "Oh no! You're not getting away with a handjob! If you really want me to be sexually better off, if you really want to do your duty, you need to give me a blowjob." What about "Oh no! You're not getting away with a handjob! If you really want me to be sexually better off, if you really want to do your duty, you need to let me give you a blowjob"?

A Bibliography of the Philosophy of Sex

The bibliography is divided into sections by topic or field, and, except for the first category of "General," all the topics and fields are listed alphabetically. Sometimes we included entries that are non-philosophical but essential to the field of the philosophy of sex. In the case of some important anthologies, we listed some of their crucial essays as their own entries. The sections are listed in the following order:

General
Abortion, Contraception, Circumcision, Procreation, Sex Assignment
BDSM
Consent, Power, and Rape
Fantasy and Masturbation
Internet and Technology
Kant (including Objectification) and Other Historical Philosophers
LGBTQ
Marriage and Relationships
Pornography
Promiscuity and Casual Sex
Prostitution
Sexual Harassment
Sexual Perversion
Virtue

GENERAL

Abramson, Paul R. *Sex Appeal: Six Ethical Principles for the 21st Century*. Oxford: Oxford University Press, 2010.

Abramson, Paul R., and Steven D. Pinkerton, eds. *Sexual Nature Sexual Culture*. Chicago: University of Chicago Press, 1995.

Alexander, W. M. "Philosophers Have Avoided Sex." *Diogenes* 72 (Winter 1970), 56–74. Reprinted in *The Philosophy of Sex*, 2nd ed., edited by Alan Soble, 3–19. Savage, Md.: Rowman & Littlefield, 1991.

Ariès, Philippe, and André Béjin, eds. *Western Sexuality: Practice and Precept in Past and Present Times*. New York: Blackwell, 1985.

Ashcraft, Donna M. "The Psychology of Love and Sex." In *Philosophy: Sex and Love*, edited by James Petrik and Arthur Zucker, 303–28. Farmington Hills, Mich.: Macmillan Reference USA, 2016.

Atkinson, Ronald. *Sexual Morality*. London: Hutchinson, 1965.

Atkinson, Ti-Grace. *Amazon Odyssey*. New York: Links Books, 1974.

Baker, Robert, and Frederick Elliston, eds. *Philosophy and Sex*, 1st ed. Buffalo, N.Y.: Prometheus, 1975.

Baker, Robert, and Frederick Elliston, eds. *Philosophy and Sex*, 2nd ed., Buffalo, N.Y.: Prometheus, 1984.

Baker, Robert B., Kathleen J. Wininger, and Frederick A. Elliston, eds. *Philosophy and Sex*, 3rd ed. Amherst, N.Y.: Prometheus, 1998.

Baker, Robert B. and Kathleen J. Wininger, eds. *Philosophy and Sex*, 4th ed. Amherst, N.Y.: Prometheus, 2009.

Belliotti, Raymond. *Good Sex: Perspectives on Sexual Ethics*. Lawrence, Kans.: University Press of Kansas, 1993.

Benn, Piers. "Is Sex Morally Special?" *Journal of Applied Philosophy* 16:3 (1999), 235–45.

Bernard, Michael E. "Sex." In *Rationality and the Pursuit of Happiness: The Legacy of Albert Ellis*, 127–54. Chichester, U.K.: Wiley-Blackwell, 2011.

Blackburn, Simon. *Lust: The Seven Deadly Sins*. New York: Oxford University Press, 2004.

Bruce, Michael, and Robert M. Stewart. *College Sex: Philosophers with Benefits*. Malden, Mass.: Wiley-Blackwell, 2010.

Brundage, James A. *Law, Sex, and Christian Society in Medieval Europe*. Chicago: University of Chicago Press, 1987.

Bullough, Vern L., and Bonnie Bullough. *Sexual Attitudes: Myths and Realities*. Amherst, N.Y.: Prometheus, 1995.

———, eds. *Human Sexuality: An Encyclopedia*. New York: Garland, 1994.

Buss, David M. *The Evolution of Desire*. New York: Basic Books, 1994.

Butler, Judith. *Bodies That Matter: On the Discursive Limits of "Sex."* New York: Routledge, 1993.

———. *Gender Trouble: Feminism and the Subversion of Identity*. New York: Routledge, 1990.

———. *Undoing Gender*. New York: Routledge, 2004.

Bristow, Joseph. *Sexuality*, 2nd ed. London: Routledge, 2011.

Browne, Jude, ed. *The Future of Gender*. Cambridge: Cambridge University Press, 2007.

Cahill, Ann J. "Recognition, Desire, and Unjust Sex." *Hypatia* 29:2 (2014), 320–36.

Califia, Pat. *Public Sex: The Culture of Radical Sex*. Pittsburgh, Pa.: Cleis Press, 1994.

———. *Speaking Sex to Power: The Politics of Queer Sex*. San Francisco: Cleis Press, 2002.

Clatterbaugh, Kenneth. *Contemporary Perspectives on Masculinity: Men, Women, and Politics in Modern Society*. Boulder, Colo.: Westview Press, 1997.

Colker, Ruth. "Feminism, Sexuality, and Authenticity." In *At the Boundaries of Law*, edited by Martha A. Fineman and Nancy S. Thomadsen, 135–47. New York: Routledge, 1991.

———. "Feminism, Sexuality, and Self: A Preliminary Inquiry into the Politics of Authenticity." *Boston University Law Review* 68:1 (1988), 217–64.

Davidson, Arnold. *The Emergence of Sexuality: Historical Epistemology and the Formation of Concepts*. Cambridge, Mass.: Harvard University Press, 2001.

Davis, Murray. *Smut: Erotic Reality/Obscene Ideology*. Chicago: University of Chicago Press, 1983.

Devine, Philip E., and Celia Wolf-Devine, eds. *Sex and Gender: A Spectrum of Views*. Belmont, Calif.: Wadsworth/Thomson Learning, 2003.

Diamond, Jared. *Why Is Sex Fun? The Evolution of Human Sexuality*. New York: Basic Books, 1997.

Digby, Tom. *Love and War: How Militarism Shapes Sexuality and Romance*. New York: Columbia University Press, 2014.

Dillon, M. C. *Beyond Romance*. Albany, N.Y.: SUNY Press, 2001.

Diorio, Joseph A. "Feminist-Constructionist Theories of Sexuality and the Definition of Sex Education." *Educational Philosophy and Theory* 21:2 (1989), 23–31.

Dufourmantelle, Anne. *Blind Date: Sex and Philosophy*. Translated by Catherine Porter. Urbana, Ill.: Illinois University Press, 2007.

Duggan, Lisa, and Nan D. Hunter. *Sex Wars: Sexual Dissent and Political Culture*. New York: Routledge, 1995.

Dworkin, Andrea. *Intercourse*. New York: Free Press, 1987.

Eadie, Jo, ed. *Sexuality: The Essential Glossary*. London: Arnold, 2004.

English, Deirdre, Amber Hollibaugh, and Gayle Rubin. "Talking Sex: A Conversation on Sexuality and Feminism." *Socialist Review* 11:4 (1981), 43–62.

Enns, Diane. *Love in the Dark: Philosophy by Another Name*. New York: Columbia University Press, 2016.

Epstein, Louis M. (1948) *Sex Laws and Customs in Judaism*. New York: Ktav, 1967.

Farley, Margaret. "Sexual Ethics." In *Encyclopedia of Bioethics*, edited by Warren Reich, 2365–75. Revised edition, vol. 5. New York: Simon & Schuster Macmillan, 1995.

Fausto-Sterling, Anne. *Sexing the Body: Gender Politics and the Construction of Sexuality*. New York: Basic Books, 2000.

Feder, Ellen K., Karmen MacKendrick, and Sybol S. Cook, eds. *A Passion for Wisdom: Readings in Western Philosophy on Love and Desire*. Upper Saddle River, N.J.: Prentice Hall, 2004.

Ferber, Abby L., Kimberly Holcomb, and Tre Wentling, eds. *Sex, Gender, and Sexuality: The New Basics*. New York: Oxford University Press, 2009.

Firestone, Shulamith. *The Dialectic of Sex: The Case for Feminist Revolution*. New York: Bantam Books, 1970.

Foster, Gary, ed. *Desire, Love, & Identity: Philosophy of Sex and Love*. New York: Oxford University Press, 2017.

Foucault, Michel. *The History of Sexuality. Vol. 1: An Introduction*. New York: Vintage, 1976.

———. *The History of Sexuality. Vol. 2: The Use of Pleasure*. New York: Pantheon, 1985.

———. *The History of Sexuality. Vol. 3: The Care of the Self*. New York: Vintage, 1986.

Fuchs, Eric. *Sexual Desire and Love: Origins and History of the Christian Ethic of Sexuality and Marriage*. Translated by Marsha Daigle. New York: Seabury, 1983.

Fuchs, Wolfgang. "Love and Lust after Levinas and Lingis." *Philosophy Today* 52:1 (2008), 45–51.

Garry, Ann. "Why Are Love and Sex Philosophically Interesting?" *Metaphilosophy* 11:2 (1980), 165–77. Reprinted in Alan Soble, ed., *The Philosophy of Sex*, 2nd ed., 21–36. Savage, Md.: Rowman & Littlefield, 1991.

Gilbert, Paul. *Human Relationships: A Philosophical Introduction*. Oxford: Blackwell, 1991.

Giles, James. *The Nature of Sexual Desire*. Westport, Conn.: Praeger, 2004; and Lanham, Md.: University Press of America, 2008.

———. "A Theory of Love and Sexual Desire." *Journal for the Theory of Social Behavior* 24:4 (1995), 339–57.

Goldman, Alan H. "Pleasure." In *Philosophy: Sex and Love*, edited by James Petrik and Arthur Zucker, 79–101. Farmington Hills, Mich.: Macmillan Reference USA, 2016.

———. "Sexual Ethics." In *A Companion to Applied Ethics*, edited by R. G. Frey and Christopher H. Wellman, 180–91. Oxford: Blackwell, 2003.

Gruen, Lori, and George F. Panichas, eds. *Sex, Morality, and the Law*. New York: Routledge, 1997.

Gudorf, Christine E. *Body, Sex, and Pleasure: Reconstructing Christian Sexual Ethics*. Cleveland, Ohio: Pilgrim Press, 1994.

Halwani, Raja. "Love and Sex." In *The Oxford Handbook of the Philosophy of Love*, edited by Christopher Grau and Aaron Smuts. New York: Oxford University Press, forthcoming.

———. *Philosophy of Love, Sex, and Marriage: An Introduction*. New York: Routledge, 2010.

———. "Sex." In *Philosophy: Sex and Love*, edited by James Petrik and Arthur Zucker, 29–52. Farmington Hills, Mich.: Macmillan Reference USA, 2016.

Hamilton, Christopher. "Sex." In *Living Philosophy: Reflections on Life, Meaning, and Morality*, 125–41. Edinburgh: Edinburgh University Press, 2002. Reprinted in *The*

Philosophy of Sex, 5th ed., edited by Alan Soble and Nicholas Power, 99–116. Lanham, Md.: Rowman & Littlefield, 2008.

Harbin, Ami. "Sexual Authenticity." *Dialogue: Canadian Philosophical Review* 50:1 (2011), 77–93.

Hauskeller, Michael. *Sex and the Posthuman Condition.* Basingstoke, U.K.: Palgrave Macmillan, 2014.

Heinämaa, Sara. "The Sexed Self and the Mortal Body." In *Birth, Death, and Femininity: Philosophies of Embodiment*, edited by Robin May Schott, 73–97. Bloomington, Ind.: Indiana University Press, 2010.

Hock, Roger R. *Human Sexuality.* Upper Saddle River, N.J.: Pearson/Prentice Hall, 2007.

Hunter, J. F. M. *Thinking about Sex and Love.* New York: St. Martin's Press, 1980.

Irigaray, Luce. (1977) *This Sex Which Is Not One.* Translated by Catherine Porter. Ithaca, N.Y.: Cornell University Press, 1985.

Jackson, Stevi, and Sue Scott, eds. *Feminism and Sexuality: A Reader.* New York: Columbia University Press, 1996.

Jacobsen, Rockney. "Arousal and the Ends of Desire." *Philosophy and Phenomenological Research* 53:3 (1993), 617–32.

Jagger, Jill. *Judith Butler: Sexual Politics, Social Change and the Power of the Performative.* London: Routledge, 2008.

Jeffreys, Sheila. *Anticlimax: A Feminist Perspective on the Sexual Revolution.* New York: New York University Press, 1990.

Jordan, Mark D. *The Ethics of Sex.* Oxford: Blackwell, 2002.

Jung, Patricia Beattie, Mary E. Hunt, and Radhika Balakrishnan, eds. *Good Sex: Feminist Perspectives from the World's Religions.* New Brunswick, N.J.: Rutgers University Press, 2001.

Kalbian, Aline. *Sexing the Church: Gender, Power, and Contemporary Catholic Ethics.* Bloomington, Ind.: Indiana University Press, 2005.

Kaplan, Morris. *Sexual Justice: Democratic Citizenship and the Politics of Desire.* New York: Routledge, 1997.

Kaye, Sharon, ed. *What Philosophy Can Tell You About Your Lover.* Chicago: Open Court, 2012.

Kershnar, Stephen. "The Morality of Faking Orgasms." *International Journal of Applied Philosophy* 26:1 (2012), 85–104.

Koertge, Noretta. "Constructing Concepts of Sexuality: A Philosophical Commentary." In *Homosexuality/Heterosexuality: Concepts of Sexual Orientation*, edited by David McWhirter, Stephanie Sanders, and June Reinisch, 387–97. New York: Oxford University Press, 1990.

Kolnai, Aurel. *Sexual Ethics: The Meaning and Foundations of Sexual Morality*, edited and translated by Francis Dunlop. Aldershot, U.K.: Ashgate, 2005.

Kuefler, Matthew, ed. *The History of Sexuality Sourcebook.* Peterborough, Ont.: Broadview Press, 2007.

LaChance Adams, Sarah, Christopher M. Davidson, and Caroline R. Lundquist, eds. *New Philosophies of Sex and Love: Thinking Through Desire.* Lanham, Md.: Rowman & Littlefield, 2017.

Laqueur, Thomas. *Making Sex: Body and Gender from the Greeks to Freud.* Cambridge, Mass.: Harvard University Press, 1990.

Lauer, Christopher. *Intimacy: A Dialectical Study.* New York: Bloomsbury Academic, 2016.

Laumann, Edward O., John H. Gagnon, Robert T. Michael, and Stuart Michaels. *The Social Organization of Sexuality: Sexual Practices in the United States.* Chicago: University of Chicago Press, 1994.

Lebacqz, Karen, ed., with David Sinacore-Guinn. *Sexuality: A Reader.* Cleveland, Ohio: Pilgrim Press, 1999.

Leidholdt, Dorchen, and Janice C. Raymond, eds. *The Sexual Liberals and the Attack on Feminism.* New York: Teachers College Press, 1990.

LeMoncheck, Linda. *Loose Women, Lecherous Men: A Feminist Philosophy of Sex.* New York: Oxford University Press, 1997.

Lingis, Alphonso. *Libido: The French Existential Theories.* Bloomington, Ind.: Indiana University Press, 1985.

Lomardo, Marc. "James Baldwin's Philosophical Critique of Sexuality." *Journal of Speculative Philosophy* 23:1 (2009), 40–50.

Lunceford, Brett. "Smeared Makeup and Stiletto Heels: Clothing, Sexuality, and the Walk of Shame." In *College Sex: Philosophers with Benefits*, edited by Michael Bruce and Robert M. Stewart, 51–60. Malden, Mass.: Wiley-Blackwell, 2010.

MacKinnon, Catharine A. *Feminism Unmodified: Discourses on Life and Law.* Cambridge, Mass.: Harvard University Press, 1987.

Maglin, Nan Bauer, and Donna Perry, eds. *"Bad Girls"/"Good Girls": Women, Sex, and Power in the Nineties.* New Brunswick, N.J.: Rutgers University Press, 1996.

Marcuse, Herbert. (1955) *Eros and Civilization: A Philosophical Inquiry into Freud.* Boston: Beacon Press, 1966.

Marietta, Don E., Jr. *Philosophy of Sexuality.* Armonk, N.Y.: M. E. Sharpe, 1997.

May, Larry. *Masculinity & Morality.* Ithaca, N.Y.: Cornell University Press, 1998.

May, Larry, Robert Strikwerda, and Patrick D. Hopkins, eds. *Rethinking Masculinity: Philosophical Explorations in Light of Feminism.* Lanham, Md.: Rowman & Littlefield, 1996.

McDowell, Ashley. "Thinking about Thinking about Sex." In *College Sex: Philosophers with Benefits*, edited by Michael Bruce and Robert M. Stewart, 145–57. Malden, Mass.: Wiley-Blackwell, 2010.

McEvoy, Adrianne Leigh, ed. *Sex, Love, and Friendship: Studies of the Society for the Philosophy of Sex and Love, 1993–2003.* Amsterdam: Rodopi, 2011.

McKinnon, Rachel. "Gender, Identity, and Society." In *Philosophy: Sex and Love*, edited by James Petrik and Arthur Zucker, 175–98. Farmington Hills, Mich.: Macmillan Reference USA, 2016.

McWhorter, Ladelle. *Bodies and Pleasures: Foucault and the Politics of Sexual Normalization.* Bloomington, Ind.: Indiana University Press, 1999.

Miller, Kristie, and Marlene Clark, eds. *Dating: Flirting with Big Ideas.* Malden, Mass.: Wiley-Blackwell, 2010.

Money, John. *The Adam Principle: Genes, Genitals, Hormones, and Gender: Selected Readings in Sexology.* Buffalo, N.Y.: Prometheus, 1993.

Moore, Gareth. "Sexual Needs and Sexual Pleasures." *International Philosophical Quarterly* 35:2 (1995), 193–204.

Morgan, Seiriol. "Sex in the Head." *Journal of Applied Philosophy* 20:1 (2003), 1–16. Reprinted in *The Philosophy of Sex*, 6th ed., edited by Nicholas Power, Raja Halwani, and Alan Soble, 101–22. Lanham, Md.: Rowman & Littlefield, 2013.

Moulton, Janice. "Sexual Behavior: Another Position." *Journal of Philosophy* 73:16 (1976), 537–46. Reprinted in *The Philosophy of Sex*, 2nd ed., edited by Alan Soble, 63–71. Savage, Md.: Rowman & Littlefield, 1991; 3rd ed., edited by Alan Soble, 31–38. Lanham, Md.: Rowman & Littlefield, 1997; 4th ed., edited by Alan Soble, 31–38. Lanham, Md.: Rowman & Littlefield, 2002; 5th ed., edited by Alan Soble and Nicholas Power, 45–54. Lanham, Md.: Rowman & Littlefield, 2008; and 6th ed., edited by Nicholas Power, Raja Halwani, and Alan Soble, 47–55. Lanham, Md.: Rowman & Littlefield, 2013.

Nagel, Thomas. *Concealment and Exposure: And Other Essays.* Oxford: Oxford University Press, 2002.

Nancy, Jean-Luc and Adele van Reeth. *Coming.* New York: Fordham University Press, 2017.

Nelson, James B. *Embodiment: An Approach to Sexuality and Christian Theology.* Minneapolis: Augsburg, 1978.

Nelson, James B., and Sandra P. Longfellow, eds. *Sexuality and the Sacred: Sources for Theological Reflection.* Louisville, Ky.: Westminster John Knox, 1994.

Newman, Micah. "A Realist Sexual Ethics." *Ratio* 28:2 (2015), 223–40.

Nozick, Robert. "Sexuality." In *The Examined Life*, 61–67. New York: Simon & Schuster, 1989.

Nye, Robert A., ed. *Sexuality*. New York: Oxford University Press, 1999.

Padgug, Robert. "Sexual Matters: On Conceptualizing Sexuality in History." *Radical History Review* 20 (Spring/Summer 1979), 3–23.

Pagels, Elaine. *Adam, Eve, and the Serpent*. New York: Vintage, 1988.

Paglia, Camille. *Sexual Personae: Art and Decadence from Nefertiti to Emily Dickinson*. New Haven, Conn.: Yale University Press, 1990.

Peiss, Kathy, Christina Simmons, and Robert Padgug, eds. *Passion and Power: Sexuality in History*. Philadelphia: Temple University Press, 1989.

Petrik, James, and Arthur Zucker, eds. *Philosophy: Sex and Love*. Farmington Hills, Mich.: Cengage Learning, 2016.

Pettman, Dominic. *Creaturely Love: How Desire Makes Us More and Less Than Human*. Minneapolis: University of Minnesota Press, 2017.

Pinku, Guy. "Exploring the Association between Love and Sex." In *College Sex: Philosophers with Benefits*, edited by Michael Bruce and Robert M. Stewart, 158–68. Malden, Mass.: Wiley-Blackwell, 2010.

Posner, Richard A. *Sex and Reason*. Cambridge, Mass.: Harvard University Press, 1992.

Power, Nicholas, Raja Halwani, and Alan Soble, eds. *The Philosophy of Sex*, 6th ed. Lanham, Md.: Rowman & Littlefield, 2013.

Primoratz, Igor. *Ethics and Sex*. London: Routledge, 1999.

———, ed. *Human Sexuality*. Aldershot, U.K.: Dartmouth, 1997.

Pruss, Alexander. *One Body: An Essay in Christian Sexual Ethics*. Notre Dame, Ind.: University of Notre Dame Press, 2012.

Punzo, Vincent. *Reflective Naturalism: An Introduction to Moral Philosophy*. New York: Macmillan, 1969.

Radakovich, Anka. *Sexplorations: Journeys to the Erogenous Frontier*. New York: Crown, 1997.

Randall, Hilary E., and E. Sandra Byers. "What Is Sex? Students' Definitions of Having Sex, Sexual Partner, and Unfaithful Sexual Behaviour." *Canadian Journal of Human Sexuality* 12:2 (2003), 87–96.

Ranke-Heinemann, Uta. *Eunuchs for the Kingdom of Heaven: Women, Sexuality and the Catholic Church*. New York: Penguin, 1990.

Reeve, C. D. C. *Love's Confusions*. Cambridge, Mass.: Harvard University Press, 2005.

Richards, Bradley. "Sexual Desire and the Phenomenology of Attraction." *Dialogue: Canadian Philosophical Review* 54:2 (2015), 263–83.

Richter, Alan. *Dictionary of Sexual Slang*. New York: John Wiley & Sons, 1993.

Richter, Duncan. "Sex." In *Anscombe's Moral Philosophy*, 139–66. Lanham, Md.: Lexington Books, 2011.

Roach, Catherine M. "Love: Bondage and the Conundrum of Erotic Love." In *Happily Ever After*, 119–41. Indianapolis, Ind.: Indiana University Press, 2016.

———. "Sex: Good Girls Do, or, Romance Fiction as Sex-Positive Feminist Mommy Porn." In *Happily Ever After*, 78–103. Indianapolis, Ind.: Indiana University Press, 2016.

Robinson, Paul. *The Freudian Left: Wilhelm Reich, Geza Roheim, Herbert Marcuse*. New York: Harper and Row, 1969.

———. *The Modernization of Sex: Havelock Ellis, Alfred Kinsey, William Masters and Virginia Johnson*. New York: Harper and Row, 1976.

Rogers, Eugene F., Jr., ed. *Theology and Sexuality: Classic and Contemporary Readings*. Oxford: Blackwell, 2002.

Rubin, Gayle S. "Thinking Sex: Notes for a Radical Theory of the Politics of Sexuality." In *Pleasure and Danger: Exploring Female Sexuality*, edited by Carole S. Vance, 267–319. London: Routledge and Kegan Paul, 1984.

Rubin, Lillian B. *Erotic Wars: What Happened to the Sexual Revolution?* New York: Farrar, Straus and Giroux, 1990.

Russell, Bertrand. *Marriage and Morals*. London: George Allen and Unwin, 1929.

Sanders, Stephanie A., Brandon J. Hill, William L. Yarber, Cynthia A. Graham, Richard A. Crosby, and Robin R. Milhausen. "Misclassification Bias: Diversity in Conceptualisations about Having 'Had Sex.'" *Sexual Health* 7:1 (2010), 31–34.

Sanders, Stephanie, and June Reinisch. "Would You Say You 'Had Sex' If . . . ?" *Journal of the American Medical Association* 281:3 (January 20, 1999), 275–77.

Sclater, Shelley Day, Fatemah Ebtehaj, Emily Jackson, and Martin Richards, eds. *Regulating Autonomy: Sex, Reproduction, and Family*. Oxford: Hart, 2009.

Scruton, Roger. *Sexual Desire: A Moral Philosophy of the Erotic*. New York: Free Press, 1986.

Secomb, Linnell. *Philosophy and Love: From Plato to Popular Culture*. Bloomington, Ind.: Indiana University Press, 2007.

Seidman, Steven. *Embattled Eros*. New York: Routledge, 1992.

———. *The Social Construction of Sexuality*. New York: W. W. Norton, 2010.

Semp, Jennifer A. and Andrew I. Cohen. "Love for Sale: Dating as a Calculated Exchange." In *Dating: Flirting with Big Ideas*, edited by Kristie Miller and Marlene Clark, 37–48. Malden, Mass.: Wiley-Blackwell, 2010.

Shaffer, Jerome A. "Sexual Desire." *Journal of Philosophy* 75:4 (1978), 175–89. Reprinted in *Sex, Love, and Friendship*, edited by Alan Soble, 1–12. Amsterdam: Rodopi, 1997.

Shelp, Earl E., ed. *Sexuality and Medicine*. Vol. 1, *Conceptual Roots*. Dordrecht: Reidel, 1987.

———. *Sexuality and Medicine. Vol. 2, Ethical Viewpoints in Transition*. Dordrecht: Reidel, 1987.

Shrage, Laurie. "Do Lesbian Prostitutes Have Sex with Their Clients? A Clintonesque Reply." *Sexualities* 2:2 (1999), 259–61.

Shrage, Laurie, and Robert Scott Stewart. *Philosophizing about Sex*. Peterborough, Canada: Broadview Press, 2015.

Singer, Irving. *The Goals of Human Sexuality*. New York: Schocken Books, 1973.

———. *Philosophy of Love: A Partial Summing-Up*. Cambridge, Mass.: MIT Press, 2009.

———. *Sex: A Philosophical Primer*. Lanham, Md.: Rowman & Littlefield, 2001.

Soble, Alan. "Philosophy of Sex." In *Encyclopedia of Philosophy*, edited by Donald Borchert, 2nd ed., vol. 7, pp. 521–32. New York: Macmillan/Thomson, 2006.

———. *The Philosophy of Sex and Love: An Introduction*. St. Paul, Minn.: Paragon House, 1998.

———. *The Philosophy of Sex and Love: An Introduction*, 2nd ed. St. Paul, Minn.: Paragon House, 2008.

———. *Sexual Investigations*. New York: New York University Press, 1996.

———, ed. *Eros, Agape, and Philia: Readings in the Philosophy of Love*. New York: Paragon House, 1989; reprinted with corrections St. Paul, Minn.: Paragon House, 1999.

———, ed. *The Philosophy of Sex: Contemporary Readings*. 1st ed. Totowa, N.J.: Rowman & Littlefield, 1980; 2nd ed., Savage, Md.: Rowman & Littlefield, 1991; 3rd ed., Lanham, Md.: Rowman & Littlefield, 1997; 4th ed., Lanham, Md.: Rowman & Littlefield, 2002.

———, ed. *Sex from Plato to Paglia: A Philosophical Encyclopedia*. Westport, Conn.: Greenwood, 2006.

———, ed. *Sex, Love, and Friendship: Studies of the Society for the Philosophy of Sex and Love, 1977–1992*. Amsterdam: Rodopi, 1997.

Soble, Alan, and Nicholas Power, eds. *The Philosophy of Sex*, 5th ed. Lanham, Md.: Rowman & Littlefield, 2008.

Solomon, Lewis D. *The Jewish Tradition, Sexuality, and Procreation*. Lanham, Md.: University Press of America, 2002.

Solomon, Robert C. "Sexual Paradigms." *Journal of Philosophy* 71:11 (1974), 336–45. Reprinted in *The Philosophy of Sex*, 2nd ed., edited by Alan Soble, 53–62. Savage, Md.: Rowman & Littlefield, 1991; 3rd ed., edited by Alan Soble, 21–29. Lanham, Md.: Rowman & Littlefield, 1997; and 4th ed., edited by Alan Soble, 21–29. Lanham, Md.: Rowman & Littlefield, 2002.

Solomon, Robert C., and Kathleen M. Higgins, eds. *The Philosophy of (Erotic) Love*. Lawrence, Kans.: University Press of Kansas, 1991.

Stafford, J. Martin. *Essays on Sexuality and Ethics*. Solihull, U.K.: Ismeron, 1995.

Stein, Edward, ed. *Forms of Desire*. New York: Routledge, 1992.

Steintrager, James A. *The Autonomy of Pleasure: Libertines, License, and Sexual Revolution*. New York: Columbia University Press, 2016.

Stewart, Robert M., ed. *Philosophical Perspectives on Sex and Love*. New York: Oxford University Press, 1995.

———. "Meaningful Sex and Moral Respect." In *College Sex: Philosophers with Benefits*, edited by Michael Bruce and Robert M. Stewart, 187–97. Malden, Mass.: Wiley-Blackwell, 2010.

Stimpson, Catharine R., and Ethel Spector Person, eds. *Women: Sex and Sexuality*. Chicago: University of Chicago Press, 1980.

Stuart, Elizabeth, and Adrian Thatcher, eds. *Christian Perspectives on Sexuality and Gender*. Grand Rapids, Mich.: Eerdmans, 1996.

Sullivan, Clayton. *Rescuing Sex from the Christians*. New York: Continuum, 2006.

Sullivan, John P. "Philosophizing about Sexuality." *Philosophy of the Social Sciences* 14:1 (1984), 83–96.

Swidler, Arlene, ed. *Homosexuality and World Religions*. Valley Forge, Pa.: Trinity Press, 1993.

Taverner, William J., and Ryan W. McKee, eds. *Taking Sides: Clashing Views in Human Sexuality*. New York: McGraw-Hill, 2010.

Taylor, Roger. "Sexual Experiences." *Proceedings of the Aristotelian Society* 68 (1967–1968), 87–104. Reprinted in *The Philosophy of Sex*, edited by Alan Soble, 1st ed., 59–75. Totowa, N.J.: Rowman & Littlefield, 1980.

Thomas, Keith. "The Double Standard." *Journal of the History of Ideas* 20:2 (1959), 195–216.

Thurber, James, and E. B. White. *Is Sex Necessary?* New York: Harper and Brothers, 1929.

Tiefer, Leonore. (1995) *Sex Is Not a Natural Act and Other Essays*, 2nd ed. Boulder, Colo.: Westview, 2004.

Trevas, Robert, Arthur Zucker, and Donald Borchert, eds. *Philosophy of Sex and Love: A Reader*. Upper Saddle River, N.J.: Prentice-Hall, 1997.

Vance, Carole S., ed. *Pleasure and Danger: Exploring Female Sexuality*. London: Routledge and Kegan Paul, 1984.

Vardy, Peter. *The Puzzle of Sex*. London: Fount, 1997.

Verene, Donald, ed. *Sexual Love and Western Morality*. 1st ed. New York: Harper and Row, 1972; 2nd ed. Boston: Jones and Bartlett, 1995.

Vetterling-Braggin, Mary, ed. *"Femininity," "Masculinity," and "Androgyny": A Modern Philosophical Discussion*. Totowa, N.J.: Rowman & Littlefield, 1988.

Vlemnick, Jens de, and Eran Dorfman, eds. *Sexuality and Psychoanalysis: Philosophical Criticisms*. Leuven, Belgium: Leuven University Press, 2010.

Warnke, Georgia. *Debating Sex and Gender*. New York: Oxford University Press, 2011.

Watson, Francis. *Agape, Eros, Gender: Towards a Pauline Sexual Ethics*. Cambridge: Cambridge University Press, 2000.

Weber, Jonathan. "Sex." *Philosophy* 84:2 (2009), 233–50.

Weeks, Jeffrey. *Invented Moralities: Sexual Values in an Age of Uncertainty*. New York: Columbia University Press, 1995.

———. *The Languages of Sexuality*. Milton Park, U.K.: Routledge, 2011.

———. *Sexuality and Its Discontents*. London: Routledge and Kegan Paul, 1985.

———. *The World We Have Won: The Remaking of Erotic and Intimate Life*. London: Routledge, 2007.

Weeks, Jeffrey, and Janet Holland, eds. *Sexual Cultures: Communities, Values and Intimacy*. New York: St. Martin's, 1996.

West, David. *Reason and Sexuality in Western Thought*. Cambridge: Polity, 2005.

Whiteley, C. H., and Winifred N. Whiteley. *Sex and Morals*. New York: Basic Books, 1967.

Williams, Mary E., ed. *Sex*. Farmington Hills, Mich.: Greenhaven Press, 2006.

Wilson, Edward O. "Sex." In *On Human Nature*, 125–54. Cambridge, Mass.: Harvard University Press, 1978.

Wilson, John. *Love, Sex, and Feminism: A Philosophical Essay*. New York: Praeger, 1980.

Wojtyła, Karol [Pope John Paul II]. *Love and Responsibility*. New York: Farrar, Straus and Giroux, 1981.

Wood, David. *Carnal Hermeneutics*. New York: Fordham University Press, 2015.

Zheng, Robin. "Why Yellow Fever Isn't Flattering: A Case Against Racial Fetishes." *Journal of the American Philosophical Association* 2:3 (2016), 400–419.

ABORTION, CONTRACEPTION, CIRCUMCISION, PROCREATION, SEX ASSIGNMENT

Adams, Sarah LaChance and Caroline R. Lundquist, eds. *Coming to Life: Philosophies of Pregnancy, Childbirth, and Mothering*. Oxford: Oxford University Press, 2012.

Alward, Peter. "Abortion Rights and Paternal Obligations." *Public Affairs Quarterly* 26:4 (2012), 273–92.

Anscombe, G. E. M. "Contraception and Chastity." *The Human World*, No. 7 (1972), 9–30. Reprinted (with criticisms and a rebuttal) in *Ethics and Population*, edited by Michael Bayles, 134–53. Cambridge, Mass.: Schenkman, 1976.

———. "You Can Have Sex without Children." In *Ethics, Religion and Politics*, 82–96. Minneapolis: University of Minnesota Press, 1981.

Archard, David, and David Benatar, eds. *Procreation and Parenthood: The Ethics of Bearing and Rearing Children*. Oxford: Oxford University Press, 2010.

Baird, Robert M., and Stuart E. Rosenbaum. *The Ethics of Abortion: Pro-Life vs. Pro-Choice*, revised ed. Buffalo, N.Y.: Prometheus Books, 1993.

Beckwith, Francis J. *Defending Life: A Moral and Legal Case against Abortion Choice*. New York: Cambridge University Press, 2007.

Beis, Richard H. "Contraception and the Logical Structure of the Thomist Natural Law Theory." *Ethics* 75:4 (1965), 277–84.

Benatar, David. *Better Never to Have Been: The Harm of Coming into Existence*. Oxford: Clarendon Press, 2006.

———. "The Limits of Reproductive Freedom." In *Procreation and Parenthood: The Ethics of Bearing and Rearing Children*, edited by David Archard and David Benatar, 78–102. Oxford: Clarendon Press, 2010.

Benatar, David, and Michael Benatar. "Between Prophylaxis and Child Abuse: The Ethics of Neonatal Male Circumcision." In *Cutting to the Core: The Ethics of Contested Surgeries*, edited by David Benatar, 23–45. Lanham, Md.: Rowman & Littlefield, 2006.

Benatar, David, and David Wasserman. *Debating Procreation: Is It Wrong to Reproduce?* Oxford: Oxford University Press, 2015.

Berlatsky, Noah, ed. *Abortion*. Farmington Hills, Mich.: Greenhaven Press, 2011.

Boonin, David. *A Defense of Abortion*. Cambridge: Cambridge University Press, 2003.

Boonin-Vail, David. "A Defense of 'A Defense of Abortion': On the Responsibility Objection to Thomson's Argument." *Ethics* 107:2 (1997), 286–313.

Boylan, Michael. "The Abortion Debate in the Twenty-First Century." *Medical Ethics*, 2nd ed., edited by Michael Boylan, 203–17. Chichester, U.K.: Wiley-Blackwell, 2014.

Brake, Elizabeth. "Fatherhood and Child Support: Do Men Have a Right to Choose?" *Journal of Applied Philosophy* 22:1 (2005), 55–73.

———. "Willing Parents: A Voluntarist Account of Parental Role Obligations." In *Procreation and Parenthood: The Ethics of Bearing and Rearing Children*, edited by David Archard and David Benatar, 151–77. Oxford: Clarendon Press, 2010.

Brody, Baruch. "Thomson on Abortion." *Philosophy and Public Affairs* 1:3 (1972), 335–40.

Cahill, Lisa Sowle. "Grisez on Sex and Gender: A Feminist Theological Perspective." In *The Revival of Natural Law: Philosophical, Theological and Ethical Responses to the Finnis-Grisez School*, edited by Nigel Biggar and Rufus Black, 242–61. Aldershot, U.K.: Ashgate, 2000.

Callahan, Daniel. *Abortion: Law, Choice, and Morality*. New York: Macmillan, 1970.

Callahan, Joan C. "The Fetus and Fundamental Rights." *Commonweal* (April 11, 1986), 203–7. Reprinted, revised, in *The Ethics of Abortion: Pro-Life vs. Pro-Choice*, edited by Robert M. Baird and Stuart E. Rosenbaum, revised ed., 249–62. Buffalo, N.Y.: Prometheus, 1993.

Callahan, Sidney. "Abortion and the Sexual Agenda." *Commonweal* (April 25, 1986), 232–38. Reprinted in *The Ethics of Abortion: Pro-Life vs. Pro-Choice*, edited by Robert M. Baird and Stuart E. Rosenbaum, revised ed., 111–21. Buffalo, N.Y.: Prometheus, 1993; and in *The Philosophy of Sex*, edited by Alan Soble, 3rd ed., 151–64, and 4th ed., 177–90. Lanham, Md.: Rowman & Littlefield, 1997 and 2002, respectively.

Cannold, Leslie. "The Ethics of Neonatal Male Circumcision: Helping Parents to Decide." In *Cutting to the Core: The Ethics of Contested Surgeries*, edited by David Benatar, 47–61. Lanham, Md.: Rowman & Littlefield, 2006.

Cohen, Carl. "Sex, Birth Control, and Human Life." In *Philosophy and Sex*, edited by Robert Baker and Frederick Elliston, 2nd ed., 185–99. Buffalo, N.Y.: Prometheus, 1984.

Cohen, Howard. "Abortion and the Quality of Life." In *Feminism and Philosophy*, edited by Mary Vetterling-Braggin, Frederick Elliston, and Jane English, 429–40. Totowa, N.J.: Rowman & Littlefield, 1977.

Colb, Shelby F., and Michael C. Dorf. *Beating Hearts: Abortion and Animal Rights*. New York: Columbia University Press, 2016.

Corea, Gena. *The Mother Machine: Reproductive Technologies from Artificial Insemination to Artificial Wombs*. New York: Harper and Row, 1986.

Daar, Judith. *The New Eugenics: Selective Breeding in an Era of Reproductive Technologies*. New Haven, Conn.: Yale University Press, 2017.

Dadlez, E. M., and William L. Andrews. "Federally Funded Elective Abortion: They Can Run, but They Can't Hyde." *International Journal of Applied Philosophy* 24:2 (2010), 169–84.

David, Dena S. "Genital Alteration of Female Minors." In *Cutting to the Core: The Ethics of Contested Surgeries*, edited by David Benatar, 63–75. Lanham, Md.: Rowman & Littlefield, 2006.

DeGrazia, David. *Creation Ethics: Reproduction, Genetics, and Quality of Life*. Oxford: Oxford University Press, 2012.

Denis, Lara. "Abortion and Kant's Formula of Universal Law." *Canadian Journal of Philosophy* 37:4 (2007), 547–80.

Diorio, Joseph A. "Contraception, Copulation Domination, and the Theoretical Barrenness of Sex Education Literature." *Educational Theory* 35:3 (1985), 239–54.

Dreger, Alice Domurat. "'Ambiguous Sex'—or Ambivalent Medicine? Ethical Issues in the Treatment of Intersexuality." *Hastings Center Report* 28:3 (1998), 24–35.

———. "A History of Intersex: From the Age of Gonads to the Age of Consent." *Journal of Clinical Ethics* 9:4 (1998), 345–55. Reprinted in *Philosophy and Sex*, 4th ed., edited by Robert B. Baker and Kathleen J. Wininger, 372–86. Amherst, N.Y.: Prometheus Books, 2009.

Dura-Vila, Victor. "Parental Obligation, Adoption, and Abortion." *Journal of Value Inquiry* 47:1–2 (2013), 29–47.

Dworkin, Ronald. *Life's Dominion: An Argument about Abortion, Euthanasia, and Individual Freedom*. New York: Knopf, 1993.

Feder, Ellen K. "Reassigning Ambiguity: Parental Decisions and the Matter of Harm." In *Making Sense of Intersex: Changing Ethical Perspectives in Biomedicine*, 88–109. Indianapolis, Ind.: Indiana University Press, 2014.

Ferracioli, Laura. "On the Value of Intimacy in Procreation." *Journal of Value Inquiry* 48:3 (2014), 349–69.

Finnis, John M. "Law, Morality, and 'Sexual Orientation.'" *Notre Dame Law Review* 69:5 (1994), 1049–76.

———. "Natural Law and Unnatural Acts." In *Human Sexuality*, edited by Igor Primoratz, 5–27. Aldershot, U.K.: Dartmouth, 1997.

Flanagan, Matthew. "Some Critical Reflections on Abortion and Virtue Theory." In *Virtues in Action: New Essays in Applied Virtue Ethics*, edited by Michael W. Austin, 102–116. Basingstoke, U.K.: Palgrave Macmillan, 2013.

Francis, Leslie, ed. *The Oxford Handbook of Reproductive Ethics*. New York: Oxford University Press, 2017.

Geach, Mary. "Marriage: Arguing to a First Principle in Sexual Ethics." In *Moral Truth and Moral Tradition: Essays in Honour of Peter Geach and Elizabeth Anscombe*, edited by Luke Gormally, 177–93. Dublin: Four Courts Press, 1994.

Gillis, Marin. "Parallels between the Ethics of Embryonic Stem Cell Research and Abortion." In *Science and Ethics: Can Science Help Us Make Wise Moral Judgments?* edited by Paul Kurtz, 106–17. Amherst, N.Y.: Prometheus Books, 2007.

Glover, Jonathan. *Choosing Children: Genes, Disability, and Design*. Oxford: Clarendon Press, 2006.

Greasley, Kate. *Arguments about Abortion: Personhood, Morality, and Law*. New York: Oxford University Press, 2017.

Grisez, Germain, Joseph Boyle, John Finnis, William E. May, and John C. Ford. *The Teaching of "Humanae Vitae": A Defense*. San Francisco: Ignatius Press, 1988.

Hanrahan, Rebecca. "The Decision to Abort." *International Journal of Applied Philosophy* 21:1 (2007), 25–41.

Harris, John, and Søren Holm. "Abortion." In *The Oxford Handbook of Practical Ethics*, edited by Hugh LaFollette, 112–135. New York: Oxford University Press, 2003.

Hegab, Moustafa H. "Abortion: Medical and Moral Aspects in Islamic Perspectives." In *Looking Beneath the Surface: Medical Ethics from Islamic and Western Perspectives*, edited by Hendrik M. Vroom et al., 177–86. Amsterdam: Rodopi, 2013.

Heyes, Cressida. "Changing Race, Changing Sex: The Ethics of Self-Transformation." In *"You've Changed": Sex Reassignment and Personal Identity*, edited by Laurie Shrage, 135–54. Oxford: Oxford University Press, 2009.

Holbrook, Daniel. "All Embryos Are Equal? Issues in Pre-Implantation Genetic Diagnosis, IVF Implantation, Embryonic Stem Cell Research, and Therapeutic Cloning." *International Journal of Applied Philosophy* 21:1 (2007), 43–53.

Hopkins, Patrick D. "Can Technology Fix the Abortion Problem? Ectogenesis and the Real Issues of Abortion." *International Journal of Applied Philosophy* 22:2 (2008), 311–26.

Houle, Karen L. F. *Responsibility, Complexity, and Abortion: Toward a New Image of Ethical Thought*. Lanham, Md.: Lexington Books, 2015.

Hull, Richard T., ed. (1990) *Ethical Issues in the New Reproductive Technologies*. Amherst, N.Y.: Prometheus, 2005.

Hursthouse, Rosalind. "Virtue Theory and Abortion." *Philosophy and Public Affairs* 20:3 (1991), 223–46.

John Paul II (Pope). "*Evangelium Vitae*." *Origins* 24:42 (1995), 689–727.

Kaczor, Christopher. *The Ethics of Abortion: Women's Rights, Human Life, and the Question of Justice*. New York: Routledge, 2011.

Kamm, Frances Myrna. *Creation and Abortion: A Study in Moral and Legal Philosophy*. Oxford: Oxford University Press, 1992.

Kipnis, Kenneth and Milton Diamond. "Pediatric Ethics and the Surgical Assignment of Sex." *Journal of Clinical Ethics* 9:4 (1998), 398–410. Reprinted in *Philosophy and Sex*, 4th ed., edited by Robert B. Baker and Kathleen J. Wininger, 387–405. Amherst, N.Y.: Prometheus Books, 2009.

Kirsch, Julie. "Is Abortion a Question of Personal Morality?" *International Journal of Applied Philosophy* 27:1 (2013), 91–99.

Kornegay, R. Jo. "Hursthouse's Virtue Ethics and Abortion: Abortion Ethics without Metaphysics?" *Ethical Theory and Moral Practice* 14:1 (2011), 51–71.

Krimsky, Sheldon. *Stem Cell Dialogues: A Philosophical and Scientific Inquiry into Medical Frontiers.* New York: Columbia University Press, 2017.

Lee, Patrick. *Abortion and Unborn Human Life,* 2nd ed. Washington, D.C.: Catholic University Press of America, 2010.

Liao, S. Matthew. "Biological Parenting as a Human Right." *Journal of Moral Philosophy* 13:6 (2016), 652–668.

———. "Time-Relative Interests and Abortion." *Journal of Moral Philosophy* 4:2 (2007), 242–56.

Lindemann, Hilde. "'. . . But *I* Could Never Have One': The Abortion Intuition and Moral Luck." *Hypatia* 24:1 (2009), 41–55.

Lowe, Pam. "Contraception and Heterosex: An Intimate Relationship." *Sexualities* 8:1 (2005), 75–92.

Lu, Matthew. "Abortion and Virtue Ethics." In *Persons, Moral Worth, and Embryos: A Critical Analysis of Pro-Choice Arguments,* edited by Stephen Napier, 101–24. Dordrecht: Springer Netherlands, 2011.

Luper, Steven. "Abortion." In *The Philosophy of Death,* 197–218. Cambridge: Cambridge University Press, 2009.

Manninen, Bertha Alvarez. "Pleading Men and Virtuous Women: Considering the Role of the Father in the Abortion Debate." *International Journal of Applied Philosophy* 21:1 (2007), 1–24.

———. "Pro-Choice Philosopher Has Baby: Reflections on Fetal Life." In *Motherhood: The Birth of Wisdom,* edited by Sheila Lintott, 41–51. Malden, Mass.: Wiley-Blackwell, 2010.

Marquis, Don. "Why Abortion Is Immoral." *Journal of Philosophy* 86:4 (1989), 183–202.

———. "Abortion Revisited." In *The Oxford Handbook of Bioethics,* edited by Bonnie Steinbock, 395–415. Oxford: Oxford University Press, 2007.

Martin, Christopher F. J. "Are There Virtues and Vices That Belong Specifically to the Sexual Life?" *Acta Philosophica* 4:2 (1995), 205–21.

Merino, Noël, ed. *Birth Control.* Farmington Hills, Mich.: Greenhaven Press, 2011.

Meyers, Chris. *The Fetal Position: A Rational Approach to the Abortion Issue.* Amherst, N.Y.: Prometheus Books, 2010.

Meyers, Diana Tietjens. "Artifice and Authenticity: Gender Technology and Agency in Two Jenny Saville Portraits." In *"You've Changed": Sex Reassignment and Personal Identity,* edited by Laurie Shrage, 155–74. Oxford: Oxford University Press, 2009.

Murphy, Timothy F. "Abortion and the Ethics of Genetic Sexual Orientation Research." *Cambridge Quarterly of Healthcare Ethics* 4:4 (1995), 340–50.

Napier, Stephen, ed. *Persons, Moral Worth, and Embryos: A Critical Analysis of Pro-Choice Arguments.* Dordrecht: Springer, 2011.

Nicholson, Susan T. *Abortion and the Roman Catholic Church.* Knoxville, Tenn.: Religious Ethics, 1978.

Noonan, John T. "An Almost Absolute Value in History." In *Medical Ethics,* 2nd ed., edited by Michael Boylan, 184–89. Chichester, U.K.: Wiley-Blackwell, 2014.

———. *Contraception: A History of Its Treatment by the Catholic Theologians and Canonists.* Enlarged ed. Cambridge, Mass.: Harvard University Press, 1986.

———, ed. *The Morality of Abortion.* Cambridge, Mass.: Harvard University Press, 1970.

Oshana, Marina. "Autonomy and the Partial-Birth Abortion Act." *Journal of Social Philosophy* 42:1 (2011), 46–60.

Overall, Christine. "Sex/Gender Transitions and Life-Changing Aspirations." In *"You've Changed": Sex Reassignment and Personal Identity,* edited by Laurie Shrage, 11–27. Oxford: Oxford University Press, 2009.

———. *Why Have Children? The Ethical Debate.* Cambridge, Mass.: MIT Press, 2012.

Paden, Roger. "Abortion and Sexual Morality." In *Sex, Love, and Friendship,* edited by Alan Soble, 229–36. Amsterdam: Rodopi, 1997.

Parker, Michael. "An Ordinary Chance of a Desirable Existence." In *Procreation and Parenthood: The Ethics of Bearing and Rearing Children*, edited by David Archard and David Benatar, 57–77. Oxford: Clarendon Press, 2010.

Paul VI (Pope). "*Humanae Vitae.*" *Catholic Mind* 66 (September 1968), 35–48. Reprinted in *Philosophy and Sex*, 2nd ed., edited by Robert Baker and Frederick Elliston, 167–83. Buffalo, N.Y.: Prometheus, 1984.

Perry, Michael J. "Abortion." In *The Political Morality of Liberal Democracy*, 123–37. Cambridge: Cambridge University Press, 2010.

Pius XI (Pope). "On Christian Marriage" ("*Casti Connubii*"). *Catholic Mind* 29:2 (1931), 21–64.

Prusak, Bernard G. "The Costs of Procreation." *Journal of Social Philosophy* 42:1 (2011), 61–75.

Purdy, Laura M. "Assisted Reproduction, Prenatal Testing, and Sex Selection." In *A Companion to Bioethics*, 2nd ed., edited by Helga Kuhse and Peter Singer, 178–92. Malden, Mass.: Wiley-Blackwell, 2009.

———. "Exporting the 'Culture of Life.'" In *International Public Health Policy and Ethics*, edited by Michael Boylan, 91–106. New York: Springer Verlag, 2008.

Rachels, Stuart. "The Immorality of Having Children." *Ethical Theory and Moral Practice* 17:3 (2014), 567–82.

Rapaport, Elizabeth, and Paul Segal. "One Step Forward, Two Steps Backward: Abortion and Ethical Theory." In *Feminism and Philosophy*, edited by Mary Vetterling-Braggin, Frederick Elliston, and Jane English, 408–16. Totowa, N.J.: Littlefield Adams, 1977.

Reiman, Jeffrey. "Abortion, Infanticide, and the Asymmetric Value of Human Life." *Journal of Social Philosophy* 27:3 (1996), 181–200. Reprinted in *Philosophy and Sex*, 3rd ed., edited by Robert B. Baker, Kathleen J. Wininger, and Frederick A. Elliston, 261–78. Amherst, N.Y.: Prometheus Books, 1998.

Rieder, Travis N. "Procreation, Adoption and the Contours of Obligation." *Journal of Applied Philosophy* 32:3 (2015), 293–309.

Roberts, Melinda A. *Abortion and the Moral Significance of Merely Possible Persons: Finding Middle Ground in Hard Cases*. Heidelberg: Springer, 2010.

Robertson, John A. "Norplant, Forced Contraception, and Irresponsible Reproduction." In *Should Parents Be Licensed? Debating the Issues*, edited by Peg Tittle, 211–23. Amherst, N.Y.: Prometheus Books, 2004.

Rulli, Tina. "Preferring a Genetically-Related Child." *Journal of Moral Philosophy* 13:6 (2016), 669–98.

Seipel, Peter. "Is There Sufficient Common Ground to Resolve the Abortion Debate?" *Journal of Value Inquiry* 48:3 (2014), 517–31.

Shotwell, Alexis. "Practicing Freedom: Disability and Gender Transformation." In *Against Purity: Living Ethically in Compromised Times*, 139–64. Minneapolis: University of Minnesota Press, 2016.

Shrage, Laurie. *Moral Dilemmas of Feminism: Prostitution, Adultery, and Abortion*. New York: Routledge, 1994.

———, ed. *"You've Changed": Sex Reassignment and Personal Identity*. Oxford: Oxford University Press, 2009.

Silverstein, Harry. "On a Woman's 'Responsibility' for the Fetus." *Social Theory and Practice* 13:1 (1987), 103–19.

Simkulet, William. "Abortion, Property, and Liberty." *Journal of Ethics* 20:4 (2016), 373–83.

Smith, Holly M. "Intercourse and Moral Responsibility for the Fetus." In *Abortion and the Status of the Fetus*, edited by W. B. Bondeson, H. T. Engelhardt Jr., S. F. Spicker, and D. H. Winship, 229–45. Dordrecht: Reidel, 1983.

Soble, Alan. "More on Abortion and Sexual Morality." In *Sex, Love, and Friendship*, edited by Alan Soble, 239–44. Amsterdam: Rodopi, 1997.

Solomon, Robert. "Sex, Contraception, and Conceptions of Sex." In *Thirteen Questions in Ethics*, 2nd ed., edited by G. Lee Bowie, Meredith W. Michaels, and Kathleen Higgins, 95–107. Fort Worth, Tex.: Harcourt Brace, 1992.

Spriggs, Merle and Julian Savulescu. "The Ethics of Surgically Assigning Sex for Intersex Children." In *Cutting to the Core: Exploring the Ethics of Contested Surgeries*, edited by David Benatar, 79–96. Lanham, Md.: Rowman & Littlefield, 2006.

Steffen, Lloyd, ed. *Abortion: A Reader*. Eugene, Ore.: Wipf & Stock, 2010.

Steinbock, Bonnie. *Life Before Birth: The Moral and Legal Status of Embryos and Fetuses*. 2nd ed. New York: Oxford University Press, 2011.

———. "Mother-Fetus Conflict." In *A Companion to Bioethics*, 2nd ed., edited by Helga Kuhse and Peter Singer, 149–60. Malden, Mass.: Wiley-Blackwell, 2009.

Teichman, Jenny. "Intention and Sex." In *Intention and Intentionality: Essays in Honour of G. E. M. Anscombe*, edited by Cora Diamond and Jenny Teichman, 147–61. Ithaca, N.Y.: Cornell University Press, 1979.

Thomson, Judith Jarvis. "A Defense of Abortion." *Philosophy and Public Affairs* 1:1 (1971), 47–66.

Tooley, Michael, Celia Wolf-Devine, Philip E. Devine, and Alison M. Jaggar. *Abortion: Three Perspectives*. New York: Oxford University Press, 2009.

Vacek, Edward C. "Contraception Again—A Conclusion in Search of Convincing Arguments: One Proportionalist's (Mis?)understanding of a Text." In *Natural Law and Moral Inquiry*, edited by Robert P. George, 50–81. Washington, D.C.: Georgetown University Press, 1998.

Varden, Helga. "A Feminist, Kantian Conception of the Right to Bodily Integrity: The Cases of Abortion and Homosexuality." In *Out from the Shadows: Analytical Feminist Contributions to Traditional Philosophy*, edited by Sharon L. Crasnow and Anita M. Superson, 33–58. Oxford: Oxford University Press, 2012.

Vogelstein, Eric. "Metaphysics and the Future-Like-Ours Argument Against Abortion." *Journal of Ethics* 20:4 (2016), 419–34.

Warren, Mary Anne. "Abortion." In *A Companion to Bioethics*, 2nd ed., edited by Helga Kuhse and Peter Singer, 140–48. Malden, Mass.: Blackwell-Wiley, 2009.

Watt, E. D. "Professor Cohen's Encyclical." *Ethics* 80 (1970), 218–21.

Whitehead, Mary Beth, and Loretta Schwartz-Nobel. *A Mother's Story: The Truth about the Baby M Case*. New York: St. Martin's Press, 1989.

Wilcox, John T. "Nature as Demonic in Thomson's Defense of Abortion." *The New Scholasticism* 63:4 (1989), 463–84.

Wilkinson, Stephen. *Choosing Tomorrow's Children: The Ethics of Selective Reproduction*. Oxford: Oxford University Press, 2010.

Willis, Ellen. "Abortion: Is a Woman a Person?" In *Beginning to See the Light*, 205–11. New York: Knopf, 1981. Reprinted in *Powers of Desire: The Politics of Sexuality*, edited by Ann Snitow, Christine Stansell, and Sharon Thompson, 471–76. New York: Monthly Review Press, 1983; and in *The Philosophy of Sex*, edited by Alan Soble, 3rd ed., 165–69, and 4th ed., 191–95. Lanham, Md.: Rowman & Littlefield, 1997 and 2002, respectively.

Wilson, George B. "Christian Conjugal Morality and Contraception." In *Population Ethics*, edited by Francis X. Quinn, 98–108. Washington, D.C.: Corpus, 1968.

Wolf-Devine, Celia. "Abortion and the Feminine Voice." *Public Affairs Quarterly* 3:3 (1989), 81–97. Reprinted in *The Problem of Abortion*, 3rd ed., edited by Susan Dwyer and Joel Feinberg, 160–74. Belmont, Calif.: Wadsworth, 1997; and in *Sex and Gender: A Spectrum of Views*, edited by Philip E. Devine and Celia Wolf-Devine, 163–72. Belmont, Calif.: Wadsworth, 2003.

Yeung, Anthony. "Abortion and the Potential Person Argument." In *New Essays in Applied Ethics: Animal Rights, Personhood and the Ethics of Killing*, edited by Hon-Lam Li and Anthony Yeung, 132–52. Basingstoke, U.K.: Palgrave Macmillan, 2007.

Zaner, Richard M. "A Criticism of Moral Conservatism's View of *In Vitro* Fertilization and Embryo Transfer." *Perspectives in Biology and Medicine* 27:2 (1984), 201–12.

BDSM

Airaksinen, Timo. *The Philosophy of the Marquis de Sade*. London: Routledge, 1995.

Bartky, Sandra Lee. "Feminine Masochism and the Politics of Personal Transformation," *Women's Studies International Forum* 7:5 (1984), 323–34.

Beckmann, Andrea. *The Social Construction of Sexuality and Perversion: Deconstructing Sadomasochism*. Basingstoke, U.K.: Palgrave Macmillan, 2009.

Burr, Viv, and Jeff Hearn, eds. *Sex, Violence and the Body: The Erotics of Wounding*. Basingstoke, U.K.: Palgrave Macmillan, 2008.

Califia, Pat. "Feminism and Sadomasochism." *Heresies*, No. 12 ["Sex Issue"]: 3–4 (1981), 30–34. Reprinted in *Feminism and Sexuality: A Reader*, edited by Stevi Jackson and Sue Scott, 230–37. New York: Columbia University Press, 1996.

———. *Macho Sluts*. Los Angeles: Alyson Books, 1988.

———. *Public Sex: The Culture of Radical Sex*. Pittsburgh, Pa.: Cleis Press, 1994.

———, ed. *The Lesbian S/M Safety Manual*. Boston: Lace Publications, 1988.

Card, Claudia. "Review Essay: Sadomasochism and Sexual Preference." *Journal of Social Philosophy* 15:2 (1984), 42–52.

Chancer, Lynn S. "From Pornography to Sadomasochism: Reconciling Feminist Differences." *Annals of the American Academy of Political and Social Science* 571:1 (2000), 77–88.

———. *Sadomasochism in Everyday Life: The Dynamics of Power and Powerlessness*. New Brunswick, N.J.: Rutgers University Press, 1992.

Chavez, Maria, Chris Gavaler and Nathaniel Goldberg. "Loving Lassos: Wonder Woman, Kink, and Care." In *Wonder Woman and Philosophy: The Amazonian Mystique*, edited by Jacob Held, 188–97. Chichester, U.K.: Wiley-Blackwell, 2017.

Corvino, John. "Naughty Fantasies." *Southwest Philosophy Review* 18:1 (2002), 213–20.

Cross, Patricia A., and Kim Matheson. "Understanding Sadomasochism: An Empirical Examination of Four Perspectives." *Journal of Homosexuality* 50:2–3 (2006), 133–66.

Estes, Yolanda. "BDSM: My Apology." In *Desire, Love, and Identity: Philosophy of Sex and Love*, edited by Gary Foster, 158–66. Ontario: Oxford University Press, 2017.

Fitzpatrick-Hanly, Margaret Ann, ed. *Essential Papers on Masochism*. New York: New York University Press, 1995.

Foucault, Michel. "What Did Sade Write?" In *Language, Madness, and Desire: On Literature*, 97–114. Minneapolis: University of Minnesota Press, 2015.

Gebhardt, Paul. "Fetishism and Sadomasochism." In *Sex Research: Studies from the Kinsey Institute*, edited by M. Weinberg, 156–66. New York: Oxford University Press, 1976.

Hopkins, Patrick D. "Rethinking Sadomasochism: Feminism, Interpretation, and Simulation." *Hypatia* 9:1 (1994), 116–41. Reprinted in *The Philosophy of Sex*, 3rd ed., edited by Alan Soble, 189–214. Lanham, Md.: Rowman & Littlefield, 1997.

———. "Simulation and the Reproduction of Injustice: A Reply." *Hypatia* 10:2 (1995), 162–70.

Kenney, Shawna. *I Was a Teenage Dominatrix: A Memoir*. New York: Retro Systems Press, 1999.

Khan, Ummni. "S/M in Showbiz." In *Vicarious Kinks: S/M in the Socio-Legal Imaginary*, 117–83. Toronto: University of Toronto Press, 2014.

Kleinplatz, Peggy J., and Charles Moser, eds. *Sadomasochism: Powerful Pleasures*. New York: Harrington Park Press, 2006.

Laccetti, Nicholas. "Calvary and the Dungeon: Theologizing BDSM." In *Queer Christianities: Lived Religion in Transgressive Forms*, edited by Kathleen T. Talvacchia, Michael F. Pettinger, and Mark Larrimore, 148–59. New York: New York University Press, 2015.

Langdridge, Darren, and Meg Baker, eds. *Safe, Sane, and Consensual: Contemporary Perspectives on Sadomasochism*. Basingstoke, U.K.: Palgrave Macmillan, 2007.

Linden, Robin Ruth, Darlene R. Pagano, Diana E. H. Russell, and Susan Leigh Star, eds. *Against Sadomasochism: A Radical Feminist Analysis*. East Palo Alto, Calif.: Frog in the Well, 1982.

Mann, Jay, and Natalie Shainess. "Sadistic Fantasies." *Medical Aspects of Human Sexuality* 8:2 (1974), 142–48.

Nielsen, Morten Ebbe Juul. "Safe, Sane, and Consensual—Consent and the Ethics of BDSM." *International Journal of Applied Philosophy* 24:2 (2010), 265–88.

Noyes, John K. *The Mastery of Submission: Inventions of Masochism*. Ithaca, N.Y.: Cornell University Press, 1997.

Reik, Theodor. *Masochism in Sex and Society*. Translated by M. H. Beigel and G. M. Kurth. New York: Grove Press, 1962.

Sade, The Marquis de. *Justine, Philosophy in the Bedroom, and Other Writings*. Translated by Richard Seaver and Austryn Wainhouse. New York: Grove Press, 1965.

Samois, ed. *Coming to Power: Writings and Graphics on Lesbian S/M*, 1st edition, Palo Alto, Calif.: Up Press, 1981; 2nd ed., Boston: Alyson Publications, 1982.

Shattuck, Roger. *Forbidden Knowledge: From Prometheus to Pornography*. San Diego: Harcourt Brace, 1996.

Stallings, L. H. "Make Ya Holler You've Had Enough: Neutralizing Masculine Privilege with BDSM and Sex Work." In *Funk the Erotic: Transaesthetics and Black Sexual Cultures*, 88–121. Urbana-Champagne, Ill..: University of Illinois Press, 2015.

Stear, Nils-Hennes. "Sadomasochism as *Make-Believe*." *Hypatia* 24:2 (2009), 21–38.

Vadas, Melinda. "Reply to Patrick Hopkins." *Hypatia* 10:2 (1995), 159–61. Reprinted in *The Philosophy of Sex*, 3rd ed., edited by Alan Soble, 215–17. Lanham, Md.: Rowman & Littlefield, 1997.

Weinberg, Jill D. *Consensual Violence: Sex, Sports, and the Politics of Injury*. Berkeley, Calif.: University of California Press, 2016.

Weinberg, Thomas S., ed. *S&M: Studies in Dominance & Submission*. Amherst, N.Y.: Prometheus, 1995.

CONSENT, POWER, AND RAPE

Abdullah-Khan, Noreen. *Male Rape: The Emergence of a Social and Legal Issue*. Basingstoke, U.K.: Palgrave Macmillan, 2008.

Alcoff, Linda Martín. "Discourses of Sexual Violence in a Global Framework." *Philosophical Topics* 37:2 (2009), 123–39.

Anderson, Peter B., and Cindy Struckman-Johnson, eds. *Sexually Aggressive Women: Current Perspectives and Controversies*. New York: Guilford, 1998.

Anderson, A. Scott. "Conceptualizing Rape as Coerced Sex." *Ethics* 127:1 (2016), 50–87.

———. "The Enforcement Approach to Coercion." *Journal of Ethics and Social Philosophy* (online) 5:1 (2010).

Archard, David. "Informed Consent: Autonomy and Self-Ownership." *Journal of Applied Philosophy* 25:1 (2008), 19–34.

———. "'A Nod's as Good as a Wink': Consent, Convention, and Reasonable Belief." *Legal Theory* 3:3 (1997), 273–90.

———. *Sexual Consent*. Boulder, Colo.: Westview, 1998.

———. "The Wrong of Rape." *The Philosophical Quarterly* 57: 228 (2007), 374–93.

Baber, H. E. "How Bad Is Rape?" *Hypatia* 2:2 (1987), 125–38. Reprinted in *The Philosophy of Sex*, 2nd ed., edited by Alan Soble, 243–58. Savage, Md.: Rowman & Littlefield, 1991; 3rd ed., edited by Alan Soble, 249–62. Lanham, Md.: Rowman & Littlefield, 1997; 4th ed., edited by Alan Soble, 303–16. Lanham, Md.: Rowman & Littlefield, 2002.

———. "How Bad Is Rape?—II" (Revised version of "How Bad Is Rape?"). In *The Philosophy of Sex*, 6th ed., edited by Nicholas Power, Raja Halwani, and Alan Soble, 485–501. Lanham, Md.: Rowman & Littlefield, 2013.

Belliotti, Raymond. "A Philosophical Analysis of Sexual Ethics." *Journal of Social Philosophy* 10:3 (1979), 8–11.

Bogart, John H. "On the Nature of Rape." *Public Affairs Quarterly* 5 (1991), 117–36.

Bourke, Joanna. *Rape: Sex, Violence, History.* Emeryville, Calif.: Shoemaker & Hoard, 2007.

Brison, Susan J. *Aftermath: Violence and the Remaking of a Self.* Princeton, N.J.: Princeton University Press, 2002.

Burgess, Ann Wolbert, ed. *Rape and Sexual Assault: A Research Handbook.* New York: Garland, 1985.

Burgess-Jackson, Keith. *Rape: A Philosophical Investigation.* Aldershot, U.K.: Dartmouth, 1996.

———, ed. *A Most Detestable Crime: New Philosophical Essays on Rape.* New York: Oxford University Press, 1999.

Cahill, Ann J. *Rethinking Rape.* Ithaca, N.Y.: Cornell University Press, 2001.

———. "Unjust Sex vs. Rape." *Hypatia* 31:4 (2016), 746–71.

Calhoun, Laurie. "On Rape: A Crime against Humanity." *Journal of Social Philosophy* 28:1 (1997), 101–9.

Campo-Engelstein, Lisa. "Rape as a Hate-Crime: An Analysis of New York Law." *Hypatia* 31:1 (2016), 91–106.

Card, Claudia. "Rape as a Terrorist Institution." In *Violence, Terrorism, and Justice,* edited by R. G. Frey and Christopher Morris, 296–319. New York: Cambridge University Press, 1991.

———. "Rape as a Weapon of War." *Hypatia* 11:4 (1996), 5–18.

Caringella, Susan. *Addressing Rape Reform in Law and Practice.* New York: Columbia University Press, 2009.

Cave, Eric M. "Unsavory Seduction." *Ethical Theory and Moral Practice* 12:3 (2009), 235–45.

Cowling, Mark, and Paul Reynolds, eds. *Making Sense of Sexual Consent.* Aldershot, U.K.: Ashgate, 2004.

Dadlez, E. M., William L. Andrews, Courtney Lewis, and Marissa Stroud. "Rape, Evolution, and Pseudoscience: Natural Selection in the Academy." *Journal of Social Philosophy* 40:1 (2009), 75–96.

Davis, Michael. "Setting Penalties: What Does Rape Deserve?" *Law and Philosophy* 3:1 (1984), 61–110.

Dixon, Nicholas. "Alcohol and Rape." *Public Affairs Quarterly* 15:4 (2001), 341–54.

Doniger, Wendy. "Sex, Lies, and Tall Tales." *Social Research* 63:3 (1996), 663–99.

Dougherty, Tom. "Sex, Lies, and Consent." *Ethics* 123:4 (2013) 717–44.

———. "*Yes Means Yes*: Consent as Communication." *Philosophy and Public Affairs* 43:3 (2015), 224–53.

DuToit, Louise. *A Philosophical Investigation of Rape: The Making and Unmaking of the Feminine Self.* New York: Routledge, 2009.

Estrich, Susan. "Rape." In *Feminist Jurisprudence,* edited by Patricia Smith, 158–87. New York: Oxford University Press, 1993.

———. *Real Rape: How the Legal System Victimizes Women Who Say No.* Cambridge, Mass.: Harvard University Press, 1987.

Fischel, Joseph J. *Sex and Harm in the Age of Consent.* Minneapolis: University of Minnesota Press, 2016.

Foa, Pamela. "What's Wrong with Rape." In *Feminism and Philosophy,* edited by Mary Vetterling-Braggin, Frederick Elliston, and Jane English, 347–59. Totowa, N.J.: Rowman & Littlefield, 1977. Reprinted in *Philosophy and Sex,* 3rd ed., edited by Robert B. Baker, Kathleen J. Wininger, and Frederick A. Elliston, 583–93. Amherst, N.Y.: Prometheus Books, 1998.

Francis, Leslie P., ed. *Date Rape: Feminism, Philosophy, and the Law.* State College, Pa.: Pennsylvania State University Press, 1996.

French, Stanley G., Wanda Teays, and Laura M. Purdy, eds. *Violence against Women: Philosophical Perspectives.* Ithaca, N.Y.: Cornell University Press, 1998.

Golash, Deirdre. "Power, Sex, and Friendship in Academia." *Essays in Philosophy* 2:2 (January 2001), http://commons.pacificu.edu/eip/vol2/iss2/8 (accessed March 4, 2012). Reprinted in *The Philosophy of Sex*, edited by Alan Soble and Nicholas Power, 5th ed., 449–58. Lanham, Md.: Rowman & Littlefield, 2008.

Hampton, Jean. "Defining Wrong and Defining Rape." In *A Most Detestable Crime: New Philosophical Essays on Rape*, edited by Keith Burgess-Jackson, 118–56. New York: Oxford University Press, 1999.

Harrison, Ross. "Rape: A Case Study in Political Philosophy." In *Rape: An Historical and Social Enquiry*, edited by Sylvana Tomaselli and Roy Porter, 41–56. New York: Basil Blackwell, 1986.

Hasday, Jill. "Contest and Consent: A Legal History of Marital Rape." *California Law Review* 88 (October 2000), 1373–1505.

Heberle, Renée J., and Victoria Grace, eds. *Theorizing Sexual Violence*. New York: Routledge, 2009.

Hickman, Susan, and Charlene L. Muehlenhard. "By the Semi-Mystical Appearance of a Condom: How Young Women and Men Communicate Sexual Consent in Heterosexual Situations." *Journal of Sex Research* 36:3 (1999), 258–72.

Hurd, Heidi. "The Moral Magic of Consent." *Legal Theory* 2:2 (1996), 121–46.

Husak, Douglas. "The Complete Guide to Consent to Sex: Alan Wertheimer's *Consent to Sexual Relations*." *Law and Philosophy* 25:2 (March 2006), 267–87.

Husak, Douglas N., and George C. Thomas III. "Date Rape, Social Convention, and Reasonable Mistakes." *Law and Philosophy* 11:1 (1992), 95–126.

———. "Rapes without Rapists: Consent and Reasonable Mistake." In *Philosophical Issues 11: Social, Legal, and Political Philosophy*, edited by Ernest Sosa and Enrique Villanueva, 86–117. Oxford: Blackwell, 2001.

Jenkins, Katharine. "Rape Myths and Domestic Abuse Myths as Hermeneutical Injustices." *Journal of Applied Philosophy* 34:2 (2017), 191–205.

Kennedy, Duncan. "Sexual Abuse, Sexy Dressing, and the Eroticization of Domination." In *Sexy Dressing Etc.: Essays on the Power and Politics of Cultural Identity*, 126–213. Cambridge, Mass.: Harvard University Press, 1993.

Kittay, Eva Feder. "Ah! My Foolish Heart: A Reply to Alan Soble's 'Antioch's "Sexual Offense Policy": A Philosophical Exploration.'" *Journal of Social Philosophy* 28:2 (1997), 153–59. Reprinted in *The Philosophy of Sex*, 5th ed., edited by Alan Soble and Nicholas Power, 479–87. Lanham, Md.: Rowman & Littlefield, 2008.

Lamond, Grant. "Coercion." *A Companion to Philosophy of Law and Legal Theory*, edited by Dennis Patterson, 642–53. Malden, Mass.: Wiley-Blackwell, 2010.

Leone, Bruno, ed. *Rape on Campus*. San Diego: Greenhaven, 1995.

Manson, Neil C. "How Not to Think about the Ethics of Deceiving into Sex." *Ethics* 127:2 (2017), 415–29.

Marsh, Jeanne C., Alison Geist, and Nathan Caplan. *Rape and the Limits of Law Reform*. Boston: Auburn House, 1982.

Matthews, Steve. "Addiction, Competence, and Coercion." *Journal of Philosophical Research* 39 (2014), 199–234.

May, Larry, and Robert Strikwerda. "Men in Groups: Collective Responsibility for Rape." *Hypatia* 9:2 (1994), 134–51. Reprinted in *Philosophy and Sex*, 3rd ed., edited by Robert B. Baker, Kathleen J. Wininger, and Frederick A. Elliston, 594–610. Amherst, N.Y.: Prometheus Books, 1998; and 4th ed., edited by Robert B. Baker and Kathleen J. Wininger, 477–94. Amherst, N.Y.: Prometheus Books, 2009.

McGlynn, Clare, and Vanessa E. Munroe, eds. *Rethinking Rape Law: International and Comparative Perspectives*. Abingdon, U.K.: Routledge, 2010.

McGowan, Mary Kate. "On Silencing and Sexual Refusal." *Journal of Political Philosophy* 17:4 (2009), 487–94.

McGregor, Joan. *Is It Rape? On Acquaintance Rape and Taking Women's Consent Seriously*. Aldershot, U.K.: Ashgate, 2005.

Muehlenhard, Charlene L., Sharon Danoff-Burg, and Irene G. Powch. "Is Rape Sex or Violence? Conceptual Issues and Implications." In *Sex, Power, Conflict: Evolutionary and Feminist Perspectives,* edited by David M. Buss and Neil M. Malamuth, 119–37. Oxford: Oxford University Press, 1996. Reprinted in *Philosophy and Sex,* 3rd ed., edited by Robert B. Baker, Kathleen J. Wininger, and Frederick A. Elliston, 621–39. Amherst, N.Y.: Prometheus Books, 1998.

Muehlenhard, Charlene L., and Lisa C. Hollabaugh. "Do Women Sometimes Say No When They Mean Yes? The Prevalence and Correlates of Women's Token Resistance to Sex." *Journal of Personality and Social Psychology* 54:5 (1988), 872–79.

Muehlenhard, Charlene L., Irene G. Powich, Joi L. Phelps, and Laura M. Givsi. "Definitions of Rape: Scientific and Political Implications." *Journal of Social Issues* 48:1 (1992), 23–44.

Muehlenhard, Charlene L., and Jennifer L. Schrag. "Nonviolent Sexual Coercion." In *Acquaintance Rape: The Hidden Crime,* edited by A. Parrot and L. Bechhofer, 115–28. New York: John Wiley, 1991.

Murphy, Jeffrie. "Some Ruminations on Women, Violence, and the Criminal Law." In *In Harm's Way: Essays in Honor of Joel Feinberg,* edited by Jules Coleman and Allen Buchanan, 209–30. Cambridge: Cambridge University Press, 1994.

Nenadic, Natalie. "Sexual Abuse, Modern Freedom, and Heidegger's Philosophy." *Social Philosophy Today: Poverty, Justice, and Markets,* edited by Nancy E. Snow, 111–26. Charlottesville, Va.: Philosophy Documentation Center, 2011.

Paglia, Camille. *Sex, Art, and American Culture.* New York: Vintage, 1992.

Parrot, Andrea, and Laurie Bechhofer, eds. *Acquaintance Rape: The Hidden Crime.* New York: John Wiley, 1991.

Peterson, Susan Rae. "Coercion and Rape: The State as a Male Protection Racket." In *Feminism and Philosophy,* edited by Mary Vetterling-Braggin, Frederick Elliston, and Jane English, 360–71. Totowa, N.J.: Littlefield Adams, 1977.

Petrik, James. "Autonomy, Sex, and Coercion: The Problem of Nonconsensual Sex." In *Philosophy: Sex and Love,* edited by James Petrik and Arthur Zucker, 271–302. Farmington Hills, Mich.: Macmillan Reference USA, 2016.

Pineau, Lois. "Date Rape: A Feminist Analysis." *Law and Philosophy* 8 (1989), 217–43. Reprinted in *The Philosophy of Sex,* 6th ed., edited by Nicholas Power, Raja Halwani, and Alan Soble, 461–83. Lanham, Md.: Rowman & Littlefield, 2013.

Primoratz, Igor. "Sexual Morality: Is Consent Enough?" *Ethical Theory and Moral Practice* 4:3 (2001), 201–18.

Prins, Baukje. "Sympathetic Distrust: Liberalism and the Sexual Autonomy of Women." *Social Theory and Practice* 34:2 (2008), 243–70.

Reitan, Eric. "Date Rape and Seduction: Towards a Defense of Pineau's Definition of 'Date Rape.'" *Southwest Philosophy Review* 20:1 (2004), 99–106.

———. "Rape as an Essentially Contested Concept." *Hypatia* 16:2 (2001), 43–66.

Remick, Lani Anne. "Read Her Lips: An Argument for a Verbal Consent Standard in Rape." *University of Pennsylvania Law Review* 141:3 (1993), 1103–51.

Sachs, Benjamin. "Why Coercion Is Wrong When It Is Wrong." *Australasian Journal of Philosophy* 91:1 (2013), 63–82.

Schulhofer, Stephen J. "The Gender Question in Criminal Law." *Punishment and Rehabilitation,* 3rd ed., edited by Jeffrie Murphy, 274–311. Belmont, Calif.: Wadsworth, 1995.

———. *Unwanted Sex: The Culture of Intimidation and the Failure of Law.* Cambridge, Mass.: Harvard University Press, 1998.

Shafer, Carolyn M., and Marilyn Frye. "Rape and Respect." In *Feminism and Philosophy,* edited by Mary Vetterling-Braggin, Frederick Elliston, and Jane English, 333–46. Totowa, N.J.: Littlefield Adams, 1977.

Shields, William, and Lea Shields. "Forcible Rape: An Evolutionary Perspective." *Ethology and Sociobiology* 4:3 (1983), 115–36.

Silliman, Matthew C. "The Antioch Policy, a Community Experiment in Communicative Sexuality." In *Date Rape: Feminism, Philosophy, and the Law,* edited by Leslie Francis, 167–75. University Park, Pa.: Pennsylvania State University Press, 1996. Reprinted in *Philosophy and Sex,* 3rd ed., edited by Robert B. Baker, Kathleen J.

Wininger, and Frederick A. Elliston, 661–67. Amherst, N.Y.: Prometheus Books, 1998.

Soble, Alan. "Antioch's 'Sexual Offense Policy': A Philosophical Exploration." *Journal of Social Philosophy* 28:1 (1997), 22–36. Reprinted, revised, in *The Philosophy of Sex*, 5th ed., edited by Alan Soble and Nicholas Power, 459–77. Lanham, Md.: Rowman & Littlefield, 2008.

———. "In Defense of Bacon." *Philosophy of the Social Sciences* 25:2 (1995), 192–215. Reprinted, revised, in *A House Built on Sand: Exposing Postmodernist Myths about Science*, edited by Noretta Koertge, 195–215. New York: Oxford University Press, 1998.

Sommers, Christine Hoff. *Who Stole Feminism? How Women Have Betrayed Women.* New York: Simon & Schuster, 1994.

Spivak, Andrew L. *Sexual Violence: Beyond the Feminist-Evolutionary Debate.* El Paso, Tex.: LFB Scholarly Publishing, 2011.

Stinchcombe, Arthur L., and Laura Beth Nielsen. "Consent to Sex: The Liberal Paradigm Reformulated." *Journal of Political Philosophy* 17:1 (2009), 66–89.

Taylor, Chloë. "Disciplinary Relations/Sexual Relations: Feminist and Foucauldian Reflections on Professor-Student Sex." *Hypatia* 26:1 (2011), 187–206.

———. "Foucault, Feminism, and Sex Crimes." *Hypatia* 24:4 (2009), 1–25.

Thornhill, Randy, and Craig Palmer. *A Natural History of Rape: Biological Bases of Sexual Coercion.* Cambridge, Mass.: MIT Press, 2000.

Tomaselli, Sylvana and Roy Porter, eds. *Rape: An Historical and Cultural Inquiry.* New York: Blackwell, 1986.

Travis, Cheryl Brown, ed. *Evolution, Gender, and Rape.* Cambridge, Mass.: MIT Press, 2003.

Tumulty, Maura. "Illocution and Expectations of Being Heard." *Out from the Shadows: Analytical Feminist Contributions to Traditional Philosophy*, edited by Sharon L. Crasnow and Anita M. Superson, 217–44. Oxford: Oxford University Press, 2012.

Warshaw, Robin. *I Never Called It Rape: The Ms. Report on Recognizing, Fighting, and Surviving Date and Acquaintance Rape.* New York: Harper and Row, 1988.

Watkins, Christine, ed. *Date Rape.* Detroit, Mich.: Greenhaven Press, 2007.

Weinberg, Jill D. *Consensual Violence: Sex, Sports, and the Politics of Injury.* Berkeley, Calif.: University of California Press, 2016.

Wertheimer, Alan. *Coercion.* Princeton, N.J.: Princeton University Press, 1987.

———. *Consent to Sexual Relations.* Cambridge: Cambridge University Press, 2003.

West, Robin. "Sex, Law, and Consent." In *The Ethics of Consent: Theory and Practice*, edited by Franklin G. Miller and Alan Wertheimer, 221–50. Oxford: Oxford University Press, 2010.

Williams, Reginald. "Feminism and Rape." *Public Affairs Quarterly* 29:4 (2015), 419–33.

FANTASY AND MASTURBATION

Bennett, Paula, and Vernon A. Rosario, eds. *Solitary Pleasures: The Historical, Literary, and Artistic Discourses of Autoeroticism.* New York: Routledge, 1995.

Budapest, Zsuzsanna E. "Self-Blessing Ritual." In *Womanspirit Rising: A Feminist Reader in Religion*, edited by Carol P. Christ and Judith Plaskow, 269–72. San Francisco: Harper and Row, 1979.

Burger, John R. *One-Handed Histories: The Eroto–Politics of Gay Male Video Pornography.* New York: Haworth, 1995.

Cornog, Martha, ed. *The Big Book of Masturbation: From Angst to Zeal.* San Francisco.: Down There Press, 2003.

Dodson, Betty. "How I Became the Guru of Female Sexual Liberation." In *Personal Stories of "How I Got Into Sex": Leading Researchers, Sex Therapists, Educators, Prostitutes, Sex Toy Designers, Sex Surrogates, Transsexuals, Criminologists, Clergy, and*

More . . ., edited by Bonnie Bullough, Vern L. Bullough, Marilyn A. Fithian, William E. Hartman, and Randy Sue Klein, 122–30. Amherst, N.Y.: Prometheus, 1997.

———. *Liberating Masturbation: A Meditation on Self-Love*. New York: Betty Dodson, 1978.

Elders, M. Joycelyn. "The Dreaded M Word. It's Not a Four-Letter Word." *Nerve* (June 26, 1997), www.nerve.com/dispatches/elders/mword (accessed March 3, 2012).

Engelhardt, H. Tristram, Jr. "The Disease of Masturbation: Values and the Concept of Disease." *Bulletin of the History of Medicine* 48 (Summer 1974), 234–48.

Fortunata, Jacqueline. "Masturbation and Women's Sexuality." In *The Philosophy of Sex*, edited by Alan Soble, 1st ed., 389–408. Totowa, N.J.: Rowman & Littlefield, 1980.

Francis, John J. "Masturbation." *Journal of the American Psychoanalytic Association* 16:1 (1968), 95–112.

Groenendijk, Leendert F. "Masturbation and Neurasthenia: Freud and Stekel in Debate on the Harmful Effects of Autoeroticism." *Journal of Psychology and Human Sexuality* 9:1 (1997), 71–94.

Haynes, James. "Masturbation." In *Human Sexuality: An Encyclopedia*, edited by Vern Bullough and Bonnie Bullough, 381–85. New York: Garland, 1994.

Hershfield, Jeffrey. "The Ethics of Sexual Fantasy." *International Journal of Applied Philosophy* 23:1 (2009), 27–49.

Jordan, Mark D. "Masturbation, or Identity in Solitude." In *The Ethics of Sex*, 95–104. Oxford: Blackwell, 2002.

Kahr, Brett. *Who's Been Sleeping in Your Head? The Secret World of Sexual Fantasy*. New York: Basic Books, 2008.

Kielkopf, Charles. "Masturbation: A Kantian Condemnation." *Philosophia* 25:1–4 (1997), 223–46.

Laqueur, Thomas. *Solitary Sex: A Cultural History of Masturbation*. New York: Zone Books, 2003.

Moore, Gareth. "Natural Sex: Germain Grisez, Sex, and Natural Law." In *The Revival of Natural Law: Philosophical, Theological and Ethical Responses to the Finnis-Grisez School*, edited by Nigel Biggar and Rufus Black, 223–41. Aldershot, U.K.: Ashgate, 2000.

Neu, Jerome. "An Ethics of Fantasy?" *Journal of Theoretical and Philosophical Psychology* 22:2 (2002), 137–57.

Sarnoff, Suzanne, and Irving Sarnoff. *Sexual Excitement/Sexual Peace: The Place of Masturbation in Adult Relationships*. New York: M. Evans, 1979.

Satlow, Michael L. "'Wasted Seed': The History of a Rabbinic Idea." *Hebrew Union College Annual* 65 (1994), 137–69.

Soble, Alan. "Kant and Sexual Perversion." *The Monist* 86:1 (2003), 57–92.

Tiefer, Leonore. "Review of Suzanne Sarnoff and Irving Sarnoff, *Sexual Excitement/ Sexual Peace: The Place of Masturbation in Adult Relationships*." *Psychology of Women Quarterly* 8:1 (1983), 107–9.

Van Driel, Mels. *With the Hand: A Cultural History of Masturbation*. Translated by Paul Vincent. London: Reaktion Books, 2012.

INTERNET AND TECHNOLOGY

Adeney, Douglas. "Evaluating the Pleasures of Cybersex." *Australasian Journal of Professional and Applied Ethics* 1:1 (1999), 69–79.

Ali, Rami. "A New Solution to the Gamer's Dilemma." *Ethics and Information Technology* 17:4 (2015), 267–74.

Attwood, Feona, ed. *Porn.com: Making Sense of Online Pornography*. New York: Peter Lang, 2010.

Bartel, Christopher. "Resolving the Gamer's Dilemma." *Ethics and Information Technology* 14:1 (2012), 11–16.

Ben-Ze'ev, Aaron. *Love Online: Emotions on the Internet*. Cambridge: Cambridge University Press, 2004.

———. "Virtual Relationships: Love and Sex in Cyberspace." In *Philosophy: Sex and Love*, edited by James Petrik and Arthur Zucker, 353–84. Farmington Hills, Mich.: Macmillan Reference USA, 2016.

Botz-Bornstein, Thorsten, ed. *The Philosophy of Viagra: Bioethical Responses to the Viagrification of the Modern World*. Amsterdam: Rodopi Press, 2011.

Brinkman, Bo. "Dating and Play in Virtual Worlds." In *Dating: Flirting with Big Ideas*, edited by Kristie Miller and Marlene Clark, 167–79. Malden, Mass.: Wiley-Blackwell, 2010.

Bruce, Michael. "The Virtual Bra Clasp: Navigating Technology in College Courtship." In *College Sex: Philosophers with Benefits*, edited by Michael Bruce and Robert M. Stewart, 40–50. Malden, Mass.: Wiley-Blackwell, 2010.

Collins, Louise. "Emotional Adultery: Cybersex and Commitment." *Social Theory and Practice* 25:2 (1999), 243–70.

———. "Is Cybersex Sex?" In *The Philosophy of Sex*, edited by Alan Soble and Nicholas Power, 5th ed., 117–31. Lanham, Md.: Rowman & Littlefield, 2008.

Cooper, Al, ed. *Cybersex: The Dark Side of the Force*. New York: Brunner–Routledge, 2000.

———, ed. *Sex and the Internet: A Guide Book for Clinicians*. New York: Brunner-Routledge, 2002.

Guilfoy, Kevin. "Man's Fallen State: St. Augustine on Viagra." In *The Philosophy of Viagra: Bioethical Responses to the Viagrification of the Modern World*, edited by Thorsten Botz-Bornstein, 57–70. Amsterdam: Rodopi Press, 2011.

Harmon, Justin L. "Dwelling in the House That Porn Built: A Phenomenological Critique of Pornography in the Age of Internet Technology." *Social Philosophy Today: Freedom, Religion, and Gender*, Volume 28, edited by Jeff Gauthier, 115–30. Charlottesville, Va.: Philosophy Documentation Center, 2012.

Holt, Martin. "Virtual Decadence." In *Analecta Husserliana: The Yearbook of Phenomenological Research, Volume XC: Logos of Phenomenology and Phenomenology of the Logos, Book Three*, edited by Anna-Teresa Tymienieca, 373–401. Dordrecht: Springer, 2006.

Hughes, Donna M. "The Use of New Communications and Information Technologies for Sexual Exploitation of Women and Children." *Hastings Women's Law Journal* 13:1 (2002), 129–48.

Kessler, Suzanne J. *Lessons from the Intersexed*. Piscataway, N.J.: Rutgers University Press, 1998.

Kiesbye, Stefan, ed. *Sexting*. Detroit, Mich.: Greenhaven Press, 2011.

Levmore, Saul and Martha C. Nussbaum, eds. *The Offensive Internet: Privacy, Speech, Representation*. Cambridge, Mass.: Harvard University Press, 2010.

Levy, Neil. "Virtual Child Pornography: The Eroticization of Inequality." *Ethics and Information Technology* 4:4 (2002), 319–23.

Luck, Morgan. "The Gamer's Dilemma: An Analysis of the Arguments for the Moral Distinction between Virtual Murder and Virtual Pedophilia." *Ethics and Information Technology* 11:1 (2009), 31–36.

Luck, Morgan, and Nathan Ellerby. "Has Bartel Resolved the Gamer's Dilemma?" *Ethics and Information Technology* 15:3 (2013), 229–33.

Maheu, Marlene M., and Rona B. Subotnik. *Infidelity on the Internet: Virtual Relationships and Real Betrayal*. Naperville, Ill.: Sourcebooks, 2001.

Parisi, Luciana. *Abstract Sex: Philosophy, Biotechnology, and the Mutations of Desire*. London: Continuum, 2004.

Parikka, Jussi, and Tony D. Sampson, eds. *The Spam Book: On Viruses, Porn, and Other Anomalies from the Dark Side of Digital Culture*. Cresskill, N.J.: Hampton Press, 2009.

Patridge, Stephanie L. "Pornography, Ethics, and Videogames." *Ethics and Information Technology* 15:1 (2013), 25–34.

Samama, Claude-Raphael. "Desire and Its Mysteries: Erectile Stimulators between Thighs and Selves." In *The Philosophy of Viagra: Bioethical Responses to the Viagrifica-*

tion of the Modern World, edited by Thorsten Botz-Borstein, 127–44. Amsterdam: Rodopi Press, 2011.

Young, Gary. "Enacting Taboos as a Means to an End; but What End? On the Morality of the Motivations for Child Murder and Paedophilia within Gamespace." *Ethics and Information Technology* 15:1 (2013), 13–23.

KANT (INCLUDING OBJECTIFICATION) AND OTHER HISTORICAL PHILOSOPHERS

Airaksinen, Timo. *The Philosophy of the Marquis de Sade*. London: Routledge, 1995.

Alexander, W. M. "Sex and Philosophy in Augustine." *Augustinian Studies* 5 (1974), 197–208.

Anderson, Clelia Smyth, and Yolanda Estes. "The Myth of the Happy Hooker: Kantian Moral Reflections on a Phenomenology of Prostitution." In *Violence against Women: Philosophical Perspectives*, edited by Stanley G. French, Wanda Teays, and Laura M. Purdy, 152–58. Ithaca, N.Y.: Cornell University Press, 1998.

Baker, Robert B. "'Pricks' and 'Chicks': A Plea for 'Persons.'" In *Philosophy and Sex*, 1st ed., edited by Robert B. Baker and Frederick A. Elliston, 45–64. Buffalo, N.Y.: Prometheus, 1975. Reprinted in *Philosophy and Sex*, edited by Robert B. Baker, Kathleen J. Wininger, and Frederick A. Elliston. 3rd ed., 281–97, along with "'Pricks' and 'Chicks': A Postscript after Twenty-Five Years," 297–305. Amherst, N.Y.: Prometheus, 1998.

Baron, Marcia. "Love and Respect in the *Doctrine of Virtue*." In *Kant's Metaphysics of Morals: Interpretive Essays*, edited by Mark Timmons, 391–408. New York: Oxford University Press, 2002.

Baumrin, Bernard. (1975) "Sexual Immorality Delineated." In *Philosophy and Sex*, 2nd ed., edited by Robert B. Baker and Frederick A. Elliston, 300–311. Buffalo, N.Y.: Prometheus, 1984.

Beckman, Frida. *Between Desire and Pleasure: A Deleuzian Theory of Sexuality*. Edinburgh: Edinburgh University Press, 2013.

Beckman, Frida, ed. *Deleuze and Sex*. Edinburgh: Edinburgh University Press, 2011.

Belliotti, Raymond. *Good Sex: Perspectives on Sexual Ethics*. Lawrence, Kans.: University Press of Kansas, 1993.

Bencivenga, Ermanno. "Kant's Sadism." *Philosophy and Literature* 20:1 (1996), 39–46.

Boros, Gabor. "The Passions." *The Oxford Handbook of Philosophy in Early Modern Europe*. Oxford: Oxford University Press. 2011.

Brake, Elizabeth. "Justice and Virtue in Kant's Account of Marriage." *Kantian Review* 9 (March 2005), 58–94.

Brecht, Bertolt. (1938) "On Kant's Definition of Marriage in *The Metaphysic of Ethics*." In *Poems 1913–1956*, edited by John Willett and Ralph Manheim, with Erich Fried. Revised ed. Translated by John Willett, 312. New York: Methuen, 1987.

Cahill, Ann J. "The Difference Sameness Makes: Objectification, Sex Work, and Queerness." *Hypatia* 29:4 (2014), 840–56.

———. *Overcoming Objectification: A Carnal Ethics*. New York: Routledge, 2011.

———. "Why 'Derivatization' Is Better Than 'Objectification.'" In *The Philosophy of Sex*, 6th ed., edited by Nicholas Power, Raja Halwani, and Alan Soble, 335–57. Lanham, Md.: Rowman & Littlefield, 2013.

Carr, David. "Freud and Sexual Ethics." *Philosophy* 62:241 (1987), 361–73.

Clark, Maudemarie. "Will to Power and Sexuality in Nietzsche's Account of the Ascetic Ideal." *Inquiry* 60:1–2 (2017), 96–134.

Cooke, Vincent M. "Kant, Teleology, and Sexual Ethics." *International Philosophical Quarterly* 31:1 (1991), 3–13.

Critchley, Simon. "Philosophical Eros." *Journal of Philosophical Research* 40 (supplement) (2015), 149–57.

Denis, Lara. "From Friendship to Marriage: Revising Kant." *Philosophy and Phenomeno-logical Research* 63:1 (2001), 1–28.

———. "Kant on the Wrongness of 'Unnatural' Sex." *History of Philosophy Quarterly* 16:2 (1999), 225–48.

Draeger, John. "Can Girls Go Wild with Self-Respect?" *College Sex: Philosophers with Benefits*, edited by Michael Bruce and Robert M. Stewart, 198–208. Malden, Mass.: Wiley-Blackwell, 2010.

Dragona-Monachou, Myrto. "Eros: An Unexpected God of the Stoic Cosmopolis." *Journal of Philosophical Research* 40 (supplement) (2015), 159–79.

Estes, Yolanda. "J. G. Fichte's Account of Human Sexuality: Gender Difference as the Basis of Human Equality within a Just Society." *Social Philosophy Today: Gender, Diversity, and Difference*, Volume 25, edited by John R. Rowan, 63–74. Charlottes-ville, Va.: Philosophy Documentation Center, 2009.

———. "Mutual Respect and Sexual Morality: How to Have College Sex Well." *College Sex: Philosophers with Benefits*, edited by Michael Bruce and Robert M. Stewart, 209–19. Malden, Mass.: Wiley-Blackwell, 2010.

Freud, Sigmund. (1912) "On the Universal Tendency to Debasement in the Sphere of Love." In *The Standard Edition of the Complete Psychological Works of Sigmund Freud*, edited by James Strachey, vol. 11, 177–90. London: Hogarth Press, 1953–74.

Gaca, Kathy L. *The Making of Fornication: Eros, Ethics, and Political Reform in Greek Philosophy and Early Christianity.* Berkeley, Calif.: University of California Press, 2003.

Giles, James. "Sartre, Sexual Desire, and Relations with Others." In *French Existential-ism: Consciousness, Ethics, and Relations with Others*, edited by James Giles, 155–73. Amsterdam: Rodopi, 1999.

Gregor, Mary J. *Laws of Freedom: A Study of Kant's Method of Applying the Categorical Imperative in the Metaphysik der Sitten.* New York: Barnes & Noble, 1963.

Halwani, Raja. "Virtue Ethics, Casual Sex, and Objectification." In *The Philosophy of Sex: Contemporary Readings*, 5th ed., edited by Alan Soble and Nicholas Power, 337–49. Lanham, Md.: Rowman & Littlefield, 2008.

Hampton, Jean. "Defining Wrong and Defining Rape." In *A Most Detestable Crime: New Philosophical Essays on Rape*, edited by Keith Burgess-Jackson, 118–56. New York: Oxford University Press, 1999.

Haslanger, Sally. "On Being Objective and Being Objectified." In *A Mind of One's Own: Feminist Essays on Reason and Objectivity*, edited by Louise Antony and Charlotte Witt, 85–125. Boulder, Colo.: Westview, 1993.

Herman, Barbara. "Could It Be Worth Thinking about Kant on Sex and Marriage?" In *A Mind of One's Own*, edited by Louise Antony and Charlotte Witt, 49–67. Boulder, Colo.: Westview, 1993.

Jütten, Timo. "Sexual Objectification." *Ethics* 127: 1 (2016), 27–49.

Kielkopf, Charles. "Masturbation: A Kantian Condemnation." *Philosophia* 25:1–4 (1997), 223–46.

Kneller, Jane. "Kant on Sex and Marriage Right." In *The Cambridge Companion to Kant and Modern Philosophy*, edited by Paul Guyer, 447–76. Cambridge: Cambridge Uni-versity Press, 2006.

Korsgaard, Christine M. "Creating the Kingdom of Ends: Reciprocity and Responsibil-ity in Personal Relations." *Philosophical Perspectives* 6 (1992), 305–32.

Lamascus, Lorelle D. *The Poverty of Eros in Plato's Symposium.* New York: Bloomsbury Academic, 2016.

Landau, Iddo. "Two Notions of Objectification." *Philosophy Today* 51:3 (2007), 312–19.

Langton, Rae. *Sexual Solipsism: Philosophical Essays on Pornography and Objectification.* Oxford: Oxford University Press, 2009.

Lear, Jonathan. "Ironic Eros: Notes on a Fantastic Pregnancy." *Journal of Philosophical Research* 40 (supplement) (2015), 181–90.

LeMoncheck, Linda. *Dehumanizing Women: Treating Persons as Sex Objects.* Totowa, N.J.: Rowman & Littlefield, 1984.

Lorenz, Hendrik. *The Brute Within: Appetitive Desire in Plato and Aristotle.* Oxford: Clarendon Press, 2006.

Ludwig, Paul W. *Eros and Polis: Desire and Community in Greek Political Theory.* Cambridge: Cambridge University Press, 2002.

Madigan, Timothy. "The Discarded Lemon: Kant, Prostitution and Respect for Persons." *Philosophy Now* 21 (Summer/Autumn 1998), 14–16. Reprinted in *Prostitution: On Whores, Hustlers, and Johns,* edited by James E. Elias, Vern L. Bullough, Veronica Elias, and Gwen Brewer, 107–11. Amherst, N.Y.: Prometheus, 1998.

Maitra, Ishani. "Subordination and Objectification." *Journal of Moral Philosophy* 10:1 (2013), 87–100.

Marino, Patricia. "The Ethics of Sexual Objectification: Autonomy and Consent." *Inquiry* 51:4 (2008), 345–64.

Moscovici, Claudia. *From Sex Objects to Sexual Subjects.* New York: Routledge, 1996.

Mosser, Kurt. "Kant and Feminism." *Kant-Studien* 90:3 (1999), 322–53.

Nussbaum, Martha C. "Objectification." *Philosophy and Public Affairs* 24:4 (1995), 249–91. Reprinted in *The Philosophy of Sex,* 3rd ed., edited by Alan Soble, 283–321, and 4th ed., 381–419. Lanham, Md.: Rowman & Littlefield, 1997 and 2002, respectively. Revised in her *Sex and Social Justice,* 213–39. New York: Oxford University Press, 1999.

Obdrzalek, Suzanne. "Socrates on Love." *Bloomsbury Companion to Socrates,* edited by John Bussanich and Nicholas D. Smith, 210–32. London: Bloomsbury Academic. 2013.

O'Neill, Onora. "Between Consenting Adults." *Philosophy and Public Affairs* 14:3 (1985), 252–77. Reprinted in *Constructions of Reason: Explorations of Kant's Practical Philosophy,* 105–25. Cambridge: Cambridge University Press, 1989.

———. "Kantian Ethics." In *A Companion to Ethics,* edited by Peter Singer, 175–85. Oxford: Blackwell, 1991.

Papadaki, Evangelia. "Sexual Objectification: From Kant to Contemporary Feminism." *Contemporary Political Theory* 6:3 (2007), 330–48.

———. "What Is Objectification?" *Journal of Moral Philosophy* 7:1 (2010), 16–36.

Pearson, Giles. *Aristotle on Desire.* Cambridge: Cambridge University Press. 2012.

Ramakrishnan, Ketan H. "Treating People as Tools." *Philosophy and Public Affairs* 44:2 (2016), 133–65.

Rousselot, Pierre, Alan Vincelette, and Pol Vandevelde, eds. *The Problem of Love in the Middle Ages: A Historical Contribution.* Milwaukee, Wisc.: Marquette University Press, 2001.

Sample, Ruth. "Sexual Exploitation and the Social Contract." *Canadian Journal of Philosophy, "Feminist Moral Philosophy,"* Supp. 28 (2003), 189–217.

Sartre, Jean-Paul. (1943) *Being and Nothingness: An Essay on Phenomenological Ontology.* Translated by Hazel E. Barnes. New York: Philosophical Library, 1956.

Schaff, Kory. "Kant, Political Liberalism, and the Ethics of Same-Sex Relations." *Journal of Social Philosophy* 32:3 (2001), 446–62.

Secomb, Linnell. *Philosophy and Love: From Plato to Popular Culture.* Bloomington, Ind.: Indiana University Press, 2007.

Singer, Irving. "Benign Romanticism: Kant, Schlegel, Hegel, Shelly, Byron." In *The Nature of Love, vol. 2: Courtly and Romantic,* 376–431. Chicago: University of Chicago Press, 1984.

———. "The Morality of Sex: Contra Kant." *Critical Horizons* 1:2 (2000), 175–91. Reprinted in *Explorations in Love and Sex,* 1–20. Lanham, Md.: Rowman & Littlefield, 2001; and *The Philosophy of Sex,* edited by Alan Soble, 4th ed., 259–72. Lanham, Md.: Rowman & Littlefield, 2002.

Soble, Alan. "Kant and Sexual Perversion." *The Monist* 86:1 (2003), 57–92.

Sparshott, Francis. "Kant without Sade." *Philosophy and Literature* 21:1 (1997), 151–54.

Sreedhar, Susanne, and Julie Walsh. "Locke, the Law of Nature, and Polygamy." *Journal of the American Philosophical Association* 2:1 (2016), 91–110.

Stephens, William O. "What's Love Got to Do with It? Epicureanism and Friends with Benefits." In *College Sex: Philosophers with Benefits*, edited by Michael Bruce and Robert M. Stewart, 77–90. Malden, Mass.: Wiley-Blackwell, 2010.

Toon, Mark. *The Philosophy of Sex According to St. Thomas Aquinas*. Washington, D.C.: Catholic University of America Press, 1954.

Waldron, Jeremy. "When Justice Replaces Affection: The Need for Rights." *Harvard Journal of Law and Public Policy* 11 (1988), 625–47.

Young, Charles. "Aristotle on Temperance." *The Philosophical Review* 97:4 (1988), 521–42.

LGBTQ

(for same-sex marriage, see "Marriage and Relationships")

Abelove, Henry, Michèle Aina Barale, and David M. Halperin, eds. *The Lesbian and Gay Studies Reader*. New York and London: Routledge, 1993.

Allen, Jeffner, ed. *Lesbian Philosophies and Cultures*. Albany, N.Y.: SUNY Press, 1990.

Bailey, Cathryn. "Embracing the Icon: The Feminist Potential of the Trans Bodhisattva, Kuan Yin." *Hypatia* 24:3 (2009), 178–96.

Baird, Robert M., and M. Katherine Baird, eds. *Homosexuality: Debating the Issues*. Amherst, N.Y.: Prometheus, 1995.

Ball, Carlos A. *The Morality of Gay Rights: An Exploration in Political Philosophy*. New York: Routledge, 2003.

Baril, Alexandre. "Needing to Acquire a Physical Impairment/Disability: (Re)Thinking the Connections between Trans and Disability Studies through Transability." *Hypatia* 30:1 (2015), 30–48.

Beemyn, Brett, and Mickey Eliason, eds. *Queer Studies: A Lesbian, Gay, Bisexual, and Transgender Anthology*. New York: New York University Press, 1996.

Berlatsky, Noah, ed. *Homosexuality*. Detroit, Mich.: Greenhaven Press, 2011.

Bersani, Leo. "Is the Rectum a Grave?" *October*, 43 (Winter 1987), 197–222.

Bettcher, Talia Mae. "Appearance, Reality, and Gender Deception: Reflections on Transphobic Violence and the Politics of Pretence." In *Violence, Victims, and Justifications*, edited by Felix Ó Murchadha, 175–200. Bern: Peter Lang, 2006.

———. "Evil Deceivers and Make-Believers: Transphobic Violence and the Politics of Illusion." *Hypatia* 22:3 (2007), 43–65.

———. "Trans Identities and First-Person Authority." In *"You've Changed": Sex Reassignment and Personal Identity*, edited by Laurie Shrage, 98–120. Oxford: Oxford University Press, 2009.

———. "Transwomen and the Meaning of 'Woman.'" In *The Philosophy of Sex*, 6th ed., edited by Nicholas Power, Raja Halwani, and Alan Soble, 233–50. Lanham, Md.: Rowman & Littlefield, 2013.

———. "Without a Net: Starting Points for Trans Stories." *American Philosophical Association Newsletter on Philosophy and Lesbian, Gay, Bisexual, and Transgender Issues* 10:2 (Spring 2011), 2–5.

Bialystock, Lauren. "Transgender Inclusion in Single-Sex Competition: The Case of Beauty Pageants." *Social Theory and Practice* 42:3 (2016), 605–35.

Bily, Cynthia A., ed. *Homosexuality: Opposing Viewpoints*. Detroit, Mich.: Greenhaven Press, 2009.

Bloodsworth-Lugo, Mary K., and Carmen Lugo-Lugo. *Containing (un)American Bodies: Race, Sexuality, and Post-9/11 Construction of Citizenship*. Amsterdam: Rodopi, 2010.

Bogaert, Anthony F. *Understanding Asexuality*. Lanham, Md.: Rowman & Littlefield, 2015.

Boswell, John. *Christianity, Social Tolerance, and Homosexuality*. Chicago: University of Chicago Press, 1980.

————. "Revolutions, Universals, and Sexual Categories." *Salmagundi*, Nos. 58–59 (Fall 1982/Winter 1983), 89–113.

Bradshaw, David. "A Reply to Corvino." In *Same Sex: Debating the Ethics, Science, and Culture of Homosexuality*, edited by John Corvino, 17–30. Lanham, Md.: Rowman & Littlefield, 1997.

Braswell, Harold. "My Two Moms: Disability, Queer Kinship, and the Maternal Subject." *Hypatia* 30:1 (2015), 234–50.

Browne, Kath, Jason Lim, and Gavin Brown, eds. *Geographies of Sexualities: Theory, Practices and Politics.* Aldershot, U.K.: Ashgate, 2007.

Byne, William, and Edward Stein. "Ethical Implications of Scientific Research on the Causes of Sexual Orientation." *Health Care Analysis* 5:2 (1997), 136–48.

· Calhoun, Cheshire. *Feminism, the Family, and the Politics of the Closet: Lesbian and Gay Displacement.* Oxford: Oxford University Press, 2000.

————. "Separating Lesbian Theory from Feminist Theory." *Ethics* 104:3 (1994), 558–81.

Califia, Patrick. *Sex Changes: The Politics of Transgenderism.* San Francisco: Cleis Press, 2003.

Card, Claudia. *Lesbian Choices.* New York: Columbia University Press, 1995.

————. *On Feminist Ethics and Politics.* Lawrence, Kans.: University Press of Kansas, 1999.

————, ed. *Adventures in Lesbian Philosophy.* Bloomington, Ind.: Indiana University Press, 1985.

Cárdenas, Micha. *Trans Desire.* New York: Atropos Press, 2010.

Cerankowski, Karli June, and Megan Milks, eds. *Asexualities: Feminist and Queer Perspectives.* New York: Routledge, 2014.

Colene Hume, Maggi. "Sex, Lies, and Surgery: The Ethics of Gender-Reassignment Surgery." *Dialogue* 53:2–3 (2011), 140–48.

Colter, Ephen Glenn, Wayne Hoffman, Eva Pendleton, Alison Redick, and David Serlin, eds. *Policing Public Sex: Queer Politics and the Future of AIDS Activism.* Boston: South End Press, 1996.

Cooley, D. R. "Non-Heterosexuals in Heterosexual Marriages as a Form of Spousal Abuse." *International Journal of Applied Philosophy* 21:2 (2007), 161–79.

Corvino, John. "Analyzing Gender." *Southwest Philosophy Review* 17:1 (2000), 173–80.

————. "Homosexuality and the Moral Relevance of Experience." In *Ethics in Practice*, edited by Hugh LaFollette, 2nd ed., 241–50. Oxford: Blackwell, 2001.

————. "Homosexuality and the PIB Argument." *Ethics* 115:3 (2005), 501–34.

————, ed. *Same Sex: Debating the Ethics, Science, and Culture of Homosexuality.* Lanham, Md.: Rowman & Littlefield, 1997.

————. *What's Wrong with Homosexuality?* Oxford: Oxford University Press, 2013.

Crompton, Louis. *Homosexuality and Civilization.* Cambridge, Mass.: Harvard University Press, 2003.

Currah, Paisley, Richard M. Juang, and Shannon Price Minter, eds. *Transgender Rights.* Minneapolis: University of Minnesota Press, 2006.

Currah, Paisley, and Lisa Jean Moore. "'We Won't Know Who You Are': Contesting Sex Designations in New York City Birth Certificates." *Hypatia* 24:3 (2009), 113–35.

Daper, Heather, and Neil Evans. "Transsexualism and Gender Reassignment Surgery." In *Cutting to the Core: Exploring the Ethics of Contested Surgeries*, edited by David Benatar, 97–110. Lanham, Md.: Rowman & Littlefield, 2006.

De Cecco, John P. "Definition and Meaning of Sexual Orientation." *Journal of Homosexuality* 6:4 (1981), 51–67.

Diamond, Lisa M. *Sexual Fluidity: Understanding Women's Love and Desire.* Cambridge, Mass.: Harvard University Press, 2009.

Dover, Kenneth. (1978) *Greek Homosexuality.* Updated and with a New Postscript. Cambridge, Mass.: Harvard University Press, 1989.

Dreger, Alice Domurat. *Hermaphrodites and the Medical Invention of Sex.* Cambridge, Mass.: Harvard University Press, 1998.

Duberman, Martin, ed. *A Queer World: The Center for Lesbian and Gay Studies Reader.* New York: New York University Press, 1996.

Elliot, Patricia. *Debates in Transgender, Queer, and Feminist Theory: Contested Sites.* Farnham, U.K.: Ashgate, 2010.

Finnis, John. "Law, Morality, and 'Sexual Orientation.'" *Notre Dame Law Review* 69:5 (1994), 1049–76.

———. "Natural Law and Unnatural Acts." In *Human Sexuality,* edited by Igor Primoratz, 5–27. Aldershot, U.K.: Dartmouth, 1997.

———. "The Wrong of Homosexuality." *The New Republic* (November 15, 1993), 12–13. Reprinted in *The Philosophy of Sex,* edited by Alan Soble and Nicholas Power, 5th ed., 135–39. Lanham, Md.: Rowman & Littlefield, 2008.

Fojas, Camilla. *Zombies, Migrants, and Queers: Race and Crisis Capitalism in Pop Culture.* Urbana-Champaign, Ill.: University of Illinois Press, 2017.

Frye, Marilyn. "Lesbian 'Sex.'" In *Willful Virgin: Essays in Feminism, 1976–1992,* 109–19. Freedom, Calif.: Crossing Press, 1992.

Garber, Marjorie. *Bisexuality and the Eroticism of Everyday Life.* New York: Routledge, 2000.

———. *Vice Versa: Bisexuality and the Eroticism of Everyday Life.* New York: Simon & Schuster, 1995.

Gilbert, Miqqi Alicia. "Defeating Bigenderism: Changing Gender Assumptions in the Twenty-First Century." *Hypatia* 24:3 (2009), 93–112.

Glick, Elisa. "Feminism, Queer Theory, and the Politics of Transgression." *Feminist Review* 64 (Spring, 2000), 19–45.

Gonsiorek, John C., and James D. Weinrich, eds. *Homosexuality: Research Implications for Public Policy.* Newbury Park, Calif.: Sage Publications, 1991.

Greenberg, David F. *The Construction of Homosexuality.* Chicago: The University of Chicago Press, 1988.

Hale, C. Jacob. "Are Lesbians Women?" *Hypatia* 11:2 (1996), 94–121.

———. "Leatherdyke Boys and Their Daddies: How to Have Sex Without Men and Women." *Social Text* 52/53 15:3&4 (1997), 223–36.

———. "Tracing a Ghostly Memory in My Throat: Reflections on FTM Feminist Voice and Agency." In *"You've Changed": Sex Reassignment and Personal Identity,* edited by Laurie Shrage, 43–65. Oxford: Oxford University Press, 2009.

Hall, Donald E., and Maria Pramaggiore, eds. *Representing Bisexualities: Subjects and Cultures of Fluid Desire.* New York: New York University Press, 1996.

Halperin, David M. *One Hundred Years of Homosexuality and Other Essays on Greek Love.* New York: Routledge, 1990.

Halwani, Raja. "Essentialism, Social Constructionism, and the History of Homosexuality." *Journal of Homosexuality* 35:1 (1998), 25–51.

Halwani, Raja, Carol V. A. Quinn, and Andy Wible, eds. *Queer Philosophy: Presentations of the Society for Lesbian and Gay Philosophy, 1998–2008.* Amsterdam: Rodopi, 2012.

Hamer, Dean, and Peter Copeland. *The Science of Desire.* New York: Simon & Schuster, 1994.

Herdt, Gilbert. *Sambia Sexual Culture: Essays from the Field.* Chicago: University of Chicago Press, 1999.

Heyes, Cressida J. "Changing Race, Changing Sex: The Ethics of Self-Transformation." *Journal of Social Philosophy* 37:2 (2006), 266–82.

Hines, Sally. *TransForming Gender: Transgender Practices of Identity, Intimacy and Care.* Bristol, U.K.: Policy Press, 2007.

Hines, Sally, and Tam Sanger, eds. *Transgender Identities: Towards a Social Analysis of Gender Diversity.* New York: Routledge, 2010.

Hoagland, Sarah Lucia. *Lesbian Ethics.* Palo Alto, Calif.: Institute of Lesbian Studies, 1988.

Hope, Debra A., ed. *Contemporary Perspectives on Lesbian, Gay, and Bisexual Identities.* New York: Springer, 2009.

Horlacher, Stefan, ed. *Transgender and Intersex: Theoretical, Practical, and Artistic Perspectives*. Basingstoke, U.K.: Palgrave Macmillan, 2016.

Hutchins, Loraine, and Lana Kaahumanu, eds. *Bi Any Other Name*. Los Angeles: Alyson Publications, 1991.

Jordan, Jeff. "Is It Wrong to Discriminate on the Basis of Homosexuality?" *Journal of Social Philosophy* 25:1 (1995), 39–52. Reprinted in *Philosophy and Sex*, 3rd ed., edited by Robert B. Baker, Kathleen J. Wininger, and Frederick A. Elliston, 177–89. Amherst, N.Y.: Prometheus Books, 1998; and 4th ed., edited by Robert B. Baker and Kathleen J. Wininger, 184–96. Amherst, N.Y.: Prometheus Books, 2009.

Jordan, Mark D. *Recruiting Young Love: How Christians Talk about Homosexuality*. Chicago: University of Chicago Press, 2011.

Jung, Patricia, and Ralph Smith. *Heterosexism: An Ethical Challenge*. Albany, N.Y.: State University of New York Press, 1993.

Kaplan, Morris B. *Sexual Justice: Democratic Citizenship and the Politics of Desire*. New York: Routledge, 1997.

Kapusta, Stephanie Julia. "Misgendering and Its Moral Contestability." *Hypatia* 31:3 (2016), 502–19.

Kheshti, Roshanak. "Cross-Dressing and Gender (Tres)Passing: The Transgender Move as a Site of Agential Potential in the New Iranian Cinema." *Hypatia* 24:3 (2009), 158–77.

Klein, Fritz, Barry Sepekoff, and Timothy Wolf. "Sexual Orientation: A Multi-Variable Dynamic Process." *Journal of Homosexuality* 11:1&2 (1985), 35–50.

Klesse, Christian. *The Spectre of Promiscuity: Gay Male and Bisexual Non-Monogamies and Polyamories*. Aldershot, U.K.: Ashgate, 2007.

Koertge, Noretta, ed. *The Nature and Causes of Homosexuality: A Philosophic and Scientific Inquiry*. New York: Haworth Press, 1981.

———, ed. *Philosophy and Homosexuality*. New York: Harrington Park Press, 1985.

Koppelman, Andrew. *The Gay Rights Question in Contemporary American Law*. Chicago: University of Chicago Press, 2002.

———. "Homosexual Conduct: A Reply to the New Natural Lawyers." In *Same Sex: Debating the Ethics, Science, and Culture of Homosexuality*, edited by John Corvino, 44–57. Lanham, Md.: Rowman & Littlefield, 1997.

———. "Homosexuality and Infertility." In *The Philosophy of Sex*, edited by Alan Soble and Nicholas Power, 5th ed., 141–54. Lanham, Md.: Rowman & Littlefield, 2008.

Kosofsky Sedgwick, Eve. *Epistemology of the Closet*. Berkeley, Calif.: University of California Press, 1990.

Lane, Riki. "Trans as Bodily Becoming: Rethinking the Biological as Diversity, Not Dichotomy." *Hypatia* 24:3 (2009), 136–57.

Lee, Rosa. *Why Feminists Are Wrong: How Transsexuals Prove Gender Is Not a Social Construction*. Philadelphia: Xlibris Corp., 2006.

LeVay, Simon. *Queer Science*. Cambridge, Mass.: MIT Press, 1996.

———. *The Sexual Brain*. Cambridge, Mass.: MIT Press, 1993.

Levin, Michael. "Homosexuality, Abnormality, and Civil Rights." *Public Affairs Quarterly* 10:1 (1996), 31–48.

———. "Why Homosexuality Is Abnormal." *The Monist* 67:2 (1984), 251–83. Reprinted in *The Philosophy of Sex*, 3rd ed., edited by Alan Soble, 95–127. Lanham, Md.: Rowman & Littlefield, 1997.

Lugo-Lugo, Carmen R., and Mary K. Bloodsworth-Lugo, eds. *A New Kind of Containment: "The War on Terror," Race, and Sexuality*. Amsterdam: Rodopi, 2009.

Mayo, David. "An Obligation to Warn of HIV Infection?" In *Sex, Love and Friendship*, edited by Alan Soble, 447–53. Amsterdam: Rodopi, 1997.

McKinnon, Rachel. "Stereotype Threat and Attributional Ambiguity for Trans Women." *Hypatia* 29:4 (2014), 857–72.

McWhirter, David, Stephanie Sanders, and June Reinisch, eds. *Homosexuality/Heterosexuality: Concepts of Sexual Orientation*. New York: Oxford University Press, 1990.

Mead, Margaret. "Bisexuality: A New Awareness." In *Aspects of the Present*, edited by Margaret Mead and Rhoda Metraux, 271–86. New York: William Morrow and Co., 1980.

Mohr, Richard. *Gay Ideas*. Boston: Beacon Press, 1992.

———. *Gays/Justice*. New York: Columbia University Press, 1988.

———. *The Long Arc of Justice: Lesbian and Gay Marriage, Equality, and Rights*. New York: Columbia University Press, 2005.

———. *A More Perfect Union*. Boston: Beacon Press, 1994.

Moore, Gareth. "Natural Sex: Germain Grisez, Sex, and Natural Law." In *The Revival of Natural Law: Philosophical, Theological and Ethical Responses to the Finnis-Grisez School*, edited by Nigel Biggar and Rufus Black, 223–41. Aldershot, U.K.: Ashgate, 2000.

———. *A Question of Truth: Christianity and Homosexuality*. New York: Continuum, 2003.

Morton, Donald, ed. *The Material Queer: A LesBiGay Cultural Studies Reader*. Boulder, Colo.: Westview Press, 1996.

Murphy, Timothy F. *Gay Science: The Ethics of Sexual Orientation Research*. New York: Columbia University Press, 1997.

———. "Homosexuality and Nature: Happiness and the Law at Stake." *Journal of Applied Philosophy* 4:2 (1987), 195–204.

———, ed. *Gay Ethics: Controversies in Outing, Civil Rights, and Sexual Science*. Binghamton, N.Y.: Haworth, 1994.

———, ed. *Reader's Guide to Lesbian and Gay Studies*. Chicago: Fitzroy Dearborn Publishers, 2000.

Myerson, Marilyn, Sara L. Crawley, Erica Hesch Anstey, Justine Kessler, and Cara Okopny. "Who's Zoomin' Who? A Feminist, Queer Content Analysis of 'Interdisciplinary' Human Sexuality Textbooks." *Hypatia* 22:1 (2007), 92–113.

Namaste, Viviane. "Undoing Theory: The 'Transgender Question' and the Epistemic Violence of Anglo-American Feminist Theory." *Hypatia* 24:3 (2009), 11–32.

Neu, Jerome. "Sexual Identity and Sexual Justice." *Ethics* 108:3 (1998), 586–96. Reprinted in *The Philosophy of Sex*, 5th ed., edited by Alan Soble and Nicholas Power, 213–25. Lanham, Md.: Rowman & Littlefield, 2008.

Nussbaum, Martha. "Platonic Love and Colorado Law: The Relevance of Ancient Greek Norms to Modern Sexual Controversies." *Virginia Law Review* 80:7 (1994), 1515–1651.

———. *From Disgust to Humanity: Sexual Orientation and Constitutional Law*. Oxford: Oxford University Press, 2010.

Overall, Christine. "Trans Persons, Cisgender Persons, and Gender Identities." In *The Philosophy of Sex*, 6th ed., edited by Nicholas Power, Raja Halwani, and Alan Soble, 251–67. Lanham, Md.: Rowman & Littlefield, 2013.

Penney, James. *The World of Perversion: Psychoanalysis and the Impossible Absolute of Desire*. Albany: SUNY Press, 2006.

Pollock, Anne. "Queering Endocrine Disruption." In *Object-Oriented Feminism*, edited by Katherine Behar, 183–99. Minneapolis: University of Minnesota Press, 2016.

Prager, Dennis. "Homosexuality, the Bible, and Us—A Jewish Perspective." *The Public Interest*, No. 112 (Summer 1993), 60–83.

Pronk, Pim. *Against Nature? Types of Moral Argumentation Regarding Homosexuality*. Grand Rapids, Mich.: W. B. Eerdmans, 1993.

Reamer, Frederic G., ed. *AIDS & Ethics*. New York: Columbia University Press, 1991.

Rich, Adrienne. (1980) "Compulsory Heterosexuality and Lesbian Existence." In *Blood, Bread and Poetry*, 23–75. New York: W. W. Norton, 1986.

Richards, David A. J. *Women, Gays, and the Constitution: The Grounds for Feminism and Gay Rights in Culture and Law*. Chicago: University of Chicago Press, 1998.

Robinson, Paul. *Gay Lives: Homosexual Autobiography from John Addington Symonds to Paul Monette*. Chicago: University of Chicago Press, 1999.

Romaya, Bassam. "The Straight Sex Experiment." In *College Sex: Philosophers with Benefits*, edited by Michael Bruce and Robert M. Stewart, 28–39. Malden, Mass.: Wiley-Blackwell, 2010.

Roof, Judith. "Gender Is as Gender Does: On the Rebound." In *What Gender Is, What Gender Does*, 223–34. Minneapolis: University of Minnesota Press, 2016.

Rosario, Vernon A., ed. *Science and Homosexualities*. New York: Routledge, 1997.

Ross, Michael W., and Jay P. Paul. "Beyond Gender: The Basis of Sexual Attraction in Bisexual Men and Women." *Psychological Reports* 71:3 (1992), 1283–90.

Rubin, Henry. *Self-Made Men: Identity and Embodiment among Transsexuals*. Nashville, Tenn.: Vanderbilt University Press, 2003.

Ruse, Michael. *Homosexuality: A Philosophical Inquiry*. New York: Blackwell, 1988.

Ruti, Mari. "Queer Theory and the Ethics of Opting Out." In *The Ethics of Opting Out: Queer Theory's Defiant Subjects*, 13–43. New York: Columbia University Press, 2017.

———. *The Age of Scientific Sexism: How Evolutionary Psychology Promotes Gender Profiling and Fans the Battle of the Sexes*. New York: Bloomsbury Academic, 2015.

Samar, Vincent J. *The Right to Privacy: Gays, Lesbians, and the Constitution*. Philadelphia: Temple University Press, 1991.

Samons, Sandra L. *When the Opposite Sex Isn't: Sexual Orientation in Male-to-Female Transgender People*. New York: Routledge, 2009.

Schaff, Kory. "Kant, Political Liberalism, and the Ethics of Same-Sex Relations." *Journal of Social Philosophy* 32:3 (2001), 446–62.

Scheman, Naomi. "Queering the Center by Centering the Queer." In *Feminists Rethink the Self*, edited by Diana Tietjens Meyers, 124–62. Boulder, Colo.: Westview Press, 1997.

Scott-Dixon, Krista. "Public Health, Private Parts: A Feminist Public-Health Approach to Trans Issues." *Hypatia* 24:3 (2009), 33–55.

Shotwell, Alexis, and Trevor Sangrey. "Resisting Definition: Gendering through Interaction and Relational Selfhood." *Hypatia* 24:3 (2009), 55–76.

Shrage, Laurie, ed. *"You've Changed": Sex Reassignment and Personal Identity*. Oxford: Oxford University Press, 2009.

Snorton, C. Riley. "'A New Hope': The Psychic Life of Passing." *Hypatia* 24:3 (2009), 77–92.

Snyder, Jane M. *Lesbian Desire in the Lyrics of Sappho*. New York: Columbia University Press, 1997.

Soble, Alan. "Kant and Sexual Perversion." *The Monist* 86:1 (2003), 57–92.

Spriggs, Merle, and Julian Savulescu. "The Ethics of Surgically Assigning Sex for Intersex Children." In *Cutting to the Core: Exploring the Ethics of Contested Surgeries*, edited by David Benatar, 79–96. Lanham, Md.: Rowman & Littlefield, 2006.

Stafford, J. Martin. "Love and Lust Revisited: Intentionality, Homosexuality and Moral Education." *Journal of Applied Philosophy* 5:1 (1988), 87–100.

———. "The Two Minds of Roger Scruton." *Studies in Philosophy and Education* 11 (1991), 187–93.

Stein, Edward. *Forms of Desire: Sexual Orientation and the Social Constructionist Controversy*. New York: Routledge, 1990.

———. *The Mismeasure of Desire: The Science, Theory, and Ethics of Sexual Orientation*. Oxford: Oxford University Press, 2001.

———. "The Relevance of Scientific Research about Sexual Orientation to Lesbian and Gay Rights." *Journal of Homosexuality* 27:3–4 (1994), 269–308.

Storms, Michael D. "Theories of Sexual Orientation." *Journal of Personality and Social Psychology* 38:4 (1980), 783–92.

Storr, Merl, ed. *Bisexuality: A Critical Reader*. London: Routledge, 1999.

Stryker, Susan, and Stephen Wittle, eds. *The Transgender Studies Reader*. New York: Routledge, 2006.

Sullivan, Andrew. *Love Undetectable: Reflections on Friendship, Sex, and Survival*. New York: Knopf, 1998.

———. *Virtually Normal: An Argument about Homosexuality*. New York: Knopf, 1995.

Systma, Sharon, ed. *Ethics and Intersex*. New York: Springer, 2006.

Thomas, Laurence M., and Michael E. Levin. *Sexual Orientation and Human Rights*. Lanham, Md.: Rowman & Littlefield, 1999.

Vacek, Edward. "A Christian Homosexuality?" *Commonweal* (December 5, 1980), 681–84.

Varden, Helga. "A Feminist, Kantian Conception of the Right to Bodily Integrity: The Cases of Abortion and Homosexuality." *Out for the Shadows: Analytical Feminist Contributions to Traditional Philosophy*, edited by Sharon L. Crasnow and Anita M. Superson, 33–58. Oxford: Oxford University Press, 2012.

Warner, Michael. *The Trouble with Normal: Sex, Politics, and the Ethics of Queer Life*. New York: The Free Press, 1990.

Weeks, Jeffrey. *The Languages of Sexuality*. Milton Park, U.K.: Routledge, 2011.

Weinberg, Martin S., Colin J. Williams, and Douglas Pryor. *Dual Attraction: Understanding Bisexuality*. Oxford: Oxford University Press, 1994.

Weise, Elizabeth Reba, ed. *Closer to Home: Bisexuality and Feminism*. Seattle: Seal Press, 1992.

Weithman, Paul J. "Natural Law, Morality, and Sexual Complementarity." In *Sex, Preference, and Family: Essays on Law and Nature*, edited by David M. Estlund and Martha C. Nussbaum, 227–46. New York: Oxford University Press, 1997.

Wilkerson, William S. *Ambiguity and Sexuality: A Theory of Sexual Identity*. New York: Palgrave Macmillan, 2007.

———. "Is It a Choice? Sexual Orientation as Interpretation." *Journal of Social Philosophy* 40:1 (2009), 97–116.

———. "What Is Sexual Orientation?" In *The Philosophy of Sex*, 6th ed., edited by Nicholas Power, Raja Halwani, and Alan Soble, 195–214. Lanham, Md.: Rowman & Littlefield, 2013.

Williams, Craig A. *Roman Homosexuality: Ideologies of Masculinity in Classical Antiquity*. New York: Oxford University Press, 1999.

Wittig, Monique. *The Lesbian Body* [*Le Corps Lesbien*]. Translated by David Le Vay. Boston: Beacon Press, 1973.

Zylan, Yvonne. *States of Passion: Law, Identity, and the Social Construction of Desire*. Oxford: Oxford University Press, 2011.

MARRIAGE AND RELATIONSHIPS

Almond, Brenda. *The Fragmenting Family*. Oxford: Clarendon Press, 2006.

Anapol, Deborah M. *Love without Limits: The Quest for Sustainable Intimate Relationships*. San Rafael, Calif.: IntiNet Resource Center, 1992.

———. *Polyamory in the 21st Century: Love and Intimacy with Multiple Partners*. Lanham, Md.: Roman & Littlefield, 2010.

Arroyo, Christopher. "Same-Sex Marriage, 'Homosexual Desire,' and the Capacity to Love." *International Journal of Applied Philosophy* 25:2 (2011), 171–86.

Baird, Robert M., and Stuart E. Rosenbaum, eds. *Same-Sex Marriage: The Moral and Legal Debate*. Amherst, N.Y.: Prometheus, 1997.

Baltzly, Dirk. "The Wrongness of Adultery: A Neo-Aristotelian Approach." In *Sex and Ethics: Essays on Sexuality, Virtue, and the Good Life*, edited by Raja Halwani, 190–201. Basingstoke, U.K.: Palgrave Macmillan, 2007.

Baltzly, Vaughn Bryan. "Two Models of Disestablished Marriage." *Public Affairs Quarterly* 28:1 (2014), 41–70.

Barash, David P., and Judith Eve Lipton. *The Myth of Monogamy: Fidelity and Infidelity in Animals and People*. New York: Henry Holt, 2001.

Barker, Meg, and Darren Langdridge, eds. *Understanding Non-Monogamies*. New York: Routledge, 2011.

Barnhart, Joseph. E. and Mary Ann Barnhart. "Marital Faithfulness and Unfaithfulness." *Journal of Social Philosophy* 4:2 (1973): 10–15.

————. "The Myth of the Complete Person." In *Feminism and Philosophy*, edited by Mary Vetterling-Braggin, Frederick Elliston, and Jane English, 277–90. Totowa, N.J.: Rowman & Littlefield, 1977.

Barry, Peter Brian. "Same-Sex Marriage and the Charge of Illiberality." *Social Theory and Practice* 37:2 (2011), 333–57.

Bayles, Michael D. "Marriage, Love, and Procreation." In *Philosophy and Sex*, 2nd ed., edited by Robert Baker and Frederick Elliston, 130–45. Buffalo, N.Y.: Prometheus Books, 1984; 3rd ed., edited by Robert B. Baker, Kathleen J. Wininger, and Frederick A. Elliston, 116–29. Amherst, N.Y.: Prometheus Books, 1998.

Bennett, Christopher. "Liberalism, Autonomy, and Conjugal Love." *Res Publica* 9:3 (2003), 285–301.

Bergoffen, Debra B. "Marriage, Autonomy, and the Feminine Protest." In *The Philosophy of Simone de Beauvoir: Critical Essays*, edited by Margaret A. Simmons, 92–112. Bloomington, Ind.: Indiana University Press, 2006.

Boswell, John. *Same-Sex Unions in Premodern Europe*. New York: Villard, 1994.

Bradley, Gerard V. "What's in a Name? A Philosophical Critique of 'Civil Unions' Predicated Upon a Sexual Relationship." *The Monist* 91:3–4 (2008), 606–31.

Brake, Elizabeth. "Is Divorce Promise-Breaking?" *Ethical Theory and Moral Practice* 14:1 (2011), 23–39.

————. "Justice and Virtue in Kant's Account of Marriage." *Kantian Review* 9 (March 2005), 58–94.

————. "Marriage, Morality, and Institutional Value." *Ethical Theory and Moral Practice* 10:3 (2007), 243–54.

————. "Minimal Marriage: What Political Liberalism Implies for Marriage Law." *Ethics* 120:2 (2010), 302–37.

————. *Minimizing Marriage: Marriage, Morality, and the Law*. New York: Oxford University Press, 2012.

————, ed. *After Marriage: Rethinking Marital Relationships*. New York: Oxford University Press, 2016.

Brennan, Samantha, and Bill Cameron. "How Many Parents Can a Child Have? Philosophical Reflections on the 'Three Parent Case.'" *Dialogue: Canadian Philosophical Review* 54:1 (2015), 45–61.

Brooks, Thom. "The Problem with Polygamy." *Philosophical Topics* 37:2 (2009), 109–22.

Brophy, Brigid. "Monogamy." In *Don't Never Forget: Collected Views and Reviews*, 28–31. London: Jonathan Cape, 1966.

Buccola, Nicholas. "Finding Room for Same-Sex Marriage: Toward a More Inclusive Understanding of a Cultural Institution." *Journal of Social Philosophy* 36:3 (2005), 331–43.

Bullough, Vern L. and Bonnie Bullough. "Love, Sex, and Marriage: A Problem Area." In *Promethean Love: Paul Kurtz and the Humanistic Perspective on Love*, edited by Timothy Madigan, 143–56. Uxbridge, U.K.: Cambridge Scholars Press, 2006.

Callahan, Joan. "Same-Sex Marriage: Why It Matters—At Least for Now." *Hypatia* 24:1 (2009), 70–80.

Callahan, Sidney. "Why I Changed My Mind: Thinking about Gay Marriage." *Commonweal* (22 April 1994), 6–8.

Cannon, Loren. "Trans-Marriage and the Unacceptability of Same-Sex Marriage Restrictions." *Social Philosophy Today: Gender, Diversity, and Difference*, Volume 25, edited by John R. Rowan, 75–90. Charlottesville, Va.: Philosophy Documentation Center, 2009.

Card, Claudia. "Gay Divorce: Thoughts on the Legal Regulation of Marriage." *Hypatia* 22:1 (2007), 24–38. Reprinted in *The Philosophy of Sex*, 6th ed., edited by Nicholas Power, Raja Halwani, and Alan Soble, 177–93. Lanham, Md.: Rowman & Littlefield, 2013.

Carr, David. "Chastity and Adultery." *American Philosophical Quarterly* 23:4 (1986), 363–71.

Cave, Eric M. "Harm Prevention and the Benefits of Marriage." *Journal of Social Philosophy* 35:2 (2004), 233–43.

Chauncey, George. *Why Marriage? The History Shaping Today's Debate Over Gay Equality*. New York: Basic Books, 2004.

Cicovacki, Predrag. "On Love and Fidelity in Marriage." *Journal of Social Philosophy* 24:3 (1993), 92–104.

Clark, Elizabeth A. "'Adam's Only Companion': Augustine and the Early Christian Debate on Marriage." *Recherches Augustiniennes* 21 (1986), 139–62.

Collins, Louise. "Emotional Adultery: Cybersex and Commitment." *Social Theory and Practice* 25:2 (1999), 243–70.

Connelly, R. J. "Philosophy and Adultery," in *Adultery in the United States*, edited by Philip E. Lampe, 131–64. Amherst, N.Y.: Prometheus Books, 1987.

Conrad, Ryan, ed. *Against Equality: Queer Critiques of Gay Marriage*. Lewiston, Maine: Against Equality Publishing Collective, 2010.

Constantine, Larry L., and Joan M. Constantine. *Group Marriage: Marriages of Three or More People, How and When They Work*. New York: Macmillan, 1973.

Cooley, D. R. "Non-Heterosexuals in Heterosexual Marriages as a Form of Spousal Abuse." *International Journal of Applied Philosophy* 21:2 (2007), 161–79.

Coontz, Stephanie. *Marriage: A History*. London: Penguin, 2006.

Corvino, John. "Homosexuality and the PIB Argument." *Ethics* 115:3 (2005), 501–34.

Corvino, John, and Maggie Gallagher. *Debating Same-Sex Marriage*. Oxford: Oxford University Press, 2012.

Cott, Nancy. *Public Vows: A History of Marriage and the Nation*. Cambridge, Mass.: Harvard University Press, 2000.

Crookston, Emily M. "Love and (Polygamous) Marriage?" *Journal of Moral Philosophy* 12:3 (2015), 267–89.

Curzer, Howard J. "An Aristotelian Critique of the Traditional Family." *American Philosophical Quarterly* 47:2 (2010), 135–48.

Dean, Craig R. "Fighting for Same Sex Marriage." In *Gender Basics*, edited by Anne Minas, 275–77. Belmont, Calif.: Wadsworth, 1993.

Denis, Lara. "From Friendship to Marriage: Revising Kant." *Philosophy and Phenomenological Research* 63:1 (2001), 1–28.

Diorio, Joseph. "Sex, Love, and Justice: A Problem in Moral Education." *Educational Theory* 31: 3–4 (1982), 225–35. Reprinted in *Eros, Agape, and Philia*, edited by Alan Soble, 273–88. St. Paul, Minn.: Paragon House, 1989.

Duran, Jane. "The Problem of Polygamy: Moral Constraints and Attitudes." *International Journal of Applied Philosophy* 29:2 (2015), 191–98.

Ellis, Albert. *The Civilized Couple's Guide to Extramarital Adventure*. New York: Wyden, 1972.

Elliston, Frederick. "Gay Marriage." In *Philosophy and Sex*, edited by Robert Baker and Frederick Elliston, 2nd ed., 146–66. Buffalo, N.Y.: Prometheus, 1984.

Emens, Elizabeth F., "Monogamy's Law: Compulsory Monogamy and Polyamorous Existence," *New York University Review of Law and Social Change* 29:2 (2004), 277–376.

Eskridge, William N., Jr. *The Case for Same-Sex Marriage: From Sexual Liberty to Civilized Commitment*. New York: Free Press, 1996.

Feit, Mario. *Democratic Anxieties: Same-Sex Marriage, Death, and Citizenship*. Lanham, Md.: Lexington Books, 2011.

Ferguson, Ann. "Gay Marriage: An American and Feminist Dilemma." *Hypatia* 22:1 (2007), 39–57.

Finnis, John M. "The Good of Marriage and the Morality of Sexual Relations: Some Philosophical and Historical Observations." *American Journal of Jurisprudence* 42 (1997), 97–134.

———. "Marriage: A Basic and Exigent Good." *The Monist* 91:3–4 (2008), 388–407.

Francoeur, Robert T., Martha Cornog, and Timothy Perper. *Sex, Love, and Marriage in the 21st Century: The Next Sexual Revolution*. San Jose, Calif.: toExcel, 1999.

Freeman, M. D. A. "Not Such a Queer Idea: Is There a Case for Same Sex Marriages?" *Journal of Applied Philosophy* 16:1 (1999), 1–17.

Friedman, Lauri S., ed. *Gay Marriage*. Detroit, Mich.: Greenhaven Press, 2010.

Galupo, M. Paz, ed. *Bisexuality and Same-Sex Marriage*. London: Routledge, 2009.

Garrett, Jeremy R. "History, Tradition, and the Normative Foundations of Civil Marriage." *The Monist* 91:3–4 (2008), 446–74.

———. "Marriage Unhitched from the State: A Defense." *Public Affairs Quarterly* 23:2 (2009), 161–180.

———. "Public Reasons for Private Vows: A Response to Gilboa." *Public Affairs Quarterly* 23:3 (2009): 261–73.

———. "Why the Old Sexual Morality of the New Natural Law Undermines Traditional Marriage." *Social Theory and Practice* 34:4 (2010), 591–622.

Geach, Mary. "Marriage: Arguing to a First Principle in Sexual Ethics." In *Moral Truth and Moral Tradition: Essays in Honour of Peter Geach and Elizabeth Anscombe*, edited by Luke Gormally, 177–93. Dublin: Four Courts Press, 1994.

Geach, Mary Catherine. "Lying with the Body." *The Monist* 91:3–4 (2008), 523–57.

Gilboa, David. "Same-Sex Marriage in a Liberal Democracy: Between Rejection and Recognition." *Public Affairs Quarterly* 23:3 (2009), 245–60.

———. "Marriages, Services, and Contracts: A Reply to Garrett." *Public Affairs Quarterly* 23:4 (2009), 325–36.

Girgis, Sherif, Ryan T. Anderson, and Robert P. George. *What Is Marriage? Man and Woman: A Defense*. New York: Encounter Books, 2012.

Gray, John Scott. "Rawls's Principle of Justice and Its Application to the Issue of Same-Sex Marriage." *Southern African Journal of Philosophy* 23:2 (2004), 158–70. Reprinted in *Philosophy and Sex*, 4th ed., edited by Robert B. Baker and Kathleen Wininger, 197–212. Amherst, N.Y.: Prometheus Books, 2009.

Gregor, Thomas. "Sexuality and the Experience of Love." In *Sexual Nature Sexual Culture*, edited by P. Abramson and S. Pinkerton, 330–50. Chicago: University of Chicago Press, 1995.

Gregory, Paul. "Against Couples." *Journal of Applied Philosophy* 1:2 (1984), 263–68.

———. "Eroticism and Love." *American Philosophical Quarterly* 25:4 (1988), 339–44.

Halwani, Raja. "Virtue Ethics and Adultery." *Journal of Social Philosophy* 29:3 (1998), 5–18. Reprinted in *Ethics for Everyday*, edited by David Benatar, 226–39. Boston: McGraw-Hill, 2002.

———. *Virtuous Liaisons: Care, Love, Sex and Virtue Ethics*. Chicago: Open Court, 2003.

Higgins, Kathleen Marie. "How Do I Love Thee? Let's Redefine a Term." *Journal of Social Philosophy* 24:3 (1993), 105–11.

Jordan, Jeff. "Is It Wrong to Discriminate on the Basis of Homosexuality?" *Journal of Social Philosophy* 25:1 (1995), 39–52. Reprinted in *Philosophy and Sex*, 3rd ed., edited by Robert B. Baker, Kathleen J. Wininger, and Frederick A. Elliston, 177–89. Amherst, N.Y.: Prometheus Books, 1998; and 4th ed., edited by Robert B. Baker and Kathleen J. Wininger, 184–96. Amherst, N.Y.: Prometheus Books, 2009.

Ketchum, Sara Ann. "Liberalism and Marriage Law." In *Feminism and Philosophy*, edited by Mary Vetterling-Braggin, Frederick Elliston, and Jane English, 264–76. Totowa, N.J.: Rowman & Littlefield, 1977.

Klesse, Christian. *The Spectre of Promiscuity: Gay Male and Bisexual Non-Monogamies and Polyamories*. Aldershot, U.K.: Ashgate, 2007.

Koppelman, Andrew. "The Decline and Fall of the Case against Same-Sex Marriage." *University of St. Thomas Law Journal* 2:1 (2004), 5–32.

———. *The Gay Rights Question in Contemporary American Law*. Chicago: University of Chicago Press, 2002.

———. "Marriage." In *Philosophy: Sex and Love*, edited by James Petrik and Arthur Zucker, 199–216. Farmington Hills, Mich.: Macmillan Reference USA, 2016.

———. *Same Sex, Different States: When Same-Sex Marriages Cross State Lines*. New Haven, Conn.: Yale University Press, 2006.

Lankford, Ronald D., Jr., ed. *Polygamy*. Detroit, Mich.: Greenhaven Press, 2009.

Lee, Patrick K. "Marriage, Procreation, and Same-Sex Unions." *The Monist* 91:3–4 (2008), 422–38 (with a reply by Adéle Mercier [439–441] and a rejoinder by Lee [442–45]).

Lesser, A. H. "Love and Lust." *Journal of Value Inquiry* 14:1 (1980), 51–54.

Liberto, Hallie. "The Problem with Sexual Promises." *Ethics* 127: 2 (2017), 383–414.

Macedo, Stephen. *Just Married.* Princeton, N.J.: Princeton University Press, 2015.

Mahoney, Jon. "Liberalism and the Polygamy Question." *Social Philosophy Today: International Law and Justice,* Volume 23, edited by John R. Rowan, 161–74. Charlottesville, Va.: Philosophy Documentation Center, 2008.

Mann, Bonnie. "Gay Marriage and the War on Terror." *Hypatia* 22:1 (2007), 247–51.

March, Andrew F. "Is There a Right to Polygamy? Marriage, Equality and Subsidizing Families in Liberal Public Justification." *Journal of Moral Philosophy* 8:2 (2012), 246–72.

———. "What Lies Beyond Same-Sex Marriage? Marriage, Reproductive Freedom and Future Persons in Liberal Public Justification." *Journal of Applied Philosophy* 27:1 (2010), 39–58.

Margolis, Joseph and Clorinda Margolis. "The Separation of Marriage and Family." In *Feminism and Philosophy,* edited by Mary Vetterling-Braggin, Frederick Elliston, and Jane English, 291–301. Totowa, N.J.: Rowman & Littlefield, 1977.

Marquis, Don. "What's Wrong with Adultery?" In *What's Wrong? Applied Ethicists and Their Critics,* edited by David Boonin and Graham Oddie, 231–38. New York: Oxford University Press, 2005.

Martin, Mike W. "Adultery and Fidelity." *Journal of Social Philosophy* 25:3 (1994), 76–91.

McCluskey, Colleen. "An Unequal Relationship Between Equals: Thomas Aquinas on Marriage." *History of Philosophy Quarterly* 24:1 (2007), 1–18.

McMurtry, John. "Monogamy: A Critique." *The Monist* 56:4 (1972), 587–99. Reprinted in *Philosophy and Sex,* 2nd ed., edited by Robert Baker and Frederick Elliston, 107–18. Amherst, N.Y.: Prometheus, 1984.

———. "Sex, Love, and Friendship." In *Sex, Love, and Friendship,* edited by Alan Soble, 169–93. Amsterdam: Rodopi, 1997.

Mendus, Susan. "Marital Faithfulness." *Philosophy* 59: 228 (1984), 243–52. Reprinted in *Eros, Agape, and Philia,* edited by Alan Soble, 235–44. New York: Paragon House, 1989; and *Philosophy and Sex,* 4th ed., edited by Robert B. Baker and Kathleen J. Wininger, 116–26. Amherst, N.Y.: Prometheus Books, 2009.

Mercier, Adéle. "On the Nature of Marriage: Somerville on Same-Sex Marriage." *The Monist* 91: 3–4 (2008), 407–21.

Miller, Dale E. "Florists, Same-Sex Weddings, and Mill's Doctrine of Liberty." *Public Affairs Quarterly* 30:4 (2016), 287–312.

Mohr, Richard D. "The Case for Gay Marriage." *Notre Dame Journal of Law, Ethics, and Public Policy* 9 (1995), 215–39.

———. *The Long Arc of Justice: Lesbian and Gay Marriage, Equality, and Rights.* New York: Columbia University Press, 2005.

———. *A More Perfect Union.* Boston: Beacon Press, 1994.

Morris, John C. *First Comes Love? The Changing Face of Marriage.* Cleveland, Ohio: Pilgrim Press, 2007.

Nagle, Jeanne. *Same-Sex Marriage: The Debate.* New York: Rosen Publishing, 2010.

Nussbaum, Martha, and David M. Estlund, eds. *Sex, Preference, and Family: Essays on Law and Nature.* New York: Oxford University Press, 1997.

O'Driscoll, Lyla. "On the Nature and Value of Marriage." In *Feminism and Philosophy,* edited by Mary Vetterling-Braggin, Frederick Elliston, and Jane English, 249–63. Totowa, N.J.: Rowman & Littlefield, 1977; and *Philosophy of Sex and Love: A Reader,* edited by Robert Trevas, Arthur Zucker, and Donald Borchert, 130–37. Upper Saddle River, N.J.: Prentice Hall, 1997.

Ouellette, Alicia. "Moral Reasoning in Judicial Decisions on Same-Sex Marriage." In *Philosophy and Sex,* 4th ed., edited by Robert B. Baker and Kathleen J. Wininger, 168–83. Amherst, N.Y.: Prometheus Books, 2009.

Perry, Michael J. "Same-Sex Unions." In *The Political Morality of Liberal Democracy*, 138–55. Cambridge: Cambridge University Press, 2010.

Piper, Mark. "Adultery." In *Philosophy: Sex and Love*, edited by James Petrik and Arthur Zucker, 217–42. Farmington Hills, Mich.: Macmillan Reference USA, 2016.

Polikoff, Nancy D. *Beyond Gay and Straight Marriage: Valuing All Families under the Law*. Boston: Beacon Press, 2008.

Puka, Bill. "Relations at a Distance." In *College Sex: Philosophers with Benefits*, edited by Michel Bruce and Robert M. Stewart, 61–74. Malden, Mass.: Wiley-Blackwell, 2010.

Quinn, Carol. "What Ulrichs Knew: Resurrecting the Nineteenth-Century Debate on Same-Sex Marriage." *International Journal of Applied Philosophy* 29:1 (2015), 1–17.

———, ed. [Issue on Same-Sex Marriage] *American Philosophical Association Newsletter on Philosophy and Lesbian, Gay, Bisexual, and Transgender Issues* 4:1 (Fall 2004).

Rajczi, Alex. "A Populist Argument for Legalizing Same-Sex Marriage." *The Monist* 91:3–4 (2008), 475–505.

Randles, Jennifer M. "Intimate Inequalities and Curtailed Commitments: The Marriage Gap in a Middle-Class Marriage Culture." In *Proposing Prosperity? Marriage Education Policy and Inequality in America*, 81–105. New York: Columbia University Press, 2017.

Rapaport, Elizabeth. "On the Future of Love: Rousseau and the Radical Feminists." *Philosophical Forum* 5:1–2 (1973/74), 185–205. Reprinted in *The Philosophy of Sex*, 1st ed., edited by Alan Soble, 369–88. Totowa, N.J.: Rowman & Littlefield, 1980; and *The Philosophy of (Erotic) Love*, edited by Robert C. Solomon and Kathleen M. Higgins, 372–90. Lawrence, Kans.: University Press of Kansas, 1991.

Reitan, Eric. "Political Liberalism, State Neutrality, and Same-Sex Marriage." *Public Affairs Quarterly* 30:4 (2016), 313–34.

Robson, Ruthann. "A Mere Switch or a Fundamental Change? Theorizing Transgender Marriage." *Hypatia* 22:1 (2007), 58–70.

Rosewarne, Lauren. *Cheating on the Sisterhood: Infidelity and Feminism*. Santa Barbara, Calif.: Praeger/ABC-CLIO, 2009.

Rubin, Roger H. "Alternative Lifestyles Revisited, or Whatever Happened to Swingers, Group Marriages, and Communes?" *Journal of Family Issues* 22:6 (2001), 711–16.

Sadler, Brook J. "Public or Private Good? The Contested Meaning of Marriage." In *Social Philosophy Today: The Public and the Private in the Twenty-First Century*, Volume 26, edited by John Rowan, 23–38. Charlottesville, Va.: Philosophy Documentation Center, 2010.

———. "Rethinking Civil Unions and Same-Sex Marriage." *The Monist* 91:3–4 (2008), 578–605.

Samar, Vincent J. *The Right to Privacy: Gays, Lesbians, and the Constitution*. Philadelphia: Temple University Press, 1991.

Schaff, Kory. "Equal Protection and Same-Sex Marriage." *Journal of Social Philosophy* 35:1 (2004), 133–47.

Sclater, Shelley Day, Fatemeh Ebtehaj, Emily Jackson, and Martin Richards, eds. *Regulating Autonomy: Sex, Reproduction and Family*. Oxford: Hart Publishing, 2009.

Scruton, Roger. "Meaningful Marriage." In *Political Philosophy: Arguments for Conservatism*, 81–102. London: Continuum, 2007.

Shanley, Mary Lyndon, ed. *Just Marriage*. New York: Oxford University Press, 2004.

Shrage, Laurie. *Moral Dilemmas of Feminism: Prostitution, Adultery, and Abortion*. New York: Routledge, 1994.

Small, Meredith F. *What's Love Got to Do with It? The Evolution of Human Mating*. New York: Anchor, 1995.

Sreedhar, Susanne, and Julie Walsh. "Locke, the Law of Nature, and Polygamy." *Journal of the American Philosophical Association* 2:1 (2016), 91–110.

Stafford, J. Martin. "Love and Lust Revisited: Intentionality, Homosexuality and Moral Education." *Journal of Applied Philosophy* 5:1 (1988), 87–100.

———. "On Distinguishing between Love and Lust." *Journal of Value Inquiry* 11:4 (1977), 292–303.

Stallings, L. H. "Marvelous Stank Matter: The End of Monogamy, the Marriage Crisis, and Ethical Slutting." In *Funk the Erotic*, 122–46. Urbana-Champaign, Ill.: University of Illinois Press, 2015.

Steinbock, Bonnie. "Adultery." In *The Philosophy of Sex*, 2nd ed., edited by Alan Soble, 187–92. Savage, Md.: Rowman & Littlefield, 1991.

Strasser, Mark. *Legally Wed*. Ithaca, N.Y.: Cornell University Press, 1997.

———. *On Same-Sex Marriage, Civil Unions, and the Rule of Law: Constitutional Interpretation at the Crossroads*. Westport, Conn.: Praeger, 2002.

Strasser, Mark Philip, Traci C. West, Martin Dupuis, and William A. Thompson, eds. *Defending Same-Sex Marriage*. Westport, Conn.: Praeger, 2007.

Strauss, Gregg. "Is Polygamy Inherently Unequal?" *Ethics* 122:3 (2012), 516–44.

Stroll, Avrum. "A Defense of Same-Sex Marriage." *Public Affairs Quarterly* 23:4 (2009), 343–56.

Sullivan, Andrew, ed. *Same-Sex Marriage: Pro and Con*. New York: Vintage, 2004.

Sunstein, Cass, and Richard H. Thaler. "Privatizing Marriage." *The Monist* 91:3–4 (2008), 377–87.

Taylor, Richard. *Having Love Affairs*. Buffalo, N.Y.: Prometheus Books, 1982.

———. *Love Affairs: Marriage and Infidelity*. Amherst, N.Y.: Prometheus Books, 1997.

Vannoy, Russell. "Can Sex Express Love?" In *Sex, Love, and Friendship*, edited by Alan Soble, 247–57. Amsterdam: Rodopi, 1997.

———. *Sex Without Love: A Philosophical Exploration*. Buffalo, N.Y.: Prometheus, 1980.

Vernallis, Kayley. "Bisexual Marriage." In *The Philosophy of Sex*, 6th ed., edited by Nicholas Power, Raja Halwani, and Alan Soble, 215–32. Lanham, Md.: Rowman & Littlefield, 2013.

———. "Bisexual Monogamy: Twice the Temptation but Half the Fun?" *Journal of Social Philosophy* 30:3 (1999), 347–68.

Vernon, Jim. "Free Love: A Hegelian Defense of Same-Sex Marriage Rights." *The Southern Journal of Philosophy* 47:1 (2009), 69–89.

Walsh, Anthony. "Love and Sex." In *Human Sexuality: An Encyclopedia*, edited by Vern Bullough and Bonnie Bullough, 369–73. New York: Garland, 1994.

Wardle, Lynn D., ed. *What's the Harm? Does Legalizing Same-Sex Marriage Really Harm Individuals, Families, or Society?* Lanham, Md.: University Press of America, 2008.

Wardle, Lynn D., Mark Strasser, William C. Duncan, and David Orgon Coolidge, eds. *Marriage and Same-Sex Unions: A Debate*. Westport, Conn.: Praeger, 2003.

Wasserstrom, Richard. "Is Adultery Immoral?" In *Philosophy and Sex*, 2nd ed., edited by Robert Baker and Frederick Elliston, 93–106. Buffalo, N.Y.: Prometheus Books, 1984.

Weaver, Bryan R. "Marriage and the Norm of Monogamy." *The Monist* 91:3–4 (2008), 506–22.

Wedgwood, Ralph. "Same-Sex Marriage: A Philosophical Defense." In *Philosophy and Sex*, 3rd ed., edited by Robert B. Baker, Kathleen J. Wininger, and Frederick A. Elliston, 212–30. Amherst, N.Y.: Prometheus Books, 1998.

Wellington, A. A. "Why Liberals Should Support Same-Sex Marriage." *Journal of Social Philosophy* 26:3 (1995), 5–32.

Westlund, Andrea C. "The Reunion of Marriage." *The Monist* 91:3–4 (2008), 558–77.

Williams, Reginald. "Same-Sex Marriage and Equality." *Ethical Theory and Moral Practice* 14:5 (2011), 589–95.

Wilson, Mike. *Divorce*. Detroit, Mich.: Greenhaven Press, 2009.

Wojtyla, Karol (Pope John Paul II). *Love and Responsibility*. Translated by H. T. Willetts. New York: Farrar, Straus, and Giroux, 1981. 2nd printing 1994.

Woodcock, Scott. "Five Reasons why Margaret Somerville Is Wrong about Same-Sex Marriage and the Rights of Children." *Dialogue: Canadian Philosophical Review* 48:4 (2009), 867–87.

Wreen, Michael J. "What's Really Wrong with Adultery." In *The Philosophy of Sex*, 2nd ed., edited by Alan Soble, 179–86. Savage, Md.: Rowman & Littlefield, 1991.

PORNOGRAPHY

Aberdein, Andrew. "Strange Bedfellows: The Interpenetration of Philosophy and Pornography." In *Porn: How to Think with Kink*, edited by Dave Monroe, 22–34. Wichester, U.K.: Wiley-Blackwell, 2010.

Adler, Amy. "The Perverse Law of Child Pornography." *Columbia Law Review* 101 (March 2001), 209–73.

Allen, Amy. "Pornography and Power." *Journal of Social Philosophy* 32:4 (2001): 512–31.

Altman, Andrew. "The Right to Get Turned On: Pornography, Autonomy, Equality." In *Contemporary Debates in Applied Ethics*, edited by Andrew I. Cohen and Christopher Heath Wellman, 307–18. Malden, Mass.: Blackwell Publishing, 2005.

Antony, Louise. "Pornography and the Philosophy of Language." In *The Philosophy of Pornography: Contemporary Perspectives*, edited by Lindsay Coleman and Jacob Held, 147–75. Lanham, Md.: Rowman & Littlefield, 2016.

Assiter, Alison, and Avedon Carol, eds. *Bad Girls and Dirty Pictures*. London: Pluto Press, 1993.

Attwood, Feona, ed. *Porn.com: Making Sense of Online Pornography*. New York: Peter Lang, 2010.

Bach, Theodore. "Pornography as Simulation." In *Porn-Philosophy for Everyone: How to Think with Kink*, edited by Dave Monroe, 52–65. Wichester, U.K.: Wiley-Blackwell, 2010.

Baird, Robert M., and Stuart E. Rosenbaum, eds. *Pornography: Private Right or Public Menace?* Buffalo, N.Y.: Prometheus, 1991.

Baldwin, Margaret. "The Sexuality of Inequality: The Minneapolis Pornography Ordinance." *Law and Inequality: A Journal of Theory and Practice* 2:2 (1984), 629–53.

Bartel, Christopher. "The 'Fine Art' of Pornography? The Conflict between Artistic Value and Pornographic Value." *Porn-Philosophy for Everyone: How to Think with Kink*, edited by Dave Monroe, 153–65. Wichester, U.K.: Wiley-Blackwell, 2010.

Bauer, Nancy. *How to Do Things with Pornography*. Cambridge, Mass.: Harvard University Press, 2015.

Beauvoir, Simone de. "Must We Burn Sade?" Translated by Annette Michelson. In *The Marquis de Sade: The 120 Days of Sodom and Other Writings*, compiled by Austryn Wainhouse and Richard Seaver, 3–64. New York: Grove Press, 1966.

Berger, Fred R. "Pornography, Sex, and Censorship." *Social Theory and Practice* 4:2 (1977), 183–209. Reprinted in *The Philosophy of Sex*, 1st ed., edited by Alan Soble, 322–47. Totowa, N.J.: Rowman & Littlefield, 1980.

Berns, Walter. "Dirty Words." *The Public Interest*, 114 (Winter 1994), 119–25.

Bradley, Joy Simmons. "In the Arms of the Angel: Playfulness, Creativity, and Porn's Possibilities." In *The Philosophy of Pornography: Contemporary Perspectives*, edited by Lindsay Coleman and Jacob Held, 261–75. Lanham, Md.: Rowman & Littlefield, 2016.

Brison, Susan. "The Price We Pay? Pornography and Harm." In *Contemporary Debates in Applied Ethics*, edited by Andrew I. Cohen and Christopher Heath Wellman, 319–32. Malden, Mass.: Blackwell Publishing, 2005.

Brod, Harry. "Pornography and the Alienation of Male Sexuality." *Social Theory and Practice* 14:3 (1988), 265–84. Reprinted in *The Philosophy of Sex*, 2nd ed., edited by Alan Soble, 281–99. Savage, Md.: Rowman & Littlefield, 1991.

Brown, Beverley. "Pornography and Feminism: Is Law the Answer?" *Critical Quarterly* 34:2 (1992), 72–82.

Burger, John R. *One-Handed Histories: The Eroto-Politics of Gay Male Video Pornography*. New York: Haworth Press, 1995.

Burstyn, Varda, ed. *Women against Censorship*. Vancouver: Douglas and McIntyre, 1985.

Butler, Judith. *Excitable Speech: A Politics of the Performative*. New York: Routledge, 1997.

Butterworth, Dianne. "Wanking in Cyberspace: The Development of Computer Porn." In *Feminism and Sexuality: A Reader*, edited by Stevi Jackson and Sue Scott, 314–20. New York: Columbia University Press, 1996.

Carse, Alisa L. "Pornography: An Uncivil Liberty?" *Hypatia* 10:1 (1995), 156–82.

Caught Looking, Inc., eds. *Caught Looking: Feminism, Pornography, and Censorship*. East Haven, Conn.: Long River Books, 1992.

Chancer, Lynn S. "From Pornography to Sadomasochism: Reconciling Feminist Differences." *Annals of the American Academy of Political and Social Science* 571:1 (2000), 77–88.

Christensen, Ferrel M. "The Alleged Link between Pornography and Violence." In *The Handbook of Forensic Sexology: Biomedical and Criminological Perspectives*, edited by J. J. Krivacska and J. Money, 422–48. Amherst, N.Y.: Prometheus, 1994.

———. "Cultural and Ideological Bias in Pornography Research." *Philosophy of the Social Sciences* 20:3 (1990), 351–75.

———. *Pornography: The Other Side*. New York: Praeger, 1990.

Click, Melissa. "Fifty Shades of Postfeminism: Contextualizing Readers' Reflections on the Erotic Romance Series." In *Cupcakes, Pinterest, and Ladyporn*, edited by Elana Levine, 15–31. Urbana-Champaign, Ill.: University of Illinois Press, 2015.

Cohen, Joshua. "Freedom, Equality, Pornography." In *Justice and Injustice in Law and Legal Theory*, edited by Austin Sarat and Thomas R. Kearns, 99–137. Ann Arbor: University of Michigan Press, 1996.

Coleman, Lindsay. "The Gentle Side of Pornography: A Contemporary Examination of Pornography's Depiction of Love and Friendship." In *The Philosophy of Pornography: Contemporary Perspectives*, edited by Lindsey Coleman and Jacob Held, 199–208. Lanham, Md.: Rowman & Littlefield, 2016.

Coleman, Lindsay, and Jacob M. Held, eds. *The Philosophy of Pornography: Contemporary Perspectives*. Lanham, Md.: Rowman & Littlefield, 2016.

Cornell, Drucilla, ed. *Feminism and Pornography*. Oxford: Oxford University Press, 2000.

Cruz, Ariane. *The Color of Kink: Black Women, BDSM, and Pornography*. New York: New York University Press, 2016.

———. "Sisters Are Doin' It for Themselves: Black Women and the New Pornography." In *The Philosophy of Pornography: Contemporary Perspectives*, edited by Lindsay Coleman and Jacob Held, 225–48. Lanham, Md.: Rowman & Littlefield, 2016.

Dines, Gail. *Pornland: How Porn Has Hijacked Our Sexuality*. Boston: Beacon Press, 2010.

Dworkin, Andrea. *Life and Death*. New York: Free Press, 1997.

———. *Pornography: Men Possessing Women*. New York: Perigee, 1981.

Dworkin, Andrea, and Catharine A. MacKinnon. *Pornography and Civil Rights: A New Day for Women's Equality*. Minneapolis: Organizing Against Pornography, 1988.

Dworkin, Ronald. "Women and Pornography." *New York Review of Books*, October 21, 1993, 36–42. Reply to letter, *New York Review of Books*, March 3, 1994, 48–49.

Dwyer, Susan, ed. *The Problem of Pornography*. Belmont, Calif.: Wadsworth, 1995.

Easton, Susan M. *The Problem of Pornography: Regulation and the Right to Free Speech*. London: Routledge, 1994.

Eaton, A. W. "Pornography." In *Philosophy: Sex and Love*, edited by James Petrik and Arthur Zucker, 243–70. Farmington Hills, Mich.: Macmillan Reference USA, 2016.

———. "A Sensible Anti-Porn Feminism." *Ethics* 117:4 (2007), 674–715.

Ezzell, Matthew B. "Porn Makes the Man: The Impact of Pornography as a Component of Gender and Sexual Socialization." In *The Philosophy of Pornography: Contemporary Perspectives*, edited by Lindsay Coleman and Jacob Held, 17–34. Lanham, Md.: Rowman & Littlefield, 2016.

Ferguson, Frances. *Pornography, the Theory: What Utilitarianism Did to Action*. Chicago: University of Chicago Press, 2004.

Finlayson, Lorna. "How to Screw Things with Words." *Hypatia* 29:4 (2014), 774–89.

· Garry, Ann. "Pornography and Respect for Women." In *Philosophy and Women*, edited by Sharon Bishop and Marjorie Weinzweig, 128–39. Belmont, Calif.: Wadsworth, 1979.

———. "Sex, Lies, and Pornography." In *Ethics in Practice: An Anthology*, 2nd ed., edited by Hugh LaFollette, 344–55. Malden, Mass.: Blackwell, 2002.

Gibson, Pamela Church, and Roma Gibson, eds. *Dirty Looks: Women, Pornography, Power*. London: BFI Publishing, 1993.

Grebowicz, Margret. "Democracy and Pornography: On Speech, Rights, Privacies, and Pleasures in Conflict." *Hypatia* 26:1 (2011), 150–65.

Gubar, Susan, and Joan Hoff, eds. *For Adult Users Only: The Dilemma of Violent Pornography*. Bloomington, Ind.: Indiana University Press, 1989.

Harmon, Justin L. "Dwelling in the House That Porn Built: A Phenomenological Critique of Pornography in the Age of Internet Technology." *Social Philosophy Today: Freedom, Religion, and Gender*, Volume 28, edited by Jeff Gauthier, 115–30. Charlottesville, Va.: Philosophy Documentation Center, 2012.

Hartley, Nina and Jacob Held. "Porn, Sex, and Liberty: A Dialogue." In *The Philosophy of Pornography: Contemporary Perspectives*, edited by Lindsay Coleman and Jacob Held, 179–98. Lanham, MD.: Rowman & Littlefield, 2014.

Held, Jacob M. "One Man's Trash is Another Man's Pleasure: Obscenity, Pornography, and the Law." In *Porn-Philosophy for Everyone: How to Think with Kink*, edited by Dave Monroe, 119–29. Chichester, U.K.: Wiley-Blackwell, 2010.

———. "Pornography as Symptom: Refocusing the Anti-Pornography Debate on Pornification and Sexualization." In *Philosophy in the Contemporary World: The Journal of the Society for Philosophy in the Contemporary World* 20: 1 (2013), 15–27.

———. "The Problem with the Problem of Pornography: Subordination, Sexualization, and Speech." In *The Philosophy of Pornography: Contemporary Perspectives*, edited by Lindsay Coleman and Jacob Held, 73–88. Lanham, MD.: Rowman & Littlefield, 2014.

———. "What Is and Is Not Porn: Sex, Narrative, and *Baise-moi*." In *Sex and Storytelling in Modern Cinema: Explicit Sex, Performance, and Cinematic Technique*, edited by Lindsay Coleman, 25–48. London: I. B. Tauris, 2016.

Heyman, Steven J. "Pornography." In *Free Speech and Human Dignity*, 184–205. Yale University Press, 2008.

Hiber, Amanda, ed. *Child Pornography*. Detroit, Mich.: Greenhaven Press, 2009.

Hill, Judith M. "Pornography and Degradation." *Hypatia* 2:2 (1987): 39–54.

Hoffman, Eric. "Feminism, Pornography, and Law." *University of Pennsylvania Law Review* 133: 2 (1985), 497–534.

Hornsby, Jennifer. "Disempowered Speech." *Philosophical Topics* 23:2 (1995), 127–47.

———. "Pornography and 'Speech.'" In *The Philosophy of Pornography: Contemporary Perspectives*, edited by Lindsay Coleman and Jacob Held, 129–46. Lanham, Md.: Rowman & Littlefield, 2016.

———. "Speech Acts and Pornography." *Women's Philosophical Review* 10 (November 1993), 38–45.

Hunter, Nan D., and Sylvia A. Law. "Brief Amici Curiae of Feminist Anticensorship Task Force et al., in *American Booksellers Association v. Hudnut*." In *Feminist Jurisprudence*, edited by Patricia Smith, 467–81. New York: Oxford University Press, 1993.

Itzin, Catherine, ed. *Pornography: Women, Violence and Civil Liberties*. Oxford: Oxford University Press, 1992.

Jacobson, Daniel. "Freedom of Speech Acts? A Response to Langton." *Philosophy and Public Affairs* 24:1 (1995), 64–79.

Jarvie, Ian C. "Pornography and/as Degradation." *International Journal of Law and Psychiatry* 14 (1991), 13–27.

———. *Thinking about Society: Theory and Practice*. Dordrecht: Reidel, 1986.

Jensen, Robert. *Getting Off: Pornography and the End of Masculinity*. Cambridge, Mass.: South End Press, 2007.

Kaite, Berkeley. *Pornography and Difference*. Bloomington, Ind.: Indiana University Press, 1995.

Kappeler, Susanne. *The Pornography of Representation*. Minneapolis: University of Minnesota Press, 1986.

Kendrick, Walter. *The Secret Museum: Pornography in Modern Culture*. Berkeley, Calif.: University of California Press, 1996.

Kershnar, Stephen. "Is Violation Pornography Bad for Your Soul?" *Journal of Social Philosophy* 35 (2004), 349–66. Reprinted, revised, in *Sex, Discrimination, and Violence: Surprising and Unpopular Results in Applied Ethics*, 21–40. Lanham, Md.: University Press of America, 2009.

————. "Pornography, Health, and Virtue." *Sex and Ethics: Essays on Sexuality, Virtue, and the Good Life*, edited by Raja Halwani, 202–14. Basingstoke, U.K.: Palgrave Macmillan, 2007.

Kimmel, Michael S., ed. *Men Confront Pornography*. New York: Crown, 1990.

Kipnis, Laura. *Bound and Gagged: Pornography and the Politics of Fantasy in America*. New York: Grove Press, 1996.

————. "(Male) Desire and (Female) Disgust: Reading *Hustler*." In *Cultural Studies*, edited by Lawrence Grossberg, Cary Nelson, and Paula A. Treichler, 373–91. New York: Routledge, 1992.

Kittay, Eva Feder. "Pornography and the Erotics of Domination." In *Beyond Domination*, edited by Carol C. Gould, 145–74. Totowa, N.J.: Rowman & Allanheld, 1984.

Langton, Rae. *Sexual Solipsism: Philosophical Essays on Pornography and Objectification*. Oxford: Oxford University Press, 2009.

Levin, Abigail. *The Cost of Free Speech: Pornography, Hate Speech and Their Challenge to Liberalism*. Basingstoke, U.K.: Palgrave Macmillan, 2010.

————. "Pornography, Hate Speech, and Their Challenge to Dworkin's Egalitarian Liberalism." *Public Affairs Quarterly* 23:4 (2009), 357–73.

Lynn, Barry W. "'Civil Rights' Ordinances and the Attorney General's Commission: New Developments in Pornography Regulation." *Harvard Civil Rights-Civil Liberties Law Review* 21:1 (1986), 27–125.

MacKinnon, Catharine A. *Only Words*. Cambridge, Mass.: Harvard University Press, 1993.

————. "Pornography Left and Right." In *Sex, Preference, and Family: Essays on Law and Nature*, edited by David M. Estlund and Martha C. Nussbaum, 102–25. New York: Oxford University Press, 1997.

————. "Sexuality, Pornography, and Method: 'Pleasure Under Patriarchy.'" *Ethics* 99:2 (1989), 314–46.

————. "Vindication and Resistance: A Response to the Carnegie Mellon Study of Pornography in Cyberspace." *Georgetown Law Journal* 83 (1995), 1959–67.

MacKinnon, Catharine A., and Andrea Dworkin, eds. *In Harm's Way: The Pornography Civil Rights Hearings*. Cambridge, Mass.: Harvard University Press, 1997.

Maes, Hans, ed. *Pornographic Art and the Aesthetics of Pornography*. Basingstoke, U.K.: Palgrave Macmillan, 2013.

Maes, Hans, and Jerrold Levinson, eds. *Art and Pornography: Philosophical Essays*. Oxford: Oxford University Press, 2012.

Maitra, Ishani. "Subordination and Objectification." *Journal of Moral Philosophy* 10:1 (2013), 87–100.

Marinucci, Mimi. "What's Wrong with Porn?" *Porn-Philosophy for Everyone: How to Think with Kink*, edited by Dave Monroe, 130–39. Chichester, U.K.: Wiley-Blackwell, 2010.

Mason-Grant, Joan. *Pornography Embodied: From Speech to Sexual Practice*. Lanham, Md.: Rowman & Littlefield, 2004.

McCormack, Thelma. "If Pornography Is the Theory, Is Inequality the Practice?" *Philosophy of the Social Sciences* 23:3 (1993), 298–326.

McElroy, Wendy. *XXX: A Woman's Right to Pornography*. New York: St. Martin's Press, 1995.

McGowan, Mary Kate. "Conversational Exercitives and the Force of Pornography." *Philosophy and Public Affairs* 312 (2003), 155–89.

McGowan, Mary Kate, Alexandra Adelman, Sara Helmers, and Jacqueline Stolzenberg. "A Partial Defense of Illocutionary Silencing." *Hypatia* 26:1 (2011), 132–49.

McGowan, Mary Kate, Ilana Walder-Biesanz, Morvareed Rezaian, and Chloe Emerson. "On Silencing and Systematicity: The Challenge of the Drowning Case." *Hypatia* 31:1 (2016), 74–90.

Monroe, Dave, ed. *Porn-Philosophy for Everyone: How to Think with Kink.* Chichester, U.K.: Wiley-Blackwell, 2010.

Morgan, Robin. "Theory and Practice: Pornography and Rape." In *Going Too Far: The Personal Chronicle of a Feminist,* 163–69. New York: Random House, 1977.

Nathan, Debbie. *Pornography.* Toronto: Groundwood Books, 2007.

Nenadic, Natalie. "Heidegger, Feminism, and Pornography." In *The Philosophy of Pornography: Contemporary Perspectives,* edited by Lindsay Coleman and Jacob Held, 105–25. Lanham, Md.: Rowman & Littlefield, 2016.

Ost, Suzanne. *Child Pornography and Sexual Grooming.* New York: Cambridge University Press, 2009.

Parent, W. A. "A Second Look at Pornography and the Subordination of Women." *Journal of Philosophy* 87:4 (1990), 205–11.

Paul, Pamela. *Pornified: How Pornography Is Damaging Our Lives, Our Relationships, and Our Families.* New York: Henry Holt and Company, 2005.

Power, Nicholas. "Cheap Thrills: A Call for More Pornography." In *The Philosophy of Sex,* 6th ed., edited by Nicholas Power, Raja Halwani, and Alan Soble, 539–57. Lanham, Md.: Rowman & Littlefield, 2013.

Rea, Michael C. "What Is Pornography?" *Noûs* 35:1 (2001), 118–45.

Reid, Kyla, and Tinashe Dune. "Buy My Love: On Sex Workers, Gold Diggers, and 'Rules Girls.'" In *Dating: Flirting with Big Ideas,* edited by Kristie Miller and Marlene Clark, 101–13. Malden, Mass.: Wiley-Blackwell, 2010.

Richlin, Amy, ed. *Pornography and Representation in Greece and Rome.* New York: Oxford University Press, 1992.

Rimm, Marty. "Marketing Pornography on the Information Superhighway: A Survey of 917,410 Images, Descriptions, Short Stories, and Animations Downloaded 8.5 Million Times by Consumers in over 2000 Cities in Forty Countries, Provinces, and Territories." *Georgetown Law Journal* 83 (1995), 1849–934.

Russell, Diana E. H. "Pornography and Rape: A Causal Model." *Political Psychology* 9:1 (1988), 41–73.

———, ed. *Making Violence Sexy: Feminist Views on Pornography.* New York: Teachers College Press, 1993.

Ryder, Dylan and Dave Monroe. "The Jizz Biz and Quality of Life." In *Porn-Philosophy for Everyone: How to Think with Kink,* edited by Dave Monroe, 11–21. Chichester, U.K.: Wiley-Blackwell, 2010.

Sarracino, Carmine and Kevin M. Scott. *The Porning of America: The Rise of Porn Culture, What It Means, and Where We Go from Here.* Boston: Beacon Press, 2008.

Saul, Jennifer. "On Treating Things as People: Objectification, Pornography, and the History of the Vibrator." *Hypatia* 21:2 (2006), 45–61.

———. "Pornography, Speech Acts, and Context." *Proceedings of the Aristotelian Society* (2005–2006), 229–48.

Saunders, Kevin W. *Degradation: What the History of Obscenity Tells Us about Hate Speech.* New York: New York University Press, 2011.

Segal, Lynne, and Mary McIntosh, eds. *Sex Exposed: Sexuality and the Pornography Debate.* New Brunswick, N.J.: Rutgers University Press, 1993.

Shrage, Laurie. "Exposing the Fallacies of Anti-porn Feminism." *Feminist Theory* 6: (2005), 45–65.

Skipper, Robert. "Mill and Pornography." *Ethics* 103:4 (1993), 726–30.

Soble, Alan. "Bad Apples: Feminist Politics and Feminist Scholarship." *Philosophy of the Social Sciences* 29:3 (1999), 354–88.

———. "The Mainstream Has Always Been Pornographic." *Bridge*, No. 12 (October–November 2004), 33–36.

———. "Pornography: Defamation and the Endorsement of Degradation." *Social Theory and Practice* 11:1 (1985), 61–87.

———. *Pornography: Marxism, Feminism, and the Future of Sexuality.* New Haven, Conn.: Yale University Press, 1986.

———. *Pornography, Sex, and Feminism.* Amherst, N.Y.: Prometheus, 2002.

———. "Pornography and the Social Sciences." *Social Epistemology* 2:2 (1988), 135–44. Reprinted in *The Philosophy of Sex*, 5th ed., edited by Alan Soble and Nicholas Power, 433–47. Lanham, Md.: Rowman & Littlefield, 2008.

Spector, Jessica, ed. *Prostitution and Pornography: Philosophical Debate about the Sex Industry.* Stanford, Calif.: Stanford University Press, 2006.

Stark, Cynthia A. "Is Pornography an Action? The Causal vs. the Conceptual View of Pornography's Harm." *Social Theory and Practice* 23:2 (1997), 277–306.

Stoltenberg, John. *Refusing to Be a Man: Essays on Sex and Justice.* Portland, Ore.: Breitenbush, 1989.

Stoner, James R., and Donna M. Hughes, eds. *The Social Costs of Pornography: A Collection of Papers.* Princeton, N.J.: Witherspoon Institute, 2010.

Strossen, Nadine. *Defending Pornography: Free Speech, Sex, and the Fight for Women's Rights.* New York: Scribner, 1995.

Strub, Whitney. *Perversion for Profit: The Politics of Pornography and the Rise of the New Right.* New York: Columbia University Press, 2011.

Tisdale, Sallie. "Talk Dirty to Me." *Harper's Magazine* (February 1992), 37–46. Reprinted in *The Philosophy of Sex*, 5th ed., edited by Alan Soble and Nicholas Power, 419–31. Lanham, Md.: Rowman & Littlefield, 2008.

Tong, Rosemarie. "Feminism, Pornography, and Censorship." *Social Theory and Practice* 8 (1982), 1–17.

———. "Women, Pornography, and the Law." In *The Philosophy of Sex*, 2nd ed., edited by Alan Soble, 301–16. Savage, Md.: Rowman & Littlefield, 1991.

Tucker, Scott. "Gender, Fucking, and Utopia: An Essay in Response to John Stoltenberg's *Refusing to Be a Man.*" *Social Text*, No. 27 (1990), 3–34.

Turley, Donna. "The Feminist Debate on Pornography: An Unorthodox Interpretation." *Socialist Review* 16:3–4 (1986), 81–96.

Vadas, Melinda. "A First Look at the Pornography/Civil Rights Ordinance: Could Pornography Be the Subordination of Women?" *Journal of Philosophy* 84:9 (1987), 487–511.

———. "The Manufacture-for-Use of Pornography and Women's Inequality." *Journal of Political Philosophy* 13:2 (2005), 174–93.

———. "The Pornography/Civil Rights Ordinance v. the BOG: And the Winner Is . . . ?" *Hypatia* 7:3 (1992), 94–109.

Valverde, Mariana. "Beyond Gender Dangers and Private Pleasures: Theory and Ethics in the Sex Debates." *Feminist Studies* 15:2 (1989), 237–54.

Ward, David. "Should Pornography Be Censored?" In *Classic Philosophical Questions*, edited by James A. Gould, 504–12. New York: Prentice Hall, 1995.

Watson, Lori. "Pornography and Public Reason." *Social Theory and Practice* 33:3 (2007), 467–88.

Weitzer, Ronald, ed. *Sex for Sale: Prostitution, Pornography, and the Sex Industry.* New York: Routledge, 2010.

Williams, Linda. *Hard Core: Power, Pleasure, and the "Frenzy of the Visible."* Berkeley, Calif.: University of California Press, 1989.

———. "Second Thoughts on Hard Core: American Obscenity Law and the Scapegoating of Deviance." In *Dirty Looks: Women, Pornography, Power*, edited by Pamela Church Gibson and Roma Gibson, 46–61. London: BFI Publishing, 1993.

Williams, Linda, ed. *Porn Studies.* Durham, N.C.: Duke University Press, 2004.

Woollard, Fiona. "Cheating with Jenna: Monogamy, Pornography, and Erotica." *Porn-Philosophy for Everyone: How to Think with Kink*, edited by Dave Monroe, 93–104. Wichester, U.K.: Wiley-Blackwell, 2010.

PROMISCUITY AND CASUAL SEX

Barker, Meg, and Darren Langdridge, eds. *Understanding Non-Monogamies.* New York: Routledge, 2010.

Birkhead, Tim. *Promiscuity: An Evolutionary History of Sperm Competition.* Cambridge, Mass.: Harvard University Press, 2000.

Chen, Sisi, and George T. Hole. "Sex and Socratic Experimentation." In *College Sex: Philosophers with Benefits*, edited by Michael Bruce and Robert M. Stewart, 17–27. Malden, Mass.: Wiley-Blackwell, 2010.

Ellis, Anthony. "Casual Sex." *International Journal of Moral and Social Studies* 1:2 (1986), 157–69.

Elliston, Frederick. "In Defense of Promiscuity." In *Philosophy and Sex*, 1st ed., edited by Robert Baker and Frederick Elliston, 223–43. Buffalo, N.Y.: Prometheus Books, 1975.

Groneman, Carol. *Nymphomania: A History.* New York: Norton, 2000.

Halwani, Raja. "Casual Sex, Promiscuity, and Temperance." In *Sex and Ethics: Essays on Sexuality, Virtue, and the Good Life*, edited by Raja Halwani, 215–25. Basingstoke, U.K.: Palgrave, 2007.

———. "Virtue Ethics, Casual Sex, and Objectification." In *The Philosophy of Sex*, 5th ed., edited by Alan Soble and Nicholas Power, 337–49. Lanham, Md.: Rowman & Littlefield, 2008.

Kelly, Conor. "Sexism in Practice: Feminist Ethics Evaluating the Hookup Culture." *Journal of Feminist Studies in Religion* 28:2 (2012), 27–48.

Klesse, Christian. *The Spectre of Promiscuity: Gay Male and Bisexual Non-Monogamies and Polyamories.* Aldershot, U.K.: Ashgate, 2007.

Kristjansson, Kristjan. "Casual Sex Revisited." *Journal of Social Philosophy* 29:2 (1998), 97–108.

Ley, David J. *Insatiable Wives: Women Who Stray and the Men Who Love Them.* Lanham, Md.: Rowman & Littlefield, 2009.

Wolf, Naomi. *Promiscuities: The Secret Struggle for Womanhood.* New York: Random House, 1997.

PROSTITUTION

Anderson, Clelia Smyth, and Yolanda Estes. "The Myth of the Happy Hooker: Kantian Moral Reflections on a Phenomenology of Prostitution." In *Violence against Women: Philosophical Perspectives*, edited by Stanley G. French, Wanda Teays, and Laura M. Purdy, 152–58, 231–33. Ithaca, N.Y.: Cornell University Press, 1998.

Anderson, Scott A. "Prostitution and Sexual Autonomy: Making Sense of the Prohibition of Prostitution." *Ethics* 112:4 (2002), 748–80.

Archard, David. "Criminalizing the Use of Trafficked Prostitutes: Some Philosophical Issues." In *Demanding Sex: Critical Reflections on the Regulation of Prostitution*, edited by Vanessa E. Munroe and Marina Della Giusta, 149–62. Aldershot, U.K.: Ashgate, 2008.

Cahill, Ann J. "The Difference Sameness Makes: Objectification, Sex Work, and Queerness." *Hypatia* 29:4 (2014), 840–56.

Christina, Greta, ed. *Paying for It: A Guide by Sex Workers for Their Clients.* Oakland, Calif.: Greenery Press, 2004.

"Code of Ethics for Prostitutes." *Coyote Howls* 5:1 (1978), 9.

Davidson, Julia O'Connell. "Prostitution and the Contours of Control." In *Sexual Cultures: Communities, Values and Intimacy,* edited by Jeffrey Weeks and Janet Holland, 180–98. New York: St. Martin's, 1996.

Delacoste, Frédérique, and Priscilla Alexander, eds. *Sex Work: Writings by Women in the Sex Industry.* Pittsburgh: Cleis Press, 1987.

De Marneffe, Peter. *Liberalism and Prostitution.* Oxford: Oxford University Press, 2010.

Ditmore, Melissa Hope, Antonia Levy, and Alys Willman, eds. *Sex Work Matters: Exploring Money, Power, and Intimacy in the Sex Industry.* London: Zed Books, 2010.

Elias, James E., Vern L. Bullough, Veronica Elias, and Gwen Brewer, eds. *Prostitution: On Whores, Hustlers, and Johns.* Amherst, N.Y.: Prometheus, 1998.

Ericsson, Lars O. "Charges against Prostitution: An Attempt at a Philosophical Assessment." *Ethics* 90:3 (1980), 335-66.

Estes, Yolanda. "Moral Reflections on Prostitution," *Essays in Philosophy* 2:2 (2001), http://commons.pacificu.edu/eip/vol2/iss2/10. Revised, reprinted as "Prostitution: A Subjective Position," in *The Philosophy of Sex,* 5th ed., edited by Alan Soble and Nicholas Power, 353–65. Lanham, Md.: Rowman & Littlefield, 2008.

Garb, Sarah H. "Sex for Money Is Sex for Money: The Illegality of Pornographic Film as Prostitution." *Law and Inequality* 13:2 (1995), 281–301.

Gauthier, Jeffrey. "Prostitution, Sexual Autonomy, and Sex Discrimination." *Hypatia* 26:1 (2011), 166–86.

Green, Karen. "Prostitution, Exploitation and Taboo." *Philosophy* 64 (1989), 525–34.

Jaggar, Alison. "Prostitution." In *The Philosophy of Sex,* 2nd ed., edited by Alan Soble, 259–80. Savage, Md.: Rowman & Littlefield, 1991.

Kupfer, Joseph. "Prostitutes, Musicians and Self-Respect." In *Prostitutes, Musicians, and Self-Respect: Virtues and Vices of Personal Life,* 141–57. Lanham, Md.: Lexington Books, 2007.

———. "What Is Wrong with Prostitution?" In *Explorations of Value,* Volume 55, edited by Thomas Magnell, 213–20. Amsterdam: Rodopi Press, 1997.

Liberto, Hallie Rose. "Normalizing Prostitution versus Normalizing the Alienability of Sexual Rights: A Response to Scott A. Anderson." *Ethics* 120:1 (2009), 138–45.

Marshall, S. E. "Bodyshopping: The Case of Prostitution." *Journal of Applied Philosophy* 16:2 (1999), 139–50.

Meyers, Diana Tietjen. "Feminism and Sex Trafficking: Rethinking Some Aspects of Autonomy and Paternalism." *Ethical Theory and Moral Practice* 17:3 (2014), 427–41.

Miriam, Kathy. "Stopping the Traffic in Women: Power, Agency and Abolition in Feminist Debates over Sex-Trafficking." *Journal of Social Philosophy* 36:1 (2005), 1–17.

Nagle, Jill, ed. *Whores and Other Feminists.* New York: Routledge, 1997.

Overall, Christine. "What's Wrong with Prostitution? Evaluating Sex Work." *Signs* 17:4 (1992), 705–24.

Pateman, Carole. "Defending Prostitution: Charges against Ericsson." *Ethics* 93:3 (1983), 561–65.

———. "Sex and Power." *Ethics* 100:2 (1990), 398–407.

———. *The Sexual Contract.* Stanford, Calif.: Stanford University Press, 1988.

Primoratz, Igor. "What's Wrong with Prostitution?" *Philosophy* 68 (1993), 159–82.

Reid, Kyla, and Tinashe Dune. "Buy My Love: On Sex Workers, Gold Diggers, and 'Rules Girls.'" In *Dating: Flirting with Big Ideas,* edited by Kristie Miller and Marlene Clark, 101–14. Malden, Mass.: Wiley-Blackwell, 2010.

Shrage, Laurie. "Do Lesbian Prostitutes Have Sex with Their Clients? A Clintonesque Reply." *Sexualities* 2:2 (1999), 259–61.

———. "Is Sexual Desire Raced? The Social Meaning of Interracial Prostitution." *Journal of Social Philosophy* 23:1 (1992), 42–51.

———. *Moral Dilemmas of Feminism: Prostitution, Adultery, and Abortion.* New York: Routledge, 1994.

———. "Prostitution." In *Philosophy: Sex and Love,* edited by James Petrik and Arthur Zucker, 151–74. Farmington Hills, Mich.: Macmillan Reference USA, 2016.

———. "Prostitution and the Case for Decriminalization." *Dissent* (Spring 1996), 41–45.

———. "Should Feminists Oppose Prostitution?" *Ethics* 99:2 (1989), 347–61. Reprinted in *The Philosophy of Sex: Contemporary Readings*, 3rd ed., edited by Alan Soble, 323–38. Lanham, Md.: Rowman & Littlefield, 1997; 4th ed., edited by Alan Soble, 435–50. Lanham, Md.: Rowman & Littlefield, 2002.

Spector, Jessica, ed. *Prostitution and Pornography: Philosophical Debate about the Sex Industry.* Stanford, Caif.: Stanford University Press, 2006.

Stewart, Robert M. "Moral Criticism and the Social Meaning of Prostitution." In *Philosophical Perspectives on Sex and Love*, edited by Robert Stewart, 81–83. New York: Oxford University Press, 1995.

Varden, Helga. "A Kantian Conception of Rightful Sexual Relations: Sex, (Gay) Marriage, and Prostitution." *Social Philosophy Today: Science, Technology, and Social Justice*, Volume 22, edited by John Rowan, 199–218. Charlottesville, Va.: Philosophy Documentation Center, 2007.

Vicente, Agustin. "Prostitution and the Ideal State: A Defense of a Policy of Vigilance." *Ethical Theory and Moral Practice* 19:2 (2016), 475–87.

Weitzer, Ronald, ed. *Sex for Sale: Prostitution, Pornography, and the Sex Industry.* New York: Routledge, 2010.

SEXUAL HARASSMENT

Altman, Andrew. "Making Sense of Sexual Harassment Law." *Philosophy and Public Affairs* 25:1 (1996), 36–64.

Christensen, Ferrel M. "'Sexual Harassment' Must Be Eliminated." *Public Affairs Quarterly* 8:1 (1994), 1–17.

Cohen, Jean L. "Personal Autonomy and the Law: Sexual Harassment, Privacy, and the Dilemmas of Regulating 'Intimacy.'" In *Privacies: Philosophical Evaluations*, edited by Beate Rössler, 73–97. Stanford, Calif.: Stanford University Press, 2004.

Crosthwaite, Jan, and Graham Priest. "The Definition of Sexual Harassment." *Australasian Journal of Philosophy* 74:1 (1996), 66–82.

Crouch, Margaret A. "Sexual Harassment in Public Places." In *Social Philosophy Today: Gender, Diversity, and Difference*, Volume 25, edited by John Rowan, 137–48. Charlottesville, Va.: Philosophy Documentation Center, 2009.

———. "The 'Social Etymology' of 'Sexual Harassment.'" *Journal of Social Philosophy* 29:3 (1998), 19–40.

———. *Thinking about Sexual Harassment: A Guide for the Perplexed.* New York: Oxford University Press, 2000.

Dershowitz, Alan M. "The Talmud as Sexual Harassment." In *The Abuse Excuse and Other Cop-outs, Sob Stories, and Evasions of Responsibility*, 251–53. Boston: Little, Brown, 1994.

Dodds, Susan M., Lucy Frost, Robert Pargetter, and Elizabeth W. Prior. "Sexual Harassment." *Social Theory and Practice* 14:2 (1988), 111–30.

Francis, Leslie Pickering, ed. *Sexual Harassment as an Ethical Issue in Academic Life.* Lanham, Md.: Rowman & Littlefield, 2001.

Gallop, Jane. *Feminist Accused of Sexual Harassment.* Durham, N.C.: Duke University Press, 1997.

Hajdin, Mane. *The Law of Sexual Harassment: A Critique.* Selinsgrove, Pa.: Susquehanna University Press, 2002.

———. "Sexual Harassment and Negligence." *Journal of Social Philosophy* 28:1 (1997), 37–53.

———. "Sexual Harassment in the Law: The Demarcation Problem." *Journal of Social Philosophy* 25:3 (1994), 102–22.

Hughes, John C., and Larry May. "Sexual Harassment." *Social Theory and Practice* 6:3 (1980), 249–80.

Kenrick, Douglas T., Melanie R. Trost, and Virgil L. Sheets. "Power, Harassment, and Trophy Mates: The Feminist Advantages of an Evolutionary Perspective." In *Sex, Power, Conflict: Evolutionary and Feminist Perspectives*, edited by David M. Buss and Neil M. Malamuth, 29–53. New York: Oxford University Press, 1996.

Klatt, Heinz-Joachim. "Regulating 'Harassment' in Ontario." *Academic Questions* 8:3 (1995), 48–58.

Landau, Iddo. "Is Sexual Harassment Research Biased?" *Public Affairs Quarterly* 13:3 (1999), 241–54.

LeMoncheck, Linda, and Mane Hajdin. *Sexual Harassment: A Debate*. Lanham, Md.: Rowman & Littlefield, 1997.

LeMoncheck, Linda, and James P. Sterba, eds. *Sexual Harassment: Issues and Answers*. New York: Oxford University Press, 2001.

MacKinnon, Catharine A. *Sexual Harassment of Working Women*. New Haven, Conn.: Yale University Press, 1979.

McBride, William L. "Sexual Harassment, Seduction, and Mutual Respect: An Attempt at Sorting It Out." In *Feminist Phenomenology: Contributions to Phenomenology*, vol. 40, edited by Linda Fisher and Lester Embree, 249–66. Dordrecht: Kluwer, 2000.

Paludi, Michele A., ed. *Sexual Harassment on College Campuses: Abusing the Ivory Power*. Revised ed. Albany, N.Y.: State University of New York Press, 1990.

Patai, Daphne. *Heterophobia: Sexual Harassment and the Future of Feminism*. Lanham, Md.: Rowman & Littlefield, 1998.

Paul, Ellen Frankel. "Sexual Harassment as Discrimination: A Defective Paradigm." *Yale Law and Policy Review* 8:2 (1990), 333–65.

Robinson, Paul. "'Dear Paul': An Exchange between Student and Teacher." In *Opera, Sex, and Other Vital Matters*, 219–37. Chicago: University of Chicago Press, 2002.

Rocha, James. "The Sexual Harassment Coercive Offer." *Journal of Applied Philosophy* 28:2 (2011), 203–16.

Roiphe, Katie. *The Morning After: Sex, Fear, and Feminism on Campus*. New York: Little, Brown, 1993.

Sanday, Peggy Reeves. *A Woman Scorned: Acquaintance Rape on Trial*. New York: Doubleday, 1996.

Saul, Jennifer. "Stop Thinking So Much About 'Sexual Harassment.'" *Journal of Applied Philosophy* 31:3 (2014), 307–21.

Stan, Adele M., ed. *Debating Sexual Correctness*. New York: Delta, 1995.

Superson, Anita M. "A Feminist Definition of Sexual Harassment." *Journal of Social Philosophy* 24:1 (1993), 46–64.

Taylor, James Stacey. "Autonomy, Responsibility, and Women's Obligation to Resist Sexual Harassment." *International Journal of Applied Philosophy* 21:1 (2007), 55–63.

Tuana, Nancy. "Sexual Harassment: Offers and Coercion." *Journal of Social Philosophy* 19:2 (1988), 30–42.

Wall, Edmund, ed. *Sexual Harassment: Confrontations and Decisions*. Buffalo, N.Y.: Prometheus, 1992. Revised ed., 2000.

SEXUAL PERVERSION

(for perversion and virtual issues, see "Internet and Technology")

Adler, Amy. "The Perverse Law of Child Pornography." *Columbia Law Review* 101 (March 2001), 209–73.

Alcoff, Linda Martín. "Dangerous Pleasures: Foucault and the Politics of Pedophilia." In *Feminist Interpretations of Michel Foucault*, edited by Susan J. Hekman, 99–135. University Park, Pa.: Pennsylvania State University Press, 1996. Reprinted in *Philosophy and Sex*, 3rd ed., edited by Robert Baker, Kathleen Wininger, and Frederick Elliston, 500–529. Amherst, N.Y.: Prometheus Books, 1998.

Baltzly, Dirk. "Peripatetic Perversions: A Neo-Aristotelian Account of the Nature of Sexual Perversion." *The Monist* 85:1 (2003), 3–29.

Benvenuto, Sergio. *What Are Perversion? Sexuality, Ethics, Psychoanalysis.* London: Karnac Books, 2016.

Berger, Anne E. "When Sophie Loved Animals." In *Demenageries: Thinking (of) Animals after Derrida*, edited by Anne Emmanuelle Berger and Marta Segarra, 97–124. Amsterdam: Rodopi Press, 2011.

Bullough, Vern L., and Bonnie Bullough. *Sin, Sickness, and Sanity: A History of Sexual Attitudes.* New York: Garland, 1977.

Califia, Pat. "A Thorny Issue Splits a Movement." *Advocate* (October 30, 1980), 17–24, 45.

Conrad, Peter, and Joseph W. Schneider. *Deviance and Medicalization: From Badness to Sickness.* St. Louis, Mo.: C. V. Mosby, 1980. Expanded edition, Philadelphia, Pa.: Temple University Press, 1992.

Davidson, Arnold. "Conceptual History and Conceptions of Perversions." In *Philosophy and Sex*, 3rd ed., edited by Robert B. Baker, Kathleen J. Wininger, and Frederick A. Elliston, 476–86. Amherst, N.Y.: Prometheus, 1998.

———. "Sex and the Emergence of Sexuality." *Critical Inquiry* 14:1 (1987), 16–48.

De Lauretis, Teresa. *The Practice of Love: Lesbian Sexuality and Perverse Desire.* Bloomington, Ind.: Indiana University Press, 1994.

Denis, Lara. "Kant on the Wrongness of 'Unnatural' Sex." *History of Philosophy Quarterly* 16:2 (1999), 225–48.

De Sousa, Ronald. "Norms and the Normal." In *Freud: A Collection of Critical Essays*, edited by Richard Wollheim, 196–221. Garden City, N.Y.: Anchor Books, 1974.

Eggington, William. *Perversity and Ethics.* Stanford, Calif.: Stanford University Press, 2006.

Ehman, Robert. "Adult-Child Sex." In *Philosophy and Sex*, 2nd ed., edited by Robert Baker and Frederick Elliston, 431–46. Buffalo, N.Y.: Prometheus, 1984.

———. "What Really Is Wrong with Pedophilia?" *Public Affairs Quarterly* 14:2 (2000), 129–40.

Finkelhor, David. "What's Wrong with Sex between Adults and Children?" *American Journal of Orthopsychiatry* 49:4 (1979), 692–97.

Freud, Sigmund. (1905) "Three Essays on the Theory of Sexuality." In *The Standard Edition of the Complete Psychological Works of Sigmund Freud*, translated and edited by James Strachey, vol. 7, 125–45. London: Hogarth Press, 1953–1974.

Frye, Marilyn. "Critique [of Robert Ehman]." In *Philosophy and Sex*, 2nd ed., edited by Robert Baker and Frederick Elliston, 447–55. Buffalo, N.Y.: Prometheus Books, 1984. Reprinted, revised, as "Not-Knowing about Sex and Power," in *Willful Virgin*, 39–50. Freedom, Calif.: Crossing Press, 1992.

Gates, Katharine. *Deviant Desires: Incredibly Strange Sex.* New York: Juno Books, 2000.

Geraci, Joseph, ed. *Dares to Speak: Historical and Contemporary Perspectives on Boy-Love.* Swaffham, U.K.: Gay Men's Press, 1997.

Gert, Bernard. "A Sex Caused Inconsistency in DSM-III-R: The Definition of Mental Disorder and the Definition of Paraphilias." *Journal of Medicine and Philosophy* 17:2 (1992), 155–71.

Gert, Bernard, and Charles M. Culver. "Defining Mental Disorder." In *The Philosophy of Psychiatry: A Companion*, edited by Jennifer Radden, 415–25. New York: Oxford University Press, 2004. Reprinted in *The Philosophy of Sex*, 3rd ed., edited by Alan Soble, 57-66; and 4th ed., 57–66. Lanham, Md.: Rowman & Littlefield, 1997 and 2002, respectively.

Gray, Robert. "Sex and Sexual Perversion." *Journal of Philosophy* 75:4 (1978), 189–99.

Hensley, Christopher, and Richard Tewksbury, eds. *Sexual Deviance: A Reader.* Boulder, Colo.: L. Rienner Publishers, 2003.

Hiber, Amanda, ed. *Child Pornography.* Detroit, Mich.: Greenhaven Press, 2009.

Humber, James. "Sexual Perversion and Human Nature." *Philosophy Research Archives* 13 (1987–1988), 331–50.

Irvine, Janice M. *Disorders of Desire: Sex and Gender in Modern American Sexology*. Philadelphia: Temple University Press, 1990.

————. "Reinventing Perversion: Sex Addiction and Cultural Anxieties." *Journal of the History of Sexuality* 5:3 (1995), 429–50.

Kadish, Mortimer R. "The Possibility of Perversion." *Philosophical Forum* 19:1 (1987), 34–53. Reprinted in *The Philosophy of Sex*, 2nd ed., edited by Alan Soble, 93–116. Savage, Md.: Rowman & Littlefield, 1991.

Kaplan, Louise J. *Female Perversions: The Temptations of Emma Bovary*. New York: Anchor Books, 1991.

Kershnar, Stephen. "The Moral Status of Harmless Adult-Child Sex." *Public Affairs Quarterly* 15:2 (2001), 111–32. Reprinted, revised, in *Sex, Discrimination, and Violence: Surprising and Unpopular Results in Applied Ethics*, 1–19. Lanham, Md.: University Press of America, 2009.

————. *Pedophilia and Adult–Child Sex: A Philosophical Analysis*. Lanham, Md.: Lexington Books, 2015.

Ketchum, Sara Ann. "The Good, the Bad, and the Perverted: Sexual Paradigms Revisited." In *The Philosophy of Sex*, 1st ed., edited by Alan Soble, 139–57. Totowa, N.J.: Rowman & Littlefield, 1980.

Kincaid, James R. *Erotic Innocence: The Culture of Child Molesting*. Durham, N.C.: Duke University Press, 1998.

Kupfer, Joseph. "Sexual Perversion." In *Philosophy: Sex and Love*, edited by James Petrik and Arthur Zucker, 329–52. Farmington Hills, Mich.: Macmillan Reference USA, 2016.

————. "Sexual Perversion and the Good." *The Personalist* 59:1 (1978), 70–77.

Levinson, Jerrold. "Sexual Perversity." *The Monist* 86:1 (2003), 30–54.

Levy, Donald. "Perversion and the Unnatural as Moral Categories." *Ethics* 90:2 (1980), 191–202. Reprinted (revised and expanded) in *The Philosophy of Sex*, 1st ed., edited by Alan Soble, 169–89. Totowa, N.J.: Rowman & Littlefield, 1980.

Miller, Kristie. "I'm Dating My Sister, and Other Taboos." In *Dating: Flirting with Big Ideas*, edited by Kirstie Miller and Marlene Clark, 76–89. Malden, Mass.: Wiley-Blackwell, 2010.

————. "On the Concept of Sexual Perversion." *The Philosophical Quarterly* 60: 241 (2010), 808–30.

Milligan, Tony. "The Wrongness of Having Sex with Animals." *Public Affairs Quarterly* 25:3 (2011), 241–55.

Neu, Jerome. "Freud and Perversion." In *The Cambridge Companion to Freud*, edited by Jerome Neu, 175–208. Cambridge: Cambridge University Press, 1991.

————. "What Is Wrong with Incest?" *Inquiry* 19:1 (1976), 27–39.

Nobus, Dany, and Lisa Downings, eds., *Perversion: Psychoanalytic Perspectives*. London: Karnac Books, 2006.

Oliver, Kelly. "Innocence, Perversion, and Abu Ghraib." *Philosophy Today* 51:3 (2007), 343–56.

Ost, Suzanne. *Child Pornography and Sexual Grooming*. New York: Cambridge University Press, 2009.

Peakman, Julie. *The Pleasure's All Mine: A History of Perverse Sex*. London: Reaktion Books, 2013.

Penney, James. *The World of Perversion: Psychoanalysis and the Impossible Absolute of Desire*. Albany, N.Y.: SUNY Press, 2006.

Priest, Graham. "Sexual Perversion." *Australasian Journal of Philosophy* 75:3 (1997), 360–72.

Primoratz, Igor. "Pedophilia." *Public Affairs Quarterly* 13:1 (1999), 99–110.

————. "Sexual Perversion." *American Philosophical Quarterly* 34:2 (1997), 245–58.

Rosen, Raymond C., and Sandra R. Leiblum, eds. *Case Studies in Sex Therapy*. New York: Guilford Press, 1995.

Roudinesco, Élisabeth. *Our Dark Side: A History of Perversion*. Translated by David Macey. Cambridge: Polity, 2009.

Ruddick, Sara. "Better Sex." In *Philosophy and Sex*, 2nd ed., edited by Robert Baker and Frederick Elliston, 280–99. Buffalo, N.Y.: Prometheus Books, 1984.

Schinaia, Cosimo. *On Paedophilia*. Translated by Antonella Sansone. London: Karnac, 2010.

Slote, Michael. "Inapplicable Concepts and Sexual Perversion." In *Philosophy and Sex*, 1st ed., edited by Robert Baker and Frederick Elliston, 261–67. Buffalo, N.Y.: Prometheus, 1975.

Soble, Alan. "Kant and Sexual Perversion." *The Monist* 86:1 (2003), 57–92.

———. "Paraphilia and Distress in DSM-IV." In *The Philosophy of Psychiatry: A Companion*, edited by Jennifer Radden, 54–63. New York: Oxford University Press, 2004.

Solomon, Robert. "Sex and Perversion." In *Philosophy and Sex*, 1st ed., edited by Robert Baker and Frederick Elliston, 268–87. Buffalo, N.Y.: Prometheus Books, 1975.

Spiecker, Ben, and Jan Steutel. "A Moral-Philosophical Perspective on Paedophilia and Incest." *Educational Philosophy and Theory* 32:3 (2000), 283–91.

———. "Paedophilia, Sexual Desire and Perversity." *Journal of Moral Education* 26:3 (1997), 331–42.

Steele, Valerie. *Fetish: Fashion, Sex and Power*. New York: Oxford University Press, 1996.

Szasz, Thomas S. "The Product Conversion—From Heresy to Illness." In *The Manufacture of Madness: A Comparative Study of the Inquisition and the Mental Health Movement*, 160–79. New York: Harper and Row, 1970.

Vannoy, Russell. "The Structure of Sexual Perversity." In *Sex, Love, and Friendship*, edited by Alan Soble, 358–71. Amsterdam: Rodopi, 1997.

Zilney, Laura J., and Lisa Anne Zilney. *Perverts and Predators: The Making of Sexual Offending Laws*. Lanham, Md.: Rowman & Littlefield, 2009.

VIRTUE

Badhwar, Neera. "Carnal Wisdom and Sexual Virtue." In *Sex and Ethics: Essays on Sexuality, Virtue, and the Good Life*, edited by Raja Halwani, 134–46. Basingtoke, U.K.: Palgrave Macmillan, 2007.

Blackburn, Simon. *Lust: The Seven Deadly Sins*. New York: Oxford University Press, 2004.

Bourgault, Sophie. "Eros, Viagra, and the Good Life: Reflections on Cephalus and Platonic Moderation." In *The Philosophy of Viagra: Bioethical Responses to the Viagrification of the Modern World*, edited by Thorsten Botz-Bornstein, 9–24. Amsterdam: Rodopi Press, 2011.

Carr, David. "On the Prospect of Chastity as a Contemporary Virtue." In *Sex and Ethics: Essays on Sexuality, Virtue, and the Good Life*, edited by Raja Halwani, 89–100. Basingstoke, U.K.: Palgrave Macmillan, 2007.

———. "Two Kinds of Virtue." *Proceedings of the Aristotelian Society* 84 (1984–1985), 47–61.

Chen, Sisi and George T. Hole. "Sex and Socratic Experimentation." In *College Sex: Philosophers with Benefits*, edited by Michael Bruce and Robert M. Stewart, 17–27. Malden, Mass.: Wiley-Blackwell, 2010.

Flusser, Vilem. "Lust." *The History of the Devil*, 37–95. Minneapolis: University of Minnesota Press, 2014.

Geach, Peter T. *The Virtues*. Cambridge: Cambridge University Press, 1977.

Grabowski, John S. *Sex and Virtue: An Introduction to Sexual Ethics*. Washington, D.C.: Catholic University of America, 2003.

Halwani, Raja. "Chastity." In *The International Encyclopedia of Ethics*, edited by Hugh LaFollette, 744–47. Malden, Mass.: Wiley-Blackwell, 2013.

———. "Ethics, Virtue." In *Sex from Plato to Paglia: A Philosophical Encyclopedia*, edited by Alan Soble, 279–85. Westport, Conn.: Greenwood Press, 2006.

———, ed. *Sex and Ethics: Essays on Sexuality, Virtue, and the Good Life*. New York: Palgrave, 2007.

———. "Sexual Ethics." In *The Oxford Handbook of Virtue*, edited by Nancy Snow, forthcoming.

———. "Sexual Temperance and Intemperance." In *Sex and Ethics: Essays on Sexuality, Virtue, and the Good Life*, edited by Raja Halwani, 122–33. Basingstoke, U.K.: Palgrave, 2007.

———. "Virtue Ethics and Adultery." *Journal of Social Philosophy* 29:3 (1998): 5–18.

———. "Virtue Ethics, Casual Sex, and Objectification." In *The Philosophy of Sex: Contemporary Readings*, 5th ed., edited by Alan Soble and Nicholas Power, 337–49. Lanham, Md.: Rowman & Littlefied, 2008.

———. *Virtuous Liaisons: Care, Love, Sex, and Virtue Ethics*. Chicago: Open Court, 2003.

Kapper, Thomas. "A Question of Virtuous Sex: Would Aristotle Take Viagra?" In *The Philosophy of Viagra: Bioethical Responses to the Viagrification of the Modern World*, edited by Thorsten Botz-Bornstein, 45–56. Amsterdam: Rodopi Press, 2011.

Martin, Christopher F. J. "Are There Virtues and Vices That Belong Specifically to the Sexual Life?" *Acta Philosophica* 4:2 (1995), 205–21.

Martin, Mike W. "Love, Sex, and Relationships." In *The Handbook of Virtue Ethics*, edited by Stan van Hooft, 242–51. Durham, U.K.: Acumen, 2014.

McCluskey, Colleen. "Lust and Chastity." In *Virtues and Their Vices*, edited by Kevin Timpe and Craig A. Boyd, 115–135. Oxford: Oxford University Press, 2014.

Putman, Daniel. "Sex and Virtue." *International Journal of Moral and Social Studies* 6:1 (1991), 47–56.

Roberts, Robert C. "Temperance." In *Virtues and Their Vices*, edited by Kevin Timpe and Craig A. Boyd, 93–111. Oxford: Oxford University Press, 2014.

Taylor, Gabriele. *Deadly Vices*. Oxford: Clarendon Press, 2006.

Van Hooft, Stan. "Sex, Temperance, and Virtue." In *Virtues in Action: New Essays in Applied Virtue Ethics*, edited by Michael W. Austin, 55–69. Basingstoke, U.K.: Palgrave Macmillan, 2013.

Young, Charles. "Aristotle on Temperance." *The Philosophical Review* 97:4 (1988), 521–42.

Index

About the Editors

Raja Halwani does not quite remember how he stumbled upon the philosophy of sex, but he does remember that he has been interested in it for a long time. Being gay, his interest "naturally" started with some ethical questions having to do with homosexuality and some sexual practices often associated (correctly or incorrectly) with gay men—promiscuity, casual sex, and open relationships. Indeed, his first two publications, back in the days when he was a graduate student, were "Are One Night Stands Morally Problematic?" and "The Morality of Adultery." Convinced by the work of Alan Soble that thinking about sex is one of the most important philosophical endeavors, he has shed his guilt about publishing on sex and even brazenly used the language of virtue to often do so. Being an Arab American (originally from Lebanon), Halwani is also very much interested in issues of sex and the contemporary Middle East, often coming at them through the debate between essentialism and social constructionism. In addition, he publishes in the philosophy of art and political philosophy and is an avid fan of pop culture in general, simultaneously (or alternately?) loving it and scorning it.

Alan Soble began studying and writing about the philosophy of sex in the mid-1970s, after reading Thomas Nagel's essay "Sexual Perversion" in the *Journal of Philosophy*. His first piece in this area of philosophy was "Sexual Desire and Sexual Objects," presented at the 1978 Pacific Division meetings of the American Philosophical Association, which was held in San Francisco (shortly after his thirty-first birthday). That public appearance was followed later that year by "What Philosophers Have Been Saying about Sex" and "Masturbation," Invited Visiting Scholar lectures delivered at California State University, Sacramento, November 21–22, 1978. His reference essays on the philosophy of sex include "La morale et la sexualité," in Monique Canto-Sperber, ed., *Dictionnaire d'éthique et de philosophie morale* (Paris: Presses Universitaires de France, 1996), 1387–91; "Sexuality, Philosophy of," in Edward Craig, ed., *Routledge Encyclopedia of Philosophy* (London: Routledge, 1998), vol. 8, 717–30; "Philosophy of Sexuality" (2000, 2004, 2009), in James Fieser, ed., *The Internet Encyclopedia of Philosophy* (http://www.iep.utm.edu/sexualit/); "Sexuality and Sexual Ethics," in Lawrence C. Becker and Charlotte B. Becker, eds., *Encyclopedia of Ethics*, 2nd edition (New York: Routledge, 2001), vol. 3, 1570–77; and "Philosophy of Sex," in Donald Borchert, ed., *Encyclopedia of Philosophy*,

2nd edition (Macmillan/Thomson, 2006), vol. 7, 521–32. Among his essays published in non-philosophy journals are "Correcting Some Misconceptions about St. Augustine's Sex Life," *Journal of the History of Sexuality* 11:4 (2002): 545–69, and "A History of Erotic Philosophy," in *Journal of Sex Research* 49:2–3 (2009): 104–20 (= *Annual Review of Sex Research*, Vol. XVII).

Sarah Hoffman happened upon the philosophy of sexuality as a PhD student teaching one of her first solo philosophy courses to undergraduates and never looked back. Her interest in philosophical questions about notions such as sexual perversion and cybersex stems from a background in the philosophy of science and a fascination with behaviors labeled as deviant. She contributed entries on sexual perversion and on Andrea Dworkin to Alan Soble's encyclopedia, *Sex from Plato to Paglia* (2006). When not focused on the normally thought-to-be more corporeal and visceral matters of human sexuality, she works in the philosophy of mathematics and science. Her next project is on philosophy and psychoactive drugs.

Jacob M. Held began thinking about sex professionally while working on issues related to the First Amendment, obscenity law, and pornography. He has since published widely on pornography and was even fortunate enough to teach a course on pornography at his university, much to the chagrin of a past president and provost. Delving into the academic engagement with pornography has been eye opening, in terms of what one learns about pornography, sex, popular culture, and humanity in general, as well as what one learns about one's peers. His other interests include children's literature, horror fiction, and comics, which makes him well rounded, eclectic, or profoundly disturbed, depending on whom you ask.